SEP 1 7 2010

P9-CLF-098

WITHDRAWN

ALSO BY

SELINA HASTINGS

Nancy Mitford: A Biography

Evelyn Waugh: A Biography

Rosamond Lehmann

THE SECRET LIVES OF
SOMERSET MAUGHAM

MAURESQUE,
CAP FERRAT,
A. M.

THE SECRET LIVES OF

SOMERSET
MAUGHAM

...

A BIOGRAPHY

SELINA HASTINGS

RANDOM HOUSE | NEW YORK

ELISHA D. SMITH PUBLIC LIBRARY
MENASHA, WISCONSIN

Copyright © 2009, 2010 by Selina Hastings

All rights reserved.

Published in the United States by Random House,
an imprint of The Random House Publishing Group,
a division of Random House, Inc., New York.

RANDOM HOUSE and colophon are
registered trademarks of Random House, Inc.

This work was originally published in the United Kingdom
by John Murray Publishers, London,
in 2009, in a slightly different form.

LIBRARY OF CONGRESS CATALOGING-IN-PUBLICATION DATA
Hastings, Selina.
The secret lives of Somerset Maugham: a biography / Selina Hastings.
p. cm.
Includes bibliographical references and index.
ISBN 978-1-4000-6141-9
eBook ISBN 978-0-679-60371-9
1. Maugham, W. Somerset (William Somerset), 1874–1965.
2. Authors, English—20th century—
Biography. I. Title
PR6025.A86Z6123 2010
823'.912—dc22
[B] 2009035797

Printed in the United States of America on acid-free paper

www.atrandom.com

2 4 6 8 9 7 5 3 1

FIRST U.S. EDITION

Frontispiece photograph courtesy of the
Cecil Beaton Studio Archive at Sotheby's

Book design by Barbara M. Bachman

TO NEIL AND REIDEN JENMAN

WITH GRATITUDE AND AFFECTION

CONTENTS

. . .

THE SECRET LIVES OF

SOMERSET MAUGHAM

A BLACKSTABLE
BOYHOOD

...

FOR MUCH OF HIS LONG LIFE—HE LIVED TO BE OVER NINETY—
Somerset Maugham (1874–1965) was the most famous writer in the
world. He was known everywhere for his superb short stories and
for his novels, the immensely acclaimed, *Of Human Bondage,* becoming one of the most widely read works of fiction of the twentieth century. His books were translated into almost every known
tongue, filmed, dramatized, and sold in their millions, bringing
him celebrity and enormous wealth. Wherever he went he was pursued by journalists, eager for information: this extraordinary man
seemed to know everyone, from Henry James to Winston Churchill, from Dorothy Parker to D. H. Lawrence. His magnificent
villa in the south of France, much photographed and written about,
was a byword for luxury and elegance. On the Riviera, as in London and New York, Maugham, always elegantly dressed, looked
every inch the conventional English gentleman. And yet conventional he was not. In Maugham's outwardly respectable life there
was a great deal he was determined to keep hidden, and in old age,
when he was besieged by would-be biographers, he did his utmost
to make sure his privacy would remain intact. Evening after
evening at the Villa Mauresque, Maugham, assisted by his secretary,
went systematically through his papers, throwing every last scrap of
personal correspondence onto the fire. He also wrote to his friends
asking them to destroy any letters of his in their possession; and he
issued strict instructions to his literary executors that no biography

should be authorized, no access to his papers be allowed, and all requests for information be firmly refused.

And what were these areas of experience that it was so important to keep concealed? Mainly they were to do with his homosexuality, for Maugham lived in an era when in Britain homosexual practice was against the law. He was twenty-one at the time of the trial of Oscar Wilde in 1895, an event that traumatized a generation of men who were not by nature inclined toward marriage. And although Maugham himself did marry, and indeed fathered a child, his relations with his wife, Syrie, were wretchedly unhappy, even though he never allowed her for long to keep him apart from the great love of his life, a dissolute charmer named Gerald Haxton. Now, nearly half a century after Maugham's death, the details of his long affair with Gerald and the harrowing story of his life with Syrie have come to light. The executors of the Maugham estate in London, the Royal Literary Fund, recently rescinded the clause in his will forbidding access to his correspondence; and a transcript has been uncovered of a long and detailed recording made by his daughter, Liza, of the inside story of her father's private and domestic life. The material has turned out to be richly revealing: Liza, speaking to a close friend, was extremely frank; and ironically, Maugham's request that his letters should be destroyed ensured not only that they were kept but that most were sold for very large sums to American universities.

The story that unfolds is that of a man who after a harrowing and unhappy childhood learned early to live undercover; appropriately, in both world wars he worked for British intelligence, sometimes at considerable risk to his personal safety. He was further distanced by developing at an early age a stammer that made him agonizingly self-conscious; it inhibited him, and as an adult he formed the habit of having by his side an interpreter, a sociable, outgoing type, usually also his lover, who would make the initial contact and enable Maugham himself to keep more or less in the background. And yet for all his elaborate defenses Maugham remained intensely vulnerable; he was a passionate, difficult man, capable of cruelty as well as of great kindness and charm, but despite all his worldly success he never found what he wanted. His miserable marriage wrecked years of his existence, and the great love of his life remained unrequited.

Many of his readers associate Somerset Maugham with the British Empire and the Far East, with Maugham himself a symbol of the quintessential English gentleman, the pukka sahib, descended from generations of old established county family. Yet in fact Maugham's parents were recent arrivals among the professional middle classes, and they had lived not in England but in France: it was on French soil that Maugham's life both began and ended. Maugham's father, Robert Ormond Maugham (1823–1884), was a solicitor, the third generation to practice law in a family who were descended from farmers and small tradesmen in Westmoreland. It was Robert Maugham's grandfather who had first come to London, where he had risen no higher than a lawyer's clerk, although his son had gone on to achieve distinction not only in his legal practice but as one of the founders of the Law Society. Robert himself had done so well in the family business that in the 1840s he had moved to Paris to open a branch there, his partner, William Dixon, remaining behind to run the London office. The premises of Maugham et Dixon, *juriconsultes anglais,* were immediately opposite the British embassy, and here Maugham et Dixon prospered, especially after the firm's semiofficial appointment as legal adviser to the embassy itself.

By his mid-thirties Robert Maugham was making a good living, doing well from the boom years of Louis Napoleon and the Second Empire, when in Paris everyone seemed to be making money—*"Enrichissez-vous!"* was the cry. The population of the capital was enormously expanding, and so was the English community upon which much of the business of Maugham et Dixon naturally depended. Eventually Robert Maugham felt sufficiently well off to take a wife, and on the first of October 1863, at the age of thirty-nine, he married Edith Mary Snell, a ravishing young woman sixteen years his junior. Young Mrs. Maugham, daughter of an Indian army captain who had died when she was a baby, had lived in France most of her life. Her widowed mother had been socially superior to her husband, and it was one of her uncles who had been christened Somerset in honor of a distinguished godfather, the name to be passed on to his famous great-nephew, who never cared for it.

After the wedding the Maughams settled into an apartment at 25 Avenue d'Antin (now Avenue Franklin D. Roosevelt), a broad street lined with chestnut trees just below the *rond-point* of the Champs-Élysées. Here for nearly seven years the couple enjoyed an agreeable existence, with Robert, "lively and gregarious," working hard at his business while Edith ran the household and supervised the upbringing of the three boys who arrived in quick succession. Both Maughams were small in stature, but while Robert's appearance verged on the brutish—he was plump, with a large sallow face, yellow whites to his eyes, and a bulbous chin framed by a mustache and bushy side whiskers—Edith was doll-like and beautiful. Her hair was a rich auburn, her pale complexion flawless, her dark brown eyes large and set wide apart. When Robert and Edith were seen together, the contrast was almost risible, and they became affectionately known as "Beauty and the Beast." The Maughams enjoyed a lavish style of living, keeping a carriage, frequently attending the theater and opera, and entertaining generously. Edith dressed with style, the apartment was always filled with flowers, and the finest hothouse fruit, grapes and peaches out of season, appeared on the table. Much of the Maughams' social life inevitably revolved around the embassy, but Edith also numbered among her friends writers and painters, among them Prosper Mérimée and Gustave Doré. Regarded as the reigning beauty of the English community, Mme Maugham was one of the few foreigners whose name was listed in the annual directory *La Société et le High Life,* and after her death she was described as an habituée of the most elegant salons, *"une femme charmante, qui ne comptait que des amis dans la haute société parisienne, où elle occupait une des premières places."** Such a eulogy almost certainly owes more to flattery than fact, but it is nonethe-

---

* "a charming woman, with countless friends in Parisian high society, in which she occupies one of the highest positions."

less clear that Edith Maugham was a woman of exceptional empathy and charm.

In October 1865 the couple's first child was born, a boy, Charles Ormond, followed a year later by Frederic Herbert, and in June 1868 by Henry Neville. The youngest had barely reached his second birthday when the Franco-Prussian War broke out, shortly followed by Napoleon III's humiliating surrender in September 1870 at Sedan. With the Prussian army advancing on Paris, the Maughams, together with a large section of the English community, departed for England, leaving behind them at the Avenue d'Antin a couple of servants to look after the apartment and a Union Jack fastened to the balcony. During the terrible siege of Paris the starving populace was reduced to eating rats and animals from the zoo; as nothing could penetrate the German blockade, messages arrived from the Avenue d'Antin by carrier pigeon, one of them requesting to know whether Madame desired the summer covers to be put on the furniture in the drawing room. The five-month siege was succeeded by the bloody civil war known as the Commune, during which great swaths of the city were destroyed and more than twenty thousand people killed. But by the end of May 1871, government forces had regained control, and in August the Maughams returned to Paris, met at the Gare du Nord by their loyal manservant, François, who was able to tell them that the apartment had been left untouched by the Germans, thanks largely to their prominently displayed Union Jack.

The apartment may have remained intact, but most of the center of the city presented a scene of desolation, the Tuileries a blackened ruin, the Hôtel de Ville a heap of rubble, the Colonne Vendôme toppled to the ground. Although rebuilding began at once and progressed with speed, it was some time before the business life of the city fully recovered, and with so many English having gone for good, Robert Maugham found himself perilously out of pocket, obliged to start almost from scratch in rebuilding his practice.

In 1873 Edith again found herself pregnant. At that time the government, understandably anxious to strengthen its military might, was threatening the introduction of legislation imposing

French nationality on all boys born in France to foreign parents, a measure that would automatically make them eligible for conscription. To circumvent this, the British ambassador, Lord Lyons, had authorized the rigging up of a maternity ward on the second floor of the embassy so that the wives of those immediately connected to the Chancery could safely give birth on British soil. And here on January 25, 1874, Edith's fourth child was born, another boy, to be christened William Somerset.

The years of Somerset Maugham's early childhood were almost certainly the happiest of his life. By the time he was old enough to take notice, his three brothers, Charlie, Freddie, and Harry, had gone, sent off to school in England and coming home only for the holidays. The result was that little William led the life of a much-indulged only child, and with his father away at his office all day, returning only after the boy had been put to bed, he was in the happy position of having his adored mother entirely to himself. After the departure of his wet nurse, Willie was looked after by a French nursemaid, his "nounou," with whom he shared a bedroom, and it was she who would take him in to see his mother in the morning while she was resting after her bath, a private interlude of perfect intimacy and love, the memory of which stayed with him always, to be poignantly recalled nearly forty years later:

> [The servant] took the child over to a bed in which a woman was lying. It was his mother. She stretched out her arms, and the child nestled by her side. . . . The woman kissed his eyes, and with thin, small hands felt the warm body through his white flannel nightgown. . . .
>
> "Are you sleepy, darling?" she said.
>
> . . . The child did not answer, but smiled comfortably. He was very happy in the large, warm bed, with those soft arms about him. He tried to make himself smaller still as he cuddled up against his mother, and he kissed her sleepily. In a moment he closed his eyes and was fast asleep. . . . [T]he woman kissed him again; and she passed her hand down his body till she came to his feet; she held the right foot in her hand and felt

the five small toes; and then slowly passed her hand over the left one.

For Willie, his mother was the center of his entire existence. He loved her unreservedly and felt completely secure in her love for him. While his father remained a shadowy presence and barely impinged upon his consciousness, his mother's attention, he knew, was always his, and nothing mattered to him much that did not concern the sweet intimacy that existed between himself and her.

After visiting his mother, Willie was taken out, usually to play in the Champs-Élysées, in those days lined with private houses and luxurious apartment buildings. He and his nurse would make their way to the gardens at the end nearest the Place de la Concorde. Here there were always other children, and as he grew older Willie was allowed to play with them, dashing in and out of the shrubbery in vigorous games of *La tour prend garde* or *Balle à l'ennemi*. With his pale skin, fair curls, and large brown eyes, Willie in his black-belted suit was indistinguishable from the little French boys in their short trousers and lace-up boots who were his playmates; indeed he spoke French far more fluently than English, sometimes mixing the two. Edith was amused when one day her small son, catching sight of a horse from the window of a railway carriage, cried out, "*Regardez, Maman, voilà un 'orse.*" His first extant letter, written at the age of six and addressed to his parents, is in French: "*cher papa, chere maman, votre petit willie est heureux au jour de noel de vous exprimer ses meilleurs souhaits, et sa reconaissante affection. croyez-moi, cher papa, chere maman, votre fils respectueux, willie maugham.*"* In the afternoons, either his mother had nursery tea with him, or Willie went to the drawing room to be shown off to her guests. Occasionally he was asked to recite a fable of La Fontaine, after which, if he were lucky, some kind gentleman might tip him. On his seventh birthday one of his mother's friends gave him a twenty-franc piece, which he

---

* "dear papa, dear mama, your little willie is happy on christmas day to give you his best wishes and grateful affection. Believe me to be, dear papa, dear mama, your respectful son, willie maugham."

chose to spend on his first visit to the theater; accompanied by his eldest brother Charlie, he saw Sarah Bernhardt in an "atrocious" melodrama by Sardou, which thrilled him to the core.

Willie's education was begun at a little French day school, unlike his brothers, who had had their first lessons with English governesses at home. With his brothers away most of the year, his closest childhood friend was Violet Williams-Freeman, who had also been born in the embassy. Violet and her sister and brother were impressed by this cheerful, confident, imaginative, and rather daring little boy, and willingly appointed him their *chef du bande*. He held them spellbound with his stories and was ingenious at thinking up games. Often the children played together in the Champs-Élysées, where they ate sugared *gaufrettes* while watching the Guignol, and Willie, with an air of great innocence, delighted his companions by passing off fake sous at the kiosk selling balloons.

Violet was sometimes taken to tea on her own at the Avenue d'Antin, as Edith was her godmother. The little girl worshipped her godmother and hated to see how frail and how ill she often looked; her beautiful brown eyes were sad, and there seemed to be an aura of melancholy surrounding her, of the origins of which Violet had no idea, later speculating that perhaps there had been an unhappy love affair before Edith married. In fact illness could well have accounted for her depression, for Edith was consumptive, and depression is a familiar concomitant of tuberculosis.

As her disease progressed, Edith grew weaker. As a semi-invalid, she was advised to avoid extremes of temperature, and as summers in Paris could grow uncomfortably hot and the stifling air was considered unhealthy, she used to take the children in July to a rented house by the sea in Deauville for three months. On Saturdays, Robert Maugham took the train down from Paris to join them for a couple of days, once turning up in a "bone-shaker" car with iron tires in which he took the boys for juddering rides along the front.

When Willie was five, Edith again became pregnant. In those days it was believed that childbirth fortified women who had consumption, a theory which may have had something to do with Willie's birth in 1874, five and a half years after the arrival of Harry, the youngest of his three older brothers. This time the baby, another boy, was stillborn, and in order to recuperate, Edith, accompanied by Willie, traveled south to winter in Pau, a town at the foot of the Pyrenees. But whatever the benefits of mountain air, they were short-lived, and not long after Edith returned home her condition worsened. As his mother grew weaker, Willie's time with her was curtailed, partly no doubt in an attempt to shield him from the more harrowing symptoms of the disease. Typically, periods of paralyzing lassitude alternated with hectic bursts of energy and optimism, when for a brief period a semblance of normality could be resumed. But increasingly daily life at the avenue d'Antin came to revolve around the visits of frock-coated doctors with their sinister black bags bearing the cumbersome treatments then in vogue. Bleeding had largely been abandoned, replaced by cupping, which was thought to draw the infection out; drinking milk was also believed to be important, cow's milk, goat's milk, but best of all ass's milk, and every morning a little string of donkeys stopped at the door to provide Edith with her tonic.

Not long after the return from Pau, in the spring of 1881, Edith found she was once more expecting a child, but by this time she was too ill for there to be much hope that such a remedy could save her. Toward the end of that year she realized she was dying and that her boys would shortly be left motherless. Although eight months pregnant and desperately ill, she summoned the last of her strength and somehow managed to dress herself, putting on the bodice of a favorite white damask evening gown over a black skirt. Quietly letting herself out of the apartment, she went to have herself photographed so that her sons would always remember what their mother looked like. On January 24, 1882, Edith gave birth to a son, who was quickly baptized Edward Alan before dying the following afternoon. Less than a week later, at the age of forty-one, Edith herself died, six days after Willie's eighth birthday.

WITH HIS MOTHER'S DEATH, the world in which Willie had been so safe and happy disappeared abruptly and forever. His brothers,

who had been summoned to the deathbed, shortly afterward returned to England, and Willie was left to cope with his profound
and terrible grief as best he could. The child's love for his mother
was passionate and unreasoning, and he was never able to come to
terms with her loss. He kept her photograph beside his bed
throughout his life, together with a long tress of her hair, his two
most treasured possessions, and even in great old age Maugham
would admit that he had never recovered from his mother's death.
His father, himself utterly crushed by the loss of his wife, did what
he could to console him, but he had seen little of his youngest
son and the two were comparative strangers. As before, Robert
Maugham spent six days a week at his office, while Willie was
looked after by his mother's much-loved French maid, who now assumed the role of nurse. Willie was taken away from his little
French day school, going instead to the English clergyman of the
church attached to the embassy for his lessons. This gentleman, realizing that his pupil's English was far from adequate, made the boy
read aloud from police reports in the newspaper, details of some of
the grislier cases haunting the child for years afterward.

Only on Sundays did the boy spend any time with his father.
Robert Maugham's one indulgence was the building of a summer
house at Suresnes, a few miles west of the center of Paris, close to
the Seine and the Bois de Boulogne. On Sundays father and son,
companions in grief, would take the *bâteau-mouche* downriver to
inspect progress on the house, built in an eccentric style, part
Japanese, part Swiss chalet, painted white with red shutters, and
overlooking a splendid panorama of the Seine, the racecourse at
Longchamps, and beyond them of the whole of Paris. Robert
Maugham, described by his youngest son as having a "romantic
mind," had never forgotten the travels he had made in his youth, to
Morocco, Greece, and Asia Minor, and in his imagination his little
house near the Seine in suburban Suresnes was a villa on the
Bosporus. To emphasize the exotic effect, he had the Moorish sign
against the evil eye engraved on the windows, a sign which was fa-
mously adopted by the writer Maugham as his personal insignia.
"My father was a stranger to me when he was alive," he was later to

say. "Yet somehow that sign against the Evil Eye seems to have bound us together."

Before long the building was complete, the garden laid out and furniture delivered; but Robert Maugham had no time to enjoy it. Since his wife's death he himself had grown progressively weaker, his complexion more sallow, dogged by nausea, exhaustion, and pain, symptoms of the stomach cancer that was shortly to kill him.

On June 24, 1884, two and a half years after losing his wife, Robert Maugham himself died. He was sixty years old, and despite his long, hardworking career he left behind him less than £5,000 to be shared among his four sons. "It was the end of a home," Freddie Maugham sadly recalled. "My brothers and I were soon separated by the force of events, and therefore we did not see much of each other." Appointed the boys' guardians were the good-natured old lawyer from the London office, William Dixon, and Robert Maugham's only brother and Willie's godfather, Henry Macdonald Maugham, vicar of Whitstable in Kent. These two men came briefly over to Paris to cope with the crisis. A three-day auction was held to dispose of the contents of the apartment, personal possessions were packed and labeled, servants paid off, and all necessary arrangements made to transfer the brothers' domicile from France to England. For the three older boys, accustomed to life on the other side of the Channel, the change was not so great. But for ten-year-old Willie all was strange and unfamiliar, and it was impossible for him to imagine what he would encounter in the unknown country where he was to live from now on with his uncle and aunt.

Willie made the nine-hour journey accompanied by his faithful nurse. After the Channel steamer docked at Dover, in the midst of all the bustle of disembarkation they saw waiting for them on the quayside the sombre figure of the Reverend Henry Maugham, black-coated, bewhiskered, and severe. As they covered the twenty-odd miles to Whitstable, Willie kept close to the kindly Frenchwoman, "[the] one link with all the happiness and affection I'd known in the Avenue d'Antin. . . . my last link with my mother and all that she had meant to me." By the time they arrived at the vicarage, it was late and the travelers were exhausted. Before Willie went up to bed, however, his uncle had something to say: he announced that there was no question of being able to afford a nurse and that she was to be sent back to France as soon as possible. And the next day she was gone.

FOR THE REST OF HIS LIFE Maugham looked back on his childhood in England as a period of utter desolation. "I shall never forget the misery of those next few years," he used to say, and even in old age the memory was so painful that it gave him the "cold shudders." Indeed, in the circumstances it is hardly surprising the boy was wretched: orphaned at ten years old, still suffering agonies of grief for his mother, and placed in the care of strangers in what was in effect a foreign country. Instead of the cosseting and indulgence, of the warmth, gaiety, and lavishness of his parents' life, of their comfortable apartment and sophisticated society, he found himself in a bleak and alien environment, unloved and of importance to no one. Forty years later there appears a telling entry in his notebook: "He had had so little love when he was small that later it embarrassed him to be loved. . . . He did not know what to say when someone paid him a compliment, and a manifestation of affection made him feel a fool."

Neither his uncle nor aunt was deliberately unkind, but they were a dull, unimaginative pair, childless themselves and with no experience of dealing with children; perhaps understandably, they were nervous about having their well-regulated existence disrupted by the presence of a small boy who might well turn out to be noisy, cheeky, and rough. Willie's uncle in particular was selfish and set in his ways. As his nephew Freddie later said of him, "he was very narrow-minded and a far from intelligent cleric, and I cannot truthfully praise him as a guardian of boys." Henry Macdonald Maugham had been vicar of Whitstable for the past thirteen years, a living that he found suited him well. A lazy man, he was fortunate in having a curate, Mr. Ellman, who took much of the work of the parish off his hands. He was fortunate, too, in that his wife, Sophie, was submissive by nature and accepted without question that the comfort and convenience of her husband be considered paramount. Plump and almost pretty, her blond hair coiled in thick plaits on the crown of her head, Sophie was the daughter of a German merchant, a quiet, modest woman, straitlaced and conventional, but while prim in manner and embarrassed by any display of emotion, she had a kind heart and wanted to do her best by her nephew, as long as he in no way impinged on the well-being of her husband or the smooth running of the household.

The vicarage, two miles outside Whitstable on the Canterbury Road, was a gloomy place. The memory of the deep unhappiness suffered there weighed on Maugham for many years and provided the inspiration for his most famous work of fiction, *Of Human Bondage*. The figures of the vicar and his wife are recognizably portrayed in the novel, and much of the blame for the wretchedness of the motherless boy must be laid at their door. The Reverend Henry Maugham was not popular in the parish; snobbish, blinkered, and magnificently self-centered, he was a man who inspired neither affection nor esteem; and his timid wife unquestioningly accepted her husband at his own inflated valuation. And yet they were not bad people: the vicar was no Mr. Murdstone; it would never have occurred to him for a moment that he was not satisfactorily fulfilling his obligations toward his brother's boy. But Maugham's feelings about him and about that period of his life were tightly entangled with grief over his mother's death, with his rage at having been abandoned. Nobody could have replaced Edith Maugham, certainly not such a stiff and starchy couple as the Reverend Henry and his wife.

Yet within his own narrow limits, it is clear the vicar made an effort to be kind. In *Of Human Bondage* the episode of the young boy's arrival at the vicarage demonstrates his uncle's parsimony, but it also shows a genuine attempt to make contact with the boy:

The vicar, having said grace, cut the top off his egg.

"There," he said, handing it to Philip, "you can eat my top if you like."

Philip would have liked an egg to himself, but he was not offered one, so took what he could. . . .

"How did you like that top, Philip?" asked his uncle.

"Very much, thank you."

"You shall have another one on Sunday afternoon."

Mr. Carey always had a boiled egg at tea on Sunday so that he might be fortified for the evening service.

Nevertheless, if there was no deliberate cruelty, Henry Maugham was capable of an obtuseness that came very near it, as Maugham would describe in a later memoir, *Looking Back*. After church on the morning of his first Sunday at the vicarage, Willie is sat at the dining room table and told by his uncle to learn the collect of the day:

"I'll hear you say it at tea time," he said, "and if you say it properly you shall have a piece of cake." Then he went into his study to rest after the morning's exertions and my aunt went to lie down in the drawing-room. I was left alone. An hour or so later she went into the garden to have a stroll and as she passed the dining-room windows peeped in to see how I was getting on. My face was buried in my hands and I was crying, crying bitterly. She hurried into the dining-room and asked me what was the matter. Crying all the more, I sobbed, "I can't understand it. All those words, I don't know what they mean." "Oh, Willie," she said, "your uncle wouldn't want you to cry. It was for your own good that he wanted you to learn the collect. Don't cry." She took the prayer book away from me and I was left alone once more to sob my heart out. When the table was set for tea my uncle did not speak to me. I could see that he was cross. I think my aunt must have persuaded him that I was too young to learn a collect by heart; anyhow I was never asked to do so again.

Sophie plainly was touched by the boy's unhappiness and did what she could to make the situation better, but nevertheless she and Willie remained shy and awkward with each other. And he himself was not altogether easy: in Paris he had been spoiled by his adoring female coterie, and when crossed had quite a temper. Rather than spend time with his aunt, he much preferred to take his toys and play in the kitchen, an arrangement that suited everybody. "His aunt was not sorry. She did not like disorder, and though she recognized that boys must be expected to be untidy she preferred that he should make a mess in the kitchen. If he fidgeted his uncle was apt to grow restless and say it was high time he went to school."

The Whitstable living, worth £300 a year, included with the vicarage twenty acres of glebe land. This was not wealth, but it enabled the vicar and his wife to live respectably and in modest comfort. The household comprised a gardener, two maids, a cook, and a housemaid. In the cozy back offices it was the maids who provided Willie with a version of the warm feminine company with which he had been so happily surrounded in the Avenue d'Antin. In the two novels drawing most nearly on Maugham's own experience, *Of Human Bondage* and *Cakes and Ale,* the kindhearted maternal figure in both instances is the cook, Mary-Ann, in real life Mary-Anne Tilley. In the novels it is she who looks after the boy and whom he comes to love; she, not his aunt, who nurses him through his childhood illnesses, gives him his bath, tucks him up in bed, and tells him stories. The storytelling was important, for while he listened Willie would become wholly absorbed, forgetting his misery and his longing for his mother. As he later wrote of himself at this period, it was when he was unhappy that he wanted stories most, a form of addiction that was to stay with him for life.

As the days passed the sense of strangeness began to wear off, and by the end of the autumn of 1884 Maugham had largely grown accustomed to his new life. It was a lonely life, because his uncle considered himself a cut above most of Whitstable society, shamelessly toadying to the local squire while refusing to have anything to do with the tradesmen, or with the fishermen and their families; nor, as a pillar of the Church of England, would he speak to chapel folk, crossing the road rather than pass on the same side as the Baptist minister, Mr. Laurence, or the Wesleyan, Mr. Walter. "Old Maugham," as he was referred to behind his back, was "a cracking snob" and considered few children suitable as playmates for his nephew. A Whitstable contemporary, one of the Board School boys, recalled how isolated the child appeared. "His guardians would rigidly take care that he should be kept apart from common people," he said. "He was too remote from our way of living to encourage familiarity."

As a consequence of his enforced isolation and of the lack of love, Maugham changed from a child naturally sociable and outgoing to one guarded and withdrawn. Sometimes he was overwhelmed by sadness and a longing for his mother, but he soon learned to hide his emotions, particularly when hurt or unhappy, and could never bear to be seen crying. He spent hours playing on his own in the garden, fishing for roach in the pond or aimlessly swinging on the big five-barred gate at the end of the drive. Charlotte Etheridge, the doctor's daughter, remembered glimpsing his forlorn figure, unsuitably clad in a Frenchified velvet suit with a white lace collar, standing alone and aimless outside the house.

And there was another reason for Maugham's apartness. He had developed a bad stammer which made him painfully self-conscious. In France there had been no sign of such an impediment. Yet since Maugham's arrival in England the stammer was marked, and it caused him, and for much of his life continued to cause him, anguish and humiliation. Shy and unsure of himself, he now also had to cope with this added horror, only too well aware of how conspicuous it made him. For a child feeling his way in a foreign environment, it was particularly terrifying to be at the mercy of such a cruel encumbrance, never knowing when his speech, his chief medium of communication, might not be hideously distorted and he himself made to look slow-witted and ridiculous, laughed at as a figure of fun. Inevitably, his sense of anger and frustration was compounded by a deep, if irrational, feeling of self-disgust, a feeling unknown in his previous unclouded existence but which from now on was to remain with Maugham always. There was a memorably harrowing occasion when his uncle took him on the train to London for the day, sending him back on his own:

There was a long queue outside the third-class ticket office, so I took my place in the queue. But when it came to my turn to ask for my ticket to Whitstable I couldn't get the word out. I just stood there stammering. People behind me were getting impatient, but I still couldn't say "Whitstable." Suddenly two men stepped out of the queue and pushed me aside. "We can't wait all night for you," they said. "Stop wasting our time." So I had to go to the back of the queue and start all over again. I'll never forget the humiliation of that moment—with everyone staring at me.

ONE OF THE STRANGEST aspects of Maugham's life in Kent is the absence of any sign of communication between himself and his brothers. In Paris, it is true, he had lived like an only child and no strong bond had formed between himself and the three older boys. They had been sent to the newly founded Dover College, chosen mainly for its ease of access from France. From Dover College the eldest, Charlie, who used to take his small brother to the circus and theater during the holidays, had gone up to Cambridge to read law, while Freddie and Harry were still at school. Although Dover is only just over twenty miles from Whitstable, there seems to have been little contact with the vicarage. It is possible that the vicar discouraged visits, and entirely probable that Willie never thought to complain. Freddie was also living with a clergyman relation, the rector of Paston in Cambridgeshire, but this aunt and uncle were cheerful and affectionate and he was happy there, and it may have been only later that he discovered how miserable his brother's situation had been.

Daily life at the vicarage was strictly regulated and monotonous. The day revolved around four meals: breakfast, followed by prayers, then dinner at one o'clock, tea at five, and a cold supper (bread and butter and a little stewed fruit) at eight, followed by more prayers. This was the routine for six days of the week leading up to Sunday, the great day when the vicar delivered his sermon. This was an effort for which he required substantial bolstering in advance, a reverential hush during composition in his study, an egg beaten up in a glass of sherry at breakfast, and another egg for tea to support him through Evensong. Willie, who was not allowed to play on Sundays or make any noise, rode with his uncle and aunt to church in a hired fly that smelled strongly of stale straw. In the evening the boy again accompanied his uncle to church, this time on foot. "At first he was shy with his uncle, but little by little grew used to him, and he would slip his hand in his uncle's and walk more easily for the feeling of protection."

Apart from attending church, Maugham left the house only to escort his aunt on her occasional trips into town. There was little for him to do on these excursions except trail after her while she did her shopping, or wait fidgeting while she conducted her business at the bank, but there was often something interesting to look at. In the 1880s Whitstable, on the windswept north coast of Kent looking out over the North Sea, was still primarily a fishing community famous for its oyster beds. The harbor was always full of activity, with the coming and going of fishing boats and oyster dredgers, of shabby little colliers bringing coal from Newcastle, and luggers carrying cargoes of hay and wheat up the Thames to Tower Bridge. Leading up from the harbor was a web of narrow streets of wooden fishermen's houses, outside which on fine days the men sat smoking and mending their nets. Ocasionally Maugham was allowed inside one of these low-roofed dwellings and invited to admire some treasure brought back from the other side of the world, a lacquer box from Japan, a decorated dagger from the bazaars of Istanbul, whose owner would thrill the boy by telling him stories of the distant voyages of his youth. The lengthy high street was lined with shops displaying centuries-old Kentish names: Gann, Kemp, Cobb, Driffield. There was little wheeled traffic, and if Aunt Sophie stopped in the street to gossip with an acquaintance she rarely had to step aside for anything other than the doctor's dogcart or the baker's trap. In winter, Whitstable could be bitterly cold and the icy east wind drove people indoors. But in summer when the weather was fine the little town took on a holiday aspect, with visitors from London strolling down to the beach where they could hire a bathing machine, take a turn on the swing boats, and buy a shrimp tea for sixpence.

Gradually, as Willie grew accustomed to his new surroundings, he came to love the green and gentle Kentish countryside. The shore between Whitstable and the mouth of the Thames was wild and the marshes when overcast appeared gray and desolate, but only half a mile inland the landscape changed. Here was rich farming country, with lush pastures full of sheep, with hawthorn hedges and clumps of ancient elms, with shady lanes and wooded hills. At intervals set back from the road were the farmhouses, with their spacious barns and oasthouses overlooking the hop fields, and in clusters between them the farmworkers' cottages, their tiny gardens ablaze with wallflowers, hollyhocks and tiger lilies, with nearby the little whitewashed inns, the Jolly Sailor, the Merry Ploughman, the Crown and Anchor, their squat doorways draped in honeysuckle. In winter the wind came straight off the North Sea and sometimes it rained for days on end, but even then Maugham found something that moved him in the harshness of that barren coastline. The boy gazing out over the cold waters of the North Sea could imagine what might lie in the gray distance, even if for the present he was firmly anchored to England, with no possibility of venturing beyond.

During his first year in Whitstable it was arranged for Maugham to do his lessons at the house of Dr. Charles Etheridge, a neighbor of the Maughams and one of the town's two physicians. As the boy's education to date had been mainly in French, it was important that he should concentrate on perfecting his English, a task that was not made any easier by his newly developed stammer. In fact, however, he made greatest progress on his own, unconsciously familiarizing himself with the language during the hours he passed reading in his uncle's library, a form of recreation that was popular with the grown-ups as it kept him quiet and out of the way. Spending so much time in his own company, insensibly he formed "the most delightful habit in the world, the habit of reading. . . . Haphazard among the sermons and homilies, travels, the lives of the Saints, the Fathers, the histories of the church, were old-fashioned novels; and these [he] at last discovered. He chose them by their titles, and the first he read was *The Lancashire Witches,* and then he read *The Ad-*

mirable Crichton, and then many more. Whenever he started a book
with two solitary travellers riding along the brink of a desperate
ravine he knew he was safe." And thus Maugham discovered one of
the great passions of his life, a passion that would provide both
pleasure and inspiration, that would encourage and clarify his own
formidable skills as a storyteller, but that would also increase his
isolation: in later life he found it difficult to be in anyone's company
for more than a few hours before the longing came over him to be
alone with a book. Books were to be his great comfort and resource, his most reliable retreat. At this early stage in his development, however, Maugham was aware of none of this. "He did not
know that thus he was providing himself with a refuge from all the
distress of life; he did not know either that he was creating for himself an unreal world which would make the real world of every day
a source of bitter disappointment."

THE VICARAGE LIBRARY PROVIDED a welcome haven, but if Maugham
believed his way of life was now settled he was mistaken. In May
1885, less than nine months after his arrival in England, his world
was again turned upside down when he was sent away to school.

The King's School in Canterbury, situated in the precincts of the
great cathedral, was one of the oldest schools in the country. By the
mid-nineteenth century, however, Canterbury had become something of a backwater, and with the coming of the railways the more
prosperous Kentish families sent their sons to Eton, Harrow, and
Westminster, leaving the King's School to cater mainly to sons of
the local clergy, of the officers at the cavalry depot, and of the
better-off tradesmen and manufacturers. Yet if it could not be
ranked among one of the leading public schools, it was highly regarded within the county; Dickens paid it the compliment of sending David Copperfield to school there.

Accompanied by his uncle, Maugham made the short journey
from Whitstable to Canterbury by train. Apart from his kinder-
garten in Paris, Maugham at eleven years old had had no experience
of school and knew no other boys, and with his head filled with

alarming scenes from *Tom Brown's Schooldays,* he felt sick with apprehension. Most of all he dreaded being mocked for his stammer. On arrival they were shown into the parlor, and while waiting for the headmaster to appear, Maugham in panic blurted out, "Tell him I stammer, Uncle."

The head of the junior school was R. G. Hodgson, a giant of a man with a jovial manner. He gave the newcomers a hearty greeting, after which the vicar immediately took his leave, abandoning his nephew to his fate. Maugham's trunk and toybox were carried upstairs and he was shown where he was to sleep, in a dormitory of narrow, green-curtained cubicles each furnished with a bed, washstand, and chair. By now the day boys were assembling, and Maugham felt overwhelmed by the boisterous crowd surging into the house, all known to one another, pushing and shouting, excitedly bragging about their holidays and taking little notice of the new boy in their midst. By the end of the first morning, however, Maugham, as he had feared he would be, had become a target of derision. His stammer, immediately apparent and intensified by anxiety, was regarded as a huge joke, and in the playground boys fell over themselves imitating his stuttering speech, choking with laughter. Maugham desperately struggled not to give way to tears. "His heart beat so that he could hardly breathe, and he was more frightened than he had ever been in his life."

Even without his stammer Maugham was singularly ill-equipped for school life. Small for his age and far from robust, he suffered from a weak chest and was often unwell; indeed, he missed much of his first term through illness. Although longing to blend in, he was fatally different from the other boys: he had no parents and no friends, knew nothing of current schoolboy customs or slang, had never played cricket or football, and was still not entirely at ease with the English language. "I have never forgotten the roar of laughter that abashed me," he wrote, "when in my preparatory school I read out the phrase 'unstable as water' as though unstable rhymed with Dunstable." In this last area, his brothers' experience had been similar: they, too, were mocked for their French accents, referred to as "froggies" by their schoolfellows. Yet for them the situation was easier: not only did they have one another for company but they were far sturdier than their little brother and all three excelled at sport. Maugham in contrast was not much good at games, the sine qua non at any boys' public school, and at first was considered a dunce because his stammer made him appear inarticulate and stupid.

By the time he arrived in Canterbury, Maugham had already grown accustomed to solitude. Wholly unprepared for communal life, he hated the lack of privacy and was awkward with the ragging, the easy banter and backchat of the other fellows. The torment and ridicule he suffered over his stammer caused him to shrink into himself, and although he longed to be popular he lacked the ability to make himself liked, lacked "that engaging come-hitherness that makes people take to one another on first acquaintance." Despite these obstacles, however, Maugham did well at his work, and at the end of his three years at Hodgson's was awarded a scholarship and the privilege of wearing the scholar's black gown.

IN THE SENIOR SCHOOL Maugham found the quality of life considerably improved. By now he was on comradely terms with a good many of the boys, to whom his disability had become of little interest, and although he made no close friend he was tacitly accepted as one of the herd. It was generally recognized that Maugham was no longer an easy target. He was exceptionally observant and had a sharp wit, much appreciated by those at whom it was not directed, and this was coupled with a fiendish instinct for homing in on others' weakness. Time and again he would come out with some clever criticism to raise a laugh, not realizing that its very accuracy would cause it to rankle long after. Longing to be popular while knowing he was not, Maugham developed a singular habit, one which would eventually serve him well as a novelist. He would take as a model a boy he particularly admired and would imagine he was that boy, would talk with his voice, laugh with his laugh, imitate his gestures and mannerisms. The impersonation became so vivid in his own mind "that he seemed for a moment really to be no longer himself. In this way he enjoyed many intervals of fantastic happiness."

In schoolboy terms Maugham was clever—he had an excellent memory and won prizes in music, divinity, history, and French— so that on the whole he had little to fear from the teaching staff, with the exception of one, the bad-tempered Reverend E. J. Campbell. Nicknamed "Scraggs" for his habit of "scragging," or violently shaking boys by the neck, Campbell was a bully, both physical and mental, one of his favorite techniques being to seize a victim and force him to rub out his mistake on the blackboard with his nose. Campbell's previous post had been in Devon, at Westward Ho!, where he had taught the young Rudyard Kipling, who in *Stalky & Co.* portrays him as the hated and irascible Mr. King. Maugham's portrait is even more savage, and Campbell seen through the eyes of Philip Carey in *Of Human Bondage* is a terrifying figure:

> He began his work in a rage and ended it in a passion. . . . His large face, with indistinct features and small blue eyes, was naturally red, but during his frequent attacks of anger it grew dark and purple.

The other masters, long set in their ways, Maugham regarded with a mixture of tolerance and contempt. He found much of the teaching uninspired, the curriculum having remained unchanged for generations, with heavy emphasis on the teaching of Latin and Greek, and modern languages regarded as unimportant. As might be expected, Maugham was particularly scornful of the lessons in French, taught by masters who although they had a good grasp of grammar made no attempt to reproduce what they considered an entirely unnecessary foreign accent. None of them, in Maugham's disdainful view, could have "got a cup of coffee in the restaurant at Boulogne."

Fortunately not only for Maugham but for the entire school, in 1886 a new headmaster was appointed. At only thirty-two, the

Reverend Thomas Field arrived at the King's School full of energy and fresh ideas. A mesmerizing teacher, he was friendly and approachable, his conversation refreshingly wide-ranging and full of topical reference. As one of the high achievers, Maugham early came to the notice of Mr. Field, who was kind to him, talked to him as an adult, and encouraged him in his interests. Starved for approval and attention, Maugham eagerly responded, bestowing on Field a fervent hero worship. "I adored him," he was later to say. Field became easily the most important figure in the boy's life, and for a time his disaffection for the school diminished and he felt there was little he would not do to please such a sympathetic and imaginative headmaster.

Maugham had a highly developed visual sense, all his life being passionately interested in painting and to a lesser extent architecture, and it was while at Canterbury that he became aware of the first stirrings of an aesthetic perception. As his mood lightened and he no longer needed to dread every aspect of his day, Maugham began consciously to respond to the beauty of his surroundings. "There was a wonderfully cobwebbed feeling about their dizzy and intoxicating antiquity. . . . The whole atmosphere was strangely light and airy, full of the sound of bells and the cries of jackdaws floating around the great Bell Harry Tower." He loved the wide lawns and wisteria-clad walls of the school, the melancholy cry of the rooks in the elm trees, above all the sight of the famous cathedral grandly rooted in all its medieval magnificence. In adult life, Maugham, when in distant parts of the globe, was sometimes overcome by nostalgia when reminded of Canterbury Cathedral, when the sight of some great edifice in Russia, China, or Malaya would suddenly evoke emotional memories of his boyhood.

As conditions improved at school, so did they at home. All holidays were spent at the vicarage, but Maugham was older now and disinclined to submit so completely to his uncle's diktats. He was not in the least afraid of him, knew himself to be a great deal more intelligent, and was fairly confident of getting his own way when it mattered. For long periods now Henry Maugham was away from home, an increasingly fragile state of health obliging him to go off to the Continent for lengthy periods of recuperation. In his absence the atmosphere was noticeably relaxed and Maugham had considerable license to enjoy his independence. During the 1880s a craze for bicycling had gripped the youth of the nation, and Maugham, having persuaded his uncle to buy him one of the new safety bicycles, took a keen pleasure in riding about the countryside, exploring the network of little lanes and on warm days pedaling down to the beach with towel and bathing trunks for a swim.* By the age of fifteen Maugham, although not tall, had grown into an attractive boy, with thick dark hair, brown eyes, and a pale complexion. He had become quite a dandy, taking trouble with his clothes and priding himself on his elegant turnout in white flannels, blue blazer, and a black-and-white straw boater. Anxious to be considered grown-up, he smeared his top lip with Vaseline in the hope of encouraging a mustache, and resented being addressed still as "Master Willie."

> In fact, I did not like either of my names, and spent much time inventing others that would have suited me better. The ones I preferred were Roderic Ravensworth and I covered sheets of paper with this signature in a suitably dashing hand. I did not mind Ludovic Montgomery either.

Following the lead of his uncle and aunt, he "accepted the conventions of my class as if they were the laws of Nature." Regarding himself as a superior youth, he took on their snobbish attitudes, adopting an air of lordly patronage with the tradespeople and complaining fastidiously of the holidaymakers from London who invaded Whitstable in the summer. "We thought London people vulgar. We said it was horrid to have all that rag-tag and bob tail down from town every year."

Both at the vicarage and at school there was a heavy emphasis on religion, and Maugham could not help but be influenced by it. His uncle's speech was garnished with biblical reference, all the masters

---

* His youthful bicycling was to be vividly recalled nearly fifty years later in a crucial scene in *Cakes and Ale*.

at school were ordained, and attendance at church both in Whitstable and Canterbury was frequent and compulsory. Imbibing the pious atmosphere surrounding him, Maugham, like many children, went through an intensely religious phase, serious and devout, reading and rereading the Old and New Testaments and taking a great deal of time and trouble over his prayers. According to the version related in *Of Human Bondage,* almost certainly derived from the actual event, Philip when a boy prays to God to cure his hated affliction, in his case a clubfoot. Having been taught to believe that true faith can move mountains, it never occurs to the boy that God will not grant his petition. "He prayed with all the power of his soul. No doubts assailed him. He was confident in the word of God." In a state of rapturous excitement at the miracle about to be performed, Philip's disappointment when it fails to take place is painful and profound; bitterly disillusioned, he feels betrayed, both by his uncle and by his uncle's God. Such an incident marks the first step in Maugham's loss of faith; and yet he retained throughout his long life a strong interest in religion, in all religions, his emotional attraction toward religious belief always at war with his intellectual rejection of it, subliminally searching for a spiritual resolution that he was never able to achieve. When soon after leaving school he finally abandoned the strong and innocent faith of his boyhood, he felt it as a liberation but also as a loss. At the time hardest to accept was the knowledge that with no expectation of an afterlife he would never see his mother again.

THE KING'S SCHOOL may have prided itself on its close affiliations to the Anglican Church, but its student body was no more highminded than any other group of boys shut up for weeks at a time with scarcely a glimpse of the opposite sex. Among the two hundred boarders it is inconceivable that there did not exist the usual sexual experiment between boys, and Maugham certainly participated in this. (In later life while dining with a close friend at the Garrick Club he pointed out an elderly gentleman respectably eating his dinner as "someone I went to bed with at King's.") In both versions of Maugham's autobiographical novel, written more than twenty years apart, there is a section dealing with the hero's intense infatuation with a classmate. In the earlier novel, which was never published, the reader is left in no doubt as to the physical aspect of the crush, although in the later version Philip's sexual feelings are more obliquely conveyed, and in both instances it is his desperate need for affection that is paramount. In *Of Human Bondage* the object of his earliest passion is the handsome schoolboy Rose,★ good-natured, easygoing, and popular, the antithesis of the solitary Philip, and when Rose casually befriends him, Philip is both amazed and grateful, his gratitude transmuting into a jealous love, to which Rose is completely indifferent. It is possible that Rose's original was a boy named Leonard Ashenden, a classmate of Maugham's, who in all probability would have been known to his schoolfellows as "Ash," a single syllable, like "Rose." Tellingly, the name Ashenden is that of the narrator in *Cakes and Ale* and also of the protagonist in Maugham's collection of First World War spy stories. In a letter written in 1954 in answer to a query from the real Ashenden's widow, Maugham tells her, "I chose the name Ashenden because like Gann, and Driffield, it is a common surname in the neighbourhood of Canterbury [and] the first syllable had to me a peculiar connotation which I found suggestive."

During the Michaelmas term of 1888, when Maugham was fourteen, he suffered a bad attack of pleurisy and had to be dispatched home for the rest of the term. By Christmas he was better, but given his clinical history it was considered imprudent for him to return to school until the weather grew warmer, and so he was sent to Hyères, near Toulon in the south of France. Here he stayed with an Englishman who made his living tutoring convalescent boys; Hyères, like Pau, the town in the Pyrenees where he had been taken by his mother, was much prized for the health-giving proper-

---

★ The name Rose clearly had significance, as Maugham also gave it to the object of Stephen Carey's passion and to the irresistible heroine of *Cakes and Ale.*

ties of its mild climate. It was a strange experience for Maugham to be back in France, the country he had left four years before, whose language he had barely heard spoken intelligibly since.

When Maugham returned to school after Easter the following year, 1889, he found himself out of step. A few months is a long time in the life of a school: his old friends had made new friends, and he had been moved up to a different class, where the work was unfamiliar and the bullying of the hot-tempered Campbell seemed intensified. Maugham's hatred of the man possessed him. "I made up my mind, then and there, that I would never spend another term with that beast of a master." The plan had been for Maugham to go to Cambridge, like his brothers, and in this he was warmly encouraged by Mr. Field, who had no doubt of the boy's ability to win the necessary scholarship if he applied himself. But now his ambitions in that direction were diminished by his loathing for the school. His overwhelming desire was to leave as quickly as possible, and if that meant sacrificing his Cambridge career, then sacrifice it he would. "I was small for my age and frail, but cunning. I had no difficulty in persuading my uncle that with my delicate health it would be safer for me to spend the following winter again with the tutor at Hyères rather than take the risk of another winter in the cold and damp of Canterbury, with the happy result that at the end of that mortifying term I left the King's School for good."

Maugham had got his way, but the indications are that his relief at effecting his escape did not bring him the happiness he had anticipated. Philip Carey, desperate to leave school, also gives up his chance of the famous university. Expecting to feel nothing but excitement on his final day, he is instead tormented by regret:

> His school-days were over, and he was free; but the wild exultation to which he had looked forward at that moment was not there. He walked round the precincts slowly, and a profound depression seized him. . . . He wondered whether he had done right. He was dissatisfied with himself and with all his circumstances.

CHAPTER 2

AT ST. THOMAS'S
HOSPITAL

. . .

WITH HIS FORMAL EDUCATION COMPLETE, MAUGHAM AFTER HIS
second winter at Hyères returned home to the vicarage very much
at loose ends. At sixteen he had no idea what he wanted to do with
his life, except leave Whitstable again as quickly as possible. It was
Aunt Sophie, sympathetic to his situation, who suggested he go to
Germany to learn the language, and she wrote to relations of hers
asking them to recommend a family with whom her young nephew
could stay. The vicar approved of the scheme, no doubt relieved to
have the boy once more off his hands. "He did not much like me,"
Maugham wrote, "for which I cannot blame him, since I do not
think I was a likeable boy, and as it was my own money that was
being spent on my education, he was willing enough to let me do as
I chose." Thus it was arranged that Maugham should travel to Heidelberg, where he would lodge with a professor and his wife who
ran a pension for foreign students.

Arriving in Heidelberg on a sunny May morning in 1890,
Maugham was enchanted by what he saw of the city as he walked
up from the station, following the porter with his luggage-laden
barrow up through the narrow medieval streets and along a shady
avenue to the large white house that was to be his home for the
next year. The Herr Professor, a tall man in middle age with gray-
ing fair hair, was courteous and correct, addressing Maugham in
formal, slightly archaic English, while his wife by contrast was a

stout, red-faced little woman, bright-eyed and bustling, who chattered away in a mixture of German and broken English. At dinner
the first evening Maugham came face-to-face with his fellow guests:
a couple of American theology students, a Frenchman and a Chinese, both studying at the university, and a lanky New Englander,
James Newton, who taught Greek at Harvard and had come to
Germany to broaden his horizons. Maugham's priority was to learn
the language, and in this he was given daily tuition by the professor,
who turned out to be an excellent teacher, hitting on the clever
device of setting his pupil to translate into German one of the
Shakespeare plays he had studied at school. With his retentive memory and good ear Maugham learned quickly, and as soon as he was
reasonably proficient embarked on a study of Goethe, for whose
work his teacher had a fervent enthusiasm. Maugham also enrolled
in courses at the university, where he heard the distinguished
philosopher Kuno Fischer electrify his audiences with his discourses
on Schopenhauer, whose pessimistic theories—that the reason for
human existence is unknown, free will is an illusion, and the afterlife does not exist—came to Maugham as a revelation, further un-
dermining the last small vestiges of his religious faith.

Maugham was a keen student and spent many hours reading and
writing in his little turret room overlooking the treetops. He was
very happy. After the tedium and restrictions of school and the vicarage, he reveled in his independence and responded eagerly to the
stimulus of his new environment. He read not only the German authors to whom he was now introduced but French writers, unknown in Whitstable but whose works had filled the bookshelves at
the Avenue d'Antin: La Rochefoucauld, Racine, Stendhal, Balzac,
Flaubert, Maupassant, Anatole France. He began writing himself,
ambitiously embarking on a centenary life of the composer Meyer-
beer, but he destroyed the manuscript after it was rejected by the
first publisher to whom it was sent. The other young men at the
pension were by several years his senior, and Maugham was impressed by what seemed to him their exceptional intelligence and
sophistication. They were friendly toward him and included him in

their vigorous discussions on art, literature, and theology that often continued late into the night.

The American, James Newton, paid Maugham particular attention, kindly offering to show him the best walks within easy reach of the city. Almost daily they set off together to explore the famous ruined castle or tramp up the Königstuhl to admire the view of the Neckar valley, of the tall roofs and spires of Heidelberg, and farther off the misty outlines of Mannheim and Worms and in the distance the glinting waters of the Rhine. Sometimes they took tea in a leafy beer garden and in the evenings strolled round the Stadtgarten listening to the band. When Newton planned a fortnight's holiday in Switzerland, Maugham, having obtained his uncle's permission, accepted the older man's invitation to go with him, all expenses paid. It seemed an idyllic friendship; and Maugham later claimed it was only with hindsight he realized that his mentor's interest in him had been primarily sexual, that Newton's attentions were inspired less by generosity than by physical attraction.

Soon after their return to Heidelberg, Newton left for Berlin, his place at the pension taken by an Englishman, John Ellingham Brooks. Brooks was recently down from Cambridge and, having wasted a year failing to study law in London, had come to Germany in search of culture. Handsome, with blue eyes, a wide, sensual mouth, and wavy fair hair, Brooks was charming, kindhearted, sentimental, and vain. Passionate about literature, he talked with hypnotic intensity about his favorite authors, all new to Maugham, about Meredith, Swinburne, Walter Pater, and Omar Khayyám. He also wrote poetry himself, mostly of a pessimistic nature, which he recited while tossing back his blond locks and gazing into the middle distance with a vatic blue-eyed stare. Maugham was entranced. He sat spellbound as Brooks held forth on the glories of Italy and Greece, on Shelley and Plato and Oscar Wilde, on Cardinal Newman and Matthew Arnold. Avidly he read what Brooks told him to read, swallowed whole his unremarkable opinions, and was flattered when this charismatic character began to single him out, defending Brooks when the others ridiculed his arguments, as they not infrequently did.

Before long Brooks, like his predecessor, was inviting Maugham to accompany him on walks, during which he would boast of his aesthetic sensibility, his indifference to worldly success, and his disdain for the pitifully humdrum lives he saw his contemporaries leading. Brooks had big plans for himself, and it was only lack of time that so far had prevented his writing the important work that would ensure his place in the pantheon. Such talk was heady stuff for a lonely and intelligent boy, and when it became clear that Brooks required more of him than to be simply an admiring acolyte, Maugham was happy to oblige. Years afterward Maugham confided to a friend that he had lost his virginity to Brooks, but it seems not to have meant very much, only taking one step further the kind of activity that had been common practice at school. Indeed, for Maugham at sixteen, an impressionable and highly sexed adolescent, it was intensely exciting to be the lover of such an apparently brilliant and original young man. In time he came to see through his mentor, dismissing him as a wastrel and poseur, and his embarrassment at having been taken in led him to treat him harshly both in life and in print. But during those early days in Heidelberg, Maugham's relationship with Brooks was inspiring and added greatly to his sense of liberation, to his conviction that at last he was on the threshold of the real world.

One of Brooks's enthusiasms was for the theater, and when the winter repertory season began he and Maugham went two or three times a week to the little Stadttheater, animatedly discussing the production in the tavern afterward. Except at the age of seven when he had seen Bernhardt in Paris, Maugham before he arrived in Germany had never been to a play—the modest touring productions occasionally given in Whitstable had been considered unsuitable entertainment by the vicar—and he was now seized by a passion for the stage. The moment he entered the theater he felt excited and engaged, and the more drama he saw the more he became fascinated by the technique of playwriting, eagerly sketching out plots and writing down snatches of dialogue. Among much else, Brooks and Maugham saw several plays by Ibsen, a writer admired by the intelligentsia but regarded by most decent folk as outrageous and obscene. To Maugham, Ibsen's plays were a revelation. During his time in Germany he went several times to Munich, where it is possible in January 1891 that he was present for the first-ever production of *Hedda Gabler*. It was also in Munich that he caught his one and only sight of the great Norwegian, peacefully reading his paper over a glass of beer at the Maximilianerhof. Heavily under Ibsen's influence, he studied the dramatist's technique by translating into English German versions of Ibsen's plays, and he began experimenting with one-acters characterized by an unflinching realism and much concerned with shameful secrets and venereal disease.

Shortly before Christmas, Brooks left Germany for Florence, where he intended to immerse himself in Dante and Boccaccio, and Maugham was able to resume his studies uninterrupted. But the influence of Brooks had unsettled him, and "the delights of those easy, monotonous and exciting days in Heidelberg" began to pall. Now he was impatient to go home, assert his independence, and begin earning his living.

In July 1891, Maugham returned to Whitstable after his year's absence to find his aunt and uncle visibly diminished: both had aged, his uncle stouter and balder, Aunt Sophie wizened and obviously unwell. With no idea what to do with himself—writing as a profession was considered out of the question—Maugham asked his uncle for advice. The vicar naturally favored the church, but even he accepted that his nephew's stammer made this an unlikely proposition. Maugham's brothers had followed their father into the law; but the law, too, demanded a high level of fluency. Eventually it was Dr. Etheridge, the family doctor, who came to the rescue by suggesting that young Maugham might do worse than to train as a physician at his own alma mater, St. Thomas's Hospital. And so after a few weeks at a crammer's preparing for the necessary examination, on October 3, 1892, Maugham at the age of eighteen entered the medical school as a student.

IT HAD LONG BEEN Maugham's ambition to live in London. Since returning from Heidelberg he had chafed more than ever at the dull domesticity of Whitstable, and recently the gloomy atmosphere at the vicarage had turned even gloomier. In poor health for some time, Aunt Sophie had gone to Bad Ems in Germany in the hope that the waters would restore her, and there at the end of August 1892 she had died. Maugham had grown fond of his aunt, but he had been too much away from home to feel her loss more than slightly. Moreover he had no wish to be reminded of the harrowing bereavements of his early childhood, and now was desperate to escape. Since his school days he had been aware of the lure of London, in his imagination a city of infinite promise. A couple of boys at school had been Londoners and Maugham had been intrigued by their boasted familiarity with the seamier sides of the capital, of "the glitter of cheap restaurants, bars where men, half drunk, sat on high stools talking with barmaids; and under the street lamps the mysterious passing of dark crowds bent upon pleasure."

Such sinister glamour was little in evidence at 11 Vincent Square, a large, slightly shabby Georgian square close by the Thames Embankment, only a short distance from the Houses of Parliament. For £1 a week Maugham had two rooms on the ground floor, a bedroom at the back, and a sitting room with a bay window in the front overlooking a row of enormous plane trees and the wide green expanse of the Westminster School playing fields that the square enclosed. Here he was looked after by his landlady, Eliza Foreman, a friendly soul, cheerful and energetic, who took pride in looking after her gentlemen lodgers, for whom she provided two meals a day, a substantial cooked breakfast and a rather more frugal dinner. Maugham took trouble to make his little parlor comfortable, hanging on the wall a print of a soulful peasant girl holding a mandolin that he had found as a special offer in a Christmas edition of the *Illustrated London News*. Later, as his taste grew more sophisticated, he replaced this luscious piece of kitsch with mezzotints of paintings by Perugino, Hobbema, and Van Dyck bought for a few shillings apiece from a shop in Soho Square.

Classes at the hospital began at 9:00, and every morning Maugham woke to the sound of his landlady lighting the fire in his sitting room. Bathing hurriedly in the tin tub kept under his bed, he ate his breakfast and then walked briskly down to the Embankment, threading his way through the rush-hour crowds surging over Lambeth Bridge, then along Lambeth Palace Road to St. Thomas's. From Monday to Friday he was fully occupied, but during the first few weekends the time hung heavy and Maugham was lonely. He wandered through the National Gallery, strolled around the West End, ate his modest meals in an ABC,★ and most Saturday evenings he went to the theater. It was a relief when Monday morning dawned and he could return to regimented timetables and hospital routine.

St. Thomas's, one of the great London teaching hospitals, was founded as a charitable institution in the twelfth century for the purpose of treating the diseased poor, which seven hundred years later still remained its primary purpose. A notable distinction was conferred on the hospital when Florence Nightingale established her school of nursing there, and Miss Nightingale's dominating influence not only over her school but over the running of the entire complex ensured that high standards were rigorously maintained. At the medical school most students took the Conjoint Board of the College of Surgeons and the College of Physicians, a course costing a little over £300 per annum and stretching over five years, the winter term lasting from October to March, the summer session from May to the end of July.

The subjects of study during the first months were anatomy, biology, physics, and chemistry, and most of this Maugham found ineffably tedious. Dutifully he attended the lectures, learned hundreds of requisite facts by heart, and having equipped himself with a microscope, a mahogany instrument case, and a copy of *Heath's Dissector,* carried out his practical work in the dissecting room, which was painted an ominous red and reeked of disinfectant. This part of the course first-year students often found difficult to stomach, although Maugham never suffered from squeamishness and proved dexterous with the scalpel. The hospital provided the corpses, purchased at £5 each from the local workhouse and pre-

★ A popular chain of tea shops run by the Aerated Bread Company.

served with a mixture of vermilion and arsenic (the former to high-light the arteries, the latter to prevent putrefaction), and the students worked in pairs, clubbing together to buy their body parts, arms and legs 12 shillings and sixpence, abdomen seven and six, head and neck 15 shillings. As a guard against nausea, the lighting of cigarettes and pipes was encouraged, a privilege that naturally fostered a sociable atmosphere, and as a result "a good deal of gossip went on over the dissection of a 'part.'" Indeed at the end of the morning, when the demonstrator had left and the mangled parts been returned to the students' lockers, the dissecting room took on quite a cozy atmosphere, a home away from home where shirt-sleeved young men with a few minutes to spare could drop in for a quick smoke and a gossip.

As at school, Maugham craved popularity and acceptance, but he was still shy, still inhibited by his stammer, and although he was well disposed toward his contemporaries, there was little common ground. Those who had been to university were inclined to be standoffish, or so Maugham felt; he had no interest in the seemingly universal enthusiasm for cricket and football; neither did he wish to take part in the prodigious after-hours drinking bouts, having learned from unpleasant experience that more than a small quantity of alcohol made him sick. There were one or two handsome fellows with whom he became silently infatuated, envying their charm and high spirits, but by now he was adept at hiding his feelings. His guarded manner made any real intimacy impossible, and by his classmates he was regarded as an aloof, almost forbidding individual.

The students at St. Thomas's, like young men everywhere, talked exhaustively about sex and constantly bragged about their sexual exploits, a subject that interested Maugham a good deal. Until now his physical relations had been only with men and he felt ashamed of his lack of experience with women. One Saturday evening he walked up to the Strand to pick up a prostitute, who for £1 agreed to spend the night with him. Reassured by her youthful, almost countrified appearance, he accompanied her to a small hotel off Shaftesbury Avenue where he was led into a bare little room smelling of stale tobacco, furnished only with a chair, a washstand,

and a big wooden bed with dirty sheets. The result of the encounter was a dose of the clap, necessitating a discreet visit to one
of the house physicians for treatment. But far from embarrassment,
Maugham felt pleased with himself, proud to be able to join in
boasting with the other chaps, and perhaps privately relieved to discover he was able to function "normally."

Throughout his life an appearance of conventionality was of
profound importance to Maugham. The fact of his bisexuality had
to be kept secret from most sections of the society in which he
moved, and this need for secrecy was something that subliminally
he recognized early on. Learning in childhood how to live undercover, Maugham rarely revealed himself except to his closest intimates. His French upbringing and his stammer had set him apart
from the boys at school, and now to be categorized as an invert, as
the term then was, and thus a member of yet another unpopular
minority, would have been painfully difficult to accept. At twenty
he was well aware of his sexual orientation, of his feelings for men,
although for years he tried to pretend that such feelings were no
more than a minor aberration. "I tried to persuade myself," he said
in later life, "that I was three-quarters normal and that only a quarter of me was queer—whereas really it was the other way round."
He was struck by an incident that took place while he was going
over his dissected "part" with the demonstrator; he failed to find
the specified nerve, and when it was pointed out to him, he
protested it was in the wrong place. "I complained of the abnor-
mality, and [the demonstrator], smiling, said that in anatomy it was
the normal that was uncommon. . . . The remark sank into my
mind," wrote Maugham afterward, "and since then it has been
forced upon me that it is true of man as well as of anatomy."

PRIVATE AND SELF-CONTAINED, Maugham took little part in the
social life of the hospital. "[I] made few friends there," he recalled,
"for I was occupied with other things." Certainly medicine was of
small interest: he knew he needed to qualify, as that would provide
him with a career on which to fall back if all else failed; but

Maugham was determined to make his living by his pen, and single-minded in this pursuit, he allowed nothing and nobody to get in its way. A passionate autodidact and exceptionally disciplined and industrious, Maugham read prodigiously, not only in English literature—novels, plays, poetry—but also in French, German, Russian, and Italian. He copied out passages from Swift, Dryden, Jeremy Taylor, committing parts of them to memory. His head was filled with ideas and he covered page after page in his notebooks with outlines for stories and dramatic plots, with scraps of dialogue and with observations and reflections. "I was writing," he said, "because I could not help it." His immediate ambition was to write a play, and he continued to go regularly to the theater, often in the company of a good-looking young man whom he had first met in Heidelberg, Walter Adney Payne.

Payne's father, George Payne, was a leading figure in the London music hall, and as manager of the Tivoli in the Strand, the New Oxford on Oxford Street, and the London Pavilion in Piccadilly, he enjoyed a virtual monopoly over the West End. As Maugham, the medical student, and Payne, studying to be a chartered accountant, were both chronically short of funds, Payne senior was a valuable source of free tickets, enabling them to go nearly every Saturday afternoon to the halls. In the evening they went to the theater, where from their cheap seats in the pit they saw such memorable productions as Wilde's *A Woman of No Importance, The Second Mrs. Tanqueray* with Mrs. Patrick Campbell, and George Alexander's staging of *The Importance of Being Earnest*. On January 5, 1895, they were among the fashionable audience at the St. James's Theatre for the disastrous first night of Henry James's play, *Guy Domville,* when the distinguished author while taking his bow was humiliatingly booed off the stage. It was an agonizingly distressing scene that Maugham never forgot. "[James] was greeted with such an outburst of boos and catcalls as only then have I heard in the theatre," he wrote many years later. "He confronted the hostile audience, his jaw fallen so that his mouth was slightly open and on his countenance a look of complete bewilderment. He was paralysed. I don't know why the curtain wasn't immediately brought down."

Pictures were another passion of Maugham's, and here he had a mentor in the eccentric form of one Wentworth Huyshe. A generation older than Maugham, Huyshe had been a distinguished war correspondent for both the *New York Herald* and the London *Times*. He had lived and worked in London, Paris, and New York and had married twice, eventually settling with his wife and nine children in Essex, where he led a bohemian existence in pursuit of his many and varied interests. A friend first of Harry Maugham, Huyshe saw considerable promise in Harry's younger brother. He encouraged Maugham with his writing and took him to concerts, galleries, and museums, teaching him how to look at pictures and introducing him to new names in various branches of the arts. When Maugham's first novel was published a few years later, he inscribed a copy to Wentworth Huyshe and sent it to him with a grateful letter. "I can never forget how kind you were to me when I was a stupid boy, & you took me about & showed me things, & inspired me with all sorts of new ideas. I can honestly say that I owe a very great deal to you, and now it is a great pleasure to me to be able to send you my first-born."

Meanwhile at the hospital Maugham had moved on to study practical pharmacy and materia medica, subjects which he found marginally less tedious than anatomy, quite enjoying the business of rolling pills, mixing ointments, and grinding up powders. But it was not until he took his turn as a clerk in the Out-Patients' Department that suddenly his attention was fully engaged. Here for the first time he found his work of consuming interest, fascinated not by the range of ailments but by the men and women themselves who day after day came to the hospital for help.

Lambeth in the 1890s was one of the poorest and most overcrowded areas of London. Families tended to be large, and although infant mortality was high (deaths of the under-fives accounted for nearly 50 percent of the total mortality rate), many couples had ten, eleven, or even twelve children, with whom they lived in dark, cramped houses backing onto filthy courts with open sewers, or in overcrowded tenements where conditions were squalid in the extreme. Many of those fortunate enough to be employed worked in sweatshops, where sometimes seventeen or eighteen men and women were crammed into a tiny top-floor room, inadequately lit and heated, with water closets without water and the only ventilation coming from broken windows nailed shut, the empty panes filled up with canvas. Disease ran rife, and drink, easily available and comparatively cheap, was the most popular panacea, with the result that high levels of domestic violence were commonplace. Death from starvation was not infrequently the end for the elderly and the unemployed. Such was the population that depended on St. Thomas's for its free medical care, and with which Maugham was now in daily contact.

From early afternoon the waiting room was thronged with men, women, and children, and despite the strong odor of disinfectant the stench of unwashed bodies grew sickeningly pungent as the day wore on. The men were seen first, most suffering from chronic bronchitis, or "a nasty 'acking cough," as it was usually described, as well as venereal disease and every possible variety of drink-related disorder. With the women, aged prematurely by frequent childbirth, the main problems stemmed from malnutrition and from the split lips, black eyes, and broken ribs regularly dealt them by their drunken husbands. Maugham assisted the house physician, who allotted him the more straightforward cases to deal with on his own, and it was now that he heard the stories of these frequently harrowing lives. For the patients it was unusual to find among the hard-pressed medical staff someone who took such an interest in their personal problems, and they responded gratefully to this sympathetic young doctor with his gentle manner and expressive dark eyes. Unlike many of his colleagues, Maugham never patronized his patients: it was understanding they wanted, not pity, and through his genuine interest he came to learn more about their lives and of their teeming, claustrophobic world than did many of the highly qualified doctors who saw their patients only as medical specimens. Never before had Maugham been confronted by such a variety of character and of physical type, and he was enthralled by the narratives that day after day were spun out before him, excited by their indefinable potential. So absorbed did he become in these glimpses of life in the raw, of human nature at its most unguarded, that when he himself fell ill—with septic tonsillitis contracted after performing a postmortem on a badly decomposed corpse—in spite of being nursed in the private wing and "treated like a crowned head," he could hardly wait to resume his duties.

BUSY ALTHOUGH HE WAS at the hospital, and in his spare time immersed in his own reading and writing, Maugham nonetheless maintained his links with family and friends. One of the latter was John Ellingham Brooks, last seen in Heidelberg, who now came wafting in from the Continent, where he had been traveling extensively and writing flowery letters about love and art and the glories of Italy, particularly as seen through the eyes of Ruskin and Pater. As before in Germany, Maugham found Brooks's company inspirational, and falling again under his influence he took the opportunity of his first Easter vacation, six weeks in the spring of 1894, to visit Italy. Already the previous year at Brooks's instigation he had begun to study Italian, and now with £20 in his pocket he set off, spending a few days in Paris on the way in order to see two of his brothers, Charles and Harry, and to visit the Louvre. Fired by Pater's essay on the *Mona Lisa,* he made excitedly for Leonardo's famous portrait, but "I was bitterly disappointed. Was this the picture Pater had written about with such eloquence and in prose so ornate?" He continued on to Genoa and Pisa, and then to Florence, where he stayed for more than a fortnight. Eager to learn, Maugham made good use of his time. "I lived laborious days," as he rightly recalled, beginning each morning with a couple of hours studying Dante before setting off to see the sights, Ruskin in hand. Only in the evening did he allow himself a little recreation, wandering out after dinner in search of adventure, but according to the account written years later, "such was my innocence, or at least my shyness, I always came home as virtuous as I had gone out."

Shortly after returning from Italy, Maugham had two family weddings to attend. The first, and much the more unexpected, was that of the Reverend Henry Maugham, who, a widower for not quite two years, had proposed marriage to Ellen Matthews, the fifty-year-old spinster daughter of a Gen. Henry Matthews of Bath. The wedding took place on June 6, 1894, after which the new Mrs. Maugham was brought to Whitstable, where she was soon discovered to be a merry creature, in every way a lively contrast to her predecessor. During Aunt Ellen's occupation the vicarage became a much more cheerful house to visit, and it was clear that she made the vicar very happy.

Two weeks later, on June 21, Charlie, eldest of the four Maugham brothers, was married in London to Mabel Hardy, daughter of the animal painter Heywood Hardy. For the past five years Charlie had been working in Paris, a junior partner in the family law firm, now Sewell et Maugham, and it was here that he had met his future wife, who was studying at the Conservatoire. They returned to Paris after the wedding, where they embarked on the kind of prosperous, sociable way of life that the Maugham parents had enjoyed a generation earlier. Like his father, Charlie was good-natured and clever, while Mabel, or "Beldy" as she was known, a talented amateur artist, was vivacious and fun, both popular members of Parisian expatriate society. For a time Charlie's younger brother Harry worked with him at Sewell et Maugham, but the arrangement had not been a success. Harry was an unconventional character who had little interest in the law, his real ambition, like Maugham's, to be a writer. Gentle, kindhearted, but also thin-skinned and neurotic, Harry spent most of his spare time composing lengthy verse dramas and sitting in cafés in company with like-minded young men, artists and poets; soon he gave up any pretense of pursuing a legal career, left Paris, and after a spell in London moved to Italy. He and his younger brother had much in common, aesthetically and intellectually; they were both outsiders, shy and insecure; they were both sexually nonconformist; they both wanted to write; and yet they never became close. They were separated geographically, but also by a lack of that fraternal bond that never had the chance properly to form between Maugham and his brothers.

With Charlie and Harry living on the Continent, Maugham saw most of Freddie, the second oldest, who had remained in London

and joined chambers in Lincoln's Inn. Ironically it was their relationship that came to be most strained, the ultraconventional Freddie coming to regard his younger brother with a censoriousness
deeply resented by Maugham, who with part of himself would
have liked to have attained the ironclad respectability of his sibling.
As young men, however, this mutual hostility was mild and inter-
mittent, and they had enough of a shared past and interests in
common—the theater, golf, looking at pictures—for them to enjoy
each other's company, at least in small doses. Freddie, in adulthood
always addressed as "F.H.," was a handsome, athletic man of dour
demeanor, his icy reserve effectively concealing a sensitiveness and
vulnerability that was rarely revealed, even within the family.
In December 1896, F.H. would marry Helen ("Nellie") Romer,
daughter of a High Court judge. While F.H. appeared joyless and
austere, Nellie was affectionate, gregarious, and high-spirited, possessed of enormous charm and a rambunctious sense of humor. If
her boisterous jollity sometimes grated, F.H. nevertheless depended
on his wife for the sympathy and warmth he craved but could not
show. She and Maugham took to each other at once and quickly
became close friends, Nellie inviting her brother-in-law to family
occasions, including him in amateur theatricals, and often asking
him to tea on her own, when the two of them would gossip amicably before her husband with his blighting presence returned to the
house in the evening.

When Maugham resumed his studies at the hospital after the
summer of 1894, he moved from Out-Patients to working on the
wards, accompanying the house physician on his rounds, carrying
out tests, and writing up case notes. As before, Maugham enjoyed
contact with the patients, and yet the wards lacked the drama and
excitement of his previous post, and he welcomed the transition to
surgical clerk, assisting at operations, standing beside the surgeon
ready to hand him his instruments. If the operation were an unusual one, the theater galleries would fill up with observers, but on
most days there was not more than a handful of students watching,
which gave the proceedings a coziness that Maugham relished.

Occasionally his sangfroid deserted him, as he recounts in a description of watching an operation that painfully brought back memories of his mother's death. "The other day I went into the theatre to see a Caesarian," he wrote in his notebook for 1897.

> The operation appeared to go very well and Dr. C's face beamed when he extracted the baby. This morning I was in the ward and asked one of the nurses how she was getting on. She told me she'd died in the night. I don't know why, it gave me a shock and I had to frown because I was afraid I was going to cry. It was silly, I didn't know her, I'd only seen her on the operating table. I suppose what affected me was the passion of that woman, just an ordinary hospital patient, to have a baby, a passion so intense that she was willing to incur the frightful risk; it seemed hard, dreadfully hard, that she had to die.

The death of a mother in childbirth always touched Maugham deeply, and it was a theme that was to appear a number of times in his fiction.

In both the Easter and summer vacations of 1895 Maugham went again to Italy, this time to Capri in the company of Ellingham Brooks. Describing the island as "the most enchanting spot I had ever seen," Maugham was bewitched by the romantic beauty of the place, reveling in the warmth, the scented air, and the atmosphere of dreamy tranquillity that Capri possessed in those days when it was still a rural community with a small foreign population, visited by only a few tourists who tended to avoid the summer months. On this first visit Maugham and Brooks lodged in a modest *pensione* where four shillings a day bought board, lodging, and a view of Vesuvius from the bedroom window. Mornings were dedicated to study, after which at midday they swam off the rocks at the Bagno Timberino and basked in the sun before lazily wending their way uphill for lunch under a vine-covered pergola. Every evening after dinner they joined the throng at Morgano's, the wine shop beside the Piazza Grande. Here the expatriate community gathered to exchange news and gossip, Maugham listening intently as Brooks and his new acquaintances, writers, painters, sculptors, held forth on art, philosophy, and literature. Lacking their learning and fluency, Maugham felt himself at a disadvantage; he sat smoking and saying little, never mentioning his own attempts at composition.

> I thought it all grand. Art, art for art's sake, was the only thing that mattered in the world. . . . They were all agreed about this, that they burned with a hard, gem-like flame. I was too shy to tell them that I had written a novel and was half-way through another and it was a great mortification to me, burning as I was too with a hard, gem-like flame, to be treated as a philistine who cared for nothing but dissecting dead bodies and would seize an unguarded moment to give his best friend an enema.

Inhibited in conversation he may have been, yet the tongue-in-cheek reference to giving his best friend an enema indicates confidence in other areas. Maugham at twenty-one took care with his appearance and had begun to dress with a certain flair; with his slim build and expressive features he was an engaging young man, sexually magnetic and well aware of the glances he attracted. The powerful creative impulse, which inspired so many ideas and drove him to write for hours every night, materialized also in a sexual energy that, even while he was sitting mainly motionless and silent as during the evening sessions at Morgano's, was potent. The fact that he and Brooks were lovers would have caused little comment on Capri, where irregular relationships were accepted almost as the norm. The island had long enjoyed a reputation for tolerance toward its foreign community, many of whom were drawn there as much by the good-looking Capresi youth as by the beauty of the setting. As a later inhabitant, Compton Mackenzie, wrote of Capri, "Its reputation as a decomposer of character was classic." A blind eye was turned to the conduct of most of these exotic imports, for instance, the notorious Count Fersen, pedophile and opium addict, or the ex-vicar of Sandringham, who had arrived suddenly after trouble with choirboys at home, or Oscar Wilde's nemesis, Lord Alfred Douglas, trailing clouds of infamy and seen openly misbehaving with a pretty cabin boy on his yacht. Only occasionally did one of them go too far, like the arms magnate Friedrich Krupp, reports of whose behavior with underage boys were beginning to cause alarm, eventually resulting in his having to leave the island. In general, however, the moral climate was unusually relaxed, and to those who found the laws and attitudes of northern Europe a serious hindrance to their preferred way of life, Capri was a welcome haven. Such a one was John Ellingham Brooks, who within a couple of weeks felt so entirely at ease that he decided not to return to England but to remain on Capri for good.

Brooks's decision was timely. In the same month that he and Maugham first visited Capri, April 1895, the trial was taking place in London of Oscar Wilde. Wilde's was not the only, nor indeed the first, such trial to be exhaustively reported since the passing ten years earlier of the Criminal Law Amendment Act,[*] but it made a greater impact and reached a far wider audience on account of the fame of the accused, the social status of the accuser, the Marquess of Queensberry, and the headline-grabbing wit, flamboyance, and panache with which Wilde, fatally, conducted himself in court. Here a world was revealed of rent boys and male brothels and perverse sexual practices hitherto undreamed of by the majority of the nation's newspaper-reading population. Wilde's subsequent sentencing to two years' hard labor struck terror in the hearts of many men who had imagined that a modicum of discretion was all that was necessary to keep them out of trouble. A significant number decided there and then to leave for the Continent, and it was said that on the night after Wilde's arrest, instead of the usual sixty or so crossing from England to France, six hundred gentlemen took passage on the Channel steamers. The trial of Oscar Wilde was to cast a long shadow, and for seventy years Maugham's generation had to live with the very real fear of blackmail, exposure, public scandal, and arrest. It is unlikely that Maugham at only twenty-one fully understood the relevance of these events to his own life, but the

---

[*] The Criminal Law Amendment Act of 1885 proscribed all homosexual acts between males.

Wilde case could not fail to increase his determination to keep areas of his private life undercover, to encourage the habit of concealment.

Back in London, on the occasions when he was seen by one of his fellow students outside the hospital it was noted that he was always with the same young man, almost certainly his theatergoing friend, Walter Adney Payne. Payne, "dear companion of my lonely youth," as Maugham described him, was the first in a series of close male associates on whom throughout his life Maugham heavily depended. There is a visible pattern that runs through these relationships, beginning with a sexual affair which then evolves into an intimate friendship, with the onetime lover becoming part secretary, part companion and facilitator. Although nothing remains of any personal correspondence (on Payne's death, all letters between them were, on Maugham's instructions, destroyed), the two men were close for more than twenty years. Crucially, Payne provided an essential service: he enabled Maugham to make contact with strangers. Because of his stammer, Maugham found it next to impossible to initiate the kind of exchange so easily struck up with others in public places, and thus, knowing that he could not speak without the risk of making a fool of himself, Maugham liked to rely on someone else to start the conversation. In this respect Payne, with his good looks and pleasant manner, was the ideal companion.

Maugham was irresistibly drawn to the sexual underworld. He soon learned that a man about town never went to the music hall before nine, as that was the hour when prostitutes of both sexes arrived to ply their trade, strolling enticingly up and down among the gentlemen smoking and drinking in the promenade bar. But Maugham's early attempt at picking up a tart here, an alarmingly self-possessed young woman, ended in humiliation when she simply turned her back and walked contemptuously away from his stammered offer to buy her a drink. Outside in the Strand, trade was relatively cheap, the pricier rent boys and "daughters of joy" concentrating on prosperous Piccadilly. A slender figure in his hat and dark overcoat, Maugham, fascinated, would watch them as they sauntered along looking for custom, invisible to the ordinary couples and family parties making for omnibus and underground after an evening's blameless entertainment.

IN OCTOBER 1896 Maugham arrived at the final stage of his training at St. Thomas's, the study of obstetrics and gynecology. The first morning's lecture was memorable. "Gentlemen," the instructor began, "woman is an animal that micturates once a day, defecates once a week, menstruates once a month, parturates once a year and copulates whenever she has the opportunity." Recently a new requirement had been introduced, a course in practical midwifery, for which students were expected to be on call for a period of three weeks, and within a mile's radius of the hospital, to attend a minimum of twenty confinements. During his tour of duty Maugham was called out on sixty-three occasions. Temporarily lodged in a room opposite the main gates where he could be quickly summoned by the porter, he was rarely able to snatch more than a couple of hours' sleep, and yet he was almost unaware of his exhaustion, so absorbed was he in what he witnessed of his patients' lives. It was the first time he had worked outside the hospital precincts, and it was only now that Maugham saw for himself the frightening reality of the poverty in which large numbers struggled to exist, experienced at close quarters the noise, the stench, the overcrowding, the filthy, verminous conditions from which for many there was no chance of escape. If the head of the family were employed, then life was tolerable; if not, then the situation was desperate, and in such cases the arrival of another baby was regarded with despair. "Accidents" were not infrequent: mothers rolled on their babies while they slept, and errors of diet were not always the result of carelessness.

In a passage written fifty years later, Maugham recalls his induction into the slums of Lambeth. It was usually the husband or a small child of the expectant mother who led him through the dark and silent streets,

> up stinking alleys and into sinister courts where the police hesitated to penetrate, but where your black bag protected

you from harm. You were taken to grim houses, on each floor of which a couple of families lived and down into a stuffy room, ill-lit with a paraffin lamp, in which two or three women, the midwife, the mother, the "lady as lives on the floor below" were standing round the bed on which the patient lay. Sometimes you waited in that room for two or three hours, drinking a friendly cup of tea with the midwife and going down in the street below now and then to get a breath of air. The husband was sitting on the step and you sat down beside him and chatted.

In cases of emergency Maugham could summon help from the senior obstetric clerk, but by the time the SOC arrived it was often too late: the baby had failed to breathe or the mother had bled to death and there was nothing to be done. After nights like these it was a relief to come out at dawn into the fresh air and walk beside the Thames watching the sky turn pink and the early morning mist dissolve over the water.

It was during Maugham's training in midwifery that the idea came to him for a novel. Over the past few years he had experimented with a number of projects, his chief ambition being to write for the theater. The plays he had submitted, however, had been rejected, and so he planned instead to complete two or three novels in the hope that if these were published, managers would look more favorably on his dramatic work.

This was an exciting time in publishing. During the 1890s a number of lively new publishing houses had been founded, among them Heinemann, Hutchinson, Methuen, and the Bodley Head; and as the sway of the three-decker novel and the circulating library had recently collapsed, the way had been left clear for young writers to experiment with different and shorter forms. While browsing in the bookshops Maugham had been attracted by the Pseudonym Library, a popular series of cheap paperbound books published by the enterprising Thomas Fisher Unwin. Unwin had set up his own business in the 1870s and was notorious both for taking risks and for driving a hard bargain. Supported by, in the words of Ford Madox Ford, a "heaven-sent" team of readers that included the influential Edward Garnett and, briefly, G. K. Chesterton, Unwin had made some notable discoveries, numbering among his authors Yeats, Galsworthy, H. G. Wells, George Moore, and Joseph Conrad. Maugham sent in a couple of short stories, one of which, "A Bad Example," about a good man whose goodness leads his selfish family to regard him as mentally unbalanced,* was passed to Garnett, who advised against publication. "There is some ability in this, but not very much. Mr. Maugham has imagination and he can write prettily, but his satire against society is not deep enough or humorous enough to command attention. He should be advised to try the humbler magazines for a time, and if he tries anything more important to send it to us." As a result of this report Unwin rejected both stories, on the excuse that they were too short to stand on their own; he added, however, that if in the future Mr. Maugham chose to submit a full-length novel he would be pleased to read it. Intensely excited by this morsel of encouragement, Maugham immediately set to work.

Liza of Lambeth, or *A Lambeth Idyll,* as it was originally titled, is set in the slums with which Maugham's medical training had lately made him so familiar. Eighteen-year-old Liza Kemp is a factory girl living in a small single room with her alcoholic mother. Pretty and spirited, Liza is fond of a good time and not yet ready to settle down to a life of marital drudgery and years of childbearing. Full of ill-defined longings for love and something greater than her narrow world can offer, she allows herself to be seduced by an older, married man, by whom she becomes pregnant. Eventually she goes into labor while helplessly drunk, dying as she miscarries, with her tipsy mother watching over her, assisted by a garrulous midwife who has witnessed such a scene many times before.

As Maugham's literary taste over the past few years had been strongly influenced by John Ellingham Brooks, he might well have chosen to model his style on Brooks's beloved Pater, or on one of

---

* A theme to which Maugham was to return nearly forty years later in his final play, *Sheppey.*

the fin-de-siècle Decadents, such as Huysmans or Wilde; but in the event it was the French realists whom he chose to follow, Zola and Maupassant, the latter in particular, whose vernacular style of narrative exactly suited the unromantic nature of his subject. In an introduction to a later edition of *Liza,* Maugham wrote, "I had at that time a great admiration for Guy de Maupassant . . . who had so great a gift for telling a story clearly, straightforwardly and effectively," three adverbs which may justly be applied to *Liza,* by any standards an accomplished work of fiction and impressive indeed for a first novel. In writing *Liza,* Maugham explained, "I described without addition or exaggeration the people I had met in the Out-Patients' Department at the Hospital and in the District during my service as an Obstetric Clerk. . . . My lack of imagination . . . obliged me to set down quite straightforwardly what I had seen with my own eyes and heard with my own ears." He was later to claim that *Liza* was "the first of the realistic descriptions of the London slums that the English public had had a chance of reading," although in fact it was only one of a number published in that period giving an authentic depiction of the lives of the urban poor.

Liza of Lambeth, written in three French school exercise books, was completed in six months, and on January 14, 1897, the manuscript dispatched to Unwin. Of the three readers who were shown the text, one, Vaughan Nash, disliked it—vulgar, revoltingly frank, and lacking in romance—but the other two, of whom one was Edward Garnett, declared enthusiastically in its favor. "A very clever realistic study of factory girls and coster life," wrote Garnett. "If Fisher Unwin does not publish *A Lambeth Idyll* somebody else certainly will. . . . Mr. Maugham has insight & humour, & will probably be heard of again. . . . N.B. The conversation is remarkably well done." On the strength of these recommendations and after only one requested alteration—the changing of the word "belly" to "stomach"—a contract was signed in April between T. Fisher Unwin and William Somerset Maugham of St. Thomas's Hospital. *Liza of Lambeth* was to be published not, as originally intended, in the Pseudonym Library, but under Maugham's own name. The terms of the contract were hardly generous, but neither were they unusual: Unwin was taking a risk with an unknown author at a period when it was customary for advances to be small and royalties frequently deferred until production costs had been recovered, a slow process in this instance as Unwin failed to sell the book to the United States. The American publisher Charles Scribner, reporting back to his firm in New York, wrote, "Unwin is indeed a most troublesome person and I am glad I escaped him in London until the last day. Of the projects submitted to us by him, I myself declined the slum story."

Liza was published in September 1897, the same year as *Captains Courageous* by Rudyard Kipling, Bram Stoker's *Dracula, The Invisible Man* by H. G. Wells, and *What Maisie Knew* by Henry James, yet despite such formidable competition the unknown W. Somerset Maugham attracted considerable attention, critics on the whole applauding the author's talent while regretting his shocking subject matter. "The whole book reeks of the pot-house and is uncompromisingly depressing," wrote the reviewer in the *Daily Mail,* "but it is powerfully and even cleverly written and must be recognized as a true and vivid picture of the life which it depicts." An enthusiastic entry appeared in *The St. Thomas's Hospital Gazette,* which made a point of noticing books written by members of staff. After a review of Dr. Anderson's *Deformities of Fingers and Toes,* William Somerset Maugham was congratulated on a "great and well-deserved success [with *Liza of Lambeth,* whose] uncompromising vigour of both plot and style will appeal strongly to all lovers of realism."

Unwin, a sharp operator who thoroughly understood the value of publicity, sent the book to a number of high-profile personalities who he hoped might bring it to a wider notice, among them Basil Wilberforce, future archdeacon of Westminster, who obligingly made it the subject of his sermon one Sunday at the Abbey. Another recipient was Joseph Conrad, whose *The Nigger of the Narcissus* was also published by Unwin that year. "I've just finished reading *Liza of Lambeth,*" Conrad wrote to Unwin. "There is *any amount* of good things in the story and no distinction of any kind. It will be fairly successful I believe, for it is a 'genre' picture without any atmosphere. . . . He just looks on—and that is just what the general reader prefers. The book reminds me of [George] Du Maurier's drawings—same kind of art exactly, only in another sphere." Maugham was delighted with the attention his book was receiving, and even more delighted when after only a couple of weeks following publication he called at Paternoster Square and was told that the first edition of two thousand copies was sold out and a second already printing.

It was at this point that *Liza* came under attack. An unsigned article appeared in the literary journal *The Academy,* accusing Maugham of plagiarism, pointing out similarities between *Liza* and another "slum" novel published at the end of the previous year, *A Child of the Jago* by Arthur Morrison. Quick to defend himself, Maugham wrote to *The Academy,* "I have not yet had an opportunity of reading Mr. Arthur Morrison's books, so I cannot tell what similarity there may be between them and my own. . . . It is perhaps a little annoying to be charged with plagiarism, when my book was finished three months before the *Child of the Jago* appeared." Maugham was always notoriously vague about dates, and his statement is not strictly accurate: *A Child of the Jago* was published at the end of 1896, when Maugham had not quite completed *Liza;* yet it is unlikely he would have read Morrison's novel before finishing his own. Moreover, apart from the setting, there are few true parallels to be drawn, since Morrison's work, with its pathetic child hero, portrays a desperation, a hopelessness and violence far more savage than anything depicted by Maugham. There is, however, a strong possibility that Maugham was influenced by an earlier work of Morrison's, *Tales of Mean Streets,* a collection of short stories published in 1894, in the first of which, "Lizerunt," there are clear similarities to the later *Liza.*

The author's six complimentary copies were sent to family and friends, first among them Walter Adney Payne, inscribed to "Adney, with the author's love." Another went to Maugham's mentor, Wentworth Huyshe, and one to each of the Maugham brothers, none of whom expressed much pleasure in the present, Harry disparaging his brother's literary talent while Charlie expressed himself disgusted by the novel's content, an opinion shared by

Freddie's wife, Nellie, who noted in her diary that *Liza of Lambeth* was "a most unpleasant book." A copy was also dispatched to the vicarage, but the Reverend Henry had no time to read it for he died a few days later, aged sixty-nine, having been in poor health for some time. Maugham and Harry went down to Whitstable for the funeral on September 21, an event that was well attended by the little town, whose respect, if not affection, the vicar had won over the years. For his part, Maugham felt neither respect nor affection. Like Philip Carey, "He had no feeling for the old man, he had never liked him; he had been selfish all his life, selfish to the wife who adored him, indifferent to the boy who had been put in his charge; he was not a cruel man, but a stupid, hard man, eaten up with a small sensuality."

Finally, in October 1897, Maugham received his diploma from St. Thomas's qualifying him to practice as an MRCS (Member of the Royal College of Surgeons) and LRCP (Licentiate of the Royal College of Physicians). Somewhat to his surprise, the senior obstetric physician offered him an appointment, but with his ambition set on a career as a writer he turned it down. He had proved himself competent in medicine, and in later life he would always acknowledge the debt he owed to his training. "I think," he wrote in old age, "I learned pretty well everything I know about human nature in the 5 years I spent at St. Thomas's Hospital." Had *Liza* failed, his plan had been to take a job as a ship's doctor, which would at least have provided him with the longed-for chance to travel; as it was, the success of his novel gave him the assurance to leave medicine altogether. "I am sorry I abandoned medicine so soon," he said. "It was idiotic. Absolutely idiotic. I could just as well have written at night and avoided the desperate financial struggle I had."

After graduating, Maugham went to see Fisher Unwin, who asked him what his plans were.

> I told him that I was throwing up medicine . . . and meant to earn my living as a writer. He put his arm round my shoulder.
>   "It's very hard to earn a living by writing," he said. "Writing is a very good staff, but a very bad crutch."

I shrugged my shoulders with scorn. My first book was a success. I was full of confidence.

Unwin was at his most genial, pressing Maugham to start work on another, much longer novel about life in the slums, which now his name was known would have an even greater success than *Liza*. Maugham was unenthusiastic. "I was no longer interested in the slums once I had written a book about them," as he dismissively remarked. Instead he surprised his publisher by telling him he had already completed his next work, *The Making of a Saint,* a historical novel written during the previous summer on Capri.

Leaving the manuscript with Unwin, Maugham shortly afterward departed for Spain, where he was to stay for nearly a year, confident that by the time he returned his reputation as a professional man of letters would be established. In this expectation he was to be disappointed.

CHAPTER 3

A WRITER
BY INSTINCT

· · ·

As a boy reading in his uncle's library, Maugham had found his imagination profoundly stirred by stories and travelers' tales about foreign lands. Enthralled by *The Arabian Nights* and by several accounts of journeys through the Levant (the vicar liked to collect such works for their illustrations), he had longed to explore the exotic and unknown, a desire that remained unfulfilled while in Whitstable, where all he could do was gaze out over the cold North Sea and dream of escape. But now, done with his education, he was entirely independent, with nothing and nobody to constrain him or require his presence. "Life was before him and time of no account. He could wander, for years if he chose, in unfrequented places, among strange peoples. . . . He did not know what he sought or what his journeys would bring him; but he had a feeling he would learn something new about life and gain some clue to the mystery." Intoxicated by this unfamiliar sense of emancipation, Maugham's initial idea was to take off for a couple of years, beginning with twelve months in Spain, then going on to Italy and Greece, and finally to Egypt where he intended to become proficient in Arabic. Seductive although these plans were, however, he was levelheaded enough to realize that for a professional writer London was the marketplace, and to London he must return before too long an absence caused his name to be forgotten. Thus he decided to confine himself to the first part of his plan, an eight-month sojourn in Seville.

During his time as a medical student Maugham had read widely in Spanish literature and had fallen in love with the idea of Spain, the country that to him more than any other represented romance. And for once reality exceeded expectation, the light and warmth of southern Spain producing in Maugham an intense feeling of happiness. He arrived in Seville on December 7, 1897, and immediately fell in love with the city, the people, and the Spanish *dulcera de vivir,* reveling in a sense of liberation which up to now he had never known. "I came to it after weary years in London, heartsick with much hoping, my mind dull with drudgery; and it seemed a land of freedom," he wrote. "There I became at last conscious of my youth."

Maugham's lodgings were at 2 Calle Guzman el Bueno in the fashionable quarter of Santa Cruz, at the house of the British vice-consul, Edward Johnston, probably arranged through diplomatic contacts of his brother Charles at the law firm in Paris. Here the narrow streets were lined with large, whitewashed houses, discreetly hidden behind wrought-iron gates through which could be seen patios dense with foliage. In the heat of summer, canvas awnings shaded the street, stretching from house to house until they were taken down at evening to let in the cooler air. Maugham was glad of the quiet in which to write, for it was a peaceful district and during the day there were few sounds except for the trickle of a fountain, the occasional cry of a beggar, or the delicate *tap-tap* of a donkey's hooves on the cobbled paving. After he had finished his morning's work, Maugham explored the city; he liked to walk through the gardens and orange groves of the magnificent Alcazar and into the great Gothic cathedral where he stood transfixed before the paintings of Murillo and Zurbarán; sometimes his route took him by the government-owned cigarette factory, famous as the location of *Carmen,* just as the raucous groups of gypsy girls, the "cigarreras," came streaming out.

As his Spanish improved, Maugham entered more into the life of the city. He grew a mustache, smoked Filipino cigars, learned the guitar, and bought a broad-brimmed hat with a flat crown; he hankered for a cape lined with green and red velvet, but decided it was too expensive and bought a poncho instead; he went to the theater and to bullfights, and drank sherry in dark taverns hung with strings of sausages and hams. He was invited to private houses for dinner, where he listened to heated debates over the conduct of the Spanish-American War being fought over distant Cuba, and he took part in country picnics, where he delighted in watching the girls and young men dance the flamenco.

Maugham was captivated by the Spanish and by Spain. His perspective was highly colored and romantic, and during his months in Seville he responded eagerly to the erotic atmosphere, to the easy availability, in certain quarters, of sexual encounter. In Spain, as in France and Italy, anticlerical feeling had largely swept away the authority of the Catholic Church and the church's ancient laws against sodomy, making possible a freedom unknown in the Protestant north; and nowhere more so than in Andalusia, where the legacy of eight hundred years of Moorish occupation was evident not only in the architecture but in the relaxed Arab attitude toward homosexuality. Beneath a surface formality, courtship rituals between men and women were also conducted with unusual license. Strolling the quiet streets at night Maugham looked enviously at the cloaked young men clinging to the barred windows while they whispered passionate enticements to their girlfriends within, often with disastrous consequences.

> In Spain the blood of youth is very hot. . . . The Spaniard, who will seduce any girl he can, is pitiless . . . so there is much weeping, the girl is turned out of doors and falls readily into the hands of the procuress. In the brothels of Seville or of Madrid she finds at least a roof and bread to eat; and the fickle swain goes his way rejoicing.

In *The Land of the Blessed Virgin,* an account of his experience of Andalusia, Maugham states that while he never fell in love, he nonetheless was infatuated by a girl, a certain Rosarito, about whom he writes in a ponderously highfalutin manner:

But when I write of Spanish women I think of you, Rosarito . . . it is your dark eyes that were lustrous, soft as velvet,
caressing sometimes, and sometimes sparkling with fiery
glances. (Alas! That I can find but hackneyed phrases to describe those heart-disturbers.)

Rosarito may well have been a Rosario, or indeed never existed at
all except as a literary conceit; in a later account Maugham refers
much more convincingly to conducting numerous lighthearted affairs, and also to a passion for "a young thing with green eyes and a
gay smile," gender carefully unspecified, whose charms were sufficiently magnetic to draw him back to Seville the following year.

When describing this period, Maugham wrote that in Seville
"life was too pleasant to allow me to give an undivided attention to
literature"; nonetheless he was resolute in maintaining his usual
habit of industriousness, in eight months completing a travel book,
four short stories, and a full-length novel. It was with these in his
luggage that he arrived back in London in the autumn of 1898.

THE YOUNG MAN OF twenty-four who returned to resume his life
in England was very different from the callow graduate who had
left for Spain the previous year. Maugham had grown considerably
in confidence: he had enjoyed himself immensely in Seville; he was
personable, attractive to both men and women; and he was possessed of an enormous creative energy and appetite for hard work.
Now he was intent on taking his career forward, determined to
make of his writing a paying business. In the 1890s the literary market was rapidly expanding, focused on a large educated middle
class, with dozens of new magazines and periodicals launched every
year and more than four hundred publishing houses in London
alone. However, Maugham's start was discouraging: returning almost penniless and expecting to find waiting for him a substantial
sum in royalties earned from *Liza of Lambeth,* he was taken aback to
discover that the total came to no more than £20. The fact that

Fisher Unwin was unlikely to have made more than that himself weighed not at all with his author, who remained convinced that the publisher had pulled a fast one. As he crossly remarked, with *Liza* "[Unwin] did me thoroughly in the eye." Fortunately, he would be unlikely to have the chance to do so again, as Maugham before going abroad had appointed a literary agent, W. M. Colles, to act for him: it was Colles who would from now on negotiate with Unwin, and indeed it was Colles who had succeeded in obtaining an advance of £50 for *The Making of a Saint,* the novel written on Capri the previous summer.

Maurice Colles, a big, burly, Falstaffian figure, was one of a new breed, the role of literary agent having only recently come into existence. Predictably it was looked on with disfavor by publishers, who were accustomed to dealing directly with their authors, many of whom had a conveniently limited understanding of financial matters. One of the first literary agents was A. P. Watt, who dominated the profession for many years, but at the turn of the century Colles was almost as well known, with a number of distinguished writers on his books, Hardy, Meredith, and Arnold Bennett among them. Colles was a decent, likable man, good-humored and easy to talk to, and for most of his clients, Maugham included, it was some time before they realized the extent of his incompetence.

The Making of a Saint had made its appearance in Maugham's absence during the summer of 1898, published in June by Fisher Unwin, who had sold it to L. C. Page in the United States. Maugham had been inspired to attempt a historical novel after reading an article by the prolific Andrew Lang, who posited that the form was ideal for the young writer as story and characters were ready-made and no experience of real life was necessary. "Seduced by this bad advice," as Maugham put it, he set to work, basing his plot on an episode in Machiavelli's *History of Florence.*

In later years Maugham expressed unalloyed contempt for *The Making of a Saint;* he left it out of the collected edition of his work and went to considerable lengths to have it suppressed, and in the copy he gave his nephew, Robin, he wrote, "A very poor novel by W. Somerset Maugham." According to its author's gloomy recol-

lection, the critics received *The Making of a Saint* with coolness and
the public with indifference, although in truth the novel's reception
was far from unfavorable. One of Unwin's readers, Edward Garnett, had reported with enthusiasm, "So far as we can see Mr.
Maugham is going *strong* . . . the novel [is] a strong unusual piece
of work, full of vigour." As with *Liza of Lambeth,* a couple of re-
viewers professed themselves affronted by the explicit nature of the
love scenes, but in the main it was judged a highly creditable effort.
"[Mr. Maugham] has written a good novel," said *The Spectator,* "and
he ought some day to write much better ones."

Having given up his Vincent Square lodgings when he left for
Seville, Maugham now moved into a small flat that he shared with
his old friend Walter Payne, first in Albany Chambers, Westminster,
near St. James's Park. Shortly afterward they moved to another in
Carlisle Mansions, an apartment block behind Victoria Station, employing a maid-of-all-work to cook for them and do the housework. It was an ideal arrangement in more ways than one.
Maugham was devoted to and trusted Payne, who was amiable and
levelheaded, providing a reassuring counterbalance to his friend's
more volatile temperament; they both had a passion for the theater
and continued to go regularly to plays together; and Payne, a qualified chartered accountant with a good business sense, now agreed to
take on as a job the handling of Maugham's financial affairs, as well
as dealing with all the correspondence with publishers, agents, and
magazine editors that lay outside Maurice Colles's remit. And there
were other advantages to living with Payne: as he was out all day—
he had recently given up accountancy to read for the bar—
Maugham had the place to himself in which to write; and when
Payne returned in the evening he often brought attractive company
with him. As Maugham put it, looking back on this period with the
cold and cynical eye of his extreme old age,

He [Payne] was very good-looking, and had no difficulty in
getting girls to go to bed with him . . . small-part actresses,
shop-girls or clerks in an office. About one evening a week
Walter would arrange to go out and the girl I was then friends

with came and dined with me, after which we indulged in sexual congress. Later in the evening we dressed and went downstairs, I put her in a cab, paid the fare and made an appointment with her for the following week. There was no romance in it, no love, only appetite: on looking back, these experiences of mine seem dreadfully sordid, but after all, I was in my early twenties and my sexual proclivities demanded expression.

Determined to make his mark as quickly as possible, Maugham energetically set to work, fortunately unaware that it would be nine long years before he was to achieve any substantial success. In those days, "I had a natural lucidity and a knack for writing easy dialogue . . . to write was an instinct that seemed as natural to me as to breathe, and I did not stop to consider if I wrote well or badly." His immediate priority was to sell the works he had written in Spain, the first of which to appear was a short story, "The Punctiliousness of Don Sebastian," published in October 1898 in *Cosmopolis,* a journal printed in three languages, a third of it in English, a third in French, and a third in German. Unsurprisingly, it failed to prosper, and it folded a month after Maugham's story appeared, without paying its contributor. Bound by the terms of his contract, Maugham had no choice but to submit his work to Fisher Unwin, as the firm had first refusal of his next two books. Unwin expressed not the least interest in the sketches of Andalusia, *The Land of the Blessed Virgin,* and declined to pay the £100 Maugham was asking for his autobiographical novel, "The Artistic Temperament of Stephen Carey"; he was, however, prepared to issue the short stories as a collection, entitled *Orientations,* a decision which pleased Maugham who was anxious that these should appear before the novel. "It is true that 'Stephen Carey' is finished," he wrote to Colles, "but as it is a little strong I particularly wish to publish something milder first, so that I may not be known as a writer of the George Moore type."★

Of the six stories that make up *Orientations,* four were written in

---

★ Moore was known for novels of disturbing social realism.

Spain, while two, "A Bad Example" and "Daisy," were thoroughly reworked versions of stories Maugham had composed earlier. Edward Garnett had read the original "A Bad Example" and not cared for it, nor, with one exception, did he much care for what was put before him now. The stories, he reported, "are all a little flat, a little heavy [and] we feel that Mr. Maugham's reputation will suffer if he publishes the present collection." The exception was "Daisy," to which Garnett responded with enthusiasm, describing it as "excellent . . . *modern,* done with insight & done with spirit." If only Maugham could produce five more of this quality, "well, *that* will be a very different thing."

"Daisy" is set in Blackstable, Maugham's fictional rendering of Whitstable, and is mainly of interest for the light it sheds on the author's feelings about his boyhood. Significantly, the final version of "Daisy" was written shortly after the death of the Reverend Henry Maugham, when Maugham's memories had been vividly refreshed by attending his uncle's funeral. His portrait of Whitstable is vengeful, showing its people as mean-spirited and hypocritical; and yet there is an underlying grieving for something loved that was now lost, Maugham, like his heroine, overwhelmed by "the terrible sadness of the past."

Orientations was published in June 1899, dedicated to Mrs. Edward Johnston, wife of the vice-consul with whom Maugham had stayed in Seville. The title of the collection was dreamed up by the author, who wanted to find something suitably sententious: the word "orientations," as he rightly observed, "at the time was not very familiar to the general public." After leafing through various French moralists and failing to find a suitably relevant quotation, he decided to invent one: *"C'est surtout, par des nouvelles d'un jeune écrivain qu'on peut se rendre compte du tour de son esprit. Il y cherche la voie qui lui est propre dans une série d'essais de genre et de style différents, qui sont comme des orientations, pour trouver son moi littéraire."**

Despite an unenthusiastic notice in the *London Bookman,* describ-

---

* "Above all it is through the new work of a young writer that one is made aware of the range of his abilities. It is here he tries out the genres and the different styles that best suit him, which act as directions guiding him toward his true literary self."

ing it as "an average book, fairly readable, but with no serious interest or promise about it," *Orientations* was generally praised by the critics: "The best writing we have yet seen from Mr. W. S. Maugham," according to *The Athenaeum,* while even the previously hostile *Academy* admitted itself impressed. "Mr. Maugham begins to be interesting. This book is much better than either the shrill and hysterical *Liza of Lambeth* or the rather mediocre *Making of a Saint. . . .* [*Orientations* is] trenchant, sincere, candid, humorous, witty, and flippant. . . . Mr. Maugham . . . has an abundance of vitality, which is perhaps the scarcest thing in modern literature."

It was this abundance of vitality that was such a distinctive ingredient of Maugham's magnetism as a young man. Although he was not tall, he was strikingly attractive, with his dark hair and mustache and his pale skin. As his earnings increased, Maugham was able to spend more on clothes, and soon developed an elegant sartorial flair. In retrospect he liked to represent himself as shy and socially awkward at this stage of his life, and it is true he was always self-conscious about his lack of height. "The world is an entirely different place to the man of five foot seven from what it is to the man of six foot two," he wrote in his notebook. Yet by the time he returned from Spain, he was well able, despite his stammer, to hold his own in most company, and certainly had few inhibitions in pursuing his amorous adventures. Possessed of an urgent sexual energy, Maugham was always on the lookout for opportunity, and yet at the same time he was emotionally vulnerable, with a hunger for love and affection, "almost continuously in love," as he described himself, "from the time I was fifteen to the time I was fifty." He may have liked to see himself when young as tough and heartless, but the reality was different: in love affairs with both men and women he was almost too susceptible, and often suffered great anguish as a result. One woman with whom in his twenties he had a brief affair said of him, "He is a fearfully emotional man, sexually."

Although no overt evidence survives, there are clear indications that when Maugham was in his late teens and early twenties he experienced some powerful sexual and emotional upheavals. In the early novels sexual passion is the dominant theme; and there is one work from this period that is closely autobiographical and revealing. "The Artistic Temperament of Stephen Carey," written in Spain in 1898, was, as Maugham had warned his agent, "a little strong" as regards subject matter; and so indeed it proved, considered "too indecent for publication," even after considerable toning down. After revising his original version Maugham told Colles that "finally I have erased all that might bring a blush to the cheek of the most modest journalist," but even this was not enough to satisfy the Mrs. Grundys of the publishing world. In the event, however, Maugham came to feel profoundly grateful that the novel never appeared, as it would have made impossible the writing of the infinitely superior *Of Human Bondage*. "I should have lost a subject which I was then too young to make proper use of," he explained with hindsight. "I was not far enough away from the events I described to see them reasonably and I had not had a number of experiences that later went to enrich the book I finally wrote." When late in Maugham's life he presented the manuscript to the Library of Congress in Washington, it was on the strict understanding that it could be neither quoted from nor copied.

In later years Maugham dismissed his third novel "as merely an insignificant curiosity," an unduly harsh judgment of an immature but intriguing work that shows strong promise of a notable talent. "Stephen Carey" relates the story of the early years and young manhood of the eponymous hero, which closely, but not completely, follows the author's own experience. An orphan, Stephen is unhappy at school and in young manhood bored by his job in a lawyer's office in London. It is during his indenture that he meets and falls passionately in love with a waitress, Rose, a thin, plain young woman, good-natured and cheerfully promiscuous. Consumed by lust for Rose, Stephen is led into appalling levels of degradation, from which he eventually emerges to find salvation of a kind in marriage to an innocent and pretty cousin. "Stephen Carey" is an extraordinarily interesting document, pedestrian in the early sections, compelling once Rose enters the story, and the big central theme, Stephen's obsession with Rose, must correspond to an experience undergone by Maugham while he was studying at the hospital. Here, Rose is presented as shallow and unrefined, and yet there is something engaging about her: she is placid and prepared to be pleased—a very different type from the malevolent Mildred, her reincarnation in *Of Human Bondage.* In the later novel Maugham is dealing with a scarring sadomasochistic affair, and it is no wonder that in the earlier version, written when he was only twenty-four, he was not yet prepared to reveal it; he softened the story, blurred the edges, and inevitably turned it into something else.

Despite his failure to win the critical attention he needed to advance his career, the name Somerset Maugham was beginning to be known, and Maugham soon found himself moving in wider social circles than before. After the publication of *Liza of Lambeth,* he had been asked to a couple of bookish salons, and he had come to the attention of that literary panjandrum, Edmund Gosse, who invited him to his famous Sundays at his house near Regent's Park. Gosse, distinguished as both critic and author, wielded powerful influence; with many celebrated writers as friends, he also liked to make the acquaintance of promising newcomers, and an invitation from Gosse served as a ticket of entry to the inner circle of letters. His personal acquaintance with some eminent Victorians—Tennyson, Browning, Swinburne, Gissing—provided a fascinating link to a past age; he was formidably well read, and Maugham judged him "the most interesting and consistently amusing talker I ever knew." At Gosse's parties you might meet Henry James or Thomas Hardy, although often the room was uncomfortably overcrowded, which made it difficult to drink tea and eat cucumber sandwiches while listening intelligently to the conversation of the literati as they discussed publishers and agents and shredded the reputations of their absent colleagues. At such literary parties Maugham was particularly intrigued by the women, some dressed flamboyantly in loud patterns and big beads, others mousy little spinsters who hardly spoke above a whisper. "I never ceased to be fascinated by their persistence in eating buttered toast with their gloves on, and I observed with admiration the unconcern with which they wiped their fingers on their chair when they thought no one was looking."

Outside these predominantly literary circles, one of the most influential of Maugham's new acquaintance was that eccentric figure,
Augustus Hare. Impressed by *Liza of Lambeth,* Hare had asked a
clerical friend of his who knew Maugham to invite the young man
to dinner. The evening had been a success, and shortly afterward an
invitation was issued for a weekend in Sussex at Holmhurst, Hare's
house near St.-Leonard's-on-Sea.

Augustus Hare, part scholar, part snob, part fussy old maid, had
enjoyed his greatest success during the 1870s and '80s, when his
idiosyncratic guidebooks, in particular to Italy, France, and Spain
(*Walks in Rome, Days near Paris, Wanderings in Spain*), had been
widely read and admired. Formidably knowledgeable in his chosen
subjects, Augustus nursed a lifelong passion for the aristocracy, and
in England there was hardly a country house of importance at
which he was not an appreciative guest, his hosts flattered by the
enthusiastic interest he took in their noble mansions and their contents. Now in his sixties but looking much older with his white hair
and walrus mustache, Augustus divided his time between London,
where he dined out grandly every night, and the country, where he
led "a curious little home life very much centred on the befriending
of boys." As Maugham remarked of his new friend, "He was not
what people call a man's man" and, when entertaining, was much
more at ease in the company of middle-aged ladies, preferably titled.

Maugham grew fond of Augustus, whom he saw as "innately
and intensely frivolous [but also] kind, hospitable and generous."
The two men had a bond in that they were both survivors of
wretchedly unhappy childhoods—Augustus's appallingly so—and
Maugham, touched by the older man's kindness in taking him
under his wing, genuinely enjoyed his weekends in Sussex.
Holmhurst was far from being one of the great houses, but it was a
gentleman's residence and grander than anything Maugham had
known before. Anxious to improve himself, he was quick to learn
everything his host set out to teach him. In Augustus's view
Maugham lacked polish. It was not enough, he told him, just to sit
and listen: he must make conversational contributions of his own

and sharpen up his small talk. There were, too, some vulgar phrases of which Maugham must break the habit. Augustus was displeased to hear his young friend talk of going somewhere by bus: "I prefer to call the conveyance to which you refer an omnibus," he reproved him; he winced at another ill-bred nuance: "Yesterday when we came in from our walk you said you were thirsty and asked for a *drink* . . . A gentleman does *not* ask for a *drink,* he asks for *something to drink.*" Hare had admired *Liza of Lambeth* but he was anxious that Maugham should now leave the subject of the lower orders and acquire a knowledge of the manners and customs of the nobility and gentry. To this end he started taking his protégé with him when he called on his well-born acquaintances, encouraging them to invite his promising young friend to their parties.

Among the hostesses who at Hare's suggestion took Maugham up was Blanche Crackanthorpe, wife of the distinguished barrister and mother of the writer Hubert Crackanthorpe. At her salon in Rutland Gate, Mrs. Crackanthorpe specialized in entertaining literary celebrities, bringing together promising beginners such as Maugham with well-known figures like Hardy, Galsworthy, and Henry James. Somewhat higher up the social scale was the tuft-hunting Lady St. Helier, who at her house in Portland Place liked to mix aristocratic society with professional people, lawyers and doctors, as well as with artists and writers. A promising young writer such as William Somerset Maugham was an asset in such company, and Maugham for his part relished the opportunity to observe the upper classes in their natural habitat. It was at the end of a dazzling dinner at Portland Place that Maugham found himself sitting next to the elderly Duke of Abercorn. "Do you like cigars?" the duke asked him, taking out of his pocket a large cigar case. "Very much," said Maugham, who could rarely afford them. "So do I," continued the duke, selecting one and inspecting it carefully. "And when I come to dinner," he continued, lighting up, "I always bring my own." He snapped the case shut and returned it to his pocket. "I advise you to do the same."

Another patron of Maugham's was the wife of Basil Wilberforce, the archdeacon of Westminster who had preached a sermon on *Liza of Lambeth*. Since then Mrs. Wilberforce had taken a kindly interest in Maugham, including him in her lively parties at the house in Dean's Yard and introducing him to several fashionable hostesses, who were delighted to ask the clever, attractive, and un-attached young man to their luncheons, dinners, and dances. Maugham took pleasure in his grand new social life, even if it came at a cost: the people who entertained him were extremely well off, which he was not, obliged to economize where he could. Dining out meant dressing in white tie and tails, with kid gloves and silk top hat; as cabs were beyond his means, Maugham came and went by omnibus, with its upper deck open to the weather. When in-vited to the country for a Friday to Monday, greater expenditure was unavoidable, with half-sovereigns to be dispensed to the butler, to the footman who brought the morning tea, and often to a second footman who unpacked his bag and acted as valet. At a large house-party young bachelors were sometimes obliged to share a bed, which not infrequently led to sex. "Often it turned out to be very pleasant," Maugham recalled.

Years later, pondering on what it was that these rich and worldly people saw in him, he put the question to one of the hostesses of his youth. "You were different from other young men," she said. "Though quiet . . . you had a sort of restless vitality that was in-triguing."

A SUCCESS IN SOCIETY, Maugham found that success in his profes-sional life continued to elude him. Discouraged by having had two books turned down and reluctant to spend the winter in England, at the end of 1898 he again went abroad, first to Rome, then back to Seville, where the young creature "with green eyes and a gay smile" was still much on his mind. Leaving Andalusia after a couple of months he continued on to Morocco—a natural step after immer-sion in the Moorish culture of southern Spain—before returning to London in April 1899. After the sensual seductiveness of the Mediterranean, London appeared particularly drab: the soot and fog, the muddy streets reeking of manure, the crowds, the clatter and jangle of trams. Even more lowering to the spirit was the fact that Colles had failed to place elsewhere either of the works rejected by Unwin, "Stephen Carey" and *The Land of the Blessed Virgin;* and on top of this, a one-act play Maugham had written while in Rome, "Son & Heir," never produced or published and now lost, was also languishing from lack of interest, a particular disappointment as he was still determined on a career as a dramatist. Indeed, apart from a couple of short stories published in *Punch,* for more than two years little was heard from Somerset Maugham—until the appearance of a third novel in July 1901.

The Hero, completed between October 8, 1900, and January 14, 1901, was suggested by the Boer War, "the first rent," as Maugham later saw it, "in that great fabric, the British Empire." The war had broken out in 1899, and in 1900 with the sieges of Mafeking and Ladysmith was currently much in the news. The story tells of James Parsons, a gallant young soldier just home from the Cape, but the main theme of the novel is not war but a tormenting question of personal honor. Five years earlier, James had proposed marriage to Mary Clibborn, the girl next door, but while abroad he had become obsessed with the wife of a regimental colleague, and now feels that he would rather die than marry plain, priggish Mary when his thoughts are all of the wickedly seductive Mrs. Pritchard-Wallace. In the end, unable to resolve his dilemma, James shoots himself.

Here again the subject of physical desire was much on the author's mind. Bossy, frumpish Mary, with her good works and sensible shoes, provides the perfect foil to the unscrupulous Mrs. Wallace, whose appeal to James, it is made very clear, is based entirely on sex. "The touch of her fingers sent the blood rushing through his veins insanely; and understanding his condition, she took pleasure in touching him, to watch the little shiver of desire that convulsed his frame. . . ." In James's view, marriage without passion "is ugly and beastly," a trap to be avoided at all costs, a belief he certainly shared with his creator.

The novel, received by the critics with temperate approval, was published by Hutchinson, the three-book contract with Unwin, to Maugham's relief, having finally expired. *The Hero,* for which an advance of £75 was paid, was the first of Maugham's works to bear on its cover the Moorish sign against the evil eye, adopted by his father, Robert Maugham, after his travels in the Near East, and which was famously to become Somerset Maugham's insignia—in this case unfortunately printed upside down.

Before writing *The Hero,* Maugham had finished another novel, one for which yet again he had experienced considerable difficulty in finding a publisher. The problem was, as before, that Maugham's work was earning a reputation for impropriety, his content considered too sexually explicit, with the consequence that publishers were beginning to regard him as a risky proposition. With the new work, *Mrs. Craddock,* he was again sailing very close to the wind: not only was the subject, of female sexual desire, considered shocking, but the language, too, was found offensively frank. Publisher after publisher turned it down, including the prestigious William Heinemann; fortunately, however, the renowned critic Robertson Nicoll, a partner at Hodder & Stoughton, recognized the book's quality, and while acknowledging its unsuitability for his own imprint persuaded the more adventurous Heinemann to reconsider. This time it was read by the head of the firm himself, who agreed to take it on condition that some particularly inflammatory passages were excised. That the new novel was considered dangerously risqué had little effect in bridling Maugham, and more than a quarter of a century later the French critic Paul Dottin wrote, "Maugham will doubtless be recognised in time as one of the novelists who have contributed most to removing from the English literary vocabulary the word 'improper.' "

Mrs. Craddock is a fascinating novel, the most mature and sophisticated of Maugham's work to date. The story tells of Bertha Ley, a rich and beautiful young woman, cultured and well read, who marries one of the tenant farmers on her Kentish estate. Edward Craddock is strikingly handsome, and it is some while before the passionate Bertha realizes that although decent and well-meaning, he is also stupid, complacent, and sexually passive. The marriage quickly deteriorates, Bertha's distaste for her husband intensified after she meets a charming young cad, Gerald Vaudrey, for whom she conceives an intense infatuation. When Vaudrey throws her over, Bertha, heartbroken and humiliated, returns home, where Edward is touchingly pleased to see her. His feelings, however, are now a matter of indifference to his wife, as is his death, which occurs shortly afterward as the result of a hunting accident. The novel ends with Bertha finally grieving, not for the loss of her husband, but for the loss of the love she had for him; and with this understanding comes a sense of freedom, the last scene Bertha settling down quietly by the fire to read her book, in tranquil preparation for whatever the next stage of her life may bring.

In his remarkable portrait of Bertha, Maugham created a vital, complex, captivating, and fully rounded woman, exigent and spoiled but also sympathetic and endearing. He knows her through and through, catches every nuance of her self-deception, of her skewed falling in love, sees through her wiles, gently mocks her affectations, yet at the same time identifies wholeheartedly with every surge and current of her passionate nature, almost as though he were her alter ego, his own divided sexuality giving him a kind of double vision, a deeper insight into the feminine psyche. The influence of Flaubert is evident, with Bertha Craddock in character a close cousin of Emma Bovary. Like her French counterpart, Bertha is sensual, willful, and highly strung, and like Emma suffers agonies of boredom in her husband's company. Bertha, though, is well placed in the world, and her yearnings are not for social advancement but for romance. At the beginning she sees in Edward Craddock a romantic hero, and running parallel to her feelings of sheer carnality is her mistaken perception that the stolid farmer is a kind of noble savage whose innate sensitivity needs only to be awakened by the power of her love. Sadly, this is not the case. Edward, self-satisfied and unnoticing, ignores his wife's demands for attention, treating her outbursts of furious frustration with irritating good humor. "Women are like chickens," he is fond of repeating. "When they cluck and cackle sit tight and take no notice."

Bertha is drawn with the unerring psychological accuracy for which Maugham would become known, particularly in his treatment of women. Yet so, too, is Edward: if deserving of far less sympathy, he is nonetheless entirely credible, and the reader is shown fairly how the situation appears from his point of view. The man who supplants him in Bertha's affections, Gerald Vaudrey, is also a three-dimensional figure, and of a type, sexy, rakish, and amusing, that was attractive not only to Bertha but to her creator. (In an interview given twenty years later, Maugham admitted that of all his fictional characters, "My recollection lingers with most pleasure on a youth called Gerald Vaudrey in *Mrs. Craddock*.")

[Gerald] was certainly not at all shy, although he looked even younger than nineteen. He was quite a boy, very slight . . . with a small girlish face. . . . His hair was dark and curly; he wore it long, evidently aware that it was very nice; and his handsome eyes had a charming expression. His sensual mouth was always smiling.

Maugham knows, if Bertha does not, how dangerous such young men can be; and it is perhaps not wholly irrelevant that the novel was written very shortly after Maugham returned from his second visit to Seville, where he had gone, he said, to continue his affair with his green-eyed paramour.

Written in 1900, in the last year of Queen Victoria's reign, *Mrs. Craddock* was published in Britain at the beginning of the Edwardian age, in November 1902, not appearing in the United States until 1920. The novel was widely noticed and generally acclaimed, although several critics felt it their duty to warn readers of the daring nature of the content. "[If] you are afraid to look life in the face," said St. John Adcock in the *Bookman,* "you had better leave Mr. Maugham alone." Indeed the cuts insisted on by Heinemann had done little to blur the candid fact of Bertha's passion, and it is surprising, given the prudishness of the period, that so little was taken out. Yet even by Maugham's pessimistic standards, his fourth novel was "a substantial success." For its author, however, there remained a sense of frustration: his ambition was to write for the theater, and he still regarded his novels mainly as a means of making his name well enough known so that managers would look with favor on his drama, none of which had yet been accepted. Now, with *Mrs. Craddock* in the public eye, he was about to put this theory to the test with his first full-length play, for which he had the highest hopes.

CHAPTER 4

LE CHAT BLANC

. . .

I N HIS AUTOBIOGRAPHICAL WORK *THE SUMMING UP*, MAUGHAM, in typically self-deprecating mode, states that he began to write plays simply because "it seemed less difficult to set down on paper the things people said than to construct a narrative." There was, of course, more to it than that, but with his finely attuned ear he was quick at picking up the rhythms of colloquial speech, and in his preferred role of listener he was as intrigued by the manner in which people expressed themselves as by the content. Since the age of sixteen Maugham had been passionately interested in the theater, had read widely not only the English dramatists but French, Spanish, German, and others in translation, and he went as often as he could to see plays. It had not escaped his attention either that a success in the theater brought more substantial and immediate financial rewards than were ever likely with a novel. Maugham was to become phenomenally popular as a dramatist, his playwriting extending over three decades, bringing him fame and glamour and making him an immensely rich man. Yet such an outcome would have been hard to predict. None of his early attempts at playwriting found favor with the managers to whom they were sent, and it was only a steely determination that prevented him from giving up during ten years of rejection and discouragement. The first dramatic work by Maugham actually to be produced was a one-act play, *Marriages Are Made in Heaven*. Failing to place it in London, Maugham translated the piece into German, and as *Schiffbrüchig* (*Shipwreck*) it was staged by Max Reinhardt's company in Berlin, where it ran for a mere eight performances.

Maugham's first full-length work, *A Man of Honour,* completed in 1898, was strongly influenced by Ibsen, in his eyes the greatest of all modern dramatists. On his first visit to Italy, Maugham had taken with him a German version of *Ghosts,* familiarizing himself with the play by rendering it into English. The plot of *A Man of Honour* is recognizably Ibsenite in approach, dealing with the pressures of society, the struggle for personal integrity, and the disastrous consequences of ignoring instinct in a blind adhering to convention. But the West End was no more receptive to Maugham than it had been to Ibsen himself, and the play was turned down, first by the distinguished Johnston Forbes-Robertson and then by the American impresario Charles Frohman, who had recently taken over the Duke of York's Theatre in St. Martin's Lane. After this second rejection, Maugham made some extensive revisions before trying a completely different tack and submitting the play to the Stage Society, which to his delight accepted it for two performances in February 1903.

The Stage Society had been founded in 1899, the successor to the short-lived Independent Theatre Club set up by the pioneering J. T. Grein. Playwright, critic, and manager, Grein saw it as his mission to produce plays of artistic merit that were unlikely to prove popular in the mainstream. West End audiences in the '90s had been fed an almost exclusive fare of society drama, plays about the upper and well-to-do middle classes, preferably with a plot involving a parvenu and a shameful secret, usually that of a woman with a past. Typical titles of the period were *Lady Huntsworth's Experiment, Lady Gorringe's Necklace, Lady Epping's Lawsuit,* and *Lord and Lady Algy,* with the plays of Oscar Wilde offering the supreme example, from *Lady Windermere's Fan* to the guying of the genre in *The Importance of Being Earnest.* Jack Grein was interested in a different genre. It was Grein who in 1892 had put on *Widower's Houses,* the first-ever performance of a play by George Bernard Shaw, and Grein the previous year who had staged a single performance of Ibsen's *Ghosts,* an occasion greeted with howls of outrage. In the words of its translator, William Archer, "The shriek of execration with which this performance was received by the newspapers of the day has scarcely its counterpart in the history of criticism."

With Grein's acceptance of *A Man of Honour,* Maugham felt that at last he was within reach of the career for which he had been unsuccessfully aiming for nearly a decade. The Stage Society was a private members' club and audiences were small, but it was the only organization presenting experimental theater and consequently its productions attracted a good deal of attention. Maugham was further encouraged by the fact that a member of the committee, the eminent scholar and journalist W. L. Courtney, had offered to publish the script in the March 1903 issue of the prestigious *Fortnightly Review,* of which he was editor. This was a notable accolade: Courtney was widely respected for his flair in spotting new talent and under his editorship the *Review* was considered the leading literary journal of the day, counting among its contributors Meredith, Kipling, H. G. Wells, George Moore, and Henry James.

Described by its author as a tragedy, *The Man of Honour* deals with the wretched consequences for an honorable young man of insisting on his moral duty by marrying beneath him, by making an honest woman of the barmaid whom he has seduced. Maugham attended rehearsals, delighted to see his work come to life in the hands of an accomplished cast led by one of the initiators of the modern movement, Harley Granville Barker, shortly to become known, both as actor and director, for his association with Shaw.

The first night, on February 22, 1903, at the Imperial Theatre, Tothill Street, was well attended by friends and family and generally judged a success, although Maugham was in an agony of nerves throughout. His sister-in-law, Nellie, wrote in her diary, "Went to the first night of Willie's play . . . Very enthusiastic audience, and it was quite well acted. Willie was pale with terror!" The production attracted a gratifying amount of attention, and on the whole the playwright was thought to show promise. J. T. Grein himself, writing in *The Sunday Times,* favorably compared Maugham to the eminent dramatist Sir Arthur Wing Pinero and expressed admiration for the author's linguistic style. "Not for a long time had I heard such fine and nervous English," he stated. "Simplicity is throughout the keynote of Mr. Maugham's dramatic vein. . . . His drama is true." Max Beerbohm, who had succeeded Shaw as theater critic for the *Saturday Review,* was only slightly less complimentary. "[The second act] is admirably conceived and written; and the third act is a fine piece of emotional drama," he wrote. "[But] the rest of the play falls to pieces. Mr. Maugham becomes too bitter. . . ."

Maugham had learned some valuable lessons in stagecraft while watching rehearsals: how to shape dialogue, the importance of changing speed, how to get laughs in the right places and position the pauses; he was pleased with the level of response from the audience; and yet he was left with a feeling of frustration. The experience seemed to have advanced his career very little. The Stage Society was admirable in its way, but Maugham's ambitions were focused on a much wider horizon: the commercial theater of the West End. "I was not satisfied with the appreciation of a small band of intellectuals," he wrote. "I wanted no such audience as this, but the great public."

As a first step in this direction, Maugham sent a redrafted version of the play to Muriel Wylford, manager of the Avenue Theatre* at Charing Cross. Miss Wylford agreed to put it on for a four-week run in February 1904, together with a one-act farce Maugham had completed earlier, "Mademoiselle Zampa,"† as a curtain-raiser. The latter was a flop and had to be withdrawn, but *A Man of Honour* proved moderately popular. Max Beerbohm again wrote about it at length, considering that although it was notably inferior to the author's novels, "There is no reason to suppose that anon Mr. Maugham as playwright will not be the equal of Mr. Maugham as novelist." On the first performance the final curtain was followed by a storm of enthusiastic clapping and calls for the author. One of the actors standing by the pass door watched as Maugham took in what was happening, hardly able to believe his ears. "I can see now

* Now the Playhouse Theatre.
† Never published, and no known manuscript exists.

the shy young author, quite shaken by the cheers and prolonged applause, coming through to the stage but unwilling to take a call."

Of the three brothers it was Harry who showed the most interest in Maugham's writing for the theater. Harry, too, had ambitions as a playwright, the author of a number of plays in verse which had unfortunately met with little success. Serious and intellectual, Harry was worried by what he saw as his brother's superficiality, warning him that his ambitious social life would have a deleterious effect on his work. "Harry told me that my plays . . . were well constructed and neatly contrived but they were also trivial and shallow because the life I was leading was trivial and shallow." Plump, handsome, and permanently disheveled, Harry had never felt at home in the world; he had become increasingly reclusive, drinking too much, struggling with depression, and finding it difficult to make friends. He was a bit of a bore, according to Maugham. "He needed a lot of understanding," said Charlie's wife, Beldy, "and very few people could understand him." In 1899 Harry had left Italy, where he had been living since leaving the family law firm in Paris, and returned to England, taking rooms on Cadogan Street, Chelsea, where he led a largely solitary existence. "Very much homosexual," according to a contemporary, Harry was nervous of women and much preferred the company of men. His few friends were drawn from the bohemian circle of writers and painters of which Maugham's old mentor, Wentworth Huyshe, was the center. Years later Harry's niece Honor spoke of a well-known writer, unnamed, who told her he had been a lover of Harry's.

Harry was too sweet-natured to begrudge his younger brother his success, yet it undoubtedly added to his own feelings of inferiority. Whether it was fear of failure, unhappiness over a love affair, the threat of scandal, or simply the engulfing nature of his chronic depression, in July 1904 Harry killed himself. Freddie Maugham, "F.H.," briefly noted in his appointment diary the course of events, that on July 20 he was summoned by wire to Cadogan Street to find Harry in agony, blue in the face and gasping for breath, having swallowed nitric acid three days earlier. He took him to St. Thomas's

Hospital, where for nearly a week Harry lingered, dying on the evening of the twenty-seventh, shortly after the arrival of Charlie and Beldy from Paris. The inquest two days later determined that Harry had ended his life "while of unsound mind"; it was immediately followed by the funeral at Lambeth Cemetery. F.H. makes no mention of Maugham's being present, yet in Maugham's own version, recounted some years later, he states that it was he who was summoned, he who found Harry, he who took him to hospital. The probability is that both brothers were involved, that George Barlow, the friend who was the first on the scene, sent a wire to the two of them. Attempting suicide was a criminal offense, and as it would, therefore, have been risky to call a doctor, Maugham's medical expertise was vital; so, too, was his familiarity with St. Thomas's, where he could use his influence to persuade the authorities to keep the matter quiet. The week after the funeral Maugham went to France to stay with Charles and Beldy, and the brothers speculated endlessly about the reasons that drove Harry to his death. "I'm sure it wasn't only failure that made him kill himself," Maugham significantly concluded. "It was the life he led."

Afterward Harry's suicide was rarely referred to within the family. All four of Robert Maugham's sons suffered from depression: Charles was portrayed by his family as "pale and grave . . . melancholy . . . a rather sad man," while F.H. in his appointment diaries regularly defines his own state of mind as "depressed" and "very sad"; Maugham was an unhappy child who evolved into a deeply melancholic man, "violently pessimistic," as he described himself, and both he and F.H. in later life suffered frequently from nightmares. One of Maugham's nieces wrote of her father and her uncle Willie that "perhaps they had insulated themselves as best they could from unbearable sorrows, which resulted at times in an icy coldness which could chill and sometimes destroy human relationships." Maugham at least was fortunate in that his abundant vitality, his ambition and insatiable curiosity made his life for most of the time seem worth living. But for Harry it was not, and although Maugham could rarely bring himself to speak of it, his brother's pathetic self-destruction was to haunt him for many years.

Having turned his back on the Stage Society, Maugham believed he now understood what commercial managements were looking for, and already during the previous twelve months he had completed three plays which in his view were ideal for the West End: *The Explorer, Loaves and Fishes,* and, with Harry, *The Fortune Hunters.* And yet not one of them had been accepted. This was a grave disappointment not only in terms of establishing a reputation but also financially; at this period his only income, apart from his tiny patrimony, was generated by the occasional short story sold to a magazine. Sharing a flat with Walter Payne, Maugham was able to live modestly, but in both his professional and social life, appearances were important. He was making new friends, was admired as a promising young writer, and was beginning to be much sought after in the more intellectual social circles. Maugham liked to dress well, to give dinners on occasion, and recently he had joined a gentlemen's club, the Bath Club in Dover Street. None of this was cheap, and Maugham grew increasingly frustrated by his financial insecurity. "Times are very hard & publishers very moneyless at present," Maugham wrote to Wentworth Huyshe. "I cannot tell when the clouds will roll by!"

The easygoing Colles was continually being nagged by his client to try to interest managers in his plays, solicit commissions from journals, reissue old work, explore new sources, press for payment from dilatory editors—anything, in fact, that would bring in some money. "If you hear of anyone wanting a play translated from French, German, Italian or Spanish, or adapted, I should be glad to do it," ran a typical plea. "Also I wondered if you could get me an *Arrowsmith Annual* to do. I have sketched out a rather sensational murder story (quite proper!) somewhat in the manner of Edgar Allan Poe. . . ." "Behold three short stories," begins a businesslike communication written in July 1904. " 'The Criminal,' 2300 words, somewhat better than the others, would do for *Lloyds.* 'Flirtation,' 300 words, might suit the *D. Mail.* 'A Rehearsal,' 3000 words, is bad enough to suit anything."

His financial situation may have been precarious, but Maugham nonetheless was regarded with respect as a promising young member of the literary intelligentsia, "an honourable condition," he re-marked, "which, some years later, when I became a popular writer of light comedies, I lost." To his already heavy workload he was now invited to add the co-editorship of what was intended to be a prestigious annual anthology, a successor to *The Yellow Book,* a proj-ect on which he collaborated with the writer and illustrator Lau-rence Housman, a younger brother of the poet A. E. Housman. *The Venture,* subtitled *An Annual of Art and Literature,* boasted a distin-guished list of contributors: John Masefield, G. K. Chesterton, James Joyce, Havelock Ellis, Thomas Hardy, and E. F. Benson, with illustrators Gordon Craig, T. Sturge Moore, and Charles Ricketts. In the first number Maugham included a piece of his own, *Marriages Are Made in Heaven,* the original English version of the curtain-raiser that had been staged the previous year in Berlin. The first issue appeared, a little late, in the autumn of 1903, followed by a second in 1905, after which no more was heard or seen of *The Ven-ture.* "The whole thing was, of course, too highbrow to be popu-lar," Laurence Housman loftily concluded. "Perhaps had it been published at a guinea instead of at five shillings, it would have done better."

Among the few women writers appearing in *The Venture* was the novelist Violet Hunt, whom Maugham had first met in 1902. A woman who inspired extremes of liking and loathing, Violet, now in her forties and notorious for her turbulent love life, was tall and thin with a mass of dark hair, large eyes, a beaky nose, and a pointed chin. Born in 1862, she had been brought up among artists and poets, her father, Alfred Hunt, a landscape painter, a friend of Ruskin, Burne-Jones, Millais, and Robert Browning. Violet had modeled for Burne-Jones and Sickert, and from childhood had been encouraged to regard herself as a Pre-Raphaelite beauty. At eigh-teen she had been admired by the young Oscar Wilde, who called her "the sweetest Violet in England," and in her twenties had had a number of affairs with older men, including the diplomat and pub-lisher Oswald Crawfurd, from whom she contracted syphilis; later she became one of the many mistresses of H. G. Wells and conducted a tormenting ten-year relationship with Ford Madox Ford, eleven years her junior. A novelist of the "new woman" genre, Violet was well known as a literary hostess, with her bimonthly luncheons at the Writers' Club on Norfolk Street and her garden parties at South Lodge, her house on Campden Hill near Holland Park. Among the distinguished guests were Henry James, Ezra Pound, Joseph Conrad, Wyndham Lewis, H. G. Wells, Arnold Bennett, and D. H. Lawrence, who strolled about the lawn sipping iced coffee and encouraging their hostess in her scandalous conversation. Indeed, it was Violet's keen appetite for gossip that primarily appealed to Maugham, who was amused by her high spirits and malicious tongue; she, sexually voracious, was strongly attracted and lost little time in luring him into bed.

The physical side of the friendship was unsatisfactory and mercifully brief, Violet still suffering the aftereffects of her affair with Crawfurd. Yet the two remained fond of each other, and Maugham took to writing Violet long flirtatious letters, even confiding in her, up to a point, about his love life.

Much of the correspondence with Violet Hunt is devoted to a discussion of their literary enterprises, Maugham expanding on his own projects and offering a considered judgment of hers. In 1908 Violet dedicated to him her novel *White Rose of Weary Leaf* in graceful recognition of his dedication to her of his sketches of Andalusia, which were eventually published in 1905; unfortunately, he had neglected to ask her permission first and she had taken offense, "chiefly, I think, because it was called *The Land of the Blessed Virgin* & she could not imagine what the hell would be her business in such a country," Maugham jokingly remarked. Violet soon recovered her good humor, however, and the friendship endured, she ebullient and demonstrative, he amiable and reserved. Nearly twenty years later Maugham was to draw her portrait in *The Moon and Sixpence* as Rose Waterford. "She combined a masculine intelligence with a feminine perversity. . . . No one could say such bitter things; on the other hand, no one could do more charming ones." As she grew older, Violet grew increasingly touchy and tiresome, but Maugham always treated her with the greatest gentleness, and unlike many of her acquaintance refused to cold-shoulder her for her frequently outrageous behavior.

It was a sign of his confidence in Violet's critical judgment that Maugham asked her to read his new novel, *The Merry-Go-Round,* before he submitted it for publication, at her suggestion cutting out several whole chapters as well as undertaking some minor pruning. *The Merry-Go-Round,* somewhat reluctantly accepted by Heinemann for a royalty of £60 and as part of a package with *The Land of the Blessed Virgin,* presents a reworking of *A Man of Honour,* with the addition of two subsidiary plot lines. The second, and much the more interesting of these, describes the helpless passion of a well-to-do married woman for a venal, caddish young man, several years her junior and very much on the make. Reggie Barlow-Bassett, like Gerald Vaudrey in *Mrs Craddock,* has a sensual beauty that enslaves Grace Castillyon. From their first encounter, sitting next to him at dinner, Grace is smitten, and soon the besotted woman is lavishing money and every luxury on her worthless lover, risking her marriage and her standing in society, even though she knows he cares nothing for her and is only after what he can get. Eventually she is saved from ruin and persuaded to return to her husband by the stern intervention of Miss Ley, an outspoken spinster first encountered in *Mrs. Craddock* as standing in loco parentis to Bertha before her marriage.

Miss Ley's original was an interesting woman, Mrs. George Steevens, widow of a *Daily Mail* correspondent who died while covering the Boer War. Plain of feature but stylish—she dressed always in severe black and white—she was elderly when Maugham met her, a bright-eyed old lady full of charm and vitality, as well as outspoken and capable of stunning rudeness to those she disliked. There was an air of notoriety surrounding Christina Steevens: during her first marriage, as Mrs. Rogerson, she had been barred from polite society after her scandalous involvement in the divorce case that ruined the career of the Liberal MP Sir Charles Dilke. She once startled Henry James by confiding that she had poisoned her first husband. "If she had been beautiful and sane," James concluded, "she would have been one of the world's great wicked women." Mrs. Steevens lived at Merton Place in Surrey, on the site of the house that had once belonged to Admiral Nelson, where her precarious finances never prevented her from offering her wide circle of friends an abundant hospitality. Merton, near Wimbledon, was in easy reach of London, and a stream of visitors would drive out by hansom on Sundays for lunch or tea, in fine weather wandering through the garden and along the banks of the river. Among them were actors, writers, painters, and their hangers-on, a group that included Violet Hunt as well as others who were becoming important to Maugham, such as Max Beerbohm, Oscar Wilde's disciple Reggie Turner, and the popular playwright Henry Arthur Jones.

It was Jones who told Maugham that when he read *Liza of Lambeth* he had immediately recognized Maugham's potential as a dramatist, a flattering statement in direct contradiction of the opinion proffered by another of Mrs. Steevens's guests. While strolling one afternoon on the lawn at Merton, Maugham had had a long talk with the gentle and charming Max Beerbohm. In those days Max had not yet perfected his supremely elegant sartorial style: in Maugham's opinion, the dandyism "didn't quite come off. His very narrow shirt cuffs, protruding a good two inches out of the sleeves of his tail coat, were generally a trifle grubby, the coat needed a brushing & the trousers pressing. . . . You had the impression of a small part actor in a provincial company dressed as a swell." Max earnestly entreated Maugham to give up writing for the stage: in his opinion Maugham's talents were primarily as a novelist, and that for one capable of such subtlety of characterization the drama was too crude a medium. Of course, Max continued, there was a great deal of money to be made out of the theater by some people, but "you, my boy, are not one of those people." Maugham nodded politely and Max, "sorry for him, yet conscious of having done a good afternoon's work, briskly changed the subject." But if Max believed he had influenced his companion, he was wrong. "He little knew," said Maugham, "I was young, poor and determined."

Despite such dispiriting advice, Maugham's friendship with the witty and fastidious Max, begun at Merton, lasted a lifetime. Indeed, Maugham had much to be grateful for in Mrs. Steevens's hospitality, and he responded warmly to the old lady's liveliness and generosity, admiring her impatience with humbug and frankness in speaking her mind, both qualities he bestowed upon her fictional counterpart, Miss Ley. And in *The Merry-Go-Round* he drew on his own relationship with Mrs. Steevens in portraying that between Miss Ley and Frank Hurrell, a doctor, who both in appearance and character bears a striking resemblance to Maugham. Frank, we are told, was

> a strong man, of no very easy temper, who held himself in admirable control. Silent with strangers, he disconcerted them by an unwilling frigidity of manner . . . an extremely reserved man, few knew that Frank Hurrell's deliberate placidity of expression masked a very emotional temperament. . . .

If *The Merry-Go-Round* is not among the most distinguished of Maugham's novels, in autobiographical terms it is undoubtedly important. Not only is there a substantial element of self-portrayal in the drawing of Frank Hurrell but, more crucially, there is a revealing picture of Maugham's emotional state. In describing Grace Castillyon's passion for Reggie Barlow-Bassett, Maugham gives powerful expression to an obsession of his own, also for a much younger man. Shortly after he had completed the novel Maugham wrote to Violet Hunt, "Most of what one writes is to a greater or lesser degree autobiographical, not the actual incidents always, but always the emotions. . . . When one has to suffer so much it is only fair that one should have the consolation of writing books about it." And years later he said of this period of his life that he urgently wanted to write a novel that would make money, "because I was at the time much taken with a young person of extravagant tastes . . . I determined to write a book that would enable me to . . . hold my own with my rivals. For the young person was attractive."

Maugham was always careful to cover his tracks, and the young person in question is left unidentified, although evidence points firmly in the direction of a handsome youth named Harry Philips.

Harry was the son of the rector of Hollington in Staffordshire, and intended for an ecclesiastical career. When Maugham met him he was studying at Oxford, where he was described by a fellow undergraduate as "quite the most dazzling figure for charm, good looks, and brilliant wit that I had ever encountered." Harry, however, was proving a grave disappointment to his father. He had no interest in the church, and he regarded his time at the university as an opportunity to enjoy himself to the full and whenever possible to shock his college contemporaries by outré behavior. Like Oscar Wilde, who ten years earlier had haunted Oxford in pursuit of Lord Alfred Douglas, so Maugham became a familiar figure, strolling down the High with Harry or encountered sitting smoking in his rooms. "We took a great liking to each other," said Harry, "& I invited him to stay with my parents in Staffordshire. My Father thought him clever but did not like his views on religion." This was hardly surprising given Maugham's agnosticism and his support of Harry's determination not to enter the Church. No parental objection was made to the friendship, however, and the two men continued to see each other constantly.

In *The Merry-Go-Round,* Grace Castillyon, helplessly infatuated, is forever having to bribe Reggie to be nice to her. "She had a certain hold over him in his immense love of pleasure. She could always avoid his peevishness by taking him to the theatre; he was anxious to move in polite circles, and an invitation to some great house made him affectionate for a week." As with Reggie, so with Harry; but providing the young man with entertainment did not come cheap, and Maugham had to work at full pressure, desperate to earn money. "Money was like a sixth sense," he wrote, "without which you could not make the most of the other five." Every penny counted, and in perusing the statements sent in by Colles he allowed no detail to escape his attention. "I see that you have charged me some 15/- for postage; this you have never done before, & I don't see why you should suddenly begin," he wrote tersely in August 1904. He was relying on the new novel to rescue his finances and he stressed to Colles the importance of having the book properly publicized and promoted. "I hope," he wrote sternly, "you will impress upon Heinemann the necessity of advertising *The Merry-Go-Round* well." Unfortunately its appearance on September 19, 1904, was a flop, and in spite of a few good reviews, sales were poor, an outcome for which Maugham blamed both publisher and agent. Heinemann did no better at the beginning of the following year with *The Land of the Blessed Virgin;* this, too, failed to sell many copies in spite of a couple of appreciative notices, including one, unsigned, in *The Times Literary Supplement* by the young Virginia Stephen (later Virginia Woolf). "[Mr. Maugham] has his pen well under control," she wrote, "and he has a sincere desire to find the right word for the beauty which he genuinely loves."

As Maugham continued his ardent pursuit of the tantalizing Harry, the need for cash grew ever more pressing, and he continued to drive himself hard. "I wrote," as he put it, "with jealousy gnawing at my heart-strings." Dazzlingly attractive, Harry was much sought after, and it was mortifying to have to sit by while richer men treated him to suppers at the Savoy and lunches by the river at Maidenhead. Harry's "frivolous soul" delighted in such spoiling; he saw no reason to deny himself, and his lover's anguish was treated with an indifference that drove Maugham nearly to distraction. When in the summer of 1904 Harry came down from Oxford without a degree, vaguely inclining toward some kind of career as an artist, Maugham saw his chance and encouraged him to think seriously of training in Paris; he himself would leave London and take an apartment on the Left Bank that he and Harry could share. From the innocence of his country parish, Philips senior saw nothing wrong in the proposal: Maugham seemed a sensible chap, a hardworking writer with an established reputation who might well prove a good influence on his feckless son. Immediately Maugham put his plan into action, invigorated not only by the prospect of having his beloved boy to himself but also by the chance of breaking new ground. For more than six years he had struggled for success in London, and it suddenly seemed to look pointless and as though nothing would ever change. "It was all very nice, but I couldn't see that it was leading me anywhere," he wrote. "I was thirty . . . I was in a rut and I felt that I must get out of it. I talked the matter over with Walter Payne with the result that we got rid of the flat we had shared, sold for a song the little furniture we had and I, thrilled, went to Paris."

THROUGHOUT HIS TWENTIES Maugham had visited Paris at intervals, sometimes staying with his eldest brother, Charlie, and his young family, sometimes in a hotel, neither entirely satisfactory, as he explained to Violet Hunt. "When I am with my brother I am somewhat overwhelmed by domesticity & when I stay at a hotel I am ruined." Now in looking for somewhere to live Maugham enlisted the help of a new friend, Gerald Kelly, a young painter currently living in France whom he had met one Sunday in 1903 while staying with Charles and Beldy at the house they rented for the summer in Meudon.

Five years younger than Maugham, Gerald Kelly (of the family that published *Kelly's Directories*) was the son of a well-to-do clergyman, the vicar of St. Giles in Camberwell. Possessed of abundant nervous energy and an irascible Irish charm, Gerald was short and stocky, with finely drawn features, eyes alert behind big round spectacles, and a head of thick, untidy black hair. The formative experience of his early years had been his visits to Dulwich Picture Gallery, which first inspired his love of painting. Lacking any formal training in art, Kelly had nonetheless moved to Paris in 1901, where he bought a large studio in the rue Campagne-Première in Montparnasse, and, helped by the dealer Paul Durand-Ruel, began assiduously visiting the studios of Monet, Degas, and Cézanne, even succeeding in persuading the sculptor Rodin to take him on as an assistant. Concentrating on portraiture, with landscapes as a sideline, Kelly was beginning to become known. One of his paintings had been bought by the French government in 1903, and the following year, while still only twenty-five, he was made a member of the Salon d'Automne.

At Meudon, Maugham and Kelly had taken to each other at once, Maugham captivated by the younger man's exuberant volubility, his passion for art and ideas, while Kelly was impressed by

Maugham's intelligence, his dry sense of humor, and his wide-ranging curiosity. He was also fascinated by Maugham's appearance, which he longed to paint: "his whole face was just one colour—very pale [and] his eyes were like little pieces of brown velvet—like a monkey's eyes." The two men were very different in manner. "While I have leaned on his patience and on his wisdom, he has often been exasperated by my verbosity," Kelly wrote. Nonetheless they shared a number of common attributes: they were both tolerant and unshockable, both had a quick wit and a hot temper, although Maugham was better at controlling his; they both had a passion for travel; and they took pride in their intellectual integrity. "Both of us obstinately refused to pretend to admire what really we did not admire—even when we had been told we should admire it," said Kelly. "Willie dared to find Meredith and Pater overrated; I was bold enough to love Ingres and Manet—unfashionable judgments at the beginning of this century."

It was during this time, while he was living in Paris with Harry, that Maugham's education in the visual arts was seriously begun, and much of it he owed to Kelly. It was Kelly who lent him books and taught him how to look at paintings, exploring with him the works of the Old Masters as well as introducing him to the new. Kelly inspired his friend with his own passion for Velázquez, Maugham responding with fervor to the Spanish master's vision of Spain as well as to his uncompromising realism and profound humanity; and it was Kelly who first showed Maugham work by the Impressionists, taking him to see the collection at the Luxembourg. But despite Kelly's energetic enthusiasm, Maugham at this stage remained unimpressed: "to my shame," he wrote later, "I could not make head or tail of them." When apart, the two men wrote at length to each other about art, and after Maugham became famous, Kelly was his principal portraitist, painting him a total of eighteen times. Despite Kelly's superior knowledge, Maugham never hesitated to instruct his friend, candidly criticizing his work, pointing out where he was going wrong and taking advantage of his five years' seniority to adopt the tone of an affectionate but bossy elder brother. "My dear Gerald," he wrote in July 1905,

I am very sorry, though by no means surprised, that you have fallen ill again. It is obvious to the meanest intelligence that if you lead such a life as you led in Paris you are quite sure to be ill. . . . I cannot write to you with any patience. By the stupidest carelessness . . . you are throwing away all your chances of becoming a better painter than Tom, Dick, or Harry. For the work you do when you're not well is rotten. . . .

With Kelly, Maugham enjoyed the kind of fraternal relationship he had never formed within his own family, and although there were areas of his life that remained off-limits, his miserable childhood, for instance, and his brother's suicide, he confided in Kelly freely about almost everything else. And Kelly did the same with Maugham, on several occasions turning to him for advice when his tempestuous affairs with women went wrong. Their friendship was close and it lasted a lifetime. After Maugham's death Gerald Kelly's words were reported in *The Times:* "Willie was a duck," he said, "an absolute duck."

At Maugham's request Kelly found him living quarters near his own in Montparnasse. The apartment at number 3 rue Victor Considérant was on the fifth floor, with a view over the cemetery where Maupassant is buried, and near the great bronze Lion de Belfort. There were two rooms and a kitchen, for which the rent was 700 francs a year, the equivalent of £28; some secondhand furniture and basic utensils were purchased and a *bonne-à-toute-faire* engaged to come in the mornings to make breakfast and do the housework and laundry. Kelly's help had also been enlisted in recommending drawing classes for Harry Philips, "who has the ingenious idea of cultivating the smaller arts—costume, posters, illustration, & so forth," Maugham had written from London. The version for general consumption was that the young man was accompanying Maugham as his secretary, but as Harry frankly admitted, "I cannot say that I was his secretary, although we used that *nom de plume*. I was his companion & wrote a few notes, social & otherwise for him."

Harry's allowance was only £120 a year, and as Maugham's annual earnings amounted to barely as much, the two men were obliged to lead a frugal existence, economizing where they could and feeding themselves as cheaply as possible at the local restaurants and cafés. Despite his poverty, Maugham wished to indulge his young companion, desperately anxious to keep him happy. "He was exceedingly kind in every way," said Harry, remembering the many evenings at the theater, the excursions to Versailles, the afternoons in the Louvre and the Luxembourg. Although not much of a reader himself, Harry was impressed by Maugham's knowledge of literature and even more by his gifts as a linguist, not only in French but in German, Spanish, and Italian. Harry had the sense, or perhaps the insensitivity, to respect Maugham's reticence: vaguely aware that his early life had been unhappy, that there was a profound sadness over the death of his brother, he never probed, preferring instead to encourage the lighthearted side of his nature. "Maugham adored a laugh," Harry recalled, "& had a generous sense of humour."

Paris may have been cheaper than London, but amusements still had to be paid for, and Maugham was inflexible in keeping to the strict working routine that he had long established. After writing all morning until 12:30, he and "the Gilded Youth," as he somewhat drily referred to Harry, would go out for a modest lunch, on Sundays treating themselves to an apéritif first at the Café de la Paix.

Most evenings the two men dined at Le Chat Blanc, a little restaurant in the rue d'Odessa. Here they became part of a group of painters, writers, and sculptors to whom Gerald Kelly had introduced them. A few were French, but most were English and American, and they dined together nightly at a communal table upstairs, where over an inexpensive couple of courses and plenty of wine the rival merits of the leading artists of the day were noisily debated. These gatherings were the nearest that Maugham, in later life always careful to conform to the outward appearance of respectability, came to the bohemian way of life. Conversation often grew hotly argumentative, carried on in a fug of cigar smoke in a mixture of English and French. Among the regulars were Kelly, who would sometimes bring in his patron, Rodin, bearded and pungent; Clive Bell, a young English art student; Ivor Back, a trainee surgeon and friend of Kelly's; Penrhyn Stanlaws, the American "pretty women" painter; the Canadian Impressionist James Wilson Morrice, regarded with awe for his acquaintance with Bonnard, Matisse, Vuillard, and Lautrec; and the formidable Irish painter Roderic O'Conor, tall, swarthy, and misanthropic. "I suspect he was a tragic figure," wrote Clive Bell, one of the few who succeeded in befriending the surly Irishman, "though he kept his tragedy to himself."

It was the Irishman who interested Maugham the most, mainly because of O'Conor's friendship with Gauguin. In 1903 Maugham had been taken by Kelly to the famous Gauguin exhibition at the Galérie Vollard and had become fascinated with both the man and his work. Learning that O'Conor had spent some months with Gauguin in Brittany, Maugham was eager to ask him about it, "but unfortunately he took an immediate dislike to me which he did not hesitate to show." One evening the two men had a furious row about the merits of the poet Hérédia, during which the Irishman remained "coldly and bitingly virulent." Maugham refused to be cowed, however, and genuinely admiring O'Conor's work, he called a few days later at his studio and asked to buy a couple of small still-lifes. O'Conor was taken aback. "After a moment's hesitation, with a sullen look on his face, he mentioned a price, a very modest one, and I took the money out of my pocket and went away with the pictures in my hands." This gesture did little to improve relations, however, and O'Conor was overheard comparing Maugham to "a bed bug, on which a sensitive man refuses to stamp because of the smell and the squashiness."

This disobliging remark was relayed by another member of the group, a big, bull-like man with a savage, sensual face, flamboyantly dressed in a bejeweled red waistcoat and large silk cravat, with an enormous ring on one pudgy white hand. Aleister Crowley had been at Cambridge with Kelly, and in 1903 had married Kelly's sis-

ter, Rose. Claiming to be a master of the occult and recently created "Khan of the East," Crowley was a compulsive showoff, declaiming dramatically and making fantastic boasts of his mental and
physical prowess, and most sensationally of his supernatural powers: he himself, it appeared, had led many past lives, and was
presently reincarnated as none other than the Great Beast of the
Apocalypse; he liked to be known as Brother Perdurabo, under
which guise he dabbled in satanism and had been much involved in
the occult goings-on of the Hermetic Order of the Golden Dawn.
Crowley had experimented copiously with drugs and was indefatigable in exploring his complex sexuality, avidly pursuing every
kind of debauch with both men and women, preferably of a sadistic
and sanguinary nature. As might be expected, this preposterous
person fascinated Maugham. "I took an immediate dislike to him,"
he wrote, "but he interested and amused me." Certainly Maugham
had no wish to befriend Brother Perdurabo, but the mesmerizing
performance and undeniably sinister aura caught at his imagination,
shortly to emerge re-formed in the character of the infamous
Oliver Haddo in *The Magician*.

One of the few who saw good qualities in Crowley was the novelist Enoch Arnold Bennett, who in 1902 had moved to Paris,
where he lived with his fox terrier, Fly, in a modest apartment in
Montmartre. Like Maugham, Bennett had been introduced by Gerald Kelly to Le Chat Blanc, and had formed the habit of dining
there once a week. Both Maugham and Gerald Kelly tended to pa-
tronize Bennett, or "Enoch Arnold," as they referred to him between themselves. With his bristly mustache and rabbity teeth, they
thought he looked vulgar, "like a managing clerk in a city office,"
as Maugham snobbishly described him; behind his back they
mocked his clothes and Midlands accent, found his manners un-
couth, and dismissed his successful *The Grand Hotel Babylon* as populist tosh. Bennett's French was clumsy, whereas Maugham spoke
like a native, but at their very first meeting it was Bennett who, unforgivably, put Maugham in the wrong. As Kelly related it, at the
end of dinner,

Willie—with his impeccable French accent—said to the waitress: "Vous me donnerez un anneau," meaning that he wanted
a napkin ring. . . . "You know, Maugham," observed Bennett
heavily, "the French don't call it an 'anno,' they call it a 'rong.' "
(He meant a "rond.") Willie became quite grey with rage; to
have made this absurd mistake and thus laid himself open to
correction by a quite unspeakable individual whose knowledge of French was rudimentary!

A further cause for division was the embarrassing fact that Bennett,
like Maugham, suffered from a bad stammer, and Maugham was
well aware that the two of them at the same table struggling to get
the words out ran a high risk of looking grotesque. As he admitted,
"I am dreadfully afraid of being ridiculous."

Fortunately the amiable Bennett either failed to notice or refused to be offended by Maugham's *de-haut-en-bas* manner, enjoying his company and taking pleasure in the younger man's style.
Sometimes after dinner Maugham and Kelly would accompany
Bennett home, where he would play Beethoven to them on an upright piano. On one of these occasions Bennett startled Maugham
by making him an unexpected proposal: Would Maugham like to
share in his mistress? She spent two nights a week with him and two
nights with another gentleman, liked to take Sundays off, but was
on the lookout for someone who would take the two nights she still
had available. "I've told her about you," said Bennett. "She likes
writers [and] I'd like to see her nicely fixed up." The offer was declined.

Despite the unpromising start to the friendship, Maugham eventually became genuinely fond of Bennett, "a very lovable man" as
he described him, and he greatly admired Bennett's later masterpiece, *The Old Wives' Tale,* which he thought in its author's lifetime
never received the critical accolade it deserved. Violet Hunt, also in
Paris at that time, was one of Maugham's circle whom he introduced to Enoch Arnold, and when Maugham was otherwise engaged, she promoted Bennett to the position of favorite escort.

It was only to Violet, however, that he let down his guard and talked about his private life and emotions. At this period he was suffering a good deal of wretchedness over Harry Philips, and Violet, whose own love affairs were invariably passionate and unhappy, provided a sympathetic ear. "I never saw Maugham moved except one . . . time in Paris," she noted in her diary, almost certainly a reference to Maugham's unburdening himself about Harry's behavior. Something had happened between the two men, most probably an incident of infidelity on Harry's part, that had upset Maugham a good deal and that, as Harry later recounted, was to reappear in *Of Human Bondage*. Looking back Harry regretted his behavior. "I was somewhat ashamed," he said, "as I realized that I had hurt his feelings more than I thought." In May 1905 Harry decided to return to England for a while, leaving his lover despondent. In a letter to Kelly, temporarily absent from Paris, Maugham complained of his low spirits. "I miss you sadly," he told Gerald, "[and] I know not how I shall do when the Gilded Youth has abandoned me. . . . I am sick to death of my work & seized by panic that all my imagination has left me: sometimes I fear that I shall never be able to do any good again. I feel like a well run dry."

The work with which he was having such difficulty was a novel, *The Bishop's Apron,* a reworking of *Loaves and Fishes,* one of three plays, as yet unproduced, written after *A Man of Honour. The Bishop's Apron* is a much improved version, more complex and substantial, of what in dramatic form is a rather formulaic comedy about a snobbish clergyman with some very worldly ambitions. Theodore Spratte, vicar of St. Gregory's in South Kensington, is handsome, pompous, and vain (Maugham, it should be noted, rarely has a good word to say for the Anglican clergy). A widower, he lives with his sister and two grown-up children, devoting his energies to the busy pursuit of bettering the standing of himself and his family. If all goes as planned, his son and daughter will marry rank and money, and he himself be offered the see of Barchester, thus the reference to the episcopal vestment of the title. At first it looks as if none of his ambitions will be realized, but with typical contrariness Maugham reverses expectation, and by the last chapter the Reverend Theodore Spratte has everything he wanted and more: a bigger and better bishopric than Barchester, his daughter wed to a wealthy peer, and he himself betrothed to the well-endowed beauty his timid son failed to claim for himself.

If *The Bishop's Apron* reads a little like a novel-by-numbers, it is nonetheless an extremely efficient piece of work. Maugham was anxious to have it published as soon as possible, but not by Heinemann, condemned as culpably negligent in having failed to promote *The Merry-Go-Round*. A large share of the blame was laid also at the door of Maurice Colles, whose genial indolence had come to irritate Maugham intensely. Determined to put his affairs in the hands of someone more focused and businesslike, he talked the matter over with Arnold Bennett, another disaffected Colles client, who was now with J. B. Pinker, with whom he was much pleased; urging Maugham to follow his example, he offered to effect the introduction. "I think I have got you a new client in the person of W. Somerset Maugham," Bennett wrote to Pinker. "He seems to me a man who will make his way."

James Brand Pinker had set up his agency in 1896, having worked for a number of years on newspapers and magazines, an experience that had gained him useful contacts and an intimate knowledge of the British literary world. From his office on Arundel Street off the Strand, Pinker, clean-shaven and rosy-cheeked, dealt with the rights and contracts of a growing number of distinguished writers including Wells, Galsworthy, Conrad, Gissing, Joyce, Jack London, and Ford Madox Ford. With A. P. Watt and Curtis Brown, he was regarded as one of the leading players in the field, respected by authors and publishers alike as much for his engaging personality as for his considerable business acumen. Even William Heinemann, who had been such a vigorous opponent of the literary agent, enjoyed cordial relations with him, and indeed it was at Heinemann's suggestion that Henry James was added to Pinker's list.

Maugham's association with Pinker was to make an important difference to his professional career, and he quickly came to appreciate his new agent's dedication and expertise. Immediately, however, he was faced with the task of disengaging himself from his old agent, Maurice Colles, who was shocked and hurt by Maugham's proposed defection and by his accusations over the handling of *The Merry-Go-Round*. But Maugham was adamant. "I think we must agree to differ," he told Colles firmly. "I do not wish to enter into recriminations; but I cannot help thinking that what is obvious to me now your experience might have suggested to you then, namely, that when a publisher does not like a book & has made up his mind that it will not sell, one might just as well throw it in the Thames as let him publish it." With the old connection severed, Maugham then wrote to his new agent: knowing exactly what he wanted, he took the trouble to set out his expectations, making clear that he intended to consign all his writing to Pinker with the exception of the plays, which would be handled by the theatrical agent Reginald Golding Bright. As to *The Bishop's Apron,* he suggested it should be offered to Chapman & Hall, who had already expressed an interest in publishing Maugham, "& I imagine they will give an advance of £150 & a good royalty." But here Maugham's imagination had run away with him: Arthur Waugh, the firm's director, told Pinker there was no question of increasing his offer of exactly half that sum, £75, and with that Maugham was obliged to be content. Dedicated to Harry Philips, *The Bishop's Apron: A Study in the Origins of a Great Family* was published in a small edition in February 1906, without Maugham's evil eye insignia and with little advertisement, its critical reception, good-humored if somewhat sparse, along much the same lines as that accorded to *The Merry-Go-Round*.

Much of the correspondence with Colles and Pinker had been written by Maugham from Capri, where, having patched up his relationship with Harry, he had gone with him in July 1905 for an extended holiday. The two men had taken a little house, the Villa Valentino, and Maugham was reveling in the Mediterranean warmth and indolence and in the return of Harry's companionship. "We have been here nearly a week," Maugham wrote contentedly to Gerald Kelly in early July,

[with] nothing whatever to do from morning till night. . . . The Gilded Youth, somewhat overcome by the heat at pres-

ent, cannot make it out: he murmurs plaintively that it is such a rush to do nothing. . . . We have both suffered agonies by lying out, naked, in the sun too long on our first day. . . . G.Y.'s snowy skin suffered terribly. . . . The bathing is of course delightful; the water so warm that one can play about in it the whole morning.

Under these idyllic conditions, Maugham found it difficult to get down to work. "I have not an idea in my head," he told Kelly,

> & except that I'm rather afraid I shall never have any more in my life, I'm much pleased with myself. Only, being of a damned dissatisfied temper, it is only with difficulty that I prevent myself from making plans for the future. I find it one of the hardest things in the world to enjoy the present moment: my impulse is always to neglect it for the consideration of the wonderful things I shall do & see & feel three months hence.

One whom Maugham had looked forward to seeing again was his old friend from Heidelberg, John Ellingham Brooks, but he was disappointed to find Brooks no longer the stimulating companion he once had been. The handsome, vibrant character, so full of ideas and enthusiasm, had developed into something of a bore, his innovative theories now seeming stale and old-fashioned; his hair was thinning, he had put on weight, and his blue eyes had a slightly watery look. Having squandered his small fortune, Brooks had been rescued from penury by a wealthy American painter, Romaine Goddard, who, herself homosexual, had taken pity on him and agreed to a marriage of convenience, imagining that Brooks might provide her with pleasant companionship when she was on the island while leaving her free to follow her own distinctively bohemian life in London and elsewhere. The marriage proved a disaster, however, with Brooks shocking his wife by his grasping attitude toward money, his dreadful manners, and his insistence on a ménage à trois with a sulky peasant boyfriend forever in the background. Having married in June 1903, they formally separated a year later, Romaine buying her husband off with an income of £300 a year, a sum which was more than adequate to provide Brooks with a comfortable life of lotus-eating on Capri. As his friend E. F. Benson phrased it, "In the process of making a complete failure of his life as far as achievement of any sort went, he made himself for many years very happy."

While Maugham was writing of his summer to Gerald Kelly in Paris, Kelly was describing a passionate love affair he had embarked upon with a young dancer; he was proposing to move her in with him but wanted to know what Maugham thought of the scheme. Not much, was the answer; he gives his reasons in a letter that clearly refers to a harrowing experience of Maugham's own, and goes some considerable way to explaining his horror of the kind of relationship he depicts in both *The Man of Honour* and *The Bishop's Apron,* a relationship between two people disastrously unequal in intellect and social station. "I'm sure a lot of people will think you a devilish lucky fellow," Maugham wrote to Kelly,

[but] you must not mind if I congratulate myself rather than you. . . . I cannot help rubbing my hands & gloating because I do not stand in your shoes. . . . You wait, my boy, till you are asked when you'll be back each time you go out, & where you've been the moment you come in, till you have to put up with sulks if you don't agree to the most unreasonable things, & quarrels for the absurdest trifles. . . . Ouf! I sweat when I think of it. Women can never leave a man his freedom, they use every imaginable device to load him with chains. . . . You'll find every penny is important. Taking a woman about with one is not cheap, because one has to go in cabs instead of buses, & they have all sorts of little whims which have to be satisfied. And you'll want more money, because you'll go a great deal more to theatres & out in the evenings. You'll find that when one lives with a person of no particular education . . . time hangs rather heavily on one's hands; one racks one's brains for conversation & at last is driven to going some-

where. . . . Having said all this I give you my blessing & wish you well. . . . For myself I only hope that I shall never again be imprisoned by any passion.

The idyll on Capri failed to last the summer. At the beginning of August, Harry decided he had had enough and returned to his family in Staffordshire. "It was there I decided I was really getting nowhere & should he tire of me I would be pretty useless," Harry recalled. "His cynicism distressed me [&] I found it difficult to live with someone who believed that no one did anything without a motive." To gregarious Harry, intent on having fun, Maugham's periods of moodiness and introversion were incomprehensible, their growing lack of communication something of which Maugham himself was miserably aware; as he wrote in his notebook,

one places all one's love, all one's faculty of expansion on one person, making, as it were, a final effort to join one's soul to his. . . . But little by little one finds that it is all impossible, and however ardently one loves him, however intimately one is connected with him, he is always a stranger. . . . Then one retires into oneself and in one's silence builds a world of one's own which one keeps from the eyes of every living soul, even from the person one loves best, knowing he would not understand it.

The two men parted on good terms, however. Harry shortly afterward joined the army for a spell, before marrying a rich woman whose substantial fortune enabled him to live in idleness for the rest of his days.

WITH HARRY GONE, Maugham expected to be heartbroken; but in fact he soon recovered. Having received the first payment from Chapman & Hall for his novel, he was gratified to realize that the sum was all his to do with as he pleased. "By the time I received the money the passion that I had thought would last for ever was extinct and I had no longer the slightest wish to spend it in the way I had intended." Instead he spent it on travel, first to Tuscany with the dependable Walter Payne, then skiing in Switzerland, and in January the following year to Egypt for a couple of months. Passing through Paris only to tidy up his affairs, Maugham returned to London in the spring of 1906, extremely hard up but more determined than ever to make the breakthrough into fame and prosperity. While abroad he had written some travel articles as well as a couple of short stories, and Pinker, like Colles before him, was being urged to chase payments. "Has *The Lady's Realm* or whatever it was stumped up?" Maugham was anxiously inquiring in July. "This is the season when my tailor & hatter send in bills." Fortunately Maugham's living expenses were minimal. Payne, who continued to handle his friend's financial affairs, had taken rooms in Pall Mall, number 56, and as before, Maugham was able to make use of these, needing to rent only a bedroom next door. Here he set himself to work on a new novel, inspired by the grotesque figure from Le Chat Blanc, Aleister Crowley. *The Magician* was finished by the end of the year, but the horrific nature of its content shocked the publishers to whom it was shown, and Pinker failed to sell it.

Beginning to grow financially desperate, Maugham now resorted to the quick fix of recycling old material. He had already excavated his rejected play *The Explorer,* digging out one of its subplots for use as the short story "Flirtation," and now, like a thrifty housewife determined not to let anything go to waste, he sat down to rewrite the entire play as a novel. It was a tedious exercise, and Maugham was ashamed of the finished product. Suggested by the adventures of the great African explorer H. M. Stanley, the man who "found" Livingstone, the plot revolves around a young man's noble refusal to clear his own reputation by breaking his word to a scoundrel. *The Explorer,* dedicated "To my dear Mrs. W. G. Steevens," reads like the mechanical exercise that indeed Maugham had found it to be. "I *do not like* it," he told Violet Hunt, while to Gerald Kelly, in whose copy was inscribed the words, "Gerald Kelly from W. S. Maugham, his worst book," he wrote,

"The people were too heroic for me to live with . . . I vomited daily at the exalted sentiments that issued from their lips, & my hair stood up on end at the delicacy of their sense of honour."

By the end of the summer of 1907 Maugham was exhausted and had seen little reward for his unrelenting industry. *The Explorer* had been accepted by Heinemann but would not appear until the following year; *The Magician* had still not found a publisher; and none of the plays that had been circulating around the London managements had found any takers, despite the tenacity of Maugham's play agent, Golding Bright. But there was one glimmer of light. While in Paris Maugham had written a comedy, *Lady Frederick,* which he had designed specifically to provide a succulent part for a leading actress. At first the play met with no greater enthusiasm than its predecessors, but then suddenly Maugham's luck seemed to change: George Tyler, an American producer in Paris on the lookout for material, read it, liked it, and offered to buy an option on it for $1,000. Tyler invited Maugham to his hotel to discuss the proposition, telling him that the piece packed a hell of a punch, though it needed gingering up with a few more epigrams (within a couple of hours Maugham added twenty-four). He gave his visitor a couple of cocktails, the first of his life, "[and] Maugham told me afterwards," said Tyler, "that, when he left me that afternoon with his check for a thousand in his pocket, he was stepping on his left ear with his right hind foot. . . . He struck me as a nice young fellow with a possible future." Convinced he had a hot property, Tyler returned with the script to London, only to find that no actress, in the words of one to whom he showed it, would touch the part with a ten-foot pole. The problem was that the eponymous heroine, Lady Frederick, a fascinating adventuress not quite in her first youth, is required in the pivotal scene to appear literally and shockingly barefaced: brightly lit, wearing no makeup, and without the false hair that most fashionable women then used in considerable quantities. Under these conditions none of the big stars who might otherwise have leaped at the role would look at it: Ellis Jeffreys, the elegant and sophisticated comedienne, was appalled by the very idea; Mrs. Pat Campbell declared she had never been so insulted in her life; the American star Violet Allen said she wouldn't consider it for a moment. Charles Frohman was approached but saw little merit in the play, and so reluctantly Tyler was forced to abandon the project, "feeling pretty melancholy on Maugham's account and pretty sore on my own."

Dejected but resolute, Maugham immediately started on a new work, *Mrs. Dot,* also with a strong female lead, yet carefully designed to cause offense to nobody; this, however, was turned down on the grounds that it was too bland. "I began to think that I should never be able to write a piece that a leading lady liked," Maugham wrote despairingly, "and so tried my hand at a man's play . . . *Jack Straw.*" When this, too, failed to find favor, Maugham came near to giving up: there seemed to be nothing for it but to return to his abandoned medical career, go back to St. Thomas's for a year's revision, and then try to find a post as a ship's surgeon, which would at least give him the opportunity to travel.

It was at this point that interest was suddenly revived in *Lady Frederick*. Otho Stuart, manager of the Royal Court Theatre in Sloane Square, had had a play fail unexpectedly and was now faced with the theater dark for six weeks before his next presentation. Maugham's comedy was not at all his kind of thing, but no doubt it would adequately fill the short time available. Maugham was on his travels when he heard the news. From Sicily he wrote excitedly to Golding Bright, "Your letter filled me with exultation, & now the likelihood of an early production makes me realise that the world is not hollow & foolish." A courageous actress had been found, Ethel Irving, to play the lead, and rehearsals, which Maugham was desperate to attend, were due to start within a few days.

It was a Sunday when Bright's letter reached Maugham in Girgenti and he learned of the sudden change in his fortunes. Now he urgently needed to be in London the following Thursday. Almost penniless, he found he had enough money only for the train to Palermo and the evening packet to Naples. At Naples he disembarked on Monday morning.

I went to Cook's and found that a boat was going to Marseilles that afternoon and took a ticket, but when I offered a cheque in payment the agent firmly refused to accept anything but cash. . . . I expostulated, I raged, I stormed; and at last (I am not a dramatist for nothing) flung out of the office. . . . I went to the office of the steamship company and asked for a first class ticket to Marseilles . . . and without a word wrote a cheque for the amount due. The clerk, young and timid, looked a trifle doubtful, but my assurance was such that I think he had not the nerve to refuse; in a minute I was out of the office with my ticket to Marseilles in my pocket. But I had to get to London. . . . The shipping agents were also bankers, the banking part of the establishment being in another part of the building; I went in and walked boldly up to the desk. I took out my cheque book and the ticket I had just received.

"I'm going to Marseilles on one of your boats this afternoon. You might cash me a cheque for a fiver, will you?" I smiled ingratiatingly. . . .

I did not linger in the bank long after I had the five sovereigns in my pocket. . . . I was in great spirits, for now I had enough money to take me to Paris, and I felt confident that I could get on from there without delay. . . .

When I got to London I still had a shilling for my cab. On Thursday morning at eleven o'clock I strolled into the Court Theatre. . . .

Lady Frederick, rejected by seventeen managements, was for Maugham the first step on the path to enormous celebrity and wealth. The play, written on the back of discarded typescript because, said the author, "[I was] very short of money [and] could not afford to waste pages of good clean paper," opened on October 26, 1907. So great was its success that Maugham became famous almost literally overnight—"England's Dramatist," as he was dubbed by the press. *Lady Frederick* ran for more than a year, and by the following year, 1908, four of Maugham's plays were running concurrently in the West End, a record that for a living playwright was to remain unbroken for a generation.

CHAPTER 5

ENGLAND'S
DRAMATIST

. . .

T HE YEARS BETWEEN THE BEGINNING OF THE CENTURY AND THE
beginning of the [1914] war," wrote the distinguished theater
critic James Agate, "mark a period of the greatest dramatic energy
in this country since the Elizabethans." It was in 1907, exactly in
the middle of this productive period, that with *Lady Frederick*
Maugham enjoyed his first great triumph and laid the foundations
of his reputation as one of the most sought-after playwrights of the
age. In an era dominated by Shaw, with Galsworthy and Granville
Barker among the best known of the serious dramatists, it was
Somerset Maugham and James Barrie who for a number of years
and in terms of fashionable reputation were preeminent in the
world of West End comedy, although Barrie, despite the annual re-
vivals of *Peter Pan,* never quite approached Maugham's popularity
or earning power. This period saw the final phase of the type of society drama, witty and urbane, at which Maugham excelled: his
acute intelligence enabled him to gauge what his audiences wanted;
his expert craftsmanship delivered it. The staging of *Lady Frederick*
at the Royal Court owed a great deal to luck, but its subsequent
success was largely due to the care with which its author had
weighed and measured his ingredients. Before beginning on *Lady
Frederick,* Maugham explained,

> I reflected upon the qualities which the managers demanded
> in a play: evidently a comedy, for the public wished to laugh;

with as much drama as it would carry, for the public liked a thrill; with a little sentiment, for the public liked to feel good; and a happy ending.

Equally important, what kind of part would be most tempting to a leading lady? A beautiful adventuress with a title and a heart of gold, was the obvious answer. "Having made up my mind upon this the rest was easy."

A deft if ephemeral society comedy, *Lady Frederick* is light, sophisticated, and absolutely true to its well-established genre. Set in 1890, the action takes place in the Hôtel de Paris in Monte Carlo, where we find Lady Frederick Berolles, a charming and attractive widow in her late thirties, teetering on the verge of bankruptcy. Pleasure-loving and extravagant, she is also, despite appearances and some scandalous rumors to the contrary, a woman with a strong sense of honor. Marriage to young Charlie Mereston, a marquess with £50,000 a year, would solve all Lady Frederick's problems, and the young man is very much in love with her; but desperate though her situation is, Lady Frederick will not stoop to such a venal solution, bravely resolving to quench her youthful suitor's passion by appearing to him in her natural state. Act III, the scene that had frightened off so many actresses, opens in Lady Frederick's dressing room, the blinds pulled up to let in strong sunlight; the stage instructions describe her as "haggard and yellow and lined." In full view of the audience and Lord Mereston, the transformation is then unflinchingly effected, the false hair, the greasepaint, rouge, pencil, and powder, each step in the process mercilessly explained to an appalled Charlie Mereston. "Now for the delicate soft bloom of youth," says Lady Frederick gaily, picking up her pot of rouge. "The great difficulty, you know, is to make both your cheeks the same colour."

The ruse is successful: Mereston is persuaded to give up his pursuit and all ends happily, with the heroine agreeing to marry Paradine Fouldes, a wealthy old admirer, who as he takes her in his arms says sentimentally, "D'you suppose I don't know that behind that very artificial complexion there's a dear little woman called Betsy who's genuine to the bottom of her soul?"

Always fascinated by the feminine, Maugham was clearly intrigued by the subject of women and cosmetics, and by the moral implications involved: in the Edwardian era no respectable young lady would dream of using makeup, and even in the most sophisticated circles there was still an aura of questionable respectability about older women who were known to paint. With *Lady Frederick* Maugham had carefully calculated the impact the final act would make, and when the audience watched the leading lady, Ethel Irving, artificially construct her character's girlish complexion, they were as shocked and thrilled as audiences sixty years later when first confronted with full frontal nudity on the stage in *Hair.*

The elation and enthusiasm shown by the audience on the first night were echoed in most of the reviews. "Exhilarating entertainment," said *The Times,* while Reginald Turner in *The Academy* wrote, "a delicious evening, full of delight from start to finish. . . . [The author] was completely, splendidly successful." Such a reception naturally came as an immense relief to Maugham: when he had arrived at the theater that evening he had not known, he said, whether he should leave it "as an accomplished dramatist or an embryo bank clerk." During the performance he sat, in white tie and tails, pale and silent at the back of a box; by the end of the first act, however, it was clear that he had a hit on his hands. At the supper party he gave at the Bath Club, he was seen to be in exuberant high spirits, warmly thanking the actors, especially Ethel Irving, unanimously praised by the critics, and also Charles Lowne, who played Paradine Fouldes. Throughout his life Maugham was to remember the first night of *Lady Frederick* as the most exciting moment of his theatrical career.

Lady Frederick quickly became the talk of the town, transferring from the Royal Court to the Garrick Theatre, then to the Criterion, the New, and finally the Haymarket, where it completed an impressive run of 422 performances. The American impresario Charles Frohman, who had originally turned the play down, now "ate crow" and bought the U.S. rights for twice what he would originally have had to pay, putting it on in New York to great acclaim the following year with Ethel Barrymore in the lead.

Suddenly Maugham was much in demand as a dramatist, and his play agent, Golding Bright, was inundated with requests from eager managers for scripts that previously they had had no hesitation in declining. In quick succession Bright sold three plays that had been written earlier and turned down—*Mrs. Dot, The Explorer,* and *Jack Straw*—and was kept busy fielding requests for Maugham to undertake commissions. Exhilarated by this sudden turn in his fortunes, Maugham felt that finally he had arrived exactly where he wished to be, as a playwright, not a novelist. This moment of epiphany came to him one evening while walking past the Comedy Theatre in Panton Street:

> I happened to look up and saw the clouds lit by the setting sun. I paused to look at the lovely sight and I thought to myself: Thank God, I can look at a sunset now without having to think how to describe it. I meant then never to write another book, but to devote myself for the rest of my life to the drama.

To this end he wrote to his literary agent, J. B. Pinker, to sever the association between them, explaining that he now had so many requests for plays he would no longer have time to write stories—a letter that Pinker sensibly chose to ignore.

Maugham's next play, *Jack Straw,* opened at the Vaudeville in the Strand on March 26; this was quickly followed by *Mrs. Dot* at the Comedy on April 27; and lastly, on June 13, *The Explorer* at the Lyric. Maugham was now in the astonishing position of having four plays in the West End, with only *The Explorer* failing to make a respectable run, with a mere 48 performances against *Lady Frederick*'s 422, *Jack Straw*'s 321, and 272 for *Mrs. Dot.* "My success was spectacular and unexpected," Maugham recalled with satisfaction. His name and the titles of his plays, "the Maugham quartet," were everywhere: Walter Payne leafing through the sporting pages even came across two racehorses called "Lady Frederick" and "Mrs. Dot." "I was much photographed and much interviewed. Distinguished people sought my acquaintance. . . . I thoroughly enjoyed myself."

Predictably, Maugham, as the celebrity of the moment, was much pursued by theatrical and society hostesses. Among them was Lady St. Helier, who had originally taken Maugham up in the nineties at the request of Augustus Hare and who now began to pursue him with vigor. "Great ladies," Maugham cynically observed, "cultivate those occupied with the arts as in former times they kept buffoons." It was at Lady St. Helier's house in Portland Place that he had his sole encounter with two great literary figures, Edith Wharton and Thomas Hardy. Invited to a luncheon given in the American novelist's honor, he was led up to talk to her. Beautifully dressed and magnificently condescending, Mrs. Wharton lectured him for twenty minutes with exquisite refinement on a range of well-chosen cultural topics, until Maugham, feeling suffocated by her intellectual patronage, blurted out a question about the thriller writer Edgar Wallace. Mrs. Wharton looked at him with distaste.

> "Who is Edgar Wallace?" she replied.
> "Do you never read thrillers?"
> "No."
> Never has a monosyllable contained more frigid displeasure . . . her eyes wandered away and a little forced smile slightly curled her lips.
> "I'm afraid it's getting very late," said Mrs. Wharton.

Thomas Hardy was far more congenial. The occasion was a large, formal dinner party of eminent figures in politics and the arts.

> When the ladies retired to the drawing-room I found myself sitting next to Thomas Hardy. I remember a little man with an earthy face. In his evening clothes, with his boiled shirt and high collar, he had still a strange look of the soil. He was amiable and mild. It struck me at the time that there was in him a curious mixture of shyness and self-assurance. I do not remember what we talked about, but I know that we talked for three-quarters of an hour.

Mrs. Wharton, living in Paris, may have been unaware of Maugham's celebrity, but in London his name could hardly be avoided. J. T. Grein in *The Sunday Times* wrote, "One has to go back to the early days of Sardou★ to find a popularity similar and so sudden"; *Punch* ran a cartoon by Bernard Partridge showing the ghost of William Shakespeare scowling enviously at the sight of a wall covered in posters for Maugham's four plays; and Max Beerbohm in the *Saturday Review* hailed Somerset Maugham as "the hero of the year [whose] name is a household word even in households where the theatre is held unclean." With four plays running, why not five? Max speculated. "Five plays running simultaneously! Stupendous! . . . Yet, after all, what are five theatres among so many? Why shouldn't *all* the theatres in London be Maughamised?"

It was Grein, an energetic supporter of Maugham's since he had first produced *A Man of Honour* at the Stage Society, who wrote one of the most enthusiastic reviews of the next play, *Jack Straw,* which he described as "light as a feather and as saucy as a sparrow." An exuberant, intricately plotted piece, *Jack Straw* had been dashed off in a couple of weeks during Maugham's sojourn in Paris in 1905. The plot was suggested by a story told him by Harry Philips about some people he knew back home in Staffordshire. Thomas Twyford, a wealthy pottery manufacturer, had been cold-shouldered on moving into the neighborhood until he was taken up by Grand Duke Michael of Russia, who was leasing a house nearby. After this, according to Harry, the Twyfords "suddenly became much sought after." In the play some details were changed but the parallels were not difficult to draw, and after the play opened Harry found himself in hot water, banned from a number of houses in the locality. This experience was an early instance of what was to evolve into a familiar pattern: a story relayed to Maugham by a third party, then redesigned by him in fictional form but with so little attempt at disguise that the work's appearance frequently resulted in shocked recognition and hurt feelings. Harry Philips may have been the first but he was certainly not the last of these purveyors of tales to suffer

★ Victorien Sardou (1831–1908), a popular French playwright.

from the furious fallout consequent upon publication, a fallout that generally left Maugham himself singularly undisturbed.

AT THIS POINT in his career, Maugham as the author had little say in the matter of casting, and indeed had failed in the one attempt he made to secure a part for a friend. In *Jack Straw,* "I tried to get a small part for Sue, but could not manage it," he had written to Kelly in February 1908.

Ethelwyn Sylvia Jones, known as Sue, was a young actress, daughter of the playwright Henry Arthur Jones, who, like Maugham, had become one of Mrs. Steevens's regular visitors at Merton Place. Jones, an amusing, energetic man in his late fifties, was a farmer's son who by sheer determination had established himself in the theater; he had enjoyed considerable success during the 1890s, although his career was now on the wane. As Jones had much admired *Liza of Lambeth,* he and Maugham quickly established a rapport, with Jones voluble on the subject of the drama, talking energetically of his vision of the founding of a national theater and eager to involve the younger man in his campaign to abolish the Lord Chamberlain's punitive system of censorship.

It was one afternoon in 1906 that Jones had arrived at Merton accompanied by Sue, then a ravishing young woman of twenty-three with pale gold skin, fair hair piled high on her head, blue eyes, and a voluptuous figure. Sue had first walked on in one of her father's plays at only fourteen, after which she had served her apprenticeship in the provinces without making much of a mark. Unhappily married, she was living apart from her husband and trying to find work in the West End. Maugham was immediately captivated by Sue's luscious beauty and entrancing smile: "she had the most beautiful smile I have ever seen on a human being," he wrote; she was generous and tenderhearted and had a delicious gurgling laugh which was irresistibly sexy. The two of them flirted and talked, and Sue agreed to dine with him; after a further couple of evenings at inexpensive restaurants, Maugham took her back to his single room in Pall Mall and made love to her. While he escorted her home in a hansom afterward, she asked him how long he thought the affair would last. "Six weeks," he teasingly replied. In fact Maugham was to fall seriously in love with Sue, and their affair would continue for nearly eight years.

When he met Sue Jones that afternoon at Merton, Maugham had only recently come to the end of his relationship with Harry Philips. Reserved in manner and apparently detached, Maugham took pains to conceal the fact that he was a man of powerful, often turbulent feeling: a largely loveless childhood had made him adept at disguise. Sexually passionate, Maugham also desperately craved love, and until well into middle age was given to a series of intense infatuations. His misfortune lay in an inability ever to find affection equally returned: magnetically attractive to both sexes as a young man, he was much pursued—"I have often acted a passion that I did not feel," he admitted—and frequently in the position of having to extract himself from unwanted entanglements, "with gentleness when possible, and if not, with irritation." The irony was that he himself never experienced what he described as "the bliss of requited love." Expert at covering his tracks, Maugham left little documentary evidence of specific attachments; nevertheless there are numerous signs—references casually made in letters, fictional versions lightly disguised—of his love affairs and of an emotional neediness only partly hidden behind the reserve. When looking back in old age, Maugham declared that he had never completely let down his guard, never surrendered wholly to anyone; and yet there are indications that this was not entirely true, and that for a time with Sue Jones his carefully erected defenses were thoroughly undermined.

Apart from her sex appeal, Sue had a number of qualities which to a man as highly strung and vulnerable as Maugham were infinitely seductive. Wholly at ease with herself, she was totally accepting, possessed of a benign tranquillity, an unruffled calm that was wonderfully soothing to his spirits. She was good-humored, too, with an endearingly childlike sense of mischief; she loved to laugh, yet at other times was happy to sit in silence, not needing to be talked to or entertained. Despite her failed marriage and undistinguished career, Sue had a tremendous zest for life, her optimism and vitality a welcome counterbalance to those moods of depression and uncertainty to which her lover was prone. Most important, she possessed in abundance a maternal warmth, which for obvious reasons was irresistible to Maugham.

Unfortunately no correspondence between Maugham and Sue Jones has ever come to light, but an indelible impression has been left of Sue as the lovely, warmhearted Rosie in the novel *Cakes and Ale*. Over the years Maugham made a number of references to Rosie as the portrait of "a woman of whom I had been extremely fond for years," plainly pointing to Sue, and Gerald Kelly, in whom full details of the affair were confided, once in an interview confirmed the identification. Sue, said Kelly, "came of common family . . . and had married at the age of nineteen. . . . She led a miserable life . . . & then met Willie, the only man she ever really loved." It was his impression, Kelly added, that Willie and Sue "had a very happy love affair together. . . . She was one of the most delightful women I have ever known, I thought her wonderfully beautiful." To Maugham himself he wrote that Rosie was "the most perfectly realized woman you ever got into a book."

In *Cakes and Ale* Maugham's love affair with Sue is naturally transposed, and yet its essence is unmistakable. Here is the passage describing the first night the lovers spend together, during which the nameless narrator, a very young man at this point, takes Rosie back to his London lodgings:

> I opened the door and lit the candle. Rosie followed me in and I held it up so that she should be able to see herself. . . . The room was very small and the dressing-table was by the bed. She raised her hand and softly stroked my cheek. . . .
>
> . . . A sob broke from my tight throat. I do not know whether it was because I was shy and lonely . . . or because my desire was so great, but I began to cry. I felt terribly

ashamed of myself; I tried to control myself, I couldn't; the tears welled up in my eyes and poured down my cheeks. Rosie saw them and gave a little gasp.

"Oh, honey, what is it? What's the matter? Don't. Don't!"

. . . She rocked me back and forth as though I were a child in her arms. I kissed her breasts and I kissed the white column of her neck; and she slipped out of her bodice and out of her skirt and her petticoats and I held her for a moment by her corseted waist; then she undid it, holding her breath for an instant to enable her to do so; and stood before me in her shift. When I put my hands on her sides I could feel the ribbing of the skin from the pressure of the corsets.

"Blow out the candle," she whispered.

It was she who awoke me when the dawn peering through the curtains revealed the shape of the bed and of the wardrobe against the darkness of the lingering night. . . .

"I must get up," she said. "I don't want your landlady to see me." . . .

We dressed in silence. She did not put on her corsets again, but rolled them up and I wrapped them in a piece of newspaper. We tiptoed along the passage and when I opened the door and we stepped out into the street the dawn ran to meet us. . . .

I kissed her and I watched her walk away.

Intoxicated by his new love affair, Maugham went over to Paris to see Gerald Kelly; he told him he was "desperately in love" and that he wanted to commission Kelly to paint Sue's portrait. The result is the beautiful *Mrs. Leveaux in White,* painted in 1907, in which Sue is shown standing full length, voluptuous in a low-cut evening dress, her mouth half open, her eyes gazing languidly into the middle distance. Equally striking is a second Kelly portrait, even more candidly erotic, of Sue sitting on a sofa, again in décolleté evening dress, looking straight ahead with an expression of heavily sensual promise on her lovely face. "She posed beautifully for the picture, so patiently," said Kelly later, "and both of us did our best, and I think Willie loved the portrait."

JACK STRAW HAD BEEN RUNNING for barely a month when *Mrs. Dot* opened at the Comedy. The play was produced by the American Charles Frohman, whose theatrical empire in London was fast expanding. Frohman was one of the seventeen managers who had rejected *Lady Frederick,* and not wishing to make the same mistake twice was quick to make an offer for *Mrs. Dot,* securing Marie Tempest for the title role and the well-known producer Dion Boucicault to direct. Witty and stylish, the play opened on April 27, 1908, to a favorable reception from the critics, nearly all of whom singled out Marie Tempest for particular praise.

No one interested in the theater could now be unaware of Maugham's prominence, a prominence that inevitably attracted a certain amount of envy. Arnold Bennett, who had had a play produced for the Stage Society earlier in the year, wrote in his journal for April 29, "Noticed in myself: A distinct feeling of jealousy on reading yesterday and to-day accounts of another very successful production of a play by Somerset Maugham—the third now running." And one evening when dining alone in his club Maugham overheard two men at the next table discussing him. "D'you know him at all?" said one. "I suppose he's about as swollen-headed as he can be." "Oh, yes," said the other. "He can't get a hat big enough to fit him." The truth was rather different: in fact Maugham was remarkably unchanged by his success, although inevitably his level-headed manner struck some observers as a form of vanity. He was pleased by the acclaim, of course, but he had worked hard through ten long years to achieve it and he saw very clearly the nature of that achievement: he had discovered a knack, a facility for writing light comedy that audiences found amusing; it was not an ability he rated very highly, nor did he see himself continuing with it for very long, but while there was a demand and he enjoyed the exercise, he planned to make the most of it: after all, the effort involved could hardly be described as arduous when a play could be turned out in less than a month. "I regularly wrote one act in five days," he recalled, "took the week-end off, and wrote the second and third acts in the same time. Then I gave five days of the fourth week to revising what I had written."

For Maugham the most significant change brought about by success was financial: for the first time in his life he was free of money worries, and the relief was enormous. His plays had not yet made him rich, as they were soon to do, but the popularity of *Lady Frederick* marked the point at which he left poverty behind him. "I hated poverty," he wrote in his notebook for 1908. Fond of his creature comforts, he had never been attracted by the colorful squalor of bohemian life, and being in debt had always troubled him. On a number of levels money meant a great deal to Maugham, and few people in his opinion fully understood "the great, the insinuating . . . the overwhelming significance of money in the affairs of life." Money ensured his artistic independence, insulated him from unwelcome intrusion, enabled him to travel where and when he pleased, and provided him with the considerable level of luxury in which he chose to live; more than that, for a man who from childhood had been wholly lacking in emotional security, financial security became a vitally important substitute. That it was a subject that interested him profoundly is shown by the many references to money in Maugham's work, in his correspondence, and also in his conversation. "Sometimes after an evening with Willie," said the writer Beverley Nichols, "one felt that one had been dining with a stockbroker." In 1908, the immediate result of his newly affluent status was that he could afford to leave his single room in Pall Mall and, still with the faithful Walter Payne, move into a smart little flat in Mayfair, at 23 Mount Street, off Park Lane.

Aware that he must quickly capitalize on his current popularity, Maugham immediately set to work making the final alterations to the scripts he still had in hand, and on June 13, 1908, the curtain went up on his fourth play, *The Explorer*. Shortly also to be published as a novel, *The Explorer* after numerous rejections in the past had eventually been accepted by Lewis Waller, one of the most successful actor-managers of his day. Persuading Waller of *The Ex-*

plorer's potential had not been easy, and the play had been submitted and substantially rewritten four times before it was eventually accepted. It was Maurice Colles who had dealt with the earliest version back in 1903, which he failed to sell, and when Maugham severed his connection with the agency he naturally assumed that Colles's part in the business was over. But now here was Colles claiming commission, a claim that his ex-client felt was wholly unjustified. "Practically nothing remains of the play which you tried to place," Maugham told him. "If you who are concerned with the Authors Society in protecting authors from dubious claims, consider you have one in this case, I shall lose my faith in responsible agencies." But Colles did consider he had a claim and was not prepared to be put off, successfully suing for the money in court, the case of *Colles v. Maugham* heard in the High Court of Justice, King's Bench Division, with the plaintiff awarded a payment of £21.10s.

The trouble Maugham had with *The Explorer* closely followed on trouble he encountered with the publication of his new novel, although in this instance the affair was settled without legal intervention. *The Magician,* written in 1906, was inspired by the monstrous figure of Aleister Crowley, Gerald Kelly's brother-in-law and one of the regulars at Le Chat Blanc. The work had been accepted by Methuen, with Maugham signing an agreement for three novels for each of which he would be paid an advance of £75. It was not until *The Magician* was actually set up in print that the head of the firm read it and was so profoundly shocked that publication was canceled forthwith. "I have always thought that publishers should never learn to read," Maugham crossly remarked. However, he was sufficiently shaken by the reaction to remove the name of the book's dedicatee, Gerald Kelly, from the manuscript in order to protect his friend from association with an obscene work. The book was then sold to William Heinemann, which proved to be a move of considerable consequence: Heinemann remained Maugham's publisher for the rest of his life. At the time the Heinemann deal was struck, Maugham's name was on hoardings all over London and it occurred to Methuen's director that it might be timely to remind their author that he still owed them three novels. Maugham was outraged. "I, as you know, make a point of cultivating the *beau geste,*" he told Gerald Kelly, "& in a few moving words told him that he could go to hell."

Methuen's rejection of *The Magician* cannot have come as a complete surprise, as Maugham had been uneasy for some time about the story's reception. As early as October 1906 he had written to Pinker, "I wanted to consult you about taking out the chapter in the lunatic asylum. I do not want to horrify people more than need be." *The Magician* is in the fullest sense a horror story, and there is little sign that Maugham reined himself in, on the contrary relishing going to the limits in terms of terror and taste. In Paris at the turn of the century there was a considerable vogue for the occult, a vogue greatly encouraged by the novels of the Decadent writer Huysmans. According to Maugham, "[*The Magician*] would never have been written except for the regard I had for Joris-Karl Huysmans." Strong echoes can be found, too, of other practitioners of the genre such as Mary Shelley and Edgar Allan Poe, and, more recently, of H. G. Wells's savage and sadistic story, *The Island of Doctor Moreau.*

The dominating figure in the novel, the Magician himself, is Oliver Haddo, possessed of all of Aleister Crowley's vanity and bombast. The story begins in Paris with Arthur Burdon, an English doctor, come to visit his fiancée, Margaret, who is staying with her friend, Susie, prior to her forthcoming marriage. The two women, together with a French savant, Dr. Porhoët, take Arthur to dine at their local restaurant. Here the lively company of writers and artists is suddenly silenced by the arrival of Haddo. Haddo, a man of "vast obesity," immediately draws the attention of everyone in the room with his dramatic stance and flamboyant delivery, although he fails to impress Arthur with his ludicrous claims to be a master of the magic arts. When Haddo informs the company that he is known as the Brother of the Shadow, Arthur, looking at the man's immense girth, makes a facetious rejoinder.

This turns out to be a fatal mistake. Haddo, enraged by the ridicule, decides on a terrible revenge, casting a spell over Margaret so that she becomes obsessed by him, gripped by an overwhelming sexual passion. Helpless, Margaret leaves the heartbroken Arthur and marries Haddo. One night in London, Susie and Arthur find themselves at a dinner party, where it is clear that Margaret is in desperate need of rescue. Eventually, with the help of Dr. Porhoët, Susie and Arthur track her down to Skene, Haddo's Staffordshire estate. True to tradition, the place is bleak and remote, with terrible rumors circulating as to what is going on inside the house. In the end the forces of evil are defeated, although Margaret dies in the process, and Skene, with its wicked Magician and the loathsome horrors it contains, is destroyed by fire.

To those in the know it was obvious whence Maugham had drawn much of his inspiration, his portrait of the regulars at Le Chat Blanc (Le Chien Noir in the novel) depicted with little attempt at camouflage. "I hear that Maugham has crucified us of the White Cat in a new satirical novel," the painter Roderic O'Conor, who appears as O'Brien, wrote gloomily to Clive Bell. But as might be expected, the most extravagant reaction came from the Magician himself, Aleister Crowley, who was infuriated (or pretended to be), and at the same time perversely flattered, by Maugham's wicked caricature, describing the novel as "an appreciation of my genius such as I had never dreamed of inspiring." He had come across the book by chance, he said.

> The title attracted me strongly, *The Magician*. The author, bless my soul! No other than my old and valued friend, William Somerset Maugham, my nice young doctor whom I remembered so well from the dear old days of the Chat Blanc. So he had really written a book—who would have believed it!

In a review for *Vanity Fair* signed "Oliver Haddo," and later in his memoirs, Crowley attacked Maugham, accusing him of plagiarism, of not only plundering his life but of transposing without acknowledgment long passages from books on the occult that Maugham had found in the studio of Crowley's brother-in-law, Gerald Kelly. "I had never supposed that plagiarism could have been so varied, extensive and shameless."

Crowley had a point. The portrait of Haddo is undeniably drawn from life, and yet, repulsive though he is, it is Haddo who provides the novel's powerful nexus. As to the rest, the adventure story works well enough, and as might be expected, the theme of sexual degradation is treated with enthralling veracity; but in artistic terms what sinks the story is exactly what Crowley objected to, Maugham's incorporating hefty chunks from works on the Kabbalah, the Seven Genii, the Keys of Solomon, and "the many things in the East which are inexplicable by science." None of this really interested him—he thought it all "moonshine"—and it shows, his lazy extracts making those parts of the book cumbrous and dull. When Maugham showed the manuscript to Violet Hunt she put her finger on just this fault, and in acknowledging her reservation he wrote, "I daresay you are quite right in saying that the trail of the lamp is over it all, but it was deliberately that I gave so many dates & authorities. . . . I wanted to impress upon the reader the fact that all those things had been seriously believed in their time, & I was very anxious to prevent the book from being a mere shocker." Crowley's detailed cataloguing of *The Magician*'s plagiarized passages did little to endear him to its author: after Gerald Kelly painted Crowley's portrait, Maugham suggested he submit it to the Royal Academy, "with the title SON OF A BITCH (arrangement in black & green)."

The Magician was published in November 1908 to mixed reviews, some castigating the author for obscenity, others congratulating him for providing such "a real thrill of horror." By this time Maugham's reputation was standing high, very different from the position he had occupied only twelve months before. With Barrie, Pinero, Alfred Sutro, and other notable playwrights he was one of the founders of the Dramatists' Club; he was made a member of the Garrick, the long-established gentlemen's club in Covent Garden for actors and men of letters; and he was among seventy notable signatories, including Shaw, Barrie, Galsworthy, Pinero, Yeats, and Wells, of a letter to *The Times* complaining about theater censorship. On December 1 that year, Maugham was one of 180 guests at a dinner held at the Ritz, the purpose to honor Robbie Ross, the loyal friend and executor of Oscar Wilde—and also, indirectly, to rehabilitate eight years after his demise the reputation of Wilde himself.

MAUGHAM'S PRESENCE THAT DECEMBER evening at the Ritz is significant, a gesture of homage to a figure whose impact on his life and writing, although largely unexpressed, was considerable. Maugham never wrote about Wilde—too dangerous a subject— and yet Wilde's influence was formative: as a medical student at St. Thomas's he had read *Salome* and *The Picture of Dorian Gray* and seen *The Importance of Being Earnest;* echoes of Wilde appear unmistakably in much of his early dramatic work; and in *The Magician,* a novel with an indisputably Wildean flavor, there is a substantial, if unattributed, quotation, "I am amorous of thy body, Iokanaan!" Wilde's declared belief that "It is not for anyone to censure what anyone else does, and everyone should go his own way, to whatever place he chooses, in exactly the way that he chooses" was one to which Maugham wholeheartedly subscribed and that he constantly returned to in his work. The exposure of Wilde's homosexuality and its terrible consequences, the loss of family, of home, of reputation, had made a deep impression on Maugham, who could hardly avoid seeing a number of potential parallels in his own situation. Haunted by the tragedy and fascinated by the man, he was strongly attracted by Wilde's social and literary circles, many members of which were present that night at the Ritz, several of whom were to become important as friends of his own.

Key among them were the guest of honor himself, Robbie Ross, and his old friend, Reginald Turner, who together had accompanied Wilde to France after his release from prison. Ross was a small, neat man with a tidy mustache, discreetly homosexual—he had been Wilde's first male lover—with a roguish sense of humor and infectious laugh. As art critic of *The Morning Post* and director of a small gallery, the genial Ross was knowledgeable about paintings, in particular the French Impressionists, a subject guaranteed to interest Maugham, who found this recent acquaintance most engaging. "You are a perfect dear," he wrote to Ross the day after the dinner, "and I'm so glad to have known you." Reggie Turner had become a friend after Maugham had written to thank him for an appreciative review of *Lady Frederick*. Teasingly referred to by Wilde as "the boy-snatcher of Clement's Inn," Reggie was spinsterish by temperament and unfailingly decorous in mixed company, if capable of delirious promiscuity in all-male gatherings. "The most amusing man I have known," according to Maugham. Max Beerbohm in describing Reggie's wit remarked that he was not very responsive to other people's humor, a comment that worried Reggie, who asked Maugham if he thought it were true. "I didn't want to hurt his feelings, so I said, 'Well, Reggie, you never laugh at any of my jokes.' He blinked . . . & puckered up his ugly little face, & with a grin replied, 'But I don't [think] they're funny.' " It was Reggie who had encouraged Beerbohm to join the Wilde circle, but while Max immensely admired Wilde, he never quite became an intimate: unlike Reggie Turner and Ross, he was not homosexual and had no wish to follow in that direction, although he was happy to join in the general talk of straight men as "mulierasts" and of man's love for man as "the love that dares not speak its name."

Max and Reggie Turner had been inseparable since they were undergraduates at Oxford, and it was a compliment to Maugham that he was now invited to join their clique. Reggie had an apartment on the edge of Berkeley Square, only a couple of minutes' walk from Maugham on Mount Street and the Beerbohm family on Upper Berkeley Street, where Max lived with his mother and sisters. It was at Reggie's flat one afternoon that Maugham first met H. G. Wells, who had been lunching with Reggie and had returned to the flat to continue their conversation. Wells, regarded as one of the country's leading intellectuals, was then at the height of his fame, and Maugham, uncomfortably aware of the trivial nature of his own celebrity, felt wrong-footed and subtly patronized. "I received the impression that he looked upon me with a sort of offhand amusement as he might have looked upon Arthur Roberts or Dan Leno."* Some of the jolliest evenings in the company of Max

* Music-hall comedians.

and Reggie were spent with the eccentric Mrs. Steevens. All three young men had been regular visitors to Merton Place, which Mrs. Steevens had recently left, moving to Kensington, where her generous if somewhat chaotic hospitality continued undiminished. Maugham remembered her Tuesdays as particularly lively:

> They were very gay parties, chiefly because Reggie kept us all laughing our heads off. Max did not say much, but when he did, you remembered it. It was pretty sure to be witty or caustic. When the evening came to an end we drove on the top of a bus to go to our respective homes.

An important friendship Maugham made among the "Oscarians" was with Ada Leverson, who had also been present the night of Ross's dinner. A faithful friend to Wilde, who called her his "Sphinx," Ada Leverson had stood by him when the scandal broke and was one of the few to greet him early in the morning on his release from jail. A fine-featured, soft-spoken woman in her forties, Ada, separated from her husband, was regarded as the Egeria of a mainly homosexual coterie that included Robbie Ross, Reggie Turner, Max Beerbohm, and Lord Alfred Douglas. Attracted by and attractive to effeminate young men—she had once tried, unsuccessfully, to seduce Aubrey Beardsley—she was much loved as a discreet and unshockable confidante, treasured as a gifted if somewhat eccentric hostess. "Her conversation was artificial, in several senses elusive, chaotic and often captivatingly absurd," as one of her devotees described it. At her little house near Hyde Park, the Sphinx, though far from well off, held delightful soirées. Obliged to supplement her income, Ada had written a couple of novels, and she contributed articles to *Black & White* and *Punch*. One of her circle, Robert Hichens, author of *The Garden of Allah,* encouraged her to try her hand at writing plays. *"Write a light comedy at once,"* he wrote to her in 1908. "I wish it, I command it. Cut out Somerset Maugham."

There was little chance of that, but the friendship between Ada

Leverson and Maugham soon became warm. As in the case of Violet Hunt, a strong emotional attachment developed on the side of the Sphinx, who found this handsome, clever young man disturbingly attractive: she wrote to him constantly, filled his room with flowers when he was ill, and gave him a lucky charm to keep about his person. "My dear Sphynx," he wrote to her, using his own idiosyncratic spelling of the word, "It is too kind of you to send me that lovely horse-shoe. I will wear it on my watch-chain, watch-chain; & the flowers in my hair, my hair. You see your kindness throws me into a lyric rapture. . . ." She invited him to dinner and the opera, attended all his plays, and relied on him to criticize her work. In 1908 she dedicated to him her novel *Love's Shadow,* "a great honour," as he rightly recognized. "[Maugham's] visits were looked forward to eagerly," her daughter recalled, "and a large photograph of him became part of her personal surroundings." For his part Maugham was fond of the Sphinx, knew of her feelings, and played the relationship skillfully, indulging in a delicate flirtatiousness that scrupulously stopped just short of anything more serious. The two of them had a number of interests in common: the writing business—the Sphinx, too, was a client of J. B. Pinker—and also the theater. Her association with Wilde was of consuming interest to Maugham, who was touched when she gave him her own precious first edition of Wilde's poem *The Sphinx,* in which, inscribing it for Maugham, she had written lines beginning "Oh dark tormenting face of beauty, loved . . ." Maugham was curious about Lord Alfred Douglas, unforgettably encountered thirteen years ago during his first visit to Capri, to whom he hoped Ada would introduce him. "I wish you would ask me to meet Bosie one day," he wrote to her in December 1908.

Shortly after this, in January 1909, Maugham's next play opened, and the Sphinx, anxious to promote her friend's career, wrote to Lord Alfred, who was then editor of *The Academy,* asking if she might review it for his journal. He agreed, on condition that there was to be no "log-rolling," no writing " 'something nice' . . . because the author happened to be a friend." Unfortunately this is exactly what the piece turned out to be, and Douglas returned it with a sharp rebuke. "My dear Sphinx, I am very sorry, but this article won't do at all," he began.

> It is a much too obvious "puff" of a personal friend of yours. . . . Maugham's play may be quite amusing and worth seeing and all that, but your criticism would have applied to a really great comedy like one of Oscar's, the sort of thing that only appears once in 20 years. . . . When you asked me to dinner to meet him I began to be rather suspicious. I have been living in London on and off for the last 10 years, and if Maugham, whom I remember meeting years ago at Capri, was so anxious to meet me it is a pity he did not do so before I became Editor of a paper which is capable of being very useful to him.

The play in question was *Penelope,* with Marie Tempest again in the title role. Witty and urbane, the plot centers on the worldly wiles employed by a doctor's wife to win back her husband from his tiresome and tenacious mistress. The theme was not original: Barrie had used something like it the year before in *What Every Woman Knows,* as had Sardou in his popular 1883 farce, *Divorçons!;* but according to Maugham, *Penelope* was chiefly inspired "by the young woman . . . with whom I was having an affair," a statement that opens up the intriguing possibility that Sue Jones dealt with her lover's extramural liaisons in a similar manner. Whatever the actuality, it provided an excellent scenario, and with its topical relevance presented audiences with a work that was thoroughly up to date. In *Penelope,* and in his next play, *Smith,* Maugham for the first time dealt with the modern woman in the modern age, exchanging the grandeur, opulence, and Victorian values of *Lady Frederick* and *Jack Straw* for bridge parties, telephones, mansion flats, and light, bright sitting rooms furnished in floral chintz.

Penelope, which was to prove yet another popular success, had been commissioned by Charles Frohman, who was now to figure significantly in the promotion of Maugham's reputation as a dramatist. For Frohman the theater was his life, and within the profession he was both liked and respected, regarded as a fair man whose word was his bond. It was largely as a result of his efforts that a system of exchange for successful plays was set up between London, Paris, and New York, with the emphasis on London as the source of all that was best in contemporary drama: a much-repeated saying of Frohman's was that he would rather earn £15 in London than $15,000 in New York. By the early 1900s Frohman held a virtual monopoly on importing British drama to the United States, responsible for bringing to America works by Barrie, Pinero, and Oscar Wilde. Thus his enthusiasm for the plays of Somerset Maugham was crucial to Maugham's establishing himself across the Atlantic. The collaboration between the two had begun well, with Frohman producing *Lady Frederick* in New York and *Mrs. Dot* in London, followed by his commissioning of *Penelope*. "I want to tell you how glad I am that *Penelope* is a success," Maugham wrote to him three weeks into the run. "It is always rather nervous work to accept a commission."

At this period of his life Maugham, while never stagestruck, found he enjoyed his involvement in the process of putting on a play. He liked attending rehearsals, where he appeared always immaculately dressed, and he was one of the few authors whose presence was welcomed, as he was prepared to settle quietly in the stalls without interfering, always willing to pencil in any changes that might be required. Maugham loved the pared-down working atmosphere, with the auditorium in darkness and the stage bare; and he relished the easy camaraderie, the gossip and banter in stuffy gaslit dressing rooms, "the hurried lunch at a restaurant round the corner with a member of the cast, and the cup of strong bitter tea, with thick bread and butter, brought in by the charwoman at four o'clock." The only moment to be dreaded was the first night, when Maugham always suffered agonies from nerves. "I tried to go to my own first nights as though they were somebody else's," he wrote, "but even at that I found it a disagreeable experience. . . . Indeed I should never have gone to see my plays at all, on the first night or any other, if I had not thought it necessary to see the effect they had on the audience in order to learn how to write them." The opening night of *Penelope* was the last time he took a bow in response to cries of "Author!," as he had recently been stung by a newspaper article complaining that he was promoting himself too energetically. "I read that I had neither decorum nor decency [and] I determined not again to appear before the curtain."

Maugham counted among his friends a number of playwrights, Henry Arthur Jones, St. John Ervine, Alfred Sutro, and, after a less than promising start, Harley Granville Barker; he enjoyed "talking shop" with colleagues and discussing the techniques of the trade. He and Sutro, for instance, regularly read each other's plays and proffered advice, Sutro proving particularly helpful over the writing of *Smith,* while Maugham gave good advice with Sutro's comedy, *The Perplexed Husband.* In actors, on the other hand, Maugham was never much interested outside the confines of the theater. He admired the profession's talent and courage and was frequently amused by a gift for mimicry or anecdote, but in private life he found the companionship of actors unrewarding. In a sentence deleted from his 1938 memoir, *The Summing Up,* he wrote, "I have never been able to look upon actors as human beings."

The one exception, of course, was the beautiful Sue Jones, to whom he remained passionately attached. Sue was as delightful and alluring as ever, and yet there was something elusive about her, and Maugham found it frustrating that he seemed to be making little progress, that sweet and generous as Sue was to him, she appeared to be equally sweet and generous to everyone else. However, Maugham did what he could to keep Sue happy: having failed to land a role for her in *Jack Straw,* he now used his growing influence to secure the part of the maid, Peyton, in *Penelope.* Maugham had no illusions about Sue's capabilities: "she was not a particularly good actress," he said, "but good enough for me to be able to get her understudies or small parts"; and as Peyton she looked adorable in her maid's uniform, even winning a pat on the back from *The Sunday Times,* which referred to "the stoic and impeccable maid of Miss Ethelwyn Arthur Jones." Her lover had done her a better turn than he realized: this modest success resulted in Sue's being asked to join Beerbohm Tree's Shakespeare season at His Majesty's. Here she soon caught the roving eye of Tree himself, who in an attempt to undercut his rival told Sue over supper at the Savoy one evening that she was wasting her time with Maugham as "he's a queer," information that left Sue remarkably unfazed.

Gerald Kelly's friendship was crucial to Maugham in his affair with Sue, fond as Kelly was of Sue and closer than anyone else to Maugham. The affection between the two men remained undented even after Maugham discovered that Kelly had slept with Sue, his friend's "odious treachery" referred to by letter in a self-consciously jocular tone. Increasingly it was being impressed upon Maugham that Sue was by nature promiscuous, and that she regularly slept not only with him but with a dismayingly large number of his acquaintances, including not only Kelly but also Walter Payne and Ivor Back, Kelly's chum from Le Chat Blanc. "All my friends had been to bed with her," Maugham wrote, with understandable exaggeration. "That sounds as though she was something of a wanton. She wasn't. There was no vice in her. . . . It wasn't lasciviousness. It was her nature." Quite simply, Sue enjoyed sex, had no moral inhibitions about it, and took it for granted when a man invited her to dinner that she would go to bed with him afterward. As Kelly put it, Willie "[was] the only man she ever really loved [but] this did not keep her from continuing her promiscuous ways." But now Maugham, who, as he justly admitted, was fairly promiscuous himself, began to believe that he might want to marry Sue. For a while he had been passionately in love and he still adored her: Did it matter that she was not exclusively his? Now that the physical side of the affair had become over time less urgent, was sexual jealousy really an issue? "There was no one I liked better," he reasoned, "[and] why should I bother . . . that she had been to bed with so many of my friends? . . . [N]otwithstanding her moral looseness, she was a very good and a very sweet woman." He was now in his mid-thirties, and if he was going to settle down, he should do it before long; Sue had recently obtained a divorce from her husband, and without exactly putting it into words gave the impression she would not be averse to marrying again; so the time seemed to be right.

It was a courageous decision to make, but like most men of his class and generation whose sexual tastes were unorthodox, Maugham set enormous store by an appearance of conventionality. While by no means wishing to suppress his homosexual tendencies, he was encouraged by the fact that he could also find women attractive, and this misled him into believing that he was, as he put it, three-quarters "normal" and only a quarter "queer." Marriage might swing the balance further in the desired direction, and would at least allow him to pass as straight in polite society. Sue's accepting nature was an important part of her appeal, and so was the fact that she was from a theatrical milieu, with the theater's traditional tolerance of the irregular and nonconformist, a tolerance Maugham knew very well he was unlikely to find among his own kin. Both his surviving brothers, Charles and F.H., were solidly established husbands and fathers, both hardworking lawyers, both pillars of bourgeois respectability. After Harry's shocking suicide, all evidence of undesirable friendships in that quarter had been successfully hushed up, and clearly it was unthinkable that anything of the kind could be allowed to surface again within the family. Maugham, ever the outsider, had little wish to lead the life his brothers led, six days a week in the office and a bucket-and-spade holiday once a year; and yet there was a part of him that felt a strong urge to conform, to play the role of English gentleman, with a wife to run his home, entertain his friends, and provide him with children.

In conventional society Maugham's ambidexterity was unsuspected, and his good looks, growing fame, and attractive diffidence in manner charmed many. Both men and women found his appearance intriguing, and women were particularly fascinated by him, by his way of seeming to give them his undivided attention, apparently absorbed in their every word. There was, too, a slight air of mystery about his personality and his emotional focus that unquestionably added to his glamour. Ada Leverson in one of her novels drew a portrait of him at this period remarkable for the acuteness of its observation. In *The Limit,* the character closely based on Maugham is "Gilbert Hereford Vaughan," known to his friends as "Gillie":

He behaved like anybody else, except that perhaps his manner was a little quieter than the average. Unless one was very observant . . . he did not at first appear too alarmingly clever. He had one or two characteristics which must have at times led to misunderstandings. One was that whatever or whoever he looked at, his dark opaque eyes were so full of vivid expression that women often mistook for admiration what was often merely observation.

Discreet reference is made to a secret private life, the nature of which is of great interest to many an unattached young lady hoping to ensnare him, and the Sphinx deals cleverly with the subject by inventing an entanglement with an innkeeper's daughter, which has to be kept from the public gaze. The appearance in the story of Gladys, "who is coarse and common," may well indicate something of Ada's feelings about Sue, who was likely to have been resented as the young and beautiful object of Maugham's affections.

Like *Penelope,* the theme of Maugham's next play, *Smith,* has echoes of a work by Barrie, his 1902 play, *The Admirable Crichton,* in which the servant turns out to be an infinitely superior being to his masters. In *Smith* it is a pretty young parlormaid whose integrity is in such striking contrast to the venality and selfishness of her employers that she wins the heart of the hero, the young man of the family. *Smith,* produced by Frohman at the Comedy Theatre, had its first night on September 30, 1909, the third Maugham play to be staged that year; *Penelope* had opened in January, and in March *The Noble Spaniard,* an adaptation by Maugham of a French farce, *Les Gaietés de Veuvage,* by Ernest Grenet-Dancourt.

WITH SO MANY DEMANDS on his time, Maugham found it increasingly necessary to leave London in order to write. Sometimes he would run down to Brighton for a few days and put up at the Metropole, and there was an inn at Taplow in Buckinghamshire that he liked as it was near a golf course, and golf had become something of a passion. With writing such a sedentary occupation, Maugham was aware that exercise was important: he was vain about his figure, but more important, he needed to keep fit in order to bolster the fragile health that had been his since childhood and that left him vulnerable particularly to respiratory and lung infections. To this end he rode, he walked, he played squash at the Bath Club once a week, but there were few pastimes he enjoyed more than a game of golf. When working on *Penelope* he had found a hotel in an idyllic setting, Varenna, on the shores of Lake Como, which became a favorite location mainly on account of its excellent golf course.

Maugham's desire to travel, his wanderlust, was to be one of the great driving forces of his life, as necessary to his writing as solitude and quiet. In a letter to Kelly he described it as "that aching to be off & abroad which I know so well." It was a theme that constantly recurs in the correspondence between them. "I am neither so happy, nor so amused, nor so comfortable on my travels as I am in London," Maugham told him, "& yet I cannot get over the restlessness that drives me forth." Right into extreme old age, it was this restlessness which compelled him to be frequently on the move, and whenever he could spare time from his professional commitments he would take off. In 1908, as well as to Varenna, he went to Madrid, Constantinople, Bursa, Capri, and Corfu; in 1909 to Paris, Antwerp, and Brussels, and for a walking holiday in the Peloponnese; in 1910, the year of his first visit to the United States, he was also in the south of France, Milan, Athens, and Venice. "Really it is with the greatest difficulty that I can keep that purple patch out of my letter," he wrote to Kelly from Greece. "Birds are singing all round me. There is a wood just below, olive-trees & cypresses, poplars breaking into leaf, & fig-trees; & then rolling hills, ramp upon ramp, snow-capped in the distance & all rosy in the setting sun. . . . it is all beautiful."

Sometimes Walter Payne went with him, but more often he was on his own. In cities he liked to go to the theater and spend hours in picture galleries, the contents of which would be discussed at length in letters to Kelly. Other matters were touched on, too. In their different ways both men fully appreciated the freedom of being out of reach of the pressures of English society. Kelly in Paris reveled in the intoxicating sense of liberty brought about by escape from what he described as "the fantastic conventions and prejudices that surrounded people's sex-experiences in London." For obvious reasons this applied in even greater measure to Maugham. Brought up in France, he was frequently reduced to a state of exasperation by English prudishness. "To me England has been a country where I had obligations that I did not want to fulfil and responsibilities that irked me," he wrote. "I have never felt entirely myself till I had put at least the Channel between my native★ country and me." Whenever the chance offered he took it. "An amiable person has offered to take me on a motor tour through France," he wrote cheerily to Kelly in 1907, confident his friend would understand the situation. At sea en route to Naples in 1907 he had reported, "I met an Egyptian pasha who fell a victim to my charms & made me proposals of a nature which could not be mistaken. . . . [Though] I declined with a haughty gesture, I could not remain insensible to the compliment." In 1909 he went with Reggie Turner to Florence, like Capri home to a sizable community of homosexual expatriates; they stayed in an apartment on the Lung'Arno, where they were joined by the novelist Louis Marlow and a young friend of Marlow's, and Reggie held center stage with his stories about the late, great Oscar. Reggie, "a living link with Oscar and all those ancient buggeries," as Marlow described him, liked and admired Maugham. "He's very good," Reggie would allow. "But not as good as Oscar. Not like Oscar. Oh, no, he'd never be like Oscar!"

It was in Varenna in October 1909 that Maugham wrote most of his next play, *The Tenth Man,* which was something of a departure from form. With the exception of *A Man of Honour* and *The Explorer,* all Maugham's dramatic work so far had been lighthearted social comedy. Only one play, "Mrs Beamish,"† had failed to find a

---

★ Although born in the British embassy and thus technically on British soil, in literal terms France was Maugham's native country, but he always regarded himself as English to the core.

† "Mrs. Beamish," about a respectable middle-aged couple forced into revealing the shocking fact that they are not married and that their priggish son is therefore illegitimate, was never produced or published and exists only in manuscript, in the Library of Congress in Washington.

producer; the others, from *Lady Frederick* to *Smith,* had been popular with audiences and highly rewarding in financial terms for their
author. Maugham had been candid, perhaps too candid, about his
facility in turning out this kind of material, not troubling to conceal how effortlessly ideas came to him, how easily and quickly the
plays were written. Rather rashly he had given a newspaper interview in which he expressed his impatience with tragedy and with
the weighty play of ideas, lightheartedly arguing that it was most
unwise for playwrights to take themselves seriously as the first,
perhaps the only, aim of the playwright was to entertain. Such self-
deprecating mockery was misplaced, and was widely misunderstood by the critics. Max Beerbohm was one of several who went
on the attack. "If light comedy is the only form that he cares to
practise now, let him devote himself to that, by all means. But it is
hardly gracious in him to gibe at other men who, conscientiously,
but unremuneratively, are treading the path to which his own first
ambitions led him."

But Maugham knew what he was doing: he understood his audiences and knew how to provide them with what they wanted. As
the critic Desmond MacCarthy wrote of Maugham's plays, "They
were just cynical enough to make the sentimental-worldly think
themselves tough-minded while they were enjoying them, and just
brilliant enough to satisfy a London audience's far from exacting
standard of wit." Popular success, however, did not mean he was
unaffected by adverse criticism, and over the years he repeatedly returned to a defense of his stance. "The critics accused me of writing
down to the public," he wrote in his autobiographical work, *The
Summing Up.* "I did not exactly do that [but I] wrote my comedies
with those sides of myself only that were useful to my purpose.
They were designed to please and they achieved their aim." It was
during the early years of his fame as a dramatist that he believed his
rejection by the intelligentsia began, a rejection that continued to
rankle, despite frequent denials, through the rest of his life. "The
intelligentsia, of which I had been a modest, but respected member,
not only turned a cold shoulder on me . . . but flung me, like Lu-
cifer, headlong into the bottomless pit. I was taken aback and a trifle

mortified." In an attempt to redress the balance, with his next two plays, *The Tenth Man* and *Grace,* he deliberately set out to change tack and return to more serious treatment and themes. Unfortunately, neither was successful, and it was over two years before Maugham felt able to return to playwriting. "I am tired & bored," he wrote to Golding Bright at the end of 1909. "After this I am going to give play-writing a rest for some time. Four plays in the last two years & eight productions! I really think I have the right to slack off for a few months."

AT THIRTY-SIX, Maugham was riding high and enjoying his life immensely. "I was happy, I was prosperous, I was busy," as he rightly remarked; he was also famous, and everyone wanted to know him. Under a sedate exterior, the fashionable playwright was energetic and high-spirited, capable of a flippant gaiety that was as unsuspected as it was engaging. Described as "one of London's wittiest bachelors and most indefatigable dancers," he was deluged with invitations and seen everywhere: in white tie and tails at dances and first nights; two-stepping in Spanish fancy dress at the Chelsea Arts Ball; joining a vigorous barn dance at a charity evening at Covent Garden. He attended luncheons and dinners in Mayfair and Kensington, the next afternoon, immaculate in frock coat, top hat, and spats, calling, as etiquette demanded, on his hostess of the night before. Gerald Kelly brilliantly captured Maugham at this period in his portrait *The Jester.* Recently returned to London, Kelly had taken a studio in Knightsbridge, and here Maugham had called on him one day wearing morning dress and a gray topper. "[He] had started to dress himself in a very dapper way," Kelly recalled, "and came in delightedly to show me his grey hat." On a chair in front of an ornate Coromandel screen, the playwright is seen in the painting sitting bright-eyed and alert, one leg casually crossed over the other, hat slightly tilted, shoes shining, gloves immaculate, one hand resting on a slender gold-tipped cane, the perfect picture of the Edwardian dandy, the debonair man-about-town.

With a substantial income at his disposal, Maugham had bought for £8,000 an eight-hundred-year lease of an elegant five-story Georgian house, number 6 Chesterfield Street, right in the heart of Mayfair, jokingly referred to as "the house that Frohman built." Here he planned to move with Walter Payne, but first there was a great deal of work to be done on it and furniture to buy: "your house is being entirely redecorated," he told Frohman. "You will not know 6 Chesterfield Street when you come." Maugham's greatest pleasure was in buying pictures for the house, including an Orpen, a couple of landscapes by Wilson Steer, and, on the advice of Sir Hugh Lane, the connoisseur and founder of the Municipal Gallery of Modern Art in Dublin, a theatrical scene by Samuel de Wilde; this was followed by the purchase of a Zoffany, for £22, of David Garrick and Mrs. Cibber in *Venice Preserv'd,* and a small version of Reynolds's *Garrick Between Comedy and Tragedy,* both paintings once owned by Sir Henry Irving. These two pictures were the first in what was to grow into a notable collection of over forty theatrical paintings, some picked up in junk shops for only a few pounds, eventually donated to the National Theatre.

Between periods of intensely concentrated work, Maugham continued his busy and glamorous social life, as always fascinated to observe the morals and mores of the sophisticated circles in which he was invited to take part, all stored away as useful material for his fiction. As the critic Desmond MacCarthy wrote of him, Maugham moved through London society "with the reserve and detachment of a professional man of letters." Maugham was intrigued to learn, for instance, that the upper classes "still talked as though to run the British Empire were their private business. It gave me a peculiar sensation to hear it discussed, when a general election was in the air, whether Tom should have the Home Office and whether Dick would be satisfied with Ireland." Among his recent acquaintance was an ambitious political hostess, daughter of Lady St. Helier and wife of a wealthy member of Parliament. With Dorothy Allhusen, Maugham conducted the same kind of affectionate, flirtatious friendship that he maintained with other older women friends such as Ada Leverson and Violet Hunt. ("My dear Mrs. Allhusen, You are a faithless woman. You promise me with all the earnestness in

the world that you will write to me, though you have left me without so much as a picture postcard. . . . I miss you very much.") The
Allhusens had a large country house at Stoke Poges in Buckinghamshire, and here Maugham became a frequent guest at weekend
house parties, where there was always an interesting mix of politi-
cians, writers, and eminent members of the armed forces. "Thank
you so much for my jolly week-end," he wrote to his hostess after
one such occasion. "It is just the sort of rest I like, getting so tired
that you go to bed for the remainder of the week."

It was at Stoke Court that Maugham first met Winston Churchill, then a Cabinet minister in Asquith's government and recently
married to Dorothy Allhusen's cousin Clementine Hozier. There
was a golf course nearby and the two men often played together in
the afternoon, returning to the house for a substantial tea followed
by a glittering formal dinner. It was late one night when the ladies
had retired to bed and the men, changed into smoking jackets, were
talking over their brandy and cigars that Churchill was startled by
an intervention of Maugham's: a young man, very full of himself,
had been holding forth at length, in the writer's view talking complete nonsense, when suddenly Maugham broke in and with one
sentence, witty but devastating, silenced him. Everyone burst out
laughing, but the next morning Churchill came up to Maugham as
he was peacefully reading the Sunday papers. "I want to make a
compact with you," he said. "If you will promise never to be funny
at my expense, I will promise never to be funny at yours."

Gratified although he was to be in such demand, and much as he
relished seeing this side of life, Maugham was by no means at everyone's beck and call. In February 1910 he felt obliged to rebuke Ada
Leverson, who had made the mistake of presuming too much on
her intimacy by allowing a friend of hers whom Maugham did not
know to approach him. "My dear Sphynx, Pray thank your friend
for her kind invitation," he began.

I will not accept it. It is a very impertinent thing to invite a
total stranger to dine with you. There are certain recognized
methods of making the acquaintance of anyone one wants to

know & I do not see why they should be neglected because I happen to be a writer. . . .

Three months later, on May 6, when the London season had barely begun, the death of Edward VII was announced, technically bringing to an end the Edwardian era, although it was to continue in all but name until 1914. Maugham was in Italy most of that month, writing to Violet Hunt that he was glad to be out of England "during the dreary time of public mourning," when theaters were doing little business and society was in the doldrums. It was fortuitous that at this time he was preparing to make his first journey across the Atlantic. For some while Frohman had been urging him to come. *Mrs. Dot, Smith,* and *Penelope* had opened in New York, and *Lady Frederick,* as Maugham proudly told Pinker, "is one of the greatest successes they have had lately in America." Originally having planned to go to the States the previous year, he had been forced by illness to postpone the trip. Now, however, he was ready. "I am sailing by the Caronia on the 22nd of October," he wrote to Frohman, full of high spirits, picturing himself setting out to sea, he said, "like Christopher Columbus in conquest of America."

CHAPTER 6

SYRIE

. . .

O N OCTOBER 22, 1910, MAUGHAM SAILED FROM LIVERPOOL ON the SS *Caronia,* one of the largest and most elegant vessels in the Cunard fleet. The days of traveling on the cheap were over: from now on, whenever possible during the next half century, Maugham was to journey *en prince,* enjoying a standard of comfort that nowhere was to be more sumptuously provided than by the European liners on the North Atlantic route. The crossing took six days, and on arrival in New York, Maugham went straight from the noise and bustle of the pier to his hotel, the deluxe St. Regis on Fifth Avenue in the heart of midtown Manhattan. Built in 1903, the St. Regis was the first of the high-rise hotels, regarded as the last word in grandeur and modernity, with electric elevators, bedside telephones, and even a primitive form of air-conditioning. Nearby on Fifth Avenue the old order was imposingly represented by the monolithic mansions of the Astors and Vanderbilts, while all around was evidence of the new, with fast-rising skyscrapers, neon signs, honking motor traffic, the subway, electric trams, and an elevated railway.

Maugham's name was already familiar: four of his plays had been produced on Broadway with well-known actresses in the leading roles, Ethel Barrymore, Mary Boland, Marie Tempest, and Billie Burke. Thanks to Charles Frohman's enthusiastic welcome and a number of prominent introductions, Maugham found himself invited everywhere. He quickly became quite a celebrity, with his courteous manners, "English" reserve, and exquisitely tailored clothes. *The New York Times,* taking note of the "host of social entertainments [given] in his honor," observed that "Mr. Maugham [is] the most socially popular English playwright that has visited America in years."

One New Yorker on whom he made an unforgettable impression was his "Mrs. Dot," Billie Burke. A vivacious redhead, Billie Burke had begun her career singing in music halls in England at the age of fourteen and was now a popular comedienne working to establish herself as a straight actress, an ambition considerably furthered by her success in Maugham's play. To her, Maugham's elegance was more Parisian than Bond Street, with his finely fitted suits, beautifully made shoes, and gray silk top hat. Maugham, who liked the company of pretty women, was entertained by the actress's high spirits and flattered by her obvious admiration. After the show the two would often go dancing together, deciding one evening to go to the nightclub at the Astor. "We were not members and it was late, about 2 A.M.," Billie Burke remembered, "[but] over we went [and down] the red-carpeted grand staircase of the Hotel Astor ballroom. . . . I can permit myself to say 'made an entrance,' for no actress in her right mind would attempt less in descending a great staircase on the arm of Somerset Maugham." In her memoirs she recalled "his great smouldering brown eyes," adding wistfully, "Ah yes, Mr. Maugham, so you had, and I was a little in love with you, sir."

Miss Burke was not the only one to be smitten. After all, here was a man, handsome, famous, and rich, whose subject was marriage, and yet he was not married. It was inevitable that a number of women came to consider Maugham as ideal husband material, and he was frequently teased by matchmaking ladies anxious to be the one to find the playwright a wife. But his private life was tightly guarded: his continuing relationship with Sue Jones was known only to a few, and he kept his penchant for members of his own sex even more of a secret.

A friendship Maugham was particularly anxious to renew while in New York was with a fellow playwright, the twenty-four-year-old Edward (Ned) Sheldon, known as the Boy Wonder of Broadway. Sheldon, son of a wealthy Chicago real estate dealer, had made a sensation by writing two immensely successful plays, one while he was still at Harvard. Sheldon was clever, sensitive, charming, and urbane; he was also wealthy and very handsome; and he, like Maugham, was somewhat ambivalent in his sexuality. In 1909 he had visited Europe, which was probably when the friendship began. Maugham found him intensely attractive and hoped for a more physical relationship, but Sheldon was evasive, with the result that "there was never the least frankness between them upon the subject of sex." Nonetheless the two men became devoted friends, with Maugham when in New York often staying at Sheldon's exotically furnished apartment on Gramercy Park.

From New York Maugham went for a few days to Boston, where he dined with Henry James, then staying with his recently widowed sister-in-law in Cambridge. Maugham had met James on a couple of occasions in London and had been intrigued by him, if slightly irritated by the atmosphere of *"cher maître"* that surrounded him, by the great man's expectation of reverence and homage. Maugham's attitude to James's work over the years was to grow increasingly equivocal, a mixture of impatience and admiration, impatience with what he saw as a lack of that empathy essential to a novelist and admiration for a superb technique. "The great novelists, even in seclusion, have lived life passionately," Maugham wrote. "Henry James was content to observe it from a window." Nonetheless he found James good company, witty when in the mood, and he was pleased to see him again, enjoying the intimate evening *à trois,* although it was obvious that James on this occasion was in a nervous and unhappy frame of mind: grieving over the death of his brother, William, he was also pining to return to England, restless and ill at ease in the land of his birth. As Maugham prepared to leave, James insisted on accompanying him to the corner where he would catch the streetcar back to Boston.

I protested that I was perfectly capable of getting there by myself, but he would not hear of it, not only on account of the kindness and the great courtesy which were natural to him, but also because America seemed to him a strange and terrifying labyrinth in which without his guidance I was bound to get hopelessly lost. . . . The street-car hove in sight and Henry James was seized with agitation. He began waving frantically when it was still a quarter of a mile away. He was afraid it wouldn't stop, and he besought me to jump on with the greatest agility of which I was capable. . . . I was so infected by his anxiety that when the car pulled up and I leapt on, I had almost the sensation that I had had a miraculous escape from certain death. I saw him standing on his short legs in the middle of the road, looking after the car, and I felt that he was trembling still at my narrow shave.

Upon his arrival in England in December 1910, Maugham was immediately faced with two conflicting demands: his work, and the decoration and furnishing of Chesterfield Street. The first and most urgent requirement was to put the finishing touches to *Loaves and Fishes,* which was due to go into rehearsal after Christmas. Written as long ago as 1903, *Loaves and Fishes* had failed to arouse any interest at the time, and having subsequently been reshaped as a novel, *The Bishop's Apron,* was now returned to the form for which it had originally been intended. It opened at the Duke of York's on February 24, yet despite a polished Frohman-Boucicault production and an enthusiastic first night, it ran for only a few weeks. "I think it possible that the public is just tired of me," Maugham told Gerald Kelly.

That is an eventuality to which I have always looked forward, & it leaves me calm. I can give them a rest for a year or two, & then they will have forgotten, & come back to my work with avidity. I have put into three years & a half what most dramatists would have given ten years to, & it would not be surprising if my characteristics have become tedious.

Fortunately Maugham could easily afford to step back and consider his position. For the past fifteen years, since the writing of

Liza of Lambeth, he had worked unceasingly, producing an astonishing quantity of material; now, thanks to the large sums coming in every week from both sides of the Atlantic and to Walter Payne's prudent investments, he could allow himself some leisure. For such a prolific and successful writer, the failure of this recent production, regrettable, of course, was no serious matter. Frohman was unconcerned; indeed, was offering the enormous sum of £10,000 for a new play as a vehicle for Billie Burke, but Maugham was uninterested in the proposal and turned it down. Financially Maugham was well off, and as he told Kelly, "I shall still be able to pay for the house without touching my capital."

The workmen were finally on the point of leaving, and Maugham was anxious to give the house his full attention. He and Walter Payne were to continue their amicable arrangement of cohabiting, Payne having left the bar in order to take over his late father's music hall and theatrical business. The two men, with the assistance of a decorator friend, a Mr. Howard, now threw themselves into the creation of an elegant town house. "Howard has been very kind to us," Maugham reported to Kelly. "His advice has been extremely useful, & his taste seems excellent [although] I do not share his admiration for the massive & gilded: the only thing I am quite sure I like gilded is sin." Kelly, who on his friend's recommendation was spending some months in Spain, received a stream of letters asking him to find various ornaments—pottery, glass, pictures, fabric. In pride of place opposite the fireplace in the drawing room was Kelly's *Jester,* "one of the best things you have done," as Maugham told him. "Everyone who comes expresses admiration of the house [, and] my own room, the long one upstairs, is a great success." This was Maugham's writing room, and in contrast to the lower floors was sparsely equipped, a wide, bare room with two narrow sash windows facing the street and in the center a rough deal table serving as a desk. The finished results were entirely satisfactory. "I have never been so comfortable in my life," Maugham declared.

With the house more or less completed, Maugham became aware of the familiar restlessness taking hold. At Easter he went to

Paris, in June to Le Touquet, and then he made a short trip to the Balearics before returning to London to prepare for another visit to New York in the autumn. But now he was longing to go farther, his mind filled with visions of the Far East. One mooted project involved Kelly, who was planning a lengthy sojourn in Burma. "I have half a mind to join you in Burmah for a little," Maugham wrote to him, "& shall try & persuade you to come on to China with me." But escape was not to prove as easy as in his imaginings it seemed.

FOR THE PAST FIVE YEARS Maugham had been wholly engaged with the theater, but now his interest had waned. True, there were still minor commissions to be fulfilled: a preface for an edition of his plays to be published by Heinemann in September, and two adaptations from the French. Yet more and more he felt himself drawn toward the writing of a novel. "After submitting myself for some years to the exigencies of the drama I hankered after the wide liberty of the novel," he wrote. "I knew the book I had in mind would be a long one and I wanted to be undisturbed, so I refused the contracts that managers were eagerly offering me and temporarily retired from the stage. I was then thirty-seven." His theme was predominantly autobiographical, much the same as that attempted at twenty-four in "The Artistic Temperament of Stephen Carey," the story of his childhood and young manhood and of a degrading sexual obsession. This time, however, with greatly increased maturity and confidence, it would be approached without flinching and with an uncompromising adherence to psychological truth. The subject began increasingly to absorb him, the compulsion he felt under to write different from anything he had previously known; his memories were literally forcing themselves upon him—"choking" was the word he used: "I had all that stuff choking me, occupying my thoughts by day & my dreams by night, and I wanted to be free of it."

In order to begin on the work undisturbed he went to stay at the

Sunningdale Golf Club in Berkshire, from where he reported that he was making good progress.

> It is a great satisfaction to sit down to it every morning & peg away, without having to bother about whether it is long or dull, or whether this will get across the footlights or whether an actress will ever be able to say the other. I am afraid it will be much longer than I could wish, but there is no help for it: I have so much to say. . . .

From then on over the next two and a half years came regular reports that the book was almost finished—and yet somehow the end continued to lie just out of reach, an unfamiliar experience for Maugham, accustomed to completing a work in a matter of weeks. The novel was begun in the autumn of 1911, but it was not until the autumn of 1914 that it was delivered to Heinemann, scheduled for publication the following August.

Such an unusually long period of gestation was due not only to the size of the project but also to Maugham's reluctance to stay sequestered for more than a few days at a time: there were simply too many distractions. The winter season of 1911, the first after the coronation of George V, was particularly brilliant: The Russian ballet, with Pavlova and Nijinsky, was in London, and there were new plays by Sutro, Shaw, and Arnold Bennett, all attended by Maugham. Another diversion at this time was a brief love affair with a Russian woman, Princess Alexandra Kropotkin, the daughter of Prince Peter Kropotkin, the anarchist intellectual then living in exile in London. "Sasha" Kropotkin was a big, voluptuous woman, handsome, with high cheekbones, a wide mouth, and slightly protuberant dark eyes. Clever, serious, and intense, a friend of socialists such as William Morris and Bernard Shaw, Sasha moved in a circle of Russian artists and revolutionaries, and in this period of European fascination with all things Russian, Maugham found it exciting at her parties to make such close contact with Russian history and literature, to meet Diaghilev and Pavlova, to drink vodka and discuss Tolstoy and Dostoevsky with passionate intensity. The two of them went over to Paris for a few days where they stayed at a little hotel on the Left Bank; they visited the Louvre and the Comédie Française and went dancing in a Russian nightclub, and Sasha ate her way through a number of enormous meals with an appetite that slightly appalled her lover.* Maugham introduced her to his brother Charles, who was visibly impressed that Willie should be on such intimate terms with a real live princess. "He simply couldn't believe I was fucking anyone so grand," as Maugham somewhat indelicately phrased it. The affair provided a pleasant interlude, ending after a few weeks "without acrimony on either side," leaving Maugham free to travel. In March 1912 he went to Spain for six weeks, and in August and September made a tour of the Continent, beginning in Paris and ending in Rome. He was back in London in November but left again the following month for New York in order to undertake an unusual piece of research, nothing at all to do with his novel, but for a new play. Entitled *The Land of Promise,* this was first staged in the United States in November 1913, opening in London the following February, where a successful run at the Duke of York's was brought to an abrupt end by the outbreak of war. It was only then that Maugham put the finishing touches to his novel.

Of Human Bondage is a flawed and magnificent work, showing all the strengths as well as the weaknesses of Maugham as novelist. At three hundred thousand words and filling sixteen medium-sized notebooks in manuscript, it is the longest and also the most intensely personal of all Maugham's novels, written with an astonishing vitality and drive. "The teeming memories" that had been so insistently pushing at his consciousness were of his own boyhood and youth, the story of which provides the main plot, a linear narrative told in a style deliberately spare and unadorned: there is none of the softening and prettification that found their way into "Stephen Carey." The dominant theme is of the hero's journey

---

* Maugham drew on this episode for his short story "Love and Russian Literature" in the *Ashenden* collection.

toward self-discovery, mainly through the terrifying experience of a masochistic sexual obsession; he believes his search to be for the meaning of life, for the figure in the carpet, which turns out to be as elusive as in Henry James's famous story, although here the revelation that there is no meaning comes as an immense liberation. "His insignificance was turned to power . . . for, if life was meaningless, the world was robbed of its cruelty."

The hero, Philip Carey, is a small boy and already fatherless when the story begins with the harrowing death of his mother in childbirth. The boy is put in the charge of his uncle, the vicar of Blackstable in Kent, a selfish, unloving man, and of his German wife, Louisa. As soon as he is old enough Philip is sent to board at the King's School, Tercanbury, where he is wretchedly unhappy. At sixteen he goes for a year to Heidelberg, and then to study art in Paris, eventually returning to London to train as a doctor at St. Luke's Hospital.

Philip and one of his fellow students form the habit of dropping in at a nearby tea shop, and it is here that Philip first sets eyes on his nemesis. Mildred, one of the waitresses, is a pasty-faced young woman with an offensively offhand manner. At first annoyed by her snubbing indifference, Philip gradually finds himself perversely attracted, excited by her obvious contempt: "it was absurd to care what an anaemic little waitress said to him; but he was strangely humiliated." And so his destructive obsession takes hold. He courts Mildred slavishly, begs for her attention, lavishes whatever presents and treats he can afford on her, and the more scornfully she treats him, the more abjectly he crawls back for more. The few times she carelessly allows him to make love to her, his desire, instead of being slaked, burns stronger than ever. He clearly sees that Mildred is stupid, vulgar, humorless, and avaricious; he despises himself for his passion but is helpless in its grip. Mildred taunts him, bores him, enrages him; they quarrel violently; sometimes he wants to kill her; but away from her he can think only of seeing her again, of begging her forgiveness, of meekly accepting the humiliations she heaps upon him. She leaves him twice for other men before Philip finally comes to his senses and leaves her.

Ironically, although Philip has freed himself from Mildred, it is now that he reaches the nadir of his existence. Through an unwise investment of his tiny patrimony, he loses all his money and is left penniless. Not only can he not afford to continue his training, he cannot pay his rent, nor, after the few shillings in his pocket are spent, can he afford to buy food. Unable to find work and desperate with hunger, he starts sleeping rough, fortunately rescued at this point by a kindly character, Thorpe Athelney, who procures him a job in a large linen draper's on Oxford Street. Philip endures months of drudgery on the shop floor, but then his uncle dies, he is left enough money to complete his medical training, and the story ends with his proposing marriage to Thorpe Athelney's eldest daughter.

Of Human Bondage is an extraordinarily compelling work, standing comparison with some of the best of Maugham's contemporaries, with Bennett, Gissing, and George Moore, as well as with an important earlier influence, Samuel Butler's *The Way of All Flesh,* a novel much admired by Maugham. Throughout, it is evident that Maugham draws widely from his own experience: even apart from the boyhood sections and the dominant central theme of the affair with Mildred, there are numerous places, situations, and subsidiary characters recognizable from life. There is one vividly described sequence, however, which was created entirely from a secondhand account, the passage dealing with Philip's job as a shop assistant. With no experience of such work himself, Maugham commissioned an account from Gilbert Clark, a young actor who had been employed at the Piccadilly department store Swan & Edgar's. At Maugham's request Clark wrote a six-thousand-word description of his experience, for which he was paid thirty guineas. "Willie used my stuff practically word for word," Clark later recalled with satisfaction.

There was no need for outside assistance, however, in treating the theme at the heart of the novel, that of Philip's bondage, his masochistic obsession with the hateful Mildred. The identity of the original of this curiously androgynous character is a mystery: a Lambeth prostitute, according to one theorist, a tea shop waitress, in the view of another, while Maugham's onetime lover, Harry Philips,

who might be expected to know, definitely asserted that "she" was a
boy. What is certain is that he or she once existed and that Maugham
must have met her when he was very young, since her prototype is
Rose in "Stephen Carey," written as early as 1898. The likelihood is
that in the later novel Maugham added to the portrait various attributes and incidents culled from subsequent experience. Harry
Philips when he read the novel recognized one such incident, "undoubtedly an episode in our friendship not very creditable to me
which he attributed to her [Mildred]." Every detail of Philip's en-
slavement rings true. His degradation is relentlessly mapped out, his
lust, his abject devotion, his tormented self-loathing. Mildred is diabolical, yet at the same time Maugham allows us to see that she is to
be pitied. One of Maugham's greatest strengths as a novelist is his
ability to create three-dimensional characters, women as well as
men, interacting with one another. Mildred, so cold and callous
with Philip, is pathetic in her relations with other men. Equally,
Philip himself is depicted with ruthless honesty, eager, vulnerable,
tenderhearted, but also priggish, self-pitying, and capable of a subtle
sadism; when wishing to hurt Mildred, "he exercised peculiar skill
in saying little things which he knew would wound her; but which
were so indefinite, so delicately cruel, that she could not take exception to them."

Despite its flaws, *Of Human Bondage* is a major achievement.
Maugham, who usually cultivated a fastidious detachment, shows
in this work a personal commitment that was unusual, sweeping the
reader up in his own passionate intensity. Always an astute judge of
his own work, Maugham knew that this novel was of a different
caliber from anything he had previously produced. He also knew
that his standing was such that he was now free wholly to please
himself. As he explained to Heinemann,

> I am aware that in the past I have compromised too much with
> what others have thought the public taste. . . . Many writers
> are forced by poverty to consider whether this or that will
> hurt the sale of their books . . . but I think it would be dis-
> graceful if I allowed any such thoughts to influence me. There

are very few of us who can afford to break the bonds which the circulating libraries have placed on the contemporary English novel (bonds which have made it an object of contempt on the continent) and it behoves such as can to do so.

The choice of a title proved difficult, and a list of several was compiled: *The Road Uphill, Experience, The Broad Road, A Winter's Day, The Day's March,* none of which seemed exactly right. Heinemann was in favor of *Life's Thoroughfare,* which Maugham thought commonplace. "I am sorry to have been so fussy," he wrote, "but the book is my ewe-lamb, and I want to get away from the obvious." Eventually Maugham fixed on *Beauty from Ashes,* a misquotation from Isaiah 61 ("to give unto them beauty for ashes"), but finding this had recently been used, decided instead to take the title of one of the books in Spinoza's *Ethics. Of Human Bondage* was published by Doran in the United States on August 12, 1915, a day later by Heinemann in England. George Doran expressed his unqualified admiration for the work, recording in his memoirs, "Were I given freedom of choice as to that book which I would first choose to have written had I the genius and wit, it would be *Of Human Bondage.*"

In the press the critical reception was at first rather more muted. With Europe embroiled in war, readers were hardly in the mood for long, serious novels, and on both sides of the Atlantic, reviews were respectful rather than excited. Then at the very end of the year a notice appeared in *The New Republic* by the distinguished novelist Theodore Dreiser placing the work in a different bracket altogether. "Here is a novel . . . of the utmost importance," Dreiser wrote, "unmoral, as a novel of this kind must necessarily be . . . a gorgeous weave, as interesting and valuable at the beginning as at the end." Somerset Maugham, he concluded, was indeed "a great artist." From this point *Of Human Bondage* climbed steadily in terms of critical evaluation, although it was not until the 1920s, when it was rediscovered following the enormous success of Maugham's novel *The Moon and Sixpence,* that it attained canonical status, in 1934 made into a film with Leslie Howard and Bette Davis, and for nearly half a century widely regarded as a classic.

But this was all in the future. When Maugham began writing *Of Human Bondage* in 1911 his novels were considered a minor part of the oeuvre, his reputation based on his remarkable success as a playwright. His publishers, Heinemann and Doran, nevertheless regarded his name a prestigious addition to their lists. George Doran, who came over to London twice a year to buy books, numbering both Hugh Walpole and Arnold Bennett among his authors, regarded his association with Maugham and Heinemann as "two of the most notable, satisfying contacts of my publishing life." Maugham's dealings with Doran were solely about business, but with William Heinemann he was on more intimate terms, the two men having much in common. Like Maugham, Heinemann was small, with a slight stutter; he was a gifted linguist, with a passion for music, painting, and drama (both Pinero and Ibsen appeared under his imprint). It was often said that his genius for friendship was equaled only by his genius for publishing, a judgment supported by a list of authors that included Conrad, Kipling, Robert Louis Stevenson, Galsworthy, Beerbohm, Henry James, and H. G. Wells.

The fact that Somerset Maugham would outsell them all could hardly have been predicted in 1915, although in the theater, both in the West End and on Broadway, he was undoubtedly regarded as a very valuable property indeed; his intention to abandon writing plays had not unnaturally been received with gloom by Charles Frohman. Three years earlier, in reply to a courteous inquiry from Maugham about his health, Frohman had replied he was unwell, "partly on account of the weather, but more especially because you are not doing any work." Finally Frohman had decided to confront the issue. "I want a new play from you," he announced. "All right," said Maugham. "Why not rewrite *The Taming of the Shrew* with a new background?" The more Maugham thought about it, the more the idea appealed, and as he turned it over in his mind a memory came back to him of an aunt with whom he used to stay in Tunbridge Wells: Aunt Julia had had a paid companion who had moved to Canada to live with her brother on a farm. "I well remembered the shock it caused my elderly relative when her former companion ('very well connected, my dear') wrote and told her that she had married one of the hired men." It was this recollection that provided the starting point, the idea explored further by Maugham's going out to see for himself what that way of life was like. Perhaps it was Aunt Julia's companion who herself acted as his hostess on her bleak prairie farm, where at the end of 1912 Maugham arrived from Toronto via New York to spend a month in the bitter winter cold of the Canadian midwest.

After the comfort and modernity of Manhattan the primitive conditions encountered in Manitoba provided a harsh contrast, and yet Maugham could not help but be intrigued by his rough surroundings, reporting that despite "a good deal of discomfort and tedium" he found "that curious and intense life . . . most interesting." Back in New York at the end of December, he described his experience in a letter to the actress Mabel Beardsley, sister of Aubrey:

> My God, what a life they lead . . . surrounded by the snowy prairie, cut off from their neighbours & absorbed with the struggle of getting three meals a day. Husbands & wives get to such a pitch of irritability that they will pass weeks without speaking to one another. In one house in which I stayed the wife had killed herself, in another there hung a strange gloom of impending madness. I was glad to get away. But it was an interesting experience, & the prairie, even under the snow, had a curious fascination which lingers in my memory.

The resulting play was peculiarly topical, its title, *The Land of Promise,* a deliberate evocation of the phrase familiar from advertisements aimed at attracting British settlers to Canada. Norah, the "Shrew," has for the past ten years led a wretched existence as a paid companion in Tunbridge Wells. When the play opens her employer has just died, and Norah, completely penniless, decides to join her brother on his farm in Canada. Here the refined Norah is so miserable that in despair she offers herself as wife to one of the hired men. Frank, the Petruchio figure, strong and manly, with an

enjoyably sardonic sense of humor, agrees to take her, but only on
certain conditions. "I give her board and lodging and the charm of
my society," he says. "And in return she's got to cook and bake and
wash and keep the shack clean and tidy." Predictably, the first night
of their married life is tempestuous, with Norah at first haughtily
refusing to obey her husband's orders and Frank determined to sub-
due her. Eventually he flings open the bedroom door and Norah,
recognizing defeat, slowly walks through it. (When the film version
of *The Land of Promise* was made in 1917, this scene was censored,
with Frank spending his wedding night sleeping on the floor.) In
the last act, six months have passed and we see the shack transformed, muslin curtains at the windows, flowers on the table, and
Norah and Frank obviously on affectionate terms. Norah's brother
arrives with a letter offering her a place as companion to another
old lady in England. "For God's sake take it," he urges her. But
Norah has changed: here in this harsh land of promise there is
struggle and hardship but also the hope of a worthwhile future;
more important, she has fallen in love with her husband.

The Land of Promise is a strong piece of drama, courageous in its
treatment of sexual dominance and submission, particularly at a
time when female suffrage and emancipation were much in the
news. As Maugham realized, conveying the play's message depended enormously on how the two main characters were inter-
preted. In Norah, as well as courage and passion there is a deep
hidden sadness rooted in an unexpressed terror of facing a future as
a penurious spinster; and it is important that Frank, although un-
mannered, is basically decent and kind. We know from the scene
played out between them when they first meet that there is a strong
mutual attraction, and it is this, and Frank's good-heartedness despite his tough talk, that prevents the climax from appearing brutal
and unpleasant. In the scene leading up to what virtually amounts
to marital rape, the subtext must reveal that Norah's fury with
Frank comes as much from fury with herself for physically desiring
him. If this is not made evident, then the play fails.

The Land of Promise opened in Washington in November 1913
before transferring to New Haven, Connecticut, finally coming

into New York on Christmas Day. Billie Burke as Norah was a guaranteed draw. As Maugham told Gerald Kelly, "the audience of course knew nothing of the play, they just came to see the star." Unfortunately, Miss Burke, blind to the troubling complexities of Norah's character, saw the piece as a straightforward romantic comedy and Norah as a feisty little firebrand who by perkiness and pouting finally gets her man. Needless to say, this made nonsense of the role: "the leading part loses by being played as a romantic ingénue," Maugham complained, cross that his play was being "[so] rottenly acted . . . by that little slut." That Billie Burke herself was unhappy is made clear in her memoirs. "*The Land of Promise,*" she recalls,

> was a beautifully written but dreary kind of play for me. My costumes were not fetching—one black dress and another of a particularly ugly blue—and the problems of Canadian farmers did not interest New York audiences. It was full of integrity and all that . . . but the change of character was perhaps too sudden for me. . . . Some other established dramatic actress could have carried this play, but I could not.

In the States the notices were generally good, although there was a certain amount of umbrage taken north of the border. "No Canadian man would dream of ordering his wife about," protested the *Daily Bulletin* in Edmonton. "If there is one thing Canadian men do well, it is the way they treat their wives." By March the following year, indignation had reached such a pitch that the planned tour of Canada had to be canceled.

IN ORDER TO OVERSEE the American production of *The Land of Promise,* Maugham had arrived in New York on November 15, 1913. But on this, his third visit to the United States, he had had an additional purpose in mind. Sue Jones was also due to arrive in America, having landed a small part, obtained for her by Maugham, in Ned Sheldon's play *Romance,* which had had a successful run on

Broadway and was now playing at the Princess Theatre in Chicago. Maugham had missed saying good-bye to Sue before he left England and was determined not to miss her again, for he had finally made up his mind to make her his wife. In a telling passage in *The Summing Up* he describes his attitude toward marriage at this stage in his life:

> If I meant to marry and have children it was high time I did so. . . . It seemed a necessary motif in the pattern of life that I had designed, and to my ingenuous fancy (for though no longer young and thinking myself so worldly wise, I was still in many ways incredibly naïve) it offered peace . . . peace that would enable me to write all I wanted to write without the loss of precious time or disturbance of mind; peace and a settled and dignified way of life.

In terms of society, Maugham could have married well above his station: such an attractive and successful man was considered a good "catch," and by no means only in theatrical circles. But Sue was the woman he wanted: he loved her, and he knew despite her promiscuity that she loved him. When not on tour, Sue sometimes discreetly stayed at Chesterfield Street, and Maugham had grown used to the safe haven of her warm and welcoming presence.

Before leaving England, Maugham made his preparations with care. He bought an expensive engagement ring, two large pearls encircled by diamonds, and planned his schedule so that after fulfilling his commitments in New York he could stay in Chicago with Sue during the obligatory fortnight she would need to work out her notice with the company. After this there would be a quiet registry office wedding, and then the two of them would leave at once for a long honeymoon voyage to Tahiti and the South Seas. On the day that Sue's ship was due to arrive in New York, Maugham went down to the pier to meet it. Amid the noise and bustle of disembarkation he caught sight of her almost at once, talking to a tall, handsome young man who quickly disappeared. Sue was delighted to see him and kissed him warmly but was unable to linger, as the train for Chicago was leaving within the hour. For the next couple of weeks Maugham was kept busy with his play, but at the beginning of December he went up to Chicago, taking a room at the same hotel in which Sue was staying. He telephoned to arrange a time to meet and she sounded delighted to hear him, agreeing to have supper with him after the performance. At about half past ten Sue rang to say she was ready, and Maugham went to her small suite. Looking wonderfully beautiful, she gave him her usual loving embrace and started to tell him about the play, but something was wrong: she seemed restless, uneasy, at moments almost on the edge of hysteria. She barely touched the supper that had been ordered, and soon Maugham rang for the waiter to take it away. Deciding this was the moment, he said quietly, "I've come to ask you to marry me."

> [Sue] paused for what seemed to me quite a long time. Then, "I don't want to marry you," she said. I was taken aback. . . . "D'you mean it?" I asked. "Yes." "Why not?" I asked. "I just don't want to." . . . I took out of my pocket the engagement ring I had bought and handed it to her. "I got this for you." She looked at it. "It's very pretty," she said. . . . She handed it back to me. . . . "If you want to go to bed with me you can," she said, "but I won't marry you." I shook my head: "No, I won't do that." We sat in silence for a while. I broke it by saying, "Well, there's nothing more to be said, is there?" "No," she answered. I could see that she wanted me to go. I put the ring back in my pocket, got up, kissed her and bade her good-night.

Although the above description was written nearly fifty years later, fifty years during which the memory had remained ineradicably etched in Maugham's mind, it tallies closely with the letter he sent to Gerald Kelly from New York immediately after his return there from Chicago:

> My schemes for going round the world have come to nothing. I went up to Chicago to see Susan & found her in a very hys-

terical condition, & I can do nothing with her, I will tell you more in detail when we meet; poor thing, her nerves, her digestion, everything has gone wrong; it is an effect America often has on people, & the only thing for her is a rest cure, but I cannot induce her to be sensible & get back to England & have me.

In his memoir, *Looking Back,* Maugham depicts himself walking down Piccadilly soon after his return to London and catching sight of an *Evening Standard* placard on which in large capitals were the words ACTRESS MARRIES EARL'S SON. "I guessed at once who the actress was and bought a paper. I was right." In fact Sue had married in Chicago on December 13, while Maugham was still in New York and less than a fortnight after rejecting his proposal. Her new husband was Angus McDonnell, a younger son of the Earl of Antrim, and Maugham guessed that McDonnell had been the good-looking fellow passenger to whom he had seen her talking when disembarking from the ship; he also guessed, rightly, that McDonnell had made her pregnant ("I knew how careless she was in these matters"), which would explain Sue's nervousness and the so-called digestive disorders that he had attributed to stress.

Apart from Kelly, Maugham told almost no one what had happened. Adept at concealment, he gave little sign of his disappointment, although in fact the loss of Sue Jones was a blow from which he took a long time to recover and never ceased regretting: even after many years, the mention of her name never failed to stir deep emotion. He had loved her truly, believing that he and she could have made a happy, if not wholly conventional, life together. Of course he would have strayed, and probably so would she, but still they might have made it work. Fortunately he could not foresee that with the loss of Sue Jones all hope of such contentment was gone for good.

HEAVYHEARTED, MAUGHAM IMMEDIATELY set about driving himself harder than ever. *The Land of Promise* was doing excellent business, and Frohman was urging him to deliver four more plays for the following season. His life was not all work, however, for it was now that he encountered again a woman he had met shortly before leaving for America. He had found her amusing and attractive, but thought little more about her until chance again brought her into view. A brief lighthearted affair with no ties attached seemed the ideal prescription to alleviate his sadness over Sue. Little did he know that he was about to enter the longest, most miserable, and most bitterly destructive relationship of his life.

It began harmlessly enough one evening in the autumn of the previous year, 1913, shortly before Maugham sailed for New York. He had been sitting reading in his top-floor study on Chesterfield Street when a neighbor, Mrs. Carstairs, telephoned to ask him a favor: she and her husband had invited a couple of friends to dine and go to the theater, and at the last minute one had dropped out: would Maugham take his place? "It happened that I had nothing to do and hadn't seen the play," Maugham recalled, "so I said I would be glad to come." At the Carstairs' house he was shown into the drawing room and introduced to his fellow guest. Mrs. Wellcome, in her mid-thirties, was striking rather than conventionally pretty, with a wide mouth, slightly prominent nose, creamy complexion, and big brown eyes. It was obvious she found him attractive, and consequently during dinner he was at his wittiest and most entertaining. As they prepared to leave for the theater, Mrs. Wellcome whispered flatteringly, "I wish we didn't have to go to this play. I'd like to listen to you talking all night." The next afternoon, during the obligatory call on his hostess, Maugham mentioned that he had found her friend very charming. Syrie Wellcome was the wife of the enormously wealthy Henry Wellcome, the American pharmaceutical manufacturer, Mrs. Carstairs told him; the marriage had not been happy, and the couple were now living apart.

A few days later at the opera Maugham caught sight of Syrie Wellcome sitting in the stalls and went to speak to her. She was obviously pleased to see him, explaining that she was sorry she was unable to invite him to visit her as she was temporarily living in an "odious" flat near Marble Arch while her new house in Regent's

Park was being decorated. "She hoped I would come to the house-warming party she intended to give as soon as she moved in." It was shortly after this that Maugham left for America to oversee rehearsals of *The Land of Promise* and to ask Sue Jones to marry him.

The London production of *The Land of Promise* opened at the Duke of York's Theatre on February 26, 1914, by coincidence the same night that Syrie had chosen for her housewarming. Maugham sent her two seats in the front row of the stalls, intending to go to her reception as soon as he could get away from the theater. Tense and nervous as always on a first night, Maugham was irritated to see Syrie slide into her seat late, several minutes after the curtain had gone up, and he almost decided to cut her party, but having refused other invitations in order to accept this, he had nothing else to do, and so he made his way up to 4 York Terrace in Regent's Park. It was a good party, with an orchestra and a crowd of lively, fashionably dressed people, many of whom congratulated him on the play. Maugham, high on his success, thoroughly enjoyed himself, dancing several times with his hostess and not returning home until the small hours. "After that," he said, "I saw Syrie almost every day."

Syrie Wellcome was not quite the conventional society woman that she appeared. Born in 1879, five years younger than Maugham, Syrie was a daughter of the great reformer Thomas Barnardo, founder of the Dr. Barnardo's Homes for destitute children. The eldest girl in a family of six, Gwendoline Maud, in adult life always known as Syrie, had had an unusual upbringing. Both Barnardo and his wife, also called Syrie, although within the family referred to as "the Begum," were members of an American religious sect, the Open Plymouth Brethren. Devoutly evangelical, an ardent member of the temperance movement, Dr. Barnardo laid heavy emphasis on daily Bible readings and prayers, on strict punctuality and obedience, and on the spurning of worldly pleasures: drinking, smoking, and visits to the theater were all forbidden. Barnardo was a brilliant businessman and made a great deal of money, but spent it faster than it accrued, mainly on his various charities. A flamboyant personality, aggressive, obstinate, arrogant, and overbearing, he was also capable of considerable charm and personal kindness: he was treated warily by his children, but he was also loved, particularly by his elder daughter, who inherited a number of her father's traits, notably a hot temper, a steely determination to have her own way, and a talent for commerce that was to stand her in remarkably good stead later in life.

When Syrie was seventeen the Barnardos moved from the East End of London to a large house in the suburbs, where the Begum, in many ways more practical than her husband, started giving occasional parties so that her daughter might have the chance to meet some suitable young men. It was Barnardo's intention that Syrie should train to be a missionary and go to China, a choice of career that could not have been further from her own ambitions. Syrie loved social life and longed to leave home, where the atmosphere was gloomy and repressive; she loathed the emphasis on religion and had not the faintest interest in her father's good works. Marriage was the obvious way out, and after a brief flirtation with a local youth, Syrie, encouraged by her mother, focused her attention on a wealthy American, a friend of Dr. Barnardo's, who had rented a house in the neighborhood.

Henry ("Hal") Wellcome, a handsome, well-built man of forty-six with blue eyes and a bushy ginger mustache, was immensely rich. Like Thomas Barnardo, whom he much admired, he possessed a strong instinct toward altruism and bettering the lot of his fellow man, the great goal of his life the eradication of disease in impoverished parts of the world. He had long been settled in England, and his pharmaceutical company, Burroughs Wellcome Ltd., established in London, had become hugely successful, the first manufacturers of the compressed pill, or "tabloid," which was to revolutionize Western medicine. Wellcome enjoyed female company, although he had never had the time to seriously contemplate marriage. Syrie, however, attractive and vivacious, definitely caught his fancy, and she on her side found him good fun: he kept a canoe on the river and was always ready for a party, and she was excited by the marked attentions he paid her. Most important, she saw in Wellcome an escape route from the suffocating atmosphere of home as well as an entrée into the world of the sophisticated and well-to-do of which she longed to be part.

But at the end of the summer Wellcome left for abroad without anything having been said, and it looked as if the big fish had escaped the net. Swift action was necessary, and the wily Begum, knowing that Wellcome was bound for a research trip to the Sudan, dispatched her daughter in pursuit. No one could have been more surprised than Hal Wellcome in Khartoum to see the delightful Miss Barnardo disembark one day from a Nile steamer with a befrilled and parasoled party of sightseeing English ladies. The ruse was successful, and Syrie returned to England engaged, becoming Mrs. Henry Wellcome at a quiet ceremony in St. Mark's Church, Surbiton, on June 2, 1901.

The marriage was a disaster almost from the start. Wellcome was a man of the highest principle, intelligent, energetic, and sociable, if happier when dealing with large groups than with individuals. He was also set in his ways, wholly dedicated to his work, and as a powerful player in his field who was frequently consulted by governments and heads of state, he was accustomed to deference and inclined to be dictatorial. In marrying the daughter of his public-spirited old friend he believed he had found the ideal wife, high-minded, biddable, and self-denying, eager to devote herself to pleasing him and to promoting his numerous charitable interests. This was a serious miscalculation. Syrie, frivolous and self-indulgent, envisaged a high-spending married life in which she would preside over some of the capital's most elegant soirées, with regular vacations at fashionable Continental resorts. Her fantasy soon faded. The Wellcomes' first married home was a rented house in Kent, where Syrie found herself acting as hostess not to *gens du monde* but to gray-haired professors and their dowdy wives, who sat in the garden drinking tea and discussing diphtheria. When the Wellcomes went out it was invariably to attend crowded functions in hot hotel banqueting rooms, where young Mrs. Wellcome was required to sit on a platform stupefied with boredom while distinguished scientists made lengthy speeches prior to an endless series of presentations of cups, medals, and diplomas. Worse were the trips abroad. Instead of Le Touquet or Biarritz, Wellcome, who was completely indifferent to physical comfort, took his wife rattling around little-known parts of Europe on an obsessive search for objects for his collection of medical instruments and artifacts, which was eventually to number over one million items. For months at a time they drove over terrible roads in a car that was frequently breaking down, at night putting up in primitive inns, by day trailing around dusty shops and museums or crowded, noisy bazaars. Wellcome considered these expeditions a tremendous adventure; his wife detested every minute.

There were other areas of incompatibility, but of these nothing was said, Syrie only later confiding to one or two intimates her distaste for her husband's sexual demands. With his ginger hair now turning gray, his walrus mustache, red face, and paunch, and the heavy smell of cigars lingering on his breath, Wellcome at nearly fifty was unlikely to appear an attractive prospect to a young woman of twenty-one. It was more than that, however: there were hints of beatings and brutality, of sadistic tendencies, of pain inflicted in the bedroom that privately appalled her.

In June 1903, shortly after returning from a long tour of Canada and the United States, Syrie gave birth to a son, Mounteney. Both husband and wife doted on the boy, although his arrival, instead of bringing his parents together, acted to drive them further apart. Syrie, with a small baby to care for, objected to being made to continue with her husband's demanding program, nor was she slow in making her objections clear. She sulked, he was irritable, and there were some ferocious rows, with Wellcome by no means always coming off best. He was proud of his chic young wife, but he expected total obedience and grew increasingly resentful of what he regarded as a culpable failure in her duty toward him; he was not pleased, either, that increasingly she seemed to prefer the company of other, younger men, to whom she was obviously most appealing.

In 1909 the Wellcomes were again in America, by this time on noticeably bad terms. After visiting New York, Washington, and

California, they traveled to Ecuador, where they stayed at the American Legation in Quito. Wellcome, at the request of the United States government, was to inspect the sanitary conditions of the disease-infested Panama Canal Zone, a project enormously appealing to him, less so to his wife. Also staying at the Legation was an American financier, Archer Harman, and it was with Harman that Henry Wellcome suddenly and furiously accused his wife of adultery. Syrie vehemently denied it, but her husband refused to listen, and the scenes between them grew so violent that Syrie, frightened, left for New York. The pair neither saw nor spoke to each other again. A legal separation was brokered, with a generous personal settlement for Syrie of £2,400 a year, and custody of Mounteney until the age of eleven, during which time all his expenses would be met by his father. Whatever had or had not happened between Syrie and Harman, Wellcome was convinced of his wife's guilt and considered her a deeply immoral woman; he never forgave her, and remained morbidly miserable for the rest of his life. He forbade her name or his nine-year marriage to be mentioned in his presence, and he passed straight to his lawyers Syrie's emotional letters, most of them filled with plaintive requests for more money and anxiety about Mounteney's health.

After the shock of the breakup subsided, Syrie reveled in her freedom, dividing her time between London and Paris. For the first time in her life she was her own mistress, well provided for and able to indulge her taste for luxury and an artistic bent revealed in her stylish clothes and furnishings and an almost theatrical flair for entertaining. Her father having died in 1905, Syrie moved her mother in to live with her at York Terrace, glad of the veneer of respectability that the maternal presence would provide. For there was no doubt about it: Mrs. Wellcome was not quite respectable. Although she had escaped the stigma of divorce, she was nonetheless looked at slightly askance by the more fastidious sections of society: not only was she guilty of desertion but there was subsequent evidence of flighty behavior, including a passionate affair with a glamorous young hussar. Other wealthy admirers incuded the duc de Gramont and one of the Bourbon princes, as well as the American department store tycoon Gordon Selfridge, who reportedly paid the rent for the house in York Terrace (for which, it was also reported, Syrie had had a doormat made reading WELLCOME). It was Selfridge, too, it was said, who helped subsidize Syrie's expensive wardrobe, her lavish entertaining, and the wages of a sizable domestic staff, a butler and personal maid, cook, kitchen maid, car and chauffeur, which could scarcely have been afforded on the £200 a month allowed her by Wellcome.

At the time she began the affair with Maugham, Syrie was growing anxious. Selfridge was losing interest; she was in her mid-thirties, "a courtesan just past her prime"; and although she enjoyed her life, she was beginning to crave security. Wellcome might divorce her at any time, none of her rich lovers had offered to marry her, and with middle age approaching she felt the need of respectable status and a large disposable income. Syrie also desperately wanted another child. Her devotion to Mounteney was visceral and deep; she had looked after him, worried over his delicate health and backwardness at school, and taken him with her whenever she could on her excursions abroad. But Wellcome had grown increasingly obdurate about his son, and when in 1912 Mounteney was sent to boarding school, his father began severely to limit Syrie's access, causing acute anguish not only to her but to the boy, who had always been very close to his mother.

Thus in 1913, when Willie Maugham came into her life, he appeared to be everything Syrie wanted, "the most charming man in London," rich, fashionable, and unattached. It was not long before Syrie determined to have him, and if that meant she had to do all the running, then that was what she would do.

Three or four weeks after the housewarming in 1914, during which time she and Maugham had seen each other daily, Syrie announced she was going to Paris, where she had the use of an apartment on the Quai d'Orsay, and suggested Maugham should come, too. They traveled separately, and on arrival he telephoned from his hotel to arrange to take her to dinner, afterward going back to her apartment, where for the first time they made love. The next morning Maugham returned to London, and when Syrie followed a few days later they fell into an agreeable routine of dining almost every evening at York Terrace, after which they would go to bed. "It was all very delightful," said Maugham. "In the circles in which we moved it was an understood thing that I was Syrie's lover. . . . I was proud of her and pleased with myself." Her compliments were expert, she was sexy, and he delighted in her gaiety and vitality, appreciating the fact that she was always beautifully dressed and groomed, her instinctive chic an aspect he took particular pleasure in showing off. (After Maugham brought Syrie to call on his sister-in-law, Nellie, one of his little nieces recorded in her diary, "Uncle Willie brought Mrs. Welcome [sic] to tea in a very funny hat.") Maugham sometimes accompanied Syrie on shopping expeditions on Bond Street, and enjoyed watching her slender figure parade in silk negligées and diaphanous tea gowns. Syrie entertained frequently and with panache, with Maugham now a permanent fixture on her guest list.

All this was good fun. Maugham knew that Syrie was impressed by him, and that his connection with the stage gave her a cachet with her friends; but he regarded their relationship as no more than a lighthearted affair between two sophisticated adults, neither of whom wanted any serious entanglement. So completely was he off his guard that he laughed when Syrie told him she was "madly in love." He was touched, and his vanity flattered, if he did not for a moment take the declaration literally.

Then something happened that might have warned Maugham that the situation was far more serious than he had believed. He and Syrie were walking in Richmond Park when to his astonishment Syrie announced she wanted to have his child. Maugham was appalled: he had a weakness for babies and hoped one day to have children of his own, but not by this woman whom he did not love and with whom he had no intention of settling down. In the plainest possible terms he set out the immense difficulties, legal and social, of bringing into the world an illegitimate child, but Syrie brushed them aside, explaining that one of her brothers, married but childless, would be delighted to bring the baby up; then after three or four years she could adopt it and no one would be any the wiser. The plan was deceptively simple—so simple that for a moment Maugham was tempted—but then reason prevailed. He told Syrie that it was out of the question, he would have nothing to do with it, and she must not think of it again.

The following month, April 1914, Syrie invited Maugham to join her and a couple of friends in Biarritz. When after a few days the friends left, Syrie suggested that she and Maugham should drive over the border into Spain, a country he loved and about which he had told her so much. Maugham was instantly wary: it was one thing to conduct an affair with a married woman behind closed doors, but flagrantly to travel alone with her, without a third party as chaperon, was asking for trouble: he had no wish to compromise Syrie's reputation, nor did he wish to become involved in any punitive action that Wellcome might choose to bring against his wife. But Syrie reassured him: she and her husband had agreed to an amicable arrangement, she explained, whereby each was free to enter into other relationships. And so they set off, stopping the first night at León before going on to Santiago de Compostela. For the first time Maugham made love to Syrie without protection, carelessly leaving the precautions to her. After nearly a week in Compostela they drove to Paris and caught the Golden Arrow to London.

It was not long after his return home that Maugham received a shock. Syrie telephoned one morning and said she must see him urgently. When he arrived at her house he found her in bed, looking pale and tearful. She began to cry and told him she had had a miscarriage. "I didn't want to tell you till I was certain," she wept. Maugham was stunned, as he had understood her to have given up all idea of having a baby, but he said nothing of his disquiet; he sat down by her bed, held her hand and did his best to comfort her, drying her tears with his handkerchief. "Would you like to bring the affair to an end?" she whispered. "Do you want to finish it?" She was ill and unhappy; he knew of the painful situation over Mounteney, and he felt desperately sorry for her. "Of course not," he said. "Why should I?" Within a short time Syrie had completely recovered, and over the next few weeks the couple resumed their familiar routine as though nothing had happened, dining and dancing, going to parties together, and lunching at the Ritz. Of Maugham's friends, only Gerald Kelly was let into the secret. "I have got a great deal to tell you," Maugham wrote. "But I dare not write it. I shall tell you of a very curious development, but in the most dreadful confidence."

Maugham believed that he had had a lucky escape; he was perfectly happy to continue seeing Syrie in the short term, especially while she was still emotionally fragile, but the incident had shaken him, and it made him realize that as far as he was concerned the affair had no real future. Fond though he was, he was beginning to feel a little bored by Syrie's company, uneasy at her dependence on him and fretting to be free. Although Wellcome appeared to show no inclination to divorce his wife, the possibility that he might made Maugham distinctly nervous. For safety's sake he decided the best plan was to disappear for a while, and so he left London to spend the month of July with Gerald Kelly on Capri.

It was a short but idyllic period of respite. The two men stayed at the Villa Cercola, a little white-walled house above the town that was shared by the novelist E. F. ("Dodo") Benson and Maugham's old friend from Heidelberg, John Ellingham Brooks. Benson, whose discreetly homoerotic novel, *Colin,* vividly evokes this period on Capri, came over from England as often as he could, while Brooks was a permanent resident, the arrangement convenient because, as one of their neighbors delicately phrased it, "they had tastes in common besides literature, which made Capri a desirable retreat for them both." The villa, facing south and luxuriantly draped in passionflower and plumbago, had a terrace running along its front and a big studio out at the back; lizards basked on the walls, the orange trees were in flower, and leisurely meals, cooked by the amiable Seraphina, were eaten under the shade of a vine-covered pergola in the garden. Mornings were devoted to study, Maugham working on the first draft of a new play, after which the four men walked down to the Bagno Timberino, where they swam in the translucent water, sunbathed, and eyed the local Capresi youth, as beautiful and as obliging as ever. Following a siesta in the shuttered cool of the house, Maugham had a lesson in Russian, given him by an eccentric émigré from Odessa who came to the villa every afternoon, after which there was usually a game of tennis or a stroll up the slopes of Monte Solaro; and after dinner a short walk to Morgano's in the piazza to drink and play cards with the regulars, among them a newly arrived couple, the novelist Compton Mackenzie and his wife.

The Mackenzies had taken the Villa Rosaio on Anacapri, and there was a considerable amount of to-ing and fro-ing between the two households, the main focus for Maugham being the English newspapers that were regularly delivered there. "The bundle of papers that arrived by every post from England attracted him, and he did not pretend otherwise," Faith Mackenzie recalled. "I did a drawing of him, showing nothing but a chair, an open newspaper and a pair of crossed legs, and called it 'Somerset Maugham dines with friends.'" Compton Mackenzie, who had recently become something of a celebrity with the publication of his novel *Sinister Street,* relished the company of his fellow writers, even if he was sometimes made uncomfortable by the malicious teasing of Brooks by Benson and Maugham, who in his opinion "treated poor Brooks very badly." It was easy to see why Brooks got on their nerves: fatter and balder than before, his weak, handsome face burned a rich terra-cotta, Brooks was otherwise unchanged; lazy, amiable, and self-centered, he bored the others by insisting on reading aloud from his translation of Hérédia, endlessly fiddled at but never finished, and tormented them by banging away badly at Beethoven on his upright piano. "He had fine perceptions," wrote Benson, "[and] somewhere beneath the ash of his laziness there burned the authentic fire [but] he was inexcusably indolent."*

The peaceful bachelor routine of the Villa Cercola was suddenly shattered at the beginning of August, first by the outbreak of war on the fourth, and second by a telegram from Syrie in Rome an-

---

* After Brooks's death on the island in 1929 Maugham wrote a story, "The Lotus Eater," which was largely based on Brooks and his life on Capri. "He was of no use to anybody," he writes of the Brooks character, "but on the other hand he did nobody any harm. His only object was his own happiness, and it looked as though he had attained it" (*Collected Short Stories,* vol. 4 [Vintage, 2000], p. 221).

nouncing her imminent arrival on the island. Maugham was appalled, his obvious panic infecting the other members of the household. Brooks rushed off "in a great flutter" to report the news to the Mackenzies, telling them that Maugham had got himself involved with a woman and was terrified he was going to have to marry her. "I don't know what I shall do if Maugham brings a wife to the Cercola," Brooks wailed. "I don't think Benson will like it at all either." Mackenzie, too, was shocked, and implored Maugham to stand firm. With this support behind him, Maugham immediately wired back begging Syrie not to come as he and Kelly were on the point of leaving for England. Syrie ignored the cable and arrived off the boat in Capri (much as she had arrived off the boat in pursuit of Wellcome fifteen years earlier in Khartoum), only to find Maugham, just as he had said, on the point of departure. Her brief stay can hardly have been passed in an easy atmosphere: none of them wanted her there, least of all Maugham.

London was a city in a state of chaotic preparation for war, the excitement and euphoria of the first few days having been quickly subsumed in the confusion of mobilization. At forty, Maugham was too old to enlist,* but he was passionately patriotic. "To me the very shape of England on the map is significant," he wrote, trying to analyze his own particular brand of nationalism. "It is an emotion compact of pride and longing and love . . . an emotion which makes sacrifice easy." He was determined to take an active part in the conflict before it ended, as surely it would, by the end of the year. Many of his literary colleagues, H. G. Wells and Arnold Bennett among them, regarded their contribution in literary terms, writing about the war either, like Wells, from home or, like Bennett, by going out to northern France to describe for his readers conditions on the front. But for once Maugham had not the least desire to write: it was action he wanted. Assuming his fluent French was his greatest asset, he contacted his old golfing partner, Winston Churchill, then First Lord of the Admiralty, to offer his services,

---

* Conscription, for unmarried men between eighteen and forty-one, was not introduced until January 1916.

and was disappointed when Churchill's reply enclosed a letter to be presented to a department head in Whitehall. With no intention of spending the war behind a desk, Maugham ignored this and applied instead to the Red Cross, which was on the point of sending a detachment of ambulances to the front and in need of interpreters. The maverick Sir Frederick Treves, surgeon-extraordinary to Queen Victoria and a distinguished veteran of the Boer War, had been appointed head of Red Cross personnel at the War Office, and under his galvanizing influence a steady stream of doctors, nurses, orderlies, drivers, and stretcher bearers was daily crossing the Channel to France. Their contribution was vital, but it was the flexible, almost amateurish nature of the Red Cross, dependent on assorted, sometimes eccentric groups of volunteers at every level of ability, that appealed to the nonconformist streak in Maugham's nature as well as to his spirit of adventure.

By the third week in October, his application accepted, Maugham was in uniform and ready to leave. Before he could do so, however, there had been a wretchedly unhappy interview with Syrie, during which she told him that she was again pregnant. Maugham was horrified. He felt that this time there was no question but that he had been deliberately trapped; he was angry and dismayed, too upset to be able to disguise his feelings. Syrie, expecting sympathy, was badly shaken by his stony-faced reaction. She burst into tears, sobbing that it was only because she loved him that she wanted to have his child. "She made me feel a brute," Maugham recalled. Despite his sense of outrage, he wanted to behave honorably; although he had tired of the affair, he still retained an affection for Syrie, and there was something in the plight of a pregnant woman that never failed to touch him. Nonetheless he was adamant that he would not be panicked into promising any kind of permanent alliance. They talked, and gradually a relative calm was restored, and Maugham was able to set out exactly what he was prepared to do. "At last I promised that when she could no longer conceal her condition, I would fetch her and take her to some place where she could be confined." And with that, Syrie was obliged to be content.

Maugham landed in Boulogne on October 19, reporting with other uniformed volunteers to the Hôtel de Paris, where the Red Cross had set up headquarters. Rows of canvas-covered ambulances were parked along the quays, and the whole town was seething with khaki; everywhere groups of men roamed the streets in an aimless attempt to pass the time before orders were received. Fierce fighting was taking place only a few miles away at Ypres on the Belgian border, and the sound of gunfire rumbled and thundered intermittently day and night. With the British Expeditionary Force engaged in a desperate struggle to hold back the German advance, the casualty rate was appalling, the numbers of dead and wounded quickly reaching the tens of thousands. Maugham's unit was moved out of Boulogne almost at once to join up with an American Red Cross group in the French zone, its job to transport the wounded from the field to the casualty clearing stations just behind the line; from there they would be taken to base hospitals in towns a few miles farther away, to Doullens, Amiens, Montdidier. The weather was cold, the rain relentless. "There are no candles & nothing but tallow dips," Maugham reported to Gerald Kelly, "the roads are horrible, *pavé* with three feet of mud on either side so that if a convoy forces you down nothing but a team of horses will drag you up again." The makeshift clearing stations, set up in churches and barns on the edge of the battlefield, were overcrowded and chaotic, but the conditions in the hospitals were little better, all of them overwhelmed by the sheer numbers of wounded, staffed by exhausted medics, with inadequate supplies and a basic lack of hygiene that made them breeding grounds for infection.

For Red Cross volunteers like Maugham, frequently required to go on to the field of battle, sometimes under fire, the work was demanding and dangerous. Often the call came at night, when in the freezing cold a convoy of ambulances would have to make their way without headlights in the pitch dark, along muddy, cratered roads lit only by the flare of gunfire, to pick up their casualties, six stretchers stacked in the back of each vehicle, to be unloaded as gently as possible on arrival at their destination. Maugham's duties were various, as stretcher bearer, driver, and interpreter, his knowledge of both French and German proving invaluable in communications between the English medical staff and their patients. On one such occasion he found himself in a hospital housing two or three hundred wounded, its overcrowded wards airless and stinking of blood and excrement.

> There was one German prisoner with whom I talked a little. He had had his leg cut off and was under the impression that it would not have been amputated if he had been French. The dresser asked me to explain to him that it was necessary to save his life, and with graphic detail explained to me in what a state the leg was.

On another night, after a period of intense fighting near Montdidier, orders came to bring the ambulances to the village church. As the darkened vehicles drew up one after the other and the stretchers were unloaded, the already dead were thrown on a heap outside the door, while the living were laid in rows on the straw-covered floor. The only light came from candles placed on the altar.

> Conversation mingled with groans of pain and the cries of the dying. One young boy, horribly wounded and desperately afraid, kept screaming *"Je ne veux pas mourir,"* while three soldiers standing by him tried to comfort him: one whose hand he held caressingly passed his other hand over the boy's face. . . .*"Mais non, mon vieux, tu guériras."* . . . But he went on screaming, *"Je ne veux pas mourir"* till he died.*

Some of the volunteers were severely shaken by the constant shelling and traumatized by the sights they were forced to witness, the horrific wounds sustained by many of the casualties, torn apart by the murderous weaponry employed by both sides. But Maugham, brave and unsqueamish, was often exhilarated by enemy action. "I saw a battle between aeroplanes the other day which was

---

* "I don't want to die" . . . "No, old chap, you'll get better."

the most horribly thrilling thing I have ever seen," he told Alfred Sutro, while to William Heinemann he wrote from Dunkirk, "I was lucky enough the other day to witness the shelling by the Germans of some French batteries. . . . It was splendid to see the bursting shells & the great eruption of earth as the Jack Johnson★ buried itself in the ground. . . . On the way home they were shelling the Ypres road which I had to drive down, but missing it with admirable regularity. I went & looked at one of the holes. It was positively enormous." The carnage was frightful, after one engagement alone three hundred dead and sixteen hundred wounded; but with his medical training Maugham never flinched, his practical attitude combined with a notable gentleness and compassion resulting in his soon being asked to apply his long-forgotten skills, cleaning wounds, painting on iodine, and tying bandages. "I had done no work of this kind for many years," he recorded in his notebook, "and at first felt embarrassed and awkward, but soon I found I could do the little that it was possible to do. . . . I have never seen such wounds."

IN THE SAME UNIT with Maugham was the critic Desmond Mac-Carthy, a charming, indolent, erudite companion, only three years younger, with whom Maugham was to form a valued friendship. Elected an Apostle at Cambridge, MacCarthy knew such influential figures as Bertrand Russell and E. M. Forster, and through his friendship with Lytton Strachey, Leonard Woolf, and Clive Bell had early become involved with the Bloomsbury group. His theater reviews, particularly his writings on Shaw, were widely admired, as was his introduction for Roger Fry's famous Post-Impressionist exhibition of 1910. MacCarthy was to become a shrewd critic of Maugham's fiction, which he admired, the only one of the Bloomsbury intellectuals to pay it any serious attention. Writing on Maugham in the 1930s, he perceptively noted, "The war had a most important influence on the development of his talent. . . . He learnt then how good it was for his talent to travel and to be alone."

★ A German artillery shell named after the American boxing champion.

Maugham and MacCarthy had crossed over from England together, and on arrival in Boulogne had been warned, as writers,
against sending back reports to the press, although neither had the
least intention of doing anything of the sort. Eager for action, they
found that between periods of intense activity were long periods of
idleness, and both were grateful to find in the other a kindred spirit.
"We are either rushed off our legs or bored & idle," as Maugham
explained, and it was a great resource to have MacCarthy for company. When they could get away the two men dined together or
pottered about sightseeing in the various towns and villages in
which they were billeted. Maugham had a lucky escape one day in
the Grande Place in Ypres: he had just moved to look more closely
at the ruins of the medieval Cloth Hall when the wall against which
he had been leaning was blown up by a German shell. "It makes
sightseeing a matter of some delicacy," as he remarked in a letter to
Gerald Kelly. Their unit was constantly on the move. Near Ypres
the men stayed in a convent, fifteen to twenty in a room sleeping on
straw pallets on the floor; at Doullens, Maugham was more comfortably installed in the house of a retired shopkeeper and his wife;
at Steenvoorde near the Belgian border the accommodation was a
grim little hotel with disgusting food and no bath. Yet Maugham
found he was nonetheless enjoying himself.

> The work was hard and tedious. But what a delight it was to
> have no responsibility! I had no decisions to make. I did what I
> was told, and having done it my time was my own. . . .
> I enjoyed my liberty. There was a sensual, almost voluptuous,
> quality in the pleasure of it.

He was not, however, entirely cut off from his professional duties.
While stationed at Malo near Dunkirk, MacCarthy walked into
Maugham's tiny bedroom and found him marking the proofs of his
novel by the light of a single candle. MacCarthy, himself congeni-
tally disorganized, was struck by the neatness of the scene, the long
strips of paper tidily arranged on the narrow bed, the very few corrections that had been made. "When I remarked on it, he replied

that he always went over his work carefully [in manuscript] before he sent it to the printer."

By the end of November it was clear that the war was not going to be over soon, and Maugham wrote to Syrie urging her to think again about terminating her pregnancy, now into its third month, as this was no time to have a baby. "She took no notice of my letter," he recorded grimly. "She was determined to have the child." Reluctantly Maugham decided he must return to England, heavy-hearted because he had no wish to involve himself further with Syrie and her situation—but even more because he had recently met the man who for the next thirty years was to be the center of his life.

CHAPTER 7

CODE NAME "SOMERVILLE"

...

Sнокctly aften arniving in Boulogne in Octoben 1914, maugham's unit had joined with a group of American Red Cross volunteers, among whom was a young man of twenty-two. Gerald Haxton, with his gray-blue eyes, sleek light brown hair, and neatly trimmed mustache, was a slender, handsome youth. Speaking flawless French with no trace of an American accent, Haxton was a charming, gregarious fellow, out to enjoy himself. In common with many of his transatlantic contemporaries, he had volunteered for the ambulance service because, unlike the military, it offered excitement and risk without the necessity of a long, dull period of training first, its members classed as officers but without the responsibility of command. By chance he and Maugham were both working in the same makeshift hospital in one of the local châteaux, and Gerald recognized the well-known playwright whose picture he had seen in the paper. Maugham was trying to soothe a badly wounded British soldier who was crying out for water, which the doctors had forbidden him to have. "I'm sorry, but is there anything else I can do to help? Can I write a letter home for you?" "Raite a lettah?" the soldier sneered in a ghastly imitation of Maugham's accent. "Not on your life!" It was at this point that Gerald intervened, walking over to give the man a cigarette and tell him a few dirty stories to distract him from his pain. That night he and Maugham found themselves standing on a balcony overlooking the garden, talking of what they would do when the war was over. Maugham said he wanted to write and to travel: what did Gerald want? "From you or from life?" the young man asked provocatively. "Perhaps both," Maugham replied. "They might turn out to be the same thing." Haxton unhesitatingly made clear that what he was interested in was "fun and games . . . someone to look after me and give me clothes and parties." The two of them then went up to Gerald's room, where he had a bottle of gin, "and that's how it all began."

Although it was brief, both knew their meeting had been significant. Maugham was immediately smitten by this attractive young man, who in both looks and personality was precisely the type he found most irresistible, a bit of a chancer, raffish, self-indulgent, and good-natured. Like Reggie Barlow-Bassett in *The Merry-Go-Round* and Gerald Vaudrey in *Mrs. Craddock,* Haxton was a sexual opportunist, well aware of the potency of his own animal magnetism. In an atmosphere charged with danger, emotions ran high, with the ethos of close male camaraderie fostering intense friendships, friendships that in the trenches, as with boys at school, not infrequently led to something more.* It was in such an electric atmosphere that Maugham's long love affair with Gerald Haxton started.

FRUSTRATINGLY, THERE ARE FEW records relating to Gerald's life and circumstances before they met in 1914, and Maugham was careful to conceal or destroy as much as he could that referred to their subsequent relationship. What is certain, however, is that that relationship was the most important of his life, although among Maugham's friends and family, opinion would always remain sharply divided as to the character and influence of Gerald himself. Even in appearance there was something paradoxical, his face tanta-

---

* After the Battle of Vimy Ridge, for instance, this limerick went the rounds:
  In his bath mused the Marquess of Byng,
  Ah, Vimy Ridge such memories bring!
      That lovely young trooper—
      I mean, Gladys Cooper—
  My goodness, that *was* a near thing!

lizingly hard to read, with one eye cheerfully mischievous, the other full of threat. Some saw him as a benevolent charmer whose good humor did much to counter the older man's irritability and bouts of depression: "[he] charmed the birds from the trees . . . [and] Willie was always enraptured by him," said the writer Arthur Marshall, while the critic Raymond Mortimer found Gerald "jolly and delightful, always the life and soul of the party." There were others, however, who regarded Gerald Haxton almost as the devil incarnate. "Shifty," "disreputable," "a cad," "just this side of being a crook" are the words and phrases that repeatedly occur; the writer Peter Quennell, who memorably described Haxton as being "very masculine . . . with a hard tarty face," was one of many who judged his influence to have been wholly deleterious, holding him responsible for introducing the previously fastidious Maugham to some of the most sordid areas of the homosexual underworld. But perhaps most revealing is the portrait Maugham himself drew of Gerald as Rowley Flint in the 1941 novella *Up at the Villa*. "He had an air of dissipation and people who didn't like him said he looked shifty [but] what Rowley Flint had which explained everything was sex appeal . . . there was something that swept you off your feet, a sort of gentleness behind the roughness of his manner, a thrilling warmth behind his mockery . . . and the sensuality of his mouth and the caress in his grey eyes."

Born on October 6, 1892, in the same month that Maugham started his studies at St. Thomas's Hospital, Gerald Frederick Haxton was the son of a leading writer and editor on the *San Francisco Examiner,* who with his second wife left California to settle in Paris, where Gerald was born. When the boy was still very young his parents separated and his mother, Sara Haxton, moved to London, where she and Gerald led an impoverished existence in lodgings in St. John's Wood. It is probable that Gerald never saw his father again. Certainly money was in short supply, and in letters to a woman friend Sara complains that she has no one to advise her over Gerald's education, which plainly indicates the absence of a father figure in the boy's life. This was a deprivation from which he must have suffered, especially as his mother was in poor health and rarely had the energy or resources to go out or entertain. Sara did her best for her son, but it was a dull existence, and no doubt by adolescence Gerald was fretting to escape, oppressed by his mother's anxiety, her constant complaints of colds and neuralgia, and her suffocating dependence.

Apart from these few details, no other traces have emerged of Gerald Haxton's early years. The next sighting is in 1915, when, a year after meeting Maugham, Gerald got into trouble. On November 13, while Maugham was abroad, Gerald, aged twenty-three, was arrested with another man in a Covent Garden hotel and charged with six counts of gross indecency.* Both were acquitted, but the judge, convinced that Gerald was a bad lot, had him registered as an undesirable alien, forced to leave the country and banned from ever setting foot in Britain again.

But for now this was all in the future. At the beginning of January 1915, Maugham, summoned by Syrie, left his unit and returned to England. The two of them met in Dover, and from there went by train to neutral Italy, to Rome, where Maugham had decided Syrie could give birth "without anyone knowing anything about it." An apartment had been found near the Pincio, and here they settled to await the birth of their child. It was not a happy time for either. Maugham had no wish for a child by a woman he did not love; and painfully missing Gerald and worried about his exposure to danger at the front, he felt not particularly inclined to respond sympathetically to Syrie's complaints and constant demands for attention. He at least had his writing—he was at work on a play— and there was golf when the weather permitted, whereas Syrie, shut up in the apartment all day, was wholly dependent on his company: she spoke no Italian, showed no interest in reading, sewing, or sightseeing, and apart from Maugham saw no one except for the English doctor. To both the days seemed interminable. "It is bitterly cold here, raining & miserable, & I regret the pleasant hardships of Flanders," Maugham wrote gloomily to Heinemann, while to Gerald Kelly he expressed more specific anxieties: "If only I am

---

* The legal term covering all homosexual acts with the exception of sodomy.

able to write here & under these conditions. Oh, what a perfect fool I am! But the only thing is to set my teeth & go through with it."

As the time for Syrie's confinement drew near, Maugham wrote to her mother, asking her to come out to Rome. He had yet to meet Mrs. Barnardo, and he was apprehensive about her reaction to his living in sin with her daughter, but there was no need for disquiet: during her years in the East End the Begum had seen it all, and later while staying in York Terrace she had grown accustomed to turning a blind eye to certain aspects of Syrie's behavior. "She took it as the most natural thing in the world," Maugham reported with relief. During the evening of May 4, Syrie went into labor: it was soon clear that all was not well, and at midnight the doctor was so worried he called an ambulance to take her to hospital in the Via Lancisi. Here, on May 6, under the name "Mrs. Wells," Syrie was delivered of a daughter by cesarean section: Elizabeth Mary, always known as Liza after *Liza of Lambeth,* her father's first novel. A few days later the doctor told Syrie that she would never be able to conceive again, news that reduced her to despair: despite her age, nearly thirty-six, and her uncertain situation, she longed for more children, a longing intensified by the painful separations from her son, Mounteney. "She cried bitterly," said Maugham. "I did my best to console her. That was all I could do." Three weeks later Syrie had recovered sufficiently to travel, and on June 9 the four of them arrived back in London, Maugham returning to Chesterfield Street and Syrie, the Begum, and baby Liza to a nearby hotel, as the house in York Terrace had been rented out.

IN MAUGHAM'S LUGGAGE WAS his new play, *Our Betters,* which he had worked hard to complete, knowing how anxious Frohman had been to see it. But suddenly Frohman was no longer there. On May 1 he had sailed from New York on the Cunarder *Lusitania,* but seven days later, just off the Irish coast, the ship had been torpedoed with a loss of nearly two thousand lives, Charles Frohman's among them. From the accounts of survivors it appears that the impresario had behaved with singular sangfroid, handing his life jacket to an-

A lonely child, guarded and withdrawn.

Robert Maugham,
hard-working legal adviser
to the Paris Embassy.

The charming and
beautiful
Edith Maugham.

The Rev. Henry Maugham,
"a far from intelligent cleric."

Kindhearted
Aunt Sophie.

*Willie and his uncle
outside the vicarage.*

"Life was before him . . ."

*Maugham as a pupil at the
King's School, Canterbury.*

Willie, Charlie, and Harry Maugham
at St. Moritz.

The acerbic
F. H. Maugham
in middle age.

The painter Gerald Kelly,
a lifelong friend.

Kelly's portrait of the irresistible Sue Jones.

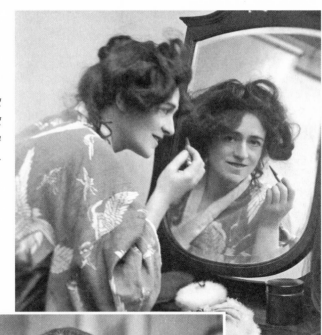

Ethel Irving shocking audiences in Lady Frederick.

Gladys Cooper, Maugham's favorite actress, in The Sacred Flame.

Syrie Wellcome, lively, stylish, and unstoppably ambitious.

The Maughams with Liza at Le Touquet.

Gerald Haxton, "charming but very naughty."

Maugham leaving New York aboard RMS Aquitania.

Eddie Knoblock, Maugham, Hugh Walpole, and Gerald Haxton with Douglas Fairbanks in Hollywood.

A. S. Frere
in his office
at Heinemann.

Eddie Marsh,
ruthless
"diabolizer."

*Maugham with Liza
at her wedding to
Vincent Paravicini.*

The Villa Mauresque.

Maugham and Haxton in Central Park, New York.

other passenger and remaining coolly on deck to finish his cigar. With a flourish that may owe more to journalistic flair than to fact, his last words were reported to have been a quotation from *Peter Pan,* "To die would be an awfully big adventure." The news of Frohman's death was a sad shock to Maugham, who had come to like and trust this dedicated man of the theater; there was, however, no time to lose in putting into action plans for the play's production. "I am very glad to know that everything is to be continued just as though poor C.F. were still alive," Maugham wrote to Frohman's business partner, Al Hayman.

In the tradition of Restoration comedy, *Our Betters* follows the path set by Goldsmith and Sheridan but with a reach considerably extended, the twin pivots of the action not London and the country but England and the United States. Its world is that of the dollar princesses who migrated from America to marry into the more impoverished sections of the British upper class. Leader of this flamboyant flock is the fascinating Lady Grayston, who, bored by her dull baronet husband, consoles herself with a series of lovers, the current incumbent the millionaire Arthur Fenwick, owner of a chain of department stores. Pearl Grayston's little sister, Bessie, has recently arrived in England, and Pearl plans to marry her off to young Lord Bleane. Bessie, however, has a mind of her own, and although initially dazzled by the splendor of her surroundings, is soon repelled by the cynicism, greed, and flagrant immorality of her wealthy compatriots and returns with relief to America.

Our Betters, "a dazzling icy glitter," as one critic described it, is a highly polished, highly expert comedy of manners, chic, sophisticated, and extremely amusing—just the play, in fact, to appeal to a war-weary London public. Unfortunately, that public was to be denied it. The Foreign Office, nervous about upsetting the sensibilities of its most powerful potential ally, suddenly decided that such a depiction of transatlantic vulgarity was anti-American and banned it. Instead of being premiered in London, *Our Betters* opened in March 1917 in New York, where, ironically, it was a resounding success. Despite a few expressions of outrage at the immorality of the theme—"morally sordid" and "offensive" according to the *New*

York Dramatic Mirror—critics loved it and audiences came flocking. Louis Kronenberger, later drama critic for *Time* magazine, wrote that "no playwright since Vanbrugh . . . had drawn so harsh and unredeemed a picture of London society as Maugham did in *Our Betters* . . . one of the best testimonials to American push ever written." When in 1923 the play eventually arrived in London, it was rated just as highly. Desmond MacCarthy praised it as "mercilessly amusing," while the influential James Agate acclaimed it "one of the most brilliant plays which has ever fallen from the pen of an English dramatist . . . a magnificent piece of satire, and the work of a master of the theatre."

In the program for the London production of *Our Betters* there was printed a curious little note from the playwright: "Owing to various rumours which were circulated when the play was produced in America, the author wishes to state that the characters in it are entirely imaginary," a statement owing more to a fear of libel than a respect for the truth. The "various rumours" that six years earlier had raced around New York referred to the close similarity between Arthur Fenwick, Lady Grayston's lover, and Syrie's lover, Gordon Selfridge, the department store tycoon. By his own later account Maugham had based the one on the other without troubling himself very much about differentiating between the two, even underlining the parallel by giving the fictional version the name of another big London store, Fenwick, and endowing him with all of Selfridge's well-known bombast and sentimentality. Of these Maugham had learned during the long weeks when he and Syrie were in Rome awaiting the birth of Liza, and Syrie had told him stories about her former admirers, chief among whom was Selfridge. "She was very amusing about him," it transpired. According to Syrie, "[Selfridge] had fallen madly in love with her and had offered to settle five thousand a year on her. She refused," Maugham recorded, adding drily, "I did not know what to believe and what, with the hope of impressing me, she invented." In the play the besotted old man lavishes presents and money on Lady Grayston, for which she has an insatiable appetite, but makes her wince by insisting on addressing her as "girlie":

PEARL: I wish you wouldn't call me girlie, Arthur, I do hate it.

FENWICK: That's how I think of you. . . . I just say to myself, She's my girlie, and I feel warm all over. . . .

It did not pass unnoticed that Gordon Selfridge, a famous first-nighter, gave the first night of *Our Betters* a miss.

IF MAUGHAM HAD BELIEVED that by taking Syrie abroad he could keep their relationship undercover, he was soon to be disabused. After the acrimonious separation from his wife, Henry Wellcome had appeared to show little interest in her activities, indifferent to whom she saw or what she did as long as she behaved herself during those times when she had care of Mounteney. But in fact Wellcome was not indifferent, and his bitterness over Syrie's departure had calcified over the years into a determination to divorce her as soon as the ideal opportunity arose. When Wellcome learned of Syrie's affair with the celebrated playwright, he knew he had got her just where he wanted: Maugham was rich and he was unmarried,★ and the scandal of being judged the guilty party in such a high-profile divorce should ensure the ruin of Syrie's reputation forever. As early as January 1912 Wellcome's lawyers had started gathering evidence, hiring private investigators to track the couple's movements, for instance, at the Imperial Hotel, Hythe, where the two of them were observed spending the night, "[Mr. Maugham] and Mrs. Wellcome occupying adjoining bedrooms." By the time Maugham and Syrie returned to London after the birth of Liza, Wellcome's legal team was already in Rome collecting information, and with the help of the British consul, interviewing witnesses, including the nurses at the hospital and the English doctor who had attended "Mrs. Wells" during her confinement.

Maugham, meanwhile, knew nothing of this, his mind set on re-

---

★ Wellcome might have chosen to cite Gordon Selfridge, but Selfridge was married with four children, and, crucially, was a member of the same Freemasons' lodge as Wellcome.

turning to some kind of war work. "I was at a loose end," he complained. "and nobody seemed to want me." It was Syrie who came to the rescue: one of her girlfriends was the mistress of a Major (later Captain) John Wallinger, an officer in the foreign section of the Secret Service bureau (later SIS, the Secret Intelligence Service), and it was arranged that the four of them should dine together one evening. Wallinger, who supervised a network of British agents in Germany and Switzerland, was impressed by Maugham and offered him a job in Geneva. It was arranged that he would go out there at the end of the year.

By this time matters were coming to a head at home, for it was now that Syrie received a letter from Wellcome's attorney stating her husband's intention to divorce her and to cite Maugham as corespondent. For Syrie this was an entirely desirable development: she longed to be rid of Wellcome, and she was far too tough a character to care very much about damage to her reputation as a consequence of divorce as long as she could be assured of remarriage at the end of it. For Maugham, however, who had always believed Syrie's assertion that Wellcome had no wish to change the status quo, the news was devastating. The case, unquestionably, was indefensible: he was to be publicly identified as corespondent and he knew very well it would be considered disgraceful if he refused to wed Syrie after it. He felt trapped, deceived, and very angry. Syrie, who had persisted in ignoring the fact that Maugham had never shown any wish to marry her, now felt frightened by his reaction, terrified that he might somehow renege on what she saw as his irrefutable obligation toward her. Desperately she sought a way to win his sympathy.

One evening Maugham was dining quietly with a doctor friend in Chesterfield Street when Syrie telephoned; she told him she had taken an overdose of sleeping pills and that he must come at once. The two men immediately went to her hotel, where the doctor, as Maugham put it, "got busy," while he telephoned the Begum, asking her to come and look after her daughter for a couple of days until she was fully recovered.

Frustratingly for Syrie, Maugham remained unmoved by her

staged attempt at suicide, still reluctant to make the final commitment. In order to prepare himself for the forthcoming case he consulted a leading divorce lawyer, Sir George Lewis, who told him
candidly that his situation was bleak: the evidence against him was
incontrovertible and Wellcome was preparing to make the most of
it, his one concession, agreed at Maugham's particular request, that
there should be no mention of the child, Liza, in court. Lewis
strongly advised Maugham to buy Syrie off: he had formed a poor
opinion of her, seeing her simply as a gold digger, an aging adventuress in search of a large income. "You'd be a fool to marry her,"
he told his client, suggesting that instead he offer to give £20,000
or £30,000, which, with the £1,000 a year Wellcome had promised
if she did not remarry, would keep her in comfort for the rest of
her life. Maugham was powerfully tempted, and yet his sense of
honor was strong; he could not quite bring himself to abandon
Syrie, for whom he still had a residual fondness and who was, after
all, the mother of his child. There was another consideration, too,
one that he may not have chosen to discuss with Lewis. Syrie was
aware of his homosexuality and even had the names of some of the
men he had slept with: ruthless as he knew her to be, it was not impossible that she might use this information to blackmail him.
"D'you *want* to marry her?" Lewis asked irritably. "No," Maugham
replied, "but if I don't I shall regret it all my life." Lewis shrugged
his shoulders. "Then there's nothing more to be said."

It was after this final interview with Lewis that in November
1915 Maugham left for Switzerland to begin his espionage work for
Wallinger, and here shortly before the case was due to be heard that
Syrie joined him, hoping to avoid the publicity that the divorce
would inevitably attract. It was a miserable period for both:
Maugham was obliged to be constantly on the move, leaving Syrie
by herself for days at a time; when he returned she was either irritable and resentful, or, in the face of his frigid politeness, tearful and
clinging, constantly declaiming her love, imploring him to tell her
what she was doing wrong and whether he still had any feeling for
her. They bickered endlessly. "If we were married it would all be
different," Syrie told him. "B-b-but it might be worse," Maugham

grimly replied. One evening he went to the theater and was wryly amused to see enacted on stage an almost exact replica of his own predicament. In *Amoureuse* by Georges de Porto-Riche, a husband is driven frantic by his wife's cloying devotion, her egotism, her over-sensitivity to his moods, the way she will never let him read or work in peace. He explodes in an outburst of bitter complaint to a bachelor friend:

> Tu n'as pas encore perdu le droit d'être seul! . . . [Ta maîtresse] n'est pas jalouse, obsédante et questionneuse. . . . Elle ne se penche pas sur ton épaule, quand tu écris une lettre . . . elle n'opère point par de petites phrases vagues, insinuantes, qui n'ont l'air de rien, mais qui se glissent dans l'esprit et entament le courage. . . . Et si, par hazard, tu dines dehors sans elle, tu ne la retrouves pas à minuit, éveillé dans son lit, le visage im-mobile, mais la voix altérée et l'oeil plein de jalousie. . . .*

"It positively made my blood run cold as I sat & watched," Maugham confided to Kelly.

The case finally came to court in February 1916, by which time both respondent and corespondent were back in London, Maugham having returned from Geneva as he was obliged to be on hand for the final rehearsals of a new play. If he had hoped to avoid public-ity, the timing could hardly have been worse: the case was heard on February 14, less than a week after the opening night of *Caroline,* a glamorous occasion, widely reported, ensuring that the play-wright's name was already prominently in the public eye. In the cir-cumstances the press were remarkably restrained, however, mainly confining themselves to briefly summarizing the evidence and re-porting the judgment, which granted Wellcome a decree nisi and

---

* You haven't lost the right to be alone! . . . [Your mistress] isn't jealous, obsessively curious. . . . She doesn't lean over your shoulder when you're writing a letter . . . she doesn't insinuate with those vague little phrases which seem to mean nothing but which lower the spirits and undermine one's courage. . . . And if by chance you go out to dinner without her, you don't come back at midnight to find her awake in bed, her face expressionless but with a broken voice and an eye full of jealousy. . . .

custody of Mounteney. Maugham himself returned almost at once to Geneva, while Syrie retired to a clinic to rest for a few days before going to Paris, which she planned to make her headquarters for the following twelve months. "You will be doubtless seeing her in a few weeks," Maugham wrote to Kelly, "& she will tell you the very sensible plan which we have elaborated. I think you will agree on its wisdom." The details of this "very sensible plan" remain obscure; what is clear, however, is that Maugham's frame of mind was rather less tranquil than indicated in his letter to Kelly. To his brother F.H. he was more open about the stressful nature of the recent ordeal:

> The whole matter has been a great distress & worry to me, but I try to console myself by thinking it is only through undergoing all varieties of human experience, however distressing some of them may be, that a writer can hope in the end perhaps to produce work of permanent value. I fancy the worst of my troubles are over, but what the final result of the misadventure will be only time can show, and in any case the future can not possibly have in store any worse harassment than I have undergone during the last eight months.

It was perhaps fortunate that Maugham could not foresee the long misery of his future with Syrie, and at least for the moment he was able to put most of his anxiety behind him and take pleasure in the dazzling success of his latest theatrical venture.

Produced by Dion Boucicault at the New Theatre, *Caroline* was an instant hit, a dexterous and supremely efficient piece of the kind Maugham could now write with one hand tied behind his back. "I have never had such an enormous success as *Caroline*," Maugham boasted to his brother. "We play to over £2000 a week, which Dion Boucicault tells me is the largest sum he has known a comedy to earn in his whole experience of the theatre." Originally titled *The Unattainable,* the play's eponymous heroine, played by Irene Vanbrugh, is a grass widow whose husband, stationed abroad for the past ten years, suddenly dies, leaving her free to marry Robert, a delightful KC with whom she has long conducted an enjoyable and entirely blameless *amitié amoureuse*. Nothing, it seems, could be more suitable, but Robert and Caroline find to their dismay that neither regards the prospect with pleasure, and gradually they arrive at the realization that their great attraction for each other lies in Caroline's unattainability. Despite the efforts of their friends to see them made man and wife, Caroline eventually contrives to return to the status quo ante by "discovering" that the announcement of her husband's death was a mistake and therefore she and Robert can happily return to their old relationship.

"Light as a feather," said *The Sunday Times,* "the quintessence of natural gaiety" according to the *Daily Mail, Caroline* nonetheless derives from some painful areas of experience. The shadow of Syrie is darkly apparent, with the fast-approaching threat of marriage, so deftly avoided in the play, providing a somber resonance, first heard in an exchange between Caroline and her maid, Cooper:

> COOPER: Well, ma'am, my belief is that men don't want to marry. It's not in their nature. You 'ave to give them a little push or you'll never bring them to it.
>
> CAROLINE: And supposing they regret it afterwards, Cooper?
>
> COOPER: Oh, well, ma'am, it's too late then.

WITH *CAROLINE* SET FOR a long run, Maugham returned on his own to Switzerland to resume his duties in Geneva. His job there, working for British military intelligence, was already well under way, having materialized after his introduction to Major Wallinger over dinner the previous summer. Wallinger had taken to Maugham, and Maugham to Wallinger, who struck him as both unscrupulous and astute, both essential qualities in a spymaster.

An ex-superintendent in the Indian police, Wallinger in 1915 had been brought in to work for the Secret Intelligence Service (SIS), supervising a network of British agents in Germany and Switzerland. So far his operation had met with little success: a keen reader of spy stories, Wallinger had adopted a number of familiar ruses, including disguising his agents as waiters, but such elementary ploys were quickly rumbled by the Swiss authorities, who, fiercely protective of their precious neutrality, were quick to arrest and expel any foreign nationals whose conduct threatened to undermine it. Recently Wallinger had suffered further losses, with one agent denouncing another to the police, who then betrayed two more in his turn; a fifth man had had to be withdrawn after suffering a nervous breakdown, and it was this man whom Maugham had been taken on to replace.

To Wallinger, Maugham appeared to have not only excellent credentials but the ideal cover, that of a writer retiring to the peace and quiet of a neutral country in order to write. His main function, Wallinger explained, would be to act as a facilitator rather than a producer of secret intelligence, relaying messages to and from a network of agents who were working within Germany, in Frankfurt, Koblenz, Trier, and Mainz. "If you do well you'll get no thanks," Wallinger warned him, "and if you get into trouble you'll get no help," conditions that Maugham accepted unquestioningly. The whole idea of becoming a spy appealed to him enormously. Long a master of disguise, happiest when he could remain undercover, Maugham had no difficulty with the prospect of playing a part; a diffident man, he always preferred listening to talking, and his fascination with other people's lives had developed in him an unusual level of perception. His natural affinity for intelligence work was revealed to a wider public when after the war he wrote a series of stories about his espionage activities, known as the Ashenden stories after the name he gave his protagonist, closely modeled on himself.

In the late autumn of 1915 Maugham, code name Somerville, had arrived in Geneva, his base the imposing Grand Hôtel d'Angleterre on the banks of the lake. It was immediately obvious that the placid Swiss city had been turned by the war into a hotbed of international intrigue, packed with a moving population of spies and revolutionaries from the various warring nations taking advantage of the safety of the neutral country in their midst. The lobby of the Angleterre became at certain times of day a babel of European tongues, with a smattering of Russian, Turkish, and Arabic besides; and when Maugham dined alone in the evenings he enjoyed identifying other guests who like himself were not quite what they seemed: a Bulgarian working for British intelligence, a prostitute who reported back to Berlin, an Egyptian known to be engaged in anti-British activities, and a German count, Karl Gustav Vollmoeller,* whom Maugham had known as a playwright in London before the war.

Despite the somewhat feverish atmosphere, Maugham found that his own duties were on the whole fairly safe and routine, although he usually carried a small revolver in his pocket as a precaution. A large part of his job involved debriefing his agents on their return from sorties into Germany, issuing instructions, and paying their wages. Having made careful note of what he was told and adding his own observations, he would then write a detailed report that he transmitted in code. This was a cumbersome business. "I know nothing so tedious as coding and decoding," says Maugham as Ashenden. In addition, on two mornings a week Maugham walked over to the market in the Place du Bourg-de-Four and bought half a pound of butter from an old peasant woman. As she gave him his change she slipped a piece of paper into his hand, the contents of which if discovered would have landed both of them in the dock; it was discreetly done, however, and for Maugham the only real moment of risk was the walk back to his hotel with the paper in his pocket, a distance he tried to cover as quickly as possible. More hazardous was the weekly journey he made on the little steamer across Lake Geneva to Thonon on the French side, where he met and conferred with a colleague and received orders from London. As this was a round-trip beginning and ending in Switzerland, it was conveniently not marked in his passport, but nonetheless Maugham could never be sure he was not being followed, either by an enemy agent or by the secret police, who would not hesitate to arrest and run out of the country any foreigner found to be engaged in espionage. To avoid attracting attention on these crossings

---

* Vollmoeller became best known after the war for his screenplay for the Marlene Dietrich film *Der Blaue Engel* (*The Blue Angel*) and for his collaboration with Max Reinhardt on the play *Der Mirakel* (*The Miracle*).

Maugham resisted going below to the warmth of the saloon, preferring to remain on deck where he would be less noticeable. But
even wrapped in a fur-lined overcoat and muffler, with his hat
pulled well down over his ears, the bitter cold chilled him to the
bone. In winter the lake was often stormy, and the gusts of sleet
blowing down from the mountains cut right through him, and he
would think longingly of the warmth of his hotel room, of a hot
bath and dinner in front of the fire with his book and his pipe.

The regularity of his timetable led to a certain tedium in an existence that Maugham described as being in many respects "as orderly
and monotonous as a city clerk's." This was not without advantage,
however, as it left him plenty of time for his own work: his greatest
anxiety while he was writing *Caroline* had been that he should be
discovered and arrested before he had time to finish it. "Geneva, the
centre of all rumours," as he described it to Kelly a few weeks after
his arrival, "is very quiet & peaceful, & there is nothing in the
world to do. . . . I write every morning . . . I walk about or ride
gently in the afternoons; & in the evening go to the play or make a
fourth at bridge." It was, as he admitted, a satisfactory way of life in
many ways, sufficiently filled, sufficiently varied, with plenty of
time to write and read; "it was absurd to think that under these circumstances he could possibly be bored and yet, like a little lonely
cloud in the sky, he did see in the offing the possibility of boredom."

There were occasions, however, when boredom was dispelled,
and "Somerville" found himself required to play a more active role.
His first mission, undertaken immediately on arrival in Switzerland, was investigating an Englishman, married to a German
woman and living in Lucerne, who was suspected of being in the
pay of the enemy. Under the pretext of taking German lessons
from the man's wife, Maugham observed him carefully for a couple
of weeks before concluding that he was almost certainly a traitor. A
trap was set: Maugham, following instructions, "indiscreetly" let
slip to his new acquaintance that he had connections in the Censorship Department in London. As intended, this information was
duly relayed back to German Intelligence by the Englishman, who

then, pretending that he wanted to go back home to look for war work, asked Maugham to furnish him with an introduction to his friends in the Department. Shortly afterward the unsuspecting prey was arrested and dispatched to England for interrogation.

At another time Maugham was sent by Wallinger to Basle to check on an agent of whom there were suspicions of a different kind. "Gustav," a Swiss businessman, was supposed to be making regular sorties into Germany under cover of his legitimate business, and on his return sending reports via Geneva to British intelligence. Again Wallinger's suspicions were proved correct, as Maugham mainly by clever questioning managed to discover that in fact "Gustav" had never left the security of Basle, ingeniously concocting his reports from German newspapers and the gossip he picked up in restaurants and beer cellars. In February 1916 another job came through, this time on the instructions of none other than Captain Sir Mansfield Cumming, head of the foreign section of the Secret Service Bureau. Cumming passed on his suspicions to Major Walter Kirke, chief of covert operations, that "Bernard," one of Maugham's agents, "had been doing us down" by taking large sums of money without sending in a single genuine report. Again Maugham was dispatched to find out what was going on, a scene he was later to describe in his postwar collection of autobiographical spy stories, *Ashenden*. The two men meet as usual in a café:

[Ashenden] gave him his orders and was prepared to finish the interview.

"Very good," said Bernard. "But before I go back to Germany I want two thousand francs."

"Do you?"

"Yes, and I want them now, before you leave this café . . ."

"I'm afraid I can't give it to you." . . .

The spy leaned forward and, not raising his voice, but speaking so that only Ashenden could hear, burst out angrily:

"Do you think I'm going on risking my life for that beggarly sum you give me? Not ten days ago a man was caught at Mainz and shot. Was that one of your men?"

"We haven't got anyone at Mainz," said Ashenden, carelessly, and for all he knew it was true. He had been puzzled not to receive his usual communications from that place and Bernard's information might afford the explanation. "You knew exactly what you were to get when you took on the job, and if you weren't satisfied you needn't have taken it. I have no authority to give you a penny more."

"Do you see what I've got here?" said Bernard.

He took a small revolver out of his pocket and fingered it significantly.

"What are you going to do with it? Pawn it?"

With an angry shrug of the shoulders he put it back in his pocket. . . .

What happened to these men, to the "Bernards" and "Gustavs," once their deceptions were found out Maugham rarely had the opportunity to discover; he was, as he put it, "no more than a tiny rivet in a vast and complicated machine."

Maugham remained in Switzerland for nearly eight months, returning to England in May 1916. By now he was in poor health; vulnerable to chest infections, he had suffered from exposure during his weekly crossings of Lake Geneva throughout the winter. He was also anxious and depressed: Wellcome was granted a decree absolute on August 30, and there was now no legal barrier to his marrying Syrie: ultimately, as he very well knew, escape was impossible, but at least he could postpone the inevitable for a little while longer. "I wanted to recover my peace of mind shattered through my own foolishness and vanity," he wrote. "I was willing to marry Syrie, but, the circumstances being as they were, I was not prepared to be rushed into it." Two plays of his, *Caroline* and *Our Betters*, were to be produced in the States, and so in October 1916 Maugham sailed to New York, intending to oversee rehearsals and also cope with the business of transferring his plays from Frohman's firm, which had proved ineffective since the death of its founder, to John Rumsey, an associate of Maugham's British play agent, Golding Bright.

New York six months before America's entry into the war seemed curiously alien, the streets brightly lit, shops full of luxury goods, and theaters and restaurants doing brisk business. The war seemed distant, with most of the newspapers giving greater prominence to the defeat of the Boston Red Sox in the World Series than to the terrible slaughter of the Battle of the Somme. Maugham was taken aback by the prevalence of pro-German feeling, with many agreeing with President Wilson's conviction that Britain's imperialist ambitions were as objectionable as Germany's. "There is a great deal of sympathy with Germans," he told Kelly, "[especially] among the more intelligent part of the population, the professors, literary men, & such like. For the rest there is great admiration of the French, but none of the English. . . . I think if the Germans were fighting alone against the English sympathy would be for the most part on the side of Germany." Maugham had wanted to find more war work, hoping to be sent to Russia, but by now his state of health was too precarious, what he called his "recurrent lung ailment" making it essential that he take some time, preferably in a warm climate, to convalesce. For many years he had wished to visit the South Seas, having long had an idea in his mind for a novel about Gauguin, and now, freed from his war work, here at last was the opportunity.

THE VOYAGE WOULD BE LONG and Maugham had no wish to travel alone. Despite their lengthy separation, he had stayed in touch with that dangerously attractive young man Gerald Haxton, currently at loose ends in Chicago, and he lost no time in suggesting that Gerald should accompany him to Polynesia in the nominal role of secretary, like Harry Philips before him, an offer that was enthusiastically accepted. Shortly before they were due to depart from Manhattan, a telegram suddenly arrived from Syrie announcing her imminent arrival, accompanied by child and nursemaid. Since his return from Geneva, Maugham for Syrie had been conspicuous by his absence, disappearing first to Paris, then to New York. Unsurprisingly, Syrie was beginning to panic: the decree absolute having been granted, there was no reason why they should not be married immediately,* and if Maugham intended to evade his responsibilities in that direction then she had no choice but to confront him and insist that he keep his word. In a cold fury Maugham went down to the pier to meet her. They were both tense, Maugham because Syrie was the last person on earth he wanted to see, she terrified that he was somehow going to give her the slip. Having escorted her back to her hotel, he told her at once that he was on the point of leaving, that he would be away for several months, and that he had no intention whatever of changing his plans. At this Syrie became hysterical and made a violent scene, which further repelled Maugham. When she eventually calmed down he assured her that he would not renege and that they would be married as soon as he returned. And with that Syrie was forced to be satisfied.

It was with an enormous sense of liberation that Maugham, accompanied by Gerald, boarded the train to San Francisco, where they were to embark on the first leg of their long sea voyage, the first of many to be undertaken together over the next quarter century. Maugham was in high spirits, setting off "[to look] for beauty and romance," and, he added feelingly, "glad to put a great ocean between me and the trouble that harassed me." Since boyhood, when he had read Melville and Pierre Loti and the Polynesian novels of Robert Louis Stevenson, Maugham's imagination had been fired by dreams of the South Seas; later as a young man in Paris he had been mesmerized by the pictures of Gauguin's Tahitian period, and while listening to Roderic O'Conor talking about Gauguin during those evenings in Le Chat Blanc he had become fascinated by the man as well as his work, for the past several years mulling over an idea for a novel based on the painter's life. "I was convinced," Maugham wrote, "that by going to Tahiti I could get just the material I wanted to enable me to set to work." He had tried to go as early as 1913, when he had hoped to take Sue Jones with him

---

* In *Looking Back* Maugham writes of this period, "The divorce had not been made absolute, and I could not have married Syrie just then even had I wanted to." But in fact it had and he could.

as his wife, but those plans had come to nothing. Now he was setting off at last, and with a companion, Gerald Haxton, who was already the focus of his emotional life.

The distance to be covered was immense, and it was at sea that it first became clear what an important asset Gerald Haxton was to be. Gregarious by nature, Gerald effortlessly made friends with his fellow passengers, with whom he was more than happy to pass hours drinking, talking, and playing poker, afterward reporting back to Maugham the stories they had to tell. Maugham himself, intensely curious and ever on the lookout for good material, was nonetheless chary of intimacy and by nature reserved. "On a journey by sea, however long," he wrote, "I would never have spoken to anyone unless someone had first spoken to me." But with Gerald so "ebulliently, irrepressibly friendly," Maugham felt released from the strain of social obligation, able to enjoy listening and watching, although he was always affable, always ready to stand his round and take a hand at cards. For Maugham a game of cards was an absorbing pastime, but for Gerald it was almost a way of life: a reckless, high-risk gambler, he was happy to spend most of the day in a fug of cigarette smoke gambling in the saloon, while Maugham joined the others only at meals and in the evening, spending much of his time on deck writing in his notebook and reading. The vast blue emptiness of the Pacific Ocean affected him profoundly, as mile after mile went by without sight of another living soul: "not a tramp, not a sailing vessel, not a fishing-boat . . . it is an empty desert; and presently the emptiness fills you with a vague foreboding."

Among the four hundred passengers there was one who made himself particularly agreeable, indeed who was to become a friend for life. Bertram Alanson, three years younger than Maugham, was from a wealthy German Jewish family, originally Abrahamson, that owned coffee plantations in Guatemala, where "Bert" Alanson had grown up and attended university. A gifted financier, Alanson in San Francisco had been the youngest man on the stock exchange floor; now a senior partner in the family firm of investment brokers, he lived in considerable style in a house overlooking the Bay.

He was tall and distinguished in appearance, with a passion for golf and Italian opera, as well as for Spanish history and literature, all interests guaranteed to recommend him to Maugham. Alanson was by nature a hero-worshipper, and within days he became infatuated with Maugham, excited by his celebrity and impressed by the older man's charm and sophistication. The two of them talked for hours, Alanson fascinated by the breadth of Maugham's knowledge and experience, Maugham delighted to find someone whose financial expertise he could endlessly draw on. He was soon to assign to Alanson total control over his investments, a gesture of confidence that was to have enormous rewards. Their friendship began and remained entirely cloudless, and looking back on it many years later, Maugham wrote that no one could have had "a more devoted, generous, considerate friend than dear Bert."

THE LONG SEA VOYAGE was to take in Hawaii and Samoa, then veer south to Fiji, Tonga, and New Zealand before heading north to Tahiti on the return leg to California. Their first port of call was Honolulu, where they arrived on November 14, 1916, and stayed for three weeks, awaiting the arrival of the *Sonoma,* a small steamship bound for Australia on which they had booked onward passage. Haxton and Maugham, with Alanson for a while in tow, took the opportunity to explore the island thoroughly. The two men were fascinated by the contrast between downtown Honolulu, a modern American city, and the rough red-light district of Iwilei, openly catering to every variety of sexual taste. On their last night, there was a police raid in Iwilei, and the following day, a few minutes before the *Sonoma* was due to sail, a young woman came hurrying up the gangplank, clearly in a state of panic. She was a Miss Sadie Thompson, it turned out, an Iwilei prostitute in flight from the law. Once at sea she quickly regained her equanimity, antagonizing her fellow passengers, among them a doctor and his wife and an American missionary couple, by playing loud ragtime on her gramophone and drunkenly keeping open house in her cabin for the ship's crew. From Honolulu the *Sonoma* sailed to Pago Pago in

Western Samoa, and here the new arrivals were obliged to remain for some days as there was an epidemic of measles in the town. Holed up together in the same squalid boardinghouse, confined indoors by the drenching monsoon rain, Maugham and his fellow travelers continued to suffer from the brazen behavior of the "hot lallapalooza from Honolulu," as one of her boyfriends called her. The missionary was particularly enraged, eventually complaining to the governor about her, thus providing Maugham with a crucial episode in what was to become his most famous short story, "Rain."

Maugham's first experience of the tropics took powerful hold of his imagination. In Pago Pago, Apia, Papeete, Suva, Savaii, wherever he went he was entranced by the exotic beauty of his surroundings while at the same time remaining intensely alert to the sometimes tragic, often mundane, unexpectedly suburban life of the colonial community. Pago Pago in Western Samoa, then under American jurisdiction, displayed exactly this juxtaposition. Once inside the barrier reef the ship entered a large and beautiful lagoon surrounded on three sides by a dramatic backdrop of towering volcanic escarpment covered in lush green vegetation. Along the shoreline were white sand beaches and slender coconut palms, beyond them groves of mango and avocado, interspersed with brilliant bursts of hibiscus, oleander, and white tiare. Here and there stood little groups of native huts, with their high thatched roofs like beehives; the Samoans themselves were tall and graceful, the men bare-chested, dressed in brightly colored pareos, while the young women wore their long black hair loose, often crowned with a wreath of heavily scented tiare. But also to be seen from the harbor were two or three trim little bungalows, a Protestant church, the local club, tennis courts, and a modest Government House standing in a neatly kept garden, the Stars and Stripes flapping languidly from a flagstaff.

Maugham's exploration of Samoa and beyond coincided with the rainy season, and during their first few days in Pago neither he nor Gerald was prepared for the shock of a tropical climate, the stiflingly high temperatures, and the hours a day of deluging rain.

With the rain came a breathless heat, sultry and suffocating. The two men dressed in the thinnest of thin shirts and suits of light linen duck, in the evening adopting the local habit of wearing only shirt and pareo. At night they slept naked under mosquito nets, though the nets were often full of holes that the insects diabolically penetrated. During the day, in between downpours, they swam in the freshwater pools, drove in a pony and trap along the wide grassy roads that cut through the plantations, and went to pay homage at Vailima, where Robert Louis Stevenson spent his last years. Maugham responded immediately to the languorous, numinous eroticism he had first seen in the paintings of Gauguin. Sex was everywhere: young couples made love in full view and without embarrassment, and at bedtime he often found a dark-eyed *vahine* lying naked and willing under his mosquito net—to be given a handful of coins and briskly shooed away. Everything was open and on offer, and after dark Gerald especially liked to prowl off in search of the all-night saturnalias regularly to be found taking place by the seashore.

While spellbound by the prelapsarian beauty of the islands, by the deep blue of the lagoon, the brilliant colors of the vegetation, the immensity of the southern sky at night, Maugham was at the same time intensely interested in the more domestic aspects of life in the tropics, his most valuable material coming from the traders, half-castes, planters, doctors, and missionaries with whom he fell into conversation. The dapper, dark-haired Englishman and his "rather handsome travelling companion" soon became familiar to the regulars who drank at the English Club or on the veranda of the local hotel. As on board ship, so here, too, it was Gerald who struck up the acquaintance, Gerald, hanging out in the billiard room or bar, who first got to know these often eccentric characters with their strange, sometimes terrible histories. Maugham was enthralled. As he expressed it in his memoir *The Summing Up,*

> I entered a new world, and all the instinct in me of a novelist went out with exhilaration to absorb the novelty. . . . I was like a naturalist who comes into a country where the fauna are

of an unimaginable variety. . . . Few of them had culture. They had learnt life in a different school from mine and had come to different conclusions. . . . They were often dull and stupid. I did not care. They were different. . . . They seemed to me nearer to the elementals of human nature than any of the people I had been living with for so long, and my heart leapt towards them as it had done years before to the people who filed into the out-patients' room at St. Thomas's.

Although he stayed in each place for only a matter of weeks, Maugham was quick to absorb the social and cultural nuances, the rivalries, the snobbishness, the delicate balance in relations between native and European, between native and half-caste. Everywhere he went he made detailed notes of the people he met: "I rarely went to my ship's cabin or lagoon-side hotel room without writing down a description of a special scene . . . or of some conversation with a special character that I might be able to use in a future story"; and gradually, "from a hint or an incident or a happy invention, stories began to form themselves round certain of the most vivid of them." Indeed it was now that his interest in writing short stories was strongly revived, and his collection of tales of the South Seas, *The Trembling of a Leaf,* eventually published in 1921, marked a triumphant return to the genre of which he was to become a master.

Maugham found inspiration at almost every turn, and as his detailed note taking makes clear, it was this search for inspiration that lay behind his lifelong passion for travel: his restlessness, his wanderlust was largely driven by an insatiable need to feed the voracious demands of his imagination. As he was to write years later, "the writer cannot afford to wait for experience to come to him; he must go out in search of it." Again and again the first tracings of a story can be detected in the jottings in the notebooks, as in the four short paragraphs in which Maugham describes the American missionary couple, a Mr. and Mrs. Woodrow, and the brazen Miss Thompson, whom he had encountered on the ship from Honolulu. The missionaries were on their way back to the Gilbert and Ellice islands, and Maugham had been struck by the dour and cadaverous appearance of Woodrow, and by the vindictive intolerance of his wife.

> [Mrs. Woodrow] spoke of the depravity of the natives in a voice nothing could hush, but with a vehement, unctuous horror; she described their marriage customs as obscene beyond description. She said that when first they went to the Gilberts it was impossible to find a single "good" girl in any of the villages. She was very bitter about the dancing.

In buoyant contrast to this proselytizing pair is Miss Thompson, "pretty in a coarse fashion . . . she wore a white dress and large white hat, and long white boots from which her calves, in white cotton stockings, bulged." From these brief jottings Maugham constructed "Miss Thompson,"* the brilliant and terrifying story that was shortly to be retitled and known to the world as "Rain." In Maugham's own words, he wanted "to have Sadie [Thompson] and the missionary experience an emotional collision that would be as shocking in print as censorship at the time would permit," an ambition that was to be amply fulfilled. Written with impressive restraint, the story is set within the claustrophobic confines of a shabby little guesthouse in Pago. The plot follows the grimly self-righteous missionary, Mr. Davidson, as with sadistic zeal he pursues the prostitute, his declared intention to save her immortal soul. Against the background of an unceasing tropical deluge the drama is played out, with the man of God bullying and hectoring his victim until she is at last convinced of her sinfulness and begs Davidson to bring her to the arms of Jesus. It is during his final interview with Sadie that the missionary, consumed by lust, succumbs, thus destroying himself and for Sadie all belief in the goodness of both God and man.

After leaving the missionaries and Miss Thompson in Samoa, the two men continued their voyage south, to Fiji, Tonga, and as far as

---

* With his usual indifference to such matters, Maugham did not trouble to give the fictional version of Miss Thompson a different name.

New Zealand. By the time they turned north toward Tahiti they had sailed in many different kinds of vessels, from American steamship to open cutter to the rusty little traders laden with bananas and copra that regularly plied between the islands; once they spent seven days in an open rowing boat. Most memorable was the passage between Pago and Apia aboard a shabby schooner reeking of paraffin; in a dimly lit cabin the Chinese cook served a supper of meatballs and tinned apricots, followed by tea with condensed milk. "After supper we went on deck," Maugham recorded.

> After a while three or four members of the crew came up and sat down smoking. One had a banjo, another a ukulele and a concertina. They began to play and sing. . . . A couple of them stood up and danced. It was a strange, barbaric dance . . . sensual, sexual even. . . . At last they grew tired and stretched themselves out on the deck and slept, and all was silence.

On February 11, 1917, they finally reached Tahiti in French Polynesia. This was the island that it had long been Maugham's ambition to visit, impatient to see for himself the place where only fifteen years earlier the great Paul Gauguin had come to paint. In Papeete, the capital, they stayed at the Tiare Hotel, a somewhat eccentric establishment run by Louvaina Chapman, an immensely fat part-Tahitian woman known throughout the South Seas and beyond for her character and charm. The hotel was only five minutes' walk from the waterfront, which pleased Gerald, who liked to hang about there eyeing the brown-skinned sailors in their scarlet loincloths while Maugham pursued his researches. At first it was difficult to find anyone who had much to say about Gauguin, though Maugham was able to talk to Émile Levy, a pearl merchant who had known the painter, and also Captain "Winny" Brander, who had discovered Gauguin's body shortly after his death in 1903. But in fact the best source turned out to be Louvaina Chapman herself, who had befriended Gauguin and was able to provide Maugham with several interesting details as well as a crucial introduction to a female chieftain at Mataiea, about thirty-five miles outside Papeete, who proffered the astonishing information that there were paintings by Gauguin in a house not far away. The owner of what turned out to be a shabby two-room bungalow was "a flat-nosed, smiling dark native," who was delighted to invite his visitors in. Maugham immediately recognized the artist's work. It transpired that in 1892, Gauguin, ill with the syphilis that was eventually to kill him, had been taken in and cared for by a local farmer, and in gratitude had painted pictures on the glass panels of three interior doors. Two of the panels had been badly damaged, scratched and picked at by children, but the third, representing a sensual Tahitian Eve, dark-haired and half naked, a heavy green breadfruit in her hand, was still in a reasonable state of preservation, and it was this panel Maugham immediately offered to buy. His host, uninterested in the painting, was willing to sell, but only at a price that would cover replacing the door.

"How much will it cost?" I asked.

"A hundred francs."

"All right," I said, "I'll give you two hundred."

I thought I had better take the picture before he changed his mind, so we got the tools from the car . . . unscrewed the hinges and carried the door away.

Once back in Papeete the door was carefully packed to be shipped via New York to London, eventually to be installed in Maugham's writing room in the Villa Mauresque, where it remained, one of his most treasured possessions, until it was sold shortly before his death.

Maugham and Gerald left Tahiti on April 8, 1917, two days after the United States entered the war. In San Francisco there was a telegram from Gerald's mother urging him to enlist. He and Maugham took leave of each other, not knowing when they would meet again, Gerald departing to join the United States Army, Maugham to be reunited with Syrie in New York.

Throughout his long liaison with Gerald Haxton, Maugham was to run the gamut of emotion—passion, love, tenderness, fury, frustration, boredom, misery, despair—but at this stage, after their sojourn in the South Seas, Maugham was happy, at the start of what one of his close friends described as "the first completely beautiful, completely appropriate love affair he had ever had." Maugham had surrendered to this young man, who on almost every level had proved to be an ideal companion, adventurous, resourceful, easygoing, with a good sense of humor and, like Maugham, a vigorous sexual appetite. It was only Haxton with whom Maugham could talk through the stories he was evolving in his mind. True, Gerald was inclined to drink too much, and when intoxicated his temper could turn nasty, revealing a seam of anger that sober he kept buried. Like his fictional alter ego, Rowley Flint in *Up at the Villa,* when Gerald was drunk "he was noisy and boastful and vulgar and quarrelsome. . . . [A]fter two or three drinks there was no holding him. . . . Sometimes I couldn't help flying into a passion with him and then we'd have an awful row." But most of the time he was "kind and gentle and sweet," and for both sides the relationship was rewarding. For his part Gerald looked up to Maugham, partly as a father figure, something crucially missing in his growing up, and also as someone who was more experienced, more sophisticated, and who would introduce him to the kind of life for which he had longed, a life as far removed as possible from the tedium and genteel poverty of his childhood with his mother in St. John's Wood. Under Maugham's protection he was indulged and doted on, he was financially secure, and also, by means of his natural sociability, his love of talk, he had found a purpose, a crucial role to play.

In his memoir *Looking Back,* Maugham acknowledged the importance of Gerald's contribution. "But for him," he wrote, "I should never have got the material on our journey to the South Seas that . . . enabled me to write the short stories which later I published in a volume called *The Trembling of a Leaf.*"★ Of the six tales, which all appeared first in magazines before they were collected in

---

★ The title comes from a quotation of Sainte-Beuve: *"L'extrême félicité à peine séparée par une feuille tremblante de l'extrême désespoir, n'est-ce pas la vie?"* ("In life only a trembling leaf separates great happiness from extreme despair").

book form, it was, ironically, "Rain," by far the most successful, that was repeatedly rejected until finally taken by H. L. Mencken's magazine *The Smart Set* only a few months before *The Trembling of a Leaf* appeared. All the stories, fluent, colorful, and dramatically succinct, proved popular, but "Rain" was to make a sensation: "a sheer masterpiece of sardonic horror, beyond criticism," ran a typical notice. A showcase both for the author's loathing of intolerant religiosity and for his unillusioned view of the weakness of human nature, "Rain" has been reprinted again and again, earning its author more than $1 million in royalties. It has been rewritten as a play, turned into a musical, nearly made into a ballet by Roland Petit for the Paris Opéra, and filmed no fewer than three times, with Gloria Swanson (1928), Joan Crawford (1932), and Rita Hayworth (1953) in the part of Sadie Thompson; in 1946 there was an all-black film version entitled *Dirty Gertie from Harlem;* and shortly before her death, Marilyn Monroe was signed to play Sadie in an adaptation for television. Among its many admirers was James Michener, author of the Pulitzer Prize–winning *Tales of the South Pacific.*★ "One of the evil limitations put upon anyone who wants to write about the South Pacific is that he must stop reading Maugham," Michener wrote.

> [But] I must admit that before I start to do any writing about this vast area I usually take down *"Rain"* and reread those first three paragraphs to remind myself of how completely one can set a physical stage in a few absolutely correct observations. I hold those passages to be about the best beginning of a mood story extant.

BUT IN 1917 THIS was yet to come. When Maugham parted from Gerald after their six months together he was faced with returning to New York and to Syrie. He had promised he would marry her,

★ It was on Michener's *Tales of the South Pacific* that Rodgers & Hammerstein based their phenomenally successful musical *South Pacific.*

and now, reluctantly, he had come to fulfill that promise. Had he said nothing else on the subject, Maugham's personal distaste for the concept of the married state could have been deduced from his work. The plot of his play *Caroline,* for instance, is posited on the assumption that love flourishes best outside wedlock and that the institution of marriage is a killjoy and a trap. In "The Fall of Edward Barnard,"* one of the short stories in *The Trembling of a Leaf,* we are asked to applaud the hero's escape from marriage in Chicago to a blissful single life in the South Seas. And in *The Moon and Sixpence,* a novel shot through with anger, written only a year after Maugham's return from Polynesia, he tells the story of the ruthless rejection of marriage and family by an artist whose creativity has been smothered by domesticity. "There is no object more deserving of pity," the narrator feelingly remarks, "than the married bachelor." But in fact there is no need to search for clues, as Maugham had little hesitation in making his feelings plain. In a letter written only three years into the marriage, he explained to Syrie his view of the situation at the time of their wedding with a candor bordering on the brutal:

> I felt that I had been put in a position which I did not for a moment anticipate was a possibility. I knew that I had made a perfect fool of myself, but I thought I had also been made a perfect fool of. . . . I married you because I was prepared to pay for my folly and selfishness, and I married you because I thought it the best thing for your happiness and for Elizabeth's welfare, but I did not marry you because I loved you, and you were only too well aware of that.

In such circumstances it is hardly surprising that the wedding itself was an unjoyous occasion. The formalities took place before a judge in New Jersey at three o'clock in the afternoon of May 26, 1917, all arrangements having been made by Maugham's friend and

---

* The plot of *The Fall of Edward Barnard* was later expanded and reworked in *The Razor's Edge.*

fellow playwright Ned Sheldon. Sheldon was one of the witnesses; the other was Alexandra Colebrooke, wife of a backwoods British peer and a friend of Syrie's. The bride gave her age as thirty-two, instead of thirty-seven, but all the groom later recalled of the ceremony was of standing before the judge, "who first sentenced the drunk in front of us, then married us, then sentenced the drunk behind us." During the brief exchange of vows Maugham felt so overcome with loathing for his bride that he could hardly bring himself to look at her. Afterward there was a small reception at the Brevoort Hotel near Gramercy Park, attended by a handful of Maugham's theatrical acquaintances gathered to celebrate the "doomed entanglement," as one of them termed it, after which the newly married pair retired to a suite at the Devon in midtown Manhattan.

Most of June was spent in New York, with Maugham much involved with theatrical business, after which husband and wife left for a seaside holiday in East Hampton, accompanied by two-year-old Liza and a nanny. It was here on Long Island at the beginning of July that Maugham received an unexpected telephone call from a family friend, William Wiseman, asking if he was interested in discussing some possible war work. Maugham was instantly intrigued.

Captain Sir William Wiseman, a young English baronet still in his early thirties, had been recruited by Mansfield Cumming to work for the American branch of the Secret Intelligence Service. With the myriad animosities between the two countries, the position was a delicate one, but Wiseman, a charming and subtle diplomatist, was making a success of it. By the time the United States entered the war, on April 6, 1917, he had already built up a formidable network of contacts, establishing close links with his American opposite numbers in Intelligence as well as between the British Foreign Office and the Department of State in Washington. For both governments it was now an urgent priority to keep Russia in the war. Of the two revolutionary parties, it was the more moderate Mensheviks, under the leadership of Alexander Kerensky, who were committed to continuing the fight, while the Bolsheviks under Lenin were agitating for peace at any price. It was thus

Kerensky and his coalition provisional government that the Allies were anxious to back. To this end Wiseman was mounting a secret operation designed to offer support to Kerensky, whose position, under attack by an increasingly vociferous Bolshevik minority, was beginning to look worryingly insecure. Wiseman needed to appoint an emissary who would go to Petrograd, hold talks with the prime minister and his colleagues, discreetly disseminate propaganda, and regularly report back on the volatile political situation. Somerset Maugham, with his experience in espionage, seemed the ideal choice.

Maugham was astonished by Wiseman's suggestion, flattered, and immediately tempted by the proposal. The prospect of seeing for himself the country of Tolstoy, Chekhov, and Dostoevsky was powerfully appealing; so, too, was the opportunity of involving himself once again in the war; and not entirely to be discounted was the additional satisfaction that such a mission would remove him at least for a time from his marital responsibilities. Against this was the fact that Maugham was far from well. Although his health had temporarily improved during the months in the tropics, it had deteriorated since his return, and now he was always tired, slept badly, was feverish, and frequently coughed up blood; recently an X ray had confirmed what he already suspected, that he was in the early stages of tuberculosis. Maugham was also worried about Gerald, from whom he had heard nothing since the young man had left the States to undergo military training in South Africa; the likelihood of any future communication from Haxton reaching him in Russia was extremely small. The opportunity now offered, however, was too good to miss, and after forty-eight hours' reflection, Maugham accepted Wiseman's proposal.

The next few weeks were busy, Maugham going by train from Long Island to New York to confer with Wiseman, book his passage, obtain visas, and make all the other necessary arrangements for travel. As before, Maugham was given the code name Somerville, his official identity again that of a writer at work, this time a journalist reporting for the British press. Before leaving, there was one final detail that needed clarification. "I do not know whether it

is intended that I should have any salary for the work I am undertaking," Maugham wrote to Wiseman.

> I will not pretend that I actually need one, but in Switzerland
> I refused to accept anything and found afterwards that I was
> the only man working in the organization for nothing and
> that I was regarded not as patriotic or generous but merely as
> damned foolish. If the job carries a salary I think it would be
> more satisfactory to have it; but if not I am not unwilling to
> go without. I leave the matter in your hands.

Wiseman took the point, and agreed to provide both salary and expenses.

Having said good-bye to Syrie, Maugham left for San Francisco,
where on July 28 he was due to embark. Concealed in a belt under
his shirt he carried bills of exchange for the enormous sum of
$21,000, to be disbursed as he saw fit in the furtherance of Allied
interests. His traveling companions were three friendly Americans,
en route to Petrograd to join the staff of the United States embassy
there, as well as Emanuel Voska, a secret agent helping to organize
Slav resistance to the Central Powers, and a trio of Czech associates
who would act as liaison between Maugham and Tomás Masaryk,
founder and future president of Czechoslovakia. During the journey it was understood that Maugham would pretend to regard the
Czechs as complete strangers. It was also understood that "Somerville" was acting as a private agent who, as before in Switzerland,
could, and undoubtedly would, be disavowed by his employers at
the first sign of trouble. From California the ship sailed to Yokohama in Japan, giving Maugham his first sight of the Far East, a part
of the world that in later years never failed to fascinate. "It was tantalizing," he told Gerald Kelly, "to get no more than a brief glimpse
of it." At Yokohama he transferred to a Russian ship as far as Vladi-
vostok, where he boarded a crowded trans-Siberian train for the
eleven-day journey to Petrograd. On arrival in the capital, Maugham
went with Voska straight to his hotel, the Europa on Nevsky
Prospekt, in order to rest—he had been feverish and unwell on the

train—and prepare for a meeting with the British ambassador on the following day.

When Maugham arrived in Petrograd at the end of August 1917, he found the city in a state of turmoil. Six months previously, the February Revolution had forced the abdication of the czar, since when there had been an anarchic period of riot and confusion. Along the broad streets tanks and armored cars had become a familiar sight, and there was often the sound of gunfire. With the relentless German advance against an army perilously short of arms and apparel, Russian soldiers were deserting in droves, many to be seen roaming the streets, desperate and dangerous. Fighting frequently broke out between the cossacks, loyal to the provisional government, and the Bolsheviks, demanding that the government should go. Crime was rife, restless crowds surged day and night along the city streets, and there was an acute shortage of all basic supplies; every morning from before dawn, long queues of women wrapped in shawls and head scarves waited patiently for deliveries of bread, milk, sugar, and tobacco. The great imperial capital, with its magnificent mansions, its canals and bridges, its gilded domes and spires, was already beginning to look dingy and dilapidated. Yet despite the crisis there was a level of normality: trams were running, and carriages and motorcars still plied up and down fashionable Nevsky Prospekt and Morskaia Street, with their shops and restaurants and grand hotels; theaters and concert halls were open for business as usual, and the cinematographs displayed huge posters of Charlie Chaplin, Douglas Fairbanks, and Mary Pickford; cafés were jammed with customers, even if there was little on offer except a sandwich and a glass of tea.

Near the Hermitage on Palace Embankment, opposite the Peter and Paul Fortress, stood the British embassy, a magnificent eighteenth-century edifice built by Catherine the Great. It was here that Maugham duly presented himself on the day after his arrival. At Wiseman's request, only the vaguest explanation had been provided by London for Maugham's presence in Petrograd: according to the Foreign Office cable, "Mr. Somerset Maugham is in Russia on a confidential mission with a view to putting certain phases of the Russian situation before the public in the United States." Despite this uninformative statement it was naturally expected that the embassy should offer him any assistance he required, specifically in the transmission of reports, to be sent in code to the British consul in New York. Shown into a sumptuously upholstered anteroom hung with massive portraits of Queen Victoria, Edward VII, George V, and Queen Mary, Maugham was left to himself for a considerable period before the ambassador chose to make his entrance; by this time he had worked himself into a nervous state, his stammer intensified by the frigid courtesy with which he was received. Sir George Buchanan was a formidable presence. Tall and lean, with silver-gray hair, a monocle, and a mustache, Sir George in his black tail coat and gray trousers looked the perfect cardboard cutout of an ambassador. "In his cold and uninteresting way he was really a very handsome fellow," Maugham grudgingly noted, smarting from the chilliness of his reception. For it was instantly and acidulously made clear that the well-known writer was a far from welcome visitor. Sir George, a skillful and distinguished diplomat, was under enormous pressure trying to keep a balance between the various warring factions as well as working to persuade a wavering Kerensky to stay in the war. Now here was this inexperienced amateur arriving on the scene, who not only was to be allowed direct access to Kerensky himself, but whose encrypted cables were to be sent on by the embassy in a code it could not read and without the ambassador's being made privy to their content. It was this last in particular that Sir George regarded as a grave affront. "I realized," wrote Maugham after the interview was over, "that I could not count on much help in that quarter."

For Maugham the most pressing undertaking was to obtain entrée to the prime minister, and with this in mind he made contact with his old flame, Alexandra ("Sasha") Kropotkin. Madame Lebedev, as she now was, had left England to return to Russia in order actively to involve herself in the revolution. An enthusiastic supporter of the provisional government, she knew Kerensky well and was more than willing to provide an introduction. The reality proved disappointing. Once a dynamic and effective leader, Kerensky, still only thirty-six, was a sick man; ensconced in his office in the Winter Palace, he had lost the vision and decisiveness that once defined his leadership, allowing himself to be easily influenced and constantly changing his mind. He knew he was losing his grip and was terrified by the prospect, which now seemed imminent, of defeat. "[Kerensky] looked very unhealthy," Maugham recorded.

> He seemed fearfully on edge. . . . His speech was rapid and emphatic; and his nervousness made me nervous too. . . . The final impression I had was of a man exhausted. . . . He was more afraid of doing the wrong thing than anxious to do the right one.

Maugham's impression on this first meeting, that the Menshevik leader was unworthy of Allied support, was fortified by an incident he witnessed shortly afterward. Maugham and Sasha Lebedev were in the audience at a vast conference held one wet September evening in the Alexandrovsky Theatre. The theater was brightly lit and the boxes filled with foreign diplomats, while at long tables on stage sat members of the presidium. Toward the start of proceedings Kerensky strode out from the wings and began to address the audience; then suddenly he stopped as if struck as a voice in the audience started to heckle. According to one observer, "in the middle of his speech [he] rushed from the platform and burst into tears. . . . It seemed incredible that this man was holding the reins of great seething Russia." Maugham was equally unimpressed. "I've never seen a man on a public platform whose face actually looked green," he recalled. "If I'd been sitting closer I could have smelt the fear."

This humiliating performance notwithstanding, Maugham continued to confer with Kerensky, their meetings taking place once a week at the Mjedved, the finest restaurant in the city. "With Sasha acting as hostess and interpreter," he recalled, "I provided my guests with quantities of caviare at the expense of the two governments who had sent me to Petrograd, and they devoured it with relish." Afterward the conversation would continue in Sasha's apartment, with Kerensky pacing the room and haranguing Maugham as though he were at a public meeting. The situation facing the provisional government was growing increasingly desperate: abroad the Allies were pressuring Kerensky to continue with the war, while within the country the masses, facing famine and the approach of winter, were demanding peace. For Kerensky the Englishman was becoming an increasingly crucial contact in his dealings with the Allied powers. The American ambassador, an ex–grain merchant from St. Louis, rarely put his head above the parapet, while His Britannic Majesty's representative was proving impossibly obdurate: at a recent meeting Sir George Buchanan had made it plain that no further help could be expected from his government until the disorganization in the army, and indeed in the country at large, was substantially resolved. Furious and frustrated, Kerensky had turned his back on the ambassador and stalked out of the room, a Napoleonic touch, as Buchanan drily described it, but one that if theatrical in effect was awkward in result, leaving the Russian leader with no direct line to Downing Street other than that provided sub rosa by Somerset Maugham.

Maugham, meanwhile, was diligently filing his reports, spending long evenings in his hotel encrypting information, an unwieldy process that it was impossible to hurry. According to the elaborate code with which he had been equipped, Kerensky was to be identified as "Lane," Lenin as "Davis," Trotsky as "Cole," and Sir George Buchanan as "Dewar," while the British government appeared under the guise of "Eyre & Co."; if a password were asked for, it was "Friend of Mr. King in New York." His briefings were highly rated by Wiseman, who knew he could rely on Maugham, now the chief British agent in the field, to send back assessments that were both accurate and politically astute. On September 24, Wiseman cabled in cipher to Sir Eric Drummond at the Foreign Office in London,

> I am receiving interesting cables from Maugham. . . . [He] asks if he can work with British intelligence officer at Petrograd, thereby benefiting both and avoiding confusion. I see no objection. . . . He is very discreet. . . .

As before in Switzerland, Maugham had a team of agents under his control, to be employed as he thought fit. He dispatched a couple of his men to Sweden and Finland to investigate rumors of an alliance between those countries and the Central Powers; and he made strenuous if ultimately unsuccessful efforts to infiltrate one of his agents into Bolshevik secret meetings, an aim eventually achieved by the Americans. He himself kept closely in touch with a wide range of contacts in Petrograd. There was Voska, of course, and the remarkable Tomás Masaryk, "gently spoken, absent-minded and undramatic," whose Czech organization was run with impressive efficiency; Maugham recommended substantial financial support for Masaryk's Slav Press Bureau, recognizing its importance as a front for anti-German propaganda as well as for more covert operations. Maugham also conferred at length with Boris Savinkov, Kerensky's war minister. Described by Maugham as the most extraordinary man he ever met, Savinkov had been responsible for some spectacular assassinations of imperial officials, and was crucial to the Allies as a firm believer in the reorganization of the army and continuation of the war.*

At first Maugham was optimistic, believing in the resolve of those at the top and impressed by the general good humor of the crowds in the street, but it was not long before disillusion set in. By the end of September he was already convinced that the cause was hopeless: Kerensky was weak, Lenin and the Bolsheviks were rapidly gaining ground, and there was a general mood of defeatism among the provisional government that it was impossible to counter. Looking back, Maugham wrote, "The endless talk when action was needed, the vacillations, the apathy when apathy could only result in destruction, the high-flown protestations, the insincerity and half-heartedness that I found everywhere sickened me with Russia and the Russians."

And yet, the political situation apart, there was a great deal to be

---

* Savinkov makes an anonymous appearance in Maugham's 1944 novel, *The Razor's Edge,* in which the narrator describes himself drinking "a glass of Russian tea in a prim parlour in Petrograd while a soft-spoken little man in a black coat and striped trousers told me how he had assassinated a grand duke."

learned and enjoyed, and Maugham was determined to make the most of his time, exploring the city and immersing himself in the language and literature of the country. Every morning he had a lesson in Russian, and he read avidly, the great novelists of the past as well as contemporary authors such as Kuprin, Korolenko, Sologub, and Mihail Artzybashev. He went to the ballet, to concerts, and to the theater. (Among the plays on offer was an unknown Russian comedy, which Maugham attended out of curiosity: as the plot unfolded it began to seem increasingly familiar, and glancing at his program he saw the author's name listed as "Mum," the title of the play *Jack Straw.*) In fine weather he took long walks, and one day, strolling around the precincts of the ancient Lavra monastery at the end of Nevsky Prospekt, he was overwhelmed by a powerful feeling of nostalgia:

> I felt homesick. I stood on the steps of the great church, looking at the long line of the monastery buildings . . . but I saw the long nave of Canterbury cathedral with its flying buttresses and the central tower more imposing and lovely to my moved eyes than any tower in Europe.

The homesickness was made worse by the fact that letters were sparse, arriving at irregular intervals in the diplomatic bag. To his friend and fellow dramatist Eddie Knoblock, Maugham wrote,

> I am longing for news of England & have very little; so pray give me half an hour of your time & send me all the current gossip. It seems incredible that one of these days we shall all settle down again to normal existence & read the fat, peaceful *Times* every morning, & eat porridge for breakfast & marmalade.

But the one friend of whom Maugham yearned to have news was Gerald Haxton, from whom he had heard nothing since before he left for Russia. All he knew was that Gerald had sailed for South Africa, but as the weeks passed without any word he began to fear the worst, that his ship had been sunk and that Gerald was dead. In fact Gerald was still at sea: on October 26, 1917, his ship, the Japanese *Hitachi Maru,* had been captured near the Maldives in the Indian Ocean by the notorious German raider *Wolf.* For the next five months *Wolf,* with her cargo of two hundred prisoners, sailed on a circuitous route north, finally reaching her home port of Kiel in the last week of February 1918. From here Gerald was transported to the prison camp at Güstrow in northern Germany, where he remained until the cessation of hostilities the following November.

Meanwhile, in Petrograd, Maugham took pains to find agreeable society for his spare time. The Europa was filled with Allied agents and there was a good deal of cheerful congress between them, especially after the arrival of the English suffragette Emmeline Pankhurst, who every afternoon kept open house, making tea on a Primus stove in her room for anyone who cared to drop in. With basic supplies growing increasingly scarce—an apple now cost $2.50, and bread was made mainly from acorns and straw—everyone was hungry and talked obsessively about food, about roast beef and roast lamb and real coffee with sugar and cream. Nonetheless, as Voska put it, "we in the Hotel Europa . . . managed at times to enjoy ourselves and forget the revolution. . . . [We] caught the Russian mood—'*Nitchevo!*' ['it doesn't matter!']—and went about our business as calmly as the natives."

The city was full of foreign visitors, diplomats, observers, journalists, and businessmen, including a large number of Americans. One of these was an American banker come to arrange a loan to the Kerensky government; garrulous, self-satisfied and naïve, the man was also curiously endearing, and Maugham came to enjoy his company, and was consequently distressed when the banker was killed in a street shooting, an incident recalled in the Ashenden story "Mr. Harrington's Washing." Also among those come to witness the revolution was a glamorous young American couple recently married, John Reed and Louise Bryant, both writers, both convinced Marxists.* Reed, who was to write a classic account of

* The 1981 film *Reds,* starring Diane Keaton and Warren Beatty, was based on Reed's life with Bryant.

the October revolution, *Ten Days That Shook the World,* had spent time in Mexico with the rebel leader Pancho Villa, and his articles on the subject had caught Maugham's attention. Interested to learn more, he invited the pair to lunch and questioned Reed not only about Mexico but about his prosperous middle-class background and conversion to radicalism. Maugham was in a jocular mood and, glancing about with an air of mystery, whispered to Louise, "You won't reveal you had lunch with a British Secret Agent, will you?"—a suggestion that struck her as so preposterous she burst out laughing. "It couldn't have been funnier if he'd said he was an ambassador of the Pope," she remarked afterward.

An acquaintance closer to home was the novelist Hugh Walpole. Classified unfit for military service, Walpole had first arrived in Russia to work for the Red Cross and was now heading a small intelligence-gathering service, grandly entitled the Anglo-Russian Propaganda Bureau, of no great utility or efficiency although much relied on by the British embassy. Maugham and Walpole had first met in London in 1911, and both were now pleased to pursue the friendship. Walpole, possessed of the fatal facility of the second-rate, was astonishingly prolific; he was also insatiably ambitious, desperate to be accepted by the great and the good and determined to make his mark as a distinguished man of letters. Shameless at self-promotion, he flattered famous writers by sending gushing fan letters, always including a request for a meeting so that he could continue the blandishment in person; and when in receipt of a bad review he never failed effusively to thank the critic concerned for his helpful comments. Bumptious and vain he certainly was, also thin-skinned and embarrassingly sentimental, and many found irritating his craving to be loved; and yet Walpole was not a bad sort: he was friendly and enthusiastic and, except concerning the productions of his own pen, was a perceptive critic. Naturally he was thrilled to have come across such a well-known figure as Somerset Maugham, and he gleefully recorded their meetings in his diary. "Delightful lunch with Willie Maugham. He most amusing" was the entry for October 27, and after a concert a few days later, "Evening with Willie Maugham who was his old delightful self—amusing, clever and extraordinarily kind."

Maugham also enjoyed these encounters. It was good to talk to someone who was so well read, who moved in much the same world, and with whom he had a number of friends in common. There was the added recommendation of Walpole's rampant homosexuality. Pink-cheeked and bespectacled, Hugh pursued a vigorous sex life; "I am very sensual but pious and pure if that sensuality is gratified," he observed of himself contentedly. He was always falling in love, and was famous in queer circles as the only man ever to have gotten Henry James into bed, a story relished and frequently dined out on by Maugham. Indeed, Maugham relished Hugh's whole performance, if not quite in the way Walpole imagined. Flattered by his companion's concentrated attention as he happily chattered away, boasting of his successes and confiding the highs and lows of his busy emotional history, Hugh failed to realize how closely he was being observed; aware he was making an impression, it never crossed his mind that that impression might be ridiculous. Later Maugham was to make devastating use of Walpole in his fiction, but for the time being all was harmonious between them, and Hugh was blissfully happy with his kind new friend.

Walpole was intrigued by Maugham's observations on the rapidly changing political scene. "He watched Russia as we would watch a play, finding the theme, and then intent on observing how the master artist would develop it," he wrote. But now the play was drawing to a close. By mid-October it was obvious to all that the Bolsheviks would soon be in power, and Wiseman, realizing that Maugham as "the secret agent of reactionary imperialism" was a marked man, decided to have him recalled. When Kerensky learned of Maugham's imminent departure, he summoned him to the Winter Palace and charged him with delivering a message to the prime minister, Lloyd George. The crux of the message, which was to be memorized, not written down, was a plea that Britain should offer peace to Germany, but a peace without annexations or compensation—in other words, on terms which would make it impossible for the Germans to accept. By thus intensifying anti-

German feeling, Kerensky believed he would have some chance of keeping his mutinous army in the field. "I must make the Russian soldiers understand what they are fighting for," he said. "We haven't got boots or warm clothes or food . . . I don't see how we can go on. Of course, I don't say that to the people. I always say that we shall continue whatever happens, but unless I have something to tell my army it's impossible." A couple of other clauses were added, including the usual request for more guns and ammunition, as well as a demand that Sir George Buchanan be replaced, as "the Ambassador does not seem able to get into sympathetic relations with the new conditions." As soon as the meeting ended, Maugham sent a coded communication to London, and within hours he received the reply that to ensure total secrecy a destroyer would be sent to Christiania (now Oslo) in Norway to bring him home.

That same evening, October 22, 1917, Maugham left Petrograd by train from the Finland Station on the first stage of his journey. By this time he was more than ready to go. Not only was there little prospect of achieving anything with Kerensky—two days after his departure saw the outbreak of Lenin's Bolshevik Revolution, "the ten days that shook the world," during which Kerensky was overthrown—but he himself was seriously unwell. With his lungs badly infected, he was feverish and exhausted, and with the food shortages grown daily more acute he was also malnourished: arriving in Christiania with a day to wait, he bought a pound of chocolates, which he ate there and then in the street. After a rough crossing to the north of Scotland, he reached London on November 17 and immediately telephoned Downing Street to make an appointment for the following day. Lloyd George was extremely cordial, expressing his pleasure at meeting the distinguished writer whose plays he so much enjoyed. He talked about these a little, then moved on to expound on the war and the current situation, and Maugham began to form the impression that the prime minister had a shrewd idea of what he had to say and was determined not to let him say it. Finally, in desperation, Maugham took a paper out of his pocket on which, contrary to instruction, he had written down

Kerensky's message and thrust it at Lloyd George, who scanned it hastily. "I can't do that," he said, handing it back. "What shall I tell Kerensky?" Maugham asked. "Just that I can't do it," he repeated, then rising to his feet explained he had a cabinet meeting to attend and left the room.

Back in his hotel room, Maugham pondered what he should do next. His immediate concern was the state of his health, and from St. Thomas's he obtained the name of an eminent lung specialist, who confirmed the diagnosis of tuberculosis and told him he must go immediately to a sanatorium. Scarcely had he had time to take in this information when on November 20 he was called to a debriefing, held in the office of the editor of the *Times* and chaired by the Lord Chief Justice, Rufus Isaacs; among others present were Gen. Sir George McDonough, director of British military intelligence; Gordon Auchincloss, secretary to President Wilson's power broker, Col. E. M. House; and, to Maugham's surprise, William Wiseman, recently returned from America. Frightened his stammer would get the better of him, Maugham handed his report to Wiseman to read aloud. It received little comment, for, as the Foreign Office representative, Sir Eric Drummond, noted on his copy, "I fear this [is] of only historical interest now." Depressed by the fact that all his efforts had been in vain, Maugham wrote of his Russian mission, "I failed lamentably," although in retrospect, he added, "it seems to me at least possible that if I had been sent six months before I might quite well have succeeded." His superiors, however, were impressed by his performance and more than ready to give him further employment. Wiseman suggested he might act as liaison with Polish groups in London and Paris; but more immediately there was a job for him in Bucharest, where he would be required to undertake the same kind of work as before, lending support not to the Mensheviks but to the Cossacks, and encouraging Romania to continue the fight.

As before, Maugham was flattered to be asked and, excited by the opportunity, tempted to accept. This time, however, he knew he was in no condition to travel.

[I thought] that it was only sensible, since I might crack up, to say that I was suffering from tuberculosis and the doctors advised me to go to a sanatorium, but if they could find no one more trustworthy to do the job, I was perfectly willing to take it on. Rufus Isaacs looked at me. He smiled. "In that case I don't think we ought to ask you to go," he said. "Go to your sanatorium and I hope you'll get well very soon."

Maugham followed his specialist's advice, repairing to a sanatorium in the north of Scotland. It was to be nearly two years before his recovery was complete, and there was no question but that he had begun treatment only just in time. Nevertheless, part of him regretted his decision to turn the Romanian offer down: "I knew . . . that I had made a bad mistake. I should have risked the danger and even though I hadn't been of much use the adventure would have been interesting."

CHAPTER 8

BEHIND
THE PAINTED VEIL

...

B Y THE TIME MAUGHAM LEFT LONDON FOR SCOTLAND AT THE END
of November 1917, he was a very sick man. Nordrach-on-Dee, just
outside Banchory in Aberdeenshire, was a huge private sanatorium
dedicated to the treatment of pulmonary tuberculosis. Opened in
1900, it was based on the German model, established at Nordrach in
the Black Forest, which had pioneered the open-air treatment of
TB. Although it was so far north, the winter climate on Deeside
was relatively mild, and patients were exposed to the bracing Scottish air twenty-four hours a day, with the windows, overlooking
smooth green lawns and a thick canopy of conifers, remaining wide
open at all times. Besides fresh air, the basic tenets of the cure were
bed rest, gentle, graduated exercise, large amounts of nourishing
food, and a complete absence of stress. The founder, Dr. David
Lawson, was insistent that the sanatorium must be a haven of tranquillity, with compulsory naps after meals, a nurse to each patient,
and no unnecessary movement allowed: in severe cases even putting
the arms behind the head was forbidden for fear of stretching the
lungs. Visitors were discouraged, especially in the early weeks of a
patient's stay. Such ministrations were not cheap—around £3,000 a
year; nor was the success rate impressive: many patients died, and
others remained at Nordrach for years without visible improvement; but until the discovery of antibiotics in the 1940s it was the
best treatment available.

Maugham would remain based at Banchory for over a year, and for the first few weeks he barely moved from his bed, exhausted by the symptoms of the disease that had killed his mother and that now had him in its grip. Gradually, however, his condition improved, and before long he was able to take pleasure in his peaceful invalid life, loving the hours spent lying in bed, relieved of all pressure and responsibility. "I delighted in the privacy of my room with the immense window wide open to the starry winter night," he wrote. "It gave me a delicious sense of security, aloofness and freedom." By degrees, as his strength returned, he began to enter more actively into the routine of the sanatorium. Between 11:00, when he rose, and when he retired to bed at 4:00, he mingled with the other patients, took some of his meals with them, played cards, and even, on fine days, sat outside wrapped in rugs on the veranda. Little did these men and women know of what consuming interest they were to the writer in their midst. To Eddie Knoblock, Maugham wrote cheerfully,

> There is something that would appeal to your passion for the macabre in the way the tuberculous fall in love with one another, have scenes, scandals, & all the paraphanalia [sic] of the drama; & you cannot imagine the effectiveness of threatening your beloved that you will have a hemorrhage (I never could spell the damned word) if she does not turn a consenting ear to your entreaties.

During the first few months, Maugham found it impossible to work, but as usual he was avid for news from London, impatient to know what was going on, in the war, in the theater, among his colleagues and friends. "The post is always the great thrill of the day," as he told Alfred Sutro, "& the recipients of letters are the envy of all around." One interesting event was the opening of a new play of his on January 26, 1918, at the Globe. Written during the previous year, *Love in a Cottage* is an inconsequential little piece which treats with a familiar theme,★ that of the rich widow who teases her mer-

---

★ Previously explored both in "Cupid and the Vicar of Swale" and in *The Bishop's Apron*.

cenary suitors by allowing them to propose before revealing that if she remarries she loses her fortune. "Meant to be nothing but pure entertainment," as the author admitted, the piece had been commissioned by Marie Löhr, who had started in management and was for the first time both producer and star. Described by Desmond MacCarthy in the *New Statesman* only a few years later as "a play so negligible that I am no longer sure of its name," *Love in a Cottage* racked up a respectable run of 127 performances, largely thanks to Miss Löhr's sparkling rendition.

Lacking strength for the physical effort of writing, Maugham was ceaselessly active in his imagination, thinking over his adventures of the past couple of years and planning new work. Closest to hand was the material gleaned from his fellow patients, a number of whose private dramas were eventually retailed in the short story "Sanatorium." Yet richer by far were his own recent adventures, the people and situations he had come across, both mundane and extraordinary, during his work for the intelligence services in Switzerland and Russia. With the nature of that work so secret, and with the war still in progress, there was no question of publishing anything for some time to come. The matter nonetheless was much on his mind, and it was now that he began to compose that seminal series of spy stories, personal, factual, and realistic, based on the exploits of his fictional alter ego, Ashenden. The Ashenden collection, "a very truthful account of my experiences during the war when I was in the Secret Service," was not to appear for another ten years, held up by "[Willie's] mysterious bosses in the Foreign Office," as his publisher explained it. According to a report there were originally thirty-one stories, but when Maugham showed them to Winston Churchill in draft, Churchill insisted that fourteen be destroyed, as he considered them in breach of the Official Secrets Act.

Some years after Maugham's death, his friend the art historian Kenneth Clark recalled that "[Maugham] often spoke about the Intelligence Service, which he greatly enjoyed. I suppose he liked the light that it shed on human nature." The truth of this remark is emphatically borne out by *Ashenden*. Maugham was fascinated not so much by action and adventure as by the effect of these unusual situations on the people involved. He was never tempted to glamorize his assignments, never lost the cool clinical eye that rested so dispassionately on his surroundings. Similarly, although a committed patriot unquestioningly dedicated to his country's cause, Maugham was well aware of the moral double standards involved. In "The Flip of a Coin," he describes a mission of Ashenden's that, if successful, will result in the deaths of a number of innocent men; it is he, the man on the ground, who will have to do the deed, obeying the instructions of superiors who choose not to know how the deed is done. He reflects with disgust on their hypocrisy:

> They desired the end, but hesitated at the means. . . . Though ready enough to profit by the activities of obscure agents of whom they had never heard, they shut their eyes to dirty work so that they could put their clean hands on their hearts and congratulate themselves that they had never done anything that was unbecoming to men of honour.

It is this clear-eyed vision that largely accounts for the extraordinary impact that *Ashenden* made on the writing of espionage fiction. The spy story as a genre had emerged at the beginning of the twentieth century, with Erskine Childers's 1903 novel *The Riddle of the Sands* still standing as one of the supreme examples of its class. Among the most popular practitioners were John Buchan with *The Thirty-nine Steps,* and the hugely bestselling William Le Queux and E. Phillips Oppenheim, both of whom specialized in tales that were unashamedly escapist and melodramatic. Their protagonists are superman-heroes, invariably engaged in missions of terrifying importance, foiling political assassination or delivering international spy rings to London, frequently dodging violent death in their desperate struggles against the diabolical enemies of king and country, whom they always brilliantly outwit. These are highly charged adventure stories with no interest at all in representing reality, and the contrast with *Ashenden* could hardly be greater. Ashenden himself is an engaging character, in almost all respects the exact reflection of his creator—he even gives his address as Chesterfield Street,

Mayfair—a solitary man, private, detached, but also incurably in-quisitive. Unlike other storybook spies of his era, Ashenden is a very fallible human being, fond of his creature comforts, at times irritable, sometimes scared, and although an experienced traveler an inveterate sufferer from train fever. Crucially, Ashenden, like Maugham, enjoys the opportunity of acting a part:

> He was travelling with a brand-new passport in his pocket, under a borrowed name, and this gave him an agreeable sense of owning a new personality. He was often slightly tired of himself. . . .

With the possible exception of Joseph Conrad's *The Secret Agent,* which is more a political than a spy novel, Maugham was the first to write about the business of espionage as in actuality it was. He was also jointly first, with his fellow novelist, Compton Mackenzie, in having himself worked as a spy; but whereas Mackenzie recycled his Secret Service experiences in Greece as unalloyed farce,★ Maugham depicted the world of undercover intelligence as not only morally dubious but frequently monotonous and dull. Although this ap-proach was to come as a shock to many readers, Maugham set the tone for an entirely new generation of British spy fiction. "The modern spy story began with Somerset Maugham's *Ashenden,"* wrote the critic and crime writer Julian Symons, a statement with which many distinguished followers of the genre agreed, writers such as Eric Ambler, Graham Greene (who described *Ashenden* as "that witty and realistic fiction"), Len Deighton, and John le Carré. Ambler stated that he was "strongly influenced by the *Ashenden* ethos," while le Carré wrote, "The Ashenden stories were certainly an influence in my work," adding, "I suppose that Maugham was the first person to write about espionage in a mood of disenchantment and almost prosaic reality." Across the Atlantic, too, Maugham's un-

---

★ Mackenzie's book, *Greek Memories,* was withdrawn after publication in 1932, and he was prosecuted under the Official Secrets Act.

flinching realism attracted admirers. In 1950 the crime writer Raymond Chandler, creator of Philip Marlowe, wrote to Maugham,

> *Ashenden* is unique. . . . There are no other great spy stories—none at all. I have been searching and I know. . . . There are a few good tales of adventure with a spying element . . . but they always overplay their hand. Too much bravura, the tenor sings too loud. They are as much like *Ashenden* as the opera *Carmen* is like the deadly little tale that Mérimée wrote.

Ashenden: or The British Agent was eventually published in 1928, by Heinemann in England, and Doubleday, Doran, in the United States. Dedicated to Gerald Kelly, the book was slow in winning the acclaim it was eventually to achieve; this was partly due to the fact that for a war-weary public, interest in the war was slow to revive (Erich Maria Remarque's *All Quiet on the Western Front,* Robert Graves's *Goodbye to All That,* and R. C. Sherriff's play *Journey's End* were not to appear until the following year); and also because at that era few aficionados of the genre were prepared for such a low-key treatment. Most critics agreed with *The New York Times,* whose reviewer judged *Ashenden* to be "a specimen of Somerset Maugham writing in second gear," although there were one or two more forthright expressions of disapproval. The least charitable notice appeared in *Vogue,* written by D. H. Lawrence. Maugham's characters, if well observed, are fakes, Lawrence wrote. "We find they are nothing but puppets, instruments of the author's pet prejudice. The author's pet prejudice being 'humour,' it would be hard to find a bunch of more ill-humoured stories, in which the humour has gone more rancid." Despite such lack of enthusiasm at its first appearance, *Ashenden* has gone on to flourish: it has been published in numerous editions, translated into many languages; it has provided the basis of a play (to date unproduced), and a film, *Secret Agent,* by Alfred Hitchcock, with John Gielgud, Peter Lorre, and Madeleine Carroll; most intriguingly, it was used as a handbook by the intelligence services, for several years required reading for entrants into

MI5 and MI6, as well as apparently inspiring a study of British spy fiction on the part of Soviet military intelligence: as its author remarked, "a strange outcome for a series of tales that were written *merely* to entertain." But perhaps the ultimate accolade was awarded during the Second World War, when the stories were referred to in a broadcast by Dr. Goebbels, the German minister for propaganda, who cited them as a typical example of British cynicism and brutality.

Meanwhile, as the long Scottish winter gave way to spring, Maugham gradually felt his health improve, and to his great delight he was given leave by his doctors to go south for the summer, on condition that he return in the autumn for further treatment. "Madame," as Maugham referred to Syrie, came up to Banchory to visit him, full of the news that she had taken a house in the country for three months. Charles Hill Court was handsome and spacious, with a large garden and a pleasant study in which Maugham could work undisturbed. The house was near Hindhead in Surrey, an attractive area of woods and heath and gentle hills, within easy reach of London. But there was another reason why the location had been chosen: fifteen-year-old Mounteney was at school in Hindhead, and his mother, who continued to suffer acute anguish at the separation imposed by her ex-husband, hoped that being so near might give her an opportunity of seeing him. She had continued to petition for increased access, but her requests were always refused by Wellcome, even though he himself was continuously abroad and Mounteney obliged to spend his holidays with one of the masters. Great emphasis was laid by Wellcome's lawyers on the importance of ensuring that Mounteney should never in any circumstances come into contact with Maugham, a prohibition that achieved little except to make circumstances even more difficult for Syrie. At least she now had her daughter, three-year-old Liza, whom she adored. Maugham, too, was fond of the little girl, despite his frequently expressed disappointment that she had not been born a boy, and during their summer in the country the three of them managed to enjoy a relatively amicable time together, Syrie happy to have her husband returned to her, he delighted to be released from the sanatorium. Privately, however, he saw little to look forward to in his marital situation. "What will happen in the future I cannot tell," he wrote resignedly. "I can only hope for the best & leave it at that."

Although he was still weak and tended to tire easily, Maugham was pleased to discover one or two congenial Surrey neighbors, in particular the writer Robert Hichens, whom he had come across previously in London. Hichens, a novelist, playwright, and music critic, was a friend of Max Beerbohm and had known Henry James and Oscar Wilde; *The Green Carnation,* his novel satirizing Wilde and the aesthetes of the 1890s, had been a great *succès de scandale,* although he had made his fortune with a bestselling romance, *The Garden of Allah*. Recently Hichens had set up house with a Swiss novelist, John Knittel; Knittel had a wife and children, but to Hichens this was no obstacle, and like a number of confirmed bachelors of the period, E. M. Forster for one, Hugh Walpole for another, he was content for his emotional and domestic life to revolve around a married man whose wife and offspring became part of the extended family. Maugham was delighted to see Hichens, and he, Hichens, and John Knittel rode together almost every day. They played tennis and croquet, with Syrie making up a foursome, and in the evenings the two couples dined together, cheerfully animated after drinking John Knittel's terrifyingly strong cocktails.

Now and again visitors came down from London, including Hugh Walpole, who spent a couple of nights at Charles Hill. After getting to know Maugham in Petrograd, Walpole was surprised to see what kind of a woman his friend had married. She was nice enough, Hugh recorded in his diary, but it was difficult to understand what Maugham saw in her, "[as] I should have thought that she was over-sentimental for his cynicism." What interested him more on this occasion, however, was the fact that his friend was hard at work on a novel.

The novel Maugham was working on while at Charles Hill in the summer of 1918 was *The Moon and Sixpence,* the story inspired by the life of Paul Gauguin. The similarities between Gauguin and Charles Strickland, the artist in the book, are marked: like Gauguin, Strickland is a respectable stockbroker with wife and children who abandons his family to live in poverty for the sake of artistic freedom; both painters settle in Tahiti, remaining in the South Seas for the rest of their lives; Gauguin, ravaged by syphilis and drug addiction, was eventually killed by a heart attack, while Strickland dies of leprosy. To tell his story Maugham employs a first-person narrator, a device he had not used since *The Making of a Saint* twenty years earlier, but one on which he was increasingly to rely, especially in his short stories. Here the unnamed "I" has only a minor part in the action, his main function to comment and observe. A young writer closely modeled on Maugham himself, with the same youthful priggishness, dry humor, and enjoyable streak of malice, he is taken up by Mrs. Strickland, an ordinary woman of limited means with ambitions as a literary hostess. When to everyone's astonishment her dull stockbroker husband suddenly abandons his family and career to live as an impoverished artist in Paris, it is the narrator to whom Mrs. Strickland appeals for help.

Arrived in Paris, the narrator finds a very different Strickland from the man he had met in London, ruthless and irascible, unmovably set on his course and with no interest whatever in the life he has left behind. The narrator has an artist friend in Paris, Dirk Stroeve, a foolish fellow and an abominable painter, who is nonetheless generous and kindhearted. Just as the penniless Gauguin was selflessly cared for by his friend Émile Schuffenecker, and repaid him by seducing his wife, so Strickland is cosseted by Stroeve, whom he similarly traduces. Some years later the narrator travels to Tahiti, and it is here on the island he learns that the painter has recently died; in the South Seas, Charles Strickland had at last found fulfillment, living with a native girl and creating the disturbing but glorious masterpieces for which he was to become posthumously famous. Back in London, meanwhile, Mrs. Strickland enjoys her role as keeper of the flame, since her husband's death living comfortably on the sale of his pictures while tastefully displaying a few colored reproductions of his work on her sitting room wall. "They must be very pleasant to live with," says one of her guests politely. "Yes; they're so essentially decorative," she complacently replies. (Understandably, this depiction of the artist's wife caused some distress to Mme Gauguin when she read it.)

The phrase "essentially decorative" was a dig at Gerald Kelly, whom Maugham used to tease by declaring that his, Maugham's, prime interest in art was decorative. Indeed, the novel owes a great deal to Kelly, as it was Kelly who had introduced Maugham to Gauguin's work, and it was with Kelly that he had first met Roderic O'Conor, who had known Gauguin well and whose snarling aggressiveness is faithfully reproduced in the character of Strickland. Kelly suspected that he himself had served as the inspiration for Stroeve, the chocolate-box painter. "I am always sure," he cheerfully admitted, "that all Willie's bad painters are portraits of myself." But in this he was wrong: the character of Stroeve is modeled on Maugham's fellow novelist, Hugh Walpole, who fortunately failed to recognize himself in the plump, silly creature, whose work was "hackneyed and vulgar beyond belief." Had Walpole discovered his contribution, no doubt there would have been a squeal of anguish, if nothing like the anguish he suffered later when coming face-to-face with himself as Alroy Kear in *Cakes and Ale*.

Published by Heinemann in April 1919, *The Moon and Sixpence* is a minor novel that has always found greater favor with the general reader than with the critics. The exotic Tahitian setting made an obvious appeal to a world only recently emerged from war, and the theme was an interesting one, that of the nature of genius, of the conflict between the ruthlessness of the creative artist and the bourgeois society he escapes. In the book this society is portrayed with a delicately satirical touch, Maugham drawing on his own experience as a young writer at Violet Hunt's salon on Campden Hill. His portrait of Violet as the novelist Rose Waterford is essentially affectionate, which is not something that could be said of his portrayal of Mrs. Strickland, depicted with a subtle venom that betrays much about the author's own feelings of entrapment by marriage and the conventions of society. Mrs. Strickland, we are told, "had the true instinct of the nice woman that it is only really decent for her to live on other people's money," while the misogynistic anger in many of Strickland's outbursts lies close to strong buried feelings in Maugham. This being so, it is disappointing that the novel's greatest flaw lies in the portrayal of Charles Strickland himself, who comes over not only as a brute but a bore, and in whose sudden transformation from dutiful paterfamilias to blazing, foul-mouthed genius it is difficult to believe. As Katherine Mansfield wrote in *The Athenaeum,* "We must be shown something of the workings of his mind; we must have some comment of his upon what he feels, fuller and more exhaustive than his perpetual: 'Go to hell.' " Despite such reservations, when in July the book came out in America its success was immediate and overwhelming: with an initial print run of only five thousand copies, it had sold close to a hundred thousand by the end of the year, its success resulting also in a huge and unexpected revival of interest in Maugham's earlier work, *Of Human Bondage.*

After leaving Hindhead at the end of August, the Maughams spent a couple of months on Chesterfield Street, Maugham's old friend Walter Payne having moved out at the end of the summer to make room for the family. He and Maugham continued to keep closely in touch, however, and when Payne took a house in Regent's Park, Maugham gave him some paintings, including one of his portraits by Gerald Kelly. Payne was to marry twice; his first wife was much liked by Maugham, but the second, a Hungarian divorcée, was loathed. The friendship survived nonetheless, and Payne until his death in 1949 continued to advise Maugham on his financial affairs.

IN NOVEMBER MAUGHAM RETURNED for further treatment at Nordrach-on-Dee. Although still under par, he felt invigorated and full of plans for the future. With the war finally over, he could hardly wait once more to go on his travels. "I am making my plans to conquer the Far East," he told Kelly. "How splendid it will be to set off, with adequate funds in one's pocket & what time one needs, for God knows where." During his previous stay in the sanatorium he had been too ill to write, but now he could hardly bear to stop, composing four plays in an eighteen-month period, *Caesar's Wife,*★ *Home & Beauty, The Circle,* and *The Unknown.*

By the time the first of these, *Caesar's Wife,* went into rehearsal in February 1919, Maugham was back in London and able to attend. His presence in the dimly lit auditorium, however, was found somewhat daunting by the play's leading lady, Fay Compton, who was having trouble remembering her lines. "He wasn't nasty about it," she said, "but he would stop and say, 'We *must* have the correct words!' " In the end it was Miss Compton, after the piece opened at the Royalty on March 27, who was recognized to be largely responsible for the success of a production that otherwise had few memorable qualities. Inspired by Mme de Lafayette's famous novel, *La Princesse de Clèves,* about a married woman's renunciation of illicit love, *Caesar's Wife* is set in contemporary Cairo, where the beautiful young wife of the British consul develops a passion for her husband's attaché. Everyone concerned behaves with the utmost virtue and nobility and the situation is eventually saved with honor all around. As Maugham explained in his introduction to the published version, he had so often been reproached for concentrating on unpleasant people that he wanted to write a work "in which all the characters were estimable." This is, perhaps predictably, what makes the result so bland.

During the previous summer at Hindhead, Maugham had held long discussions with Syrie about their future. Their marriage was an incontrovertible fact; it was far from ideal, but, considered calmly, the arrangement held advantages for both sides: for Syrie, propriety and financial security, for Maugham the façade of respectability that one side of his nature craved; also, as parents there were important responsibilities which had to be shouldered together. Surely the two of them could work out a tolerable modus vivendi? Syrie had wanted to live in her house in Regent's Park, originally paid for by Gordon Selfridge, but Maugham, squeamish about the association, insisted that they settle on Chesterfield Street. However, what had provided a commodious bachelor estab-

★ Originally entitled *The Keys to Heaven.*

lishment for himself and Walter Payne now seemed uncomfortably cramped. The house was five-storied but narrow, and in order to make space for a nursery, Maugham had had to give up his airy top-floor study, instead making do with a small parlor on the first floor overlooking the street; this was not perfect and he was vulnerable to interruption, but at least there was just enough space for the big writing table to which its owner was so attached.

It was here in the house in Mayfair that the Maughams' married life properly began, and at first it appeared that the couple were making a success of it: they were seen together at parties, galleries, and first nights—including, in 1919, the first nights of two of Maugham's own plays—and they frequently entertained at home. The Maughams "gave dinner parties to end all," recalled one of their friends. Naturally enough, Maugham's brother F.H. and his wife, Nellie, were delighted to see him settle down, the last of the surviving brothers to marry, and Syrie was made warmly welcome in Rutland Gate. The three nieces, Kate, Honor, and Diana, had always felt fond of their uncle Willie, who was kind, talked to them as equals, and tipped a generous half sovereign at every meeting, and now they were fascinated by their aunt and dazzled by her chic. The girls' clothes were bought off the peg at Bourne & Hollingsworth, whereas Syrie's were made in Paris by Lanvin and Chanel, and it was thrilling when she gave them her barely worn castoffs and taught them about style. "I had naturally bad taste, running to pleats, bows, frills and rosebuds," Kate recalled, "[and] Syrie tried to train my eye." Even F.H. had a soft spot for his sister-in-law. Frigidly polite toward his wife and a forbidding figure to his children, F.H. was a different character altogether with Syrie, gallant and charming. The two of them sometimes lunched together, and when Maugham was abroad, F.H. would sometimes dine with Syrie at Chesterfield Street.

Yet if in public the Maughams behaved as though on the best of terms, in private all was not so serene. The basic problem was twofold: the couple had almost nothing in common, and Syrie had made the fatal mistake of falling in love with her husband. This complicated everything, for it placed an added strain on the relationship that it was quite unable to bear. Maugham was shy, reticent, and highly disciplined, and shrank from any form of emotional demonstration; Syrie by contrast was emotional, volatile, and self-indulgent, and enjoyed nothing more than making dramatic scenes, preferably last thing at night. "*Don't* make me a scene!" became a familiar plea of Maugham's. Extravagantly sociable, she adored parties and hated being alone, completely insensitive to her husband's desire for periods of silence and solitude. "Syrie simply didn't understand how important his writing was to Maugham," said a woman friend of hers. "She would try to get him to take her to Henley or some such place when he wanted the morning completely to himself." Nor did she realize how taxing a day's work could be: sometimes after Maugham had been writing all day he would come down to dinner dead tired, only to find a noisy group of his wife's friends, none of whom he knew, who had been invited in for the evening. Once the guests had gone, the rows would begin, sometimes continuing until two or three in the morning, Maugham eventually retreating to bed exhausted before having to get up early the next day to write amusing dialogue for the current play, while Syrie, if she chose, could lie in until luncheon. With her remarkable eye for décor and design, Syrie loved buying pretty things for the house, and she spent a fortune on clothes, two subjects about which she was happy to chatter for hours. "You have driven me to talk to you practically about nothing but frocks and furniture," her husband exploded in one of his many fits of exasperation, "and if you knew how sick I am of both these subjects!"

She loved smart, rather raffish society, and was ill at ease with many of her husband's old friends, Gerald Kelly chief among her dislikes. When she moved into Chesterfield Street she had insisted on the removal of *The Jester,* Kelly's glorious portrait of Maugham as a young man, which had hung over the fireplace in the drawing room;* she had the painting returned to the artist, and made no secret of the fact that she found the man himself a fearful bore: when Kelly came to dine Syrie often slipped away in search of more

---

* In 1933 it was bought for the Tate by the Chantry Bequest.

amusing company elsewhere. And indeed, when in the company of her husband's fellow authors she tried to join in the literary talk, faking her way with all-purpose expressions of enthusiasm, which set Maugham's teeth on edge, irritating him beyond measure when he heard her gushing about books he knew perfectly well she had never opened. He found it infuriating that she neither could nor would leave him in peace and seemed stubbornly to resist every attempt on his part to find something to occupy her time: she never read, had no interest in cards, quickly gave up on the notion of charity work, and the traditional feminine occupations of knitting and needlework held no appeal for her whatsoever.

What Syrie wanted was her husband's approval and attention, and one of the few areas in which she got it was the theater. This was an interest shared, and here Syrie briefly came into her own. When at work on a play Maugham often read aloud passages of dialogue to her, and he was pleased when she occasionally attended rehearsals, more than once taking her with him when he had productions opening in New York. He particularly valued her advice on sets and costumes: during the preparations for *Caesar's Wife,* for example, it was Syrie who took Fay Compton shopping for her clothes. "I didn't have a voice in it at all," the actress recalled. "Syrie took over and that was that. Maugham had perfect faith in her taste in dress and he was quite right." Before an opening, Maugham was always in an acute state of nervous tension, leaving it to Syrie to make final arrangements for the cast party after the performance. And it was she who took pity on the first-night queues, sending down sandwiches and thermoses of soup to people waiting for long hours to buy cheap tickets in the pit and gallery.

The frequent scenes Syrie staged, the endless reproaches, the daily testing and questioning of Maugham's feelings for her, maddening to him, were all symptoms of her emotional insecurity, her huge desire to be loved. As a friend of Maugham's later remarked, "I think that if Syrie hadn't fallen in love with him, the marriage would have lasted." The fact that she was in love made her desperate for any show of affection. It also made her physically demand-

ing, demands which her husband found increasingly difficult to satisfy. For Syrie, Maugham was the best lover she had ever known,
but she had long lost any attractiveness for him. His wife's sexual
demands, he told a man friend, "were insatiable, intolerable," and
to another he confided that he found physical relations with Syrie a
great effort and when in bed with her was obliged to draw heavily
on his imagination. Faced with his wife's increasingly bitter reproaches, which were undoubtedly fueled by intense sexual frustration, Maugham was driven to lay some uncomfortable facts before
her. "I was forty-three when we married [and] you were not very
young either," he bleakly reminded her.

> You cannot forget the circumstances under which we married.
> I think under these circumstances you should be very well sat-
> isfied if you get from your husband courtesy and considera-
> tion, kindness and affection; but really you cannot expect
> passionate love.

Underlying all these scenes and arguments was of course the absent figure of Gerald Haxton. In February 1919, Haxton, released
from his POW camp in Germany, had illicitly arrived in London
hoping to see Maugham, but he had been quickly picked up by the
authorities and deported before the two men could meet. He would
never set foot in the country again. Haxton was nonetheless an
enormous, and profoundly threatening, presence in the Maugham
marriage, the true basis of all their rows. Whereas Sue Jones had
known about Maugham's homosexuality and tolerated it, Syrie
knew and was tormentedly jealous. Had the object of her husband's
affections been a woman, she might have found a way of dealing
with her; had he been a gentle, effeminate young man, she might
have befriended him; but as Syrie sensed long before she met Gerald, this charismatic young cad with whom her husband was so obsessed was a dangerous enemy, and one whom she had small chance
of defeating.

While recuperating in his Scottish sanatorium, Maugham had
spent much time planning a voyage with Gerald to the Far East, and

now that the war was over he was increasingly impatient to be off. His lucrative theatrical business, however, kept him in London throughout most of 1919, with the first night of *Caesar's Wife* in March, *Home and Beauty* opening in August in both London and New York,★ and *The Unknown* soon to go into rehearsal.

In addition, there was the upheaval of moving. The confined quarters of Chesterfield Street had finally been exchanged for a much larger house, 2 Wyndham Place in Marylebone. Here at last Syrie was able to give free rein to her restless energy and decorative talents, overseeing the furnishing of a house primarily intended as a setting for an ambitious program of high-level entertaining. Maugham did his best to keep out of the way, spending much of his time at the Garrick when not writing or at rehearsal, or wandering around the auction houses looking at pictures; occasionally he brought an old friend, such as Sutro or Walpole, back to the house for dinner. One such evening was noted by Walpole in his diary. The evening had been pleasant, he wrote, but "[Willie] looks ill and bored. I'm afraid the marriage is not a great success."

Away from the domestic arena, however, Maugham was riding high, much in the news with the opening at the end of August of his new play. A fast, frivolous, and brilliantly funny farce, *Home and Beauty* turns on its head a particularly unhappy aspect of the time, that of women deprived of husbands by four years of war. It was precisely the right play to entertain a war-weary public, hungry for frivolity and fun. The topical themes—rationing, the black market, the scarcity of servants—the glorious silliness of the farcical situations, and the wit and rapidity of the repartee delighted London audiences;† even the cynicism implicit in the absolute refusal to take anything seriously was accepted as a tremendous joke. This was just

---

★ In the States the play was known as *Too Many Husbands*. The line "England, Home and Beauty," from which Maugham took his title, came from *The Death of Nelson,* a popular song commemorating the Battle of Trafalgar, a subject that, it was decided, had rather less resonance in New York than it did in London.

† New Yorkers, on the other hand, less affected by the war and its aftermath, saw little to amuse them in the play, which closed after only two weeks.

as the author intended, any darker, more personal relevance a matter for himself alone. "The difference between men and women," says the heroine's mother, "is that men are not naturally addicted to matrimony. With patience, firmness, and occasional rewards you can train them to it just as you can train a dog to walk on its hind legs. But a dog would rather walk on all fours and a man would rather be free."

"A delightful entertainment," was the critical consensus, a play of "style, wit, elegance . . . a little masterpiece of polite merriment." The leading role of Victoria was taken by Gladys Cooper, a thirty-year-old actress whose cool, classical beauty concealed a sterling common sense and an excellent head for business. Although she had been on the stage since she was seventeen, Gladys had no great natural talent; as one of her colleagues put it, for Gladys acting was simply something she did for a living; she worked hard at it, however, was utterly reliable, and eventually, as Maugham wrote later, "succeeded in turning herself from an indifferent actress into an extremely accomplished one." She was to portray three further Maugham heroines, in *The Letter, The Sacred Flame,* and *The Painted Veil.* The two became firm friends, Maugham a great admirer of Gladys's self-discipline and determination as well as of her luminous blond beauty. The roles of Leslie Crosbie in *The Letter* and of Stella in *The Sacred Flame* were both written with Gladys in mind, and as Maugham himself admitted, the knowledge that she would be playing these parts "more or less unconsciously" colored his depiction of them.

ONCE THE PLAY WAS settled into its run, Maugham felt able at last to depart for the long-planned expedition to the Far East. The journey, of which he kept detailed notes, was to take more than six months. Leaving from Liverpool in August 1919, he went to New York, then by train across country, collecting Gerald in Chicago before continuing to the West Coast for embarkation. They sailed first to Hong Kong, after which they traveled on to Shanghai and

Peking and finally to Mukden in the north, returning home by way of Japan and the Suez Canal.

China was fascinating territory for Maugham, a country that "gives you everything," as he was later to declare. At the time of his visit the nascent republic was in a state of flux: since the overthrow of the imperial dynasty in 1912, most of the country had fallen into the hands of feuding warlords, with a deep division opening up between on the one hand an almost medieval feudal economy and on the other a rebellious student movement committed to modernization and reform. The government in Peking was precarious and ineffective, largely ignored at home although officially recognized abroad, with all the major powers maintaining embassies in the capital. For Maugham this was his first experience of being in a foreign country unable to speak the language, and outside the major cities he was largely dependent on the services of an interpreter, a restriction of minimal importance in his case, as his consuming interest was in the expatriate milieu, in the behavior of Westerners living uprooted within Chinese society. As before in Polynesia, the Americans and Europeans he encountered, the lives of doctors, diplomats, traders, missionaries, and their women, were the subject of his closest scrutiny, and his notes are full of their stories: the consul, the taipan, the desperate-to-be-married spinster, the missionary who had come to hate his calling, the agent of British-American Tobacco driven half mad by homesickness, the saintly mother superior in her white-walled convent who talked nostalgically of her family home in the south of France. One of the few exceptions was an interview with a Chinese, a renowned scholar and expert on Confucius. Long retired, this ancient gentleman with gray pigtail and discolored teeth had for many years been secretary to one of the empress dowager's greatest viceroys; educated at Oxford and Berlin, he spoke fluent English, and he sufficiently unbent, after some lavish flattery, to discourse on history, on philosophy, and with considerable fervor on the relationship between his country and the West. "You have thrust your hideous inventions upon us," he fiercely harangued his somewhat startled visitor, "[but] do you not know that we have a genius for mechanics? . . . What will become of your superiority when the yellow man can make as good guns as the white?"*

Although travel within the country was often cumbersome and slow, Maugham and Haxton covered vast distances. Accompanied by a team of bearers, blue-clad coolies in big straw hats carrying their luggage balanced on poles over the shoulder, they experienced a wide variety of transport. Sometimes they were carried by litter, or jogged along astride tough little ponies; for days at a time they walked, at night putting up in rough country inns, sometimes sleeping on the bare earth floor; and for fifteen hundred miles they sailed by sampan along the upper reaches of the Yangtze, on as far as Chengdu, from whose crenellated walls could be seen the snowy mountains of Tibet. Maugham was entranced by the beauty of the country, by the vivid green of the paddy fields, the little tree-covered hills, the graceful bamboo thickets that lined the side of the road. He transcribed his impressions while they were still fresh in his mind, often while actually on the move, scribbling his notes while being carried in a chair or moving downriver in a sampan. On their way the two men visited shrines and temples, they sat in teahouses and opium dens; they watched peasants in the fields plowing with lumbering water buffalo, passed women on the road tottering along on tiny bound feet; by the river at night they saw fleets of junks, their sails ghostly in the moonlight; and once in remote country a group of Mongol tribesmen clattered by, dressed in black silk coats and trousers and boots with turned-up toes.

On occasion the sight was less picturesque. Walking up to inspect a hillside graveyard they came upon a little tower, gruesome evidence of the Chinese custom of disposing of unwanted baby girls. "At its foot were a number of rough baskets thrown about in disorder," Maugham wrote.

> I walked round and on one side saw an oblong hole, eighteen
> inches by eight, perhaps, from which hung a stout string. From

---

* The old scholar's outburst as recorded in the notebook is given almost word for word to the character Lee Tai Cheng in the 1922 play *East of Suez*.

the hole there came a very strange, nauseating odour. . . . It was a baby tower. The baskets were the baskets in which the babies had been brought . . . let down gently by means of the string. The odour was the odour of putrefaction. A lively little boy came up to me while I stood there and made me understand that four babes had been brought to the tower that morning.

The contrast between rural China and the great cities of Peking, Shanghai, and Hong Kong could hardly have been more marked. Hong Kong, the first port of call for Maugham and Haxton, was emphatically British, clean, efficient, and redolent of home, with its clubs, race course, tennis courts, and comfortable, chintz-covered sitting rooms where white-coated servants brought in cocktails and olives on the dot of six. Shanghai, commercial and cosmopolitan, was very different in character, with the great banks and businesses lining the Bund, streets jammed with motor traffic, with a busy nightlife centered on the restaurants and nightclubs run mainly by a glamorous White Russian population in flight from the recent revolution. Here, as in the other major metropolises, every kind of sexual delicacy was provided, the famous boy brothels in particular popular with Europeans. The ancient walled capital, Peking, was yet another world altogether, "an experience that really enriches the soul," as Maugham testified, "one of the pleasantest places in the world to spend the rest of one's life." Here there were cities within cities, the Forbidden City, the Imperial City, the Chinese City, each enclosed by its own massive wall surrounding temples and palaces, lakes, gardens, pagodas, and a rabbit warren of houses. In each, the broad tree-lined streets and imperial palaces were surrounded by an infinite network of tiny *hutungs,* or alleyways; a doorway in a blank wall might open onto a series of cool courtyards fragrant with flowering shrubs, or onto an overcrowded slum stinking of rotting refuse. As Maugham remarked, "very nasty smells" were often overwhelming: sewers were a rare luxury; instead, open drains ran in the street and the night soil was wheeled out every morning to be spread outside the city walls and used as fertilizer. Unlike noisy Shanghai, there were few cars in Peking, the most common form of transport the rickshaw, silent on its pneumatic tires and the soft-shod feet of its runner. Most foreigners lived within the legation compound, where there were clubs and a couple of European-style hotels. Expatriate social life was frenetic, with racing, day-long picnics, dances, and luncheons, as well as diplomatic dinner parties, to many of which, as a distinguished visitor, Maugham was naturally invited, their pomposities and protocol meticulously transcribed.

Shortly before returning home Maugham wrote to his agent, Golding Bright, "I have got a good deal of material in one way and another (besides having a very good time)." The material referred to was to provide the basis for three works: a play, *East of Suez;* a novel, *The Painted Veil;* and a collection of sketches, *On a Chinese Screen.* The latter was the first to be ready for publication, and when it was in typescript Maugham sent it for expert appraisal to H. I. Harding, a well-known sinologist and second secretary at the British embassy in Peking. Harding read the typescript with care and made a number of corrections:

> p. 124 I am inclined to criticize the epithet "familiar." I do not know that the habit of poisoning relatives one dislikes is commoner in China than in England. . . .
>
> p. 126 may I object to the epithet *singular*? The Chinese may strike us as singular, weird, funny, curious, strange, mysterious, etc, but at the same time we strike the inexperienced Chinese in just the same way. . . .

Maugham was grateful, even if he did not agree with all the emendations. "Your suggestions are most helpful & of the forty-one you made I am taking thirty-six," he told Harding. "[But] once or twice I think you have misapprehended my meaning: for instance I did not call the Chinese singular because they are Chinese but because of artistic capacities which do surely distinguish them from other peoples. . . ."

On a Chinese Screen appeared in 1922, received with acclaim on both sides of the Atlantic. Gerald Gould in the *Saturday Review* congratulated the author on the subtlety of his observation. "His descriptions are not so much natural as psychological . . . he shows us the actual effect of China on minds with preconceptions similar to ours; and thus we learn the 'feel' of that ancient and alien civilization."

The second work to come out of the Chinese experience was the novel *The Painted Veil;* although it was not published until 1925, the idea for it, as so often with Maugham, lay maturing in his mind for several years before he felt ready to set it down on paper. The theme was inspired both by an episode from Dante's *Purgatorio,** remembered from his first visit to Italy, and by a notorious scandal concerning an Englishwoman in Hong Kong that he was told while on his travels. It was, he said, "the only novel I have written in which I started from a story rather than from a character. . . . [The characters], constructed from persons I had long known in different circumstances . . . were chosen to fit the story I gradually evolved."

The plot concerns the marriage of the ill-matched Walter and Kitty Fane. The couple first meet in London when Walter comes home on leave from his job as a government bacteriologist in China. Shy, scholarly, and introspective, Walter is not at all Kitty's type, but at twenty-five and still unmarried, pretty, frivolous Kitty is afraid of being left on the shelf and so agrees to marry the besotted Walter, who proudly takes his new wife back to Hong Kong. Here, to Kitty's relief, life among the British colony turns out to be tremendously good fun. True, her husband is a dull stick, but there are compensations, chief among them the handsome assistant colonial secretary, Charles Townsend, charming, gregarious, and devilishly flirtatious.

Soon Kitty and Townsend are embarked on a thrilling affair, she as obsessed with the vain, charismatic Charlie as she foolishly assumes he is with her. But then one afternoon they are discovered by Walter; in a cold fury he presents Kitty with a murderous ultimatum: either she accompany him upcountry to distant Mei-tan-fu, a

---

* In Book V, there is the story of the gentlewoman from Siena whose husband, suspecting her of adultery, takes her to his castle in the Maremma, hoping that the noxious vapors from the marshes will kill her.

town in the grip of a deadly cholera epidemic, or he will divorce her, citing Charlie Townsend as corespondent. Initially Kitty seizes on the latter alternative, but in a mortifying scene in Townsend's office she is made to see that she has been horribly mistaken and that her lover has not the least intention of involving himself in such a damaging scandal. She must be a sensible girl, he tells her, pull herself together and go along with Walter to Mei-tan-fu.

It is during the bleak and terrible weeks spent in the devastated little town that Kitty finally comes to understand the reality of her situation. The love Walter had for her has turned to unrelenting hatred, the love she thought she had from Townsend was worthless, her own existence has been selfish and shallow. Gradually, as she sees Walter's heroic work to save lives, she begins to look outward, even volunteering to work among the orphans cared for in a convent run by French nuns. Finally Walter succumbs to cholera and dies, apparently unreconciled, leaving Kitty to return a much wiser woman to Hong Kong. Yet Maugham has her measure and is too much of a realist to leave it at that; despite herself, his weak-willed heroine succumbs for a second time to Townsend's casual seduction, eventually departing for England humiliated and full of self-loathing.

The portrait of Kitty Fane is one of Maugham's finest fictional achievements. As with Bertha Craddock more than twenty years before, he displays an extraordinary empathy, an ability to create a woman as seen not from a man's perspective but from that of the woman herself; he completely inhabits and possesses Kitty, knows her from the inside, down to the very nerves and fiber of her being. Apart from her prettiness, she is an ordinary little thing, silly, self-absorbed, and not overendowed with intelligence. And yet Maugham shows sympathy for her, for her loveless upbringing, for her terror at ending up as a penurious spinster, and for her boredom with her husband's inept bedroom technique. No wonder Townsend's confident lovemaking overwhelms her; and there is no doubt at all that the author knows precisely what he is talking about when he describes the almost physical pain Kitty suffers in her craving for sex with big, bad Charlie Townsend.

Intriguingly, there is a great deal of the author himself in Walter Fane. Maugham once said that he had based the character largely on that of his brother F.H., and it is true that in appearance and in manner there are strong similarities. But so there are to Maugham. Here is Maugham describing Walter: "He was self-conscious. When there was a party and everyone started singing Walter could never bring himself to join in. He sat there smiling to show that he was pleased and amused, but his smile was forced. . . . You could not help feeling that he thought all those people enjoying themselves a pack of fools." And here is Maugham on himself: "Convivial amusement has always somewhat bored me. When people sit in an ale-house or, drifting down the river in a boat, start singing I am silent. . . . I do not much like being touched, and I have always to make a slight effort over myself not to draw away when someone links his arm in mine." There are, too, visible parallels between the home life of the Fanes and that of the Maughams, with both husbands, taciturn by nature, married to chatterboxes. Like Syrie, Kitty was "willing to chatter all day long."

[Walter's] silence disconcerted her. He had a way which exasperated her of returning no answer to some casual remark of hers. It was true that it needed no answer, but an answer all the same would have been pleasant. If it was raining and she said: "It's raining cats and dogs," she would have liked him to say: "Yes, isn't it?" He remained silent.

MAUGHAM ARRIVED HOME ON April 18, 1920, his luggage filled with treasures: porcelain, Ming figures, Chinese silks; for Syrie a gold and jade necklace and a heap of chinchilla to make a cloak; a white squirrel fur coat and little blue coolie suit for five-year-old Liza. But although he was immediately caught up in the busy demands of his London life, Maugham's overriding desire was to leave again as early as possible. For the previous half year he had been living at close quarters with Gerald, and the abrupt change to marital domesticity was unpalatable in the extreme. Maugham still believed that every effort should be made to retain at least a veneer of harmony, that it was important to keep up appearances, and that he and Syrie should do their utmost to make the relationship work, as much for Liza's sake as for their own; and while he was at a safe distance of nine thousand miles, he was able to view the prospect of cohabiting with his wife in a mood of relative equanimity. Yet when faced with the reality of life in Wyndham Place, resignation seemed more difficult. Syrie, craving love, yearning for openness and warmth, was made miserable by her husband's emotional detachment, indeed his apparent inability to show any interest in her at all. Inevitably she resorted to tears and reproaches, made scenes, and gave way to wild accusations and bouts of furious temper, to such a degree that sometimes Maugham dreaded coming home. "I seem to live in an atmosphere of complaints which I have never been used to and which I cannot think are reasonable," he wrote to her in a letter.

> Do you know that no one in all my life has said the things you have said to me? No one has ever complained of me and nagged me and harassed me as you have. How can you expect me to preserve my affection for you? You have terrorized me. . . . Just think that at the age of forty-six, a strong, healthy enough man, I should often have to go and have a cocktail in order to face you. . . . You have lived all your life among people who say the most awful things to one another, but I haven't. It humiliates me. It makes me miserable.

Syrie felt excluded from her husband's life, and understandably resented the fact that he went abroad so often, for so long, and chose to travel with a companion other than his wife. She longed to go with him, she told him, longed to explore the remote regions of the world. But here again Maugham was adamant. He was not a globetrotter, he said, moving from one luxury hotel to another. "You are very pleasant to travel with," he conceded, "but I go with a special object . . . and you unfortunately get between me and the impressions I am gathering. I go to seek ideas and when I am with you I get none. I am very sorry, but that is the brutal fact."

Behind closed doors the quarrels continued, although as before the two of them put on a good face in public. Syrie was a gifted and imaginative hostess, a quality much appreciated by Maugham, who also enjoyed social life, if on a rather less exuberant level. There were luncheon parties, small dinners for old acquaintances, and big evening receptions notable for their lavishness and glamour, with marvelous food and copious quantities of champagne. Here Syrie was in her element, although not all of Maugham's friends found her entirely sympathetic: "Syrie had a very heartless side," said one; "it was easy to be fascinated by Syrie, less easy to love her," wrote another; "her sparkling eyes could be sharp, and the pert expression and staccato, high-pitched voice was not to everyone's liking"; while a third was even critical of her love of entertaining. "Her hospitality did not spring from warmth of heart, but from an inability to be long alone," he wrote, not wholly inaccurately. "Left to herself, she soon grew bad-tempered."

On August 9, four months after Maugham returned from China, his play *The Unknown* opened at the Aldwych. A curiously unsatisfactory work, it returns to territory covered in the 1901 novel, *The Hero*. The characters are the same, but instead of a struggle between sex and duty, here the hero's struggle is with his religious faith. In spite of a strong cast headed by Basil Rathbone, *The Unknown* was taken off after less than two months, the general opinion concurring with that of the critic in *The Times,* who wrote that the argument was shallow and the play itself "a little dull and lacking in drama."

Maugham, meanwhile, was absorbed in new projects, his head full of his impressions of China. When his study door was closed, between the hours of nine and twelve, the household knew he was not to be disturbed. This was a frustrating time for Liza, who was excited to have her father home and longed for his attention. "I was a little frightened of him as a forbidding father," she recalled, "but also I always loved his being back." With his strong sense of the importance of continuing the family line, Maugham had always hoped one day for a son, and in this sense Liza had been a disappointment. Nonetheless Maugham was fond of children, and since his time as a medical student had had a weakness for babies and the very young, with whom he was unusually patient and gentle. He found his daughter to be a touching little figure, small and slight with a sweet, pale face and huge dark eyes; he loved her, wanted to do the best for her, and yet his feelings were painfully complicated by the fact that she was so much her mother's creature. (Significantly, Maugham for years insisted on referring to his daughter as "Elizabeth," whereas Syrie, and everybody else, called her "Liza.") Syrie doted on Liza and spoiled her shamelessly, indulging her with expensive clothes and toys and keeping her with her as much as she could. The little girl naturally enjoyed this cosseting, but whereas she knew she could depend on her mother, her father was the fascinating unknown, and his rare presence in her life was greatly prized. Maugham's own early life had been singularly lacking a father figure: he had scarcely known his own father, and his uncle the vicar was unloving and remote; without a role model he found himself awkward in that role, well intentioned but not quite knowing what to do. "I think he must have had a picture of what fathers should be like," said Liza later, "[but] it was all a bit studied." Unlike Syrie, her father was not a great provider of treats, never took her to the pantomime, for instance, or the circus, or even for an ice at Gunter's in nearby Berkeley Square; but there were trips to the zoo, and sometimes he rode with her, or let her accompany him on a walk, when he would tell her stories. But he never revealed anything about himself or about his own childhood. Most enjoyable to both was the "happy ritual," as Liza described it, of his coming upstairs in the evening to read aloud to her once she was tucked up in bed. Maugham was charmed by the sight of the little girl in her pajamas, pink from her bath, her hair in two tight plaits, eagerly waiting for his visit. "He never stammered when he read," said Liza, "which was really extraordinary."

Young though she was, Liza could not but be aware, however subconsciously, of the tensions in the house when her parents were in residence together. Sometimes she heard sounds of fearful rows, sounds which terrified her, and she would creep away afterward to hide so that no one should ask why she was crying. One symptom of anxiety manifested itself in the child's reluctance to eat: fussy and difficult at mealtimes, she often drove her governess to distraction by refusing to finish whatever was on her plate. During the whole of one cold winter when Maugham was abroad Liza was given her breakfast by herself in his study, the warmest room in the house. Filled with despair at the sight of the sausage and bacon in front of her, she waited until the maid had left the room, then quietly hid every last scrap of the fatty food behind the rows of books on the shelves. This subterfuge continued undetected for weeks, until her father eventually returned to find a disgusting smell and dozens of his precious volumes covered in putrefying grease and ruined beyond repair. Not unnaturally, he was extremely angry.

Throughout the summer of 1920 Maugham had dutifully played the part of husband and father, but now he was planning to escape. The relationship with Syrie had become so wretched that it was imperative he make a serious decision as to the future. The couple were hopelessly incompatible and deeply unhappy. Maugham had recently begun to feel suicidal, and this had shocked him into realizing that something must be done. It was, after all, he who had the upper hand, as was made very clear during the debate he held with his wife on the subject. "There are only two courses open to us now," he told Syrie flatly, when a couple of weeks later he put in writing the points made in their discussion. "You must either accept the claim I made then for freedom and go and come when I like, for as long as I like and as often as I like in peace and without scenes; or else separation . . . I have said little enough of Elizabeth," he continued, "but you know how constantly she is in my thoughts. . . . For her sake, as well as for yours and mine, I should like us to continue to live together if you can only bring yourself to a willing compromise."

Syrie had little option but to agree, however much she may have disliked the terms. Certainly she had plenty of time to think them over, as shortly after delivering his ultimatum her husband again left to go abroad, this time remaining away for more than a year.

CHAPTER 9

A WORLD OF
VERANDA AND PRAHU

. . .

U NLIKE MANY OF HIS PEERS, MAUGHAM FOR MOST OF HIS LONG
life retained an unusual ability to move with the times. As a writer of
fiction he stayed surprisingly up to date both in his choice of themes
and in the sometimes startling modernity of his approach, his short
stories in commercial terms becoming a global phenomenon, translated into almost every language. Yet even more remarkable for a
writer born in the mid-Victorian era, Maugham early became established as a valuable property in the motion picture industry. His own
attempts at writing scenarios were undistinguished, his personal interest in the medium was limited, and he found most of the people
involved in the business unlikable, yet it was through film that his
work became famous to millions, many of whom knew nothing at all
about his books. Throughout the 1920s and '30s and during the Second World War, Maugham spent considerable time in Hollywood,
rarely with pleasure, and although personally involved in the process
on a number of occasions, he never cared for the film versions of his
fiction. When invited to watch Garbo in *The Painted Veil,* he recoiled
in horror. "I cannot imagine that anything is likely to take me to see
the film. I cannot bear seeing my works when they are made into pictures." Nonetheless he was canny enough to realize that here was a
fabulous source of income, to be exploited at every opportunity.

The first call to Hollywood came in 1920, from the pioneering film
producer Jesse L. Lasky, who during a recent swoop on London had
signed up a number of well-known authors, including Maugham,

Eddie Knoblock, Henry Arthur Jones (father of Sue Jones), Arnold Bennett, and Elinor Glyn. Lasky had started his company in 1912 in partnership with his brother-in-law Samuel Goldwyn, and their first employee had been Cecil B. DeMille, who was then a little-known stage director. In 1916 Lasky had joined forces with the newly formed Paramount Pictures, the most powerful studio of the silent era. Although the talkies were still some way off (the first talking picture, *The Jazz Singer,* was not released until 1927), Lasky and Goldwyn were convinced that distinguished writers were essential to their enterprise, and they spent vast sums importing eminent authors to California, assuming they could easily be taught how to create plot and delineate character in terms of the silent cinema. The experiment, although costly, was ultimately a failure: the writers, whose skills were verbal, not visual, were baffled by the new medium, and most were wholly unable to adapt. Eddie Knoblock, for example, in a screenplay for DeMille, went down in Hollywood legend for the unhelpful line, "Words fail to describe the scene that follows."

Maugham, although accustomed to writing dialogue for the stage, did little better. He with Gerald Haxton arrived in Hollywood in November 1920, and immediately found himself part of a group effort, obliged to listen to the director, producer, other writers, and even the actors themselves, for none of whom he had much respect: he privately referred to DeMille as "the obscene Cecil." Assuming he would be delivering stories for $15,000 to $20,000 a time, he was disappointed that the only deals he was able to make were the sale of the rights to his 1918 play, *Love in a Cottage,*★ and a $15,000 commission for a script which in the event was never used. "I look back on my connection with the cinema world with horror mitigated only by the fifteen thousand dollars," he would later tell Knoblock. Ironically, during his lifetime Maugham was to have more works adapted for film than any other writer in the language.†

★ Altered almost beyond recognition, it was released in 1922 under the title *The Ordeal*.

† At the time of this writing there have been ninety-eight versions, for film and television, of works by Somerset Maugham. His nearest rival is Conan Doyle, with ninety-three film adaptations of the Sherlock Holmes stories.

If dealing with the studio was frustrating, outside working hours there were considerable compensations. Even during Prohibition, Southern California was an agreeable place in which to pass a few weeks. In the early 1920s, Hollywood still had something of the atmosphere of a subtropical village, with small farms, lemon and orange groves, and here and there empty plots of land overgrown with sagebrush and wildflowers. Then as now, there was something surreal about the film world, about the illusion and artificiality that pervaded even everyday life, as Maugham discovered when walking down Sunset Boulevard and finding himself suddenly surrounded by cowboys and Indians or ladies of the harem. Even more bizarre was an incident that resulted in his first-ever appearance on celluloid. When out for a stroll one morning he joined a small crowd that had gathered to watch the shooting of a scene for a movie. Suddenly,

I was shoved roughly into the front of a crowd by a bullying assistant director, who yelled at me: "Look excited!" A pack of oddly garbed American bobbies were rushing pell-mell down the street. I think they called them "The Keystone Cops." So I became an actor, but without pay.

Among the many members of the film colony to whom Maugham was introduced was the comedian Charlie Chaplin, a legendary figure in Hollywood and one of the highest paid, and most famous, men in the world. Chaplin was in the process of making his first independent feature, *The Kid,* a semiautobiographical story drawing on his childhood experience of extreme poverty in the tenements and workhouses of Walworth and Lambeth. This was an area Maugham knew well from his time at St. Thomas's, and the two men formed an immediate bond, Maugham entranced by Chaplin's knockabout humor and genius for mimicry; but behind the exuberant clowning Maugham sensed a profound melancholy, a nostalgia for the life of the London slums, for a warmth and liveliness unknown in the affluent avenues of Los Angeles. One night the pair took a long walk together, two short Englishmen, dapper and dark-haired, strolling in a haze of tobacco smoke and talking, talking, as they made their way toward the poorest quarter of the city; here, among squalid row houses and dingy little shops, Chaplin's face lit up and he exclaimed in a cheerful voice, with its curious half-cockney intonation, "Say, this is the real life, isn't it? All the rest is just sham." When Sam Goldwyn gave a dinner for the first private screening of *The Kid,* Maugham was one of the guests, delighted to join in the tremendous ovation that greeted Chaplin's poignant work.

It was purely by chance that Maugham, before he left Hollywood, struck one of the most lucrative deals of his career. A fellow guest at his hotel was John Colton, a young American playwright, who one evening asked if he might borrow something to read. Maugham offered him the galley proofs of his South Seas story, "Miss Thompson," as yet unpublished, and the next morning Colton came down to breakfast in a great state of excitement, saying he had been enthralled by the story and might he please adapt it for the stage. As the piece had been rejected by a number of periodicals before its eventual acceptance by *The Smart Set,* Maugham had no great hopes for it and equably agreed to Colton's proposal: nothing to be paid for the rights, as Colton was hard up, but a fifty-fifty split on any profit. They shook hands and Maugham thought little more about it, until a few weeks later when the story appeared in the magazine and made an enormous splash, with offers coming in for film and play rights worth thousands of dollars. Whatever his private regrets, Maugham stuck by his agreement, and the following year saw Colton's play produced in New York, retitled *Rain* and with the popular star Jeanne Eagels in the lead. *Rain* was an outstanding success, running for the better part of a year on Broadway, followed by a long tour and further productions throughout the States, eventually grossing more than $3 million. The extraordinary trajectory continued, with film rights sold for $150,000 and the play staged in England in 1925 by Basil Dean at the Garrick Theatre. Dean's first choice for leading lady had been the beautiful but volatile Tallulah Bankhead, who had pursued the part with some avidity, but when Maugham attended the first two days of rehearsal he was so disappointed by Miss Bankhead's performance that he insisted she be replaced. Humiliated and furious, the actress threw a volcanic tantrum in Basil Dean's office, then flounced out of the theater, went straight back to her flat, wrote a histrionic suicide note, and swallowed a very small handful of aspirin. Fortunately she awoke next morning with no ill effects, although she left an exhausted author and director in her wake. Tallulah caused "more bother than you can imagine," Maugham reported. "She used every scrap of influence she had to sway me and when finally I put my foot down I was the object of the obloquy of all her friends." The production continued with the less well known Olga Lindo as Sadie, who gave a performance that, if reliable, was fatally lacking in sex appeal, a quality possessed in abundance by the husky-voiced Miss Bankhead. Some years later Maugham admitted that the greatest mistake of his professional life had been preventing Tallulah from appearing in *Rain*.★

AFTER THEIR STAY IN HOLLYWOOD, Maugham and Gerald Haxton left Los Angeles in February 1921, going first to San Francisco, where they spent a few days with the financier Bert Alanson, whom they had first encountered en route to Hawaii in 1916. On February 21 they sailed for Honolulu and from there to Australia before setting out on the final leg of the voyage to Singapore.

To the vast majority of his readers, Somerset Maugham has come to be associated with the latter days of the British Empire, and in particular with the British Empire in the Far East. Just as Kipling is identified with India and the Raj, so is Maugham identified with the Malayan archipelago. Those famous tales of his set on rubber estates, on remote outstations, in the card rooms of the local club, those stories of incest and adultery, of sex-starved missionaries and alcoholic planters, of footsteps in the jungle and murder on the ve-

---

★ Immediately after her well-publicized dismissal by Basil Dean the actress was cast in Noël Coward's play *Fallen Angels:* on the first night she changed her line, "Oh dear, rain" to "My God, *rain*!," which predictably brought the house down. Tallulah did finally get to play Sadie, to great acclaim, in the 1935 revival in New York.

randa, are what remain in the minds of many as the very image and epitome of Maugham's fictional territory. As Cyril Connolly once wrote,

> If all else perish, there will remain a story-teller's world from Singapore to the Marquesas that is exclusively and forever Maugham, a world of veranda and prahu which we enter, as we do that of Conan Doyle's Baker Street, with a sense of happy and eternal homecoming.

In fact Maugham spent relatively little time there, six months in 1921 and four months in 1925; but from these journeys came a couple of short-story collections, *The Casuarina Tree* and *Ah King,* which contain some of Maugham's most accomplished work, written during the years when he was roaming the world with Gerald Haxton and at his most fecund and creative.

The world that Maugham portrays in these two books is that of a still extensive empire, but an empire that had been substantially weakened by the First World War. Up to 1914 the 12 million square miles of the land on which the sun never set seemed almost impregnable, the confidence of the British in their innate superiority by and large accepted as unquestioningly by the ruled as by the rulers. As one colonial administrator put it, "Most English households of the day took it for granted that nobody could be always right, or ever quite right, except an Englishman. The Almighty was beyond doubt Anglo-Saxon [and] dominion over palm and pine . . . was the heaven-conferred privilege of the Bulldog Breed." The colonial possessions were to be administered first and foremost for the benefit of Britain, but kindly administered, naturally: "nobody but the most frightful bounder could possibly question our sincerity about that—but firmly too, my boy, firmly too, lest the school-children of Empire forget who were the prefects and who the fags." During the war, however, this image of imperial infallibility was badly cracked, and the fags were treated to the unedifying spectacle of the prefects being killed by the hundreds of thousands, indeed coming close to humiliating defeat. At the same time the prestige of the white man, of paramount importance in governing territories far too extensive to be controlled by force, was further undermined by the arrival of the cinema, revealing to audiences throughout the British-ruled part of the globe a view of the master race as variously licentious, criminal, or clownish. In an attempt to counter these regrettable influences it was decided by the governing élite that a tightening of regulations, with an increased emphasis on moral rectitude, was essential. As George Orwell, employed in the colonial civil service in Burma, wrote of this period, "A sahib has got to act like a sahib . . . it is the condition of his rule that he shall spend his life in trying to impress the 'natives.' " Inevitably such a policy resulted in strains and stresses in certain areas of expatriate society. And it was this society that provided such a fertile field for Maugham, who at the end of March 1921 landed in its midst.

At the time of Maugham and Haxton's arrival in Malaya the country was going through a period of relative prosperity, mainly due to the prewar rubber boom caused by the expansion of the motor industry in America. There was a general air of confidence and stability throughout the region, comprising the three Straits Settlements of Singapore, Penang, and Malacca, which were directly under British rule, as well as the four Federated Malay States administered by Britain, the sultanates of Selangor, Perak, Negeri Sembilan, and Pahang, with Kuala Lumpur the capital. Despite the upheavals caused by the war, there was still a general belief that British rule would last indefinitely, with the daily round continuing much as before and a standard of living, improving all the time. Even the poorest planter now ran a car in place of a pony and trap, a cold storage company had opened in Singapore, and two big modern hotels had recently gone up in Kuala Lumpur, where there were a railway station, some good shops, a cinema, tearoom, golf course, polo ground, and racetrack. The British presence was divided into two groups, the Malayan Civil Service on the one hand, and the professional and technical departments on the other, with the former in social terms considering itself a definite cut above the latter: a large proportion of the MCS, which in the upper echelons provided the ruling class of Residents and District Officers, were products of the major public schools and universities, whereas most of the rest, planters, tin miners, doctors, engineers, were not. Maugham in his notebook described the attitude of planters toward government officials as "a combination of awe, envy, contempt and petulance." Such a situation naturally gave rise to a certain amount of divisiveness and insecurity, and there was a good deal of competitive talk about which school one had gone to, one's regiment, and one's relations back home; a titled family connection, however distant, was universally accepted as the trump card.

The European settlement of the FMS, predominantly British, was extremely sparse: on some of the more isolated rubber estates a planter could go for months, years even, without seeing another white face. The mail arrived by river once a month, bringing letters and books, as well as magazines and newspapers that were at least six weeks out of date. To some, like Mr. Warburton in *The Outstation,* it was a matter of vital importance that despite his solitude standards should be rigidly maintained:

> Most people living in out-of-the-way places when the mail comes tear open impatiently their papers and taking the last ones first glance at the latest news from home. Not so Mr. Warburton. His newsagent had instructions to write on the outside of the wrapper the date of each paper he dispatched. . . . His head-boy's orders were to place one on the table every morning in the veranda with the early cup of tea and it was Mr Warburton's especial delight to break the wrapper as he sipped his tea, and read the morning paper. It gave him the illusion of living at home. Every Monday morning he read the Monday *Times* of six weeks back, and so went through the week. On Sunday he read the *Observer.* Like his habit of dressing for dinner it was a tie to civilization.

Even in the towns the expatriate population was small, which intensified the strong sense of community, the conscious desire to stick together and to reproduce as nearly as possible the way of life as it had been lived back home. Nearly every little town boasted its

Anglican church, its cricket pitch and mock-Tudor tavern, and the wives, the memsahibs, went to great lengths to teach their Chinese cooks how to make bread sauce, parsley stuffing, Welsh rarebit, and steak-and-kidney pie. However hot and steamy the weather, in bungalows throughout the colony breakfast was tea, porridge, and bacon and eggs or kippers, followed by toast and marmalade; a typical dinner consisted of tomato soup, cold asparagus smothered in bottled salad dressing, roast chicken (invariably overcooked), mashed potatoes, and tinned peas, with tinned fruit salad for dessert.

At the heart of all expatriate social life was the club. It was here that the locals gathered in the cool of the evening to talk and play tennis and generally relax among themselves, relieved of the effort of maintaining the dignified demeanor the white man was expected to adopt in his dealings with the native. Offices closed at 4:00 P.M., which allowed for a couple of hours of golf or tennis before the sun set, after which the men, changed out of their sports clothes or their shorts and sun helmets, congregated in the bar. Here, served by white-coated servants in scarlet sashes, they downed a few stiff drinks, a couple of *pahit*s (gin and bitters), or two or three good *stengah*s (whisky and soda), while on the veranda their mems smoked, gossiped, complained about the heat and their servants, and leafed through newly arrived issues of *Punch, The Lady,* and *The Illustrated London News.* A perennial topic was "home" and where to live when the time came to retire. Home leave was granted every five or six years, passionately looked forward to but often a disappointment in the event. For months people excitedly planned what they were going to do: London, with its shops, theaters, restaurants—they were going to have the time of their lives! But frequently after a couple of weeks,

> they were more lonely than in the jungle. It was a relief when at a theatre they ran across someone they had known in the East . . . and they could fix up an evening together and have a good laugh and tell one another what a grand time they were having.

No such dissatisfactions would be admitted, of course, once back at the club. In Kuala Lumpur there were three clubs, the biggest, the Selangor, possessing a billiard room, card room (almost everybody played bridge), reading and tiffin (luncheon) rooms, a hairdresser and barber, and two bars, from one of which women were excluded. There were weekly dances to music provided by a windup gramophone, occasional fancy dress balls, and jolly amateur dramatics and smoking concerts, with classical music on the whole avoided but lots of songs from the current West End shows enthusiastically performed by fellows who had recently returned from London on leave. Most evenings the Resident dropped in for a game of cards, and at regular intervals gave an official dinner party at the Residency, where, in tropical temperatures, the men in stiff shirts and tails, the women in long dresses, ate their roast beef and Yorkshire pudding to the strains of a medley from Gilbert and Sullivan played by a regimental band on the veranda. "They are bored with themselves, bored with one another," was Maugham's impression. "They look forward to their freedom from bondage and yet the future fills them with dismay."

Although the colony prided itself on maintaining a high level of racial harmony, there was on the whole little interest in indigenous customs or culture. In the FMS, members of the non-European population were generally referred to as "natives" or "Asiatics," usually in a tone of vague contempt, although any incident of maltreatment of a native by a white man was severely frowned upon. Social interaction was rare, except with the local sultans, who were treated with due deference as their willing cooperation was essential to the imperial purpose. For people of mixed race the situation was especially tricky. Whereas a blind eye was turned to white men visiting brothels and using native prostitutes, it was very definitely not done to appear in public with a Eurasian or Asian woman on your arm. Interracial marriages were vigorously discouraged, and half-castes had a difficult time of it, accepted as equals by neither one side nor the other. Eurasians spoke English with an accent known as "chee-chee," regarded as comical by Europeans, and many went to considerable lengths to conceal their racial origins. Such a one is Izzart in *The Yellow Streak*. An old Harrovian, handsome and stylish, member of a distinguished regiment during the war, Izzart has a shameful secret: his mother is of mixed blood. His insecurity on this account and his desperate anxiety to conceal his origins are brilliantly delineated by Maugham:

> [Izzart] wondered whether by any chance the men at Kuala Solor with whom he was so hail fellow well met suspected that he had native blood in him. He knew very well what to expect if they ever found out. They wouldn't say he was gay and friendly then, they would say he was damned familiar; and they would say he was inefficient and careless, as the half-castes were, and when he talked of marrying a white woman they would snigger.

If it was tacitly accepted that white men consorted with native women, the subject, if not the practice, of interracial homosexuality was taboo, this despite the fact that a career in the colonies attracted an unusually high proportion of men who had good reason for wishing to avoid marriage at home. It was unspoken but well known that opportunities for a wide variety of casual sex were far greater overseas than in Britain, and the Far East in particular was seen as offering unparalleled largesse. As soon as an Englishman was east of Suez a new world opened before him, from the *terrassiers,* the boys working the hotel terraces in Cairo and Port Said, to the all-male brothels of Karachi and Tientsin, the easy acceptance of homosexual practices in Siam, and the willing youth of Peshawar on the northwest frontier, where it was said that "to get a boy was easier than to pick flowers by the wayside." Much the same liberal sexual climate existed in the FMS, and Maugham used to say that the most memorable sexual experience of his life had been a moonlit night on a sampan with a boy in Malaya.

Within the British administration of the Malay States, a notable exception to the policy of racial separateness had existed before the war in the custom of concubinage, of white men living with Malay or Chinese mistresses, a custom that had of necessity been widely accepted, as so few European women had been prepared to endure the hardships of life in the East. But in the prosperous postwar period the situation began to change, with more and more men bringing their wives out from home. These were often unsophisticated young women who were ignorant of the world into which they were now introduced, and for some, the discovery that their husbands had had an Asian mistress, and sometimes children, came as a profound shock. Naturally such a state of affairs was meat and drink to Maugham, always intensely interested in sexual relationships, and he describes exactly such an instance in *The Force of Circumstance*. Doris, newly wed and only recently arrived in Malaya, is blissfully happy with her husband, Guy, and entranced by the exotic surroundings in which she finds herself on their remote outstation. The best part of the day is when Guy returns from his work in the courthouse, and after a game of tennis they sit companionably together looking out at the peaceful river and at the palm trees on the opposite bank:

> The blinds on the verandah were raised now and on the table between their two long chairs were bottles and soda-water. This was the hour at which they had the first drink of the day and Guy mixed a couple of gin slings. . . . He took her hand and pressed it.
> "Are you happy here, darling?"
> "Desperately."
> She looked very cool and fresh in her linen frock.

Gradually, however, Doris begins to be disturbed by the menacing presence of one of the native women from the kampong, who with her three half-caste children has taken to hanging around outside the bungalow. When she asks Guy about her he at first prevaricates, before finally admitting that the woman had been his mistress for ten years and that the children are his. Doris is appalled. Unable to overcome her revulsion, she tells Guy the marriage is over and that she must return to England. Guy pleads with her, but as nothing he says has any effect, he has no choice but to agree, while knowing

that Doris's departure will break his heart. And yet he is not to be
left entirely unconsoled. As he sits alone after seeing his wife off to
Singapore a small boy sidles into the room.

> It was the elder of his two sons.
> "What do you want?" said Guy. . . .
> "My mother sent me. She says, do you want anything?"
> Guy looked at the boy intently. . . .
> "Tell your mother to pack up her things and yours. She
> can come back."
> "When?" asked the boy impassively. . . .
> "To-night."

Yet if the men were fallible, so, too, were the women. Men who
brought wives with them to the tropics "had real trouble on their
hands," according to Maugham. "White women were scarce, and
bachelors were fair game to the neglected wives of overworked civil
servants or planters." Part of the trouble was boredom. With their
husbands out all day, the mems had almost nothing to do, unless they
were among the few prepared to interest themselves in local charities
or community work. Many found themselves enjoying a far higher
standard of living than they had been used to at home, with even the
lowest-grade civil servant allotted a spacious bungalow and four or
five servants to look after him. Thus domestic responsibilities were
few, and as it was not done for a mem to go to market herself, almost
her only duty was to order the meals, leaving hours to fill until her
husband came home. As a handbook of the period explained,

> The chief disadvantage for ladies is often the lack of interest-
> ing occupation during the day. In the larger towns, where
> there are European stores, it is possible for a lady to go shop-
> ping during the morning, or to visit friends, but in the smaller
> stations or on estates or mines, life is apt to be monotonous.
> The climate is unsuited to housework, and too much sewing
> or reading may have its effect on the eyesight. A lady will
> therefore often find that time hangs heavily on her hands. . . .

Not unnaturally, love affairs were regarded by some as a welcome diversion—if few ended as badly as that of Mrs. Proudlock, wife of a schoolmaster in Kuala Lumpur. In 1911 Ethel Proudlock was charged with murder, having shot dead William Steward, manager of a tin mine in Salak, who she claimed had turned up one evening when her husband was out and tried to rape her. The court, however, was unpersuaded by her account, concluding that Steward had been her lover whom she had killed in a jealous rage after discovering he was living with a Chinese mistress. Mrs. Proudlock was sentenced to hang, but after an impassioned petition had been signed by friends and supporters, she was eventually granted a free pardon by the sultan.

It was Mrs. Proudlock's lawyer, E.A.S. Wagner, who in Kuala Lumpur ten years later described the case to Maugham. Immediately alert to its possibilities, Maugham constructed a fictional version, "The Letter," in which he keeps fairly closely to the framework of events as described in court but adds an ingredient of his own. In the real case no concrete evidence was found of an intimate relationship between Mrs. Proudlock and Steward, but in the story a letter is produced, written by Leslie Crosbie, that leaves little room for doubt that Hammond was her lover. Up to that moment her lawyer had been convinced she had nothing to worry about and that he would have no trouble in establishing her innocence. But the letter changes all that: she is guilty, and unless this damning evidence is destroyed she will be convicted. The incriminating document is in the hands of Hammond's Chinese mistress; the Chinese woman is prepared to sell, but only for an outrageous sum, and the lawyer has no choice but to ask for the money from Leslie's nice, stupid, utterly trusting husband, who has never for one moment doubted his wife's virtue. When he hears the sum required, a terrible realization begins to take hold.

> Crosbie grew very red. His mouth sagged strangely.
> "But . . ." he could not find the words, his face now was purple. "But I don't understand . . . You don't mean to say they'd find her guilty?" . . .

Then something seemed to dawn in that slow intelligence of his.

"The Letter," which first appeared in *Hearst's International* in 1924 before its publication two years later in *The Casuarina Tree,* was to become one of Maugham's best-known short stories, mainly thanks to its stage and screen adaptations.* Ironically, the one part of the world where it was not popular at all was in Malaya. A member of the Malayan Civil Service who arrived in the country shortly afterward wrote of Maugham's passage through the FMS that "[it] was clearly marked by a trail of angry people. The indignation aroused by his play, *The Letter,* . . . was still being voiced in emotional terms when I came by. It was also charged against him that he abused hospitality by ferreting out the family skeletons of his hosts and putting them into his books." Other, similar accusations followed, and Maugham was so stung by them that for the American edition of *The Casuarina Tree* he added a tetchy postscript in self-defense:

> Some of the smaller communities in the countries washed by the China Sea are very sensitive, and their members are much agitated if, in a work of fiction, a hint is given that the circumstances of their lives are not always such as would meet the approval of the suburban circles in which contentedly dwell their cousins and their aunts. . . . [But] because a reader, unprofitably employing a useless leisure, recognises in a character one trait, mental or physical, of someone he knows and is aware the author has met, it is silly to put the name of this person to the character described and say: here is a portrait.

Such a surly tone was unlikely to soothe hurt feelings, and more than a decade later, resentment at Maugham's depiction of the

---

* Maugham himself dramatized it for a production at the Playhouse in 1927, with Gladys Cooper playing Leslie Crosbie; in 1929 there was a silent-screen version with Jeanne Eagels, and in 1940 the famous Warner Bros. film directed by William Wyler with Bette Davis in the lead.

colony was still rumbling around the FMS. "It is interesting to try to analyze the prejudice against Somerset Maugham which is so intense and widespread in this part of the world," began an article in *The Straits Budget* in June 1938.

> The usual explanation is that Mr. Maugham picks up some local scandal at an out-station and dishes it up as a short story. . . . The second cause is disgust at the way Mr. Maugham has explained the worst and least representative aspects of European life in Malaysia—murder, cowardice, drink, seduction, adultery. . . . always the same cynical emphasis on the same unpleasant things. No wonder that white men and women who are living normal lives in Malaysia wish that Mr. Maugham would look for local colour elsewhere.

At first taken aback, in time Maugham grew relatively indifferent to such accusations, to local fury over those "masterpieces of disloyalty and betrayal," as they were regarded by many decent, uxorious, well-meaning servants of empire. Maugham never denied that he traveled in order to find stories or that the stories he found formed the foundation of his tales. Most of his characters were based on real people, as he admitted:

> I tried to make use of them, and their problems, as capably as I knew how. That I didn't portray them, or their emotional circumstances, as attractively as they imagined them to be, earned me, of course, considerable criticism and hatred. On my return visits to many of those places a lot of doors were rudely slammed in my face, I was publicly insulted, and some even threatened to do me bodily harm. But I learned to accept all that. . . .

Both he and Gerald were good listeners, adept at drawing people out, and time and again discovered for themselves the truth of the observation that people talk to strangers in a way they never would to family and friends. While in a bar, or on a club veranda, or staying upcountry with some lonely District Officer, Maugham heard the extraordinary dramas in these seemingly ordinary lives: "sitting over a siphon or two and a bottle of whisky [within] the radius of an acetylene lamp . . . a man has told me stories about himself that I was sure he had never told to a living soul. . . . I have in this way learned more about men in a night than I could have if I had known them for ten years." It was thus he learned of the incestuous affair between brother and sister that he describes in "The Book-Bag"; the case of the alcoholic husband murdered by his wife in "Before the Party" was inspired by a couple he met at dinner one evening in Singapore; the basis of "The Force of Circumstance," of a wife's discovery of her husband's illegitimate half-caste children, was told him by a trader staying in the same upcountry rest house; while it was Gerald who heard about the scandal that was to reappear as "Footprints in the Jungle." The two men were in Sumatra, and Maugham had arranged to meet Haxton for dinner, but as usual Gerald had lingered in the bar drinking, and Maugham, tired of being kept waiting, began eating on his own. Just as he was finishing, Gerald lurched into the dining room. "I'm sorry, I'm sorry," he said. "I know I'm drunk, but I've got a corking good story for you," and out came the shocking sequence of events surrounding "the Cartwrights," as they appear in the story, who on the face of it had seemed just another nice elderly couple innocently enjoying a few rubbers of bridge during their evening at the club.

It is at the end of the postscript to *The Casuarina Tree,* while he was still smarting from the first accusations of betrayal, that Maugham, with a bold disregard for the facts, states that of the six stories in the collection, only one, "The Yellow Streak," was based on an actual incident, and that, he says pointedly, "was suggested by a misadventure of my own." "Misadventure" is putting it mildly, for what happened very nearly cost him his life.

IN MARCH 1921, Maugham and Haxton had arrived in Singapore, where they collected their mail, explored the city, and made the most of their letters of introduction. Singapore, one of the great ports of the East and seat of the governor of the Straits Settlements, was very different in character from the rest of the country, crowded, noisy, exotic, and morally lax. The city was half Asian— largely Chinese—and half European—predominantly British. The Asian city with its bustling street life, its open-air workshops, its markets and food stalls, temples, teahouses, and opium dens, stood in close proximity to the European district of luxury hotels, includ- ing the famous Raffles, of department stores, restaurants, and nightclubs, of huge imperial buildings housing government offices, of parks and public gardens, and of the expensive residential areas inhabited by rich Westerners and by even richer Chinese, who con- trolled most of the more profitable businesses. It was here in Singa- pore that Maugham smoked his first pipe of opium, the immediate effect a feeling of great peace and clarity of mind, unfortunately followed next morning by a cracking headache and hours of noisy retching.

From Singapore, Maugham and Haxton traveled the length and breadth of the Peninsula, staying sometimes in hotels and rest houses, sometimes with a Resident or DO, or, less comfortably, on remote outstations or rubber estates: compared to the relative lux- ury of official residencies, planters' houses, Maugham noted, were "a bit dreary, a lot of gimcrack furniture and silver ornaments and tiger skins. And the food's uneatable." They sailed widely about the is- lands of the archipelago and beyond, often taking passage on board the pearling luggers that plied their trade throughout the South Pa- cific, voyaging to Merauke in New Guinea, to Banda and the Kai Islands, to Mobiag and Thursday Island in the Torres Straits. Partic- ularly memorable was their visit to Sarawak, on the north coast of Borneo. Here in the kingdom of the white rajahs, the only oriental kingdom in world history to be ruled by an English dynasty, they were entertained by the rajah himself, the very handsome, very En- glish Vyner Brooke, whose wife, Sylvia, was the sister of the painter Dorothy Brett, a close friend of D. H. Lawrence. Anxious to ex- plore, Maugham and Haxton set off on an expedition up the Skrang River, traveling by canoe with a crew of Dayak boatmen. They themselves reclined comfortably beneath an awning, enjoying the peace and beauty of the scene, of white egrets flying low over the dark green water, of the sandy banks lined with feathery casuarinas, and beyond, sloping uphill, the jungle dense with acacia and coconut palms. Every evening they tied up by a Dayak village, spending the night in one of the thatched longhouses, each inhabited by several families, twenty to thirty people, all intensely, exhaustingly hospitable, with feasting and dancing every night that continued into the small hours.

One day while slowly moving upriver they suddenly saw an enormous tidal wave approaching, a bore, roaring toward them and rapidly increasing in volume until with a rush a great wall of water eight feet high burst over them, capsizing the canoe and throwing them into the water. Desperately, Maugham and Haxton tried to hang on to the side of the boat, but it was impossible to get a grip, and with the wave surging and storming around them, they were repeatedly submerged. Before long, Maugham, bruised, exhausted, and gasping for air, felt his strength go and knew he was in imminent danger of drowning. "I thought the best thing was to make a dash for the bank, but Gerald begged me to try to hold on. . . . I swallowed a good deal of water. . . . Gerald stayed near me and two or three times gave me a hand." After several further minutes of struggle, they heard a shout from one of the crew, who had caught hold of a thin mattress as it floated past, and with this to support them they managed to reach land. Their feet sinking into thick mud, they pulled themselves ashore and somehow succeeded in scrambling up the bank, collapsing into the tall grass at the top. Here they lay motionless for quite a while, covered in mud and too exhausted to move, until Maugham eventually summoned the strength to get up and strip off his filthy clothes, making a loincloth out of his shirt. It was then he saw to his horror that Gerald in attempting to rise had collapsed and appeared to be in the throes of a heart attack. "I thought he was going to die," Maugham recalled. There was no help at hand and nothing to be done. For what seemed like hours Maugham sat beside his lover, soothing him and talking to him, telling him that the pain would pass and everything would be all right. Eventually help arrived, and the two exhausted men were taken by canoe to a longhouse, where slowly they recovered. In retrospect Maugham was surprised that he had felt no fear, although he was intensely glad to find himself still alive. "Later in the evening when I was sitting in a dry sarong in the Dayak house and from it saw the yellow moon lying on her back it gave me a keen, almost a sensual pleasure."

For the first day or two Maugham and Haxton felt so happy at their escape that nothing else seemed to matter. But soon they began to fret for all those personal possessions that had gone to the bottom of the river and decided to return to Singapore to refit. From here in mid-August they set out again, this time to Java, where the intention was to stay for a few weeks before starting on the long voyage home. But weeks turned into months, for it was on Java that Gerald, still weak after his near-drowning, fell seriously ill with typhoid and had to be moved to a sanatorium at Garoet on the south coast. Maugham, too, was unwell, with an attack of colitis, and so they remained in the pleasant little hill town while Gerald underwent his treatment, Maugham perfectly happy as long as he could spend hours a day reading. Throughout his life Maugham referred to his love of reading as an addiction; it was, he explained "a necessity, and if I am deprived of it for a little while I find myself as irritable as the addict deprived of his drug"; wherever he was he took care to be well supplied with books, on his travels always taking a trunkful with him. But now, staying on so much longer than planned, he found to his dismay that he had nothing left, and that the only literature locally available that was not in Dutch was school textbook editions of Goethe, La Fontaine, and Racine. "I have the greatest admiration for Racine," he wrote later, "but I admit that to read his plays one after the other requires a certain effort." It was as a result of this experience that Maugham resolved never again to risk running out: he purchased a bookbag, a large canvas sack with a leather base, cumbersome but capacious, that from then on, filled to the brim, accompanied him on all his travels.

IT WAS WHILE STILL on Java that in October 1921 Maugham received some bad news. His broker in New York, Trippe & Co., had suddenly failed, with the loss of a considerable portion of his savings. "I am dreadfully put out about it," he complained, "because I had been saving all I could so as to put myself in such a position that I would never write for money again." He turned to his friend Bert Alanson, asking if he could recommend a reliable stockbroking firm in the United States, and Alanson at once offered to manage the portfolio himself: he had already made a few investments on Maugham's behalf and now suggested that he should take on the rest, working without commission as an expression of his admiration and affection. Alanson was also glad to repay a favor Maugham had done him while he was in Russia in 1917, cabling a coded warning about the fall of the rouble (AUNTIE RACHEL VERY ILL) which had saved Alanson a small fortune. Maugham for his part was grateful for Alanson's offer, although he had little idea how grateful he would have cause to be. For the next thirty-six years, from 1922 until his death in 1958, Alanson made Maugham a very rich man, turning the dividend checks that were regularly sent him into a substantial fortune. For Maugham as he grew older, money, and amassing vast quantities of it, was to become increasingly important on a number of levels: it gave him personal and artistic freedom, it allowed him to be generous when he chose and to buy silence when necessary; and the knowledge that he could afford the best of everything compensated him, up to a point, for other, less material deprivations in his youth. Money was a highly emotive area of his life in which Bert Alanson was intimately involved, giving their friendship a depth and texture it might not otherwise have possessed. Alanson was one of the few people in whom Maugham had complete trust, and his gratitude and reliance never wavered. "You are a wonderful friend," he told him in February 1921 after staying with him on his way to the Far East, and nearly thirty years later the theme was much the same. "You were as ever wonderfully good to me," Maugham wrote in 1949, "& I can never hope to repay all the care you have taken of me for so many years except by giving you my deep & sincere affection."

In the event, the failure of Trippe & Co. was not as disastrous as first appeared, and by the following year Maugham had recovered about two-thirds of his original losses. In addition, during his absence abroad a new comedy had been produced that was proving an impressive money-spinner. *The Circle,* opening on March 3, 1921, at the Haymarket, had run for nearly six months, doing excellent business, before being staged in New York in September, where it was bringing in $20,000* a week and collecting a sheaf of adulatory reviews from some highly influential critics. Well received at the time, its popularity continued to grow on both sides of the Atlantic throughout the playwright's lifetime, the American Louis Kronenberger in 1952 describing *The Circle* as "one of the very few creditable high comedies written in English in the twentieth century," while the British James Agate wrote of "this brilliant playwright" that "his technique is flawless and *The Circle* is his best play."

The Circle is a highly polished, expertly structured piece that deals with the difficulties of the survival of love within marriage, with the pressures of society, and with the triumph of character over circumstance. The action takes place in a large house in Dorset, where Arnold Champion-Cheney and his pretty young wife, Elizabeth, are expecting the arrival of Arnold's mother and her lover. Thirty years ago Lady Kitty scandalized society by running off to Italy with Lord Porteous, a married man, with whom she has been living in sin ever since. Arnold is apprehensive, still resentful at his mother's abandoning him, but Elizabeth is thrilled by the romantic love story of lovely Lady Kitty and the glamorous peer and can hardly wait to meet them. All are taken aback when the couple walk in, she an idiotic chatterbox with heavily painted face and dyed hair, he a bald, bad-tempered old man complaining about his rheumatism; it is quite clear the two are badly on each

* Approximately 10 percent of this sum would go to the playwright.

other's nerves and hardly able to exchange a civil word. Their example is not lost on Elizabeth, who had herself been intending to leave her husband and run off with a lover. Lady Kitty, when she learns of the plan, makes an impassioned speech imploring Elizabeth to stay, describing her own unhappy experience of life outside the pale. "One sacrifices one's life for love and then one finds that love doesn't last. The tragedy of love isn't death or separation. . . . The tragedy of love is indifference." In the end, however, the young lovers remain resolute and succeed in making their escape, aided in a surprising reversal by Kitty and Porteous, who underneath all the snapping and snarling are shown still to have a true fondness for each other.

In many ways *The Circle* offers a curious premise for a comedy, a fusion of romance and reality, with a bleak message underneath the frequently very funny dialogue. There is real cruelty, particularly in the exchanges between Porteous and Kitty, and little comfort to be found in any of it. When the young lovers go off together in the final scene the audience is left not knowing whether they are looking at a happy ending, a lack of resolution that on the first night attracted some boos from the gallery and that encouraged several critics to accuse the author of cynicism, an accusation with which Maugham was to grow wearily familiar. In reviewing the play both Frank Swinnerton and St. John Ervine described the cynical tendency as a flaw, although the more perceptive Desmond MacCarthy recognized it as the vital driving force behind Maugham's comedic gift, "[a] gift [that] sprang from a clear-sighted, hard-edged cynicism, rare in English writers. . . . *The Circle* is one of the best plays he has yet written [and] it is one of the most cynical."

Despite a few critical reservations, the play was a huge hit, and Maugham was relieved to be able to tell Golding Bright that *The Circle*'s popularity had restored his financial independence. Maugham's reputation had been further enhanced while abroad by the publication in Britain and America of his short-story collection *The Trembling of a Leaf*. Predictably, "Rain" was singled out as the most remarkable, but as the *Saturday Review* put it, "each separate tale is begun by inspiration and completed by artistic perfection." It was an age in which the form was popular, and the author was grat-ified by his enormous sales. "My short stories have been a very great success here & everyone is being very nice to me," he wrote to Bert Alanson, admitting that he was enjoying being lionized. Maugham found it a strange experience to return after such a long absence, away from England for over a year, and find everyone doing and saying much the same as when he had left. The first time he dropped in at the Garrick one of the members greeted him with, "'Hulloa, Maugham, have you been away?' 'Yes,' I said, 'I've been to Brighton for the week-end.' 'Ah,' he answered, 'I thought I hadn't seen you about lately.'"

Not everything had stayed the same, however, and Maugham had been grieved to learn of the death of his publisher, William Heine-mann. Heinemann at only fifty-seven had died of a heart attack in October 1920, less than three weeks after Maugham had left England. With no obvious successor in line, the firm had been stranded until Heinemann's associate director had managed to do a deal with the New York publisher F. N. Doubleday, persuading him to buy a controlling interest in the business while leaving the English com-pany intact. Doubleday, a powerful, charismatic figure, with many prominent English writers on his list, Kipling among them, had taken his son, Nelson, into the company, and it was Nelson Doubleday, a big, energetic, sporty young man, who was to form not only a close professional connection but a lifetime's friendship with Maugham.

Within a few months of Maugham's return from abroad his agent, J. B. Pinker, had also died unexpectedly, in February 1922 while on a business trip to the States. The two men had always en-joyed cordial relations and Maugham had been grateful to Pinker, who had done well for his client in the early days of their associa-tion; however, as Maugham by now was at least as well known in America as in Britain, he decided to put his business into the hands of an American agent, Charles Hanson Towne. Towne, regarded by Maugham as "one of the most agreeable persons I know in New York," was a very different type, an engaging, sophisticated man of letters, a novelist, poet, magazine editor, and columnist, a consider-able celebrity in bookish circles in Manhattan.

With the success of *The Circle* and *The Trembling of a Leaf*, Maugham was very much in the public eye, immediately swept up in an energetic round of entertaining and being entertained. He was also eager to catch up with old friends such as Walpole, Knoblock, and Kelly. Gerald Kelly, who by this period was making a good living in fashionable portraiture, had recently married, his wife, Lilian (always known as Jane), a blond and beautiful working-class girl who had been one of his models. Maugham had been delighted by the match. "I think you have done a very clever thing & I am sure you will make a great success of it, & be very happy," he had told him, recognizing that Jane's gentleness and calm would provide the necessary counterbalance to Kelly's high-strung, restless nature. Next to Kelly, Knoblock and Walpole were the friends to whom Maugham was closest. Eddie Knoblock, sweet-natured and gregarious, led a somewhat precarious professional existence, and when penury threatened, as it frequently did, he returned to Hollywood to write film scripts and recoup. Walpole, on the other hand, was going from strength to strength, popular as a novelist, a distinguished member of the literary establishment, living in an expensive flat in Piccadilly, and reveling in a glamorous if frustrating affair with the Danish tenor Lauritz Melchior. While nervous of his friend's slightly barbed teasing, Hugh nevertheless admired Maugham and craved his good opinion. The two met frequently, with Hugh eagerly noting in his diary any words of praise let drop by the older man.

A new acquaintance made at this time was with the American novelist Sinclair Lewis, over from the States on a visit to London. Lewis had become famous with the publication two years earlier of his novel *Main Street,* a work that had fascinated Maugham, with its detailed depiction of small-town life in the Middle West. During his frequent train journeys across America, Maugham had seen men of exactly this background lounging about the smoking car, "in their ill-fitting, ready-made clothes, gaudy shirts and showy ties . . . they were as strange to me as the Chinese and more impenetrable." Now having read *Main Street* he felt he understood something about them and was eager to talk to the author, inviting him to dinner at

Wyndham Place. The occasion turned out to be somewhat uncomfortable. To meet Lewis, Maugham had asked Eddie Knoblock, the painters Ambrose McEvoy* and Christopher Nevinson, the playwright and critic St. John Ervine, Osbert Sitwell, Hugh Walpole, and that exquisitely refined connoisseur and patron of the arts, Eddie Marsh. Syrie as hostess was the only woman, but even her presence failed to restrain Lewis, the guest of honor, from becoming wildly overexcited, in the words of Nevinson,

> restless, clownish, and intense. . . . Never have I met a man so sensitive and yet with such a gift of putting his foot in it. . . . After dinner, Sinclair Lewis took Eddie Marsh's monocle, stuck it in his own eye, and began parading up and down with Eddie Marsh following like a dog on a string. Then, to amuse himself, he parodied high-brow conversation in the best Oxford manner, at times imitating McEvoy's cracked voice. . . . All of us were embarrassed, as the parody was grotesquely realistic.

Eventually, to Maugham's relief, Nevinson rescued the situation by taking Lewis off to a nightclub.

The monocled Eddie Marsh was a relative newcomer in the group that evening at Wyndham Place, but in years to come he would play a unique role in Maugham's career. Only two years older than Maugham, Marsh, once described as a cross between Puck and Mme de Maintenon, was a man of impressive erudition, with a double first in classics at Cambridge and an extraordinarily retentive memory, particularly for poetry, of which given the slightest encouragement he would recite reams in his thin, slightly squeaky voice. Editor of the much-admired five-volume anthology *Georgian Poetry,* he was also a connoisseur of contemporary painting, and although of modest means had assembled an important collection of

---

* In the account of the dinner party in Nevinson's diary no first name is given for McEvoy: the probability is that it was Ambrose McEvoy, though it could have been the playwright Charles McEvoy.

works by artists such as Mark Gertler, Duncan Grant, Stanley Spencer, and Paul Nash. By profession Marsh was a civil servant and for nearly twenty years held the post of private secretary to Winston Churchill. The first letter extant from Maugham to Marsh, written in 1919, is a note of thanks for services unspecified—"My dear Marsh," Maugham had written, "Thank you very much *indeed*. I am very grateful indeed for what you have done for me"—most probably a reference to Marsh's using his influence with Churchill in obtaining an imprimatur for the Ashenden stories. Nattily dressed and insatiably social, Marsh led an impeccable bachelor existence, much given to romantic attachments to gifted and beautiful young men, Rupert Brooke being one, the actor and composer Ivor Novello another. It was through following Novello's career that Marsh had developed a passion for the theater, present at every first night, madly enthusiastic no matter how terrible the play. "Heavens!" exclaimed James Agate one evening when Marsh had loudly clapped a player's exit only minutes after the rise of the curtain, "you *can't* be enjoying it *already*!" With his scholar's mind and sharp eye for error, Marsh as a hobby had started correcting proofs for writer friends, most notably for Churchill himself, as well as for Desmond MacCarthy, Harold Nicolson, Walter de la Mare, Dorothy L. Sayers, A. A. Milne, and eventually Somerset Maugham.

AT HOME MAUGHAM WAS relieved to find that relations with Syrie were calmer and more amicable than at any time during the marriage so far. There was good reason for this: Syrie had found something to do. Bored and restless while her husband was away, she had decided to follow a bent for interior decoration, with the aim of eventually establishing herself in business. She was fortunate in her timing: up until 1914 it was almost unheard of for a respectable lady to go into retail, with interior design the preserve of the big stores such as Fortnum & Mason, Liberty's, Whiteley's, and Waring & Gillow. But with the postwar economic decline a number of ladies had set up in trade, opening smart little shops selling hats or dresses or ornamental knickknacks, thus bringing about an important change in attitude. (An article in *Vogue* commenting on this trend began, "Someone once said that a woman is either happily married or an Interior Decorator. . . .") When installed by Gordon Selfridge in York Terrace, Syrie had employed a designer, Ernest Thornton-Smith, head of the antiques department at Fortnum's, and it was Thornton-Smith to whom she now turned, asking him to take her on as an unpaid apprentice to teach her about furniture and restoration, how to deal with customers, and all the invaluable little tricks of the trade. It quickly became apparent that Syrie had found her vocation, not only in décor but as a businesswoman, tough, tenacious, and with a keen eye for a bargain; and in 1922 with borrowed capital of £400 she opened a shop, Syrie Ltd., at 85 Baker Street. Stocked initially with the contents of the house in Regent's Park, Syrie Ltd. was an immediate success, its proprietor delighting in the process of buying and selling, of attending auctions and picking up cheaply pieces that could be cleaned up, cleverly embellished, and sold at a handsome profit.

Over the next two decades the name Syrie Maugham was to become synonymous with elegant modernity. Her artistry and sense of style were to make a considerable impact on interior decoration in both Britain and the United States, with her famous all-white rooms copied widely, from Mayfair to Manhattan. "With the strength of a typhoon," wrote the photographer Cecil Beaton, "[Syrie] blew all colour before her . . . turning the world white. . . . White sheepskin rugs were strewn on the eggshell-surface floors, huge white sofas were flanked with white crackled-paint tables, white peacock feathers were put in white vases against a white wall." Syrie was even paid the compliment of being caricatured by Evelyn Waugh: in *A Handful of Dust* there are undeniable similarities between Syrie and the ruthless Mrs. Beaver, who desecrates the Gothic gloom of Hetton Abbey with natural sheepskin and white chromium plating. Syrie's emphasis on neutral color and the importance of space was regarded as exciting and new, especially in England, where the prevailing taste tended toward violently contrasting schemes in black and orange, or else tea-cozy travesties of Tudor design complete with bogus beams and inglenooks. Syrie made a workshop for herself in one of Liza's nurseries where she could practice her techniques, and soon she was pickling and bleaching tables and chairs and stripping the black lacquer off Coromandel screens with a gusto that delighted her clients and provoked shocked accusations of vandalism from the more traditional sections of the trade.

If not altogether pleased to find his wife running a shop, Maugham was relieved that Syrie's formidable energies had found an outlet other than in marital rows. And he had always admired her flair for color and design. "She has exquisite taste," he wrote in his notebook in 1922, before going on to list further good qualities:

> She is clever. She has charm. . . . She is generous and will spend her own money, to the last penny, as freely as she will spend other people's. She is hospitable. . . . In sickness she will show herself an admirable and devoted nurse. She is a gay and pleasant talker. Her greatest gift is her capacity for sympathy. She will listen to your troubles with genuine commiseration and with unfeigned kindliness will do everything she can to relieve them. . . . There is real goodness in her.

But on the other side of the coin,

> She is not only a liar, she is a mythomaniac. . . . She is grasping and will hesitate at no dishonesty to get what she wants. She is a snob. . . . She is vindictive, jealous and envious. She is a quarrelsome bully. She is vain, vulgar and ostentatious. There is real badness in her.

At this period, however, the good appeared to outweigh the bad, and while he did not entirely approve, Maugham did nothing to stop his wife's new venture. It is telling that Syrie had not turned to her wealthy husband for the capital to fund it, preferring instead to borrow from friends, less as a statement of independence than from a conviction that he would almost certainly refuse her. For when it came to his wife, Maugham kept a tight hand on the purse strings; her willful extravagance infuriated him, and refusing her money was an effective method of punishment and control. He gave her a generous annual allowance of £3,000 for clothes and personal expenses, which she was always exceeding, and her profligacy in housekeeping drove him to distraction: the gallons of cream, the case upon case of champagne, the enormous numbers of dishes prepared, never eaten, and then thrown away. One summer, having rented a house for a family holiday in Brittany, Maugham became so enraged by the food bills Syrie was running up that he refused to pay them, even though there were guests staying at the time, and Syrie was forced to borrow in order to settle the accounts. With regard to Liza, now seven, the fact that the little girl was so wrapped up in her mother eased his conscience, protecting him from feeling that he might be failing in his duties as a father; he himself in childhood had had only a tenuous relationship with his father, which may go some way to explaining a curious statement made later that year: "I have a notion that children are all the better for not being burdened with too much parental love."

While thankful that the atmosphere at Wyndham Place was less turbulent, Maugham still was not prepared to spend much time there, and at Easter he left for Italy to meet Gerald Haxton, who had been parked in Florence while awaiting the next departure for the Far East. On his return from Java, Maugham had written to his old friend Reggie Turner, who had been long settled in an apartment on the Viale Milton, asking him to take the young man under his wing. Haxton, "my constant companion on all my travels [is] a very dear friend of mine for whom I hope you will do everything you can. . . ." When Maugham arrived, he and Haxton joined a group containing Turner, Hugh Walpole, Eddie Knoblock, and the Italian publisher Giuseppe ("Pino") Orioli, who at the time was living with that crusty, charismatic figure, Norman Douglas. Douglas, admired as the author of *South Wind,* notorious as an unregenerate pedophile, was now in his fifties and after many years on Capri and then in England had settled in Florence in an attempt to recoup his fortunes after a long period of poverty and several run-ins with the law for molesting young boys. "I left England under a cloud no bigger than a boy's hand," he used to quip. His financial situation had recently become so desperate that a secret appeal had been launched by the writer Rebecca West; when she approached Maugham, he told her he would assume total responsibility, depositing enough money to provide a roof over Douglas's head for life on condition that his identity as benefactor was never revealed: Douglas, he joked, had a habit "of attaching himself to the hand that feeds him." With such dazzling conversationalists as Douglas and Reggie Turner, the three weeks in Florence passed swiftly. Turner in particular was delighted to see Maugham again, his only criticism that his old friend could be "a little arid" when it came to tipping. Haxton, the new boy, was liked by all, Walpole recording in his diary that Maugham's chum was "charming, full of kindness and shrewdness mixed."

There was no question of Maugham's staying away long, as his presence was required in London for rehearsals of his new play, *East of Suez,* a prospect regarded without much enthusiasm. "You cannot think how impatient I am to be on the wander again," he wrote to Alanson. "London is very nice to come back to, but to my mind flat & unprofitable to live in. . . . It is like an artificial comedy, amusing enough to sit through for a period, but apt to grow tedious if it lasts too long. I am feeling very much as though it were time for the curtain to fall." Far from falling, the curtain was about to go up on a costly extravaganza, a show embellished with all kinds of expensive novelty, including a spectacular Peking street scene with shops, rickshaws, sixty Chinese extras, a real Ford motorcar, and an onstage orchestra playing some twangy "Chinese" music especially commissioned from Eugene Goossens. The play, in some respects a looking-glass version of *The Painted Veil,* is set among the British colony in Peking, and in an undeniably melodramatic tone offers a rich mix of adultery, racism, suicide, and attempted murder. Produced by Basil Dean at His Majesty's, *East of Suez* opened on September 2, 1922, in London and almost simultaneously in New York. Audiences loved it, but critics on both side of the pond derided it. *The Spectator,* describing the work as crude and pretentious, declared itself shocked that Mr. Maugham could have written anything so amateurish. "Another piece of work like this and his reputation as a serious playwright will be gone!"

Fortunately for his peace of mind, Maugham had left London a few days before these notices appeared. He narrowly escaped another unpleasant press report, of a very different nature, when shortly after his departure Syrie was involved in a fatal accident. Driving down Park Lane one evening she knocked down a woman cyclist, who subsequently died of a fractured skull. Giving evidence at the inquest, Syrie swore she had never seen the cyclist, and to her enormous relief it was ruled that the death was not her fault.

BY THIS TIME MAUGHAM was thousands of miles away, again headed for the Orient. His destination this time was Burma, a British dominion rather less docile in mood than the Federated Malay States: Burma was administered not as a separate colony but as a province of India, thus relegated to second-class status in the imperial order, a fact much resented by the Burmese. Maugham had been warned to expect trouble, from headhunters, tigers, and snakes as well as from native insurgents. "We have got quite an arsenal with us," he wrote to Bert Alanson, although as it turned out the expedition, if arduous, passed off without threat. In his account of the journey, published under the title *The Gentleman in the Parlour,* Maugham makes no mention of any political issue, an omission for which he has been censured by some. By contrast, George Orwell, who was in Burma at exactly the same period, working in the Burmese police, was intensely alive to the seething resentments around him, coming to loathe what he regarded as the despotism of British rule. Orwell portrayed the colonial oppressors as at worst vicious, at best stupid and dull: a dull people, "cherishing and fortifying their dullness behind a quarter of a million bayonets." He clearly foresaw the end of empire, while Maugham appeared not so much unaware of as indifferent to the subject. In his introduction to *The Gentleman in the Parlour* he introduces the matter in a tone of slightly awkward facetiousness. "I cock a snook at the historian of the Decline and Fall of the British Empire," he writes, after rehearsing the arguments he supposes lined up against him: "Did he go through Burmah and not see how the British power was tottering?"

To such detractors, though, the reply is simple: the fall of empire was not his topic. Much of the enormous popularity of Maugham's stories stems from the fact that he knew his limitations, perfectly understood the range of his engagement: it was not the big picture that appealed to his imagination, but the small lives of unremarkable individuals struggling to create the reassuringly ordinary out of an extravagantly exotic environment.

Maugham and Haxton arrived in Rangoon from Colombo in Ceylon, sailing up the Irrawaddy on a hot, bright morning, dazzled by the sight of the great golden spire of the ancient Shwedagon pagoda glinting in the sunlight. The plan was to journey from Rangoon to Mandalay, then north into Siam and on to Bangkok, thence into Indochina and finally to Hanoi and Haiphong, where they could board a ship to Hong Kong, and from there they would sail home. Rangoon, Mandalay, Bangkok, their names so full of mystery and promise, turned out to be disappointing, hot and dusty, all three noisy modern cities with European restaurants and hotels, their crowded streets jammed with traffic, with trams, cars, gharries, and rickshaws, and little sign of the mysterious East, of the "narrow alleys [and] devious ways down which the imagination may wander." Once out into the country, however, the modern world disappeared, as they slowly progressed north and into the Shan States. Here the going was hard, as they traveled through jungle and up mountain passes, riding, or trudging along on foot, sometimes rowing upriver on ramshackle rafts, or jolting uncomfortably along mud-rutted roads in the back of a bullock cart.

The most difficult part of the journey was from Taunggyi, capital of the Shan States, to Keng Tung on the border with Siam, a distance of nearly seven hundred miles, which was to take twenty-six days to cover, Maugham and Haxton astride surefooted Shan ponies at the head of a caravan of mules transporting the luggage and equipment. As well as the team of porters, there were two Indian servants, a Ghurka manservant, Rang Lal, and a Telugu cook. Rang Lal was well trained and efficient, but the cook proved to be a problem, dirty, frequently drunk, and his cooking inept and monotonous: dinner, preceded by gin and bitters, was either curry, tinned sardines, or a stringy bird shot by one of the two white men, inevitably followed by trifle or cabinet pudding, "the staple sweets of the East." After a while, desperate for change, Maugham took matters into his own hands and showed the cook how to make corned beef hash. "I trusted that after he left me he would pass on the precious recipe to other cooks and that eventually one more dish would be added to the scanty repertory of Anglo-Eastern cuisine." Progress was slow, especially when it came to persuading the mule train across a river, the Salween or Mekong, or pushing through dense thickets of bamboo, or on foot while pulling their ponies knee-deep in mud along a forest trail. Sometimes it was suffocatingly hot and steamy, while high in the mountains it was misty and cold. Nights were spent either in circuit houses, one indistinguishable from the other with their shabby teak furniture and years-old copies of *The Strand* magazine, or in monasteries, their camp beds and mosquito nets placed among golden Buddhas brooding on their great lotus leaves in the gloaming. The journey was exhausting and occasional rest days were a necessity, instead of rising at dawn a late lie-in with tea and a cigarette, peaceful hours spent lounging in pajamas, playing patience and reading. A favorite work that Maugham had brought with him was *Du Côté de Guermantes,* and for fear of finishing it too quickly he rationed himself to thirty pages a day. "A great deal of course was exquisitely boring [but] I would sooner be bored by Proust than amused by anybody else."

Once they had crossed the small stream that marked the boundary with Siam, the landscape changed completely, and they found themselves in open agricultural country, with rice fields on either side of the road, neat little villages, and gentle hills covered with well-husbanded teak forests. Then, riding into a village at noon, Maugham suddenly felt a familiar perfumed warmth, "the harsh, the impetuous, the flamboyant" air of the south, and realized with a shock of delight that he was in the tropics. Once in Siam, everything was easy: they were welcomed by a polite village official who insisted they stay in his own spacious house, putting at their disposal a bright red Ford motorcar in which they drove off at what seemed a vertiginous speed of eight miles an hour to the nearest station to catch the train to Bangkok.

The heat in the capital was overwhelming, and soon after settling into his hotel Maugham succumbed to a bad attack of malaria, recurrences of which would dog him for many years. A doctor was called who immediately administered quinine, but at first this had no effect and Maugham's temperature soared dangerously, to over 105 degrees. But eventually the crisis came, and drenched in sweat, the patient began to recover: soon he could breathe easily, his head ached no longer, and he was free from pain. "I felt extraordinarily happy," he recalled.

From Bangkok the two travelers continued by sea to Kep on the Cambodian coast, and from there to Phnom Penh and Angkor, where the ruined, overgrown Khmer temples deep in the forest, "looming gigantic and black in the moonshine," made a powerful impression. One of the last cities on the itinerary was Saigon in French Indochina, a charming place with the air of a little provincial town in the south of France. From Saigon their route took them to the royal city of Hué, where they had an audience with the emperor, then to Hanoi, and finally to the big French naval base at Haiphong, where they boarded a steamer to Hong Kong, from there making their way via Shanghai, Yokohama, and Vancouver to New York and the welcome comfort of the *Aquitania*.

*The Gentleman in the Parlour,** Maugham's account of his adventure, is notable for the author's obvious enjoyment, his high spirits, the exuberance with which in a prose both lucid and relaxed he writes of his experiences. Maugham loved to explore, loved to be on the move, and he always found in travel not only a source of inspiration for his writing but an enormous sense of freedom, free-

---

* The title is taken from an essay of William Hazlitt's, *On Going a Journey,* in which Hazlitt describes his delight in travel, and particularly in the opportunity it provides "to shake off the trammels of the world and of public opinion—to lose our importunate, tormenting, everlasting personal identity in the elements of nature, and become the creature of the moment, clear of all ties . . . to be known by no other title than The Gentleman in the Parlour!"

dom from social, domestic, and moral constraints, and freedom as
well from the limitations of his own sometimes suffocating sense of
self. "I am often tired of myself," he wrote, "and I have a notion
that by travel I can add to my personality and so change myself a little. I do not bring back from a journey quite the same self that I
took." On this occasion he returned with copious notes on which
to base his book, the result an attractive mix of simple yet vivid descriptions of the land and the people, with a number of intriguing
histories gleaned from characters met on the road, among them a
saintly Italian priest living in a remote jungle village, a degenerate
figure who had been a fellow student of Maugham's at St.
Thomas's, and an eccentric American couple, the Wilkinses, propri-
etors of a tiny traveling circus. The Wilkinses, whom Maugham
years later still remembered as the oddest people he ever encountered, were fellow passengers aboard a squalid little steamer plying
along the Cambodian coast between Bangkok and Kep, and during
the long hot hours on deck they tell Maugham about their animals,
all of whom they regard as family:

> "I guess Egbert would like a sip of your lemonade, my dear,"
> said Mr. Wilkins.
>   Mrs. Wilkins slightly turned her head and looked at the
> monkey sitting on her lap.
>   "Would you like a sip of mother's lemonade, Egbert?"
>   The monkey gave a little squeak and putting her arm
> round him she handed him a straw. . . .
>   "Mrs. Wilkins thinks the world of Egbert," said her hus-
> band. "You can't wonder at it. He's her youngest."
>   Mrs. Wilkins took another straw and thoughtfully drank
> her lemonade.
>   "Egbert's all right," she remarked. "There's nothing wrong
> with Egbert."

There are also some mild philosophical reflections and literary mus-
ings and a few brief passages of autobiography, and as always in
Maugham's accounts of his travel abroad there flows a small subter-

ranean stream of nostalgia for the Kentish countryside of his boyhood: in Petrograd he was moved by the resemblance of the Lavra monastery to Canterbury Cathedral; in China, "the bamboos, the Chinese bamboos, transformed by some magic of the mist, look just like the hops of Kentish fields"; while in Burma a distant tributary of the Mekong recalls the little stream where as a child "[I used] to catch minnows and put them in a jam-pot." On its publication in 1930 *The Gentleman in the Parlour* was widely acclaimed. "Never was Mr. Maugham more readable or so wholly delightful as in this," declared the *New York Herald Tribune,* while Desmond MacCarthy in an essay on Maugham described the work as "sombre and beautiful, entertaining and sincere."

The one overwhelmingly significant absence in the account of this long journey is that of Gerald Haxton. From first page to last, both in *The Gentleman in the Parlour* and in the published notebooks, there is rarely the smallest indication that the author is not traveling alone. Yet Gerald was there every step of the way, his presence a crucial component of Maugham's emotional and physical well-being. It was Gerald who supervised the details of Maugham's journeys, Gerald who acted as secretary, typing Maugham's letters on a machine laboriously lugged all the way from London; and it must have been Gerald who nursed Maugham during his life-threatening attack of malaria in Bangkok. But of what he thought, what he said, how he conducted himself, Maugham made sure there was left no trace. When on the last day of the voyage the *Aquitania* docked briefly at Cherbourg, the two men took their leave of each other, Gerald disembarking in France while Maugham sailed on to Southampton and his alternate identity as respectable family man. That Haxton was much on his mind, however, is made clear in a letter written while still in mid-Atlantic to Bert Alanson. "Will you invest $5,000 in the name of Gerald Haxton," Maugham asked him. "I am making him a present of this. . . . He has been very faithful & devoted to me for many years. Of course he has not been able to save anything & I should like this to be a nucleus of some provision for him in case I die."

CHAPTER 10

SEPARATION

. . .

Iɴ ᴀ 1923 ᴀʀᴛɪᴄʟᴇ ɪɴ *VANITY FAIR*, ᴍᴀᴜɢʜᴀᴍ ɪɴ ʜɪs ꜰɪꜰᴛɪᴇᴛʜ year wrote, "middle age has its compensations . . . you feel no need to do what you do not like. You are no longer ashamed of yourself. You are reconciled to being what you are, and you do not much mind what people think of you." On his return from the Far East that year he was the epitome of such self-assurance, rich, famous, outwardly confident, and composed. Everyone wanted to know him, and in the relatively small society of 1920s London, almost everyone did. Yet in private the strain of maintaining a double life, of dividing himself between Syrie, who increasingly bored and re-pelled him, and Gerald Haxton, to whom he was wholly in thrall, was beginning to seem untenable. Maugham still looked on London as his base: it was his home, the center of his social and professional life; and yet it was also where he felt most repressed and confined. Gerald, representing freedom and adventure, was exiled on the other side of the Channel, and it was not possible for Maugham to endure his absence for long.

Arriving in London at the end of May, Maugham would be gone again by October. The four intervening months were spent in the usual industrious activity, including overseeing rehearsals for *Our Betters,* the play that had been banned during the war, complet-ing a couple of short stories, writing a new farce, *The Camel's Back,* and starting his Chinese novel, *The Painted Veil.* To add to the pres-sure, there was the upheaval of moving again, leaving Wyndham

Place for a bigger, even grander establishment barely a hundred yards south at 43 Bryanston Square. "It is simply magnif," Arnold Bennett reported after being invited to a dinner party there with Charles Towne, H. G. Wells, and Virginia Woolf, adding enviously, "The fellow's study is larger than my drawing room." In the embittered memoir of his old age, Maugham attributed the move to Syrie's "social aspirations": yet in fact it was Maugham, not Syrie, who initiated the move, although it was true she found considerable advantages in it, not only for entertaining but as a showcase for her business, a beautiful backdrop for the bibelots and "restored" pieces of furniture that were her stock in trade. It took Maugham some time to realize what was going on, why the sofa he sat on one evening would be gone the following morning, that the price of tables and chairs could be quoted on inquiry. Yet in the beginning Maugham was pleased with the move to Bryanston Square and enjoyed his handsome new house, "so roomy and spacious," as he told Bert Alanson, "and I bless *Rain* which made it possible."

Rain had also helped pay for a small flat in Paris for Gerald, at 65 rue La Fontaine, a nearer and more convenient location than Florence in which to pass the time during the inevitable periods of separation. By now the relationship had lasted almost ten years, and in the homosexual circles in which Maugham moved it was looked upon as something of a model. But there were problems nonetheless, and Maugham was never easy about leaving Gerald to cope on his own.

Haxton at thirty was fast developing into an accomplished wastrel. In childhood he had been spoiled and adored by his mother, just as now he was spoiled and adored by Maugham. He was an intelligent man, well read in both English and French, yet except briefly during the war he had never worked for his living. Unmotivated and lacking in discipline, left for long periods with nothing to do, it was all too easy for him to slide into dissipation. For a long time now Gerald had been a heavy drinker; he was also dangerously addicted to gambling, regularly running up enormous debts, all silently settled by his patron; as Maugham pragmatically phrased it, "You must expect to pay something for the amusement you get out of knowing wrong 'uns." Sexually, too, Gerald could be wildly irresponsible: "charming but *very* naughty," according to that old reprobate Norman Douglas, who might be expected to know. When in Paris he was often to be found in the shady bars and clubs of the rue de Lappe, well known as a homosexual marketplace of unusual variety and sophistication. With a natural preference for adolescent boys, Haxton was also more than ready to prey on any available female—housemaids, debutantes, married women—once even attempting to seduce Gerald Kelly's wife, Jane—and sometimes very young girls: it was one of his boasts that while in Siam he had bought a twelve-year-old girl for a tin of condensed milk. "He was a naughty boy and he grew into a wicked man," said one of Maugham's homosexual acquaintances, "[and] he took off his trousers far more frequently than most of us, in the most unlikely bedrooms."

To Maugham, Gerald was irresistible. With his vitality and daring, he alone had the power "to unlock a door inside Maugham's shut-away secret wall." Maugham was charmed by Gerald, invigorated by his company, and he also valued his intelligence, very much relying on the younger man's critical opinion of his work. According to Rebecca West, who shrewdly observed the couple over a number of years, "[Haxton] was probably the only person he really felt at home with, and from that point of view I think Willie had a right to him. . . . Gerald was exactly . . . his cup [of tea]." The relationship was complex, and not always clear to the casual witness. Those who saw them together were sometimes shocked by the insolent manner in which the younger man behaved toward the older: Gerald waving his long cigarette holder, imperiously summoning Maugham from across the room to replenish his cocktail: "the handsome young man, lolling in his arm-chair, with one bare leg thrown over the arm, holding up his glass, demanding his poison. The aging genius . . . pouring out the libation, as if he were making a sacrifice to a young god." Yet what such onlookers failed to grasp was the complicity, the nature of the bond, the elaborate rules of the sexual power games played out between them. And there was more to it than that: while Maugham was frequently exasperated by Gerald's behavior, there was a protective, paternal element in his feelings, aware as he was of the young man's vulnerability, a vulnerability that was deeply buried and invisible to most; he was bewitched, too, by his extraordinary charm; and he was touched by an unexpected gentleness that surfaced when Maugham was ill or depressed, when his lover offered those little attentions so often learned by an only child living with an ailing parent. Most of all, though, Maugham was fascinated by Haxton's dangerous edge, by the bad-boy aura that surrounded him. In a sense, Gerald was the Mr. Hyde to Maugham's Dr. Jekyll: it was Gerald who let rip, gave full rein to a sensuality and subversiveness that in the older man were in the main strictly held in check.

Compared to Haxton's appetite for risk and debauchery, Maugham's tastes seem almost prim: he liked sex and he liked a lot of it; few good-looking young men who crossed his path were left unpropositioned; but his preferred practice tended toward the straightforward and conventional. "Willie's sex life was not necessarily virtuous but it was extremely simple," remarked a homosexual friend, the writer Glenway Wescott. Once when he and Maugham were contemplating a nude painting of a man and woman making love in the "missionary" position, Maugham observed that it was a pity two males could not perform like that. "I didn't have the heart to tell him," said Wescott. Gerald's physical presence had a potent effect on Maugham, and if they were no longer, or not often, sexual partners, they continued to be intricately involved in each other's sexual activities. In the same way that Maugham when abroad relied on Gerald to go out and make contact with strangers in order to discover their stories, so he relied on him to go out and find boys to bring back to his bed. Maugham was fastidious in his tastes, recoiling from the actuality of the decadent and shady, as Haxton well understood. "Gerald Haxton was wonderful for Willie," said the film director George Cukor. "He kept him in touch with the gutter."

On August 9, 1923, Haxton's invalid mother, Sara, died. She had not seen Gerald for nearly ten years, although Maugham, like a dutiful son-in-law, had always kept in touch, visiting her in St. John's

Wood whenever he was in England. The writer Clemence Dane was later to say of "her dear friend Sally Haxton" that she "worshipped" Maugham because of what he had done for her son. "I personally had much affection for her," Maugham told Bert Alanson, "[but] it was a dreadful life she led [and] I am thankful that she is dead at last." Gerald, overwhelmed by feelings of grief and guilt, was deeply distressed, mourning his mother and wretched at the thought of the miserable existence she had led, permanently deprived of the presence of her adored only child.

The departure for the United States at the end of September thus came as a timely distraction, and during the two and a half months in New York, Maugham and Haxton enjoyed themselves, despite the fact that Maugham's new play, *The Camel's Back,* was a failure. Maugham remained unperturbed by this minor setback, however, much more interested in the signing of a contract with Ray Long, editor in chief of the Hearst magazines, including *Cosmopolitan, Good Housekeeping, Harper's Bazaar,* and *Town and Country,* for a series of short stories for $2,500 each, "a very substantial, comfortable sum," as he remarked. They went several times to the theater, once with Charlie Chaplin, and Maugham was impressed by the enthusiastic reception the star received:

> It was quite an experience to see that huge audience get up and applaud him, and when we came out through a side door in order to avoid the mob we had to fight our way through a couple of thousand people. . . . [Charlie] was frankly delighted, and I could not help thinking it must be an intoxicating experience thus to receive face to face the acclamation of the people.

Returning to London in the New Year Maugham concentrated on the writing of his novel *The Painted Veil,* due to be published the following spring. The only fiction of his in book form to appear in 1924 was a short story, "The Princess and the Nightingale." This was Maugham's contribution to a collection of two hundred miniature manuscripts by famous writers commissioned to furnish the library of Queen Mary's Dolls' House, designed by Sir Edwin Lutyens and on show that year at the British Empire Exhibition at Wembley. The contents of each little book, an inch and a half high and bound in yellow calf with the queen's bookplate inside, were transcribed in tiny writing by its author; among the contributors were Thomas Hardy, Barrie, Kipling, Hilaire Belloc, and Conan Doyle. Maugham's minuscule opus is a pretty fairy tale about a young princess befriended by a nightingale whom she comes to love so much she puts him in a golden cage so he may not fly away; but kept a prisoner the little bird can neither eat nor sing, and the princess realizes that unless she releases him he will die. "Take your freedom," she tells him at last. "I love you enough to let you be happy in your own way," a message of peculiarly personal relevance to the story's author.

With *The Painted Veil* completed, Maugham, as restless and energetic as ever, now planned a long journey to Central America in search of new material. He wrote to Bert Alanson, who had recently married, congratulating him and also asking for some introductions for Mexico. "I cannot tell you how much I am looking forward to breaking into a new hunting ground," he told him. In the event this particular hunting ground was to prove disappointing, yet it was with high hopes that in September 1924 Maugham and Haxton yet again crossed the Atlantic. On board the *Majestic* they found a number of friends, among them the young playwright Noël Coward, whom Maugham had first met at the end of the war. Despite a mutual liking and a genuine respect for each other's work, the two men were never to become close, mainly because Coward was too fond of Syrie ever to be on intimate terms with Maugham. Also among the passengers were Eugene Goossens, who had composed the music for *East of Suez,* and Basil Dean, who had directed it. In New York, Maugham was introduced to the writer and photographer Carl Van Vechten, who was to remain a friend for life. Van Vechten, a big, burly man only six years younger than Maugham, was a prominent figure in artistic and intellectual social circles. Although twice married, "Carlo," as he always signed himself, was homosexual, a dandy by nature if not in physique, specializing in a camp jokiness that Maugham found amusing. The two men met the day before Maugham and Haxton left town, and Van Vechten presented Maugham with a copy of his latest novel, *The Tattooed Countess*. Three days later Van Vechten was thrilled to receive from New Orleans "a perfectly amazing letter" from his new friend saying how much he had enjoyed it.

After a brief stay in New Orleans, Maugham and Haxton crossed the border into Mexico. "I must confess that I am disappointed with Mexico," Maugham wrote to Eddie Knoblock after a couple of cold, rainy weeks in the capital.

> I cannot find very much that's interesting except the civilisation that the Spaniards brought and if one is willing to be excited about that one is after all better off in Spain. . . . My chief object of course was to find material for stories and so far as I can see there is not the smallest likelihood of it.

In fact the time was not entirely wasted, and material was unearthed for a couple of stories, *The Man with a Scar* and *The Closed Shop,* although in both the author's lack of engagement is evident in the telling. Unlike China and Malaya, the country had no dominant expatriate community, and the foreign residents, though numerous, were too internationally varied to provide that particular colonial ambience that so fascinated Maugham.

The reaction of another English writer in Mexico at exactly this time was different. D. H. Lawrence, who was to be powerfully inspired by both the country and the people, had recently arrived in Mexico City with his wife, Frieda, and their friend, the painter Dorothy Brett, sister of Sylvia Brett, Ranee of Sarawak. Lawrence had never met Maugham, but hearing he was in town dispatched a civil note from his modest hotel. "Dear Somerset Maugham," he wrote,

> I feel that two such literary Englishmen as you and I ought not to pass as ships in the night, with a piece of wide sea in be-

tween. Would you care to come to lunch at this little place? If so, you might ring up, or leave a message.

Maugham sent a telegram refusing as he was on the point of leaving for Cuernavaca to write, a reply that upset the famously thin-skinned Lawrence, who felt he had been snubbed. "Damn his eyes and his work," he exclaimed crossly on October 25, while four days later, still brooding over the imagined slight, he wrote to a friend that Somerset Maugham, "a narrow-gutted 'artist' with a stutter," was apparently "no loss: a bit sour and full of nerves and fidgets lest he shouldn't produce a Maughnum opus with a Mexican back-ground before Christmas," adding enviously, "As if he could fail!!" The following month, when Maugham returned to Mexico City for a few days before leaving for Yucatán, the meeting finally took place. He and Haxton, Dorothy Brett, and the Lawrences were in-vited to lunch by the distinguished American anthropologist Zelia Nuttall* at Casa Alvarado, her sixteenth-century house in the sub-urb of Coyoacán. Yet what should have been a pleasurable occasion quickly turned sour. Something Gerald said offended his hostess; Dorothy Brett was predisposed against both Haxton and Maugham, having apparently received unfavorable reports from her sister in Sarawak; Maugham was in a sullen mood; and Lawrence, tense and aggressive, was infuriated by what he took to be the older writer's lack of interest in himself. As they sat down at table, Frieda Lawrence, placed next to Maugham, asked him how he liked Mex-ico. "He answered crossly: 'Do you want me to admire men in big hats?' I said: 'I don't care what you admire.' And then the lunch was drowned in acidity all around." Afterward Lawrence described Maugham as *"sehr unsympatisch"*; "I didn't like him," he concluded, "a bit rancid," an adjective that obviously struck him as apposite as he used it again four years later in his carping review of *Ashenden,* when he wrote in *Vogue* that "it would be hard to find a bunch of more ill-humoured stories, in which the humour has gone more

---

* The model for Mrs. Norris in Lawrence's novel *The Plumed Serpent.*

rancid." Maugham would return the compliment by describing Lawrence in print as "a sick man of abnormal irritability . . . warped by poverty and cankered with a rankling envy."

The Mexican trip continued to Yucatán, Cuba ("just like Atlantic City"), Jamaica, British Honduras, where they made an expedition by mule into the bush, and finally Guatemala; from Guatemala City they sailed to Hué in Indochina, continuing from there to Saigon, where they boarded a Messageries Maritimes ship for Marseilles. Shortly before sailing home, Maugham confided to Eddie Knoblock that

> [I have] arrived at the conclusion which I think is not without use that I am reaching the end of my exotic material. I have of course notes for a good many stories which I have not yet written but shall write, but I have not the capacity to assimilate much more. I have no doubt there is here and in the East a great deal which another writer could make stories of and plays [but] I have reached the end of the vein. . . . It will at all events take me four or five years to get finished with the material I now have collected.

Maugham arrived back in London at the end of March 1925 in time for the publication of *The Painted Veil*.* This, the story of Walter and Kitty Fane and of Kitty's affair with the caddish Townsend, had already run into trouble. It had first appeared in Britain serialized in *Nash's* magazine, when the two protagonists had been called not Fane, but Lane, with the unfortunate consequence of bringing a libel action from an unknown Mr. Lane, eventually settled for £250. But there was further trouble when *The Painted Veil* was published in book form, and an objection was made by the Hong Kong government over the adulterous role ascribed to the colony's assistant colonial secretary; uneasy that awkward conclusions might be drawn, they insisted that the location of the story

---

* The title is taken from a sonnet by Shelley beginning,
   Lift not the painted veil which those who live
      Call Life . . .

be altered. Thus Maugham was obliged to turn Hong Kong into the imaginary Tching-Yen, Happy Valley into Pleasant Valley, the Peak into the Mount, and Kowloon into Lushan, with all references to neighboring Canton removed (the original place-names were restored in later editions). As bad luck would have it, by the time these corrections were made, two printings of four thousand copies each had already been run off and a large number distributed to the press, all of which had to be recalled. There was a further annoyance. Despite the book's immediate jump into the bestseller list in the United States, with sales of over a hundred thousand and a number of good reviews, Maugham felt that his American publisher, George Doran, had been remiss in promoting it. For once it was not a question of finance. As Maugham explained to his agent, Charles Towne, "I am not so anxious to make a large sum of money out of a book as to have it as widely read as possible. I seek distinction rather than lucre." Yet with *The Painted Veil* Doran seemed to have been culpably inactive. "He just sent it out like a parcel of tea and let it sell on its own merits, without anything more than a perfectly mechanical and useless advertising," he complained. "I do not wish Doran to look upon me as a goose which lays regularly a golden egg," he continued, suggesting that after his contract expired,

> we go to Doran and unless he is prepared to guarantee success for my next books (which will consist of a volume or two of short stories, a travel book, and, last, a novel) make arrangements elsewhere. There is only one way I know in which a Publisher can guarantee success, and that is by giving so large an advance that it is necessary for him to do everything he can for the book in order to get his money back.

One element in *The Painted Veil* recognizable only to Maugham's inner circle is that of the portrait of his brother. Maugham admitted that he took much of the character of Walter Fane from F.H., his shyness and superciliousness, his coldness and steely self-control; but he is also visible in the person of Kitty's father, Bernard Garstin.

Garstin is a barrister, a KC, a reticent, lonely figure, given to depression who, like F.H., lives at home in a state of self-imposed isolation. Unlike Garstin, however, who is looked down on by his two daughters, F.H. was a figure of fear to his children, cold, captious, and remote. In fact the tragedy of F.H. was that his icy manner hid a craving for affection that within the family he was unable to express. Outside the house he could be lively company, and for some years he conducted a secret love affair with a woman with whom presumably he was more forthcoming than with his wife.* Yet with Nellie he was distant and fractious, and with his children he found it impossible to unbend. Kate, Honor, and Diana had learned early to keep out of their father's way, their lives centered on their warmhearted mother, who was passionately devoted to her daughters.

In 1916, when the girls were approaching adulthood, Nellie Maugham, to everyone's astonishment, gave birth to a boy. As an only son, Robert Cecil Romer, always known as Robin, might have been expected to engender some feeling of affection in his father, but he was treated with an even greater frigidity than his sisters. "My father was fifty years old when I was born," Robin wrote later, "and the half century that separated us was certainly one of the factors that made our relationship difficult." But it went further than this, and for years the boy received at his father's hands nothing but callous rejection. He was an unwanted child: even his mother treated him severely, believing that boys, unlike girls, needed to be toughened up and denied any form of indulgence. As a result Robin had a miserable childhood, spending much of his time separated from the rest of the family, looked after by a series of nurses and governesses. He was almost exactly a year younger than his cousin Liza, and sometimes Syrie would bring Liza to have tea with him in the nursery at Cadogan Square while she talked to Nellie downstairs.

The sisters-in-law had become good friends, and sitting on the

---

* According to admittedly sketchy evidence in F.H.'s pocket appointment diary, this affair seems to have come to an end in 1923.

drawing room sofa with the door closed they confided in each other, comparing the difficulties both had with their husbands. In each case, the couples were disastrously mismatched, two lively, sociable women married to clever men who were exceptionally controlled and controlling—and whose affections were engaged elsewhere. If Nellie remained in ignorance of her husband's mistress, Syrie was only too well aware of the danger represented by her long-term rival, Gerald Haxton. For several years before her marriage to Maugham, Haxton had been in the picture, but she had yet to set eyes upon him.

During the six months that her husband was abroad, Syrie's career had continued to prosper, so much so that she had been able to move her shop, Syrie Ltd., from Baker Street to fashionable Mayfair premises, 87 Duke Street, at the corner of Grosvenor Square. From here she not only continued to sell her decorative furniture but also ran a successful design business, taking on commissions to decorate rooms, apartments, and even entire houses. Recently she had built herself a house at fashionable Le Touquet on the Normandy coast, a destination that was fast becoming popular with the rich British. The Villa Eliza, surrounded by pine trees and set some way back from the sea, provided a perfect backdrop for Syrie's modernistic beige-and-white décor as well as giving her easy access to the junk and antiques shops of the Seine valley. The construction had been expensive, however, and with ready money not always available, Syrie had to do what she could to raise it. Thus, shortly before he had sailed from Hué, Maugham, to his extreme annoyance, learned that Syrie had rented out his house in Bryanston Square for the summer; she was planning to move into rented accommodation in Chelsea, he was informed, where a bed-sitting room would be prepared for his use. "Needless to say I could not work in a bed-sitting room in the King's Road," he exploded to Golding Bright, "& in any case I am too old to pig it!" Fortunately it then transpired that the tenants were postponing their arrival until July, and as Maugham had no intention of staying in London for more than two or three months, there was no reason why his plans should be affected. As the ship neared Marseilles, his thoughts increasingly focused on his homecoming and the reunion with his wife. "I do not of course know," he wrote to Eddie Knoblock, "whether it is to be war or peace; but I shall when I arrive."

As it turned out, the summer of 1925 was a combination of the two. As before, husband and wife assumed a convincing appearance of harmony. The artistic young men who had begun to gather around Syrie, such as Glyn Philpot, Rex Whistler, Cecil Beaton, and Oliver Messel, mixed well with the literary young men, novelists and playwrights, who clustered around Maugham. Once again the house in Bryanston Square was the location for some glamorous parties, where theater people, writers, publishers, painters, and designers met the more cultured members of high society; George Doran, Eddie Marsh, Jeanne Eagels, Gladys Cooper, Ivor Novello, H. G. Wells, Rebecca West, Noël Coward, and Michael Arlen mingled with the eccentric Lord Berners, with Sir John and Lady Lavery, with the theatrical peer Ned Lathom, with Sitwells and Guinnesses. On a couple of occasions the gaunt figure of D. H. Lawrence could be seen going up the steps of number 43, a fragile reconciliation between himself and Maugham having been effected by Reggie Turner. "Don't expect us to be two roses on one stem," Lawrence had warned Turner. "But perhaps he's nice, I don't pretend I know him. And if he'd like to see me, I should like to see him. Honi soit etc." Sometimes friends from abroad came to stay, one of whom was the novelist Theodore Dreiser; it had been Dreiser's review of *Of Human Bondage* that had first won the novel serious attention, and Maugham put himself out to entertain his American guest, every evening concocting the martinis fashionable in New York if still something of a novelty in London. When talking about it later, Dreiser said that he had enjoyed everything about his visit except for the awful cocktails.

But it was when the guests had gone that the rows started. Always, always the figure of Gerald Haxton loomed over their increasingly ferocious fighting. Syrie, still craving her husband's affection, was venomously jealous, tormented by the reality of Maugham's sexual relationship with the hated Haxton ("she did desperately mind . . . about the sex part," said her daughter later).

She was unable stop herself from nagging and reproaching him, working herself up into screaming, shouting rages that Maugham countered either by icy withdrawal or, when driven beyond endurance, by shouting back at her himself; more than once he hit her. These frightful quarrels★ left Maugham drained and depressed, and usually with a splitting headache. Extremely self-disciplined, a private, undemonstrative man who found it difficult to show emotion, he was profoundly shaken by being provoked to such violent outbursts, bitterly humiliated by his loss of control. Syrie, on the other hand, recovered much more rapidly: quick-tempered by nature, she had always thrived on confrontation—as her employees both at home and in the shop knew only too well—and she relished the daily drama of her volatile emotions. From Maugham's point of view, the marriage was effectively over. He and Syrie had little in common, her chic, frivolous world was not his, her aggressive acquisitiveness was anathema to him, and only traces remained of the youthful prettiness he had once so admired. Now in her late forties, Syrie, despite rigorous efforts, was growing plump; she retained her flawless complexion but it was heavily powdered, her square chin and big nose were more prominent, and her hair, styled in a modish Eton crop, was cut unbecomingly short.† It was now common knowledge that relations between the Maughams were strained to the breaking point, a topic that Syrie, with a level of vituperation that sometimes shocked her listeners, had little compunction in airing. "I realized," said one, "that what she was chiefly concerned about was doing Willie damage." Some of the couple's close friends, including Eddie Knoblock, Noël Coward, and Gladys Cooper, tried to intervene, to lower the temperature between them, but it soon became distressingly clear that nothing could be done. According to H. G. Wells, "[Syrie] was incapable of realising

★ To be vividly described a few years later in *The Constant Wife*.
† In his short story "A Man with a Conscience," Maugham describes a husband's feelings of revulsion toward the wife he is about to murder: "Marie-Louise had started a little while before having her hair cut differently, quite short, and I thought it repulsive . . . the stubble of cropped hair on her neck made me feel rather sick" (*Collected Short Stories*, vol. 4, p. 239).

Maugham's distaste for her [and] always expected a reconciliation to take place. This was impossible, as Maugham's writing about her showed."

The one area where the couple might have found some accord was in regard to their daughter; instead, the subject of Liza became one of the bitterest battlegrounds of all, and she herself described her parents' quarrels over her upbringing as "volcanic." Although doted on by her mother and in many ways overindulged, the little girl was also neglected, often lonely, and sometimes wretchedly unhappy. Apart from a couple of cousins, Robin Maugham and a little Barnardo cousin, Eilidh, who sometimes came to play, she had few friends of her own age, and now that Syrie was so immersed in her business she often appeared to forget about Liza for days at a time, leaving her in the care of one of the maids. On the first day of a seaside holiday in Dinard, Syrie, anxious to prepare the rented house for the arrival of guests, deposited her daughter on the beach and was astonished when at the end of the day a policeman turned up to deliver her child, weeping and distraught. " 'Did you have a nice day, darling?' she asked, then she saw how upset I was and was very sorry," Liza recalled. "She had been completely absorbed in what she was doing. And she was very absent-minded." It was during this same holiday that Liza for the first time witnessed a series of violent fights between her parents, including one that so frightened her she was physically sick; on other occasions their rows reduced her to hysterical crying, once covering her face with greasepaint in an attempt to disguise her tears. "I had a great feeling of insecurity," she said of this period of her life, "quite the reverse of a happy childhood."

Liza was now ten, and Syrie wanted to keep her at home, doing her lessons in a relaxed fashion with a series of governesses. At the age of eight Liza had contracted tuberculosis and been forced to spend several months confined to a spinal carriage, and this had made her mother even more determined to keep her closely under her wing; her father, however, was adamant that the child should be sent away to school. He was determined she should be properly educated, and saw it as essential that she should be removed from her mother's influence and allowed to make friends of her own age. So Syrie was overruled and the child dispatched to a boarding school in the country, a decision that caused great wretchedness to both, with Syrie constantly on the telephone with anxious instructions regarding Liza's comfort and care. One Sunday evening a group of dinner guests at Bryanston Square were embarrassed to witness their hostess provoked to such exasperation over some matter to do with Liza's schooling that she threw the receiver on the floor. When she returned to the table, her husband tauntingly remarked, "S-S-Syrie d-d-didn't really imp-p-prove matters by l-losing her t-t-temper with that wretched woman," at which Syrie, white with rage, retaliated with icy distinctness, "You said you wanted a child, but you lied. You didn't want a child, you only wanted to be a father." Rebecca West, a close ally of Syrie's who was present at this exchange, recalled, "Willie took this without protest. It was quite obvious that she was alluding to something which was understood between them." Meanwhile Liza at school was so miserably homesick that she went on a hunger strike, eventually making herself ill enough to be sent to a sanatorium. From there she ran away, caught a train to London, and turned up at the house, imploring her parents not to send her back. There was an emotional scene, but Maugham refused to be swayed and insisted that she return to school; again Liza escaped, was again returned; but when she escaped a third time Syrie could bear it no longer and resorted to trickery. She took Liza to the oculist and asked the man to put drops in her eyes to obscure her vision temporarily: unable to see, she was unable to go to school.

At this point Maugham admitted defeat and made little further attempt to influence his daughter's education other than by opening an account in her name at Bumpus's bookshop in Oxford Street, where she was allowed to buy as many books as she pleased. Under her mother's regime, Liza's schooling remained haphazard, sometimes lessons with a temporary governess, occasionally a few weeks in a school in London, Chicago, Nassau, New York, or wherever else Syrie's expanding business and peripatetic way of life happened to take her. Even in adulthood Liza's handwriting remained childish, and she never learned to spell, a fact that exasperated her father, who accused her of "writing like a chambermaid." On the other hand, she was a well-dressed and well-traveled little girl, and accustomed to the company of her mother's sophisticated social set; in a curious way she appeared much older than her years. "She had a miniature, rather touching dignity," said one of her contemporaries. "She seemed already to have entered into 'society,' and to exist there like a waif, waiting to be a few years older."

While Maugham admired Syrie's taste and flair, he loathed her ruthless commercialism. Embarrassed enough by the notion of his wife's running a shop, he found it abhorrent when she conducted business at home. (After waiting for his guests to be seated at a luncheon party one day, he drily announced, "I think I should warn you, l-l-ladies and gentlemen, to hold tight to your chairs. They are almost certainly for s-s-sale.") Publicly he dealt with it by pretending it was all a great joke, that they were so hard up Syrie had been forced to go to work selling bits of old junk, but inwardly he hated the situation, hated the flow of people in and out of the house and the disruption of his working routine. The actress Cathleen Nesbitt, who stayed for a few days in Bryanston Square, saw for herself the effect it had on him. "[Syrie] for a time used her own house as a show place for precious pieces which were always being snapped up and removed by eager clients," the actress recalled. "I confess I was rather astonished by the courtesy with which he [Maugham] accepted the constant change of surroundings!" But there came a day when Syrie went too far. One evening when Maugham came downstairs before dinner, "he found that his sacred writing desk was gone from his study, and all his papers and manuscripts laid out on a table. . . . When Syrie said cheerfully, 'There's a magnificent new desk coming tomorrow, darling,' I almost expected him to knock her down but he merely said, 'I see,' with a tight face and closed the door." The writing table was the one Maugham had used for more than twenty years, bought when he moved into his house on Chesterfield Street; an integral part of his working life, it suited him perfectly, and to him Syrie's removing it was an outrage, a brutal act, insensitive in the extreme. "He appeared to take it calmly,"

said Cathleen Nesbitt, "but I sensed a rage of fury coldly controlled." Later he was to say it was the selling of his desk that finally
caused him to end his marriage, and his anger about it remained
unassuaged until eventually finding vitriolic expression in his 1930
novel, *Cakes and Ale*.

Increasingly, Maugham was growing uneasy about his wife's
methods: there was in Syrie's character a moral coarseness that
shocked her fastidious husband. It was one thing to charge outrageous prices—she was hardly unique in the trade for that—but
there were more serious suspicions about her conduct. Already
there had been a couple of lawyers' letters demanding reimburse-
ment for a fake passed off as an antique, and she was beginning to
earn a bad reputation among her professional colleagues. "She was
tricky in business," an American decorator remembered; "I knew
Syrie slightly and hated her as did anyone who had business dealings with her: she was dishonest," said another; while a third remarked of her that Syrie was "a tough old rogue who never paid for
anything unless she had to"; "she was a schemer, hard as nails."
Needless to say, Maugham distanced himself as far as possible from
his wife's business transactions, but there was one occasion when
her lack of integrity was forcefully brought home to him. The
magnificent jade and gold necklace he had brought back for Syrie
from China in 1920 had become a great favorite and she wore it
often, having first insured it for a considerable sum. One evening
she returned to the house from a buying trip to Paris and immediately burst into tears. "I don't know how to tell you," she sobbed.
"I've lost my jade string." It appeared that she had been in the
Louvre, absorbed in matching silks, and in the crowd some clever
thief must have slipped it off her neck. Maugham consoled her as
best he could, Syrie put in a claim, and the insurance company paid
up. A few months later one of the company's employees walking
down the rue de la Paix spotted the very same necklace on display
in a jeweler's window, and on inquiry learned it had been sold to
the shop by a Madame Maugham. Fortunately Syrie escaped prose-
cution as the company, having been reimbursed, was persuaded not
to pursue the matter further.

At about the same time as the affair of the necklace, Maugham began to have suspicions of further duplicity on Syrie's part, suspicions that were confirmed by one of her girlfriends. This was almost certainly Barbara Back, wife of the surgeon Ivor Back. Barbara had originally been a supporter of Syrie's, but she had been shocked by the way Syrie talked about her husband, spreading scandalous gossip about his private life, and so she had come more and more to sympathize with Maugham. When Barbara warned him that Syrie had taken not one but two lovers, he was unsurprised. "I knew them both," he wrote sourly, "and had a very poor opinion of either." In fact Maugham cared very little how his wife conducted herself; if anything, he was pleased, recognizing that her adultery strengthened his position: she could hardly make such a fuss about his relationship with Gerald if she was in much the same position herself. But the discovery of her unfaithfulness, coming so soon after the attempted fraud over the necklace, fired his imagination, and on three separate occasions in his writing he was to use a necklace, in each case of pearls rather than jade, to stand as a symbol of sexual licentiousness and betrayal. The theme first appeared in 1925 in the short story "Mr. Know-All," then in a play in 1932, and finally in another short story about ten years after that.

The subject of divorce was now being seriously discussed between the Maughams. From Maugham's point of view there was no future in the marriage and the sooner they effected a clean break the better: he had made it clear there was to be no question of his separating from Gerald, and that he was more than happy for Syrie to divorce him, after which they could both go their separate ways. But Syrie did not wish to divorce. She enjoyed the prestige of being Mrs. Somerset Maugham, she still loved her husband, and she still hoped that somehow an amicable compromise might be found. With this in mind the obvious next step was for Syrie and Haxton to meet, a suggestion she had previously refused to consider. Thus it was decided that in August the two men should spend a week with Syrie at her house in Le Touquet. Liza, who was a silent witness to this momentous encounter, recalled it as "a disaster from the start. I shall never forget the terrible atmosphere of those few days. . . . Syrie and my father were completely and tragically incompatible in every way and that Le Touquet episode was the real beginning of the end."

THE ARRANGEMENTS HAVING BEEN MADE, Maugham did his best to feel optimistic about the proposal. Le Touquet "is really a very charming little place . . . and all kinds of amusing people go there for the summer so that I think we ought to have a very pleasant time," he wrote tentatively to Bert Alanson. Meanwhile he fortified himself for the ordeal by taking Gerald off for a couple of weeks' holiday on Capri to stay at the Villa Cercola with John Ellingham Brooks. The island was as seductive as ever, and Maugham, not for the first time, was much taken with the idea of buying a house there, a refuge to which he could retreat to work in peace; he asked Brooks to look for one in his absence, arranging access to his bank for any necessary deposit. From Capri he and Haxton went on to a spa at Brides-les-Bains in the French Alps, where they followed a strict teetotal regime and took vigorous exercise on the golf course and tennis court.

Fit and rested, Maugham and Haxton arrived at the Villa Eliza in the second week of August 1925 to find a house party in progress: Noël Coward and his handsome American lover, Jack Wilson; the former musical comedy star Gertie Millar, now the Countess of Dudley; Barbara Back; the glamorous Delavignes, brother and sister; Frankie Levesson, a Danish decorator whom Syrie was shortly to take on as manager of her shop; and Beverley Nichols, a good-looking young man with literary ambitions, very much on the make. As soon as the two newcomers entered the house the tension in the air became almost tangible. Syrie, dressed in white and heavily made up, was overvivacious, trying to conceal her nervousness by gushing embarrassingly—*"darlings!"* she greeted the couple, dramatically flinging up her arms. Maugham, in blue blazer and pale blue trousers, remained courteous but remote, while Gerald in open shirt and shorts made a point of being elaborately relaxed, lounging about smoking and picking his teeth or hovering absorbedly over the cocktail tray. "Gerald makes the *best* sidecars in the *world!*" Syrie complimented him anxiously, blowing him a kiss that he ostentatiously disregarded. After tea, Syrie, accompanied by Beverley Nichols, Haxton, and Liza, drove off to see an *antiquaire* who had a Provençal armoire she had her eye on. "She'll pickle it before you can say knife," Noël joked. Arriving back at the house, Haxton, accidentally on purpose, gave Liza a sharp push as she climbed out of the car, causing her to fall and scrape her knee.

In the evening several people came in for dinner, including the Swedish multimillionaire industrialist Ivar Kreuger, who had founded his vast fortune from matches. Watching Kreuger fumble with his lighter, Maugham made everyone laugh by saying as he proffered a matchbox, "*Mon cher ami, il paraît qu'il vous manque une allumette?*"* After dinner Noël, much relied on to make the party go, entertained at the piano, then at around midnight Haxton, already fairly drunk, took the younger guests off to the nearby casino, among them Beverley Nichols, who later described the scene. Gerald at the tables was "still very decorative," though his cheeks were flushed and his eyes glazed, and there was cigar ash all down his dinner jacket. "He caught my eye and shouted, 'Come over here, you pretty boy, and bring me luck.' Which," Beverley added prissily, "is not how I cared to be addressed." It was after three in the morning when Nichols returned to the villa, but no sooner had he crept into bed than he was joined there by Coward's boyfriend, Jack Wilson, their lovemaking terrifyingly interrupted by Coward himself crashing open the door, a furious figure in a green silk dressing gown, looking, Nichols recalled, "like the wrath of 49,000 Chinese gods." Next day Nichols felt so humiliated by what had happened that he told Syrie he had to return home at once, and to his surprise she promptly decided to leave with him, pouring out while on the boat train to London her feelings of fear and loathing for Gerald Haxton. Haxton, she said, was poisoning her husband's mind against her; he was a liar, a forger, and a cheat;

* "It seems you need a match, my friend."

he had no morals at all, and "if he thought it would be of the faintest advantage to him he'd jump into bed with a hyena."

This is Nichols's version, produced more than forty years later. By that time all three principals, Maugham, Syrie, and Haxton, were safely dead and Nichols was focused on revenging himself on Maugham, with whom at the end of the old man's life he had fallen out. His book, entitled *A Case of Human Bondage* and purportedly an analysis of the Maugham marriage, gives some telling detail of the week at Le Touquet and of Syrie's emotional state: she and Beverley were fond of each other and he was undoubtedly one of the many in whom she confided. In essence, however, the book is untrustworthy, fueled by spite and warped by deliberate distortion: for instance, Nichols in his book asserts that it was Haxton, not Wilson, who came into his room, and Maugham, not Coward, who caught them at it, a falsification he later admitted in a letter to Coward's secretary, Cole Lesley. Certainly his is a more coloratura rendition than that given at the time by Maugham, who clearly believed that the visit, despite the tense atmosphere and numerous unspoken anxieties, had not been unsuccessful. "Syrie was as nice as nice could be & is evidently eager to turn over a new leaf," he wrote to Eddie Knoblock. It appears that Maugham noticed nothing odd in Syrie's early departure with Nichols; it is plain there had been some serious talks between husband and wife, and equally plain that Maugham was determined not to move one inch from his stated position. "I hope," the letter continued, "[Syrie] will cease her complaining about me to all her friends . . . but if she complains to you, you will do me a service by reminding her that she has only to say the word & I am willing to let myself be divorced. I cannot change & she must either bear with me as I am, or take her courage in both hands & make the break."

BY THE TIME THIS letter was written, in October 1925, Maugham and Haxton were on their way back to the Far East. "I am so thrilled at getting [away] that I can think of nothing much else," Maugham had written to John Ellingham Brooks on the eve of his departure. They arrived in Singapore at the beginning of November, where they stayed for more than three weeks before traveling on to Bangkok, then to Borneo and Brunei, Maugham en route giving courteous interviews to the local press, which respectfully kept track of his progress. To accompany them on their travels Maugham had employed a servant supplied by an agency in Singapore. Ah King, a sweet-natured young man of twenty, turned out to be a marvel.*

> He could cook, he could valet, he could pack, he could wait at table. He was quick, neat and silent. . . . Nothing surprised him, no catastrophe dismayed him, no hardship ruffled him, no novelty took him unawares. It was impossible to tire him. He smiled all day long. I have never met anyone so good-humoured.

There was only one drawback: although Ah King was able to speak some English, he understood hardly a word, which made communication difficult. When at the end of six months Maugham paid him off, he saw to his astonishment that Ah King was crying.

> I stared at him with amazement . . . he had always seemed to me strangely detached . . . as indifferent to my praise as he was unconcerned at my reproofs. . . . That he had any feeling for me had never entered my head. . . . I felt a little uncomfortable. I knew that I had often been impatient with him, tiresome and exacting. I had never thought of him as a human being. He wept because he was leaving me. It is for these tears that I now give his name to this collection of stories that I invented while he was travelling with me.

The two collections of Far Eastern stories garnered during Maugham's expeditions in the 1920s, *The Casuarina Tree,* published in 1926, and *Ah King* in 1933, contain some of his finest work in the genre

---

* Ah King makes a further appearance as the devoted servant in the 1932 novel, *The Narrow Corner.*

at which he remains an acknowledged master. Fluent in style and apparently effortless, the stories are tightly constructed and minutely observed, amply demonstrating the three virtues that he himself prized highest, of lucidity, simplicity, and euphony. As a writer of fiction, Maugham was a realist: his imagination needed actual people and events to work on, and these his travels amply furnished, enabling him to explore the imperial theme from an intimately personal and domestic standpoint. During those months spent listening to strangers telling him their private dramas, "I seemed," he said, "to develop the sensitiveness of a photographic plate." He wrote about ordinary, fallible people, the kind of people he knew and understood, the white professional middle classes, and when challenged about why he never attempted to depict native life, he replied that it was because he did not believe any European could get to the inside of it.

> I felt that all the depictions that had been made of either Chinese, Indians, or Malays were merely superficial impressions combined with a lot of conventional prejudices. It is very nearly impossible for an English author to create a French character so that French readers would accept him as real. How much more difficult then would it be for an English writer to create a Chinese the Chinese would accept as plausible.

It is his oriental tales that many readers most associate with Maugham, and they were and are widely admired in his day by such distinguished literary figures as George Orwell, Evelyn Waugh, Graham Greene, Christopher Isherwood, Angus Wilson, and Anthony Burgess. Burgess, describing these two collections as containing some of the finest examples in the language, wrote, "The width of observation was something new in English fiction, as was the willingness to explore moral regions then regarded as taboo"; while Cyril Connolly, who selected *The Casuarina Tree* for his influential compilation *100 Key Books of the Modern Movement*,*

---

* *The Casuarina Tree* was listed under "The Twenties," with *Ulysses, A Passage to India, The Great Gatsby, The Sun Also Rises, To the Lighthouse,* and *Decline and Fall.*

particularly praised the author for "his mastery of form," going on to say that

> Maugham achieves an unspoken ferocity, a controlled ruth-
> lessness. . . . He tells us—and it had not been said before—
> exactly what the British in the Far East were like, the judges
> and planters and civil servants and their womenfolk at
> home. . . .

MAUGHAM RETURNED TO EUROPE in March 1926, having spent most of the voyage confined to his cabin with a recurrence of the malaria from which he had been so ill during his first visit to Bangkok. "The journey on a French boat from Saigon to Marseilles, over thirty days, has seemed terribly long," he wrote to Alanson, "& I am thankful as I write to you to see out of the window of the smoking-room the shining, sunny coast of Corsica." A letter from Syrie had just reached him, containing the information that she was currently on business in New York and had again rented out the house in Bryanston Square, news that left him feeling both angry and depressed. "I am tired of wandering about & would gladly remain quietly at home, but at present I have no home," he told Alanson; "a domestic disturbance, whether permanent or temporary I do not yet know, has left me without a roof to my head." Still feeling unwell, Maugham with Haxton retired to a comfortable hotel in Aix-en-Provence to recuperate, but the more he brooded on the situation, the more intolerable it seemed that he should be denied access to his own home, that Syrie was treating Bryanston Square as hers to do with entirely as she pleased regardless of his wishes. The plan to purchase a property abroad now became a priority, a house where he could live with Gerald and to which Syrie would have access only by invitation. Reading between the lines, he was even cautiously optimistic that his wife was beginning to come around to the possibility of a judicial separation. "I cannot but think that she has at last determined on a break," Maugham wrote hopefully to Knoblock, "though I cannot imagine what has made her reverse her very definite desire to have nothing of the sort with which I left her last autumn. If you hear anything of interest to me I am sure that you will let me know."

Maugham's arrival in London on May 3, 1926, coincided with the beginning of the general strike, when the industries of the entire nation were closed down in an attempt to force the government to increase pay for coal miners. During the ten days it lasted, a once-in-a-lifetime opportunity was provided for the educated classes to play at being train drivers, bus drivers, newspaper editors, and policemen. Even to those of a left-wing bent the chance was irresistible, and Maugham, through a friend in the Public Prosecutions Department, landed a job in Scotland Yard, "sleuthing," as he described it to Arnold Bennett. With the strike ended, the house vacated by its tenants, and Syrie returned from New York, negotiations between husband and wife began in earnest, and for once appeared to result in an agreement acceptable to both: Bryanston Square would be sold, and with the proceeds Syrie would buy a house of her own in which she would live with eleven-year-old Liza, while Maugham would look for a permanent base abroad: not on Capri, which on reflection he concluded was too difficult to reach, but in the south of France. "I have made a very agreeable arrangement with my wife," Maugham wrote to Alanson.

> She is to have her house in London & I my house on the Riviera & we are going to stay with one another as guests when it suits our mutual pleasure and convenience. I think this is the best thing for both of us & it will give me the opportunity which I need to work in pleasant surroundings & without interruption.

But instead of house hunting, he was first caught up in a series of professional projects. There were talks in progress about a film version of "Rain," a revival of *Caroline* had just opened at the Playhouse, and Maugham had a new play, *The Constant Wife,* that he was anxious to see staged; there were as well frequent requests from Ray Long for stories for Hearst magazines, and there was also some complicated business to sort out with his New York publisher, George Doran. While Maugham was abroad, Charles Towne had arranged a new contract with Doran that, to his client's irritation, appeared to tie him to the company not only for life but also on much less advantageous terms than before. "I will not conceal from you that I am extremely vexed at your having signed an agreement with Doran which gives me nothing that I wanted but on the contrary takes away what I value most dearly, my freedom of action," Maugham crossly complained.

> You seem now to have bound me hand and foot for the rest of my career as a novelist [nor] is the contract you have signed so good as the offer which Doran made me himself by letter several months ago. . . . I do not know exactly what advantage I get in receiving an advance of five thousand dollars on a novel. It is to be presumed that with such a reputation as I have any novel I write will earn that sum in royalties without any effort on the part of the publishers; and what I particularly aimed at was to force the publisher to do a little more than his best for me.

Within months, however, the cause of the quarrel became academic: Doran's firm was absorbed by Doubleday, and Towne resigned his agency to take on the editorship of *Harper's Bazaar,* a move regarded by Maugham with approval. "I am sure you will make an excellent editor and bring the greatest possible success to the magazine," he told Towne. "Though I consider you too arbitrary to be an agent I continue to think you a charming and an amiable companion."

With the house in Bryanston Square up for sale, Maugham felt disinclined to remain in London, going first to Brides-les-Bains, then to Capri, then to Salzburg for the Festival. He returned to London in August, but only for a brief interval, leaving at the end of September for the States in order to be present at the opening of *The Constant Wife.* On arrival in New York he wrote to Bert Alanson with some exciting news. After looking at a number of houses on the Riviera he had finally found one that he liked on Cap Ferrat, a rather dilapidated property that had long been left vacant as so much money was needed for its restoration. An early twentieth-century house near the top of the Cap, it had been curiously embellished by a series of pseudo-Moorish architectural features, thus accounting for its name, the Villa Mauresque. "Twenty minutes before starting for the station to take the train to Southampton and the ship for New York," Alanson was told, "the agents of the owner of the house I have been haggling over for the last six months came to see me and accepted my last offer; so that I am now the possessor of nine acres of land and a villa half way between Nice and Monte Carlo."

CHAPTER 11

THE VILLA
MAURESQUE

· · ·

THE VILLA MAURESQUE AND SOMERSET MAUGHAM, SOMERSET MAUGHAM and the Villa Mauresque: for nearly forty years the two were inextricably linked, the house the richest thread in the fabric of the legend, visited, photographed, filmed, described in countless articles, regarded with awe as the glamorous and exotic backdrop for one of the most famous writers in the world. The villa itself was of no great architectural merit, but its location was superb, overlooking the sea and hidden among trees at the top of Cap Ferrat, a thickly wooded promontory jutting out into the Mediterranean. To the west are Nice, Cannes, and the wide sweep of the Baie des Anges, while to the east lie Beaulieu, Monte Carlo, and the Italian Riviera; behind are the snow-covered peaks of the Alpes Maritimes, while before stretches the wide blue expanse of the ocean, where on a clear day the misty outline of Corsica can be glimpsed on the horizon. Here was the south, here were warmth, light, vibrant color, white houses with terra-cotta roofs and a luxuriant vegetation reminiscent of the tropics, mimosa and oleander, yucca and bougainvillea, olive and palm trees. Most of the land on Cap Ferrat had been bought in the early years of the century by King Leopold II of the Belgians, who had built himself a palace there, in 1906 adding a house nearby for his elderly confessor. This gentleman, a Monseigneur Charmeton, had spent much of his life in Algeria and understandably wished to end his days in the Moorish style to which he had become accustomed; thus, the square, whitewashed villa had

had imposed upon it horseshoe windows, a Moorish archway, a large cupola on the roof, and tacked onto one side a grandiose Venetian portico.

Maugham was entranced by his new acquisition, and considered the £7,000 he paid for it a very fair price. "I have at last found a place that pleases me more than Capri," he wrote to Gerald Kelly. "Of course at present everything is upside down and one requires the eye of faith to see what the house and garden will be like when the place is shipshape." A local architect, Henri Delmotte, was engaged to restore the house to its original shape. Indoors, a courtyard was constructed, spacious and quiet, and leading from it were a dining room and a long, high-ceilinged drawing room, in summer its tall windows kept cool and shuttered from the glare outside. From the large hall a white marble staircase ascended to a gallery around which were the bedrooms and bathrooms: as well as apartments for Maugham and Haxton, there were big double bedrooms with dressing rooms for guests, with two bachelor bedrooms on the ground floor. At the very top of the building, reached by a wooden stairway leading onto the flat roof, was Maugham's study, a private chamber apart from the rest of the house; entered through French windows, the room was airy and spacious, with wide views over the tops of pine trees to mountains and the sea. Alone in his aerie on days when the mistral was blowing, Maugham used to say it was like being on the deck of a ship.

While the builders were painting and hammering in the house, Maugham turned his attention to the steep, overgrown hillside on which it stood. He had never had a plot of his own to cultivate before, he wrote, and "I hadn't reckoned on the temptation that is afforded by a great neglected garden." When he first saw it, the land was a dense jungle of foliage, pine trees, mimosa, and aloes, with the ground beneath a tangle of wild rosemary and thyme. Once this had been cleared and cut back, the garden was properly stepped and leveled, flowering shrubs were planted, camellias, hibiscus, and bougainvillea, a lily pond was scooped out, and orange and lemon trees were set in a formal pattern on the terraces immediately outside the house. Thousands of spring bulbs were dug in, and, extremely rare for the Mediterranean, turf was laid for a grass lawn, readily admitted by Maugham to be a rich man's folly. "The great luxury on the Riviera is grass, for it will not bear the long heat of summer and must be dug up at the end of every spring and replanted every fall"; yet he had an inextinguishable nostalgia for the smooth green swards of English country houses and wished to have something of the same himself. Away from and above the house were greenhouses and a kitchen garden, and just below these a tennis court, reached by a flight of stone steps and hidden by a hedge; a long marble swimming pool was installed, with at one end a diving board and at the other, gushing water, a magnificent mask of Neptune carved by Bernini that Maugham had found in Florence. With the arrival of his furniture and other possessions from Bryanston Square, his books, theatrical pictures, and the various ornaments and objets d'art collected in the East, the Villa Mauresque soon began to feel very much like home.

There was little time to enjoy his new property, however, as Maugham's professional commitments required his presence in London, where he was involved in the preparation of two new dramatic works, *The Constant Wife* and *The Letter,* the second an adaptation he had made of his Malayan short story about Mrs. Crosbie's shooting of her lover and her subsequent trial. From the first Maugham had been determined that Gladys Cooper should take the lead part of Leslie Crosbie, and her performance more than fulfilled his expectation, so impressing him that he offered her the option on his next three plays.

Maugham had the highest regard for Gladys Cooper: he admired her beauty, her professionalism, and her no-nonsense attitude toward life in general, while she for her part had the greatest esteem for him. "I place Somerset Maugham as our finest writer for the stage," she stated in her autobiography. It was during rehearsals for *The Letter,* of which she was also coproducer, that Gladys properly came to appreciate Maugham's method, impressed by how accommodating he was with regard to making changes to his text. "The majority of authors," she wrote, "are terribly sensitive and jealous of their work, regarding every word they have written as almost a pearl beyond price. . . . Not so Somerset Maugham." He would sit in the stalls, ready with his blue pencil to cross out or rewrite whatever she or the director Gerald du Maurier wished. In large part this relaxed attitude derived from the detached view Maugham took of his dramatic work: it was the private process of composition that engaged him, not the play's evolution onstage; once the work was in the hands of the actors and director, it became something else, with which he no longer felt closely concerned. For this reason the theater was ultimately regarded as an unsatisfactory medium for a writer, as Maugham explained in a letter to Noël Coward:

> [We] have to content ourselves with at the best an approxima-tion of what we see in the mind's eye. After one has got over the glamour of the stage and the excitement, I do not myself think the theatre has much to offer the writer compared with the other mediums in which he has complete independence and need consider no one.

For Maugham, rehearsing had become dull work, attended to more from a sense of duty than because he felt crucially involved in the interpretation of his script. This attitude, verging almost on indif-ference, had been noted by the director Basil Dean, who during preparations for *East of Suez* had concluded, rightly, that it sprang from the fact that "Maugham lacked genuine enthusiasm for the theatre. . . . Throughout the rehearsals," Dean recalled,

> he remained withdrawn, neither helpful nor obstructive, never offering advice unless it was asked for. I think he found the whole business tiresome and the actors' arguments rather petty. Yet, when appealed to, he was always ready with the unconvincing response: "Oh, ex-excellent!" Once I asked him whether I might cut certain lines: "Wh-wh-why not?" he spluttered. "The st-st-stage is a w-w-workshop."

With *The Letter* doing so well on both sides of the Atlantic, and with a sellout production of *Pluie* (*Rain*) at the Théâtre de la

Madeleine in Paris, Maugham's theatrical reputation had never been higher, and much was expected of the new work, due to open in London in April 1927. But with *The Constant Wife* almost everything went wrong from the start.

In the guise of a smart little comedy of manners, *The Constant Wife* is in fact ablaze with anger, anger about the injustices and constraints of the married state, with Maugham's bitterness about Syrie just below the surface. "I'm tired of being the modern wife," says Constance. "What do you mean by the modern wife?" her sister asks, to which Constance bleakly replies, "A prostitute who doesn't deliver the goods." It is for this reason that Constance makes up her mind to earn her own money—by working as an interior decorator, interestingly enough. She harangues her husband on the subject of the meretriciousness of her previous position:

> CONSTANCE: Are you as great a fool as the average man, who falls for the average woman's stupendous bluff that just because he's married her he must provide for her wants and her luxuries, sacrifice his pleasures and comfort and convenience, and that he must look upon it as a privilege that she allows him to be her slave and bondman? . . .
>
> JOHN: You were the mother of my child.
>
> CONSTANCE: Let us not exaggerate the importance of that, John. I performed a natural and healthy function of my sex. . . . Let us face it, I was only a parasite in your house. . . .

Even more venomous is the advice Constance gives a woman friend on how to punish her husband, in words that derive directly from the author's own miserable experience:

> Refuse to speak to him, but never let him get a word of defence in edgeways. Cry enough to make him feel what a brute he is, but not enough to make your eyes swell. Say you'll leave him and run sobbing to the door, but take care to let him stop you before you open it. Repeat yourself. Say the same thing

over and over again . . . and if he answers you take no notice, but just say it again [until] at last . . . you've reduced him to desperation, when his head is aching as though it would split, when he's sweating at every pore, when he's harassed and miserable and haggard and broken. . . .

The Constant Wife was produced in 1926 in America, with Ethel Barrymore in the lead, the first time she had played in a piece by Maugham since *Lady Frederick* twenty years before. Opening in Cleveland, Ohio, on November 1, the play suffered a bad start because the actress, stricken with stage fright, repeatedly forgot her lines, obliging the assistant stage manager, George Cukor, to hide in the fireplace onstage in order to prompt her. Maugham was in the audience. "I suffered agonies," he later admitted to Cukor.

When the curtain came down for the last time I went on to the stage. Ethel flung her arms round my neck and kissed me on both cheeks. "Darling," she said. "I've ruined your play, but don't worry; it'll run for two years." And it did.

But if the play recovered after its poor beginning in the States, it was given no such chance in London. The production was booked to go into the handsome Theatre Royal, Haymarket, with a cast led by Leon Quartermaine and Fay Compton. The director, Basil Dean, was unhappy with the choice of the two stars. "Quite early in rehearsals I discovered they were not well suited to their parts," he recalled. "Maugham's cynical comedy called for the lightest of treatment. Fay's comedy style was too arch and Leo was too pedantic." Then came the news that the Haymarket was no longer available and the Strand was taken instead, a much smaller theater with a stage unsuited for any but the broadest effects. But most damaging of all was the disastrous opening on April 6, 1927, when a managerial blunder over tickets succeeded in totally disrupting the performance. The fashionably dressed gentry arrived to find their seats in the stalls occupied by cheap-ticket holders who refused to budge; violent rows broke out and order was restored only when the theater manager went up onstage to appeal for calm. "Maugham and his wife sat in a stage-box, dismayed, while the argument was going on," Dean recalled. "[And] the effect on the actors can well be imagined. Already suffering from the usual first-night nerves they were put completely out of countenance by the fracas." More disruption was to follow when at the end of the play Fay Compton came forward to make the traditional speech of thanks, and mistaking a cry of "Shut up!" from the gallery as intended for her, pointedly thanked the "civil" members of the audience, which immediately provoked loud booing from the upper regions. Unsurprisingly, the production never recovered, and the critical consensus, that "Mr. Maugham was out of form when he wrote *The Constant Wife,*" kept audiences away.

Maugham had already left the theater by the time Miss Compton made her speech, as Syrie was giving a combined first-night and housewarming party at her new address, 213 King's Road, Chelsea. The property comprised a four-story early Georgian house of great beauty, with a smaller house linked by a wide indoor passage around the corner on Glebe Place. On the first floor of the King's Road house Syrie had made a large and spectacular drawing room decorated wholly in white, with white sofas, off-white satin curtains, white velvet lamp shades, and a white carpet by Marion Dorn; behind a white brocade sofa a huge folding screen made of narrow pieces of mirror reflected great sprays of white flowers, roses, lilies, peonies, and lilac, supplied on a regular basis by a recent associate of Syrie's, the florist Constance Spry. On the floor above were apartments for herself and Liza, and on the top floor a bedroom for her husband, "nice enough," he granted, "but it had the disadvantage of being also the 'gentlemen's cloakroom,' so that when there was a party I had to put away my writing materials." Displeased by such a constraint, Maugham soon moved his quarters from the main house to the Glebe Place annex, which was quieter and more private; with this arrangement he and Syrie were in effect living apart while still appearing to be under one roof. Certainly they were regarded as joint hosts for the glamorous first-night party for *The Constant Wife,* attended by almost everyone who was anyone in theatrical and literary circles. "Crowds and crowds at the party," Arnold Bennett reported, with major stars such as Marie Tempest and Tallulah Bankhead much in evidence; altogether the evening was deemed "a great success. . . . Only Maugham and wife were a bit gloomy. . . . I hear the play is rotten."

IF IT WAS HARDLY surprising that Maugham was gloomy following the débâcle earlier in the evening, nonetheless at this point it was Syrie whose state was the more precarious. With her husband's purchase of the Villa Mauresque she had finally been forced to accept that he had chosen a way of life in which she would have little part. Unable to conceal her despair, she poured out her misery to any sympathetic friend who would listen; Rebecca West was one who spent several long afternoons sitting in a darkened room while Syrie wept over what she considered her cruel desertion; she shocked another friend, Cecil Beaton, by telling him that during a visit to New York she had been so distraught over the prospect of her marriage ending that she had "spent three whole nights in Central Park too miserable to go home." Despite a likely element of exaggeration, there is no doubt that Syrie was wretchedly unhappy and on the point of collapse. "My mother had a very bad nervous breakdown," Liza recalled of this period, a breakdown that reached its nadir during a business trip to the States. While in New York, Syrie became so frantic that she decided to go to Bermuda to try and find peace, but once there could hardly wait to leave, insisting on boarding the first ship out of the harbor, a tramp steamer with no passenger accommodation, she and Liza sleeping in chairs on the open deck as far as Nassau. The two of them stayed for several weeks in the Bahamas and here at last Syrie began to recover, Liza attending a little open-air school run by nuns, "the nicest of my collection of schools," as she remembered it.

Upon returning to England it seems that Syrie made one final attempt to persuade Maugham not to leave her. She asked him to come once more to Le Touquet, in the hope that between them they might find some form of resolution less drastic than divorce.

Little came of the meeting, except for a shocking incident involving Liza and Gerald Haxton. "I always hated Gerald Haxton and he always hated me," said Liza. Their first encounter the previous summer had been uncomfortable, the child wary of this strangely powerful friend of her father's, and he no doubt irritated by the spoiled little miss he saw being cosseted by her mother. On this second occasion Barbara Back was again staying with them, and she, Haxton, and Liza went for a drive, Liza taking with her an adored puppy she had recently been given. Suddenly in an act of possibly drunken, seemingly inexplicable cruelty, Gerald at the wheel scooped up the dog and hurled it out the window. "I was hysterical," said Liza, "and tried to throw myself out of the car after it but was held back." Months later the dog was found and returned, but the damage was done: the enmity between Haxton and the two women was irreparable, and Syrie made sure that while in her care Liza would never set eyes on Gerald again.

IT WAS AFTER THIS second visit of Maugham's to Le Touquet that Syrie finally acknowledged that her marriage was over. Her friends were told that it was she who was pressing for a divorce, mainly for her daughter's sake, it now appeared: it was painfully obvious, said Syrie, that Gerald was going through her husband's money at a terrifying rate and soon there would be nothing left for Liza. During that summer, in 1928, Syrie was staying on the Riviera with her old friend and professional rival, the flamboyant Elsie Mendl. Lady Mendl, now in her sixties and recently married to the diplomat Sir Charles Mendl, had had a long and successful career in America as Elsie de Wolfe, the first woman interior decorator, much admired for her wide knowledge of French art and culture. While Syrie was staying with the Mendls at Antibes, Maugham was nearby at the Villa Mauresque. According to his version of events, he invited Syrie to lunch with no other purpose than to show her his house, sending his car to collect her and take her back. "We lunched tête à tête," he recalled, and after lunch I took her over the premises. She was becomingly appreciative. After she had seen everything . . . I put her in my car. An hour or two later the car came back with a letter. In it she said that she wished to divorce me and hoped I would put no obstacles in the way. It took me by surprise. I thought the matter over for a day and then wrote to say I would do what she wished if she would be satisfied with a French divorce . . . because divorce in France is a simple matter and there is no publicity attached to it. Syrie agreed and the lawyers went to work.

The lawyers must have had their hands full, with a multitude of complex negotiations to be carried out on both sides. According to Maugham family record, Syrie wanted to cite Haxton as corespondent, and there are other indications that she was prepared to use his homosexuality against him ("Your mother dragged me through the mud when she divorced me," Maugham later told Liza). Eventually Syrie was persuaded to drop any such charge, a charge that would have had a devastating effect on Maugham, with the potential to ruin him professionally and socially and to prevent him from ever setting foot in England again. Evidence of his wife's adultery may well have helped his case, but as Maugham knew very well, his most effective bargaining tool was financial, and he was willing to pay a substantial price for his liberty, making over to Syrie the house on the King's Road with all its contents, the house on Glebe Place, which was put in Liza's name, the car, a Rolls-Royce, and as well a generous annuity of £2,400, with £600 a year for Liza. Syrie filed suit in Nice that autumn, and the decree was granted, on grounds of incompatibility, on May 11, 1929. "Everything is absolutely finished," Maugham wrote to Barbara Back of his twelve-year marriage, "and all there is for me to do is to hand over twelve thousand pounds and resign myself to paying six hundred pounds a quarter free of income-tax until Syrie marries again."

Thus Maugham was finally freed from a union he had come to detest. "I made a mistake when I married her," he wrote. "We, she and I, had nothing in common and by doing what was considered 'the right thing,' I brought happiness neither to her nor to myself." As the years went by, instead of fading into indifference, Maugham's feelings for Syrie grew increasingly corrosive; he hated her for the large sums of money she had cost and would continue to cost him, and he could not forgive her for the misery and humiliation she had inflicted. For a man who enjoyed the company of women, who in his fiction and his friendships was so understanding and compassionate toward them, his attitude toward his ex-wife is startling, indicative of a very deep wound indeed. Although after the divorce he seldom saw her, his distaste for Syrie turned into an active and visceral loathing. "She made my life utter hell," he would say, bitterly referring to Syrie as an "abandoned liar . . . [the] tart who ruined my life," describing her as "[opening] her mouth as wide as a brothel door" in her constant demands for money. His great hope was that she would marry again and thus relieve him of the pecuniary burden, and many joking references were made to this prospect in letters to friends. Yet Syrie never remarried, remaining financially dependent on her ex-husband until the day she died. The two of them communicated mainly through lawyers, and Maugham made it clear to interviewers that he disliked talking about his marriage; if questioned he testily dismissed the subject as "[a] very unimportant detail."

Once the divorce had gone through, the Maughams closed ranks and shut their doors to Syrie; she was no longer welcomed by F.H. and Nellie at Cadogan Square, and Liza lost touch with her cousins. Yet if seldom discussed within the family, the Maugham divorce was a subject of intense fascination to their friends, especially among the homosexual coterie. "For those who seek a moral, one stands clear: / Don't marry if you happen to be queer," giggled the aesthete Harold Acton, while a number of other young men began jockeying for position, hoping that if they played their cards right the famous writer's patronage would help their careers. One of the first in the field was Beverley Nichols. Originally a friend of Syrie's, Beverley was pretty, intelligent, highly sexed, and drivingly ambitious. He had already begun to make quite a name as a journalist,

had written a couple of novels, had big plans for himself as a dramatist, and in 1926 at the age of only twenty-five had published an autobiography, appropriately entitled *Twenty-five.* This he had
persuaded Maugham to praise in *The Sunday Times,* a considerable
achievement as Maugham almost never wrote book reviews. "He
wrote it at my request after a very lavish dinner at the Café Royal
and gave it to me as a birthday present," Beverley recalled with satisfaction. Beverley, vain and unscrupulous, was more than ready to
make himself sexually available in exchange for favors such as these;
there was no reason why men like Maugham should not "help one
up one's little ladder," as he whimsically phrased it. "Struggling to
make a living from letters, one would be a fool to ignore the kindly
attentions of the literary lions, particularly if they happen also to be
extremely rich . . . [and] Willie's attentions were very kindly indeed." Naturally Beverley was unable to resist boasting of his conquests, to, among others, Cecil Beaton, who was frankly shocked
by his revelations. "With drink Beverley's tongue was wildly lubri-
cated & I heard more that staggered me that evening than I have
during the past few years," Beaton confided to his diary.

> I, who have not been to bed with anyone but myself since I
> was at school, had come to think that the amount of people
> who actually went to bed together was very small . . . but
> Beverley disproved my beliefs with the most hair-raising sto-
> ries of the unceasing lusts of nearly all my friends. . . . [He]
> assured me, at first hand knowledge, of the homosexuality of
> Noël [Coward], Somerset Maugham, Avery Hopwood, Syd-
> ney Howard,★ Edward Knoblock—a most disturbing evening
> & a great eye opener.

Another "tarty" young man who caught the eye of Willie
Maugham at this period was a friend and colleague of Beverley's,
Godfrey Winn. Similarly ambitious, Godfrey, too, was making a

---

★ Avery Hopwood (1882–1928) was a successful playwright of the American jazz age;
Sidney Howard (1894–1946) was an English film actor.

career in journalism, specializing in cozy pieces for women's magazines about his cottage in Esher, his dog, "Mr. Sponge," and such important topics as "The Girl I Hope to Marry," "Why I Like Working with Women," and "Should Wives Have a Career?" He, too, had brought out a novel, and as luck would have it, it was exactly at this moment that he met Maugham, introduced over a game of bridge, Winn being a player of championship standard. "I have been very fortunate in my life in regard to the sponsors whom I encountered at a crucial moment," he wrote in his autobiography. "Soon after my first novel was published, I had the good fortune to come under the literary influence of Somerset Maugham." Godfrey, like Beverley, was sexy and attractive, equally willing to oblige the great man, and equally unable to resist boasting about it afterward. Unwisely, he chose to brag of his triumph during a stay at the Villa Mauresque, while at a party at the house of a neighbor of Maugham's, the beautiful Lady Kenmare, whose guests found Godfrey's claim "that Willie had fallen for him in a big way and chased him all over London" distasteful in the extreme. It may be that ultimately Maugham came to hear of the betrayal: for some years he regarded Winn as a friend, invited him to stay, advised him on his writing, and brought his work to the attention of well-disposed critics. But then something happened to sour the relationship, and in *Strictly Personal,* a wartime memoir published in 1941, Maugham, in a passage excised from the British edition, drew a contemptuous portrait of Godfrey, who appears under the name George Potter.

Yet if men like Nichols and Winn were taking advantage of Maugham, he was far too shrewd not to understand what they were after. He liked young people, liked to be surrounded by good-looking boys, and was more than prepared to help them when he could. And he for his part had never been hesitant in making his own wishes known: the brother of Constance Spry, the fashionable florist, remembered being taken aback by the unvarnished nature of the older man's approach, while the ballet dancer Anton Dolin had great trouble with him at a party of Ivor Novello's at the Savoy: "Don't be a fool," said Novello as Dolin was trying to escape. "It will mean a gold Cartier cigarette case tomorrow." The famously charming, famously charismatic young peer Napier Alington was another of Maugham's conquests, "a delicious creature," as Maugham described him after their night together. Beverley Nichols, who might be assumed to know what he was talking about, said of Maugham, "He was the most sexually voracious man I've ever known"; and Hugh Walpole, himself no laggard on the homosexual scene, told Virginia Woolf that in his view Maugham was lucky not to have been imprisoned. "You don't know the kind of life that Willie has led. I do." As Maugham was recognized wherever he went, his behavior inevitably became the subject of gossip, and not only within the queer world. It was at about this time that some disquieting information on the matter came to the attention of none other than the commissioner of the Metropolitan Police at Scotland Yard; alarmed by its content, the commissioner felt obliged to convey a message to F. H. Maugham, discreetly indicating that he should issue a warning to his younger brother. F.H., now a High Court judge and recently knighted, was acutely embarrassed by the situation; revolted by the whole subject of homosexuality, for years deliberately ignoring this aspect of his brother's nature, he found himself in the distasteful position of having to tell Willie straight out that if he did not curtail his activities while in London he would almost certainly be arrested.

AND IN THE MAIN Maugham made his contacts discreetly, ideally in safe houses belonging to like-minded friends. It was in one of these, at a stag dinner in George Street given by a wealthy collector, Robert Tritton, that in 1928 Maugham met a young man who was to become of crucial importance in his life. Alan Searle was a very youthful-looking twenty-three, a working-class boy from Bermondsey, the son of a Dutch tailor and cockney mother. With his dark eyes and thick, curly black hair, Alan was well known in certain circles as "a modified version of rough trade," a common, sexy boy who was also quick-witted, good-natured, and eager to better himself. "I was quite a dish," as he himself said. His taste was for older men, and already he had an enthusiastic following among a number of distinguished figures. "He was wonderful with elderly gentlemen," the critic Raymond Mortimer recalled. Lytton Strachey was mad about Alan, called him his "Bronzino boy"* and wrote him a series of erotic letters; Reggie Turner fell for him, as later did the composer Lennox Berkeley, and also Guy Little, a friend of Osbert Sitwell's, who was besotted by "my starry eyed little friend . . . the darlingest pet in the world," as he dotingly addressed him. Alan was currently working at a picture gallery on Brook Street, which is probably where he had met Bob Tritton. When on the day of the dinner one of Tritton's guests failed at the last moment, Alan had been whistled in to take his place, seated next to Maugham, the guest of honor. Maugham was immediately attracted by the cheeky cockney, and as was his custom began to question him about his life and ambitions. Alan told him he longed to travel, which naturally struck a chord with Maugham, who at once offered to take him on a Continental tour, suggesting they leave the party together to discuss further plans. But Alan had already made an arrangement with another guest, Ivor Novello, and to Maugham's frustration it was with Novello that he went off that night. Next day Maugham sent a wire claiming to have been very upset by Alan's treatment of him, "but if you'll have dinner with me tonight all is forgiven." They dined at Quaglino's, an evening that, said Alan, "changed the whole course of my life." Not only did the two men become lovers ("Willie was the most marvellous lover I ever had"), but that night saw the start of an association of supreme importance to them both, one which was to endure for nearly forty years.

There was no question of Alan's taking Haxton's place. Yet Maugham frequently had reason to make short trips within Europe, sometimes to see one of his plays, more often just to wander around art galleries, and neither occupation was of particular interest to Gerald. Alan, on the other hand, was an enthusiastic traveling companion

* A similar comparison is made in Proust's novel by the homosexual Baron de Charlus about the object of his infatuation, the violinist Morel: "he has become so beautiful, he looks just like a Bronzino" (*Remembrance of Things Past: The Captive*, vol. 2, translated by C. K. Scott Moncrieff [Chatto & Windus, 1941], p. 16).

and he had a passion for paintings. As he was also extremely practical, Maugham engaged Alan to act as his secretary, to deal with his correspondence in London when he was in the south of France, and also to act as gentleman's gentleman on his visits to England. Before the divorce from Syrie, whenever Maugham stayed at Glebe Place it was Alan who accompanied him. The two men kept very much to themselves: "the less Syrie knows about you the better," Maugham had told him; but the King's Road housekeeper remembered Searle, remembered remarking how young he was, and that "Mr. Maugham wouldn't have anyone else to valet him and look after him." Fascinated by Alan's background and history, Maugham questioned him about them in detail, anxious also to meet Alan's mother. But this proved impossible: she knew the kind of man who wants to take a young boy on a trip to Europe, she said, and declined the opportunity. Maugham was curious, too, about Searle's lovers, and expressed a particular wish to meet Lytton Strachey. Alan Pryce-Jones, a mutual friend, arranged a dinner for the four of them, far from successful, as it turned out. Strachey was in a sour mood from the start and Searle remained silent, while Maugham failed to engage his audience with long-winded stories about Augustus Hare.

It was shortly after this awkward occasion that Maugham went to New York to oversee the production of a new play, *The Sacred Flame*. The plot involves a young married man, Maurice, who, badly wounded in the war, wishes only to die. His adored wife, Stella, no longer in love though loving her husband, has secretly been having an affair with her brother-in-law, Colin, by whom she has recently become pregnant. Suddenly her carefully concealed condition is brutally revealed by Maurice's puritanical nurse, who announces it to the family early in the morning, having just discovered that her patient has died during the night from an overdose of chloral. She angrily accuses Stella of having administered the drug, but it turns out it was Maurice's mother, Mrs. Tabret, who gave her son the sleeping draft, honoring a private promise to help him die when his life became unendurable. It then appears that she had known all along of Stella's affair with Colin, for both of whom she has the greatest sympathy. "Perhaps we should all look upon these matters very differently," says Mrs. Tabret, "if our moral rules hadn't been made by persons who had forgotten the passion and the high spirits of youth. Do you think it so very wicked if two young things surrender to the instincts that nature has planted in them?"

The Sacred Flame is a strong and compelling drama, particularly noteworthy for the broad scope of the author's emotional intelligence. As ever, Maugham is on the side of love,* sexual, romantic, and maternal, and against the narrow-minded morality of conventional society. Quietly subversive, he demonstrates his belief in the supreme importance of tolerance, even if its exercise goes against the accepted rules. Each member of the family loves and is concerned for the others, and ironically it is only the professional carer, the nurse, with her steely adherence to "duty," who shows herself to be narrow, vindictive, and lacking in compassion. For Maugham himself, a large part of his interest in the play was also technical, experimenting with a move away from a naturalistic style and toward more formal dialogue. "Stage dialogue has been simplified out of all relation with life but that of the cocktail bar," he wrote with a sideways swipe at the rising star, Noël Coward.† It was his wish to redress the balance, "to make my characters use not the words and expressions that they would have used in real life on the spur of the moment . . . but words and expressions that they might have used if they had had time to set their thoughts in order." In the event, this proved largely unworkable; at a time when Coward was delighting audiences with the brittle colloquialism of *The Vortex* and *Hay Fever,* the actors found Maugham's style ponderous and declamatory and he was obliged to make substantial revisions.

The play, coproduced by Messmore Kendall and Gilbert Miller, opened in New York on November 19, 1928, where, largely due to the last-minute substitution of an understudy in the part of Stella, it was given a poor reception: according to *The New York Times,* it was

---

* The title is taken from Coleridge's poem "Love": "All thoughts, all passions, all delights, / Whatever stirs this mortal frame / All are but ministers of Love / And feed his sacred flame."

† "Everyone but Somerset Maugham said that I was a second Somerset Maugham," wrote Coward in his autobiography, *Present Indicative* (Methuen, 2004), p. 196.

no more than "another of Mr. Maugham's highly cultivated shilling shockers." Maugham was taken aback, and more than usually apprehensive about its staging in London. However, on the evening of February 8, 1929, well before the final curtain it was clear he had another hit on his hands. Gladys Cooper excelled as Stella, while Mary Jerrold and Clare Eames as Mrs. Tabret and Nurse Wayland, reprising the parts they had played in New York, reached new heights under Raymond Massey's direction. After several weeks of sold-out performances, *Flame* was given a further boost when the Bishop of London denounced it as shockingly immoral, thus ensuring, as Gladys Cooper delightedly recalled, "[that] our business went up by leaps and bounds, people besieging the box office for seats, and instead of the play coming off it got a new lease of life."*

IT WAS TO BE a year before Maugham set himself to writing another play, a year spent mainly in travel—Denmark, Germany, Austria, Greece, Cyprus, and Egypt—and in enjoying a long summer on the Riviera. It was only since the mid-twenties that the Riviera had become fashionable in the warmer months. For over fifty years the British, in the footsteps of Queen Victoria, had regarded the south of France as a winter resort, but recently, following the example set by a high-profile American contingent, people such as Scott and Zelda Fitzgerald, the Cole Porters, and Gerald and Sara Murphy, growing numbers of the smart set had begun to colonize the Côte d'Azur during July and August. The grand hotels in Nice and Cannes were now staying open all year, and at the end of 1922 a new fast train service was launched, the Calais-Méditerranée express, universally known as Le Train Bleu, after its smartly painted blue coaches.† Richly paneled, velvet-upholstered, famous for its luxury and haute cuisine, the first-class-only Blue Train left

---

* The same happened the following year when the play opened in Rome and was denounced by the Vatican on the front page of its official organ, *L'Osservatore Romano*.
† In 1924 Diaghilev created a ballet inspired by the train. Based on a story by Cocteau, *Le Train Bleu* had a front curtain by Picasso, music by Milhaud, and costumes by Coco Chanel.

from Calais, stopped in Paris, then, speeding through the night, arrived the following morning in the south, letting off passengers at stations along the coast—Juan-les-Pins, Antibes, Monaco—before reaching its final destination at Menton near the Italian border. Maugham was often on the Blue Train, disembarking at Beaulieu, only a short drive from Cap Ferrat. In September 1928, at the end of his first full summer at the Mauresque, he described to Bert Alanson the busy social season just ended:

> For some reason (chiefly I suppose the wretched climate of the north of Europe) the Riviera has suddenly become the fashion; the hotels have been packed & the casinos making money hand over fist. There have been parties every day & everywhere, & it really looked as though all the world were assembled here. It has been amusing, but a trifle tiring. Now it is over; the smart world vanished as though by magic on the 1ˢᵗ of September & betook themselves in a vast body, with their motor-cars, maids & valets, to Biarritz. Sheep!

If hardly one of the great showplaces, like the Fiorentina at Saint-Hospice or the Château de l'Horizon near Cannes, the Villa Mauresque had nonetheless been transformed into a dwelling of impressive luxury. Approached along a narrow road bordered by pine trees and winding up to the top of the Cap, the Mauresque stood within gates on whose white plaster posts the familiar sign against the evil eye was picked out in red. A short drive led up through terraced gardens to the white-painted house with its green shutters and tall green double doors. Immediately inside the front door was a black-floored, high-ceilinged hall, dominated by a Chinese figure of the goddess Kuan-Yin, brought back by Maugham from Peking. A large dark-green drawing room was given a somewhat baroque flavor by heavy Spanish furniture, blackamoor figures, gilded wooden chandeliers, and Savonnerie carpets; there were comfortable chairs, a couple of sofas, and a round table piled high with new books. The whitewashed dining room was comparatively small, the walls adorned with four paintings of white-skinned, coal-eyed girls by Marie Laurencin. Up the marble stairs with their white and yellow walls were the bedrooms and dressing rooms, these plainly but beautifully appointed, with muslin curtains, white silk bedspreads, and Chinese prints on the walls; each had a desk with a good supply of sharpened pencils, as well as books, fruit and flowers, bottles of mineral water, and a carved glass box of cookies beside the bed. The bathrooms were modern and luxurious, well stocked with piles of thick towels and with new soaps, oils, and essences from Floris.

Maugham's own quarters were simple to the point of austerity. In his bedroom a narrow bed jutted out crosswise from a corner near the window so he could see the garden from his pillow; behind it stood the effigy of a Spanish saint, and built into one wall was a bookcase filled with the works of favorite authors such as Hazlitt, Samuel Butler, and Henry James; there were also Grimm's *Fairy Tales,* the journals of Gide, Edward Lear's letters, poems by Yeats, and the sonnets of Shakespeare. On the bureau beside his bed, among the books, lacquered cigarette box, matches, paper knife, and spectacles, he kept the photograph of his mother. Above the bedroom floor was the flat roof reached by a wooden stairway, and here, a structure standing alone, was Maugham's study. A large square room full of light, with windows on all sides, it had an open fireplace, bookcases, a comfortable sofa on which to read, and for a desk a big seventeenth-century Spanish refectory table, lowered by several inches to accommodate the writer's short stature; the window immediately above it, looking toward Nice and the Mediterranean, had been blocked up so that there would be no distraction by the view. There were only two paintings in the room: a head of Sue Jones by Gerald Kelly, and, forming the middle panel of a triple window, Gauguin's beautiful Tahitian Eve.

Maugham was pleased with this secluded refuge, as he was pleased with the whole house, which was at last exactly as he had envisaged it. "I was prepared to spend the rest of my life there," he wrote, "and I was prepared to die in the painted bedstead in my bedroom. I sometimes crossed my hands and closed my eyes to imagine how I should look when at last I lay there dead."

—

FROM THE VERY BEGINNING, Maugham was the most hospitable of hosts. Among the earliest visitors to the Villa Mauresque were Max Beerbohm, now living in Rapallo; H. G Wells, who also had a house in the south of France; Arnold Bennett, sailing along the coast on his luxurious yacht; Walter Payne and his first wife, Phil; Desmond MacCarthy; the Gerald Kellys; Maugham's American publisher, Nelson Doubleday; and his play agent, Golding Bright. It was Bright's wife, Mary Chavelita Bright, who described the experience of staying at the villa as "the raffinement de luxe [with] perfect unfussed service," an opinion endorsed by many others, that the Mauresque was "a haven of comfort, good food, beauty and entertaining talk." And indeed Maugham knew exactly how he wanted his household run and was prepared to go to considerable trouble and expense to achieve the highest standards. With a well-trained staff of thirteen—a butler, two footmen, a *femme de chambre* to look after the ladies, a chef, kitchen maid, chauffeur, and six gardeners—the attention to detail was immaculate, the impression of ease and informality maintained by means of a discreet but tightly disciplined order behind the scenes. If guests arrived, as most of them did, by train, they were met at Beaulieu by Jean with the limousine and driven the short distance to the house. As the car drew up on the gravel, the front doors were opened by Ernest, the butler, and there in the hall would be Maugham, smiling, his arms outstretched in greeting. "The arms would drop back again to the sides without contact," as one of his neighbors, Rory Cameron, shrewdly observed, "but it was meant as a welcoming gesture."

For visitors the days were leisurely and relaxed. Ladies breakfasted in bed, awakened by the light filtering through the mosquito net and a cooing voice—"Bonjour, Madame. Madame a bien dormi?"—that accompanied the arrival of an exquisitely arranged breakfast tray with coffee, croissant, fruit, and fresh orange juice. Downstairs the men enjoyed a more substantial meal in the dining room, often preceded by an early swim or game of tennis. Mornings were spent reading on the terrace, the air fragrant with the scent of orange and lemon blossom, or strolling in the garden, or basking on linen mattresses by the pool while watching the brilliant blue dragonflies skim the surface. The pool on one side was backed by a thick hedge of pink and white oleanders behind which was a dense screen of rock and pine trees, and on the other gave onto a glorious view over Villefranche Bay. It was here that most people congregated and where much of the day was spent, swimming and sunbathing, or, if the sun became too hot, lying in the shade provided by a little natural grotto formed in the rock. Nearby was a bronze gong brought back from the East that was sounded twice a day to announce the serving of cocktails—an ice-cold Gibson, perhaps, or a very dry mint-flavored martini. During the summer lunch and dinner were usually on the terrace, both rather formal meals of several courses served by the white-coated footmen supervised by Ernest. Wines and champagne were always plentiful and excellent, and the food delicious, classic French with an interesting American accent, most of the salads and vegetables grown in the garden. Lunch might be a clear white tomato broth, followed by chicken Maryland and *pêche* Melba; for dinner there might be eggs in aspic, a fillet of beef with *sauce béarnaise,* and an exquisite *brie en gêlée,* followed by fresh figs, peaches, or *fraises du bois.* One of Maugham's favorite dishes was corned beef hash, the same corned beef hash he had taught to his drunken cook when in Burma; and in later years a great *spécialité de la maison* was an avocado ice cream, a rich concoction of crushed avocado, Barbados rum, sugar, and cream, the pears picked from trees grown from cuttings which Maugham had smuggled back in his golf bag from California, reputedly the first avocados to be grown in France. With such cuisine, it is no wonder Maugham's guests enjoyed themselves. "I am silent with pleasure at almost *every* dish that is put before me," Desmond MacCarthy wrote to his wife during a stay at the Mauresque.

The infrastructure required to maintain such levels of comfort and efficiency demanded constant supervision; Maugham was the overseer, with Gerald responsible on a day-to-day basis for the smooth running of the house. It was Maugham who interviewed the cook after dinner every evening and ordered the meals for next day. Although he ate sparingly himself, he enjoyed and was interested in culinary matters and knew precisely how a dish should be. "[Willie] always had a genius for food," said the very social Christabel Aberconway. The French chef at the Mauresque was superb, but after it was discovered he was supplementing his salary by selling surplus produce from the kitchen, he was sacked and the Italian kitchen maid, Annette Chiaramello, promoted to his place. Annette turned out to be an inspired cook, and she and her employer made an ideal team, he bringing back descriptions of dishes encountered elsewhere, she delighting him by her perfectionism as well as by her invention and flair. This area apart, it was Haxton, "the faithful watchdog," who was the majordomo: like Syrie, he was an excellent organizer and knew precisely what was wanted. As Maugham's secretary he spent part of the day in his office immediately below Maugham's study, deciphering his employer's not always legible hand and typing up manuscripts, as well as taking dictation for letters; he also dealt with the servants and made sure that the houseguests had everything they desired. During the siesta hour, in candy-pink shirt and shorts, he would sit peacefully playing patience on the shady side of the terrace. Sometimes if the weather was fine he took the house party out on the *Sara,* a comfortably converted old fishing trawler kept anchored at Villefranche; after a couple of hours' sailing, the anchor was dropped so that everyone could swim before eating the delicious picnic loaded into hampers on board. A few of Maugham's friends privately detested Gerald ("He had about him an aura of corruption," said one), but most found him a great asset. "It was Gerald Haxton," wrote Maugham's nephew, Robin, "who was largely responsible for the atmosphere of happiness and comfort" at the Villa Mauresque.

Maugham was a genial host, a benign presence whose formidable discipline was carefully concealed beneath an apparent ease of manner. In a sense, the way of life at the Mauresque summed up the two sides of his nature, on one side *luxe* and warmth and sensuousness, on the other the austerity of the artist and a rigorous self-control.

While his guests slept late and idled by the pool, for Maugham the daily routine was strict and unvarying, and nothing was allowed to derange it. At about nine in the morning, after breakfast in bed, he retired to his rooftop retreat, silent, solitary, and safe, and there he remained until just after 12:30, when he came downstairs to join his guests for a cocktail, never more than one, on the terrace before lunch. After lunch he retired for a nap and more reading, reappearing again about four to suggest tennis or golf, a swim or a game of cards before tea. He loved to walk along the grassy, tree-shaded paths accompanied by his beloved dachshunds, all named after characters in Wagnerian opera. (He was a great animal lover, and it always upset him, when preparing to leave for London,* to see the little dogs climb into his empty suitcases, hoping not to be left behind.) At some point in the day there would be a session with Gerald, dictating replies to his copious correspondence, although much of this he answered himself, scrupulously replying in longhand to his often enormous pile of fan mail. Dinner was always preceded by more cocktails, with everyone in evening dress, unless he and Haxton were alone or with one or two close friends, when Maugham sometimes favored more unconventional garb, for instance a black Mandarin's robe brought back from China, a costume in which to some he appeared curiously simian, his diminutive figure swamped by the swaths of heavy silk. Conversation was usually lively, thanks to quantities of pink champagne and the host's skill at encouraging others to talk. "Fundamentally," said Rory Cameron, "Maugham was a formal man and not given to confidences"; he could tell a good personal anecdote when required, but it was usually a polished performance, rarely the result of spontaneous expression. After dinner there was a game of bridge over a cigar, following which Gerald would take a group off for some serious gambling. Maugham rarely accompanied them, retiring to bed by eleven in order to be rested for the next morning's work.

---

* Britain imposed strict quarantine laws, which made it impracticable to bring animals into the country for short visits.

—

FOR MAUGHAM, WRITING WAS not just what he did: it was where he lived. "I have never been able to persuade myself that anything else mattered," he wrote in *The Summing Up*. While at work he was completely in control, in a world of his own making, and in extreme old age he stated that the happiest hours of his life had been experienced while seated at his desk when his writing was going well, and "word followed word till the luncheon gong forced me to put an end to the day's work." His strict adherence to only three hours a day, no more, no less, derived, rather curiously, from the example set by Charles Darwin. "[As Darwin] never worked more than three hours a day and yet proceeded to revolutionise biological science," Maugham explained, "I decided I could probably achieve what I wanted to achieve by the same amount of labour." The tools of his trade were simple: a fountain pen specially designed with a thick collar to give added weight, a bottle of black ink, and white unlined paper purchased from the Times Bookshop, of which there was always a neat stack on his desk. He wore horn-rimmed reading spectacles, and chain-smoked as he worked; in later years he took to wearing a pink elastic mitten with zip fasteners designed to protect against repetitive strain and poor circulation. While Maugham's productivity was unceasing, he always made a point of differentiating between invention and imagination. "I have always had more stories in my head than I ever had time to write," he said, but

> though I have had variety of invention . . . I have had small power of imagination. I have taken living people and put them into the situations, tragic or comic, that their characters suggested. I might well say that they invented their own stories. I have been incapable of those great, sustained flights that carry the author on broad pinions into a celestial sphere. My fancy, never very strong, has been hampered by my sense of probability.

The countless stories in his head meant he was never at a loss for a subject; indeed, most of his life was passed in a state of possession, with ideas for plays, novels, and stories dominating his thoughts, not letting him rest until he had written them down. Because he lived with his themes and characters for months beforehand, sometimes years, there was never any need for an outline, and when eventually he was ready to begin he wrote fast, not stopping for anything. While in the middle of a novel, Maugham said, his characters were more real to him than the characters of real life; he inhabited a different dimension, more vivid and more meaningful than the physical world outside.

With the first draft complete, the work of revision followed. "Then I go over very carefully all I have written & get order into the thing, look for the right words, bother myself with euphony, shorten, make what was obscure clear." The words did not always flow, and sometimes a single page had to be written and rewritten, but however difficult, the experience never failed to be wholly absorbing. Yet in the final analysis the actual process of creation, "the most enthralling of human activities," as Maugham described it, was impossible to pin down. As many writers have attested, the precise moment of alchemical reaction remains a mystery, explicable only as the work of the subconscious, of "the useful little imp that dwells in your fountain pen and does for you all your best writing." Once he had rid himself of the story by putting it on paper, once the text was revised, the proofs corrected, the final version edited and approved, there was the excitement of seeing the work in print; a brief excitement, however, as by the time the book was published and in the shops, "I am no longer interested in it and I don't really care what people say about it."

IT WAS NOT LONG after moving into the Villa Mauresque that Maugham in 1929 began work on a novel, his first since *The Painted Veil* four years before. At last in possession of his own domain, free after years of a miserable marriage, Maugham found that his imagination was all at once thronged with the places and people of his distant childhood: sitting in his study overlooking the Mediterranean his mind's eye rested on the Kentish countryside of his boyhood and the windblown streets of Whitstable; his thoughts were full of his uncle and aunt and the vicarage; and, finally released from the compulsion to write about Syrie, he returned to memories of the lovely, loving, promiscuous Sue Jones, "who had lingered in my mind for the last fifteen years and whom I could never till now find a way of disposing of." In this new work, to be entitled *Cakes and Ale,* ★ Sue appears as Rosie, the first wife of a famous novelist, Edward Driffield, who, once a simple countryman, is now a greatly revered national figure. On the book's publication, the inspiration for Driffield was immediately identified as Thomas Hardy, a fact at the time energetically denied by the author. "I swear I never thought of Hardy at all when writing the book," Maugham told the *Daily Telegraph,* although later he became more equivocal when questioned on the subject: "Oh, I don't know. I've denied it and admitted it and denied it. [There] might have been some small thread of him in the fabric. In any case, what does it matter?"

Like most novelists, Maugham was irritated by attempts to identify the "real" people behind his fictional characters; yet far more than most writers he made use of actual people with little alteration, putting them onto the page very much as they were in life, with small attempt at disguise. And nowhere in his work is this practice of verisimilitude more striking, indeed more notorious, than in *Cakes and Ale.* With the character of Edward Driffield, the parallels with Hardy (who, significantly, died in January 1928, not long before Maugham began writing his novel) are too conspicuous to be convincingly denied: both men came from humble back-

---

★ From a speech by Sir Toby Belch in *Twelfth Night,* Act II, scene iii: "Dost thou think, because thou art virtuous, there shall be no more cakes and ale?" In a letter to the critic Paul Dottin written on January 1, 1931, shortly after the novel's publication, Maugham explained, "the title is supposed to suggest the gaiety of life which my heroine's attitude at all events exemplified. If I had thought of it I might very well have called it 'Beer and Skittles.' "

grounds, both wrote novels about simple folk, both had socially ambitious lower-middle-class second wives,★ both in old age retired to their native counties, Hardy to Dorset, Driffield to Kent. Driffield at Ferne Court, like Hardy at Max Gate, became an object of pilgrimage to the literary and fashionable world; both were awarded the Order of Merit.

By early summer the book was almost done, Maugham writing cheerfully to Gerald Kelly on May 30 that "I am just finishing a novel y-clept *Cakes & Ale* or *The Skeleton in the Cupboard*." His high spirits were justified, for here Maugham is at the height of his powers, the novel a masterly work, technically dexterous and written in a sinuous, silky prose ideally adapted to the author's sardonic view of the world. From the very first sentence, written in that familiar conversational style with its air of urbane detachment, the reader is caught. "I have noticed that when someone asks for you on the telephone and, finding you out, leaves a message begging you to call him up the moment you come in, as it's important, the matter is more often important to him than to you," he begins in a deliberately casual manner.

> So when I got back to my lodgings with just enough time to have a drink, a cigarette, and to read my paper before dressing for dinner, and was told by Miss Fellows, my landlady, that Mr. Alroy Kear wished me to ring him up at once, I felt that I could safely ignore his request.

The story is told in the first person, the narrator once again William ("Willie") Ashenden, a literary gentleman to all intents and purposes the author himself. Ashenden is invited to lunch by an old

---

★ In 1944 Logan Pearsall Smith, discussing *Cakes and Ale* with Hugh Trevor-Roper, wrote, "The second Mrs. Driffield is a photo straight from life. Shortly after the book was published I sat by a 'Mrs. Thomas Hardy' at a luncheon party in Lady Noble's palace and this female's talk about social life in Dorsetshire seemed to come so directly word for word out of *Cakes and Ale* that I honestly believe that she was a sham Mrs. Hardy acting the part for fun" (*A Chime of Words: The Letters of Logan Pearsall Smith,* edited by Edwin Tribble [Ticknor & Fields, 1984], p. 86).

friend and fellow writer, Alroy Kear, a boastful, bumptious, self-satisfied fellow who has made a successful career out of his second-rate novels by assiduously sucking up to critics and cultivating the prominent. Kear has just been commissioned to write the life of the famous novelist, the late Edward Driffield, whom Ashenden knew when he was a boy. Kear's questioning takes Ashenden back to memories of his early life, of his boyhood at the vicarage with his uncle Henry and aunt Sophie, and of his friendship with Driffield and Driffield's much younger wife, Rosie. They first meet after Willie Ashenden is given a bicycle. Unsuccessfully trying to master it he runs, literally, into the Driffields. Driffield kindly offers to teach him to ride, and Willie, a priggish boy, accepts with some reluctance, aware that the couple are socially beneath him. Willie is soon won over, however, by Driffield's amiability and by Mrs. Driffield's sweet nature and sensual beauty, and he becomes a regular at the hearty teas and sing-alongs held at their cozy cottage. Idolizing Rosie, he loyally dismisses the ill-natured gossip he hears about her, and it is thus a shock when he comes across her making love in a hedgerow with the Blackstable coal merchant, a colorful, swaggering character known in the neighborhood as "Lord" George Kemp.* It is soon after this that the Driffields, heavily in debt, disappear from Blackstable.

Some years later Ashenden, now a medical student in London, by chance meets Rosie in the street. Driffield is beginning to earn a considerable reputation as a novelist, with the help of a lady highly regarded in society as a distinguished literary patron. Mrs. Barton Trafford, it appears, has marked Edward Driffield out for great things, promoting him vigorously to the critics, showing him off to her fashionable friends. Rosie, so sexy, so common, is a problem, of course (the skeleton in the cupboard), but a problem with which Mrs. Trafford knows exactly how to cope. "[Her] manner with Mrs. Driffield was perfect. . . . She was cordial, playful, and gently determined to put her at her ease. It was strange that Rosie could

---

* Mr. F. Kemp and Mr. C. M. Driffield had both been members of the Whitstable parish council under the Reverend Henry Maugham.

not bear her." Ashenden becomes infatuated with Rosie, and they enjoy a brief affair, important to Ashenden if not to Rosie, who, generous as ever, sleeps with him out of kindness. By now Ashenden has come to accept Rosie's promiscuity, but he is nonetheless stunned when Rosie suddenly runs off with none other than the Blackstable coal merchant, Lord George. Abandoned by his wife, the frail and elderly Driffield eventually moves back to Kent and, shockingly, marries his nurse. It is Amy, the second Mrs. Driffield, a tireless keeper of the flame, who after her husband's death, and assuming that Rosie, too, has died, commissions Alroy Kear to write the biography. Kear, smugly satisfied to have landed such a plum job, takes Ashenden down to Ferne Court, the Driffields' house outside Blackstable, where the widow proudly displays the great writer's study, no longer a workroom but a showplace. Harking back to a scarring incident with Syrie, Maugham has Kear explain how Amy had had to replace with new all the awful old furniture Driffield brought with him.

> "She told me the hardest job she had was with his writing-desk. I don't know whether you've noticed the one there is in his study now. It's a very good period piece. . . . Well, he had a horrible American roll-top desk. He'd had it for years, and he'd written a dozen books on it, and he simply wouldn't part with it. . . . You must get Amy to tell you the story how she managed to get rid of it in the end. It's really priceless. She's a remarkable woman, you know; she generally gets her own way."
>
> "I've noticed," I said.

Shortly afterward, Ashenden leaves for New York to oversee the production of a new play, and it is here that he meets Rosie for the last time, a contented widow in her seventies, stout, red-faced, white-haired, but with the same sweet smile. That she is alive and in full possession of the facts about her first husband's life is information unlikely to be passed on to Alroy Kear.

In a preface to a later edition of *Cakes and Ale,* Maugham wrote,

"I had long had in mind the character of Rosie. I had wanted for years to write about her, but the opportunity never presented itself." There is no doubt that he had continued to think about Sue after she refused his proposal all those years ago in Chicago; and there is even a small but crucial indication that they met at least once after this, by which time Sue had turned into the stout, red-faced woman described in the novel. In half a sentence in *The Gentleman in the Parlour,* Maugham writes that while riding through the Shan States his thoughts turned to "the yellow hair of a girl with a sweet smile, hair now grey and shingled." Now, in this intensely autobiographical novel, Maugham distills the essence of his affair with Sue, reproducing on the page, as Gerald Kelly had done on canvas, her voluptuous blond beauty as well as her amorousness and calm good nature. The scene in which Willie Ashenden for the first time makes love to Rosie and breaks down in tears, overwhelmed by emotion, has all the signs of having been drawn from life, even down to such details as Rosie's wrapping her corsets in newspaper before slipping out of the house at dawn the next morning. The portrait of Willie himself is enormously engaging, a touching young man, conventional, slightly snobbish, very conscious of his dignity and of the dashing figure he believes himself to cut in his smart new clothes.

But it is in his delineation of the London literary world that Maugham as social satirist shows himself at his most lethal and incisive. Ashenden's entry on the scene compares closely with that of the author's, when as a very young man he was invited to literary teas in South Kensington, to Edmund Gosse's at-homes in Hanover Terrace, and under the wing of Augustus Hare to dinner with hostesses such as Lady St. Helier: it was while dining with Lady St. Helier in Portland Place that in 1908 he had met Thomas Hardy. In *Cakes and Ale* there is more than a vestige of the indefatigable Lady St. Helier in the character of Lady Hodmarsh, "who neither read the books nor looked at the pictures of the people to whom she offered hospitality"; Gosse and Hare combine in the person of the influential critic Allgood Newton, who "was very amiable to the authors he met . . . and said charming and flattering things to them, but when they were gone he was very amusing at their expense." The queen of the metropolitan literati is the influential Mrs. Trafford, wife of an exquisitely scholarly civil servant; she is regarded with deference, in particular for her close friendship with a very famous writer indeed, whose letters to her after his demise Mrs. Trafford had graciously allowed to be published, her husband following up with an elegant biography, "in which he showed quite definitely how great a part of the writer's genius was due to his wife's influence." The originals of the Barton Traffords were a prominent pair, the Sidney Colvins, he the director of the Fitzwilliam Museum in Cambridge, she an intimate friend of Robert Louis Stevenson; as in the novel, after Stevenson's death Colvin produced an edition of his letters, and in such manner as to shed the most flattering light upon his wife.

The Colvins, together with Gosse, Hare, and Lady St. Helier, were all leading members of the cultural establishment and, as such, tempting targets for the irreverent streak in Maugham's nature. And yet his treatment of them is positively benign compared to that meted out to a fellow writer, his old friend Hugh Walpole. By 1930 Walpole, too, was a member of the literary elite, the self-appointed "viceroy of the literary world." He was the author of numerous popular novels, chairman of the Book Society, an indefatigable lecturer in Britain and the United States, busy on numerous boards and committees, a devoted friend to the famous (who, however, quickly found themselves dropped if their reputations declined), and above all was an assiduous promoter of his own career. Over time Maugham had grown quite fond of old Hugh, while at the same time regarding him as eminently ridiculous. In recent years, however, the ruthlessness of Walpole's self-promotion, coupled with a lack of generosity—"he was mean as cat's meat," said Maugham— had begun to repel him. Hugh, it seems, had behaved badly to a couple of good friends of Maugham's, Gerald Kelly being one; he had also, in the course of a recent and prestigious Cambridge lecture, omitted Maugham's name from a list of well-regarded contemporary novelists; and yet in none of these instances does the offense seem sufficient to inspire such a deadly attack: there must surely have been something more at the bottom of it. A clue may lie in a brief reference to the subject by the thriller writer Eric Ambler, describing a dinner party given by the publisher A. S. Frere in Albany. Maugham was present, as were Noël Coward and J. B. Priestley. In the course of the evening somebody mentioned Walpole. "I knew Hugh Walpole for a great many years," said Maugham.

> "I can tell you from my own knowledge that he behaved disgracefully to several talented young writers, one of whom I knew personally. Hugh Walpole ruined his life."
>
> He glowered at us. His meaning was plain. We all knew perfectly well that what he was really talking about was not a talented writer but a stolen boyfriend, an unrequited love and an old canker of jealousy. . . .

Maugham's depiction of Walpole as the self-serving Alroy Kear, hearty, humorless, and vain, is devastatingly true to life. "[I had] a considerable affection for Roy," Ashenden begins innocently enough, before going on to describe with relish the man in all his glorious fatuity:

> Than Roy no one could show a more genuine cordiality to a fellow novelist whose name was on everybody's lips, but no one could more genially turn a cold shoulder on him when idleness, failure, or someone else's success had cast a shade on his notoriety. . . . I could think of no one among my contemporaries who had achieved so considerable a position on so little talent.

Like Walpole, Alroy Kear is desperate to be liked, anxious to be a friend to all the world so that nothing will threaten his standing as a good fellow. When he describes the important biography he plans about Driffield, Ashenden can see all too clearly the sort of oleaginous hagiography it will turn out to be. "I'll tell you the sort of book I want to write," says Roy,

> a sort of intimate life, with a lot of those little details that make people feel warm inside, you know, and then woven in with

this a really exhaustive criticism of his literary work, not ponderous, of course, but although sympathetic, searching. . . .

Would it not be more interesting to draw the man warts and all?
Ashenden asks.

> "Oh, I couldn't . . . I must behave like a gentleman."
> "It's very hard to be a gentleman and a writer."
> "I don't see why. . . . Of course I don't deny that if I were
> thoroughly unscrupulous I could make a sensation [but]
> they'd only say I was imitating Lytton Strachey. No. I think I
> shall do much better to be allusive and charming and rather
> subtle, you know the sort of thing, and tender."

About Alroy Kear's private life Ashenden is comparatively discreet,
although there was a great deal more he could have said, as Walpole
was as boastful about his sexual conquests as about everything else.
After a vigorously active young manhood, Hugh in middle age had
contentedly settled down with a married policeman; in the past,
however, Maugham had had to listen to a great deal about Hugh's
affairs, in particular about his frustrating passion for the famous,
and very handsome, Danish tenor Lauritz Melchior, an episode
obliquely referred to in the novel thus:

> [Alroy Kear's] views on marriage were abstract, for he had
> successfully evaded the state which so many artists have found
> difficult to reconcile with the arduous pursuit of their calling.
> It was generally known that he had for some years cherished a
> hopeless passion for a married woman of rank, and though he
> never spoke of her but with chivalrous admiration, it was un-
> derstood that she had treated him with harshness.

To readers who had no personal acquaintance with Hugh Walpole
this would have meant very little, but to Hugh himself it was an
outrageous betrayal of confidence, proof positive of the deliberate
nature of Maugham's calumny.

Cakes and Ale, ranked by Maugham as his favorite among his novels, was published by Heinemann on September 29, 1930, and four days later by Doubleday, Doran in New York. A new novel by Somerset Maugham was naturally a noteworthy event; no one, however, could have foreseen the brouhaha that broke out among the cognoscenti over the caricature of Walpole as Alroy Kear, described by one commentator as "one of the most memorable literary dissections since Dickens's treatment of Leigh Hunt as Mr. Skimpole in *Bleak House.*" Hugh himself, completely unaware, had received an advance copy a few days before publication. On September 25, he had come back in the morning in a very happy mood from a visit to Cambridge, attended a meeting of the Book Society, then dined with a friend with whom he had gone to the theater. Returning home after midnight, he had started to undress when he caught sight of Maugham's book on his bedside table. Sitting on the edge of his bed in his pajamas he idly picked it up and began to read. "Read on with increasing horror," he recorded in his diary. "Unmistakeable portrait of myself. Never slept!" At 4:00 A.M., by now in a frenzy, he telephoned Maugham's publisher, A. S. Frere, imploring him to stop publication, which Frere told him he was unable to do. "I can't see any resemblance to you in any of the characters," he assured him. Walpole spent all the next day, "dreadfully upset," calling on his friends, desperate to know what was being said. Most did their best to persuade him he was imagining it, while others swore that Maugham was already strenuously denying the rumor. "But how can he," wailed Hugh, "when there are in one conversation the very accents of my voice? . . . He has used so many little friendly things and twisted them round."

Having exposed his wounds so publicly, Walpole had to suffer the further torment of knowing that everyone was talking about it, that there was much gloating, by friend and enemy alike, over his distress. "[*Cakes and Ale*] contains a most envenomed portrait of Hugh Walpole, who is out of his mind with agitation and horror," wrote Lytton Strachey to his sister, Dorothy Bussy, adding delightedly, "It is a very amusing book"; E. M. Forster in a letter to Maugham himself admitted "your laudable fiendishness fascinates me more than I can say"; Eddie Marsh gleefully observed, "I hear poor Hugh says it has finished him"; Logan Pearsall Smith, in a wickedly apt metaphor, described the novel as "the red-hot poker that killed Hugh Walpole,"★ while Arnold Bennett made matters even worse by insisting the portrait was not malicious at all but "thoroughly just, accurate and benevolent." The general view was that that ass Walpole had had it coming—he "cried aloud to be caricatured," said Beverley Nichols—and few blamed Maugham for succumbing to temptation. In the words of the philosopher Isaiah Berlin, "I can see why Maugham, why any sharp toothed person, could not resist the temptation of getting his teeth into flesh so pink & innocent, so obviously made for cannibals."

During October, numbers of reviews appeared on both sides of the Atlantic, most of them adulatory, even if several critics claimed to be taken aback by the author's blatant subjectivity. "No English writer is more transparently, more unblushingly autobiographic than Somerset Maugham," wrote Leslie A. Marchand in *The New York Times.* In *The Graphic,* Evelyn Waugh (whose *Vile Bodies* appeared the same year) praised Maugham for his "supreme adroitness and ease. . . . I do not know of any living writer who seems to have his work so much *under control* . . . he is a master for creating the appetite for information, of withholding it until the right moment, and then providing it surprisingly." As time passed, admiration for the novel continued to grow. Desmond MacCarthy, writing in 1934, called *Cakes and Ale* "a model of construction," while in the second half of the century Gore Vidal described it as a "perfect novel" and Anthony Burgess called it simply "superb."

In print no reviewer was so tactless as to notice any possible similarity between Hugh Walpole and Alroy Kear; nearly everyone, however, remarked, mostly with disapproval, on the strong resemblance between Driffield and Hardy. Disgracefully, Ashenden in the novel shows little admiration for Driffield's oeuvre, which shows some striking similarities with that of Hardy. "[Driffield] gave you

★ In Marlowe's play *Edward II,* the homosexual monarch is famously put to death impaled on a red-hot spit.

the impression of writing with the stub of a blunt pencil," says Ashenden. "[My] heart sank when he led me into the forecastle of a sailing ship or the taproom of a public-house, and I knew I was in for half a dozen pages in dialect of facetious comment on life, ethics, and immortality." Such unreverent opinion was considered an outrage, and TRAMPLING ON THOMAS HARDY'S GRAVE, HITTING BELOW THE SHROUD, and GRAVE PROFANED BY LITERARY GHOUL were typical of some of the headlines in the press. When Walpole finally got up the courage to write to Maugham, complaining of the cruel treatment he had received at his old friend's hands, Maugham was able to use Hardy as a decoy. "I am really very unlucky," his letter began.

> As you may have seen I have been attacked in the papers because they think my old man is intended to be a portrait of Hardy. It is absurd. The only grounds are that both died old, received the O.M. & were married twice. *You* know that for my story I needed this & that there is nothing of Hardy in my character. Now I have your letter. I cannot say I was surprised to receive it because I had heard from Charlie Evans [at Heinemann] . . . it had never occurred to him that there was any resemblance between the Alroy Kear of my novel & you; and when he spoke to me about it I was able very honestly to assure him that nothing had been further from my thoughts than to describe you. . . .
>
> . . . Alroy Kear . . . is made up of a dozen people and the greater part of him is myself. There is more of me in him than of any writer I know. I suggest that if there is anything in him that you recognise it is because to a great or less extent we are all the same. . . .

In his reply to this deeply disingenuous explanation,* Walpole wrote that of course he accepted Maugham's word on the matter;

---

* "Hugh was a ridiculous creature and I certainly had him in mind when I wrote *Cakes and Ale,*" Maugham admitted in a letter written to Myrick Land in 1961, long after Walpole's death. And in a preface to the 1950 edition of *Cakes and Ale* (Random House), he states, "It was true that I had had Hugh Walpole in mind when I devised the character to whom I gave the name of Alroy Kear."

although in truth he did nothing of the sort. He continued to ago-
nize over the subject, rehearsing it again and again to anyone who
would listen. The following month he went to tea with Virginia
Woolf, who described Hugh in her diary as "piteous, writhing &
wincing & ridiculous." "Indeed it was a clever piece of torture,"
she wrote of his "flaying alive" in *Cakes and Ale:*

> Hugh palpably exposed as the hypocritical booming thick
> skinned popular novelist . . . who is thick fingered & insensi-
> tive in every department. But said Hugh, turning round on his
> bed of thorns again & yet again, & pressing them further &
> further in, "That's not what I mind so much. What I mind are
> a few little things—little things that Willie & I had together—
> only he and I knew—those he has put into print. That's what
> I cant get over. . . . And he wrote to me & said he could not
> believe that I could be hurt. He said he had written without a
> thought of me. But that letter is almost worse than the book."

By the end of the year the fuss had largely died down, to the relief of both parties. The relationship between the two men continued to be amicable, at least on the surface: when Hugh's new novel,
Judith Paris, came out the following summer Maugham sent him a
jokey telegram of congratulation signed ALROY MAUGHAM. But then
the affair threatened to blow up again in May 1931 with the publication in America of a scurrilous piece of fiction, *Gin and Bitters,*
which was an overt attack on Maugham. The author, disguised
under the pseudonym, "A. Riposte," was at first assumed to be
Walpole, but in fact was a prolific if little-known writer, Elinor
Mordaunt, née Evelyn Clowes. A friend of the second Mrs. Hardy,
who had been bitterly hurt by *Cakes and Ale,*★ Mordaunt had decided to retaliate by drawing an instantly recognizable, deeply offensive portrait of Somerset Maugham in the guise of the famous

---

★ Maugham had been supplied with quantities of accurate detail about the Hardys
and about the social and domestic life at Max Gate by several visitors to the house,
among them Desmond MacCarthy and Siegfried Sassoon.

novelist Leverson Hurle. Mordaunt had traveled widely in the Far East, which gave some measure of credibility to an otherwise feeble story, but as she had never met Maugham and clearly knew nothing about him that was not in the public domain, he at first took little interest in the matter. But then it appeared that the book, under the title *Full Circle,* was now to be published in England, and not only that but by Maugham's own publisher, Heinemann. Understandably reluctant to offend their bestselling author, Heinemann offered to suppress it; Walpole, too, appalled by the prospect of the whole affair's being given a new airing, begged Maugham to take out an injunction; but it was not until F. H. Maugham, alarmed by the libelous nature of the text, strongly advised his brother to take action that Maugham decided to issue a writ. By this time, the book had been taken over by another firm, Martin Secker, who found themselves in the unfortunate position of having to withdraw it from circulation shortly after publication following the receipt of a threatening letter from Maugham's attorneys.

Within a surprisingly short time Walpole succeeded in convincing himself that after all there was little similarity between himself and Alroy Kear, although of course he could understand how a popular and successful figure such as himself might appear "to a cynic and an uneasy unhappy man like Willie." Yet despite these consoling arguments his standing in the eyes of the world never recovered from Maugham's portrayal, and after the publication of *Cakes and Ale* there were few in literary London who regarded either the man or his work with much respect: when in 1937 Walpole finally received his longed-for knighthood, the wits all said it was a consolation prize for *Cakes and Ale.* Admiration for the novel itself, however, continued to spread. "[After *Cakes and Ale*] Maugham's reputation as a novelist had no immediate parallel," wrote the critic Frank Swinnerton. "Within a few months of its publication all active novel-writers were considerably his juniors."

CHAPTER 12

MASTER HACKY

. . .

*C*AKES AND ALE WAS PUBLISHED IN 1930, AT THE START OF A decade that was to bring turmoil to the Western world, but for Maugham it was a period of ever-increasing fame and prosperity. On October 25, 1929, subsequently known as Black Thursday, the American stock market crashed, heralding the start of the Great Depression, during which millions lost their livelihoods. Maugham, however, came through relatively unscathed, his investments carefully tended by Bert Alanson. "As what I have was invested in gilt-edged securities," he told Messmore Kendall, "I do not care and am prepared to wait till things right themselves again." Everywhere there were signs of retrenchment, with theater audiences falling off and book and magazine sales disastrously in decline; and yet Maugham, as though he possessed some magic amulet, remained almost unaffected. His plays continued to be produced not only in Britain and America but globally, and for his stories he was now paid by *Cosmopolitan* and *Nash's* the astronomical sum of a dollar a word. With his publishers, too, he was exceptionally fortunate. The Depression created a crisis in the publishing industry, and yet on both sides of the Atlantic, Maugham's publishers were among the few who continued to flourish. Heinemann, under the joint directorship of Charles Evans and A. S. Frere, remained profitable and strong, while in the States, the merger in 1927 of Doubleday with George Doran had resulted in the creation of one of the most distinguished imprints in America. Under Nelson Doubleday's dynamic leadership, Doubleday, Doran by the early 1930s had grown into the largest publishing company in the English-speaking world.

Both Frere and Nelson Doubleday became personal friends of Maugham's. Frere, small and energetic, in some ways a mysterious man, evasive about his early years, had great charm as well as a genuine love and wide knowledge of literature; he was sociable and counted many writers among his close acquaintance. "He was warm, affectionate, generous and stimulating," said Frere of his famous author. "All he asked was that one should repay him with a similar loyalty and affection." On a professional level Frere was a shrewd judge, clear-sighted in assessing his most valuable property. "[Maugham] had an inestimable gift of story-telling," he said once in an interview. "His strength . . . was integrity [to his art] based on an unshakable humility. He knew he wasn't a great writer but set out to make a living by whatever ability he had." Both men understood perfectly the rules and limits of their professional relationship, the writer's job to deliver a manuscript, the publisher's to publish it, with no question of editorial interference. "In all the years I was associated with Willie I never had a cross word with him about anything connected with his work," Frere recalled.

> When I got a manuscript from Willie it went straight to the printer. I'd send him proofs and get them back within ten days and that was that. We didn't alter a comma. He used to say, when I finish the proofs I don't want anything more to do with it. He never commented on the jackets.

Nelson Doubleday enjoyed a similarly untroubled working relationship with Maugham, if in character he was very different from his English counterpart. A big, hearty, cigar-chomping heavy drinker, keen on outdoor sports, Nelson was ill at ease in society, although generous and affectionate toward his family and intimates. A reluctant reader, Nelson was first and foremost a businessman, known to be a tough operator and one of the shrewdest men in the trade. "I don't *read* books," he used to boast, "I sell 'em." He prided himself on driving a hard bargain, "but Willie," said one of Doubleday's colleagues, "can back Nelson into a corner every time." It used to amuse the editorial staff when Maugham visited the office on Long Island to watch Nelson towering over the short Englishman, "as a St. Bernard towers over a beagle . . . 'Of course I know nothing about business,' " Maugham always began, "but before the conversation is over he will have got from Nelson everything he wants—which, incidentally, is plenty."

With his enormous sales, Maugham had become one of the most famous authors alive. He was also attracting some serious critical attention, most of it, perhaps surprisingly, away from his home ground. Like his fellow novelists Charles Morgan and Rosamond Lehmann, Maugham came to be held in far greater esteem in France than in England, where it was not done in highbrow circles to take his writing seriously. In France, a professor at the University of Toulouse was one of the first in the field: in 1926, Paul Dottin published an essay on Maugham, "Le Réalisme de Somerset Maugham," which two years later was expanded into a full-length study, *Somerset Maugham et ses romans,* followed in 1937 by *Le Théâtre de Somerset Maugham.* In 1935 Maugham was made an Officier of the Légion d'Honneur for his services to literature. Soon there were other scholars eager to pay their respects, not only in France but in Germany and the United States. In Britain, by contrast, Maugham was largely disregarded by the intelligentsia. His picture was included in the Famous Writers series on the Wills cigarette cards, and yet the three most influential literary surveys published in 1930 almost wholly ignored him: *The History of English Literature* by Émile Legouis and Louis Cazamian hardly mentions his name; A. C. Ward's *Twentieth-Century Literature* refers only to the plays, while the same author's *The Nineteen-Twenties* does not notice Maugham at all.★ Extraordinarily for such a popular and prolific author, *The Oxford Dictionary of Quotations* included not a single entry for

---

★ Nearly half a century later, little had changed: in Valentine Cunningham's monumental *British Writers of the Thirties* (1988), published by Oxford University Press, the only work of Maugham's to be mentioned—briefly, inaccurately, and in parentheses—is the short story "Rain."

Maugham until the 1953 edition, when he was permitted one. It was left to a more renegade group of critics, serious intellectually but ranging outside the walls of academe, to give Maugham his due, critics such as Raymond Mortimer, Richard Aldington, and Cyril Connolly, who in *Enemies of Promise* categorized him as "last of the great professional writers."

The critique that meant most to Maugham himself was written by his old friend Desmond MacCarthy. Published as a pamphlet by Heinemann in 1934, *William Somerset Maugham: The English Maupassant* was part critical assessment, part memoir, recalling MacCarthy's first meeting with Maugham in France in 1914. Of the writer's similarity to Maupassant, MacCarthy says this: "He has a sense of what is widely interesting, because, like Maupassant, he is as much a man of the world as he is an artist . . . while at his best he can tell a story as well as any man alive or dead." Such a testimony was gratifying not only because MacCarthy was respected as a critic but also because he was a member of the Bloomsbury group, an élite by whom Maugham felt he had been unfairly cold-shouldered. Typical of their attitude was a remark of David Garnett's: "I can tell you nothing about Maugham's reputation in the Bloomsbury group," Garnett loftily told an inquirer, "because I never heard him discussed." Such dismissiveness rankled. It was not that Maugham was deluded about his professional status: "I know just where I stand," he said more than once, "in the very front row of the second rate"; but it irked him that a writer as successful as he, one moreover who, like Bloomsbury, had consistently defied public attitudes toward religion, class, and sexual morality, should be so ignominiously ignored. And yet as much as his middlebrow reputation it was his success, and the affluence that came with that success, that in the eyes of Bloomsbury placed him beyond the pale. Somerset Maugham with his villa, his swimming pool, his chauffeur-driven limousine, was the ultimate antibohemian, his luxurious style of living organically antipathetic to the high-minded inhabitants of Charleston and Gordon Square.

Three years before MacCarthy's article was published, the first bibliographical record of Maugham's work appeared, from a somewhat surprising quarter. Fred Bason was a working-class lad from Walworth who in 1931 brought out *A Bibliography of the Writings of William Somerset Maugham,** with a preface contributed by Maugham himself. An avid reader but from a very poor family, Bason from boyhood had pursued his literary heroes with vigor, hanging around outside theaters and fashionable restaurants in the hope of collecting an autograph. With Maugham he went further, and when only nineteen wrote to propose compiling a bibliography. Maugham was intrigued. "If you have a snap-shot of yourself you might send me that . . . so that I may know to what sort of boy I am writing," he told him, adding, "I hope we shall meet when next I come to London." They did meet, and the friendship flourished, despite Bason's making clear from the start that sex was not on offer (after receiving some expensive presents from Maugham, Fred wrote in a private memorandum, "We Cockneys try to repay. But not in the way he really wants—that Never Never"). At the older man's request, Bason showed him around Walworth, the neighboring borough to Lambeth and thus a nostalgic experience for Maugham; they went greyhound racing, to a boxing match, for tea with Bason's parents (Mrs. Bason knitted Maugham a cardigan for Christmas), and to the music hall at the Elephant and Castle, Maugham conspicuous in his expensive black overcoat that he was too cold to take off. He was touched by this young man from the slums with a passion for books and the theater, and over the next few years sent him tickets for his plays, as well as occasional sums of money when times were hard, and for a while gave advice on Bason's own attempts at writing, until the prolific young author grew too exigent. "No, I do not think I want to read your new play," Maugham told him in November 1931.

> I read one of yours earlier in the year. Remember that there are a great many people who want my opinion on their un-published works and in the last fortnight I have had to cope

---

* An inept and amateurish effort, later described by the scholarly Ben Abramson of the Argus Bookshop in Chicago, as "[a] dreadful work . . . full of errors" (written on an undated letter from Bason to Maugham, HRHRC).

with no less than five different authors. I think you have had your fair share for the present.

Bason's ambition was to set up his own antiquarian book business, and it was Maugham who made this possible by giving him manuscripts and signed first editions to sell on a 10 percent commission. At first all went well, until Bason overstepped the mark. First, there was a "misunderstanding" over money that should have been paid to Maugham but was spent by Fred. "You know quite well that you should not have done this," Maugham wrote in a tone of paternal reproof. "I daresay it was a temptation to you to make use of this money which did not belong to you . . . but it was not the right thing to do." No sooner was this mishap behind them than Fred earned himself a more serious rebuke, discovered selling for inflated prices to American dealers signed copies that he had assured Maugham were for personal customers only. The final break came after one of Maugham's visits to Bason's mother: here he was made to spend the entire time not only signing dozens of books but inscribing in them fulsome messages at Fred's dictation, solely to enhance their value. It was at this point that Maugham brought the association to an end: there would be no more autographed copies, the young man was told, although "you are at perfect liberty to sell the postcards I sent you or my letters to you if you can find anybody silly enough to buy them."

APPROACHING SIXTY, MAUGHAM SHOWED no sign of slowing down, with a planned schedule of work stretching far into the future. It was now that he set himself to complete what he had determined would be his four last plays, with *The Sacred Flame* the first of the quartet. As all four treated "difficult" subjects—euthanasia, for instance, in *The Sacred Flame*—Maugham suspected they were unlikely to be popular; the success of *The Sacred Flame* had come as a surprise. But at this stage he was unconcerned with writing to please: having spent nearly thirty years in the theater and written more than thirty plays, he felt that he had almost exhausted the medium and that there was no longer any enjoyment to be had out of any of it. Describing in an interview the sheer effort, "the toil and struggle" of writing a play, he went on to complain of the "awful" business of having to cooperate with actors and director. "I haven't the desire, the time, nor the physical ability to watch rehearsals, to quarrel with performers, and to cut and rewrite," he said. "[With a play] you cannot have that intimate relation there is between the writer of a book and his reader." There was also a growing conviction that he was beginning to be out of touch. "Play-writing is a young man's job," he stated in the preface to the final volume of his collected plays. "Fashions change in the theatre much more radically and more swiftly than they do in other forms of art," and younger writers, "led by the brisk but determined form of Mr. Noël Coward," were now in vogue. To underline this last point he sent Coward a photograph of himself under which he had written "a picture of a gentleman on the shelf."

At the end of March 1930 Maugham delivered the script of a new play, *The Breadwinner,* that began a five-month run at the Vaudeville on September 30, with Ronald Squire, Marie Löhr, Jack Hawkins, and Peggy Ashcroft. *The Breadwinner,* a lively if ultimately unsatisfactory piece, tells the story of Charles Battle, a stockbroker, who suddenly decides he is tired of his job and bored by his family. In a somewhat pallid replay of Charles Strickland's dramatic exit in *The Moon and Sixpence,* he walks out on the lot of them, not, like Strickland, to dedicate himself to his art but simply to start an unspecified new life on his own. Dutifully, Maugham put in time at rehearsals, and he also attended the out-of-town previews prior to the play's coming into the West End. Yet if he found the companionship of actors unrewarding, he was by no means inattentive to his cast, as an incident during the run of *The Breadwinner* shows. After the first night's performance in Eastbourne the leading man, Ronald Squire, lost his temper with a young actress whom he successfully reduced to tears. When the company assembled at the restaurant where Maugham was buying them dinner, the playwright immediately noticed Miss Hood's absence and dispatched his chauffeur to collect her, insisting he be told exactly what had happened. Somewhat shamefacedly, Squire admitted he had "given her a roasting," as he put it, whereupon Maugham coldly made clear that if the actor bullied any member of the cast again the management would lose the performing rights to the play. Nineteen-year-old Jack Hawkins, who with the others had been watching the scene open-mouthed, recalled that when Maggie Hood finally arrived, she was "red-eyed and miserable, but Willie placed her on his right at the dinner table, and spent the rest of the evening treating her as though she was the leading lady."

Since the divorce from Syrie, Maugham when in London stayed in lodgings at various locations in or near the West End. His first rented apartment was at 18 Half Moon Street, off Piccadilly, where he had rooms on the ground floor, the parlor decorated with potted ferns, with antimacassars on the chairs and romantic scenes of knights and ladies hung on the walls. One journalist who came to interview him was struck how odd it was "to see the brilliant casti-gator of modern morals against a background of Victorian plush and lace curtains." As always Maugham enjoyed his London life. "I dote really on the smell & the crowds & the colour of London," he wrote to Osbert Sitwell's companion, David Horner. "I know no place where I feel more myself; & then, it's one of the few places in the world in which you can idle with complete satisfaction." On Half Moon Street he was within walking distance of everything he needed, including his club, the Garrick, where he called in often for a drink and a hand of cards. Sundays he always kept free for a round of golf, usually followed by an evening of bridge with Barbara Back and her husband at their house near Regent's Park. Here Maugham was completely content, sitting bespectacled in a cloud of cigarette smoke at the card table, with the Backs and whoever else had been invited to play, H. G. Wells sometimes, or Gerald Kelly, or Basil Bartlett, a good-looking young actor who lived nearby. A large part of his pleasure lay in the lack of social effort required, minimal conversation, the company of old friends, and a simple supper of cold beef and baked potatoes.

Since he was a young man Maugham had had a passion for bridge, which he considered "the most entertaining game that the art of man has devised." Inevitably his stammer was a handicap: "I've lost hundreds because of that stammer," he complained. "I may have a perfectly legitimate slam in my hand, but I can't bid it— the 's' just won't come out." Nonetheless he loved the intellectual exercise of the game, the ruthlessness, the quick decisions and need for intuition and balanced judgment; and he relished the opportunity it gave him to study his partner and opponents. "The student of human nature can find endless matter for observation in the behaviour of his fellow card-players," he once wrote. "Few are so deep that you do not know the essential facts about them after a few rubbers of bridge." Just as he rated himself as a writer in the top rank of the second class, so he judged himself as a bridge player. "I do not flatter myself that I am in the first flight," he wrote to a fellow enthusiast, "although I think, without any undue vanity, that I might describe myself as fairly well-up in the second class." Maugham's hero was the American world champion, Charles Goren, and he collected all Goren's books on the subject, regarding his *Better Bridge for Better Players* as his bible. "I wish I could make a novel as absorbing as you make your books on bridge," he told Goren, with whom he occasionally played when in New York, once, to his incredulous delight, winning $12 from him at the end of an evening's play.

With his time in London limited, Maugham rarely found himself with a free evening. He entertained generously, usually at the Caprice, the Savoy, or the Café Royal, and was much sought after by fashionable hostesses, among them those two forceful leaders of the pack, Sibyl Colefax and Emerald Cunard. Lady Colefax and her husband lived at Argyll House on the King's Road, next door to Syrie; the two women disliked each other, both professionally— Sibyl Colefax was also an interior decorator—and as neighbors, since the Colefaxes' dog drove Syrie mad with its barking, and the late-night slamming of taxi doors after Syrie's parties annoyed Lady Colefax. Naturally this was of no consequence to Maugham, who liked the celebrity-chasing "Coalbox." He saw her for the good-hearted woman she was and enjoyed being one of her "lions," enjoyed mixing with the other celebrities at her salon. Here he met the Cole Porters, the Gershwins, Artur Rubinstein, H. G. Wells, Max Beerbohm, and Noël Coward, as well as figures from public life, including Winston Churchill, Chips Channon, Harold Nicolson, and the more glamorous members of the aristocracy such as Lady Diana Cooper and the Prince of Wales. Sibyl Colefax had a famous birthday book in which she asked favored friends to write, Maugham contributing a typically quizzical quotation from the symbolist poet Henri de Régnier: "*Qu'importe sa vie a qui peut par son rêve / Disposer de l'espace et disposer du temps?*"★

Many of the same people were also regular guests of Lady Cunard in Grosvenor Square, but here the atmosphere was very different. Emerald Cunard, the American widow of the shipping magnate Sir Bache Cunard, was small, exquisite, clever, and extremely chic. "Birdlike" was an adjective often applied—"she was like a little parrot," said one of her friends. Yet although Emerald might appear featherheaded, in fact she was widely read, profoundly musical, and politically astute. Her intricately orchestrated luncheon and dinner parties were brilliantly entertaining, with the hostess acting as conductor, rapping her tiny talons on the table before pointing to one of her guests—Anna Pavlova, it might be, or Sir Thomas Beecham, or the Duke of Westminster, or some promising young playwright—with the announcement that he or she was going to address the company on a subject of Emerald's choosing. Not unnaturally, some participants found the prospect daunting, but the results could be enthralling. "The talk goes rocketing round," as one friend described it, "and Emerald herself [with her] shock-tactics manages to get something out of everyone." Maugham became extremely fond of Emerald; it was a real friendship, and she was one of the few who could tease him with impunity. Once when he got up to leave an evening party unusually early, he jokingly proffered the excuse, "I have to keep my youth." "Then why don't you bring him with you?" Emerald archly inquired.

★ "What does life matter to him who in his dreams has space and time at his disposal?" (from "Au Pays Musulman").

—

DURING THESE LONDON VISITS Maugham maintained minimal contact with his ex-wife, whose recently expanded business had been badly hit by the slump. Syrie had opened branches in Chicago, Palm Beach, and Los Angeles as well as her showroom in New York, but she had been forced to close down almost all her American operations. A timely exit, perhaps, as there had been some awkward confrontations with United States Customs regarding the bringing in and taking out of the country items that turned out to be not quite as they were described on the manifest. There was also a U.S. Treasury investigation that uncovered two sets of books and some highly creative accounting. Fortunately for Maugham, such embarrassments were no longer his concern: his sole reason for communicating with Syrie was to arrange a couple of times a year, when he was in England, to see his daughter. Liza, now in her mid-teens, was prettier than ever but painfully ill at ease, and these rather formal encounters—lunch or dinner in Claridge's restaurant—were difficult for both: years later, when an American friend invited Maugham to dine at Claridge's he begged off on the grounds that it would bring back too many painful memories. Maugham, unused to the company of adolescent girls, was not always tactful with his choice of topic, as Liza recalled. "I remember being terribly hurt when he said to me when I was about fourteen that he had been bitterly disappointed that I was born a girl . . . I was frightfully upset." On a couple of occasions Maugham took Liza to the theater, which made the time pass more easily, but both were relieved when the ordeal was over and Maugham could tip Liza half a crown and put her in a taxi home. In 1931, when she was sixteen, he gave her a car, which thrilled her, enabling her for the first time in her life to have some independence from her mother. It was around this time that Liza found out about her father's homosexuality, of which until then she had known nothing. "It was the most terrible shock," she recalled.

Lord Wharncliffe, a horrible man, said to me one day, point blank, "Did you know your father's a queer?" And my father always, always believed that it was my mother who had told me. She never did but he couldn't believe it, and it was another source of great bitterness between them.

ON RETURNING FROM LONDON to the south of France, Maugham was returning to his vocation, his writing, and yet the pace of his social life hardly abated. Despite being in his late fifties Maugham had the energy and physique of a much younger man. Although his face, with its neatly trimmed mustache, was beginning to look lined and his dark eyes had shadows under them, his hair, brushed straight back, was thick and without a trace of gray, and his figure was slim. He took vigorous physical exercise every day, went for long walks over the Cap, swam, water-skied, played golf and tennis. He was invited everywhere and entertained lavishly himself, his guests ranging from the raffish to the extremely grand. Maugham was not a snob in the sense of rating people solely by social status, yet he did love dining with a duke: he was impressed by titles and by the old established aristocracy, discreetly thrilled when in the presence of royalty. At a luncheon party, Chips Channon, possessor of the most sensitive social antennae in Europe, observed Maugham's attitude toward that grand old courtier Sir Harry Stonor, noting "There was a trace of subservience in Maugham's manner to the supercilious Stonor . . . and a touch of contempt in Sir Harry's condescension to Somerset Maugham." Soon after moving to the south of France, Maugham was a guest of the Duke of Connaught, one of the sons of Queen Victoria, at a dinner given by His Royal Highness at his villa on Cap Ferrat. On another occasion the thriller writer E. Phillips Oppenheim, arriving at the Mauresque for tea, found to his surprise Maugham in smart white ducks and Gerald in his best pale pink entertaining the king and queen of Siam. "A strange little gathering," Oppenheim remarked. "Our host was chiefly occupied with the Queen, a circumstance not to be wondered at, for Her Majesty, although diminutive, is charming in face, figure and conversation."

Within his own rules of engagement Maugham was hospitable, and he thrived on intelligent talk, not always easily available in the expatriate circles of the Côte d'Azur. There were some interesting local residents, however, writers such as F. Tennyson Jesse, whose Burmese novel, *The Lacquer Lady,* naturally appealed to Maugham; there was the amusing and malicious Elizabeth Russell, author of *Elizabeth and Her German Garden;* and Michael Arlen, who after making a fortune from his bestseller, *The Green Hat,* had bought a property outside Cannes. Among Maugham's French friends one of the cleverest and most entertaining was Horace de Carbuccia, a fat, jolly, bald-headed Corsican who had a house along the coast at Sainte Maxime. Founder of the publishing house Éditions de France and editor of the violently right-wing journal *Gringoire,* Carbuccia was a brilliant, intemperate, charming, and unscrupulous man with a profound knowledge and love of literature. He and Maugham had first met in London after the war and had become friends, Carbuccia publishing a number of Maugham's stories in *Gringoire;* more important, he was instrumental in promoting Maugham on the Paris stage, arranging for the translation of four of the plays, *Rain, The Circle, The Letter,* and *The Sacred Flame.* The translator, Mme Blanchet, was a girlfriend of Carbuccia's, and as Maugham had no need of the money and Carbuccia wished to do something for his *petite amie,* it was arranged that the royalties should be divided between her and Gerald: *"J'ai un secrétaire que j'aime beaucoup,"*★ Maugham had told him. Carbuccia was delighted when Maugham moved to France, relishing the dryness of the Englishman's wit. *"Et puis, vous aimez bien la France,"* Carbuccia said to him one day. *" 'J'aime vivre en France,' répliqua-t-il avec son sens exquis des nuances."*† Maugham for his part respected Carbuccia as an editor

★ "I have a secretary of whom I am very fond."
† " 'So you like France.' . . . 'I like living in France,' he replied with his exquisite sense of nuance."

and was enormously entertained by him, while disliking his politics and knowing perfectly well that the man was a rogue. "He was a gangster who had the gangster's code of honour [but] he was a wonderful raconteur of droll, bitter stories [with] a cynical effrontery that I could not but find fascinating."

Just as clever, if very different, was the infinitely genial H. G. Wells, who had recently built a house for himself at Grasse. Since those early years before the war, when Maugham had first met Wells with Max Beerbohm and Reggie Turner, an agreeable friendship had developed between the two, Maugham fascinated by Wells's huge intelligence and mesmerizing conversation, if not a wholehearted admirer of his fiction. Now that they were neighbors, the two men saw each other often, Wells initially in the company of his attractive but tiresome mistress Odette Keun. Recently, however, H.G. had fallen in love with a beautiful Russian, Moura Budberg, and was trying to disentangle himself from Odette, while she, ferociously jealous, was doing everything in her power to stymie his new affair. Finding in Maugham a sympathetic listener, Odette poured out her hurt feelings, crucially mistaking his courteous attentiveness for partisanship. In gratitude, she inserted a fulsome dedication "To W. Somerset Maugham" in a little book she had written on England and the English:

> My dear William . . . During a time of great bewilderment, you showed me a fearless, wise and steadfast friendship for which I do not cease to be grateful. . . . I love and admire in you a genuineness of spirit and a sensitive kindness of heart which set you apart from the men and women I have known.

Shortly after the book was published, however, Odette discovered that in her absence Maugham, unforgivably, had entertained H.G. with the hated Moura at the Mauresque, an act that so enraged her that she immediately instructed her publisher to remove the dedication in future editions, writing a bitterly hurt letter to "William darling" telling him what a treacherous brute he had been:

It is not true that you are exceptionally kind; it is not true that you are exceptionally sensitive. . . . I cannot bear what I have written [in the dedication], because it is so extravagantly *false*. . . . Oh, William! Oh, William! . . . Do not answer this letter. I never want to hear from or of you again. Finished, this shallow and brittle friendship. . . .

Needless to say, such an eruption made no difference whatever to relations between the two men, with Maugham growing almost as fond of the mysterious Moura as he was of Wells himself.

The numbers of expatriates enormously increased during the summer, when crowds of exotic imports arrived on the Riviera and there was no shortage of lively company: Eugene O'Neill, for instance, the opera singer Mary Garden, Charlie Chaplin, and Alexander Woollcott, who was found to be a great addition when he rented a villa for the season at Antibes. It was Woollcott who introduced Maugham to the actress Ruth Gordon, and to Harpo Marx, of the Marx Brothers, both of whom became friends. Some years later Maugham was amused to learn that in Harpo's "library" in his house in California there were only two books, both inscribed by their authors: a copy of *Saint Joan* given him by Shaw, and *Of Human Bondage*.

By and large, friends invited to stay at the Villa Mauresque fell into two categories, the first composed mainly of married couples, the other of what one observer later described as "cosmopolitan gay." In the first group were friends like the Kellys, the Brights, Frere and his wife Pat, Alan and Poppy Pryce-Jones, Desmond MacCarthy, Jacques Raindre, a wealthy financier from Paris, and Nelson Doubleday, who had just divorced his first wife and was shortly to marry his second. Barbara Back, closest to Maugham of all his women friends, was frequently called upon to play the part of hostess, her brassy blond elegance, her love of gossip, and especially her expertise at the bridge table much admired by Maugham: presenting her with one of his novels, he inscribed it, "For Barbara, because she never calls on his diamonds to the Queen, from her appreciative partner the author." Barbara came often to the

Mauresque, usually on her own, as her flamboyant and far from faithful husband, Ivor Back, was rarely able to accompany her; this suited Maugham, who liked to have Barbara to himself. She for her part knew exactly how to handle him, with a combination of mischief and respect; he loved her earthiness and her guttersnipe humor, and he relied on her long chatty letters to provide him with all the most indiscreet gossip of the town. "Your letters are a boon & a blessing," he told her. "They bring a whiff of London down to the Riviera." Another member of the Mauresque inner circle was the novelist G. B. (Gladys Bronwen) Stern, always known as "Peter." Enormously fat with a round face and Skye-terrier bangs, Peter Stern was no beauty, but her entertaining conversation and general jolliness were considered great assets, even though Maugham was dismayed by her greed at table and not overkeen, aesthetically, on her habit of sunbathing naked. She was, however, a good sort, and he respected her critical opinion. "She is the least self-centred writer I know," he wrote to his niece Kate, "& the more one knows her the more delightful one finds her." Also included on the regular guest list were Maugham's nephew and nieces, sometimes accompanied by their father, F.H. "I think they all enjoyed themselves," Maugham wrote to Barbara Back after a family visit in June 1931. "I know the girls did. F.H. as you know would rather die than let a word of appreciation pass his austere lips."

The second group of visitors were men only, some with partners, some alone, some near Maugham's generation in age, others considerably younger. There was Osbert Sitwell, who came with his lover, David Horner, an attractive man by whom Maugham for a while was very taken; there were Harold Nicolson ("so nice, gay & easy to please"), Harold Acton, Raymond Mortimer, Noël Coward, Cecil Beaton. (A story that gleefully went the rounds was of the poet Edna St. Vincent Millay arriving at the Mauresque to find Maugham sitting on the terrace with Haxton, Beaton, and Coward. "Oh, Mr. Maugham," cried Miss Millay, clapping her hands. "This is fairyland!") Those two ambitious young men, Godfrey Winn and Beverley Nichols, were regularly invited, Winn recalling with mortification his first visit to the villa when he arrived wearing a gray flannel suit. "This is the South of France in August, not Finals Day at Wimbledon," said Maugham severely, and sent him off in the car with Gerald to buy linen shirts and trousers and a pair of espadrilles. Another good-looking young writer, Keith Winter, was reeled in after being spotted in Villefranche with the Waugh brothers, Alec and Evelyn, who were staying with their parents at the Welcome Hotel. The three young men were asked to dine. Alec with his beautiful manners made an excellent impression, while Evelyn—ingeniously affecting ignorance of Maugham's literary reputation, addressing him throughout as "Dr." Maugham—was dismissed as "odious."* The Waughs left after dinner but Winter stayed the night, returning to Villefranche the next morning, very pleased with himself, said Alec. "Willie had told him how well he used his fingers, which made me think of Strickland in *The Moon and Sixpence,* who often despised the people he was enjoying." Later that year Alec saw Maugham with Winter at a cocktail party in London. "Keith was getting a drink and he touched Willie's hand and I saw a look of real lust cross Willie's face."

On a rather different level was the friendship Maugham formed with a brilliant young don from King's College, Cambridge, George ("Dadie") Rylands. Rylands with his schoolteacher friend, Arthur Marshall, and another young Cambridge academic, Victor Rothschild, had come on holiday to Monte Carlo, where they encountered Maugham. Invited to the Mauresque, Rothschild, the only heterosexual member of the party, was somewhat taken aback by their reception. "Somerset Maugham," he wrote, "may have misunderstood the purpose of our visit, at least a stroll in the garden with Gerald Haxton led me to that conclusion." Rylands and Marshall meanwhile were duly propositioned by their host, but once that was out of the way, the pair, and Rylands in particular,

---

* Evelyn's relations with Maugham remained tricky. Some years later he was taken to stay at the Villa Mauresque by Lady Diana Cooper, an old friend of Maugham's. Describing the occasion to Harold Acton, Waugh told him he made "a great gaffe. The first evening he [Maugham] asked me what someone was like and I said: 'A pansy with a stammer.' All the Picassos on the walls blanched" (*The Letters of Evelyn Waugh,* edited by Mark Amory [Ticknor & Fields, 1980], p. 372).

soon became part of Maugham's circle. Blond, blue-eyed, pink-cheeked, and enchanting, Dadie Rylands was an ebullient, magnetic personality. A member of the Apostles at Cambridge and a habitué of Bloomsbury, Rylands was already recognized as a leading Shake-spearean scholar; he had, too, a passion for theater, for directing and acting (his performance as the Duchess of Malfi was talked about for years); and he was an inspired teacher. Although Rylands was so much younger, Maugham was soon looking to him to cor-rect his writing—"his taste appeared to me faultless," Maugham wrote in *The Summing Up*—and requiring him to give what amounted to a series of tutorials in English literature. These, as Marshall recalled, usually took place over meals:

> Lunch would have been going for about five minutes when a tentative, stammering voice would say, "D-D-D-Dadie, I have a notion that when George Eliot says in *Adam Bede* 'Our deeds determine us, as much as we determine our deeds,' what she really meant to say was . . . " and there would follow some additional thought or comment of his own. Dadie would pause and cogitate and then reply, but if Willie's remark was something of a bromide (and bromides from his lips were by no means unknown . . .), Dadie would just smile and nod and say "Yes, Willie," upon which Willie would give me a side-ways glance and just whisper "I've b-b-b-been reproved."

Maugham grew devoted to the two friends: they were quick-witted, they made him laugh, and, significantly, they were among the few young men who had no ulterior motive: they wanted noth-ing from him.

Rylands and Marshall were both struck by Maugham's benevo-lence and generosity, and also by how "marvellously entertaining" he was. They adored his jokes, "which were more frequent and fun-nier than some may imagine," and were both perfectly in tune with his astringent sense of humor: "he loved to make one laugh aloud," said Dadie. "He loved to *tease*." This is far from the image more commonly purveyed of the formidable figure with a bitingly sarcastic tongue. Maugham could be caustic: as Rebecca West remarked, "it would be idle to deny that a great many people feel a certain alarm at the sight and thought of Mr. Maugham"; but he could also be very funny, even if his wit was sometimes so dry it came over as more wounding than witty. Occasionally he was enveloped in a strange melancholy, which inevitably cast a gloom over the company. "It is exasperating that with everything to induce content I have not been able to get rid of an almost constant depression," he wrote to the pianist Harriet Cohen in 1933. "I take it hardly because in general I have high spirits and none of the misfortunes of daily life has power to affect me for more than a day or so." Maugham's shyness, too, was scarcely conducive to putting guests at their ease; his stammer was disconcerting, and he flinched from personal contact. "Willie hated to be touched except by arrangement," said the American writer Glenway Wescott. "If you touched him by surprise, he was like a shellfish quivering when you pour lemon juice over it." When relaxed, however, he could be marvelous company, the gentle malice most seductive and the famous cynicism little more than a writer's pose. Yet the benevolent mood could disappear very quickly, for Maugham's temper was largely dependent on the ups and downs of his daily relations with Gerald. This particular fact of life was impressed upon Glenway Wescott, who as a young man was brought to the Villa to meet Maugham. Blond, boyish, bookish, charming, Wescott was all that should have been found appealing, and yet everything he said was snubbed or crossly contradicted by his host, who was "carping at everyone, his eyes blazing . . . [pulling] his mouth down like a snapping turtle's. . . . 'You're another one of those young Americans who think they know everything because they've read Proust,'" Maugham tetchily remarked. The reason for Maugham's bad temper on this occasion, as Wescott later discovered, was that he had just had a fight with Haxton.

SUCH QUARRELS WERE BECOMING more and more frequent, and were beginning seriously to disrupt the "*luxe, calme, et volupté*" that had been so carefully created at the Mauresque. For Maugham it was essential that he should be in absolute control of his environment: everything must be regulated, disciplined, running on time, and it was Gerald whose job it was to keep the system in order. This, when sober, he did very well. Gerald animated the household, his vitality and exuberance a welcome counterbalance to his employer's cautious, sometimes chilly reserve. He provided a much-needed element of fun and frivolity, especially during the morning sessions around the pool, where he loved to show off his athletic figure in graceful dives into the deep end—in all-male company there was a rule at the Mauresque that everyone swam in the nude. After dinner, too, he was always ready for fun. "I lead a peculiarly quiet life, having made a vow not to go out in the evening," Maugham warned Gerald Kelly, who was arriving to stay, "but Gerald tears about from end to end of the Riviera and he will give you all the gaiety you require."

The balance of the relationship was plain, with Maugham much the more devoted of the two. "The mental domination exercised over Somerset Maugham by his friend Gerald Haxton was total and unbreakable," said Beverley Nichols, an impression also received by Arthur Marshall. "No matter how badly he behaved, Willie was always enraptured by him." Marshall recalled one afternoon when he, Rylands, and Maugham, waiting for Haxton to make up a four at tennis, suddenly saw him sauntering toward them through the trees. "Oh, here's Master Hacky now," said Maugham softly, and the expression on his face and his tone of voice showed "such affection and love, as if about a child." Almost paternal, too, was the way in which Maugham put up with behavior from Gerald that would not have been tolerated for one second from anyone else. But then that, too, was, or had been, part of the appeal, part of the delinquent type, the cocky, handsome rogue with sex appeal and charm, to which Maugham had always been attracted. That canny witness Horace de Carbuccia understood exactly what it was about, having often seen the two together in Paris as well as in the south. In Paris, Carbuccia observed,

> [Maugham] venait généralement accompagné de son secré-
> taire, un garçon d'une grande beauté, sportif, intelligent et
> sympathique. . . . Ce jeune homme était aussi dissipé, fantai-
> siste, gaspilleur et intempérant que mon ami paraissait sérieux,
> économe, sobre et discipliné. Ils s'entendaient parfaitement.★

Was this what was going on between them, an echo of some old
playfulness mutually acknowledged, when sometimes Maugham,
astonishingly, failed to react to what appeared to be outrageous
provocation? One day when Wells, Moura Budberg, and Elizabeth
Russell had come to lunch, Maugham inconsequentially remarked
that he had just had "a most h-h-h-heavenly hot bath." "And did
you masturbate?" demanded Gerald, staring at him challengingly.
The others were horror-struck, not knowing what to do or say; but
Maugham seemed unperturbed. Taking his time, he continued
calmly scooping out his avocado. "As it h-h-happens," he replied,
"n-n-n-n-no."

There were other old established patterns deeply embedded in
the relationship. As during their travels in the Far East and elsewhere when Gerald had acted as pander for Maugham, so now in
the south of France he fulfilled much the same role, cruising the sea
front, hanging out in bars, picking up young men to be brought
back to the Villa. A favorite hunting ground was the Welcome
Hotel. Villefranche was a naval base, and when the fleet was in, the
quiet family hotel overlooking the harbor was transformed into a
noisy bar and brothel, where to the sound of loud jazz sailors
danced, drank, fought, and got as much sex as they could before
their shore leave expired. Such a location was a magnet to Gerald.
One night he brought back to the Mauresque a couple of enlisted
men from the American Sixth Fleet, one of whom, while being
shown around the house, pocketed a pen from Maugham's study,

★ "[Maugham] was usually accompanied by his secretary, a young man of great
beauty, athletic, intelligent and pleasant. . . . This youth was as extravagant,
capricious, wasteful and over-indulgent as my friend appeared serious, frugal, sober,
and controlled. They got on perfectly."

and afterward cheekily sent his host a letter telling him it had been written with his own pen. Such goings-on were relatively straightforward and aboveboard: the sailors knew what they were in for and were well paid for their services. But there were rumors that Gerald sometimes went further than this, talk of involvement with a procurer in Nice, of underage boys, which if true was a potentially dangerous situation, and a serious anxiety for Maugham. He knew only too well how fatally attracted Gerald was to trouble: "just this side of being a crook," in the opinion of some.

A further anxiety lay in Gerald's addiction to gambling. From Cap Ferrat it was only a short drive to the famous casino at Monte Carlo, as well as the casinos at Nice and Beaulieu. Night after night Haxton, far from sober, would take the car and either alone or with a group of guests drive along the coast and install himself at the tables until the small hours, face flushed, cigar in hand, a glass of whisky and a pile of chips at his elbow. After a good night's play, he was wildly generous and would turn up at the Villa laden with gifts; once he came home with a Great Dane, and on another occasion he presented Maugham with a two-seater sports car bought with a single night's winnings; Maugham loved it and drove it for years. More often than not, however, there were appalling losses, and these inevitably were a cause of contention, although in the end his patron always paid up. "I'm p-p-perfectly aware that Gerald is both a drunkard and a gambler," Maugham would say, "but he does have great qualities." Yet there were some debts so large, amounting to several thousand pounds, that Gerald dared not confess them, and on more than one occasion he was forced to apply to Bert Alanson for rescue. "Thank you again for your kindness in so quickly responding to my signals of distress," Gerald wrote after a particularly bad run. "I had a most awful winter in the various casinos along the coast never getting a win at all. Fortunately this summer has smiled upon me and I have made nearly ten thousand dollars. I have decided that that is enough and will gamble no more till winter."

Promises made were easily broken, especially when alcohol played such a large part in driving Gerald's behavior. He had long been a heavy drinker, but now his drinking was frequently out of control. "He was a bad, bad, loud drunk, a big martini drinker," said one of the regulars at the Mauresque. Habitually now Haxton appeared in the morning with his eyes bloodshot, his face gray beneath his tan, sometimes wearing makeup to give himself better color; his breath reeked of alcohol despite copious quantities of peppermint mouthwash, and his hands shook while holding his cards at the bridge table. By the evening his speech was slurred, his mood on that dangerous edge between gaiety and rage which so easily explodes into violence. "*Why* do you have to drink so much?" Maugham would despairingly ask. "Because it makes life look rosier," was the defiant reply. Drunken scenes were a frequent occurrence, both depressing and enraging Maugham, who was appalled by the transformation of his beloved companion into a manic Lord of Misrule, set on destroying the balance and control so essential to the writer's existence. "You do not know what it is like, and I hope you never will, to be married to someone who is married to drink," Maugham remarked feelingly to Godfrey Winn. It had become impossible to conceal Gerald's condition, and there were some appallingly embarrassing incidents. One such occurred when the Duke of Connaught arrived for an elaborately arranged luncheon, accompanied by his sister, Princess Louise, and an aide-de-camp. To Maugham's fury, Gerald, who had been out all night, staggered in late, sweating and unshaven, and sat at the table glassy-eyed, unable to eat or speak. Sometimes he would emerge from his disgrace contrite and hungover, promising never to touch a drop again, but as soon as Maugham's back was turned he was at the drinks tray pouring himself a full tumbler of gin, to be knocked back in a single gulp.

There was no doubt that the relationship between Maugham and Haxton was under severe strain, but it was only years later and in retrospect that Maugham fully confronted the complexities involved. In a number of ways Gerald's life was full of frustration. A generation younger than Maugham (Gerald turned forty in 1932, Maugham sixty just two years later), he was a man of energy and resource who had very little to do, and no outside interests to keep him amused. Except for a small legacy from his mother, he was dependent on his patron for everything, for his salary of $2,000 a year and for his board and lodging, provided in return for duties as secretary and majordomo; every year he was allowed a holiday on his own, usually spent in Austria or Italy. Yet keeping an eye on the servants and writing letters to dictation were hardly the most rewarding occupations for an intelligent man, and there were long periods when he was by himself while his employer was in London. He could have left, but under Maugham's protection there was guaranteed security, and by now Gerald was fatally accustomed to a life of wealth and ease, to first-class travel and luxury hotels, to the company of clever, glamorous, famous people. On his own there would be nothing like that; and yet part of him resented his subservient position, perhaps even despised the person he had become. He was fond of Maugham, he enormously admired him, and at the same time he felt rebellious and penned in. "At times when I'm shut up there in that great villa all alone with him I feel I could scream," he confessed to Maugham's nephew, Robin. There were days and weeks, especially during the winter, when there was little social life, no guests came to stay, it was cold, it rained, an icy mistral blew for days on end, and Maugham was completely wrapped up in his writing. "Gerald couldn't help resenting the fact that he played only a peripheral part in Willie's life," said Robin. "Although Willie loved him desperately, he couldn't give all of himself to Gerald because he felt he had to reserve the most important part for his work." Sometimes, too, Maugham was submerged in a black melancholy that rendered him silent and remote. "He has moods when he gets depressed," said Gerald, recalling the loneliness of these desolate periods, "but then he'll say something to make me smile, or to fascinate me, and I'll forgive him everything."

Up to a point, Maugham was sympathetic about Gerald's situation. "What's wrong?" he would gently inquire. "I'm getting bored: that's what's wrong," was the sullen response. Occasionally Maugham tried to do something about it: he bought a fast motorboat, for instance, which Haxton loved, roaring out to sea at full throttle and spending hours tinkering with it in the harbor at Villefranche. But there seemed no solution to the drinking, which was fast destroying all signs of the vital, attractive man Maugham had met nearly twenty years before. To Dadie Rylands, Maugham confided his unhappiness. "Gerald now likes the bottle more than he likes me," he told him. And in the *Writer's Notebook* of this period there are lines of verse that almost certainly refer to his state of wretchedness over Gerald:

> I could not bear the thought that I should ever lose you
> Or that our lives might ever be disjoined,
> But yet I knew that in your wanton heart
> There was for me nor love nor tenderness. . . .
> Humbly I thanked you when you feigned to love me.
> I bought your grudging lips for gold.
> And now the love I thought would last till death is dead. . . .
> . . . I regret
> My pain, my rapture, my anguish and my bliss.

The sheer tedium of living with an alcoholic weighed almost as heavily on Maugham as the private misery of his deteriorating relationship; his despair over Gerald's bad behavior temporarily obscured much deeper feelings, leading him to believe, mistakenly, that his love for Haxton was exhausted. Every day was dominated by Gerald's drinking and destructiveness, and he refused to consider a cure. But then something happened that seemed to change everything. In the early autumn of 1930 Gerald, drunk, dived into a half-empty swimming pool and broke his neck. The accident took place during a party at the house of a rich American neighbor, Charlotte Boissevain, and Gerald as usual had become quickly inebriated. "I don't know about you, ducky," he had declared to his hostess, "but I'm going to have a swim." Tearing off his clothes, he had lurched off to the pool before anyone could stop him. Gerald came very near to death: his life was despaired of; but miraculously he survived. Badly damaged, with cracked vertebrae and a dislocated spine, he was rushed to Paris to be operated on. While there, encased in plaster and immobile in his hospital bed, Gerald for many weeks had no access to drink, and when he finally returned to the Mauresque it looked for quite a while as though the bad times might be over. "[Gerald] is getting more peaceful, sleeping without drugs & looking astonishingly well," Maugham wrote cheerfully to Barbara Back. "He carries his head a bit askew . . . & he cannot brush his hair yet. But there is no great harm in that. He looks like a rough & there are people who fancy that." Months passed, and still there was no sign of the bad old ways returning. "It is really very pleasant here," Maugham told Barbara. "For the first time since I bought the house I am leading an entirely peaceful life. . . . Gerald seems to like it & to be very happy."

DURING ALL HIS DIFFICULT dealings with Gerald, Maugham found immense comfort in the soothing contrast of his continuing relationship with Alan Searle. The young man was rarely out of his thoughts, Maugham writing to him from the Mauresque every two or three days, affectionate letters addressed to "Alan my lamb," "dearest Alan," "Alan my sweet," letters full of longing for his presence, of eager anticipation of the next meeting, and of concern for the boy's health and well-being. If more than a few days passed without a reply, Maugham would dispatch a teasingly reproachful note.

> Wretched creature, Why don't you write to me? Your last note was brief & you sounded ill. Were you? If so, what is the matter with you? Or is it that you just love another? . . . I'm not going to write to a filthy little beast who doesn't write to me. . . .

Alan, much given to hypochondria and self-pity, was frequently under the weather, complaining of a hundred and one minor ailments, from acne to "nerves" and chronic exhaustion, about all of which Maugham sympathized and advised, even offering to pay all Alan's medical bills. After receiving a letter in which a rare period of good health was reported, Maugham wrote,

I am so very glad to think that you are well & strong & spot-
less. I hope you will remain so. Has it occurred to you that not
a bad way to achieve so desirable an object is not to tear about
too much, to get a proper amount of sleep & not to fill your
greedy belly with masses of rich food?

At Christmas and on his birthday Alan received expensive presents,
and Alan's old admirer, Lytton Strachey, reported to a friend it was
quite clear Mr. Somerset Maugham was "*entiché* [besotted]" with
Searle, which probably "makes his relations with H[axton]
easier. . . . Perhaps he will find happiness in that direction—why
not? . . . It would be shattering for me at first, no doubt, but if it
was really a solution of his difficulties one couldn't complain." Alan
had been pressingly invited to stay at the Villa Mauresque, but his
occasional visits were inclined to be tense, as he was terrified of
Gerald, if needlessly so: Gerald never perceived Alan as a threat,
and his manner toward him remained one of benign contempt.
Much more rewarding for Alan were Maugham's sojourns in London, when for the duration of Maugham's stay Alan moved into
rented accommodation with him. By now Alan had left his job at
the Mayfair art gallery for employment that his compassionate nature found infinitely more rewarding. Through the good offices of
Guy Little, another of his old gentlemen, Alan had been taken on as
an official prison visitor at Wormwood Scrubs and Pentonville; he
was also working for the Discharged Prisoners' Aid Society and, on
a voluntary basis, for the Salvation Army in his native Bermondsey.
He earned a small supplementary income by running errands for
Maugham, making travel arrangements, booking theater tickets,
and sending over to France parcels of cigarettes and cigars from
Dunhill and bottles of Gerald's favorite White Hyacinth eau de toi-
lette from Floris.

WHATEVER HIS EMOTIONAL STATE, Maugham allowed nothing to
get in the way of his writing. "The artist should never allow his
happiness to interfere with his work," he wrote once, "for his work

is more important than his happiness." During the summer of 1931 his main undertaking was an adaptation for Gladys Cooper of *The Painted Veil,* which opened at the Playhouse on September 19. That same month saw the publication of *Six Stories Written in the First Person Singular,* the first collection to appear since *Ashenden* in 1928.

As a compilation, *First Person Singular* is typically Maugham in style and content, even if a couple ("The Round Dozen" and "The Creative Impulse") can hardly be considered Maugham at his best. There are two outstanding stories, however, "The Human Element" and "The Alien Corn." The first tells with sly humor of a beautiful divorcée who abandons her smart social circle in England for the island of Rhodes in order to live, very discreetly, with her chauffeur, a situation familiar to Maugham in the homosexual world and here efficiently transposed. The shocking truth of Betty's domestic arrangements is discovered by an old suitor of hers, who has come to stay:

> One morning when he had been in Rhodes a little over a week, he happened to be coming upstairs as Betty was walking along the passage.
> "You've never shown me your room, Betty," he said.
> "Haven't I? Come in and have a look now. It's rather nice." . . .
> His eye took in the bed-table . . . there were two or three books on it, a box of cigarettes, and on an ash-tray a briar pipe. Funny! What on earth had Betty got a pipe by her bed for?

In "The Alien Corn,"* George Bland is a young man who seems to have everything; he is good-looking, clever, and adored by his wealthy father, who proudly expects him to take over the family estate and eventually stand for parliament. But George wants none of it, his ambition being to make a career as a concert pianist; and

---

* From Keats's "Ode to a Nightingale": " . . . the sad heart of Ruth, when, sick for home, / She stood in tears amid the alien corn."

when he fails at this, he shoots himself. Here the plot, which, as the title of the collection implies, is told by a first-person narrator, is secondary to context, which is crucial. For George is Jewish. His family name, Bland, was until recently Bleikogel, and his parents, Adolph and Miriam, have determinedly translated themselves into Freddy and Muriel. At heart the struggle between George and his parents is a racial and cultural conflict, the son in order to return to his roots rejecting the hearty philistinism of the English shires so slavishly adopted by his parents.★ Finely and with precision, Maugham reveals the infinite complexities of English anti-Semitism: the casual, snobbish prejudice of the upper classes, who regard Jews as somehow, well, slightly *common;* then the Jewish anti-Semitism of those who, like George's parents, are desperate to disguise their alien origins; and finally, there is the brilliantly observed portrait of Ferdy Rabenstein, the perfect type of English society's token Jew. Rich, handsome, scholarly, charming, he is received everywhere, cleverly making himself acceptable by playing up his Jewishness, telling funny Jewish stories, and flashing the big diamond rings on his fingers. "After all, I am an Oriental," says Ferdy. "I can carry a certain barbaric magnificence." Yet at the same time and at some profound level Ferdy despises the world in which he moves:

> Though he spoke facetiously, there was in his tone the faintest possible derision and I felt, hardly felt even, the sensation was so shadowy [that] there was in the depth of his impenetrable heart a cynical contempt for the Gentiles he had conquered.

Over the next couple of years the high rate of production continued, with more short stories, two plays, and a full-length work of fiction. In the latter, *The Narrow Corner,* published in November 1932, Maugham returns under full sail to the Pacific, to the islands

---

★ In 1939 an article was published in Germany entitled "Die Rassenfrage [The Race Question] in W. S. Maugham's 'The Alien Corn' " (Zeitschrift für Neusprachlichen Unterricht XXXVIII) in which the story was used to support the Nazi thesis that racial barriers are natural and that the Jews will always remain the alien corn in any country.

of the Dutch East Indies in the Malay Archipelago. A remarkable novel, and one that has been consistently underrated by critics, *The Narrow Corner*★ is heavily imbued with mystery, with all the favorite ingredients of lust, guilt, and disillusion; clearly influenced by Conrad, it is cynical and witty, and of all Maugham's novels it evokes the most powerful sense of place. Here delineated with simplicity and restraint are a series of unforgettable impressions of the heat, the sounds, the squalor, and the lush, numinous beauty of the tropics. Much of the action takes place in and around a dilapidated bungalow in Kanda-Meria† that had once belonged to a Dutch *perkenier,* a nutmeg planter.

> It was a large, square building not on piles, but on a foundation of masonry, covered with an attap [palm leaf] roof and surrounded by a neglected garden. . . . In the cool of the evening the air was limpid. The kanari trees, in the shade of which grew the portly and profitable nutmeg trees, were enormously tall. . . . You heard the boom of great pigeons and saw them flying about with a heavy whirr of wings.

There are, too, several sequences at sea, magnificently conveyed, with a description of a terrifying sunlit storm worthy of Conrad himself. One of the chief protagonists is a medical man, and in the picture of Dr. Saunders as a passenger on board a yacht sailing between the islands there is a clear reflection of Maugham himself in similar circumstances in the past:

> Mainsail and foresail were hoisted, the anchor weighed, and they slipped out of the lagoon. There was not a cloud in the sky, and the sun beat down on the shining sea. The monsoon was blowing, but with no great force, and there was a slight swell. Two or three gulls flew round them in wide circles.

★ The title is taken from *The Meditations of Marcus Aurelius:* "Short, therefore, is man's life; and narrow is the corner of the earth wherein he dwells."
† In reality Bandanaira, a settlement on one of the Banda Islands, Indonesia, once part of the Dutch East Indies.

Now and then a flying-fish pierced the surface of the water, made a long dart over it and dived down with a tiny splash. Dr. Saunders read, smoked cigarettes, and when he was tired of reading looked at the sea and the green islands they passed.

Of the three main characters, all outcasts, two have made brief appearances in earlier works, Dr. Saunders in *On a Chinese Screen* and Captain Nichols in *The Moon and Sixpence*. Dr. Saunders, returning home to China after treating a rich patient on an outlying island, takes passage in Captain Nichols's shabby old lugger, currently conveying Fred Blake, a beautiful but sullen young Australian whose circumstances are tantalizingly obscure. After several days' sailing they put in at Kanda-Meria, and it is here, in and around the nutmeg plantation, that the crux of the drama takes place, with sexual passion and betrayal, suicide, and the revelation that Fred is on the run after having murdered a man in Sydney. The plot is taut and heavy with sexual tension, predominantly between Fred and the lovely young daughter of the plantation owner; Fred casually seduces her, whereupon her dull but decent fiancé, Erik, shoots himself. But with characteristic contrariness, Maugham reveals the girl, Louise, to be as unmoved by her deflowering as Fred himself. "She was just aching for it," Fred tells Dr. Saunders, while Louise coolly admits, "I wanted him simply frightfully. . . . And afterwards I didn't regret it. . . . I didn't really care if I never saw him again." There are further, deeper sexual currents covertly running through what Gore Vidal described as "Maugham's one and only crypto-fag novel." Fred himself, whose girlish beauty is much dwelt upon, develops a strong emotional attachment to Louise's fiancé, the manly Erik; and Dr. Saunders, through whose eyes the drama is viewed, has a close if unspoken attachment to his Chinese servant, Ah Kay, "a slim, comely youth with large black eyes and a skin as smooth as a girl's. . . ."

RETURNING FROM LONDON TO the south of France at the end of November 1931, Maugham had immediately begun work on his

next project, one to which he had inadvertently drawn a great deal
of attention. In a newspaper interview he had casually remarked
that he was approaching the end of his career as a dramatist and intended to write only two more plays. "This matter, which I supposed of concern only to myself, aroused nearly as much interest as
though a well-known prize-fighter had announced his intention of
retiring from the ring." For this reason the atmosphere on the first
night of *For Services Rendered,* on November 1, 1932, was more than
usually electric, although the audience that crowded into the Globe
full of anticipation was to leave the theater sharply divided on the
merits of what it had seen.

For Services Rendered has its roots in Maugham's loathing of war,
a loathing intensified by an acute awareness of the ominous deterio-
ration in international relations. Although at a distance from the
centers of power, Maugham was intensely alert to developments in
the political arena and often very perceptive about them. "I live on
the Continent," he told a reporter, "and every moment I see the
countries of Europe arming themselves to the teeth as hard as they
can go, and that is why I wrote my play . . . to try to protect the
new youth of today from dying in the trenches or losing five years
of their lives in a war that seems almost imminent."

The play, set in 1930, paints a bleak picture of postwar chaos and
disillusion as symbolized by the Ardsleys, the family of a country
lawyer living in a small village in Kent. The son, Sydney, awarded
the Military Cross, was blinded in action; a daughter, Eva, lost her
fiancé and now faces a frustrated middle age as the family drudge;
another daughter has married beneath her to a heavy-drinking
farmer; and the youngest girl, Lois, already twenty-six, regards her
prospects as bleak. Only the head of the family, old Ardsley, is convinced that all is well, stupidly unaware of the misery that sur-
rounds him. Harsh, bitter, and uncompromising, *For Services
Rendered* is a powerful work, at one level dealing with the destructiveness of war and at another with the devastating results of self-
delusion and of failure to take responsibility. In the Ardsley family
it is the blind brother, Sydney, who sees the situation most clearly.
"She wants a man, that's all," he states bluntly after a hysterical out-

burst from his spinster sister, Eva; and he understands his own position only too well:

> The day's long past since I was a wounded hero for whom nothing was good enough. Fifteen years is a long time. . . . They say suffering ennobles. It hasn't ennobled me. It's made me sly and cunning. Evie says I'm selfish. I am. But I'm damned artful. I know how to make people do things for me by working on their sympathy.

Maugham had no great expectations for his new work's reception, which in the event was much as he had anticipated: despite a first-rate cast, the play closed after barely two months.* Decades later, *For Services Rendered* was to be recognized as one of Maugham's finest dramas, but for the middle and upper classes of the 1930s such radical pessimism was unpalatable; at a time of political instability and acute economic depression, audiences were angry at what they saw as a lack of patriotism, and they were made uncomfortable by the author's dismal prediction for the future. "We were the dupes of the incompetent fools who ruled the nations," Sydney rages at his smug old father.

> They muddle on, muddle on, and one of these days they'll muddle us all into another war. . . . It's all bunk what they're saying to you, about honour and patriotism and glory, bunk, bunk, bunk."

The play had its supporters, although many considered the author's pacifism reprehensible, a piece "of malevolent propaganda against those who live with courage and hope," according to an editorial in the *Daily Express*. Among Maugham's friends, too, opinion was divided, the contradictions neatly distilled in an exchange of letters between two of his literary acquaintance, Louis Marlow and Llewellyn Powys. "My dear Lulu," wrote Marlow,

---

* It fared even worse in New York, where it lasted only three weeks.

Somerset Maugham's new play is remarkably fine. . . . *Incomparably* his best play . . . I was moved to tears and, for some hours afterwards, the area of my liver, spleen, kidneys and whatever else is thus affectible, remained disturbed & exhausted. I wish I could take you to see it. I have more free tickets for next Saturday—and long to see it again. Your loving Louis

To this Powys replied,

My dear Louis, *For Services Rendered* obviously has a grip of a kind but good heavens Louis I was astonished that you can think so highly of it. . . . God! I think it is a thoroughly banal and commonplace piece of work—utterly lacking in imagination, platitudinous, popular, melodramatic and without any distinction except a rather obvious Movie House Grip. If this is your idea of the tragic impact Good Luck to you! Yours, Lulu

Unruffled by the reaction, Maugham continued calmly to carry out his plan, with his last play, *Sheppey,* unlike any other in the Maugham repertoire. The plot tells of a simple man, a barber, a contented husband and father, who dreams of retiring one day from London to a little cottage near the sea in Kent. Sheppey's prospects are suddenly changed when he wins an enormous sum in the Irish Sweepstake. But instead of spending his winnings on himself and his family, Sheppey anounces he intends to follow Jesus' teaching and give everything away to the poor; underlining his point, he brings into the house two destitute characters, a thief and Bessie, a local prostitute. Such a course of action naturally appalls his wife, who persuades the family doctor to declare her husband insane.

Up to this point the play follows closely a short story, *A Bad Example,* that Maugham wrote nearly forty years earlier, but if it is extraordinary that this particular theme should have remained alive for so long in Maugham's imagination, even more extraordinary is what he now chose to do with it. The short story ends with the protagonist about to be carted off to an asylum, but in the last act of the play, Sheppey, who we know is about to be certified, is left alone onstage, where he is visited by the figure of Death, in the outward form of the prostitute, Bessie. A surreal dialogue then takes place between the two, in which before the curtain falls the reluctant Sheppey is gently but implacably prepared for his imminent demise:

> SHEPPEY: To tell you the truth, I'm feeling rather tired. I don't feel like making a journey to-night.
>
> DEATH: It's an easy one. . . .
>
> SHEPPEY: You know, I don't feel at all well. I think I ought to see the doctor.
>
> DEATH: You'll feel better presently. . . .

Sheppey opened at Wyndham's Theatre on September 14, 1933, to a somewhat bemused response. Nobody had expected anything like this. To its author it was "a perfectly straightforward sardonic comedy . . . I cannot for the life of me," he wrote, "see why it should puzzle because the theme is Jesus rather than adultery." Yet puzzle it did, and it was not only the critics who were unsure what to make of it: both the producer, Bronson Albery, and the director, John Gielgud, admitted to a degree of bewilderment. During rehearsals Albery had tried and failed to persuade the author to change the last scene, "so as to make it more palatable to the audience," while Gielgud admitted he was confused by the play's generic identity. "It seemed to be conceived in an extraordinary mixture of styles," he wrote, "with a first act of Pinero-esque comedy, a second of almost Shavian cynicism and drama, and a third of tragic fantasy." Matters were made worse by problems over casting, and in the title role the choice of Ralph Richardson turned out to be far from ideal. Noël Coward in a heartfelt letter to Maugham described Richardson's performance as "extremely false and theatrical":

> I almost bowed in acknowledgement when he occasionally condescended to drop an aitch just to show he was of humble

origin . . . his ringing, beautifully modulated voice was so dreadfully incongruous. . . . Oh Willie Willie how very very naughty of you to write a play filled with subtle implications and exquisite satire and then cheerfully allow dull witted lunatics to cast it!

Sheppey ran for only eighty-three performances, a fact which perturbed its author not at all. "[It] was the last play I ever intended to write [and] I was perfectly indifferent to its success or failure," he explained some years later. "Since then I have never had the smallest inclination to write a play. That they continue to be acted from time to time in various parts of the world, shows, I suppose, that I had some natural gift for the theatre." So it was that after a phenomenally successful career spanning more than thirty years, during which he wrote twenty-seven original plays and three adaptations, Maugham with a sigh of relief shut up shop and left the whole business behind him. Shortly after *Sheppey* closed he wrote to Coward, "I cannot tell you how I loathe the theatre," a view he continued to hold for the rest of his life. "With all its glamour, I found it a frustrating and maddening world, full of childish people," and "I can never get over my astonishment that people remain enraptured with it till ripe old age." (In a sentence deleted from his 1938 memoir, *The Summing Up,* he wrote, "I have never been able to look upon actors as human beings.") Maugham made a great deal of money from his dramatic work, which would continue to be produced, translated, and adapted for cinema and television, but creatively he knew that that seam was exhausted and it was time to turn his attention elsewhere. "I want to write novels & stories & essays," he told Bert Alanson. "[They give] one so much more scope to say what one wants to, & though of course the financial result can never be as great, it is surer; and after all no one but an idiot would at my time of life do anything but what he wants."

Maugham once famously referred to the fact that only in his playwriting had he knowingly compromised, deliberately designing his work to meet the demands of a specific audience at a specific period of time. Now, released from any such obligation, he could do precisely as he pleased, and during the next decade and beyond, far from slowing down, he was to experience a surge of energy and inspiration that was to take him in some unexpected directions. There would be an immensely ambitious novel dealing with a realm of experience of crucial significance to its author; there would be essays and criticism, emanating from a lifetime's attentive reading; and, perhaps most surprising from this most private of men, there would be works of autobiography, one of which in the eyes of many was to place him firmly and forever beyond the pale.

CHAPTER 13

THE TELLER
OF TALES

· · ·

WITH HIS CAREER AS A DRAMATIST BEHIND HIM, MAUGHAM'S working life temporarily took on a more leisurely pace. His name was constantly kept before the public, yet with relatively little effort on his part. During the 1930s several short-story collections were published, there was a Tauchnitz edition of his works, and a Pocket Edition was brought out by Heinemann, who between 1931 and 1934 also published the selected plays in six volumes. At the end of the decade, *The Circle* was being filmed in London for the new medium of television, which would have introduced Maugham to yet another audience had it not been for the order to close down the service on the outbreak of war. In 1933 Nelson Doubleday, excited by his world-famous author's phenomenal sales, commissioned a massive anthology of English prose and poetry, *The Travellers' Library,* with Maugham choosing the entries and writing a brief introduction to each section. Nelson's hunch that this was just what the market required proved correct, encouraging him to commission a short-story anthology, *Tellers of Tales,* that appeared in 1939.

But it was as a teller of tales, as a writer of short stories, that Maugham himself was most widely known and admired. With one single exception,★ all his 122 stories appeared first in magazines,

---

★ "The Book Bag" was rejected by Ray Long for *Cosmopolitan* because of the shocking nature of its subject, an incestuous affair between brother and sister.

easily accessible on newspaper stands and station bookstalls even to people who would never dream of entering a library or bookshop. "Beloved by unliterary, unofficial, unacademic humanity," as Glenway Wescott put it, Maugham, "the mahatma of middlebrow culture," exerted a hold over the popular imagination matched by few of his contemporaries. "Mr. Maugham's short stories are among the best now being written," wrote William Plomer in a review of *Ah King*. There was something infinitely seductive in the persona he frequently adopted as narrator, a narrator who both is and yet is not part of the story, a man of the world with a clear eye and sardonic sense of humor, who in a leisurely manner over a drink and a cigar settles down to confide in the reader something pretty fascinating about the kind of ordinary chap encountered any day of the week in a bar or club. "His extraordinary knowledge of human beings is like that of an experienced confessor," said Raymond Mortimer, and like a confessor, "he is never shocked." The deceptive simplicity of Maugham's method conceals a highly honed technique, as anyone who has tried to imitate it will know: in the opinion of the novelist John Fowles it is as necessary for a writer to have mastered the "Maughamesque short story . . . as it is for an artist to have mastered the art of drawing." His hallmarks were the plain style, the absolute verisimilitude, the dramatist's taut plotting and deftness with dialogue, and often the provision of the unexpected dénouement, the twist in the tale, that leaves the reader shocked and delighted. "His plots are cool and deadly and his timing is absolutely flawless," said Raymond Chandler, himself an expert in the genre. Naturally there were critics quick to condemn him for what he was not: his stories were not remarkably profound; he was never particularly inventive; and he lacked the vision, the genius, "the transforming passion," in V. S. Pritchett's words, of a Conrad or a Chekhov; and yet what he did he did superbly well, and occasionally he approached perfection.

It was with the short story that Maugham found his true métier. "I have never pretended to be anything but a story-teller," as he stated more than once. He enjoyed the form, worked hard at it, and was always on the lookout for new characters and themes. Just as he had done all those years before in the East, he continued to encourage strangers and familiars alike to describe their experiences, even if there was sometimes a high price to be paid for the process. "I find it often a very tedious business," he wrote in his notebook. "It requires a good deal of patience. . . . [Y]ou must be ready to listen for hours to the retailing of second-hand information in order at last to catch the hint or the casual remark that betrays." Knowing his method, friends were helpful in putting material in his way. Rebecca West, for instance, wrote to recommend her sister, Letitia Fairfield, who was coming to the Côte d'Azur on holiday. "She is not mondaine, she doesn't play bridge, and she is a devout Roman Catholic," Rebecca warned him. "[But] she is a doctor and a lawyer, and has worked on the L.C.C. for twenty years, and has some good prison and asylum yarns, which she tells very well."

Curiously, Maugham never seemed to find in the south of France the wealth of inspiration he uncovered elsewhere. The Riviera, that "sunny place for shady people," as he once memorably described it, serves as a background for only a handful of tales, among them "Gigolo and Gigolette," "The Lion's Skin," and the exquisitely comic "The Three Fat Women of Antibes." Perhaps he was wary of raising hackles so near home, as otherwise it is difficult to believe he would not have been tempted by the richly rewarding cast of characters dotted along the coast from Cannes to Monte Carlo. "He had a certain dreadful circle along the Riviera," said Dadie Rylands, "[a] group of very trivial, rich expatriates." Dadie, dyed-in-the-wool Bloomsbury, had nothing but contempt for such a breed, yet there was a side of Maugham that reveled in the trappings of luxury and wealth, that enjoyed being lionized by a transatlantic millionairess with a fabulous villa and a famous chef. Among his regular hostesses, almost all American, were Charlotte Boissevain; Marion, Lady Bateman; Emily Sherfesee, daughter of a meat-packing king from Chicago; Daisy Fellowes, the Singer sewing-machine heiress; the sharp-tongued Princess Ottoboni—she and her homosexual husband were known as Pédéraste et Médisance; and the notorious Lady Kenmare, who was popularly supposed to have murdered four of her five husbands ("Lady Kill-more" was Maugham's nickname for her). "He was too much im-pressed by money, and by being able to associate with millionaires as a millionaire," remarked Cyril Connolly with his customary per-spicuity, "[but] he gave the Riviera point, so that it became more than just a rest-camp for Philistines."

During the winter many of the villas were closed and their own-ers departed to London, Paris, or New York, but during the sum-mer social life became frenetic; the harbors were crammed with large yachts, the hotels were full, and chic-looking crowds shopped, strolled, sunbathed on the sand, and met for cocktails at the crowded little bars along the Croisette. With guests staying most of the summer, Maugham was glad to be able to take them to lunch and dinner at smart local restaurants such as the outrageously ex-pensive La Réserve at Beaulieu, or, grandest of all, on the terrace of the casino in Monte Carlo, where there was dancing every night and a spectacular cabaret on the stage overlooking the sea. Al-though he rarely played at the tables himself (he left that to Gerald), Maugham dined at the casino, attended the galas, and was on excel-lent terms with the raffish father of the Principality's ruler, the handsome, half-Mexican Prince Pierre of Monaco. It was at the casino one evening that Maugham saw the terrifying stunt that he later made the basis of his story "Gigolo and Gigolette." In this he gives a decidedly sour impression of the clientele, so bored and blasé they turn up night after night in the hope of seeing the cabaret artist killed while performing her dangerous act. The group's host-ess is Eva Barrett, a wealthy American.

> It was a representative Riviera party. There was an English Lord and his Lady . . . who were prepared to dine with any-one who would give them a free meal. . . . There was an Ital-ian countess who was neither Italian nor a countess . . . and there was a Russian prince who was ready to make Mrs. Bar-rett a princess and in the meantime sold champagne, motor-cars and Old Masters on commission.

While they were standing at the bar Paco Espinel passed through and stopped to shake hands with Eva Barrett. . . . It was his duty to be civil to the rich and the great. . . .

"Got a good table for me, Paco?" said Eva Barrett.

"The best." His eyes, fine, dark Argentine eyes, expressed his admiration of Mrs. Barrett's opulent, ageing charms. This also was business.

A more charitable picture is given in "The Three Fat Women of Antibes," an affectionate sendup of feminine silliness and rivalry among a trio of middle-aged ladies who take a villa together one summer in order to diet and play bridge. "It was their fat that had brought them together and bridge that had cemented their alliance." Beatrice, Arrow, and Frances (known as Frank) are very much at home on the coast, either on the beach or at the Monkey House at Eden Roc,★ "an enclosure covered with glass overlooking the sea, with a bar at the back . . . it was crowded with chattering people in bathing costumes, pyjamas, or dressing-gowns, who were seated at the tables having drinks." It is here that the friends finally face defeat: after nobly supporting each other through a tormenting fortnight of nothing but rusks, tomatoes, and hard-boiled eggs, their resolve is fatally undermined by the delicious breakfasts served every morning at the Monkey House:

> In front of Beatrice was a plate of croissants and a plate of butter, a pot of strawberry jam, coffee, and a jug of cream. . . .
>
> "You'll kill yourself," said Frank.
>
> "I don't care," mumbled Beatrice with her mouth full.

Never able to stay in one place for long, Maugham had established a pleasant annual routine, spending several weeks in London every autumn and spring,† and traveling with Gerald on the Conti-

---

★ The Hôtel Eden Roc was the inspiration for the Hôtel des Étrangers in Scott Fitzgerald's *Tender Is the Night*.

† For Maugham to retain his nonresident tax status, he could spend no more than ninety days a year in Britain.

nent for part of the summer. Venice and Florence were favorite destinations, as were Munich and Vienna, but the two unchanging fixtures each year were Salzburg in August for the music festival and Badgastein for its spa. Maugham always took care of his health, and over the years he had been a frequent visitor to spas in France and Italy, to Vichy, Abano, and Brides-les-Bains, taking Gerald with him as often as possible in order to dry him out for a few weeks. But it was Badgastein in the Austrian Tyrol that became the favorite. Lodged at the luxurious Kaiserhof the two of them ate sparingly, submerged themselves in the thermal waters, and took long walks along the Gastein valley. Maugham liked the discipline of the spa routine, enjoyed the fresh air and bracing hikes through the mountains, and as long as he could play bridge in the evening was perfectly prepared to put up with the monotony. "The cure at Bad Gastein . . . is amazing," he told Sibyl Colefax. "The place is unbelievably dull & staggeringly expensive [but] I never felt so well in my life."

From Badgastein to Salzburg was an easy drive, but here the pace was very different, the town thronged with a fashionable international society for whom the Festival was an unmissable event. Under its two leading conductors, Toscanini and Bruno Walter, the Salzburg Festival during the 1930s was at its most brilliant, with the Vienna Philharmonic and the Vienna State Opera performing throughout the day, from morning until late at night. Music meant a great deal to Maugham; he was not trained and had never played an instrument, and to professional friends, such as the pianist Harriet Cohen, he described himself as "very ignorant," yet he derived enormous pleasure from listening to music, his tastes were catholic, and he was always interested in exploring new experience. When in Paris or London, Munich or Vienna, he went regularly to concerts and the opera, but Salzburg was the great highlight in his calendar. "We went to a lovely performance of *Rosenkavalier*," he reported to Alan Searle in August 1934. "I have never heard the trio in the last act more beautifully sung; & last night *The Magic Flute*. . . . We leave here tomorrow immediately after the Verdi *Requiem*." In between performances there was a demanding social schedule, with

English, French, Germans, Italians—many of them dolled up in peasant costume, the women in dirndls, the men in shorts and feathered hats—meeting in restaurants and cafés, for picnics and for excursions on the lakes. "I am pretty well tired out," Alan was told. "Four or five hours of music every day since we arrived, lunch parties & supper parties. . . . [But] for a wonder the weather is quite lovely & all the bits & pieces are strutting about in their new Tyrolean costumes." Even Gerald had succumbed and bought a pair of lederhosen, and "expects to make a great sensation with them on the Riviera."

Gerald of course had to be left behind when Maugham went to England, and in London it was Alan Searle in whose company the writer was most often seen. The young man was generally popular with Maugham's old friends: Barbara Back was fond of him, as was Peter Stern, who invited him to dine in her chambers in Albany. When in October 1934 Maugham was asked for the first time to stay at Renishaw, Osbert Sitwell's family seat in Derbyshire, Searle was included in the invitation, welcomed by Osbert and David Horner and cosseted by Osbert's sister, Edith. Yet Maugham was careful never to cross the line by taking his lover into company that was likely to be censorious. With Gerald it was different: socially he was of the same class, he spoke with an educated accent, and his position as Maugham's secretary provided the perfect cover. But Alan was a cockney straight out of the East End. There was no question, for instance, of introducing him into the family, toward whose members Maugham had always behaved with the utmost decorum, looked up to by his nephew and nieces as an eminently respectable figure.

Of the three surviving brothers, William, the youngest, was by far the richest and most famous, a fact resolutely unacknowledged by his nearest in age, F.H., who rarely referred to any of Willie's books or plays. This was despite the fact that he himself was near the top in his own profession: in 1928 F.H. had been knighted, and in 1935 he was honored further when he was appointed a lord of appeal as Baron Maugham. The eldest brother, Charles, had been much less fortunate in life. A quiet, modest man, with "easily the nicest character of the four of us," according to Maugham, Charles had retired from his lawyer's practice in Paris and moved to London with his wife and only son, Ormond, who had been paralyzed in a childhood accident. In January 1935, Ormond died, at only twenty-five, followed six months later by his father, at seventy. In the British press Charles Maugham's death was only briefly reported, of interest solely on account of his family connections. JUDGE AND AU-THOR BEREAVED was the heading over three very short paragraphs in the *Daily Telegraph*. "Charley's death was expected," Maugham told Gerald Kelly, "but was nevertheless a shock to me since it brought back to me recollections of my earliest childhood & youth. He was a very good man, I think the best I have ever known, & wonderfully kind & unselfish & unenvious."

Charles's death made little change to the barbed relationship be-tween the two remaining brothers; there was an unspoken mutual respect but the wariness and hostility remained, although it never had any bearing on Maugham's feelings for F.H.'s children. All three girls were married, and Kate and Diana had both published novels, their uncle taking trouble to comment helpfully on their work, if privately he had little opinion of their gifts. The third sis-ter, Honor Earl, was a painter, and for some reason she and Maugham never hit it off, he dismissing her work as "quite negligi-ble" and making no secret of the fact that she bored him. The only time she got his attention, Honor recalled, was when she became a visitor at Holloway women's prison. One of the inmates there was Ruby, a prostitute, who specialized in " 'kinky clients' . . . the only time I ever managed to interest my uncle, Somerset Maugham, in anything I said was when I told him of some of Ruby's experi-ences."

But of all F.H.'s children, the one to whom Maugham became most attached was the youngest, Robin. Born in 1916, with almost a generation between himself and his sisters, Robin had endured a miserable childhood, frightened of his father and badly bullied at Eton. During those early years he retained only vague recollections of his uncle, "a well-dressed attractive man with a skin the colour of parchment, who came to visit my mother"; but from the time

Robin left school at seventeen, Maugham began to take an interest in him. He was a well-mannered boy, eager to please, and despite a short upper lip and a long, pointy nose like a shrew's, nice-looking. Maugham had always wanted a son, and until now his paternal instincts, so wretchedly warped in his relations with Liza, had emerged mainly in the protective feelings he showed toward his male lovers, not only Haxton and Searle but also young men such as Beverley Nichols and Godfrey Winn. Now there was Robin, and for this nephew Maugham began to feel a strong fatherly affection, an affection, however, in which there was a strong, if subliminal, element of sexuality. This undercurrent of erotic attraction was remarked upon over the years by a number of Maugham's homosexual friends, among them Harold Nicolson and Glenway Wescott. "I'm not saying I think there was incest," said Wescott, who saw both men at close quarters, "but Willie was infatuated with Robin, and told everyone how extraordinary he was." There was so much in Robin's situation to provoke Maugham's sympathy: he pitied his position at home, which reminded him of his own unhappy childhood, and he understood very well the boy's problems with his father. F.H. was determined his son should read for the bar, but Robin wanted to be a writer, and on this he naturally turned to his uncle for advice. And there was another, more sensitive subject on which Maugham was able to help. Robin was struggling with the problem of his sexual identity, desperately trying to persuade himself he was "normal," terrified of his father's reaction should he admit to being queer.

In the summer of 1934, after Robin's last term at school, F.H. arranged for him to go to Vienna for a couple of weeks, chaperoned by his sister Kate. Hearing of this, Maugham wrote Robin a letter that any youth might dream of receiving from a rich and worldly uncle:

> This is only to say that if you find yourself in straitened circumstances, for I imagine that life in the great city may prove a little more expensive than your sainted parents imagine, you can write to me & I will come to the rescue. Also if you get

into any hole, trouble or jamb [*sic*], I recommend you to com-
municate with me rather than with the above-mentioned
sainted parents. Having led a vicious but not unpleasant life
for a vast number of years I am conscious that there are difficulties which even the best brought-up young men cannot always avoid and being as you know a hardened cynic I have a
great tolerance for the follies of the human race.

Maugham mischievously let drop to F.H. that as it happened Gerald
was going to be in Vienna at the same time and would be pleased to
keep an eye on the young people. F.H. was furious—"the man's a
drunkard and worse"—and forbade either of his children to have
any contact with the infamous Haxton. "But, of course, we did—
quite by chance," said Robin.

We met him the first night we went to the opera, and I was
extremely disappointed, for he didn't look wicked at all: he
was a smart, dapper, lean man of forty with a small moustache, a cheerful laugh and an innocent smile. . . . But a week
later, when Gerald got blind drunk in a weinstube, I began to
appreciate that he wasn't quite as innocent as he seemed.

Nor, by the time he returned home, was Robin. "I learned many
things in Vienna at the age of seventeen," he wrote later. Gerald offered to take him to Venice for a couple of days on his own, driving
there and back in Maugham's big Voisin coupé. They shared a twin-
bedded room at the Danieli, and it was here that Gerald made his
intentions plain. Robin, shocked, pushed him off, whereupon Gerald crossly returned to his own bed. "I should have known," he
grumbled, before turning out the light and falling asleep. The next
day, to the boy's relief, no reference was made to the previous
night; on the contrary, "he was very kind to me [and] took me
sightseeing around Venice."

Robin was only a year younger than Liza, but since the Maughams' divorce the cousins, close in childhood, had been kept apart.
When Liza was seventeen, Syrie arranged for her to be presented at

court, and during her first season had thrown a memorable dance, paid for by Maugham, at the house on the King's Road. The ballroom was banked with white flowers, a parquet floor had been laid in the garden, and a coffee stall set up in Glebe Place. "I had a lovely party and enjoyed everything very, very much," said Liza, who had looked ravishing in pink and white tulle. "It was a very happy time." From the moment of Liza's début, Syrie focused on her daughter with a new intensity. To all intents and purposes Liza was an only child, her half brother, Mounteney, having been consigned to the past. (Judged to be backward after leaving school, he had been put in the care of a farming couple in Essex, and his mother was either denied access or of her own volition gave up trying to see him.) Liza was now the center of her life, and the socially ambitious Syrie was determined not only that Liza should marry soon but that she should marry well. Nothing was considered too good for Liza, and her mother with her formidable energy oversaw every detail, every moment of her day. "She was wrapped up in cottonwool," said one of Liza's friends. "She and Syrie were *very, very* close . . . far too much so."

Needless to say, Maugham had not attended his daughter's dance, and he continued to keep as much distance between himself and his ex-wife as possible. From time to time, however, he was reluctantly involved in her affairs, as when Syrie, up to her old tricks, was again found to be engaging in some fancy footwork with the Inland Revenue. "What do you think," he wrote to Barbara Back in March 1934,

> I have to appear before the income tax authorities who are claiming two thousand pounds from me for Syrie's income tax: she is swearing that during the first four years I was at the Villa Mauresque she & I were living together. A bit thick, eh?

This letter was written from Spain, from the Alhambra Palace Hotel in Granada. For some time Maugham had felt drawn to return to the subject of Spain, which since his year in Seville in the 1890s had continued to exert a powerful fascination. At ease in the language and widely read, especially in the writers of the Golden Age, his first idea had been a novel set in the sixteenth century, but now this was put aside in favor of a highly personal travel book. In February 1934 he and Gerald set off on a six-week tour in the Voisin, taking in Barcelona, Granada, Málaga, Seville, Córdoba, Toledo, and Madrid. In Córdoba they were pleased to run into Alan Pryce-Jones, who joined them on a couple of expeditions into the spectacular mountains above Granada. Pryce-Jones was surprised by Maugham's practicality: after stopping for lunch at a small inn, he was impressed to see Maugham go into the kitchen and in fluent Spanish order an excellent luncheon of raw ham, a tortilla, fish, and a good bottle of manzanilla sherry. Nonetheless the older man's company proved something of a strain, and returning to their hotel in the evening Alan found it a relief to have a cocktail alone in the bar with Gerald, that "odious charmer," as he referred to him, who regaled him with a funny story about taking the writer J. B. Priestley to a brothel in Nice.

Don Fernando, the work resulting from the expedition, is an agreeable ramble through fifteenth- and sixteenth-century Spain, an idiosyncratic introduction to Spanish history and culture interspersed with recollections of Maugham's own travels in the country as a young man. In an easy, discursive manner he considers the work of the great novelists and dramatists, of Cervantes, Calderón, and Lope de Vega, as well as the religious writers and mystics such as Saint Teresa, Saint Ignatius Loyola, and Fray Luis de León. Interspersed with these reflections are descriptions of the Spanish character and way of life, and an account of the work of the great Spanish painters, Velázquez, El Greco, and Zurbarán. From an autobiographical point of view the most interesting section is on El Greco, in which Maugham in discussing the painter's putative homosexuality revealingly sets out his own view of the characteristics of the homosexual artist:

[A] distinctive trait of the homosexual is a lack of deep seriousness over certain things that normal men take seriously. This ranges from an inane flippancy to a sardonic humour. He has a wilfulness that attaches importance to things that most men find trivial and on the other hand regards cynically the subjects which the common opinion of mankind has held essential to its spiritual welfare. . . . He has small power of invention, but a wonderful gift for delightful embroidery. . . . He stands on the bank, aloof and ironical, and watches the river of life flow on.

Published in 1935, *Don Fernando* received on the whole an indifferent reception, most critics treating it with little more than polite interest. "St. John of the Cross is not everyone's cup of tea," as Raymond Mortimer remarked in the *New Statesman*.

THE TRIP TO SPAIN had been a success, and Gerald, since recovering from his accident, had been much more like his charming old self, "kind, very considerate & easy to get on with," Maugham told Barbara. He was drinking less and concentrating more on his duties toward his employer, and as a result the quality of domestic life at the Mauresque had greatly improved. "I have been playing golf today, a lovely day, & came back very tired," Maugham wrote one evening to Alan Searle.

> Now I am writing to you after a long soak in a pine bath. Gerald has just given me a Baccardi [*sic*] cocktail & I am breaking off this little letter to drink it in peace. It was delicious, made with fresh limes from the garden. . . . Here is Ernest to announce dinner. . . . The fleet is in [he subsequently continued] & I went down the other night to have a look see; but it was lateish, & there was nothing much to reward me. . . . We are rather thinking of going down again this evening. . . .

So encouraged was Maugham by Gerald's good behavior that he began planning a journey to Central America and the Caribbean, the first long voyage since the two of them had returned from the South Pacific in 1926. However, it was at this point that matters started to deteriorate fast, and Maugham was soon confiding to Searle and Barbara his intense anxiety about Haxton: the situation was worse then ever, it appeared, with Gerald not only back on the bottle but suffering fits of delirium tremens. "Things are going very badly here & I do not know exactly what is going to happen," Maugham wrote to Searle in April 1935. "I am restless & miserable & do not know what to do." By July little had changed and Maugham admitted to feeling deeply depressed, writing to Searle in August that circumstances were desperate and that he was left with no choice but to issue Gerald with an ultimatum.

> The doctor tells me that G. is so unbalanced that I must take no notice of anything he says, but in another week he (the doctor) assures me he will be in a state sufficiently normal for me to be able to discuss the position reasonably with him. . . . I hope it will settle things for good & all. I am afraid it won't, however, & that not much will come of it. . . . Anyhow, even if the worst comes to the worst, & I don't really know what *is* the worst, the air will to some extent be cleared.

The plan seemed to work: Gerald swore he would go on the wagon, and on November 3 they finally set sail for New York on the SS *Europa,* en route for the West Indies.

The crossing was agreeable, Maugham pleased to have been allotted a large and luxurious suite, and Gerald in excellent form. "He has got off [had sex] twice during the journey & is very much pleased at having such a success," Maugham reported to Alan. Each morning a sheaf of radio telegrams was delivered with invitations to events in New York, and on arrival a swarm of journalists and photographers came on board to question Maugham about his plans. Having hoped for a quiet few days with Nelson Doubleday and his new wife, Ellen, at their house on Long Island, he was slightly dismayed by the succession of large parties the Doubledays had arranged in his honor. Returning to Manhattan, comfortably installed at the Ritz-Carlton, Maugham was immediately caught up in a whirl of more parties, of theatergoing, newspaper interviews, photograph sessions, book signings, and insistent telephone calls from studio heads in Hollywood offering "fantastic contracts," which, he said, "it gives me singular pleasure to turn . . . down." Maugham was a celebrity, recognized everywhere he went. The biographer Leon Edel remembers his excitement at catching sight of this famous man simply strolling down Madison Avenue like anyone else, "small, neat, impeccably dressed, wearing a soft hat he sometimes had to hang on to while his other hand controlled the straining leashes of his dachshunds." One of the few genuinely enjoyable social occasions was a small luncheon with Maugham's old friend, the novelist and photographer Carl Van Vechten, who had taken the opportunity of this visit to take a remarkable series of photographs of Maugham and Haxton together. And even with so much hospitality pressed upon them, Haxton remained resolutely abstemious. "Gerald," Maugham reported, "has been behaving with great prudence & I have no complaints to make whatever."

Maugham had been looking forward to the three-month voyage in the Caribbean, counting on it to provide him with interesting new material for his fiction: Rudyard Kipling, who had been there five years earlier, had recommended its potential. The reality was uninspiring. Haiti was the first stop, but the island whose exoticism and decadence was later to enthrall Graham Greene★ had little to offer Maugham. "The place is picturesque enough," he told Alan, "[but] there are no amusements of any kind." The next port of call, Martinique, was no better—"I see no sign of any material that I can make use of"—with Dominica and Trinidad equally barren. "The traders & planters can think & talk of nothing but rum which is their sole source of revenue [and] the wives are dull, dull, dull. . . . I ask you, what material can a novelist possibly hope to find in circumstances like these," Maugham wondered, gloomily concluding, "There is not the romance & excitement in the life in these islands that there is in the South Seas & in Malaya."

A longer and more considered account of the voyage was sent to a relatively new friend, Lady Juliet Duff, at whose house in Wilt-

---

★ Greene's novel about Haiti, *The Comedians,* was published in 1966.

shire Maugham had stayed on his last visit to England. Lady Juliet, now in her fifties, was the daughter of the Earl of Lonsdale and a noted patron of the arts, with a wide circle of friends in the theater and ballet worlds. Maugham was proud of his acquaintance with Lady Juliet: "You can't go higher in English society than [that]," he used to boast; and wishing to make a good impression, he took care with composing his letter, which gives an interesting picture of Maugham at work. "The West Indies are disappointing," he begins.

> They are very pretty of course, though not nearly so pretty as the islands of the South Seas, & the people who live in them are in too close touch with England or the US to have acquired the oddness which makes them when they live in places out of the beaten track so fascinating. . . . I expected Martinique to be very romantic [but] I found only mean little French fonctionnaires whose only idea was to save as much money as they could so that they could get back to France & planters whose sole conversation was the sugar out of which they make their living. They were immensely kind to me. They asked me night after night to dinner parties of twenty people, when I was placed between the women . . . who were completely silent; I started a topic of conversation, it dropped, I started another, it dropped; by the time we had finished the fish I had run dry & could think of nothing more to say. . . .

During these dull weeks among the islands there was one brief period of absorbing interest. While staying on the South American mainland at Cayenne, the capital of French Guiana, Maugham obtained permission to visit the great penal colony at Saint-Laurent-de-Maroni. This was much more to his taste. Saint-Laurent, more like a town than a prison, had a population of over six thousand entirely made up of convicts and their guards; all shipped out from France, a few were en route to far harsher conditions offshore, to one of the Îles de Salut, of which the Île de Diable (Devil's Island) was the most notorious; the majority, however, had remained at

Saint-Laurent for years, considered too passive and harmless to attempt escape. The governor lent Maugham a bungalow in which to stay for a few days, "& gave me a couple of murderers serving their sentence to look after me," he told Juliet Duff. "The director of the gaol said to me, you know, they're perfectly honest, you can leave anything about; but all the same I locked my door & my shutters when I went to bed at night." At Saint-Laurent, Maugham had "a wonderful time," conducted all over the camp and allowed to talk to the inmates. In his notebook he describes the layout of the settlement in some detail, including the sinister execution cell:

> The guillotine is in a small room within the prison. . . . To make sure that it will work well a banana stem is used for practice because it is of the same thickness as a man's neck. From the time a man is strapped up to the time his head is off, it takes only thirty seconds. The executioner gets a hundred francs for each execution.

In his interviews with the convicts, many of them murderers, the subject that interested him most was remorse, "[but] of all the men I questioned," he said, "I only found one who regretted his crime." Saint-Laurent-de-Maroni was undoubtedly the highlight of the trip. "I got one very good story★ out of my visit," he told Alan. "Grim naturally, but I think uncommon. I must be one of the few Englishmen who have seen that place."

From Cayenne, Maugham and Haxton began the long journey home, first by banana boat up the Mexican coast to California, staying for a few days in Hollywood, where Maugham was much fêted, then with Bert Alanson in San Francisco, before taking the train to New York, sailing from there at the beginning of April 1936. At

---

★ "An Official Position" tells the story of Louis Remire, a policeman from Lyons, who is serving a twelve-year sentence at Saint-Laurent for murdering his wife. Because of his good behavior he has been appointed the prison executioner. A brutal and conscientious man, he loves the job, but naturally is loathed by his fellow convicts, who devise a terrifying end to his career.

Cherbourg, as so often before, the two men parted, Gerald and the heavy luggage returning to the Mauresque, Maugham going on to London.

UPPERMOST IN MAUGHAM'S MIND was reunion with Alan Searle. "I have been thinking much of you lately, more than usual in fact," he had written from New York, "& I have got suggestions to make to you which I hope will please you." During the past five months Maugham had written every few days to Alan in England, describing the voyage ("My happiness would be complete if you were only here to share it with me") but also and at length discussing plans for Alan's future, offering advice on everything from his finances and his love affairs to his work in the prison service, and chivvying him about his health. Every page of this correspondence is permeated with Maugham's own deep feelings for the young man, while at the same time and in a fatherly fashion he is careful to put Searle's interests first, debating with scrupulous objectivity the pros and cons of Alan's various plans and ambitions. There was, for instance, a marriage proposal made to Alan by a rich older woman. "I can quite see that the prospect of unlimited money & all possible luxury . . . must be exciting & tempting," Maugham allowed,

> [but] remember that to be a rich woman's husband is a whole time job. No woman that I have ever known fails to exact her money's worth. . . . Further of course you must be prepared to give up your friends. . . .

And this last point revealed the crux of the matter:

> So far as I am concerned I should regret it if you did a thing which must necessarily separate me from you. We have been so intimate for so many years that I have got into the habit of looking upon you as a fixture in my life or what remains of it; but that is a purely selfish & personal view.

The truth was that Maugham now looked longingly upon Alan as the ideal companion. He was attractive, efficient, and sweet-natured; he enjoyed travel, was musical, and knew about and had a very good eye for pictures; unlike Gerald, Alan never got drunk, never made scenes; above all he was biddable. First and foremost Maugham was a writer, and about his writing he was ruthlessly self-protective; he needed to guard his privacy, to keep the outside world at bay. For years the role of guardian and administrator had been Gerald's, but Gerald could no longer be relied upon; not only was his behavior destroying the essential solitude and calm, but it was often he who had to be looked after, requiring an expenditure of time and emotional energy on Maugham's part that was profoundly resented. For the moment all was well, but Maugham was skeptical of any lasting reform, and he dreaded a return to the horrific experiences of the recent past. It was Gerald whom he loved, Gerald who was in his blood, but Alan whom he needed; there was no question of Maugham's abandoning Gerald, but he felt that Searle was essential to his work, and it was this strong instinct for artistic survival that was largely driving him now.

. Maugham arrived in London on April 10, 1936. "I am only coming to see you," he had written to Alan before setting out on his transatlantic crossing. The most important topic to be discussed was that of the young man's future. Alan loved his work with the Salvation Army in Bermondsey and for the Discharged Prisoners' Aid Society at Wormwood Scrubs, and he kept Maugham well supplied with stories.* On several occasions he took him to see for himself the mean streets of the East End, and once even arranged for him to visit the prison. There was no immediate possibility of Alan's working full-time for Maugham, but they talked about various schemes that in the future might allow Searle to come more often to the Mauresque. "Of course what I should like is that you should spend at least several months, a year if you thought you could, with me & making the Mauresque your headquarters. . . . It would be

---

* The plots of "Episode," "The Kite," and "The Round Dozen" were all supplied by Alan.

grand to have you there for an indefinite time & be able to go long trips here & there with you." In the meantime, Maugham had to content himself with seeing Alan on his visits to London and for occasional holidays on the Riviera.

On his way south Maugham stopped in Paris, partly at the request of Marie Laurencin, who had asked to paint his portrait. Mlle Laurencin had been to the Mauresque several years earlier to see the four pictures of hers, of graceful, pale-faced young girls, frivolous and sugary, that hung in the dining room. "*Ses Laurencins étaient jolis,*" she said approvingly. In 1934 Maugham wrote an enthusiastic preface for the catalogue to a Laurencin exhibition at the Mayor Gallery in London, for which no doubt she felt indebted. He for his part was flattered by her suggestion that he should sit for her, "but felt it only right to remind her that I was not a young thing with a complexion of milk and roses . . . but an elderly gentleman with a sallow, wrinkled skin and tired eyes." He posed in her studio during four afternoons, during which she told him the story of her life.* When she had finished she put down her brushes and looked analytically at the canvas. "*Vous savez,*" she said, "*on se plaint toujours que mes portraits ne sont pas ressemblants. Je ne peux pas vous dire à quel point je m'en fou.*"† With that, she lifted the canvas off the easel and handed it to her sitter as a present. Maugham expressed his gratitude but privately he considered his portrait was indeed a poor likeness, "lousy," as he privately described it. Later his admiration for her work diminished further and he sold his Laurencins, causing the painter considerable pique when she heard of it: he had become "*trop mondain*" ("too worldly"), she said crossly. "*J'ai dû être remplacée par un autre snobisme.*"‡

Arrived on the Riviera, Maugham spent only a few weeks at home before he returned to England. In April, Liza's engagement had been announced, her fiancé Lieutenant Colonel Vincent Par-

---

* In his 1944 novel, *The Razor's Edge,* Maugham used parts of Marie Laurencin's story, she herself bearing marked similarities to the character of Suzanne Rouvier.
† "People complain that my portraits are not a good likeness. I can't tell you how little I care."
‡ "I must have been replaced by another snobbery."

avicini, son of the Swiss minister to the Court of St. James's. Paravicini was delightful, a sweet-natured man of notable elegance and charm, but Syrie was furiously disappointed in her daughter's choice and had "fought like a steer" against the match. In Syrie's view Vincent was just another young man about town, and with neither money nor title was certainly not good enough for her daughter. On this occasion, however, Liza defied her: she loved Vincent and was determined to marry him, and Syrie had no choice but to give in. At first Maugham, too, had disapproved of Paravicini, referring to him as "Liza's Swiss waiter," but Vincent soon won him over by his charm and by a simple sense of humor that tickled Maugham immensely; it amused him, too, that his son-in-law was not remotely bookish, his preferred reading two magazines, *Farmer & Stockbreeder* and *The Connoisseur.*

The wedding, a sumptuous society occasion, took place on July 20, 1936, at fashionable St. Margaret's, Westminster, Liza, aged twenty-one, looking pale but beautiful in a white brocade dress by Schiaparelli. For the first time in years her parents appeared together, walking down the aisle arm in arm, Maugham in top hat and tails to give his daughter away. At the large reception afterward at the Swiss Legation, Maugham behaved toward his ex-wife with an immaculate courtesy. "I found myself positively in danger of falling in love with him again!" Syrie gushed. "It was the first time since our courtship that I ever knew Willie to be so wonderfully thoughtful towards me." As a wedding present Maugham had bought the young couple a house on Wilton Street, off Belgrave Square, and for her contribution Syrie had decorated it. "A perfect decorator's house," Maugham dismissively remarked when he saw the finished result. "Nothing personal about it!" For their honeymoon the Paravicinis were lent the Villa Mauresque, the first time Liza had been there, Maugham and Haxton moving out to give "the young things" a chance to be on their own.

RETURNING AT THE BEGINNING of September, Maugham settled down at the Mauresque for a brief period of intensive work before returning to London in October. His most immediate concern was to put the finishing touches to a novel, *Theatre,* the only one of Maugham's fictional works to deal with the world in which he had been intimately involved for more than thirty years. Employing the favorite plot line of the older woman in love with a worthless and much younger man, *Theatre* tells the story of Julia Lambert, a celebrated actress married to a successful theater manager, who in middle age falls for a boy scarcely older than her schoolboy son. Tom Fennell is an accountancy clerk brought in to look over the theater's books, and Julia's husband, Michael, amused to see that the boy is stagestruck, invites him to lunch to meet his famous wife. Soon Julia is helplessly and humiliatingly in love, despite the fact that Tom is revealed to be a common little snob, regarding Julia, with all her grand friends, as a useful means of advancing his career. The climax comes when he asks her to give a part in her new play to a girlfriend of his, a pretty but overconfident young woman who, Julia quickly realizes, is nowhere near as talented as she believes. During a glittering first night it is Julia's cunning upstaging of Avice, in the most literal sense, that effects the dénouement and brings the story to a satisfactory end.

There is nothing bohemian in the theatrical world that Maugham depicts, which is solidly entrenched in the upper echelons of the West End. Julia has her clothes made in Paris, dines in the most expensive nightclubs and restaurants, and is much sought after in elevated social circles. As might be expected, the theatrical milieu is faultlessly drawn, with Maugham giving a particularly well-observed portrait of his leading lady, always performing whether onstage or off, and endowed with a number of characteristics drawn from actresses such as Ethel Barrymore, Irene Vanbrugh, and Marie Tempest. *Theatre* is not one of Maugham's finest novels—he was perhaps too little engaged with the world he was depicting—but it is highly accomplished, and after its publication in March 1937 it sold well (in Britain over 22,000 copies in the first two months) despite a tepid reception by the critics.★

★ The novel was dramatized in 1941 and has been filmed twice: in 1962, with Charles Boyer and Lilli Palmer, and in 2004, as *Being Julia,* with Annette Bening and Jeremy Irons.

With *Theatre* finished, Maugham in October went again to London, where as usual his diary was crammed with appointments. He spent a weekend at Renishaw with Osbert Sitwell and David Horner, and another at Bulbridge in Wiltshire with Juliet Duff, where H. G. Wells was also staying. On October 13 he attended a dinner at the Savoy, organized by PEN,* to celebrate H.G.'s seventieth birthday, the toast proposed by Bernard Shaw. At the end of the month he attended a large dinner party given by the recently widowed Sibyl Colefax, her last before moving out of Argyll House. The guests were old friends, among them the Winston Churchills, the Duff Coopers, Artur Rubinstein, Harold Nicolson and Desmond MacCarthy, and the talk was all of "the great Simpson question," as Harold Nicolson described it, "[and the] very serious rumours that the King will make her Duchess of Edinburgh and marry." The Prince of Wales's affair with Mrs. Simpson had been the subject of scandalized gossip for the past couple of years; it was bad enough that the heir to the throne was involved with an American divorcée, but now he was insisting on marriage, which momentarily opened up the appalling possibility of this twice-married foreigner's becoming queen. Since the death of George V in January, the matter had become of urgent constitutional importance, and with the coronation only weeks away it had been made clear to the new king that he must end the relationship. Instead, he decided to abdicate. Maugham had known Wallis Simpson for years—she and her husband had had a flat off Bryanston Square— and he was distressed by the violent hostility provoked by the future king's decision to give up his throne for the woman he loved. "I am a writer & it is my instinct to put myself in other people's shoes," he told Juliet Duff,

> & I have been strangely harassed by the thought of that wretched man, unshaven, unwashed, unkempt, kicking the doors & beating his head against the walls, that people who have seen him describe; & I am shocked by the suddenness of

---

* A writers' society founded in 1921 to promote literature.

that fall, from such an amazing popularity to such a universal contempt. Now the man in the street, who worshipped him, calls him a mess & says, a good riddance to bad rubbish.

On December 11, in a corner of the public lounge at Claridge's, Maugham, Eddie Marsh, Osbert Sitwell, and Graham Greene listened to the abdication broadcast on a radio borrowed from one of the porters. By this time Wallis Simpson had left the country and fled to the south of France, where she would wait out the stressful months before her divorce was finalized and she and the Duke of Windsor, as he now became, could marry. On Christmas Day, Maugham, who had returned to the Mauresque, invited Wallis and her aunt, Bessie Merryman, to lunch, together with Bob Boothby, a slightly raffish, slightly renegade member of Parliament. Despite the obvious tensions, it was a cheerful occasion, and in the afternoon there was a game of bridge, with Maugham partnering Wallis. "I'm afraid I am not a very good partner," he said putting down his hand. "I've only got a couple of k-k-kings." "What's the use of them?" Wallis wisecracked. "They only abdicate." Throughout the following weeks, Maugham, sensitive to the pressures and problems of her situation, continued to be attentive, inviting Wallis to meals and to stay for a weekend. "I think she had a very difficult role to play," he said, "and I doubt whether any woman could have played it successfully." Finally, in March, Wallis prepared to leave Cannes to be reunited with the duke at the Château de Candé in Tours, where they would marry. "I am leaving Cannes tomorrow," she wrote to Maugham, "and I wanted to tell you again how very much I have appreciated your kindness to me since I have been here." "What many people did not understand," she said later, "was that Willie was at heart a very kind man. That Christmas I felt in the wilderness, and I have never forgotten his sympathetic understanding in those especially difficult, lonely days."

Perhaps fortunately, Gerald had not been in evidence on Christmas Day. "Gerald is in bed with a bad attack of malaria, which is awkward since there is [my lunch party] tomorrow," Maugham with a certain irritation had written to Alan Searle on Christmas

Eve. "But still I shall manage, & in a day or two more he should be quite well." Yet Gerald did not get well, indeed became so desperately ill that a nurse was employed and a specialist called in, and the local doctor was obliged to drive over three times a day. For a while it was feared he might die, but then very gradually Gerald began to grow stronger. Maugham, despite his frequent fury and exasperation, had been desperately worried, and was grateful to be consoled by Alan, who came out to stay for a couple of weeks. Searle's presence at the Mauresque impressed on Maugham the contrast between the young man's gentle, if somewhat colorless, personality and Haxton's. "[Alan] is being very sweet," Maugham told David Horner, "[but] he is never what you could call the life & soul of a party; so there is no one for me to be funny about—or with—& I wander about the garden & long to laugh." In Alan, dependable and comforting, he missed the wickedness and wit, the sheer excitement, of being with Gerald. "Searle was more pussy-cat," said one friend who knew them both, "whereas Haxton was bristlingly abrasive, like a bulldog about to break his lead."

One beneficent result of Gerald's illness was a renewed resolution on his part to keep his drinking under control. "So far as I am concerned I can do no more," Maugham told Barbara Back in a letter whose tough stance is belied by the tenderness of the final sentence:

> I have told him, & he knows it himself that if he starts drinking again he will kill himself; & if he does, it will mean that he has come to the conclusion that he would rather drink & die than not drink & live. If he really comes to that conclusion that is the end of it, I shall pension him off & resume my domicile in England; I cannot spend the few remaining years of my life acting as nurse & keeper to an old drunk. But, I have no need to tell you, I hope with all my heart that it will not come to that.

In order to keep himself busy and amused, Gerald bought a boat, a small yacht with just enough room belowdecks for a couple of bunks. The weather was beautiful, and Gerald spent nearly every day sailing, entranced by his new toy. Equally entrancing was the young cabin boy who regularly accompanied him. Louis Legrand, known as "Loulou," was a ravishing sixteen-year-old male whore, slender, blond, tanned, with a soft mouth and a sweet smile; he wore gold bangles on both wrists and spent most of the day dressed only in a minute pair of faded swimming trunks. Gerald was infatuated with him, and when not on the boat Loulou passed much of his time at the Mauresque, at the disposal not only of Haxton and Maugham, who grew very fond of the charming boy, but of any male guest who desired his services, Gerald afterward discreetly settling the bill. Both Harolds, Nicolson and Acton, became appreciative customers (*"Mon cher Lulu,"* wrote Nicolson from Paris, *"merci pour la soirée délicieuse"*); and so, during the course of the summer, did Maugham's nephew, Robin.

Under pressure from his father, Robin had gone up to Cambridge to read law, but in his spare time continued to write, sending his compositions to his uncle for criticism. Maugham saw little evidence of talent—"quite the worst play I have ever had to look at" was his opinion of a dramatic sketch—but he was determined nonetheless to help Robin and instill in him as much as he could of his own philosophy. The play, he told him on this occasion,

> is a ghastly mess [and] I think you should prepare your mind for the possibility that it will be a failure. You are so monstrously conceited that I am afraid you will find failure very difficult to bear [but] to bear failure with courage is the best proof of character that anyone can give. . . . My last piece of advice is not to let anyone see your mortification.

Robin, fascinated by what he had heard of the high life at the Mauresque, had asked if he might come and stay during his long vacation, ostensibly in order to concentrate on his writing. But when he arrived he found himself alone with his uncle, Gerald having left for Paris to collect a new car, and any hopes he might have had of plunging into glamorous Riviera society soon disappeared in the actuality of the daily routine, with Maugham, intent on his work, spending all morning in his study, in the afternoon walking around the garden with the dogs, and disappearing to bed fairly soon after dinner. There was plenty of opportunity for some frank discussion, however, with Robin particularly anxious for reassurance about his homosexuality. His uncle was both practical and bracing, advising him to accept what he was and to have as much fun as he could. "You are quite attractive," he told him. "Don't waste your assets. Your charm won't last for long." That having been said, it was important that Robin should bear in mind that being queer was no impediment to marriage, and as the only son it was his duty to marry and propagate.

This was a theme that Maugham returned to repeatedly, impressing on Robin that of the next generation it was only he who bore the family name, a responsibility that became of crucial importance when in 1938 Robin's father was appointed lord chancellor. Maugham, who for all his socialist beliefs was far from impervious to the benefits of rank, was delighted. He was intensely gratified by the prestige conferred on the family, and impressed that F.H. entirely by his own efforts should have achieved such an exalted position. "It is very wonderful, if you come to think of it," he wrote to Bert Alanson, "that an obscure young man, without money or influence to help him should by sheer merit in his profession achieve . . . the highest office in the British Empire that any lawyer can attain." As a law lord, F.H. could not pass his title on to his descendants, but as lord chancellor he was sure to be offered a hereditary peerage, an offer that Maugham was anxious he should accept, his visions for Robin's ermined future as the second Viscount Maugham revealing a profound reverence for the old aristocratic order. "There is no reason why your father should not live another ten or fifteen years," he wrote to Robin,

> & in that time you might easily have gained a considerable experience as a member of parliament & then, as a peer, would have . . . a great chance to get office or a governorship . . . to be the son of a deceased Lord Chancellor is to be very small fry, to be a peer is always to be something.

Toward the end of Robin's stay, Gerald arrived back from Paris. By chance he and Robin had run into each other in Salzburg earlier in the summer and renewed their friendship. Cheerful and relaxed, the older man had made an irresistible impression. "Well-dressed, attractive and slim," Robin recorded, "very European though he was an American . . . Gerald exuded vitality and charm and money." Friendly as ever, Haxton had taken Robin to the opera and afterward to a bierstube. Here they drank schnapps while Gerald gave him a knowledgeable summary of the local rent boys lined up along the bar before disappearing with his personal favorite, a winning fourteen-year-old always available for "Onkel Gerald." Now returned to the Mauresque, Gerald generously determined to give Robin a night to remember before he returned home. Beginning the evening at the casino in Nice, the two of them went on to a couple of backstreet bars, where they got pleasantly drunk, and then to a brothel, where Gerald paid for the young man to be expertly entertained. Finally, in the early hours of the morning, it was decided to drive over to Villefranche to look at the boat. Here they found Loulou on board, lying on one of the bunks, "his hair tousled, his limbs sprawled out in sleep, his lips slightly parted." Gerald immediately saw that Robin was smitten. "Have a good time," he winked at him, and lurching up the gangplank, he left. "Good night, ducks," he called out. "See you both in the morning."

Gerald continued, just, to keep his drinking within limits, Maugham having made plain that if he wished to retain his position he would have to make some radical reforms. The situation was not a happy one, however, and the tensions and uncertainties now inherent in the relationship made Maugham restless and uneasy, so much so that for a while he even contemplated giving up the Mauresque. But for the moment such drastic plans were shelved as he concentrated on preparing for a Far Eastern journey, this time to India, proposing to depart at the end of the year, returning the following spring. "I am tired & want a change," he told Charles Towne, "& besides, I want to get some material for a novel I have in mind to write in the future." Meanwhile, the summer passed in trips abroad—the usual visits to Munich, Salzburg, and Badgastein, as well as a disappointing excursion with Peter Stern to Scandinavia ("Sweden . . . such a boring place")—and in entertaining at home. "Yesterday Anthony Blunt & a friend Burgess came over to lunch & are coming for the week-end," Maugham reported to Searle. "Do you remember Anthony? You met him once or twice at Cambridge. He is (or was) a fellow of Trinity & is an authority on baroque."

BEFORE LEAVING FOR INDIA, Maugham was determined to finish a book of great personal importance to him, a form of memoir on which he had been working intermittently for some time. "I have put into it all I know," he told Charles Towne; but if his readers were hoping for details of a personal nature, they were to be disappointed. In its author's own words, *The Summing Up* "is not an autobiography nor is it a book of recollections": rather it is an overview of his professional career and intellectual development, and of "the subjects that have chiefly interested me during the course of my life." The first half of this personal credo deals with his boyhood and youth, and, at greater length, with his development as a writer. Here he argues for his three favorite tenets, lucidity, simplicity, and euphony, and discusses some of the authors whom he most admires: Dryden, Swift, Dr. Johnson, Hazlitt, Voltaire, Stendhal, Colette, and Maupassant, who exercised such influence over his own style of short story. Maugham also addresses his career in the theater—"I caught the colloquial note by instinct"—paying his respects to his fellow playwrights, in particular Ibsen ("the greatest dramatist the last hundred years have seen"), Chekhov, and Shaw. And with admirable detachment he analyzes his own strengths and weaknesses as a practitioner of the art to which he had dedicated his life. "I am a made writer," he states unequivocally. "I do not write as I want to; I write as I can. . . . I have had small power of imagination . . . no lyrical quality . . . little gift of metaphor . . . [but] I had an acute power of observation, and it seemed to me that I could see a great many things that other people missed." Clear-sighted about his abilities, he yet shows a certain sensitivity to the fact that he has been largely ignored by serious critics. "There are but two important critics in my own country [Desmond MacCarthy and Cyril Connolly] who have troubled to take me seriously," he complains; the rest by contrast have either ignored or dismissed him. "In my twenties the critics said I was brutal, in my thirties they said I was flippant, in my forties they said I was cynical, in my fifties they said I was competent, and now in my sixties they say I am superficial."

The second large theme in *The Summing Up* is the author's life-long exploration of philosophy and religion, which had absorbed him since boyhood. Always curious, always searching, ever eager to find a pattern or purpose to his life, Maugham for years had read diligently in the works of the great philosophers, from Plato to Bertrand Russell, from the Christian mystics to the Upanishads, looking for but never finding the certainty that would bring consolation. Here Maugham the autodidact comes to the fore, the intelligent inquirer, hopeful of enlightenment on the great questions that have preoccupied man through the ages: "what is the value of life, how he should live and what sense he can ascribe to the universe." Unable to regain the faith he lost in boyhood, he yet remains unsatisfied, puzzled by the frustration experienced by his rational self in failing to take comfort in religion. "It may be that my heart, having found rest nowhere, had some deep ancestral craving for God and immortality which my reason would have no truck with." Unable to integrate his perceptions in an all-inclusive creed, he states his conviction, in characteristically uncompromising terms, that "There is no reason for life and life has no meaning."

Although the author is at pains to remain at a dignified distance—"Never have I read an autobiography which contains so little auto," complained Peter Stern—*The Summing Up* is shot through with a sometimes startling candor. Of his experience of love he says, "Though I have been in love a good many times I have never experienced the bliss of requited love," and "I have most loved people who cared little or nothing for me, and when people have loved me I have been embarrassed," and "there are few things that cause greater wretchedness than to love with all your heart someone who you know is unworthy of love." Writing of sex, enthusiastically described as "the keenest pleasure to which the body is susceptible," he states it is his great regret that because of "a native fastidiousness" he never indulged enough, a surprising admission from one who was so deeply interested in the subject, wrote about it with such feeling, and was so tireless in its pursuit. Throughout, the writer is revealed, not always consciously, as a sensitive, vulnerable, passionate man, aloof, unillusioned, a realist rather than the cynic he was so often taken to be; he is solitary by choice ("I find social intercourse fatiguing. . . . It is a relief to me when I can get away and read a book"), a depressive capable of some happiness and much enjoyment. As one of his critics was to write, in this book there is revealed "an injured and defensive heart behind the fluent mind of the impervious man of the world."

Anxious that *The Summing Up* should be as good as he could make it, Maugham sent proofs to both Eddie Marsh and Dadie Rylands for criticism. Eddie Marsh was particularly relied upon for detailed textual editing. Recently retired from the Civil Service, Marsh had made a speciality of correcting the work of well-known authors, Winston Churchill among them. Referred to as his "diabolization," it was a process this pernickety, scholarly, kindhearted character relished. There was no question of payment, for it flattered his vanity to be consulted by famous writers ("There's glory for me!" Marsh noted in his diary after he was first approached by Maugham); he was proud of what he called "my morbid eye for detail" and loved showing off his exhaustive knowledge of grammar, derivation, and the finer points of style. Maugham's first meeting with Marsh had been during the war at a luncheon* of the Winston

---

* The word "luncheon" was something of a stumbling block between Marsh and Maugham. "Whenever I wrote *lunch,* he changed it to *luncheon.* I protested that the word was obsolete. . . . It was natural to say, I urged, 'Will you come and have lunch with me,' and so why shouldn't you use it in a book. 'But it isn't natural to me,' Eddie cried in his shrill voice, 'I won't come and have lunch with you. I will, however, if I am disengaged be pleased to come and have luncheon with you' " (*Eddie Marsh: Sketches for a Composite Literary Portrait,* compiled by Christopher Hassall and Denis Mathews [Lund Humphries, 1953], p. 29).

Churchills', but the first books of his to be diabolized were *Don Fernando* and *Theatre*. "I think you must know grammar better than anyone in England," Maugham had written gratefully after receiving back the corrected scripts. "I can't tell you how wonderfully useful I've found your notes, but, my word, some of them have made me sweat." On *The Summing Up* Marsh went to work with gusto: "p. 28 Has 'massivity' any advantage over the usual 'massiveness'? . . . p. 110 Surely three infinitives are too many? . . . p. 113 Your argument here is tantalizingly incomplete. . . ." Not all his suggestions were accepted, but most of them were, and his sharp eye demonstrably saved Maugham from error, inelegance, and some impossibly tangled lines of argument. In gratitude Maugham made a present to Marsh of some beautiful eighteenth-century emerald buttons from India to use as cufflinks. "I like to think they may have adorned the sleeve of one of the Moghuls' page boys," he told him.

While a few of Maugham's friends, hoping for personal revelations, were disappointed, by the majority of his readers *The Summing Up* was respectfully received. After publication in January 1938 (two months later in the United States), most opinion praised the work for its intellectual and emotional honesty, and for its illuminating reflections on the writer and writing, if politely dismissive of the more metaphysical passages. Generally it was perceived to be "immensely readable" (V. S. Pritchett) and "continuously entertaining" (Graham Greene), and sales figures were excellent, quickly reaching a hundred thousand in the United States, to Nelson Doubleday's satisfaction.

MEANWHILE, WITH THE BOOK completed by the end of summer 1937, Maugham returned to planning his expedition to India, arranging to rent out the Mauresque for the four months he and Haxton would be away the following year. As usual, the autumn was spent in London, where he gave a party to celebrate the birth of Liza's first child—a boy, to Maugham's delight—Nicolas Vincent Somerset. The reception, at Claridge's on December 8, was a glamorous occasion. "Never before were so many celebrities gathered together under one roof," Hugh Walpole observed, with Syrie much in evidence among them. "Willie [had] hoped she wouldn't come"; she was easy enough to avoid, however, as Maugham had taken care to surround himself with old friends including H. G. Wells, Barbara Back, Sibyl Colefax, Osbert Sitwell, Harold Nicolson, Juliet Duff, and Desmond MacCarthy.

Once this ordeal was over, Maugham concentrated on finalizing the details of his journey, his intention being to leave just before Christmas, embarking from Genoa for the five-week voyage to Bombay. Maugham had already been furnished with letters of introduction from prestigious friends, including his Riviera neighbor, the Aga Khan, and naturally expected while in Delhi to be received by the viceroy, the Marquess of Linlithgow. But then came an unexpected hitch that threw everything into confusion: the India Office refused to issue a visa to Gerald, who twenty years earlier had been categorized as an "undesirable alien." Maugham was furious. It was humiliating and outrageous; how could this be happening when his trunks were packed and it was too late to revise his plans, and how could he possibly cope without Gerald, "[who has] been to pretty well every British colony with me for the last umpteen years"? Discreet approaches were hastily made, strings pulled, and fortunately at the last minute the ban was rescinded, although it was made clear there would be no official recognition of Mr. Maugham's presence on the subcontinent. In practical terms this hardly mattered, as it was Maugham's intention to concentrate not on British but on Hindu India and on the states ruled by the Indian princes;* nonetheless the slight rankled and was not forgotten.

It may seem curious that Maugham, with his passion for travel and for the Far East, should have waited so long to visit India: by his own account the blame lay with Rudyard Kipling. He had long believed

---

* The British Raj, or Indian Empire, was divided into two regions: British India, which was administered directly by the British government, and the Princely or Native States, governed by individual rulers under the paramountcy of the British Crown.

that "so far as stories were concerned Kipling had written all the good ones," a belief he now saw was baseless: in a letter sent to E. M. Forster from Calcutta he wrote, "[I] only regret that the shadow of Kipling lurking over the country in my imagination prevented me from coming twenty years ago." Kipling had died only two years before, but in fact his world had long been gone; the British hold on India, for over a hundred years the jewel in the crown, the symbolic center of the imperial structure, was weakening by the day; the Government of India Act of 1935 was a virtual guarantee of independence in the near future, and movements for nationalization were rapidly, in some states violently, gaining ground. Yet it was not this complex political situation that concerned Maugham, nor was he this time on the prowl for stories; his main objective was to explore Hindu philosophy and religion, to meet religious leaders and teachers, and to learn what he could at first hand of a subject of passionate personal interest, one that he intended to use as the foundation for a novel, eventually to be published as *The Razor's Edge*.

After a calm and comfortable voyage, Maugham and Haxton arrived in Bombay at the beginning of January 1938, and left from there exactly three months later. Their itinerary took them first to Goa, to Trivandrum and Madura on the southernmost tip of India, then north to Madras on the east coast, to Hyderabad, up to Bidar and Nagpur in the interior, then to Calcutta and Benares, and finally to Agra, Jaipur, and Delhi, where Maugham, but not Haxton, was invited by Lord Linlithgow to lunch at Viceregal Lodge; the invitation was declined. From Delhi they returned to Bombay to board a ship bound for Naples on March 31. Despite all he had read and been told, Maugham was unprepared for the impact of India. The endless traveling was exhausting, the trains slow, the heat frequently oppressive, the social demands enervating in the extreme, yet he was fascinated by all of it, by the white beaches and empty churches of Goa, the Black Pagoda in Orissa, sunset on the Ganges at Benares, the noise and bustle of Calcutta, and in Agra by the astonishing beauty of the Taj Mahal, his own reaction to which Maugham observed with interest:

I can understand that when people say something takes their breath away it is not an idle metaphor. I really did feel shortness of breath. I had a queer, delightful feeling in my heart, as though it were dilated. I felt surprise and joy and, I think, a sense of liberation.

Gerald, on the other hand, was far more excited by the couple of days spent driving through the jungle, where he was able to get in some shooting. He had hoped for a tiger, and they waited for hours up a fifteen-foot bamboo platform in the trees, but none appeared; he shot a crocodile, however, and a peacock, which they ate that same evening for dinner. Maugham was distressed by the incident.

I have seldom seen a sight more thrilling than that peacock threading its solitary way through the jungle. My companion told the driver to stop and seized his gun.
    "I'm going to have a shot at it."
    My heart stopped still. He fired, and I hoped he'd miss, but he didn't. The driver jumped out of the car and brought back the dead bird which a moment before had been so exultantly alive. It was a cruel sight.

There was no question now, as there had been in the past, of roughing it, and wherever they went the two men were entertained in magnificent style. "[We] are living in the lap of luxury," Maugham wrote to Searle from Trivandrum, where he was a guest of the maharajah of Travancore. He and Haxton had been given a house in the palace grounds, "where we have a bed-room, dressing-room & bathroom each, a dining-room & two sitting-rooms; we are looked after by a butler & two footmen, & a large yellow car stands at the door all day with a chauffeur & a footman." And a few days later from Cochin he wrote to Juliet Duff, "we are on our way to Madras & then we go to stay with the Maharajah of Mysore & the Nizam [of Hyderabad]. I am inclined to think that I am getting a little above myself." The only drawback to this regal level of hospitality was that there was little opportunity for more private activities. "Of course no larks," Maugham regretfully told Searle, "& we are being as good as gold." Throughout the princely states they visited, Maugham's Indian hosts were discovered to be infinitely courteous, learned, charming, and generous; "as soon as the maharajas realized that I didn't want to go on tiger hunts but that I was interested in seeing poets and philosophers, they were very helpful." This was in marked contrast to the British, whom Maugham found philistine and narrow-minded. "Oh the doddering old fools who are running this country!" he lamented to Barbara from Bombay. "It is a wonder India hasn't been lost long ago." He was repelled by the instances he witnessed of the colonists' insufferably superior attitude toward Indians, particularly on the part of the women, the memsahibs, few of whom seemed to have any interest in the people, customs, or culture that surrounded them. At a tea party given by the wife of a minor official, his hostess asked him about his trip,

> and when I told her that I had spent most of my time in the Indian States, she said: "You know, we don't have anything more to do with Indians than we can help. One has to keep them at arm's length." The rest of the company agreed with her.

Such an attitude may well have accounted for Maugham's grumpy mood while staying at the magnificent British Residency in Hyderabad. Here his fellow guest was M. M. Kaye, then a young woman of thirty, later to become well known for her novel about India, *The Far Pavilions*. "I was enthralled to meet him," she recalled, "but disappointed to find him a sour and unfriendly old gentleman who stumped off fairly early to bed." By the next morning, however, Maugham's mood had improved, and "we got on like a house on fire." Encouraged, Mollie Kaye mentioned that she had just written a novel,

> but that I was afraid I would never make a writer. He asked why, in a distinctly bored voice, and I said because I wrote much too slowly and would stick for hours on end over a sentence that I couldn't get right. . . . The old boy peered at me

over the top of his spectacles exactly like an elderly tortoise, and said: "My dear young woman, that is the only thing I have heard you say that makes me think you may be a writer one day."

Maugham's quest in coming to India was to investigate the vast subject of Hindu religion in the hope of gaining an insight into a spiritual side of life that had always intrigued and at the same time eluded him. In preparation he had read widely and, armed with a sheaf of introductions, he had met and talked to numbers of scholars and priests; despite his best efforts, however, he was unable to make very much of what they told him. The experience frustrated and tantalized him. "As for getting any insight into the intense spiritual life that one finds here, there & everywhere," he wrote when halfway through his tour, "well, it is like seeing the Himalayas at night only in one flash of lightning." Doggedly he persevered. Under instruction from a yogi he tried for himself the benefits of meditation, sitting cross-legged on the floor in a darkened room and making his mind a blank. "I remained in that state for so long that I thought I must have by far exceeded the quarter of an hour [the yogi] had prescribed. I looked at my watch. Three minutes had passed." Traveling the length and breadth of the country he interviewed swamis and sadhus; he watched fakirs gouging out their eyeballs and sticking skewers through their cheeks; in Hyderabad, through the good offices of Sir Akbar Hydari, the finance minister and a friend of E. M. Forster's, he talked to an immensely distinguished Hindu holy man, but "[he only] said the things I had heard from others twenty times before." It was the same when he met a Sufi, from whom he hoped to gain some different perspective, only to find that the Muslim mystic "[spoke] of the self and the supreme self in the same strain as the Hindu teachers speak." To Maugham this was the crux of the problem, that all the Indian thinkers relayed the same doctrines in the same words:

And though you feel that it should not make you restive, for if they possess the truth, as they are convinced they do, and if the truth is one and indivisible, it is natural enough that they should repeat it like parrots, there is no denying the fact that it is irksome to listen interminably to the same statements. You wish at least they could think of other metaphors, similes, illustrations than those of the Upanishads. Your heart sinks when you hear again the one about the snake and the rope.★

At Tiruvannamalai, near Madras, Maugham visited the ashram of the famous sage Sri Ramana Maharshi, where he enjoyed the unique opportunity of talking to an English sadhu. Maj. A. W. Chadwick, a retired British army officer, currently incarnated as Sadhu Arunachala, had lived in the ashram for years, and was more than happy to discourse at length about karma and reincarnation and to describe his personal efforts "to realise the self in him in communion with the universal self, to separate the I that thinks from the self, for that is the infinite." But even with a fellow Englishman, Maugham was left little the wiser, and by the end of the interview still "could not get from him exactly what he meant." The maharshi received visitors at an audience every afternoon, and Maugham and Haxton having arrived at midday were halfway through their picnic lunch on the veranda outside Chadwick's room when Maugham suddenly fainted. Chadwick carried him indoors and laid him on his bed, where he stayed for some time, feeling too unwell to join the crowd in the central hall. The maharshi, informed of what had happened, graciously consented to come and see him, and "Bhagavan [the maharshi] and Somerset Maugham sat opposite to each other for about half-an-hour without uttering a word," Chadwick recalled.

At the end of which Somerset Maugham looked nervously across in my direction and said, "Is there any need to say any-

★ "The world is illusory, judged from the standpoint of Reality, but it is not an illusion. It is a fact of consciousness," Maugham explains. "The wise men of India are fond of using the following illustration: you see on a dark night what you take to be a snake and you run away from it; but when a light is brought, you see that what you took for a snake is in fact a rope. It was an illusion that what you saw was a snake, but it *was* a rope. . . ." (*Points of View*, p. 58).

thing?" "No," replied Bhagavan. "Silence is best. Silence is itself conversation."

He may have failed to achieve enlightenment, but so intrigued was Maugham by this first visit to India that before embarking from Bombay on the voyage home he had already determined to return the following year, a project that events far outside his control were to render impracticable. While still at sea, on board the *Conte Biancomano,* the gravity of the situation in Europe was forcefully impressed upon the passengers, as news reports arrived daily over the ship's radio of Franco and the Civil War in Spain, of the Fascist imperialism of Mussolini in Italy, and now, on March 14, of the Anschluss, of Hitler's invasion of Austria. "We have been much disturbed over the Austrian business [and] Gerald has been much in the dumps over it all because so many of his friends are affected," Maugham wrote to Alan Searle. "For a moment I was terribly afraid that it might mean a general war; but that seems now not to be the case."

Docking at Naples, they were met by Jean the chauffeur and by Alan, who was to join them on the leisurely drive back to the south of France. From Naples they went to Rome and then Florence, where the three of them were hospitably received by Harold Acton and his parents at the family villa, La Pietra. During their stay, Harold remembered, "while Gerald painted the town red, Willie sat glued to the bridge-table." Maugham also called on his old friend Reggie Turner, whom he found in a state of deep depression. The city was festooned with Fascist banners in preparation for a triumphal visit by Hitler and Mussolini, and Reggie was appalled by what he saw happening to his beloved Italy. He was also a very sick man, his famous wit and brilliant conversation almost extinguished by a cancer of the tongue, which was shortly to kill him. He was, however, able to accompany the party to Montegufoni, the Sitwells' massive medieval castle just outside Florence, where Edith was staying with her father.

Maugham finally arrived back at the Mauresque in May 1938, to enjoy what appeared in prospect another idyllic summer on the

Riviera. The weather was flawless, he was at work on a new novel, Gerald was happy planning to sail to Sicily with Loulou, and there were relays of friends coming out from England to stay: Barbara, Robin, Beverley Nichols, Raymond Mortimer and his lover, Paul Hyslop, the Paravicinis, the Actons, and Harold Nicolson. It was Nicolson that summer who captured the essence of the Mauresque magic. "It really is the perfect holiday," he told his wife, Vita Sackville-West; "the heat is intense, the garden lovely, the chair long and cool, the lime-juice at hand, a bathing pool there if one wishes to splash, scenery, books, gramophones, pretty people." At the end of one day he describes himself alone in the garden after everyone else had gone inside to dress:

> There was a lovely soft warm evening, that marvellous pink light among the pines. I went up and sat alone with Tacitus by the swimming-pool. It is surrounded by great massifs of red and white oleanders. The sun set over Cap d'Antibes. The lighthouses began to wink across a still purple sea. I stayed there until the red oleanders became invisible and only the white oleanders shone in the moon.

But then he suddenly realized the time, closed his book, descended the steps, and walked across the terrace and into the house to shave, bathe, and put on a black tie, as the newly married Duke and Duchess of Windsor were expected that night to dine. This was a slightly tense occasion, as Wallis, to her husband's fury, had been denied the title of Royal Highness, and there was thus a slight unease among the group waiting in the drawing room as to how she should be addressed. When the car was heard pulling up on the gravel, Maugham, accompanied by Liza, went into the hall to receive them. A few seconds later the duke walked into the room. "I'm sorry we were a little late," he said cheerfully, "but Her Royal Highness couldn't drag herself away." "He had said it," Nicolson recorded. "The three words fell into the circle like three stones into a pool . . . and not one eye dared to meet another."

The Mauresque may have provided a haven of beauty and tranquillity, yet all around, events were unfolding of the most sinister nature. With the threatened German invasion of Czechoslovakia there was no question of the usual expedition to Salzburg and Badgastein. "I do not think there is any danger of war," Maugham wrote to Bert Alanson, "but the Austrians have a little lost their heads just now and are behaving in such a manner that it is better for foreigners to keep out of the country." Maugham was already doing what he could to help the flood of Jewish refugees pouring into Britain and France, using his influence to find work and accommodation as well as giving substantial sums of money to Jewish charities. When approached for a donation by Herman Ould, the secretary of PEN, he sent a fairly brisk reply. "I have not waited until I received your letter to do what I could for the Austrian Jews of my acquaintance who have had to leave their country," he wrote, "and so I must ask Mr. Frischauer to be content with a cheque for ten guineas and to look upon it more as a mark of my sympathy than as a reasonable contribution to so worthy a fund."

In the third week of September, while Nazi troops were massing on the Czech border, Maugham left the Côte d'Azur for London, driven by Jean. Near Auxerre, south of Paris, the car hit a tree and overturned, leaving both occupants badly shaken, Maugham the worse off, very bruised and with a broken rib. Determined not to enter a hospital, he insisted on being taken to a Paris hotel, the France et Choiseul, where they knew him and where Alan came out to nurse him. "Alan has been an angel," Maugham told Barbara. "For two or three days I couldn't move in bed without help. Fortunately the surgeon who was looking after me was merciful enough to keep me under morphia." After a couple of weeks he was well enough to complete his journey, arriving in London at the beginning of October just as reports were coming in of Hitler's annexation of the Sudetenland. The talk everywhere was of the crisis, and of Neville Chamberlain's triumphant return from Munich, waving his piece of paper with its declaration of "peace for our time." On November 1, 1938, Maugham felt well enough to attend a dinner party of Sibyl Colefax's, among his fellow guests Max Beerbohm, Virginia Woolf, and the talented young novelist Christopher Isherwood. "That young man holds the future of the English novel in his hands," Maugham told Virginia. She, perhaps not knowing of his accident, was privately appalled by his appearance, "like a dead man," she wrote in her diary. "And his lips are drawn back like a dead man's . . . A look of suffering . . . A mechanical voice as if he had to raise a lever at each word . . . Sat like an animal in a trap: or like a steel trap. And I could not say anything that loosed his dead man's jaw."

In fact, while still in physical pain, Maugham was feeling more cheerful than he had for some time. During the past few years he had grown increasingly pessimistic about the likelihood of a lasting peace, a pessimism given full expression in his recently completed novel, *Christmas Holiday*. But now, with the signing of the Anglo-German pact confirming the two countries' stated desire "never to go to war with one another again," there was room for cautious hope. "Well, we've escaped war, & (I think) for many years," Maugham wrote to Alanson. "Things should go better now at least for a bit."

CHAPTER 14

AN EXERCISE
IN PROPAGANDA

...

Maugham always claimed not to care for the novel of ideas, the novel as polemic. "I think it an abuse to use the novel as a pulpit or a platform," he stated more than once. Yet in his new work of fiction he comes very near to doing exactly this. *Christmas Holiday,* written during 1938, is constructed primarily to carry a message, an impassioned denunciation of the malevolent forces developing within Europe, of the powerful dictatorships in Germany, Italy, and Spain. Since the beginning of the decade Maugham had been pessimistic about the possibility of maintaining a viable peace, as he had made plain six years earlier in *For Services Rendered.* Since then he had watched with acute apprehension the increasingly bitter conflict between left and right—the rise of Fascism, the widening divisions between rich and poor—and the terrifying threat that they presented, a threat that in his opinion blinkered Britain appeared dangerously slow to understand.

Christmas Holiday follows the disillusionment of Charley Mason, a naïve young Englishman come to Paris to enjoy a short holiday with Simon, his childhood best friend. But the Paris he finds himself in is a shabby, uneasy city, rank with poverty and corruption, and Simon is almost unrecognizable, transformed into a raging, power-hungry fanatic, a dictator in the making. During the next few days Simon brutally sets out to destroy Charley's innocence, to warp his instinctive tolerance and mildly socialist values. And thus when he finally returns to England, Charley feels he has been living in a nightmare, but one that "had a fearful reality which rendered all else illusory. . . . Only one thing had happened to him . . . the bottom had fallen out of his world."

Christmas Holiday is first and foremost a political allegory, in which the author employs his characters to illustrate the ideological struggles in Europe, using them to personify the nature of Fascism and the totalitarian states, and the fatal malleability of the oppressed. Unfortunately, they are all, with the exception of Charley, two-dimensional, and the lengthy relating of their various stories at secondhand grows monotonous. The only human aspect of Simon, carefully left unexplored by the author, is a strong impression that he is and always has been hopelessly in love with handsome, heterosexual Charley (thus refuting Gore Vidal's assertion that *The Narrow Corner* is Maugham's only "crypto-fag" novel). Ironically, the few scenes that at once spring vividly to life are those concerning Charley and his comically complacent family back home in London. The Masons are a little too pleased with themselves, but they are decent, tolerant people, their chief failing, in common with most of the rest of the country, a refusal to take seriously the threat of the imminent destruction of their comfortable way of life.

IN FEBRUARY 1939, when *Christmas Holiday* was published, Maugham was on business in the United States (where the novel appeared in October). As before, he was inundated with requests to broadcast—he was paid $500 for one two-minute radio talk—for interviews, articles, and short stories, and with the usual pressing offers from Hollywood. "I am now advised that Maugham will not, under any circumstances, consider a picture assignment," wrote the producer David O. Selznick. "There is no indication that he may change his mind in the future." By the time he returned to Europe, sailing from New York on the *Queen Mary,* Maugham was exhausted, eager for his annual restorative retreat. As there was no question at the present of visiting Austria and Badgastein, the spa at Montecatini was chosen instead. "Here in Italy everyone seems convinced that there will be no war," he wrote to Alanson in June, "so unless the Germans do something idiotic I think we are safe."

Back at the Villa Mauresque by July, Maugham saw no reason to alter his plans or to cancel his guests for the summer, among them Liza and her husband with a group of young friends. It was a particularly gay season on the Riviera, with a plethora of plays, open-air concerts, horse shows, fireworks, balls, and, keenly anticipated, the inauguration of the first-ever Cannes Film Festival, due to open on September 1. But by the beginning of August it was ominously apparent that no such festivity would be taking place. On August 23, with the signing of the Nazi-Soviet Non-Aggression Declaration, the atmosphere grew darker and more tense: all at once soldiers were everywhere, their tented camps erected among the trees; Cap Ferrat was converted into a highly fortified military zone, with machine gun emplacements installed along the cliffs and an antiaircraft battery at one end of the road that ran below the Mauresque. Suddenly everyone seemed to be on the move, with holidaymakers rushing to return home—there was not a place to be had on the Blue Train—and the roads jammed with traffic as heavily laden cars and trucks full of troops heading north met hordes of refugees fleeing south. Within one 24-hour period during the last week in August the Mauresque was virtually evacuated, the guests suddenly packed and gone and most of the servants departed: the kitchen maid, the footman, and his wife, all Italian, returned to Italy; Jean the chauffeur was called up, as were a couple of gardeners, while the butler, Ernest, a Swiss, was recalled to Switzerland; only Annette, the cook, and a housemaid, Nina, remained in the house. At the same time an order was posted that all private yachts must immediately leave the harbor at Villefranche. With the decision to move forced upon them, Maugham made up his mind to take the *Sara* west to Cassis, a port too small to be of interest to the navy. He and Gerald drove hurriedly into Nice to stock up on provisions, and with these stowed on board they set sail, taking with them as crew a couple of Italian boatmen too old for conscription.

The weather was perfect, and at first, Maugham recalled, "there

Maugham on the terrace with Winston Churchill and H. G. Wells.

Henry James,
criticized by Maugham
for his "triviality
of soul."

Edith Wharton,
"magnificently
condescending."

Virginia Woolf gave Maugham one of his earliest reviews.

*Robin Maugham, well mannered
and eager to please.*

Maugham shopping in Macy's.

Maugham surrounded by admirers on Cape Cod.

The writer Glenway Wescott had much in common with Maugham.

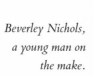

Beverley Nichols, a young man on the make.

The elegant Barbara Back,
witty and indiscreet.

Maugham with G. B. Stern, a cheerful presence at the Mauresque.

Alan Searle, the Bronzino boy.

Maugham with (clockwise from left) Dadie Rylands, Raymond Mortimer, Paul Hyslop, Gerald Haxton, Barbara Back, and Arthur Marshall (front).

By the pool: (left to right) Gerald, Raymond Mortimer,
Maugham, Paul Hyslop, and Godfrey Winn.

Breakfast in bed at the Mauresque.

Liza with her father and Bert Alanson in California.

*Ellen and Nelson Doubleday with
Maugham at Bonny Hall.*

*Haxton and Maugham riding with
friends in South Carolina.*

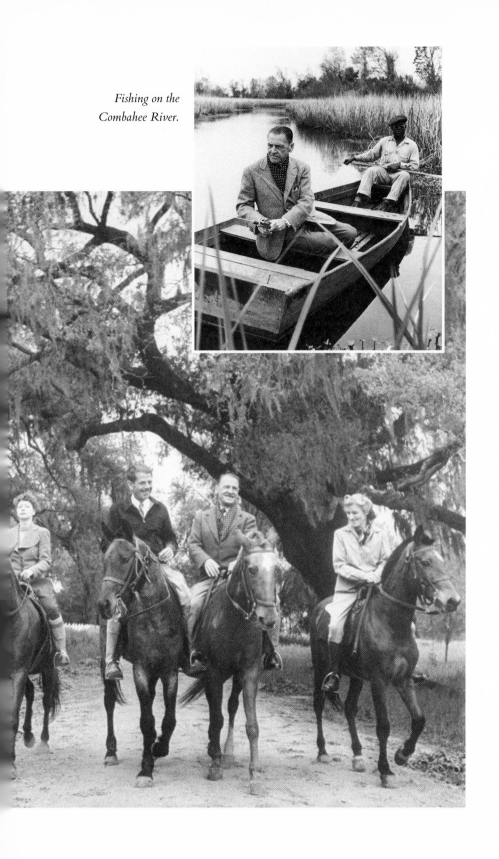

Fishing on the Combahee River.

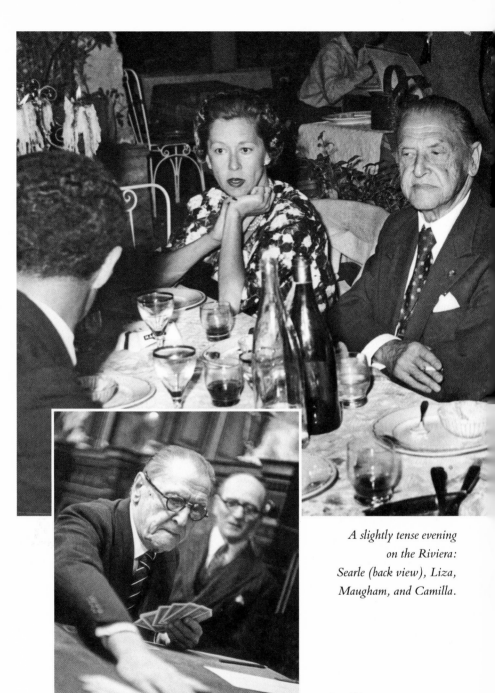

A slightly tense evening on the Riviera: Searle (back view), Liza, Maugham, and Camilla.

Bridge, "the most entertaining game that the art of man has devised."

*Alan, the perfect
nanny of Maugham's
second childhood.*

*Robin was very
attentive to his
aged uncle.*

Writing, "the most enthralling of human activities."

was a feeling of gentle excitement at the notion of getting away from the danger zone . . . I read and slept and smoked . . . enjoying the quiet after those harassing days"; the Stars and Stripes floating from the stern ensured the boat's safety. With coastal waters heavily mined, they were obliged to navigate a circuitous route, and by the third day they had sailed only as far as Bandol, a pretty fishing village halfway between Toulon and Marseilles; as there seemed little point in going farther, here they resolved to stay until the furor had died down and it was safe to return. At Bandol a routine was quickly established, with Maugham every morning rising early to go ashore and visit the market, an experience entirely new to him:

> I bought chickens with trepidation because I could never tell if that dead, featherless creature was young and tender or old and tough; I tried to pretend I knew what I was doing by poking a timid finger into its breast but the cold and clammy skin gave me goose flesh.

As the days passed, news of the international situation grew increasingly grim, with the invasion of Poland on September 1, France officially mobilized on the second, and on the third, Britain and France declaring war on Germany. With little to do, time moved slowly; the fine weather turned cold and cloudy, and Maugham grew restless, anxious to return home and discover whether any reply had arrived to the letter he had sent the Ministry of Information offering his services. With his country prepared for war, Maugham once again was eager to participate. "I am hoping [to] get some sort of work in the department I was in during the last war," he confided to Desmond MacCarthy on the *Sara*'s elegant writing paper (canary yellow, with the name of the yacht in dark blue).

> It may be that the authorities will think me useless: in that case I don't quite know what I shall do. . . . I have four novels in my head that I should like to write before I finish & if I can do nothing else I suppose the sensible thing would be to sit down & write them, but at present I am too distraught to give

them a thought; I spend my time devouring such papers as I can get hold of & turning on the radio whenever there is news.

Finally, after nearly a month away, he and Gerald decided to decamp, abandoning the boat at Bandol and ignoring the stringent restrictions recently imposed on movement between one *département* and another. Brazenly the two of them climbed into a taxi and ordered the astonished driver to take them to Cap Ferrat, a journey that, miraculously, they completed without a hitch.

Arriving unannounced, they found the house shuttered and airless, and apart from the obvious comforts of being at home, the atmosphere was melancholy. "I much fear that I shall be left to twiddle my thumbs indefinitely," Maugham wrote to his nephew, while Gerald told Robin, "Willie and I are . . . feeling very aged and on the shelf—nobody seems to want our services. He is very low and gloomy about it." Then finally a message came through from the Ministry with a definite offer of work. "This raised my spirits," said Maugham, "for it looked as though I were at last going to be given something to do."

In 1939 the Ministry of Information was in a state of some confusion, vaguely aware that well-known writers should be useful but unsure exactly how to deploy them, much time being wasted in the forming and dissolving of committees and the sending out of impractical statements of intent. Yet amid the muddle, the almost unique usefulness of Somerset Maugham in respect of Anglo-French relations had been noted: not only had the man lived in France for over a decade, but he was widely known there and held in high regard—as recently as August 1939 he had been raised to the rank of Commandeur of the Légion d'Honneur—and consequently would have access to people and information available to few outsiders. Thus he was asked, first, if he would compile a private report for the Ministry on the attitude of the French toward their British allies, and second, if he would write a series of articles to be published in Britain extolling France and the French war effort.

Immediately galvanized, Maugham packed his bags and left for

Paris. Here he made arrangements for visiting the front, paying calls on Jean Giraudoux, dramatist and diplomat, currently head of the Bureau of Information, and Raoul Dautry, minister for armaments, who provided him with the necessary introductions and laissez-passer. It was from these highly placed contacts, too, that he gleaned such information as might be discreetly transmitted to London, "private reports," as he termed them, "upon such matters as it behoved the government to be informed." Much of this information was gathered when he dined out in the evening after his day's work was done, and frequently he came away appalled by the pro-German sentiments he heard expressed. Many of the more prosperous sections of society had loathed Léon Blum and his socialist government and were terrified by the threat of Communism, openly admitting that they believed they would do better under German domination. Patriotism was regarded as a notion a civilized man should have outgrown. "What difference will it make to us if Hitler does conquer France?" they asked. "We shan't be any worse off." Others were more circumspect and took care what they said in front of the quiet, well-mannered Englishman with the dark, watchful eyes. The vehemently pro-Fascist Horace de Carbuccia, Maugham's Riviera neighbor, was one who had a shrewd idea what his old friend was up to. *"Méfiez-vous de cet Anglais,"* he claimed to have been warned. *"Il est de l'Intelligence Service. . . . Soyez assuré que s'il tire de vous un renseignement de quelque intérêt, le deuxième étage de Downing Street en sera informé le lendemain."*★

During the following month Maugham made an extensive tour. Beginning at Nancy in the east, he went first to the headquarters of General de Lattre de Tassigny, commander of the Fifth Army, where "I was entertained by generals whose composure terrified me." From there he moved up to the Maginot Line, "driving through a fog at night with no lights in a military car with a driver who doesn't know the way and goes at fifty miles an hour," he told Juliet Duff. Here he was shown over one of the massive, and reputedly impreg-

★ "Beware of that Englishman. He's in the Intelligence Service. You can be sure that any interesting information he gets out of you will be known in Downing Street the next day."

nable, fortresses that stretched along France's border with Germany. It was an impressive sight. "The officer in command told me he could hold out for six months if he were besieged," Maugham reported. "It came as something of a shock to me to see in the paper some months later that this particular fortress had been captured after four days." He was taken down a coal mine at Lens, and was conducted around several munitions factories, both in the east and near Paris; during the third week he traveled to the Charente, in the southwest, to inspect the resettlement there of half a million evacuees, French nationals, from Alsace and Lorraine. The final week was spent at sea on board two naval vessels based at Toulon. Privately, Maugham was horrified by much of what he witnessed, by the innate corruption, the lack of morale, the deep and bitter divisions between the social classes, and he found it an enormous struggle to conceal his personal reactions while for propaganda purposes presenting as positive a picture as he could. "I was determined to write nothing that was untrue," he said later, "[and] it would have caused a useless scandal to relate the facts as I saw them." To his masters at the Ministry, however, the facts were sent back unvarnished, one of the subjects of most concern the resentful attitude of the French toward British forces on French soil, regarded as insufficient in number and shockingly licentious in behavior:

> The impression I received was that there was widespread dissatisfaction with the inadequacy of British support and with the behaviour of British troops, and that such cordiality as the French thought fit to display to their allies was due to policy rather than to friendliness. . . . There was a lot to be done in the direction of improving the feeling between the B.E.F. [British Expeditionary Force] and the French.

It was as a step in this direction that Maugham wrote a series of newspaper articles, later published as a pamphlet, *France at War*,*

---

* *France at War* sold more than a hundred thousand copies between its publication in March 1940 and the fall of France in May and June, when it was withdrawn.

specifically designed to foster in Britain respect and fellow feeling for her ally across the Channel. In a tone of heartfelt admiration, these articles present an unstintingly heroic picture—a picture that was to be devastatingly undermined when less than two years later Maugham in his book, *Strictly Personal,* produced his true impressions, written to set the record straight. Considered together, *France at War* and *Strictly Personal* make an interesting study in contrasts. After touring a munitions works, for instance, Maugham in his article reverently exclaims, "I cannot attempt to describe the wonderful things I saw . . . the pains that are taken . . . every part is quite exquisitely finished. The machines that are used for the manufacture of all these lethal weapons are miracles of ingenuity"; whereas in the book he makes plain how disturbing it was to find signs in every factory of seething dissatisfaction, attempted sabotage, and frequent incidents of revolt. Similarly, he reveals two very different perspectives in his visit to the Charente, where he witnessed the meanness and hostility shown to French families who had been living near the German border and were now forcibly removed and resettled. Arriving in a strange part of the country with almost nothing, these people were deeply resented and given little help by the locals, their fellow countrymen. Straining to shine as favorable a light as possible, Maugham concentrates in his article on the industry and courage shown by the displaced persons. "There are plenty of empty houses and abandoned cottages . . . in a sad state of dilapidation [but] the refugees set to with a will to make them habitable. It is wonderful with what spirit these people, snatched away from comfortable homes, bear their lot." In fact the conditions were disgraceful.

> These wretched people had been hustled out of their houses at two hours' notice . . . put in cattle trucks and had spent three days and sometimes more, in the heat of day, in the cold of night, till they reached Poitiers and Angoulême. . . . Some fell dangerously ill on the way and not a few died. . . . They learnt after a few weeks that their houses had been looted by the soldiers who had been entrusted with their care. . . . They were

miserably housed . . . in broken-down hovels in which you wouldn't have put a pig.

For the last leg of his tour Maugham visited the naval base at Toulon, where he was invited to witness routine exercises at sea. Dividing his time between two vessels, a warship and a torpedo boat, he was struck by the casual attitude displayed by both officers and crew. In the article this relaxed deportment is tactfully described as "pleasantly democratic. . . . Orders are given in a less peremptory fashion than in our own ships [and] officers and men smoke where and when they please on board, during working hours and out of them." In *Strictly Personal,* however, Maugham confesses himself shocked: "I had not been able to help noticing the slovenliness of the men's appearance, which contrasted in so marked a manner with the trim cleanliness so conspicuous in British and American vessels, and I had been taken aback by something that looked very like lack of discipline."

Having completed his tour of inspection, Maugham returned to the Mauresque shortly before Christmas to write his articles, which were so well received that he was immediately recalled to London to discuss a parallel series, about the Home Front, to be translated into French. For the first time in his life Maugham made the journey by air, flying in extremely bad weather from Le Bourget, outside Paris, on an RAF transport plane. After long delays they finally took off, keeping low over the Channel so as not to be mistaken for enemy aircraft, finally landing at a military aerodrome somewhere in Sussex. From here he was driven by truck to the nearest town, where he managed to hire a car, as there were no trains, and "arrived in London cold, tired and hungry, but in time for late dinner at the Café Royal."

During the next three months, the spring of 1940, Maugham was forced to endure the hanging about and time wasting that was an inevitable part of the wartime experience, with the men at the Ministry unable to make up their minds exactly how to employ him. "I was like a performing dog in a circus," he wrote, "whose tricks the public would probably like, but who somehow couldn't be quite fitted into the programme." During this period two of his books were published, *Books and You,* a gathering together of three essays on favorite classics, and a collection of short stories, *The Mixture as Before* (the phrase used by doctors when writing a repeat prescription). This included some vintage Maugham, including "The Three Fat Women of Antibes," "The Lion's Skin," "The Facts of Life," but his readers expressed dismay at the author's pronouncement in his preface. "I have now written between eighty and ninety stories," Maugham states. "I shall not write any more." In fact, as he was later to make clear, the typesetter had left out an *m* and the line should have read, "I shall not write many more."

Meanwhile, his diary was filled with the usual social engagements, with weekends in the country and catching up with the family in town: Syrie had closed down her business and was temporarily living in Paris, Liza was spending as much time as she could with Vincent before he was sent overseas, and F.H. had finally been awarded the hereditary peerage for which Maugham had so fervently hoped (F.H. had enjoyed only a brief period on the woolsack, however, as to his bitter disappointment Chamberlain had replaced him as lord chancellor the day after war was declared). Robin would now inherit the title, and Maugham, anxious to make appropriate provision for his beloved nephew, arranged with Bert Alanson for a generous allowance to be paid him—"It means that the second Viscount will be able to pursue the political career on which he has set his heart," he told Alanson—as well as leaving him a large sum in his will. Regarding the latter, Maugham wrote, "Robin dear,

> I am settling $25000 on you which will be paid you immediately & without further formalities on my death. But I very strongly advise you to leave it in the care of Bert, who is both clever & honest. . . . If you die without issue I should like you, if you will, to leave the money (if you have not already squandered it) in some way that may be to the advantage of English literature; but of course I shall turn in my grave if you don't have issue. . . .

Recently Robin had been the subject of some concern to his uncle, who had heard worrying reports of the young man's heavy drinking, destructive bouts which had obliged the family doctor to forbid any alcohol at all for a while. "I am very glad," Maugham scolded him. "You were quite obviously drinking a great deal too much [and] I have had too much to do with soaks not to look with dismay upon the prospects of anyone I know becoming one." But on the outbreak of war Robin redeemed himself by immediately enlisting, joining the Inns of Court regiment. The news pleased Maugham, who wrote fondly, "I am told on all sides . . . that your buttons are brighter than any buttons in the British Army."

AT THE BEGINNING OF MAY, less than a week before the German invasion of the Low Countries, Maugham returned to the south of France. "It was very quiet on the Riviera," he recalled. Permission was received to bring the *Sara* back from Bandol to her old berth at Villefranche, but no yachts were allowed outside the harbor. There were shortages of food, of coffee in particular, a blackout was enforced, and gasoline was severely rationed, which drastically curtailed the opportunities for social life. As the Phony War, the period of relative military inactivity, continued, people grew restless and resentful. "Everyone is bored & more or less irritable," Maugham told Ellen Doubleday. "Not me! I am delighted that it is impossible to go out to dinner & if only I could afford the gas to go & play golf two or three times a week I should have nothing to complain of." But then the end came with startling suddenness. On May 28, Belgium surrendered, and in northern France the British Expeditionary Force was routed and forced to flee, the remnant rescued from the beaches at Dunkirk during the first few days of June. On June 10 Italy entered the war, four days before the Germans marched into Paris. Immediately the entire Côte d'Azur was thrown into turmoil: within a few hours 50 percent of the population of Monaco had fled and Menton and the area around it was evacuated. If, as seemed probable, the Italians occupied the Riviera, all British residents would be interned, a fate that Maugham was not prepared to contemplate: with typical sangfroid he had planned in such an event to kill himself with the sleeping pills he kept by him for just such an emergency. In order to find out what was happening he drove into Nice, where he found the consul general surrounded by a panicking crowd begging for information. After an anxious wait a message came through from the British embassy, hastily relocated to Bordeaux, that all British subjects were advised to leave the country as quickly as possible, and that two ships, now at Cannes, had been requisitioned to take them off. Passengers were to be on the quay at eight o'clock the following morning, each person permitted one small bag of personal belongings, a blanket, and enough food for three days.

That evening over a hurried dinner, plans were made for the immediate future. It was decided that Gerald, protected by the immunity conferred by his American passport, should stay on at the Villa for a few days to save what he could of the pictures and the most valuable possessions, including Maugham's notebooks and the unfinished manuscript of his new novel. Annette and Nina, both Italian, would remain where they were for as long as it was safe to do so, Maugham giving instructions that if the house had to be abandoned, his favorite dachshund, Erda, should be killed. Reckoning that the roads would be impassable by morning, he decided to leave at midnight, hurriedly packing a few clothes, three books, a blanket, and a pillow, and filling a basket with lump sugar, tea, a couple of packets of macaroni, a jar of marmalade, and a loaf of bread. "It never struck any of us," he later remarked, "that I should want a tin opener, a plate, a knife and fork, a glass and a cup." Having said good-bye to the maids, he and Gerald left the Mauresque. "We drove in silence. I was unhappy," Maugham wrote. "Every few miles a lantern was waved at us and we stopped to have our papers examined by a picket of soldiers." In Cannes, Gerald dropped Maugham at the Carlton Hotel on the Croisette, and the two men took leave of each other; as in the first war, neither knew how or when they would meet again.

The Carlton, one of the grandest hotels on the Riviera, was thronged with people, most of them in evening clothes, many of them drunk, a few hysterical. Sleep was out of the question. Early the next morning, Sunday, June 23, Maugham walked down to the harbor, where he found a scene of indescribable chaos. On the quay a dense mass of more than three thousand people, all laden with luggage, was pushing forward toward a counter where a couple of customs officers were inspecting bags. There were all types and classes, men, women, and children, some invalids come straight out of the hospital, even a few on stretchers who, refused entry, were forced to turn back. From time to time a large car would drive up and the well-dressed occupants alight to join the queue, the driver having no choice but to abandon his vehicle and toss the keys into the little crowd of locals looking on. The sun blazed overhead and the heat grew intense. In the harbor the two ships could be seen moored to bollards, not the spacious vessels envisaged but a couple of small colliers, the *Saltersgate* and the *Ashcrest,* en route to Algeria after discharging their cargoes of coal at Marseilles. It was four hours before Maugham was directed on board the *Saltersgate,* where he was told to join eighty others allotted a small space in the hold. When that evening they were finally ready to sail, there were five hundred passengers, many of them wealthy, owners of fine villas, accustomed to first-class hotels, now jammed into accommodations intended for a crew of thirty-eight. Every surface was covered in coal dust, there was hardly room to move, and Maugham, finding unbearable the crowding and stuffiness below decks, decided to sleep in the open; but the iron deck was painfully hard and it grew cold before dawn, so on the following night and thereafter he slept below.

The next morning the two ships reached Marseilles, where, after waiting all day, they received instructions to join a French convoy headed for Oran. They were at sea for a week, and the conditions on board were frightful. It was very hot, water was in short supply, the few lavatories were filthy and hopelessly inadequate, and rations were extremely limited; most of the day was spent queueing in the sun either for food (four sweet biscuits and a cube of bully beef) or for the chance of a quick wash in a bucket in which fifty people had washed before; everyone was covered in a thick paste of sweat and coal dust. Ill-equipped for the circumstances, Maugham was grateful when a kind lady gave him a scrap of towel and someone else a jam jar to hold his drinking water. As the days passed, fear of attack by torpedo and the misery caused by overcrowding intensified: four people went out of their minds and one elderly woman died. As there were neither rafts nor life belts and U-boats were known to be in the area, it occurred to Maugham to ask one of his neighbors, a retired doctor, how best to drown quickly; ever since his experience in Burma when he had nearly lost his life in a tidal wave he had had a horror of drowning. "Don't struggle," was the advice. "Open your mouth, and the water pouring into your throat will bring on unconsciousness in less than a minute." Spirits rose as the coast of Algeria came into view: word had gone around that a liner would be waiting to take everyone on to England. But after they docked at Oran a wireless message was received that there was no liner and that the captain should quickly take on what stores he could and proceed immediately under escort to Gibraltar.

Accordingly, the *Saltersgate* left that night, a Sunday, arriving in Gibraltar the following Tuesday. Rations had slightly improved as bread, fruit, and cigarettes had been brought on board, and the prospect of disembarking on British soil, of a bath, a drink, a good meal before transferring to more comfortable accommodation for the last leg of the voyage, cheered everybody up. Hopes were dashed, however, when after reaching port they were refused permission to land: thousands of refugees were already on the Rock and there was no room for more, nor was there another vessel; they would have to sail to England in the ship they were in. "Many broke down then," Maugham wrote, "[for] it was a cruel disappointment." The *Saltersgate* remained in port for three days, and eventually passengers were allowed ashore, in parties of fifty for two hours at a time. Maugham was in the last batch, and he hurried off to buy a quilt, sardines, tinned fruit, whisky, and rum. Conditions had improved by the time they were ready to leave, as more than two hundred passengers—children, the sick, and those over seventy—had been taken off, and Maugham was able to move out of the hold and into the slightly more spacious fo'c'sle, where in a corner he constructed a bed for himself by laying a couple of planks over three baskets and covering it with his quilt.

In a convoy of twelve ships, *Saltersgate* and *Ashcrest* left Gibraltar on June 28, finally reaching Liverpool on July 8. With the ship less crowded, Maugham had been able to pass the time in relative ease. Sitting cross-legged on the hard iron deck, he read Plato in the morning, and in the afternoon played patience and continued with one of the two novels he had brought with him, Thackeray's *Esmond* and Charlotte Brontë's *Villette;* after a meager supper at seven he told stories, despite his stammer, to anyone who cared to listen. Eventually the convoy came in sight of the coast of Lancashire and the mouth of the Mersey, "the blessed shores of England." After twenty days on the ship Maugham was haggard, dirty, weak, and exhausted. Arriving by train that night in London he was surprised to learn that his whereabouts had been a matter of some concern to the British press. "Among well-known people still missing in France are Mr. Somerset Maugham," the *Daily Telegraph* had reported on June 24, thus causing considerable disquiet to his family. "The telephone went all day from reporters about Willie, who has disappeared," Nellie Maugham wrote anxiously in her diary, adding on the following day, June 25, "Still no news of Willie and I do hate not knowing. The American embassy say they can't get any news from Paris, nor can the Red Cross." She was therefore relieved to read in the *Daily Mail* on July 2 that at last he had been sighted. "Somerset Maugham's countless admirers will be happy to hear that he has appeared in Gibraltar . . . E. Phillips Oppenheim, too, has escaped. . . . Only P. G. Wodehouse of our leading authors remains, as far as one can assume, in German hands." Finally, on the night of July 8, Maugham himself telephoned from the Dorchester Hotel. "Willie got home!" Nellie wrote. "He is coming to dinner tomorrow, but is too tired to speak tonight, poor darling." And on the evening following, "Willie dined here. He looks terribly tired & thin but not so bad as might be expected after his awful experiences. . . . He didn't take off his clothes for 3 weeks . . . !"

Maugham's immediate concern, after a few days' necessary respite, was to return to his war work. He made a series of propaganda broadcasts, for both home and overseas transmission, their purpose to bolster Anglo-French relations. He was also commissioned by the Ministry of Information and by *Redbook* magazine in America to write a series of articles about the war effort and life on the Home Front. On at least one occasion he took the opportunity to combine duty with pleasure by visiting Alan Searle, currently based at a military camp in Yorkshire, where he was helping to run a canteen and leisure facilities for troops off duty.

It was now that Maugham, aged sixty-six, for the first and only time in his life tried to find a cure for his stammer. Realizing that he would be increasingly called upon to speak in public and on the radio, he consulted a Dr. Leahy, a hypnotist, to whom he had been referred by his old acquaintance, Christabel Aberconway. After several sessions with Dr. Leahy, in which he was taught a method of self-hypnosis, he was surprised to find that up to a point the treatment worked: he continued to stammer in private conversation, but when performing in public he was able to speak on the whole without stumbling. Unfortunately the Leahy effect wore off after a while, but nonetheless it gave Maugham confidence, and from this time on he spoke far more fluently before an audience than when at home with his friends.

Meanwhile, in London, daily life carried on as near normally as possible under wartime conditions. Barrage balloons floated high overhead, Hyde Park was scarred with trenches, sandbags were piled against storefronts and around the statue of Eros in Piccadilly, and mailboxes, lampposts, and trees had been striped with white paint to help pedestrians find their way in the blackout. Maugham had booked a suite on the top floor of the Dorchester Hotel on Park Lane, a conveniently central location. Over the last few months this modern hotel had been experiencing a boom: built of reinforced concrete and boasting a gas-proof shelter in the basement, it was popularly supposed to be indestructible; several cabinet ministers had taken up residence, and rooms were much in demand by people coming up from the country or returning from abroad, or by Londoners too nervous to remain at home. The *Daily Express* reported that now the Dorchester bar "is to London what the Ritz bar used to be to Paris—crowded with business men, socialite women, diplomats, spies." Maugham was constantly running into old friends in the busy lobby, and a couple of days after disembarking in Liverpool he found himself face-to-face with Syrie. "Willie!" she cried, rushing up to him. "Thank God you're safe! I've been so worried!" "So I should hope," Maugham drily responded. Syrie, too, it turned out, was staying at the hotel, having left Paris shortly before the Germans arrived. News of this public encounter between the famously embattled Maughams was naturally seized upon by the gossips, who came up with any number of hilarious versions of the frightful snubs and insults that had been traded.* But in fact during this one short period, under the strains and surreal conditions imposed by war, the two managed to resume genuinely friendly relations. They met almost every afternoon for tea, where they were often joined by Liza, she and her mother fervently hoping that this is how it would be from now on. "But it didn't work that way at all," Liza sadly recalled.

At the beginning of September the air raids began, at first by day and then night after night, often starting at dusk and continuing until dawn. For the first two nights of the Blitz, Maugham stayed on the top floor, but the pounding of the antiaircraft batteries only yards away in Hyde Park became unendurable, and so from the third night he went down to the basement after dinner, joining the other residents who were camping out in pajamas and dressing gowns, huddled together on the floor with pillows and eiderdowns, sleeping as best they could until the all clear sounded between five and six in the morning. "After my three weeks on an iron deck on the *Saltersgate* this was luxury and I slept like a child," Maugham wrote. During the day, as he walked along the familiar streets of the West End, he saw the "grim sight" of the bomb damage, the pave-

---

* The most widely repeated anecdote draws on Maugham's account of the advice he was given by the doctor on board the *Saltersgate*. In the most popular version Syrie tells her husband she is planning to cross to the States and is terrified of being torpedoed. "Well, S-S-Syrie," Maugham is supposed to have replied, "I am assured that when you find yourself in the water, if you open your m-m-mouth wide, it's all over much more quickly" (*The Infirm Glory*, p. 253).

ments covered in broken glass, the gaping, smoking holes where a house or row of houses had stood, including the building in Portland Place where previously he had stayed with Alan. One afternoon with Nellie and F.H. he went to look at the mangled remains of a Messerschmitt that had crashed down into the forecourt of Victoria Station. When other duties permitted, Maugham arranged to meet friends, eagerly seized upon by that dedicated hostess Sibyl Colefax, who invited him to lunch together with Lady Diana Cooper, the journalist and secret agent Robert Bruce Lockhart, Moura Budberg, and H. G. Wells. Wells was garrulous, delivering a tedious monologue on the subject of God. "Willie Maugham was palpably bored and chewed the string of his eyeglass cord most of the time," Bruce Lockhart noted in his diary. One night, returning from a dinner party in Westminster, Maugham and Virginia Woolf were walking up Whitehall when a couple of bombers came over. "[I] shouted at [Virginia] to take cover but in the noise she couldn't hear," Maugham recalled. "She made no attempt to take cover but stood in the middle of the road and threw her arms into the air. She appeared to be worshipping the flashing sky. It was a most weird sight to watch her there, lit up now and then by the flashes from the guns." Yet on the whole, dinner engagements were rare: few cared to venture out in the evening, and the bar and restaurant at the Dorchester were always packed, everyone steadying their nerves with stiff drinks, the resulting party atmosphere providing a welcome insulation from the constant raids. "You know we've had some air raid warnings here," Maugham told Alan Searle. "The Dorchester is very gay while they last. . . . [I] spent such a nice evening, with Diana & Duff [Cooper] & Juliet [Duff]."

Duff Cooper had recently been appointed minister of information, and shortly after Maugham arrived in London he had proposed a propaganda mission to the United States, a mission which by its nature had to be very hush-hush. For Britain it was a matter of paramount importance to win American support for the war, a tough proposition as the majority of the American population was isolationist and Anglophobic and nursed a deep suspicion of anything that smacked of foreign propaganda. Memories remained vivid of the last European conflict, and most Americans were darned sure they wanted nothing to do with this one. Clearly it would be a hard task to convert an essentially unsympathetic nation into a loyal and active ally, and in furthering their cause the British government had to step extremely carefully, as any overt attempts at propaganda would be deeply resented and deleterious: since the signing in 1935 of the Neutrality Act, it had become illegal for foreign agents to conduct propaganda within the United States. In order to avoid the appearance of any suspicious activity, Lord Lothian, the British ambassador in Washington, had urged the use of well-known authors on the lecture circuit; and for this a writer such as Maugham, with a long-established reputation in the States, was considered ideal. During the nearly two and a half years before America entered the war, numbers of well-known British writers toured the country, many to great effect, but few worked harder, made more of an impact, or proved as valuable as Somerset Maugham.

Maugham agreed with alacrity to Duff Cooper's proposal. To provide himself with cover, he contacted Nelson Doubleday, who sent him a letter stating that he was urgently required in New York to arrange for the publication of his next book, a ruse that in the event deceived nobody: "W. Somerset Maugham is in this country as a British agent," blithely begins an interview in *The New York Times* that appeared soon after his arrival. Maugham left London one afternoon at the very end of September, spent the night in Bristol, and next morning caught the plane for Lisbon, taking off with an escort of Spitfires. Capital of a neutral country, Lisbon was imbued with an almost holiday atmosphere, warm and sunny, crowded with people of all nationalities, the shops stocked with food and other merchandise long unobtainable elsewhere. None of this was much enjoyed by Maugham, who found himself billeted in a filthy little pension, obliged to spend hours queueing to have his papers examined and passport stamped prior to his departure for the United States. Finally, on October 7, after several frustrating days, he was free to go, boarding the Pan Am clipper, a luxurious flying boat, for the sixteen-hour flight, via the Azores and Bermuda, to New York.

As on previous occasions Maugham stayed at the Ritz-Carlton, at Sixty-fourth and Madison, where he proposed to remain until Gerald, now making his way to Portugal, was able to join him. Currency restrictions imposed on British subjects abroad were extremely tight, but as Maugham was in America to promote the British cause it had been discreetly arranged with the Treasury that he be allowed to draw on a portion of his American royalties, thus enabling him to enjoy a rather higher standard of living than would otherwise have been the case. Almost immediately he was put to work, writing articles, making speeches, giving interviews, attending fund-raising dinners, and helping sell books for the British War Relief Bookshop. He also made a number of radio broadcasts, his first with Edward Weeks on NBC, during which, in answer to a question about great war novels, Maugham said, "Just as the best novel about the First World War, *All Quiet on the Western Front,* came out of Germany's defeat, so I hope and believe that the best book about this war will come from the same source, and for the same reason." It was an emotive reply and it received an outburst of applause from the studio audience. During the first month Maugham addressed gatherings that varied in size from three thousand in a flag-draped hotel ballroom to a hundred ladies at tea in a private house. Sometimes he was the sole speaker, at other times part of a panel with other writers, among them Louis MacNeice, Robert Sherwood, Thomas Mann, and the Austrian novelist Franz Werfel. Whatever the occasion, Maugham was careful to emphasize the ineradicable links between Britain and America. "When, in this war, we British are defending our culture, the rich and fertile culture of the English-speaking peoples, we are defending not only what is ours but what is yours," he told a large audience one night at the Waldorf-Astoria. Another reiterated theme, carefully chosen to counter the New World's dislike of the Old with all its arrogance and imperialism, was the future partnership of the two great democratic countries. The war, Maugham repeatedly stressed, was having a democratizing effect: "the crisis was destroying the class consciousness which has been one of the evils of English life. . . . [After the war] the country shall be much more democratic than ever before. Some accept it with resignation, some with joy. I myself accept it with joy." Such sentiments, genuinely held, were also directly in line with the briefings Maugham regularly received both from the embassy in Washington and from the British Information Services in New York. His masters were pleased with him. "On his arrival Maugham was given widespread and favourable publicity," it was reported to the Foreign Office in London. "He is apparently well-liked by the Press [and] is widely quoted in out of town papers."

In his free time, and while waiting for Gerald, who was currently cooling his heels in Lisbon while trying to get a seat on the flying boat, Maugham saw friends, news of them retailed in long letters to Alan Searle, to whom he wrote devotedly every week. There were the Doubledays, Alexander Woollcott, Dorothy Parker, George S. Kaufman, Carl Van Vechten, H. G. Wells, "looking old, tired and shrivelled," and the playwright Ned Sheldon, now paralyzed and blind but as saintly and charming as ever. A fellow guest at the Ritz was Emerald Cunard, "my girl Emerald" as Maugham affectionately referred to her; she had a suite five floors above his, "[where] she managed to create the nearest thing to a salon that New York has ever had"; every afternoon he went up to take tea with her, "& hob-nobbed with all the fantastic people she gathered about her."

It was with Emerald one day that Maugham met again the writer Glenway Wescott, first encountered in 1928 when Wescott had been brought to lunch at the Mauresque. On that occasion, Maugham, in a surly temper, had snubbed the young man, but now he was enchanted by him, much taken by his blond, youthful good looks and quickly finding much in common: like Maugham, Wescott was intensely interested in sex and literature and other people's lives; he was a novelist; he had lived in France, and with his lover, Monroe Wheeler, a director at the Museum of Modern Art, knew everyone in literary and artistic circles in Paris and New York. For his part, Wescott enormously admired Maugham, and the two men soon became close friends, developing an almost father-son relationship. Wescott sensed that Maugham would have liked something more, and he was grateful for the elder man's tact in not making this an issue: "though frequently complimenting me on my youthfulness, etc., he has never felt, at least never let me feel the least strain in this way. His discretion never fails." Glenway invited Maugham to spend a weekend at Stone-blossom, the country house in New Jersey he and Monroe shared, providing a welcome respite for Maugham from the pressures of war work in the city. Here they had long discussions about books, and about Glenway's writing—Maugham had reservations about Wescott's first novel, *The Pilgrim Hawk*—and Maugham encouraged Glenway to describe his sex life.

> I said that for my part I am never as eager to have intercourse with a new lover as with one I have already enjoyed, again and again and again. Somewhat to my surprise Willie said that oh, indeed, it was so for him as well.

Also in New York were Liza with her little son, and Syrie. With Vincent away in the army, Liza, newly pregnant, had come over in July and almost immediately fallen ill, for a time so ill that her hostess, Nelson Doubleday's sister, had panicked and cabled for her mother. Immediately all the old bitterness flared up between Maugham and his ex-wife: he thought his daughter should live quietly, preferably in the country, at least until after the baby was born; Syrie, on the other hand, was determined that Liza should be with her in Manhattan, and saw no reason, once she was well again, why she should not lead as active a social life as she chose. At the back of her mind was the thought that Liza, so chic and pretty, might meet a rich man who would eventually take the place of the impecunious Vincent. Liza felt torn apart. She was touched by her father's concern: "I had the feeling that he wanted to be and to remain friends with me"; but she hated the position of being yet again the cause of quarrels between her parents. "It was a very painful situation," she said. "In the end I chose to share an apartment with my mother at the Sulgrave Hotel . . . though I must say there were times when I would have preferred to be independent."

Finally, at the beginning of December 1940, Gerald arrived in New York; after several weeks in Lisbon he had eventually made the crossing by sea, having despaired of obtaining a passage on the clipper. Maugham was relieved to see him safe, but his heart sank when it immediately became obvious that Gerald was back to his bad old alcoholic ways. "I can't bear this," Maugham declared, pacing up and down. "Haven't I done enough for him? Why do I have to go through more?" If only Alan could come over and take his place; but there was no chance of that with the world in its present state.

Within a couple of weeks of Gerald's arrival, he and Maugham left for Chicago, where there were further propaganda talks to be given—to audiences that were notably less sympathetic, as Chicago was a bastion of the noninterventionist America First Committee. During the month that they spent in Illinois, the two men took off a couple of days to go to Oregon to visit a handsome, hard-drinking ex-lover of Gerald's, Tom Seyster. They took with them on the trip a thirteen-year-old English boy, Daniel Farson,★ a godson of Seyster's, who had been entrusted to their care by his aunt, with whom he was staying in Chicago as an evacuee. Farson remembered the occasion vividly: he had no idea that Maugham was a famous author and chattered brightly to him all the way on the train, Maugham listening politely, Haxton palpably bored by the child's presence. Both men seemed at a low ebb, Farson said later, and it was plain that Haxton was drinking heavily, the impression that lingered of Gerald "a large ginger moustache and violent temper when he was not mute from hangover." During their stay in Oregon, Seyster and Haxton quarreled furiously, Seyster still besotted by Gerald, who was permanently intoxicated, while Maugham remained silent and detached. Dutifully the three adults bought the boy popcorn and took him bowling and to the cinema, a strange little group to be wandering the streets, as Farson remarked: "in this small . . . town our appearance must have been disconcerting to the point of shame." When they finally returned to Chicago, Maugham drew

★ Farson later became a noted writer, photographer, and television journalist.

Farson's aunt aside and warned her that Seyster was not a suitable companion for a boy of Dan's age.

From Chicago, Maugham and Haxton traveled to California, staying with the Alansons in a rain-soaked San Francisco for three weeks, where Maugham dutifully continued his lecturing. Where Chicago had been defiantly isolationist, in California the general attitude was more difficult to define. It was "a jittery population," Maugham told his brother:

> The vast majority are ready to give all aid to Britain, but the vast majority also are very much afraid of being forced into the war [having] been frankly terrified by the stories of the bombing of London & the pictures of destruction that have been sent over. . . .
>
> [There are also] vast numbers of Republicans who cannot forgive Roosevelt his victory in November & are prepared to oppose any measure, regardless of its merits, merely because he proposes it. I wouldn't go so far as to say they would like a British defeat, but it hasn't escaped them that it would be a smack in the eye for the President. . . . Of course this is confidential; I don't let a hint of this escape me when I talk.

Exhausted after a bout of influenza, Maugham was beginning to find public speaking a strain, and it was a relief finally to reach Los Angeles, where he and Gerald stayed at the Beverly Hills Hotel and could spend at least some of the day relaxing in the sun by the pool. Here on the West Coast he skillfully played up the German threat, not to distant Europe but to territories much nearer home:

> If by any chance we are beaten, then your danger will be great. It isn't a ruined Europe that Hitler wants, it isn't an unproductive Africa; it's those great undeveloped territories of South America with their inexhaustible stores of raw material that he hankers after.

He also made a point of distancing indomitable Britain from her fallen ally, France. Describing the collapse of France as the most tragic event of the war, he laid much of the blame on the climate of corruption that had long permeated the country:

> In France there were many thousands of men of the highest integrity. There were not enough. They were swamped by men who were greedy, dishonest, selfish, and immoral. . . . The Germans have been saying for years that the French were a decadent people; they were right.*

Effective as propaganda, this was also a fact of which Maugham himself was bitterly convinced; his awareness of the atmosphere of moral decay seeps onto almost every page of *Christmas Holiday,* and the degeneracy of the French national character is a subject examined at length in *Strictly Personal:* "If a nation values anything more than freedom, it will lose its freedom, and the irony of it is that if it is comfort or money that it values more, it will lose that too." When Glenway Wescott asked Maugham what he thought France would be like after the war, he replied "in his hardest, narrowest voice . . . 'They will have eaten so much shit they will stink of it.' "

Committed to promoting his country's cause, Maugham in Los Angeles suddenly found himself cornered, faced with an offer he felt honor-bound to accept. Over the years he had persistently turned down all offers of film work, uninterested in the medium and knowing full well he lacked the requisite skills; now, however, he found himself obliged to give in. At the instigation of Brendan Bracken, the dynamic new minister of information in London, Maugham was approached by David O. Selznick with a proposal for a propaganda film about an English family in wartime. Selznick, one of the most successful producers in the business—two of his films, *Gone with the Wind* and *Rebecca,* had recently won Best Picture Oscars—was ex-

---

* Needless to say, such sentiments were ill received among the French community in California. When the director René Clair met Maugham in Hollywood, the encounter was frigid in the extreme.

cited at the prospect of at last signing up the world-famous author, so much of whose work was already on celluloid. With this particular new property Selznick was aware that he would have to tread carefully, not wishing to estrange either the film industry itself or potential audiences, for whom any hint of propaganda was something alien and sinister. "Naturally we should keep confidential from everybody other than the British authorities the fact that [the film] will have a propaganda value," he wrote in an internal memo.

Reluctantly, Maugham agreed to the deal, and by the beginning of March 1941, when he returned to New York, he had already completed the first thirty pages of *The Hour Before the Dawn*. But then followed several weeks of interruption, with lectures to be given in Chicago, Philadelphia, and Lafayette, Indiana. On March 15, Liza's baby was born, a daughter, christened Camilla. "So far I have only been allowed to see the infant through a sheet of glass," Maugham reported after visiting mother and child in New York City Hospital. "[She] has bright red hair at present & the most lovely little hands you ever saw."

At the beginning of April, Maugham went to Washington for the first night of a dramatized version of *Theatre* ("poor & poorly acted"), and in that same month a novella, *Up at the Villa,* was published by Doubleday. A slight work, with some unusually wooden dialogue, *Up at the Villa* nonetheless maintains an exciting tension, and the almost universal panning it received—"fictional drivel," his "worst novel," must have been "talking in his sleep"—is difficult to justify. In later years Maugham came to hate *Up at the Villa* and flinched when it was mentioned. "I don't want to hear a word about it!" he would angrily exclaim. "I'm ashamed ever to have done it!"—a curious response from one who was famously impervious to critical censure. But his reaction may have had more to do with a feeling of guilt: in the story, the cad Rowley Flint—"an unscrupulous scamp . . . a waster"—is in all major respects a portrait of Gerald Haxton; and there are telling similarities, too, between Gerald and the heroine's dead husband, a charmer but a soak. "He had immense vitality. He was so kind and gentle and sweet—when he was sober. When he was drunk he was noisy and boastful and vulgar and quarrelsome. . . . He was a dreadful gambler and when he was drunk he'd lose hundreds of pounds." "Why didn't you leave him?" Mary is asked. "How could I leave him?" she replies. "He was so dependent on me." These were portrayals Maugham may have bitterly come to regret, given the harrowing sequence of events that was shortly to unfold.

By the end of May, despite constant distraction, *The Hour Before the Dawn* was finally finished, and Maugham and Haxton returned to Hollywood. The story, about an upper-middle-class English family, one son a pacifist and one in intelligence, complete with a beautiful Nazi spy, appeared first in *Redbook* magazine, for which Maugham was paid $25,000; the plan was then to rework it as a film script before finally processing it into a full-length novel—by which time its author was heartily sick of the whole project: "the most tedious job I have ever done in my life."

As he had agreed to make himself available during shooting, Maugham rented a house at 732 South Beverly Glen Boulevard, in the leafy residential area of Beverly Hills. "It is two miles from the sea & so gets the cool breeze," he told Ellen Doubleday.

> It has a very nice garden & a swimming pool. It is furnished in
> Hollywood Italian, but quite unobjectionably & has a studio
> in the garden for me to work in. . . .

Relieved to be settled, Maugham started work on the screenplay, for which he had been paid $15,000, with an additional $5,000 for every week he spent on it. He was in a relatively contented frame of mind, following much the same daily routine he had established at the Mauresque: writing all morning, swimming and golf after a sleep in the afternoon, followed by an evening entertaining or being entertained. Gerald, too, was delighted to be back in California, full of good resolutions to curb his drinking while at the same time determined to enjoy himself to the full. Soon after they moved in, Liza, the children, and a nanny arrived for an extended visit. At first Liza had been nervous about accepting the invitation, as she had been frightened of Haxton since her childhood and was apprehensive about staying in the same house, but her father had assured her that Gerald was hardly drinking now and was "so good and sweet." That this was not entirely the case, Liza immediately realized. "Of course it wasn't true about his not drinking: he just did it secretly," she said. "There was a bar in the living room and he would have glasses full of drink for himself lined up under there while he served everyone else and kept a soft drink in full view." Yet there seemed to be a tacit agreement not to mention the problem. On one occasion when Liza and Maugham went with the Alansons to Lake Tahoe for a few days, they returned to find Haxton in the grip of delirium tremens. "My father seemed to accept even this from him," she resignedly remarked. Soon, however, she, too, ceased to worry, quickly swept up in a glamorous social life, out most of the day and rarely coming home until the small hours, with a constant stream of handsome young actors calling at the house to take her to parties and screenings.

Whether drunk or sober, Gerald, too, was loving the life, detailed accounts of which he sent back in affectionate letters to Louis Legrand in France. Gerald painfully missed Loulou, and he worried about his health and situation, whenever possible sending him parcels of provisions through the good offices of a friend in the Red Cross. To Loulou he described the wonderful time he was having, taking advantage of everything Southern California had to offer: sex, swimming, gambling, shopping for clothes, driving a big car, and, rather worryingly given the alcoholic intake, learning to fly. Most exciting of all, as he knew Loulou would appreciate, was actually meeting the stars. *"J'étais dans une grande soirée hier ou il y avait tout le monde de Hollywood,"* he boasted, *"Chaplin, [Ronald] Colman, [Herbert] Marshall et toutes les plus jolies femmes de cette terre. Hedy Lamarr était la plus ravissante, mais j' ai trouvé plus à mon goût Rosalind Russell et Loretta Young."*★ In another letter he described a luncheon party Maugham had given where both Douglas Fairbanks and Bette

---

★ "I was at a big party yesterday with the whole of Hollywood, Chaplin, Colman, Marshall and all the prettiest women on this earth. Hedy Lamarr was the loveliest, but I found Rosalind Russell and Loretta Young more to my taste."

Davis were present, the latter *"charmante mais très laide"*★ in Gerald's opinion. Under the circumstances, Miss Davis had reason to be charming, as it was the film of *Of Human Bondage* that in 1934 had turned around what she herself described as a "fast-disappearing career. . . . I had been wandering aimlessly until *Of Human Bondage* came along and brought me out of the fog," she said in an interview. "We have such reverence for the chance this picture gave [me] that everything in our family dates BB (Before *Bondage*) and AB (After *Bondage*)."

Predictably, Maugham was considerably less enamored of Hollywood than Gerald and Liza, regarding the film colony with much the same weary indifference as he had regarded theater folk in London. "I see something of the stars; I cannot say they greatly excite me," he languidly admitted to his niece Kate, while to Osbert Sitwell he complained of the almost total lack of culture of most actors: "one little ray of sunshine was when Mr. Cary Grant told me he didn't really think much of Cézanne," he added sardonically. To this most disciplined of men, the relaxed atmosphere, the lack of regard for punctuality, was frustrating in the extreme: it maddened him when he arrived for dinner precisely on time to find his hostess had just drifted upstairs to have a bath. The stupidity and self-regard within the acting profession, the suffocating parochialism of the industry, bored him intensely. "I meet few people who interest me," he complained. "They are cordial & hospitable . . . but I can find no one who is willing to talk to me of the things I like talking about. It is like having nothing to eat but candy." Typical of this kind of experience was an evening when the well-known actor Errol Flynn called at the house to collect Liza. For once there had been a rare Allied victory widely reported that day in the papers, and Maugham asked the star if he had seen the wonderful news. "You mean about Mickey Rooney?" came the guileless response. Occasionally Maugham tried to enliven proceedings for himself, as on the day he was taken to see Spencer Tracy filming *Dr. Jekyll and Mr. Hyde*. The star came on set costumed as Dr. Jekyll, formally

★ "charming but very ugly"

dressed, very elegant and dapper, and began his scene. "Which one is he supposed to be now?" asked Maugham in a carrying whisper, provoking a loud guffaw from the camera crew, for which Tracy never forgave him.★

Much more to Maugham's taste was the company of fellow writers, Dorothy Parker, for instance, whom he was pleased to find next to him at a dinner party, "demure in black silk, but with a demureness fraught with peril to the unwary." Among the English contingent were Aldous Huxley, the playwright John Van Druten, Gerald Heard, mystic and polymath, and Christopher Isherwood. Isherwood, now living in Los Angeles, was delighted by the reunion. "I was so pleased to see Willie again," he noted in his diary, "that old, old parrot, with his flat black eyes, blinking and attentive, his courtly politeness and his hypnotic stammer." Maugham was as much a mystery to him as he was to Maugham. In a letter to E. M. Forster, Isherwood compared the sixty-seven-year-old writer to "an old Gladstone bag covered with labels. God only knows what is inside," while Maugham referred to the lively, boyish Christopher as "that delightful, strange man whom you could never really know." The two of them had a good deal in common and relished each other's company, Maugham finding in Christopher and his compatriots the restless intelligence, the subversive wit and wide culture he had failed to find elsewhere in California. Isherwood one day invited Maugham to visit him at the MGM studios where he was working. The Marx brothers were also there, and Harpo, excited to see his old acquaintance, rushed at Maugham, the whole gang following, "screaming like devils," Christopher recalled, "[climbing] all over him, hugging and kissing him, as Willie submitted to their embraces with shy pleased smiles." At Isherwood's house in the Hollywood hills, he, Maugham, and Gerald Heard had long conversations about the Upanishads and the Hindu scriptures, about Vedanta and the ninth-century philosopher Shankara, all of

★ Twelve years later, when Spencer Tracy was in the south of France with Maugham's old friend Garson Kanin, he was adamant in refusing an invitation to dine at the Mauresque.

absorbing interest to Isherwood and Heard, both disciples of the influential California guru Swami Prabhavananda. Maugham told them that his great ambition was to return to India and write a serious book about Shankara and his teaching. "I was much moved on hearing this," Isherwood recorded, "until the news reached us, through van Druten and others, that Willie had made fun of Gerald [Heard], albeit quite affectionately, at a cocktail party next day, and deplored my wasting my time with mysticism when I ought to be writing novels."

Expecting at any moment to be called in for the filming of *The Hour Before the Dawn,* Maugham was beginning to feel frustrated, sick to death of writing propaganda and longing to start on a novel that had nothing to do with the war. As he had told Isherwood, a return to India was uppermost in his mind, his plans yearningly elaborated in letters to Alan Searle. As soon as the war ended and they could travel again, he told Alan, Gerald would return to France to put the house in order, while Alan would come out to California and from there the two of them would sail for India.

> I am afraid this is no more than wishful thinking . . . but how grand it would be if it were so! No more propaganda writing for me & a lovely journey ahead . . . & peace, peace, peace for a generation at least.

Maugham was abruptly awakened from these pleasant daydreams by a communication from David O. Selznick Productions: the screenplay of *The Hour Before the Dawn* had been judged wholly unacceptable. "I have read scripts and reviewed fiction since 1932 but never have I felt so speechless," begins one internal memorandum.

> It is impossible to credit Maugham with this formless, maundering, illiterate rubbish. It is so trite and dead; the characters are stock of the worst novelette type. I just do not know what to say or how to say it, except that for his own sake Mr. Maugham had better just tear this up and forget what must have been a bad dream.

The author was consequently informed that his services would no longer be required, a dismissal to which he reacted partly with relief and partly with extreme irritation that so much time had been wasted. "I loathe the people I am working for," he told his niece Kate, "[and] I will never again have anything to do with pictures." A film of *The Hour Before the Dawn* eventually appeared in 1944, with Veronica Lake and Franchot Tone, and disappeared again shortly afterward, while the novel was brought out only in the United States, Maugham having refused to let it be published in Britain. "I know very well it was poor & I was miserable about it," he confessed to Eddie Marsh. "I tried to console myself by looking upon it as my contribution to the war effort, but that did not help much and I prefer to think now that it will be unread in England and forgotten in America."

In mid-September, Liza and the children left California to return to New York, followed a week later by Maugham and Haxton, who completed the first part of the journey by car, driving through Texas to South Carolina. The purpose of the detour was to visit Bonny Hall, a property near Charleston belonging to Nelson Doubleday, who had offered to build Maugham a bungalow there, to be paid for out of future royalties, where his author could live and work in peace for the duration. Maugham had been delighted by the suggestion, and he was pleased by the look of the little house already almost finished. Arrived in New York, he enjoyed shopping for furniture to fill it, a welcome diversion, as the weeks passed, from the almost ceaseless drudgery of the propaganda treadmill. "Writing, writing, writing all the time," he complained to Searle. "No sooner do I get through with one job than I have to get started on another." He was gratified to be invited to join the Pulitzer Prize Committee as a judge of the drama section, the first time an Englishman had been asked to take part; however, "the result so far is that I have seen as lousy a lot of plays as it has been my misfortune to see for many years . . . the only halfway good one being Noël's [*Blithe Spirit*], [and] he not being American is not eligible."

But then suddenly everything changed. On December 7, 1941, the Japanese bombed Pearl Harbor and the United States entered the war. Maugham, who had just returned to the South, felt as though an enormous weight had been lifted off his shoulders. "Now that America is in the war my job has come to an end," he wrote with relief to Glenway Wescott. "I can't be any use in further trying to persuade the Americans that the English are not so bad after all since you've got to put up with us now if you like us or not."

IT WAS AT YEMASSEE in South Carolina that Maugham was to be based for the rest of the war. His little house, Parker's Ferry, was situated in the middle of marshland, on the banks of the Combahee River, less than an hour's drive from the Atlantic coast. It was a rural, sparsely populated region, with the nearest town, Beaufort, twenty-six miles away and Charleston, more than fifty. "The countryside [is] wild, lonely, monotonous & lovely," Maugham wrote. "I like it very much indeed & find myself happy here."

The Doubledays' handsome house, Bonny Hall, recently rebuilt but on the old plantation pattern, was at the center of an estate now turned over to the cultivation of azaleas and camellias. Two miles from the Hall and set in its own garden was Maugham's white-painted bungalow, simple in design yet spacious and comfortable, with three bedrooms and a large living room, hung with reproductions of pictures from the Villa Mauresque, that led out onto a veranda. A short distance from the house were servants' quarters and a separate small cottage that served as Maugham's study. To look after him there were a black cook and housemaid, Nora and Mary, and a gardener, Sunday, who was helped out on an irregular basis by his nephew, Religious. Maugham's innate courtesy impressed the two women, and he in turn was very taken by them. "[They] have captured my sympathy because they find me the funniest man they have ever known," he reported. "They simply bellow with laughter at my smallest joke." Nora was an excellent cook, with a repertoire of southern dishes that Maugham found much to his taste—gumbo, fried chicken, corn fritters—though she refused to cook any Yankee food, such as his favorite, Boston baked beans. As he had done with Annette at the Mauresque, Maugham immediately began to teach Nora some basic French cuisine. The Doubledays, invited to dinner shortly after his arrival, were astonished to be offered *soupe à l'oignon, truite au bleu, canard à l'orange,* and a perfect almond soufflé, all expertly served, under their host's watchful eye, by Mary and Sunday.

During the winter Nelson ran his publishing business from Bonny Hall, returning to Oyster Bay in the spring when it began to grow hot. While the Doubledays were in residence there was a great deal of coming and going of editorial staff and their wives from Garden City, resulting in a busy social program of bridge, cocktails, and dinner parties, in which Maugham on occasion joined. On the whole, however, he preferred it when the couple were on their own, when he could go up for a game of cards with Ellen in the afternoon and in the evening join Nelson for a drink before returning to his own house for dinner. Husband and wife could hardly have been more different. Nelson was a buccaneer, a big, beefy man, moody and flamboyant, an outdoorsman who loved duck shooting and churning down the river in his powerful motorboat; he was also a prodigious drinker, rarely without a glass of bourbon in his hand, unattractively referred to as his "phlegmcutter." Ellen, by contrast, was a sweet, nervous woman, completely overwhelmed by her noisy, dominating husband, hopelessly untidy and disorganized, her domestic affairs always on the brink of chaos. "Ellen ran the worst household in America," said Jerry Zipkin, a New York friend of Maugham's who visited him at Parker's Ferry. "The roast never went round, [and] if you were sitting on her left you starved. Nelson roared about what a rotten housekeeper she was, and she'd come in tears to see Willie and ask him how to run a house, since his cottage was so well organised."

As fuel was severely rationed, there was little opportunity for driving about the countryside, and when calling at Bonny Hall, Maugham and Haxton usually walked the couple of miles up to the house; otherwise they rode nearly every day, exploring the area on a couple of horses provided by Nelson, a form of exercise that

Maugham had always enjoyed. "I have grand gallops through the country," he wrote in April 1942. "The woods just now are lovely, all the young green of the green trees very gay against the dark green of the live oaks & the gray of the Spanish moss; and here and there, in great patches, white lilies, & on the canal banks, iris." For Gerald this was all very well, and for a while he amused himself fishing from the river and shooting ducks, but the nearest tavern, the Golden Eagle in Beaufort, was miles away, and with Maugham as usual absorbed in his writing he soon grew restless and bored. He was also unwell—he had recently had a bout of heart trouble—and so he decided to return to New York for treatment. Here his condition turned out to be more serious than anticipated, necessitating a three-week stay in the hospital followed by a month's convalescence in Florida.

With the United States' entry into the war, Maugham had assumed that his usefulness would end and he could devote himself to the novel that he had had in mind for over three years. But in this he was mistaken, and to his dismay he found his services constantly called upon, "roped in," as he put it, "to do stuff for America." Again he was asked to broadcast and write articles, to promote Defense Bonds and report on the local leisure facilities provided by the USO (United Services Organization) for the armed forces; one of his lowest points was reached when he was faced with having to come up with an inspiring article to encourage Americans to send vegetable seeds to Britain. "It's no good your telling me that Dean Swift wrote a very pretty piece about a broomstick," he grumbled to Eddie Marsh. "I know he did." Briefly there was even talk of sending him on a propaganda tour of Brazil, a country honeycombed with pro-German organizations, but after a brief flurry this particular project was abandoned.

Once the Doubledays had left, Maugham spent a great deal of time on his own at Yemassee, very contentedly for the most part. Except for the occasional weekend, Gerald did not return after his convalescence in Florida, having decided to go to Washington to try to find some war work of his own, a plan of which Maugham wholeheartedly approved, even though it would leave him without a secretary. "Of course I should miss him," he told Alan, "but I think he will be happier doing some such work & I think it will keep him out of mischief." Sometimes friends visited, Glenway Wescott and Monroe Wheeler among the most welcome. Maugham was impressed by Monroe's standing and scholarship, his knowledge of the art world, but he was closest to Glenway, who often came on his own and with whom Maugham felt he could talk about anything—writing, philosophy, psychology, literature, life—and with whom he relished dissecting their mutual friends. It was Glenway who picked up on the fact that Maugham was still involved in some way with "government business": "I know that people used to come to see him in Yemassee and I'd have to go out of the room," Wescott recalled, and once Maugham told him, "The day doesn't pass that I don't send some poor [pro-German] Englishman back home."*

Dorothy Parker was another visitor. She came for three weeks, "three long, long, long weeks," during which she suffered hours of tedium. Expecting to join an amusing house party, she was dismayed to find herself alone with Maugham, who offered little in the way of entertainment except endless games of bridge. "That old lady," as she described her host, " is a crashing bore." Occasionally people were asked over for cocktails, but they turned out for the most part to be "various handsome young men who were not interested in ladies but who were interested in Mr. Maugham" and thus of no use to Mrs. Parker. Presumably she managed to conceal her ennui, however, as a couple of years later Maugham contributed an admiring preface to a collected edition of her stories and verse.

A far more appreciative guest was Eleanor Roosevelt, who stayed at Yemassee after visiting the State University in North Carolina. Mrs. Roosevelt had been a fan of Maugham's since the late

---

* Maugham's involvement was obliquely acknowledged years later by Sir William Stephenson, code name Intrepid, who was head of British Security Coordination in the United States during the war. "Intrepid had a variety of friends and contacts working for him [and there] were those who subsequently made it plain that they were not opposed to being acknowledged publicly. I don't think Somerset Maugham ever made this feeling known" (*Maugham,* Ted Morgan, p. 467).

1920s; they had met more recently on one of Maugham's visits to Washington and had taken a great liking to each other, Maugham admiring the remarkable First Lady for her courage, tenacity, and strong social conscience. In 1941, when Maugham was in Washington for a production of *Theatre,* Mrs. Roosevelt had given a dinner in his honor, which was followed by a party thrown for him by her niece, Alice Longworth. The two also shared an interest in food, and the small correspondence that survives is mainly on this subject. "Dear Eleanor," begins a jocular note from Maugham, "Thank you very much for the recipe. We are going to try it immediately and if you see that my whole household has died suddenly, you will know the reason." Mrs. Roosevelt also sent Maugham the photographs she had taken during her stay at Parker's Ferry. "What a distinguished profile you have given me," he wrote appreciatively. "You are indeed a marvellous photographer & I feel that you have wasted your time being a wife & mother. You should have been a great artist & led a life of sin."

In May, when the heat in South Carolina became unbearable, Maugham went to New York, but as the temperature there was hardly less ferocious—"too hot to do anything," he complained to Alan from his suite at the Ritz, "too hot to work, too hot to play"—he moved to Martha's Vineyard, off the coast of Massachusetts, and stayed at the Colonial Inn in Edgartown. Here he was able to be quiet and cool and, most important, to work undisturbed on his novel. His sole appearance in public was at a showing of the film version of *The Moon and Sixpence,* which, as Maugham's presence on the island had become known, was given its premiere at the local movie house in Edgartown. After a couple of months he felt much restored, able to face the demanding schedule of broadcasts and lectures that awaited him during the coming autumn.

The war was constantly weighing on Maugham's mind. As an Englishman, he could not but be aware how disastrous in effect throughout 1942 was the decline of Britain's prestige, defeat following defeat, the fall of Singapore, the loss of Malaya and Burma, and the fiasco of the Eighth Army's performance in Libya. "Our stock is falling lower & lower in this country," he told Searle. "At present you hear nothing but that the English are stupid & incompetent & that all Winston has to offer is fine speeches. It is terribly discouraging & one doesn't know what to answer." Since the previous winter, both Robin and Vincent had been fighting in North Africa. Terrible reports were coming through of casualties in the Western Desert as the Eighth Army engaged with the panzer divisions of Rommel's Afrika Korps. Then in July came the news that Captain the Honourable Robin Maugham had been wounded and shipped out to a hospital in Egypt. His recovery was slow, but eventually he returned to England and was invalided out of the army, registered unfit for active service.

After an autumn in New York Maugham returned to South Carolina for the winter and spring. From there at the beginning of May 1943 he finally finished the first draft of his novel *The Razor's Edge*. "The book has been a great pleasure to me to write & I do not care if people on the whole think it good or poor. I have got it off my chest & that is all that matters to me." From the moment of its publication, nearly a year later, *The Razor's Edge* made an enormous impact. There were many adulatory reviews, and sales were immense; in the States, over a half a million copies sold by the end of the first month. Maugham expressed himself gratified by such an appreciative response to a work that was of tremendous personal importance to him. "I will not pretend that I am not staggered," he admitted to Eddie Marsh, while in October he wrote to his niece Diana, "It has given me a lot of satisfaction to have produced a novel in my old age which has had such a great success."

The Razor's Edge★ is undoubtedly one of the most interesting of all Maugham's fictional works. In it he engages the three topics that always most fascinated him: sexual passion, the mores of society, and the nature of goodness, in this case as illustrated in the division between the material and spiritual worlds. The novel opens in Chicago in 1919, with the narrator, "Maugham," spending a few weeks in the city on his way to the Far East, just as the real

---

★ The title refers to a quotation from the *Katha Upanishad:* "The sharp edge of a razor is difficult to pass over; thus the wise say the path to Salvation is hard."

Maugham had done that same year on his way to China. A wealthy acquaintance from Paris, Elliott Templeton, telephones out of the blue, explaining that he is staying with his widowed sister and inviting him to luncheon at her house. Here, as well as his hostess, Mrs. Bradley, "Maugham" meets her daughter, Isabel, and Isabel's fiancé, Larry Darrell. It is clear that Isabel, a bouncy, self-confident young woman, is passionately in love with handsome Larry, although to Maugham's experienced eye Larry seems curiously uninvolved, a quiet, smiling figure, amiable but remote. It transpires that Larry, an aviator in the war, had been badly shaken when his best friend was killed, leaving him obscurely troubled ever since. Reluctantly, Isabel agrees to his suggestion that he go on his own to Paris, on the understanding that he will use the time to pull himself together so that they may begin on the richly upholstered married life to which she avidly looks forward. Elliott Templeton, an exquisite, snobbish old queen who lives for his rarefied social life, generously offers to launch Larry in Paris—"Believe me, my dear fellow, the average American can get into the kingdom of heaven much more easily than he can get into the Boulevard St. Germain"—but to Elliott's astonishment Larry rebuffs him, instead disappearing to a shabby hotel room to pursue some mysterious course of study of his own. When eventually Mrs. Bradley and Isabel, alarmed at the absence of news, follow Larry to Paris, he in as kind a way as possible breaks off the engagement.

Ten years pass before Maugham runs into any of them again. By this time Isabel has married a prosperous banker, Gray Maturin, with whom she leads a lavishly materialistic life in Chicago, while Larry in Paris is encountered one day in the street, dressed like a tramp. Invited by Maugham to tell his story, he launches into a lengthy description of his journey toward spiritual enlightenment, from working in a coal mine to spending five years at an ashram in India. At the same time the Maturins, too, return to Paris. They have suffered badly in the crash of 1929, Gray's business completely wiped out, and are now living entirely off Isabel's uncle Elliott, who has given them his splendid apartment on the Left Bank, while he spends most of the year on the Riviera. It is Maugham who brings Larry back into their lives, to Isabel's particular delight—until she learns that he is about to be married to a girlfriend of hers from Chicago. Sophie is a drug-addicted dipsomaniac who will sleep with anyone for the price of a drink, and Larry, hooked on sacrifice and salvation, believes he can save her by making her his wife. This Isabel cannot allow: passionately possessive of Larry, she ruthlessly determines to scuttle his plan, which she does by means of a cruel trick.

Elliott, meanwhile, having magnificently held court on the Côte d'Azur, is now beginning to fail, to find himself out of date, no longer in demand. Though he is old and ill, his passion for society is yet undimmed, and thus it is a near mortal blow when he finds he is not invited to the great ball of the season, given by the Princess Novemali, a rich American.* Maugham, realizing his old friend is dying, schemes to purloin the longed-for card, his description of his encounter with the odious Edna Novemali providing an effective counterpoint to the genuinely moving scenes surrounding Elliott's death. By this time, the end of the story is in sight: Larry, divested of all earthly possessions, is happy at last and leaves for America where he plans to earn his living as a taxi driver; Isabel, well provided for by her uncle Elliott's bequest, goes back to Chicago with Gray, who is rejuvenated by the prospect of returning to work. In the final paragraph the author writes that to his surprise,

> I had written nothing more or less than a success story. For all the persons with whom I have been concerned got what they wanted: Elliott social eminence, Isabel an assured position backed by a substantial fortune . . . Gray a steady and lucrative job . . . and Larry happiness.

In answer to a question put to him about *The Razor's Edge,* Maugham said that he had had the character of Larry Darrell in his

---

* Princess Novemali is a portrait of Maugham's Riviera neighbor, the sharp-tongued Princess Ottoboni. "Ottoboni" in Italian means "eight good things," here changed by Maugham to "Novemali," "nine evils." The princess was not pleased by her appearance in *The Razor's Edge,* and for some time there was a rift in the relationship.

mind for more than twenty years, and that it was the experience of India in 1938 that revived his interest and inspired him to write his story. In fact Maugham had already used a version of the theme twice before, in *The Road Uphill,* an unpublished play, now lost, written in 1920, which has close similarities to the novel, and in the short story *The Fall of Edward Barnard,* written in 1921. Ironically, in *The Razor's Edge* it is Larry, vacuous, dull, and a little smug, who constitutes the book's flaw, while everything else, construction, characterization, setting, narrative tone, shows Maugham at his most supremely accomplished. He knows from the inside out the society he portrays, that of the nouveaux-riches Americans, intelligent, ambitious, Europeanized; and thus it is not saintly Larry who holds our attention but the ultrasophisticated figure of Elliott Templeton. In vain, snobbish, kindhearted Elliott, Maugham achieves one of his most brilliant creations, so vital and ridiculous with all his fuss and furbelows that he comes near to stealing the novel. Inevitably, after the book came out, there was much busy speculation about Elliott's original, but in the end it was Maugham's publisher who revealed that the prototype was one Henry Chalmers Roberts, a retired American diplomat. Roberts had made his first appearance in *Our Betters* as Thornton Clay, "[who] calls more countesses by their Christian names than any other man in London." "[Willie] was fascinated by him," said Frere. "[Roberts] was a pederast, knew Henry James, and was as crashing a snob as an expatriate American could be."

Maugham was in New York when *The Razor's Edge* came out, its success providing him with a brief respite from a long period of anxiety—as usual, over Gerald. In the autumn of 1943, Gerald, tired of working for almost nothing at a local radio station in Washington, had accepted instead an offer of employment from Nelson Doubleday, overseeing a staff of nearly fifty in the firm's commissary on Long Island. "Gerald is working very hard providing food for three thousand people," Maugham reported to Robin. "It is a marvel to see him getting up at six thirty to go to work and getting home just before eight. . . . He is happier than he has been for many years." But shortly afterward, a more interesting prospect came Haxton's way, which led to his returning to Washington to take up a minor post in intelligence, at the Office for Strategic Services in the State Department.

This was work Gerald thoroughly enjoyed, and he had been in the highest spirits when he came up to New York on business in November, full of talk about his new job. Maugham was struck by the extraordinary change in him. Poignantly he saw for the first time the man Gerald might have been had he not been tied all those years to his dependency on Maugham: in a way, Maugham had made Gerald's life, and in a way had ruined it, too. Once and for all Maugham made up his mind that there must be no question of Haxton's returning to his old employment and that he must be persuaded to remain in America for good. "[He] is delighted really to be on his own & absolutely independent of me," Maugham told Alan, "[and] it is a wonderful relief to me to be free of that responsibility & of the constant worry & anxiety." Now within weeks of his seventieth birthday, Maugham was anxious about the future: he wanted to write at least one more novel and had several nonfiction projects in mind, but he felt he had become an old man. He had begun to refer to himself as "the old party," and believed he might not have very much longer to live. He needed calm and routine, needed to be sure that what remained of his life should be free of the constant crises created by Gerald. Thus, after thirty years together, the two men agreed to separate, Maugham arranging with Bert Alanson for a sum of $35,000 to be settled on Haxton, which would provide him with a generous annual income. As soon as the war was over, Maugham would return to France, and Gerald's place as secretary and factotum at the Mauresque would be taken by Alan, dear Alan,

> who will give me, I think, a happiness I have not known with Gerald for ten years. . . . He has neither Gerald's vitality [nor] energy, but is sober, modest, affectionate & of a great sweetness of nature. . . . I must expect to grow progressively frailer

& less active; I want someone kind, unselfish & considerate who will look after me till my death & that I think my little Alan will be only too glad to do.

With these plans afoot and Gerald settled contentedly in Washington, Maugham at Yemassee continued his industrious output. His seventieth birthday on January 25, 1944, he spent alone, perfectly serene in his own company. He had decided to prepare his writer's notebooks for publication, and these had to be carefully perused and edited. There was also a revival of his last play, *Sheppey,* due to open in New York in April, for which Maugham had made some crucial alterations to the last act. In the event, *Sheppey* was as great a failure in New York in 1944 as it had been in London eleven years earlier, a fact that left its author relatively unmoved. "I was disappointed, but not distressed," he told Eddie Marsh, "for the play was written long ago & I have long ceased to be interested in the theatre." And by the time of its opening there was another, far more serious matter on his mind.

"I HAVE BEEN IN great trouble," Maugham wrote to Barbara Back. At the end of April, Gerald in Washington had suffered an attack of pleurisy so severe that Maugham, alarmed, had brought him to New York where he could be looked after at one of the best nursing homes in the country. Here an X ray revealed that his lungs were badly infected with tuberculosis, the dangerous disease that had haunted Maugham since his mother died of it when he was eight. Now Gerald's condition began to deteriorate with terrifying rapidity: he was feverish and suffered intense pain that could be controlled only with morphine; he had a racking cough and found it difficult to swallow; he was fast losing weight and every movement hurt him. "It was agonizing to watch him," Maugham told Barbara. Although he had been told it was unlikely Gerald would survive, Maugham believed that if he could get him out of the heat and humidity of New York and into the dry, pure air of

Colorado he just might have a chance. But the doctors refused to allow it, saying that Gerald was far too ill to be moved and was expected to die within weeks, information that was carefully kept from the patient. Maugham, who sat by his bed for hours a day, was distraught. The detachment of a short time earlier, the calm and optimism with which he had been looking forward to a future without Gerald at the Mauresque, vanished in an instant as all his old feelings of love and protectiveness came flooding back. "Though I have long known that the life he led must kill him now that he is dying I am shattered," Maugham confessed to Ellen Doubleday.

> He made life impossible for me & I was thankful when he left me, he brought shame & disgrace on me, but now I can forget all that. I only remember how devoted he was to me & how he trusted me & depended on me & how eager he was to help me. I can only think of those years when his vitality & his gift for making friends were of so much service to me. Without him I should never have written those stories which did so much for my reputation in the world of letters & it was he who helped me to get out of the commonplace life of the ordinary humdrum writer & put me in the way of gaining that wider experience of life which has made me what I am today. I can never forget that he was mixed in with some of my happiest & most fruitful years & now that it is finished, or so nearly, I cannot but weep because his long end has been so miserable & so worthless. I don't know how much I am to blame. If I had been firmer, if I had not tried to force a kind of life on him for which he was temperamentally unsuited, it may be that he would have made less of a hash of things than he has. Of course I shall get over it, one gets over everything, but just at the moment I am broken.

At last in July there was a very small improvement in Gerald's condition, and Maugham was advised that he could after all risk a journey. It was decided not to go as far as Colorado but to take him by ambulance to Saranac in upstate New York, to the famous Adirondack Cottage Sanitarium where Robert Louis Stevenson had been treated. Here in the fresh mountain air, Gerald, to Maugham's enormous relief, "[began] to breathe a little better & is in less pain"; he was still very weak and emaciated but seemed in fairly good spirits on the whole, and remarkably uncomplaining. Maugham had set great hopes on Saranac. "If we can only get through the next two or three weeks it won't be so bad," he wrote to Barbara. He was tireless in his attendance on Gerald, could not bear to think of him left to the mercy of strangers, and prepared to stay in Saranac for months if necessary, despite the fact that his hotel was comfortless and the food awful. "I can't remember that I've ever hated a place more." Morning and afternoon he went to the hospital, where he did his best to keep Gerald's spirits up. "I think going to see him twice a day & encouraging him cheers him & helps him to make a fight for it," he wrote to Barbara. "The attitude I take is that of course he is very ill, but that lots of people have had T.B., myself included & have completely recovered & I see no reason why he should not be as strong as ever in a year."

But after the initial promise, Saranac had little beneficial effect, and every day Gerald grew more frighteningly feeble, although there were occasions when he seemed briefly possessed by a frenzied energy, raging against his dying and hurling obscenities at Maugham, screaming that he had ruined his life, had kept him a prisoner, that he hated him; once while in a drugged delirium he laughed wildly at the thought of the fun he would have after Maugham himself was dead. In desperation Maugham decided to move him once more, this time to the New England Baptist Hospital in Boston, where he could be seen by specialists at the Leahy Institute. Here he was told the only chance that remained was a risky operation to remove a couple of ribs, which could best be carried out in New York. The four-hour train journey was undertaken with Gerald, heavily drugged, on a stretcher. "I am afraid he is growing weaker & weaker & I am beginning to lose hope," Maugham wrote to Eddie Knoblock from Manhattan at the beginning of October. "They say as one grows old one feels less; I wish it were true." By now Gerald was barely conscious, always in pain, on some days too ill to see even Maugham, who was in a state of tormenting indecision. "I have to face the prospect that the operation will kill him," he told his niece Diana; he was unable to make up his mind "whether to let him die by inches or to risk all on this final attempt. . . . I can hardly help wishing that he would die one night quietly in his sleep without knowing that he was in danger of death." Finally, on November 2, the operation was carried out. To everyone's surprise Gerald survived it, and although very weak and in great pain seemed to be holding on. "There is a slight hope that he may make a recovery after a fashion," Maugham reported to Alan, "but will still be very ill for a long, long time." For three days Gerald remained in a drugged semi-coma, knowing nobody, with Maugham allowed to see him for only a few minutes at a time. Then, on the morning of November 7, at the age of fifty-two, Gerald Haxton died.

Maugham was inconsolable, beside himself with grief and tormented by remorse. At the funeral on November 9, 1944, at the Episcopal Church of St. James on Madison Avenue, he broke down and wept. In response to the many letters of condolence he poured out his overwhelming unhappiness, his anguish at losing the love of his life. "Gerald's death has been a bitter blow to me & I am finding it very hard to cope with life without him. I am lost & hopeless & lonely," he told George Cukor, while to Charles Towne he wrote, "Please don't write & sympathize, letters like that just tear me to pieces. You see, I'm too old to cope with so much grief." Toward the end of December he described to Alan "the tempestuous grief that tore me to pieces . . . the last few weeks have been very hard to get through [and] I have been terribly depressed." The writer Cecil Roberts, wishing to offer his sympathy in person, was taken aback by the agony in Maugham's voice when he answered the telephone:

"I don't want to see you! I don't want to see anyone! I want to die!" he cried in a distressed voice, and put down the telephone.

Another friend, the playwright Sam Behrman, was also shocked to see how near Maugham was to complete breakdown. Behrman, who had been working on a dramatization of one of Maugham's short stories, had arranged to lunch with him in his suite at the Ritz; he naturally expected to see some sign of distress, but to his surprise there was none. "He had his habitual composed and impassive expression," Behrman recalled, as they chatted about people they knew and Maugham asked Behrman about his latest production. Finally Behrman thought he must mention Gerald. "Willie, you haven't told me," he began:

"How was it with Gerald—at the end?" I was instantly sorry. "Please," he said in a broken voice, "don't ask me that." He began to cry and left the room. It was the sudden demolition of a carefully built image.

After the funeral, all that remained was for Maugham to carry out the instructions Gerald had made in his will, a simple document in which his personal effects were left to Maugham, his money to Robin, who had become almost an honorary younger brother, and the proceeds from the sale of the flat in Paris, which had been in Gerald's name, to Louis Legrand. *"Mon pauvre Loulou,"* Maugham wrote sadly, *"Sois heureux, mon petit, et tâche de ne pas te tracasser avec des souvenirs tristes. Ça ne sert à rien et tu es trop jeune. Oublies."** As soon as the will was proved, Maugham left New York for South Carolina. With the end of the war at last in sight, he was faced with returning to France, to the Villa Mauresque, a prospect he now dreaded, he told David Horner:

I suppose I shall give it a trial, but if Gerald dead is all over the place, wandering about the garden, sitting at the card table

---

* "My poor Loulou, be happy, my little one, and try not to torment yourself with sad memories. There's no point and you are too young. Forget."

playing patience, I couldn't stand it; & so I would sell it for what I could get & buy myself a little house somewhere in the English country, Wiltshire perhaps, & settle down there for the rest of my life. That would not be for very long, for by now I am a very old party.

CHAPTER 15

THE BRONZINO
BOY

. . .

Maugham's desolation in the months following Gerald Haxton's death was impenetrable and profound. "For thirty years he has been my pleasure and my anxiety and without him I am lost and lonely and hopeless," he wrote to Noël Coward in February 1945. "It is three months since he died now and I cannot get used to it. I try to forget and a dozen times a day something I come across, something I read, a stray word reminds me of him and I am overcome with my first grief. . . . I am too old to endure so much grief. I have lived too long."* To Gerald's beloved Loulou he also wrote most poignantly of his unhappiness: *"Tout me le rappelle et je le revois souvent, trop souvent pour ma paix, dans mes rêves, ou il est toujours gai et vivace et délicieux."†* Maugham was mourning for his dead lover, but mourning, too, for his own past, for the years of travel and adventure he had shared with Haxton, and, crucially, mourning for his powers as a writer, for the artistic impulse and inspiration that wrought those experiences into novels and stories. "The best years of my life, those in which we were wandering about the world, are inextricably connected with him, & in one way & another, however indirectly, all I have written during the last thirty has something to do with him, if only that he typed my manuscripts." It was almost as if Gerald had possessed some talismanic

---

* It was this letter that gave Coward the idea for his 1966 play, *Song at Twilight*.
† "Everything reminds me of him, and I see him often, too often for my peace of mind, in my dreams, where he is always cheerful and lively and delightful."

power and without him he would no longer be able to write. And in a sense that was true: none of the work Maugham produced after Gerald's death would amount to very much.

After the funeral, Maugham had been relieved to leave New York and return to Parker's Ferry, his little house at Yemassee, but once there he was tormented by loneliness and yearned more than ever for the solace of Alan Searle's company. Yet Alan was in England and unable to leave his army canteen in Yorkshire. Maugham's plight was desperate, however, and his friends realized he could not be left to continue without companionship. Discreet approaches were made to the Foreign Office, with the result that Brendan Bracken at the Ministry of Information arranged with his opposite number in Washington to obtain permission for Maugham's nephew, Robin, to visit the States for a few months, officially to launch a magazine, *Convoy,* he had just started in Britain. It was an arrangement that was of benefit to both: Maugham was delighted to see his beloved nephew, and Robin, nearly thirty, still very jittery and unwell after his experiences in North Africa, was grateful for a period of convalescence. He arrived just before Christmas 1944, and the two men supported each other through the somewhat rambunctious seasonal celebrations under way at Bonny Hall. "I found Willie overwhelmed with misery," Robin recalled, shocked when Maugham more than once broke down in tears in front of him. He was shocked, too, to see how much his uncle had aged, still physically fit, clean-shaven now, but with his face very lined, his dark eyes hooded, and heavy creases pulling his mouth downward, giving him the appearance of an old and melancholy tortoise.

Even at his most wretched, Maugham had never stopped working, continuing to fulfill the program he had mapped out for himself. His daily stint of writing was the one reliable escape, the one drug that never failed in its effect. Just as ten years earlier he had decided to bring his career in the theater to an end with four last plays, so now he planned to write four last novels. The first of these had been *The Razor's Edge,* to be followed by two historical works of fiction, and finally by a novel about a working-class family in

Bermondsey, thus coming full circle with a return to the territory treated in *Liza of Lambeth* fifty years before. This last was never written, but already by February 1945, *Then and Now,* the first of the two historical novels, was completed and sent off to Eddie Marsh for editing.

Then and Now describes an embassy of Machiavelli to the court of Cesare Borgia, and although it conscientiously conveys the background of Renaissance Italy and the elaborate dealings and counterdealings between the two men, it is a pedestrian work; a few scenes concerning Machiavelli's attempted seduction of a beautiful young woman flicker briefly into life, but all too clearly the book reflects the despondent state of mind of its author. When it was published in 1946, however, it sold well and won some admiring reviews on both sides of the Atlantic. And there the matter might have rested had it not been for a long article in *The New Yorker* by America's most influential critic, Edmund Wilson. Unluckily, *Then and Now* was the first fiction by Maugham that Wilson had read: he had long been irritated by some of Maugham's critical judgments, particularly pertaining to Henry James, and he considered Maugham's reputation as a writer ludicrously overrated; yet by his own admission he knew nothing of any of the novels, plays, or short stories. "It has happened to me from time to time to run into some person of taste who tells me that I ought to take Somerset Maugham seriously, yet I have never been able to convince myself that he was anything but second-rate," he begins.

> [*Then and Now*] seemed to me . . . one of the most tasteless and unreadable books from which I had ever hoped to derive enjoyment, and nothing but the necessity of supplying this review could ever have taken me through it. . . .

And so on. Maugham, who had always admired Wilson,★ describing him in one of his wartime articles as "the most acute critic now

★ It was Maugham's recommendation that persuaded Nelson Doubleday in 1946 to publish Edmund Wilson's short-story collection, *Memoirs of Hecate County.*

writing in America," reacted to this devastating attack with almost superhuman sangfroid. "He has always disliked me," he told Ellen Doubleday. "[But] nobody can be liked by everyone and I bear Edmund Wilson's dislike with good humour."

On May 8, 1945, VE Day, the war in Europe was finally declared at an end, but Maugham at Yemassee was unable to feel any great exhilaration. "Everyone here is of course very much relieved & I am too," he wrote to Alan, "but my chief feeling, I think, is one of sadness for all the death & misery it has caused, so that I haven't been able to be as cheery about the surrender as most people." At the front of his mind was the prospect of a return to the freedom he had known before the war. "I am hoping restrictions upon travel will be lifted soon & that we shall all be able to go wherever we want to & when we like." He longed for Alan to come to him, and he longed to return to France, but neither was a possibility at the present.

Instead, with Robin having left to promote his journal in New York, Maugham was obliged to return to Hollywood on his own, his presence required for the filming of *The Razor's Edge*. As the screenplay commissioned by the studio had been judged unsatisfactory and jettisoned, Maugham had been asked if he would write it, a job he took on with uncharacteristic enthusiasm because his old friend George Cukor was to direct. The two men had first met in 1923 when Cukor was a young stage manager on the American production of *The Camel's Back;* six years later, Cukor had abandoned the theater for the film industry, where he had enjoyed some notable successes, among them directing Katharine Hepburn in *Little Women* and Greta Garbo in *Camille*. One of his few failures had been the film of *Our Betters* in 1933, about which Maugham had been most understanding. "[Willie] was very, very kind to me and took it philosophically, just as he did most things," Cukor recalled. Now Cukor invited Maugham to stay with him at his house off Sunset Strip, ideal for Maugham as not only was Cukor charming and intelligent but, homosexual himself, he knew all the reliable pimps and whores and was generally recognized as master of revels throughout the Hollywood fraternity. Cukor's poolside parties were particularly popular: glamorous female stars were invited to join the company for lunch, but after they left, a gang of good-looking young men, actors, waiters, motor mechanics, would arrive for an afternoon of all-male entertainment; as the wags put it, when the ladies departed the naughty boys came by to eat the leftovers. On Maugham's previous visits to Hollywood both he and Gerald had enjoyed Cukor's hospitality, and it was an additional pleasure for Maugham that he could talk about Haxton, whom Cukor had liked. Cukor for his part was fond of Maugham personally, admired him for his inimitable stagecraft, and, as he said once in an interview, always regarded it as to Maugham's credit that "Willie liked Jews."

The film rights to *The Razor's Edge* had been bought for Twentieth Century–Fox by Darryl Zanuck for the very large sum of $250,000. Understandably, Zanuck was reluctant to spend more on having the script rewritten, but when Cukor explained the situation to Maugham, the author immediately offered to do it for nothing. "[His] script was wonderful," Cukor recalled, and Zanuck, delighted, suggested the studio should buy Maugham a painting, worth anything up to $15,000. "I'd never bought a picture at such a price before and I was thrilled," said Maugham. Nervous about spending such a sum on his own, he asked Monroe Wheeler to advise him, and the two men spent several agreeable mornings visiting dealers in New York. Eventually Maugham chose a Camille Pissarro, a view of the harbor at Rouen (*Quai Saint-Sever à Rouen*) that moved him because it was the view Flaubert must often have looked at when at work on *Madame Bovary;* Monroe, however, persuaded him instead to buy a Matisse, a snow scene, which he said was a much better picture. "But I could not get the Pissarro out of my mind," Maugham wrote later. "I thought I should always regret it if I did not have it, so I exchanged the Matisse for it."

Few projects in the film world run smoothly, and in the end Maugham's script was abandoned, the film finally going into production in 1946 with Tyrone Power as Larry, Gene Tierney as Isabel, and some frightful painted backdrops of the Himalayas.

—

THROUGHOUT HIS STAY IN CALIFORNIA, Maugham continued to press for Alan to join him: he missed the comfort of his company, and he was finding it increasingly difficult to cope without a secretary. But civilian travel between Europe and America was still difficult and exit permits hard to obtain. Maugham appealed to everyone he could think of who might have influence, asking Frere to approach the foreign secretary, Ernest Bevin, on his behalf, and himself writing to Lord Halifax, the British ambassador in Washington. As a graceful gesture, Maugham had offered to present to the Library of Congress the manuscript of his most famous novel, *Of Human Bondage,* "in grateful acknowledgement of the kindness and hospitality shown by the people of this country," and who could better be entrusted with it than Alan Searle? "You would be doing me a great favour," Maugham told Halifax, "if you would ask the Foreign Office to give my secretary . . . now released from war work, the exit permit which will enable him to bring the bulky package over." Fortunately for Maugham his request was favorably regarded behind the scenes, his contribution to the British war effort standing him in good stead in Whitehall. "I know that at one time he was working privately and unofficially as a propagandist for us in the US," a Foreign Office memorandum noted. "The national interest requires us to regard Mr. Maugham as in a special category . . . and do whatever we reasonably can to help him. I think that Mr. Searle should be granted an exit permit and that we should give him a moderate degree of priority in obtaining a sea passage."

This was written in September 1945, yet it was not until December that Alan succeeded in making the crossing, docking at Hoboken, New Jersey, on Christmas Day. From there he made his way by train to South Carolina, where Maugham was waiting for him at the station. The two men had not seen each other for more than five years, during which time Maugham had written to Alan every week, had thought of him constantly, and had yearned for the presence of his sweet, sexy Bronzino boy. The first sight was something of a shock: during the war at his army canteen Alan had done himself well, and the figure that stepped down onto the platform was no longer that of the slender youth Maugham remembered but of a stout, round-faced, middle-aged man. "Alan arrived, very heavy with his chipmunk cheeks," Glenway Wescott recalled, "[and] William was grief-stricken at the loss of his looks. 'You may have looked like a Bronzino once, but now you look like a depraved Frans Hals,'" Maugham commented sourly. Nonetheless Maugham was happy and relieved to be reunited with Searle, who was to be his devoted companion for the rest of his life. Alan immediately took over all Gerald's duties and more, writing letters, telephoning, shopping, dealing with the maids. "[Alan] is a great comfort to me," Bert Alanson was told. "He is so happy to be here, & with me, that it is heart-warming."

With the war over and Alan restored to him, all Maugham's energies were concentrated on his return to France. At the end of March he and Searle went to New York, and then to Washington for a few days, where on April 20 Maugham presented his manuscript of *Of Human Bondage* to the Library of Congress. It was a prestigious occasion, every seat in the Coolidge Auditorium filled for Maugham's address, in which he talked about literature, about his own career as a novelist, and about writing *Of Human Bondage,* revealing that recently when making a recording of it he had broken down and wept while reading the passage describing the death of Philip Carey's mother: "it recalled a pain that the passage of more than sixty years has not dispelled." The main purpose of his speech, however, was to record his gratitude to the people of the United States, in particular "for the kindness and the generosity with which you received the women and children of my country when in fear of a German invasion they came to America."

At last, on May 29, Maugham and Alan sailed from New York, arriving in Marseilles in the second week of June. Looking back, Maugham used to say that the day he set foot again in France was one of the happiest of his life. When later in the summer Ellen Doubleday pressingly invited him to return to South Carolina, he was firm in his refusal. "I am very grateful to you and Nelson for having given me Parkers to live in during the war," he wrote, "but as you know I only looked upon it as a temporary residence, and though I am pleased that you should want me to come back I think it much better to tell you that I never shall. I hope occasionally to come to New York on brief visits during the rest of my life, but when all is said and done Europe is where I belong."

He and Alan took rooms at a small hotel, the Voile d'Or, overlooking the harbor at Saint-Jean, a short distance from the Villa Mauresque. Although he had received occasional reports about the state of the house, Maugham had no real idea what to expect, but to his relief the depredations were less serious than he had feared. The villa had been occupied first by the Italians, then by the Germans, who had mined the garden but otherwise done little harm; the only significant damage had been caused by the Royal Navy while attempting to shell a semaphore positioned at the top of the Cap. By paying some heavy bribes, Maugham soon assembled a team of workmen to repair the holes in the roof and to replace the shattered windows; indoors there was much repainting to be done, as well as the replacing of moth-eaten carpets and almost all the fixtures and fittings: after the Germans left, the local French, it appeared, had taken everything they could lay their hands on, including crockery, cutlery, and even the bolts from the bathroom doors. Soon the work was sufficiently advanced for furniture and pictures to be brought out of storage, and to Maugham's great gratification most of the staff returned, with Annette, who had remained at the Villa throughout the war, rejoined by Ernest, the butler, Jean, the chauffeur, and Louis, one of the gardeners.

An immediate concern of Maugham's was to fulfill Gerald's bequest to Louis Legrand. Loulou had escaped conscription because of a tubercular infection and had spent the first couple of years of the war running in and out of the Mauresque, where he had made himself not altogether popular with Annette. Now he had gone to Paris, Maugham having given him permission to live in Gerald's flat until it was sold, when the proceeds would be made over to him. Maugham had felt very tender toward Loulou, the boy so adored by Haxton, but now he found to his extreme annoyance that the young man had been up to some distinctly underhanded behavior. In compiling a list of losses incurred during the war, Maugham had included the contents of his substantial wine cellar, which had been emptied, he assumed, by the Italians. Now he learned from Annette that it was Loulou who had sold the lot to a local wine merchant. And not only that: Loulou had pocketed some personal items of Maugham's, including two favorite wristwatches. These, Maugham told him sternly, must be returned. With his confidence in Loulou shaken, Maugham felt uneasy about leaving him unsupervised in the Paris apartment, and with reason, as it turned out: the enterprising Louis was already carrying on a brisk trade. *"Cher Lulu,"* begins a besotted letter, postmarked London, from an American army officer, *"Voilà votre Colonel d'Amérique votre grand ami . . . TRES TRISTE—car son Louis est à Paris bien loin d'Angleterre. . . ."*★ That autumn Maugham himself was in London, and from there he wrote to Loulou informing him that David Posner, a young student friend from the States, would shortly be arriving in Paris and would stay in the flat until he found a place of his own. For his part, Posner had been well briefed. "[I lived] in Maugham's Paris apartment," he recalled, "ostensibly to have digs when I first arrived in France; but actually to 'spy' upon the boy who was living there, Gerald Haxton's former pickup, whose activities Maugham was afraid of (rightly, as it turned out)."

David Posner was an extraordinary episode in Maugham's life. In the spring of 1943, Posner, then a seventeen-year-old schoolboy in Lawrenceville, New Jersey, had written Maugham a letter describing himself as a poet and expressing an ardent admiration for *Of Human Bondage.* Intrigued, Maugham had invited the boy to call on him at the Ritz in New York, where he instantly found himself overwhelmed by a tidal wave of emotion, a powerful mixture of fascination and lust. David Posner was sensual and swarthy, tall, very handsome, with thick lips, olive skin, and dark curly black hair. He frankly set out to seduce the older man, and Maugham

---

★ "Here's your American Colonel, your great friend . . . VERY SAD—because his Louis is in Paris so far from England. . . ."

succumbed utterly, later delightedly boasting that he had been raped by this "gigantic Jewish poet . . . a sort of satyr." Glenway Wescott, an interested observer of the relationship, said Maugham had believed he was finished with love affairs and then "along came this little storm and he rode it in. . . . Willie was very proud of himself because this great poet violently booted sprang on him." Maugham invited Posner to stay at Yemassee, and Posner, infinitely ambitious, eagerly accepted. "I was starry-eyed," he later recalled. "I was hoping this would happen." Maugham as a lover "wasn't particularly virile," he recalled, "[and] was rather businesslike about sex, but it's equally true that there were occasions when we would spend a long time just fondling. . . . When we were alone he could be the world's most enchanting conversationalist." Maugham was so taken by the young man, and so impressed by his love and knowledge of literature, that he offered to pay part of his tuition at Harvard. They continued to see each other, and after the war, Posner, in France to study at the Sorbonne, visited the Mauresque on several occasions, until Maugham eventually became irritated by the young man's pushiness and self-regard and turned against him. "Willie just cut his head off," said Westcott. "[Posner] came and stayed at the Villa and Willie couldn't stand him."*

WHEN MAUGHAM ARRIVED in London in September 1946 he found a city seemingly drained of all vitality. Buildings stood unpainted and unrepaired, the streets were full of potholes, and bomb craters, thickly overgrown with loosestrife and willow herb, were everywhere. Life in the capital was grim, he reported to Nelson Doubleday. "People are strangely apathetic and do not seem very much interested in anything [and] the food is awful." However, most of his old friends had survived, the happiest among them Barbara Back, since her son, feared dead, had just returned from a Japanese

---

* Posner later added W. H. Auden, Thomas Mann, and André Gide, among others, to his literary conquests. He studied at the Sorbonne and at Oxford, published seven books of poetry, and taught at New York State University and the University of California. He married, fathered two sons, and died of AIDS in Florida in 1985.

prisoner-of-war camp. The family, too, was intact, Robin much improved in health, F.H. visibly aged but in manner as dry and withering as ever: he and Maugham had had some sharp exchanges after Labour's landslide victory the year before, with F.H., an entrenched Tory, vehemently opposed to his brother's socialist views. Liza had been reunited with Vincent, who had left the army as a full colonel, having been awarded the DSO for bravery under fire in North Africa; however, after such a long separation, relations between husband and wife had become strained, and now they had decided to divorce. "I hope I shall like her next husband as much as I liked the last," her father told Bert Alanson. "She pretends that she will never marry again, but I don't for a moment believe her." Liza meanwhile had gone to Switzerland to install her mother in a sanatorium, "said mother, aged 67, having contracted T.B.," Maugham wrote unfeelingly. "I am told that to get it when you are as old as that gives little hope of recovery, but my own impression is that said mother is indestructible."

Even with the punitive rates of postwar taxation, Maugham was by any standards a rich man. Since his first success as a playwright, Maugham, an honorary member of PEN since 1933, had been generous to writers, young and old, who were down on their luck, often helping anonymously when appealed to for funds; and he nearly always responded to requests from impecunious friends with a sizable check—unless, as happened on occasion, he felt they were taking advantage, when a sharp snub would be administered instead. The appeals were constant and increased in size and number as his celebrity grew. "In the last week I have had requests for loans amounting to £36,000," he complained in 1960, and a few months later, "By every post demands come by the dozen for gifts, loans, guarantees and financial assistance of every kind. I am bewildered and harassed by it all." Now that he was growing old, money was much on his mind. He had provided liberally for Liza and her children and for Robin, and when Peter Stern and then a widowed Barbara Back fell on hard times he provided for them, too. Nonetheless Maugham was complicated about money. He loved talking about it, would boast about how much he himself made, and was acutely aware of the effect his wealth had on other people. Money gave him freedom and privacy and the ability to do as he pleased, but it also gave him considerable power—power that toward the end of his life he was to wield with devastating effect.

IT WAS NOW, shortly after the war, that Maugham finalized arrangements for the establishment of a literary prize. "Millionaires & such like are always ready to give money to universities [and] hospitals . . . but will never do anything for the arts," he explained. "I was disappointed that neither Kipling nor Barrie did anything, & I suppose Shaw will leave his fortune in the same foolish way as his wife did.★ So I think I should do what I can, but not after I am dead, now." Worth £500 and administered by the Society of Authors, the Somerset Maugham Award was to be presented annually for a work of fiction, nonfiction, or poetry written by a British subject under the age of thirty-five, the money to be spent on travel. In 1947 the first announcement of this glittering prize attracted the attention of Evelyn Waugh. Mr. Maugham's proposal "of giving £500 yearly to a young writer to be spent in foreign travel" was cruelly tantalizing, Waugh complained in a letter to the *Daily Telegraph*:

> Does Mr. Maugham realize what a huge temptation he is putting before elderly writers? To have £500 of our own— let alone of Mr Maugham's—to spend abroad is beyond our dreams. . . . What will we not do to qualify for Mr. Maugham's munificence? What forging of birth certificates, dyeing of whiskers, and lifting of faces! To what parodies of experimental styles will we not push our experienced pens!

★ Charlotte Shaw directed that the bulk of her fortune be employed in improving the manners and deportment of the Irish people, a scheme described by Shaw's biographer Michael Holroyd as "Charlotte's version of the Pygmalion experiment" (*Bernard Shaw, Vol. III, 1918–1950: The Lure of Fantasy* [Chatto & Windus, 1991] p. 499).

The first year's judges were V. S. Pritchett, the historian C. V. Wedgwood, and the poet Cecil Day-Lewis, who chose as the winner for 1947 A. L. Barker with her short-story collection, *Innocents*. Although he took no part in the judging, Maugham followed the process and the subsequent careers of the winners with attention, among them, during his lifetime, Doris Lessing (1954), Kingsley Amis (1955), Ted Hughes (1960), V. S. Naipaul (1961), and John le Carré (1964).

Another venture close to his heart was the founding of a national theater, to the planning of which over the years he had contributed both time and money only to see the project postponed again and again, "overcome [by] the indifference of governments and the apathy of the public." But in the postwar period it looked as though the scheme might prove practicable at last, and Maugham redoubled his efforts to involve his fellow playwrights in the cause. "I wish I could enlist your help in interesting the British people in a National Theatre," he wrote to J. B. Priestley in 1948. "It seems to me a scandal that England should be the only European country that does not possess one." The following year the National Theatre Bill was finally passed by Parliament, a significant step forward that Maugham recognized by giving to the trustees his eighty theatrical paintings. Maugham's collection was impressive, second in importance only to that owned by the Garrick Club, and it included three oils by Zoffany, fifteen by de Wilde, and a fine version of Reynolds's famous portrait of David Garrick. The paintings were removed from the Mauresque in 1951, but have been seen only infrequently since in the building for which they were intended.

Of all Maugham's charitable bequests, that made to his old school, King's School, Canterbury, might be regarded as the most unexpected, given his wretchedness while a pupil there. And yet Maugham had always felt a nostalgia for the place, for the grounds and the ancient buildings magnificently overshadowed by the great gray cathedral; he had, too, always felt rooted in the Kentish countryside, and on a number of occasions had returned to wander around Whitstable, where more than once he was spotted tending the graves of his uncle and aunt in the churchyard. The notorious account of his school days in *Of Human Bondage* had hardly endeared him to KSC, but since his day the school had fallen on hard times, and shortly before the war the then headmaster, Canon Shirley, a vigorous and resourceful character, had written a letter to Maugham soliciting a donation, to which Maugham had generously responded. Encouraged, Shirley took pains to cultivate the connection, writing regularly, extending invitations to visit the school, and eventually enrolling Maugham on the governing body. His attentiveness paid off, and over the years Maugham gave thousands of pounds, for new buildings, for tennis courts, for pictures and furniture, and for the construction of a library that would eventually hold a large proportion of his books, eighteen hundred volumes, from the Villa Mauresque. He also presented the school with his portrait, especially commissioned from Gerald Kelly, and with the manuscripts of his first and last novels, *Liza of Lambeth* and *Catalina*. In 1952 he surprised Canon Shirley with a request that he should be buried within the precincts of the school.

When Maugham returned to Cap Ferrat from London at the end of 1946, his chief concern was to finish his novel *Catalina,* begun earlier in the year. It was to be his last full-length work of fiction, and he was particularly anxious that Eddie Marsh should work on it, although he was a little taken aback, when the manuscript was returned to him, by the extent of Marsh's diabolization. "I think you have been harsher than I have ever known you before, but I kiss the rod & I have accepted all your emendations," Maugham told him gratefully. Ten years earlier, in *The Summing Up,* Maugham had stated, "The novelist should turn to the historical novel towards the end of his career," advice that he himself had taken, with his previous work about Machiavelli and now with *Catalina.* Set in sixteenth-century Spain, the story follows the adventures of a crippled peasant girl cured by a miraculous Virgin, and while it is firmly founded in Maugham's lifelong study of Spanish history and literature it shows a substantial falling off from the energy and invention of *The Razor's Edge,* reading less like the work of an experienced novelist and more like a good school essay written by a diligent pupil who has clearly done all his homework. He himself was not at all sure how *Catalina* would be received, but both Frere and Nelson Doubleday professed themselves delighted, and with reason, for on publication in 1948 it was chosen as Book of the Month in America and in Britain had sold 93,000 copies by the end of the first week. "I cannot tell you what a relief to me it is to think that I have written my last, my very last novel," Maugham confessed to Glenway Wescott.

BY CHRISTMAS 1946, when Maugham was once more in residence, the Villa Mauresque had been almost completely restored to its luxurious prewar standard. The number of indoor staff had been slightly reduced, but under the sharp eye of Ernest the butler and of Germaine the housekeeper the same high levels of immaculate efficiency were maintained. In the kitchen Annette was once more producing delicious menus, despite the continuing shortages; pictures were rehung, the silver and china unpacked, and the statue of the Chinese goddess Kuan-Yin returned to the hall. The dachshunds, rumored to have been roasted and eaten during the occupation, were replaced by three Pekingese, to which were added a couple of pedigree poodles, Luke and Mark, a present from Lady Kenmare. The garden statues, which had had their ears and noses broken off, were repaired, the lily pond was restocked with goldfish, and the garden itself, badly damaged by shelling and completely overgrown, was carefully replanted; already some of the spring bulbs that Maugham in a moment of optimism had put in just before leaving in 1940 were beginning to show. The cars had been seized by the Italians, but in the garage now were a Citroën and a big new Buick shipped over from America. Altogether, as Maugham wrote to Ellen Doubleday, he was "very much pleased with it all. It is on the whole a much more beautiful house than it was before."

The one great change, of course, was the absence of Gerald. It was now Alan Searle who was running the house, Alan who sat opposite Maugham at the dining table, Alan who typed and telephoned in the little room beneath Maugham's rooftop study. In no time at all it seemed as if Alan had been there for years, and despite his failure to learn French, his friendly manner and talent for organization ensured the staff were happy and their duties smoothly carried out. With Searle, Maugham had no need to dread rows or to worry that he would be embarrassed in front of his guests: Alan was obedient, even-tempered, and polite, his overwhelming desire at all times to please his employer. And indeed Maugham had soon grown completely dependent on him; he trusted him, and was fond of him, and the two enjoyed a sexual compatibility that was unusually long-lasting, Alan now sleeping in Gerald's bedroom, divided only by a bathroom from Maugham's. Not everything was perfect: Alan had none of Gerald's wit, charm, or sophistication, certainly none of his elegance or style. In summer Searle trotted about the house in garishly patterned shirts, his plump thighs bulging out of a pair of tiny white shorts, and in winter he wore thick double-breasted suits that, with his crinkly dark hair and red face, gave him a curiously aldermanic appearance. Nor was Alan as intelligent as Gerald; he knew something about pictures but little else, and had no interest in reading; he did, however, have a camp sense of humor and a repertoire of comic imitations that Maugham on occasion found amusing. But if Alan's opinions were of limited interest, Maugham nonetheless needed and relied on him, and if Alan was sometimes irritating and a bore, it was a small price to pay for equanimity and peace of mind.

Although in theory Alan's position in the household was the same as Gerald's, in fact it was not: Gerald had been accepted everywhere as Maugham's social equal; Alan was working-class, he spoke with a cockney accent, and his manner was ingratiating, and this inevitably put him on a different footing. But it was not only, or even mainly, the fact that he dropped his aitches: Maugham's friends took their cue from the master of the house, and because Maugham showed Alan little respect, ordered him about, and sometimes angrily rebuked him in public, he was inevitably regarded more as a favored employee than as a friend. Most visitors to the Mauresque liked Alan, and they were glad to see Maugham so well settled. Searle was clearly the ideal companion for his later years: "as right as rain for William," said Glenway Westcott; "[the perfect] nanny of his second childhood," another friend remarked. But how did Alan regard his situation? His devotion to Maugham was never in question: "I loved him with all my heart & being," he wrote later in a private memorandum. "I didn't care about his faults & vices, I loved every facet of him." And yet all was not quite as serene as it appeared on the surface. "I am, I think, very happy, sometimes I am not sure," Alan wrote to Ellen Doubleday as early as December 1946. "Life can be very difficult, and people too."

This oblique mention of "people," carefully left unspecified, re-ferred to members of the Maugham family, for whom Alan nursed a covert but profound hostility. Liza, quite unknowingly, was the object of his most intense hatred, and from the very beginning of Alan's residence at the Mauresque there is expressed in some of his correspondence an undercurrent of venom toward her and her chil-dren of which he gave not the smallest hint when in their company. "I'm so glad you're here, dear," he would say to Liza as she arrived, "give me a little squeeze." As far as Liza was concerned, Searle seemed perfect for her father, a huge improvement on the terrifying Gerald, and she was grateful to him for his devotion; her children, too, Nicolas and Camilla, loved Alan's company, loved running up to his office where he would tell them jokes and outrageous stories in funny voices that made them laugh. "The family were all fond of Alan," said Nic. None of them had any inkling of the bitter resent-ments that lay beneath the surface, for the moment expressed only in letters to a few trusted correspondents. "Liza and the children are here," Alan wrote to Bert Alanson in the summer of 1947. "I find it a very disturbing element and do not like it at all."

In July 1948 Liza remarried, as her father had predicted she would, her new husband a Conservative member of Parliament, Lord John Hope, younger son of the Marquess of Linlithgow. It was Linlithgow who as viceroy in India in 1938 had snubbed Maugham by refusing to receive Gerald Haxton, a slight neither forgotten nor forgiven by Maugham, and John Hope was regarded with disfavor from the start. "He is a pompous donkey," he told Ellen Doubleday, "but Liza dotes on him." For the time being, however, he put a good face on it, courteously writing to his future son-in-law to welcome him into the family and sending the couple a check for a hundred thousand francs as a present. He went over to London for the wedding, where with professional ease he acted the part of proud father, managed to be civil to Syrie, and made a creditable speech at the reception at Claridge's afterward. For the second time Liza spent her honeymoon at the Mauresque, bringing with her a lavish trousseau designed by Mainbocher, which her mother had arranged to have smuggled over from New York. As John was anxious to return to Scotland for the grouse shooting, Liza left Nic and Camilla with their grandfather for the rest of the summer, "which adds greatly to the gaiety of the proceedings," Maugham told Nelson Doubleday. "I must say they are very good, but now and then rather hard work. They eat like wolves, sleep like dormice, swim like fish, and in the interval run helter-skelter about the garden like hares."

This letter was written partly in response to some ominous news from Ellen about her husband's health. Nelson had recently been diagnosed with alcoholic neuritis, his prodigious consumption of "phlegm-cutters" having finally caught up with him, although he himself was refusing to acknowledge the problem. The situation grew so bad that eventually Nelson was obliged to relinquish the presidency of Doubleday, his place in the company taken by Douglas M. Black, Nelson's lawyer and long-serving employee, for whom Maugham had considerable respect. Meanwhile Nelson's condition continued to deteriorate: he was found to have advanced lung cancer, and despite an apparently successful operation he died on January 11, 1949, five days before his sixtieth birthday. Maugham had been genuinely fond of Nelson, despite his drunkenness; he went to see him before he died, and in his letter of condolence he told Ellen how much he owed both to her husband's friendship and to his acumen. "I am not so foolish as not to be aware that I should not hold the position I do in America except for his confidence in me & his constant effort to make me better & better known. I shall always be grateful to him for that, but also, even more, for the affection he bestowed upon me."

As Nelson's involvement in the business over the last couple of years had been minimal, Maugham experienced little change in his dealings with Doubleday. Somerset Maugham was the firm's most valuable property and he was treated accordingly. It was disappointing that there were to be no more novels, but there was no question of Maugham's retiring, and his name on fiction and non-fiction alike was a guarantee of sales often in the hundreds of thousands. The quality may not have been quite what it was, but if the critics were caustic, nobody cared: reviews had long ceased to matter when marketing Maugham. In 1947 a short-story collection, *Creatures of Circumstance,* was published, which included Maugham's only Second World War story, a chilling tale set in occupied France describing the tortured relationship between a German soldier and the young French woman he has raped. The following year saw the publication of *Great Novelists and Their Novels,* introductions to ten world-class novels—among them *Pride and Prejudice, Moby-Dick, War and Peace*—accompanying shortened versions of the works, abridged by Maugham. *The Sunday Times,* in the person of the paper's foreign manager, Ian Fleming, bought the serial rights for £3,000, Fleming flying down to Nice to negotiate personally with the author; the serialization ran for fifteen weeks, resulting in a weekly increase of up to fifty thousand copies, 10 percent of the paper's circulation. In 1949 Maugham published *A Writer's Notebook,* a selection from the fifteen volumes of notes and memoranda he had kept since he was eighteen, including descriptive accounts of his travels, with the dedication, " In Loving Memory of My Friend Frederick Gerald Haxton." And in the 1950s there were two collections of essays, *The Vagrant Mood* (1952) and *Points of View* (1958).

Far from trailing off during his seventies and eighties, Maugham's career grew ever more phenomenally successful. In his old age he was regarded even in Britain as one of the Grand Old Men of English Letters, every birthday marked by newspaper articles and interviews and the arrival of literally hundreds of letters and telegrams at the Mauresque. He was the recipient of honors both at home and abroad, including honorary doctorates from the universities of Oxford, Heidelberg, and Toulouse. In 1954, at Winston Churchill's suggestion, he was appointed a Companion of Honour by the Queen, who received him in a private audience at Buckingham Palace. "[The Queen] was very nicely dressed & looked extremely pretty," Maugham told Bert Alanson. "She asked me to sit down & we sat & talked for a quarter of an hour, after which she said, It's been very nice to see you, Mr. Maugham; so I got up & she got up, we shook hands again, I bowed & retreated backwards for about three steps, then turned to reach for the door & walked out. It was all very easy & cosy." In 1961 the Royal Society of Literature elected Maugham a Companion of Literature, his fellow CLs that year being Churchill, E. M. Forster, John Masefield, and the historian G. M. Trevelyan. Such recognition was gratifying, if late in arriving and in Maugham's view inadequate. After going to Buckingham Palace to receive his CH, Maugham had lunched at the Garrick with Dadie Rylands and Arthur Marshall, who congratulated him warmly on his award. "But don't you see what the C.H. means for somebody like me?" he asked them. "It means 'well done, but . . . .' " In Maugham's inner circle it was understood that he had refused a knighthood, hoping instead for one of the most distinguished awards of all, the Order of Merit: it rankled that both Hardy and Galsworthy, inferior novelists in his opinion, had been awarded the OM, "[and as] I am the greatest living writer of English, they ought to give it to me." Undeniably there was a tacit understanding in establishment circles that Maugham's homosexuality had damaged his reputation. The nature of the relationship with Gerald Haxton had been widely known, whereas other homosexual writers, Hugh Walpole, for instance, had been far more successful in keeping their private lives private: Walpole had been knighted as long ago as 1937.

Astonishingly, Maugham, who was born in the year Disraeli succeeded Gladstone as prime minister, now found a large new audience through the medium of television. In 1948 four stories were filmed, "The Facts of Life," "The Alien Corn," "The Kite," and "The Colonel's Lady," all scripted by R. C. Sherriff, author of *Jour-*

ney's End, the famous play about the First World War. Maugham himself appears on-screen to introduce *Quartet,* his study at the Villa Mauresque painstakingly recreated at J. Arthur Rank's Gainsborough Studios in Shepherd's Bush. "You will remember how astonished I was to find the set an exact reproduction of my writing-room on Cap Ferrat," he told the director, Antony Darnborough. "When I sat down at the desk & noticed the paper knife . . . I said to myself: 'the dirty dogs, they've sneaked my paper-knife' & when I took it up I was staggered to find by its weight that it was made of, I suppose, papier maché." By today's more naturalistic standards, Maugham gives a stilted performance. With his gentle Edwardian enunciation ("looking beck"), he is plainly struggling to remember his lines and there is some frantic fiddling with the said paper knife. Nevertheless, he claimed to have enjoyed the experience of "being a movie star for a couple of days," and *Quartet* was such a success that it was followed by *Trio* ("The Verger," "Mr. Know-All," and "Sanatorium") and then by *Encore* ("The Ant and the Grasshopper," "Winter Cruise," and "Gigolo and Gigolette"), the latter nominated for the Grand Prix at the 1952 Cannes Film Festival.

There was no doubt that Maugham relished his celebrity, partly because it brought him a great deal of money, and also because it went a long way toward soothing his sense of grievance over what he considered a lack of critical acclaim. Since his television appearances he could go nowhere without being recognized, pursued by journalists and photographers, by fans and students of literature, by would-be writers asking for advice, and by literary ladies, "soulful damsels," as Maugham described them, who expected him to be "terribly sinister & cynical." When he went to the States in 1950 for the showing on CBS of *Trio,* dinners were given in his honor by the Society of Arts and Letters, which elected him an honorary member, by the Pierpont Morgan Library, and by the Library of Congress in Washington. And in 1956, at the wedding of Prince Rainier and Grace Kelly in Monte Carlo, it was Somerset Maugham whose presence among the prominent guests was among the most widely reported, his photograph one of the biggest in *Life* magazine's coverage of the event. Such recognition brought with it practical advantages, too: special rates at hotels, a swift passage through Customs at Calais, Dover, and New York, and always the best table and most unctuously mannered maîtres d'hôtel at restaurants everywhere.

Not all the appurtenances of fame were agreeable, of course, and Maugham grew increasingly resentful of the numbers of people who on the merest acquaintance made tiresome demands on his time. "People I haven't seen in thirty years write letters saying 'darling Willie we must meet,' " he complained. "They don't care a fuck about me . . . [they] simply want to show me off." He hated being used, and he exploded once when he found a couple of young men, who claimed to know one of the family, hanging about outside the Mauresque expecting an invitation to stay. "I am not a monkey in the zoo for people to come & stare at & I very much resent being treated as such," Maugham wrote furiously to his niece Kate Bruce.

> I do not know your son in law & I think he took a most impertinent liberty in telling his friends to "look me up." I shall be obliged that you see that he does not repeat a proceeding which is highly offensive to me.

Such a demanding way of life would have exhausted many a younger man, but Maugham remained exceptionally limber, lusty, and fit. "When he emerges [from the pool] and lies down to sun himself," wrote the film director Garson Kanin, "I see an old body but a firm one, wrinkled but unblemished." Always abstemious, Maugham continued to restrict himself to no more than two courses at lunch and dinner, with, at the most, a couple of cocktails beforehand. The results of such self-discipline were rewarding. Robert Bruce Lockhart at a dinner in London described the seventy-four-year-old Maugham's appearance with admiration:

> Willie arrived punctually at eight looking very dapper in a double-breasted coat of light navy-blue, black silk socks and a monocle. The figure is wonderful. He has no spare flesh, but

quite a good calf for a man of his age. He sat on the sofa with his legs tucked up.

There was to be more to it than self-discipline, however. In 1954, shortly after his eightieth birthday, Maugham spent ten days at a clinic in Switzerland run by a Dr. Paul Niehans. Overlooking Lake Geneva just outside Vevey, La Prairie offered an expensive and apparently revolutionary method of rejuvenation known as "fresh-cell therapy," in which the patient was injected with a solution made from cells taken from the fetus of a freshly killed sheep. Dr. Niehans had always declined to publish details of his research and thus was deeply distrusted by the scientific community, which was highly critical of "the whole air of hanky-panky, instant cookery, and big money" that surrounded him. But to his patients the charismatic Niehans was a genius, a savior, consulted by large numbers of famous people who had complete faith in his treatment as well as in his absolute discretion. Among the many clients who booked into La Prairie in search of a lost youth were Noël Coward, Gloria Swanson, Marlene Dietrich, Konrad Adenauer, Thomas Mann, the Aga Khan, Wilhelm Furtwängler, Christian Dior, and Charlie Chaplin. By far the most important of Niehans's patients was Pope Pius XII, who was treated under conditions of great secrecy in the Vatican, Niehans flying to Rome for the first consultation, it was said, accompanied by two heavily pregnant ewes. When Maugham arrived in Switzerland with Alan, who was also to undergo the treatment, he received the red-carpet reception from Niehans, who invited the two men to dine at his house and gave them a tour of the clinic, the abattoir, and the laboratories. He explained the procedure in detail, that in the space of an hour the sheep was slaughtered, the fetus removed, and the tissue sliced, minced, mixed with saline solution, and injected by means of a large horse syringe into the patient's buttocks. A three-week stay was the norm, but after only ten days Maugham announced he had had enough and returned to France, with strict instructions not to smoke or drink for the following three months. "I feel strange," he reported after returning to the Mauresque. "Not ill, nor especially well, simply—strange."★ Alan, on the other hand, was delighted to notice an immense surge in his own virility, an effect to which he drew attention on every possible occasion. "We had Willie Maugham and his catamite Searle to lunch," Diana Cooper told Evelyn Waugh. "They both had the 'cell' treatment in Switzerland [and] Searle has become a garrulous Tom Cat . . . I heard him say . . . in a cockney-pansy voice, 'My dear you can't imagine what it's like—I wake up to find myself under a *tent*'—here an obscene gesture was made, denoting a fabulous erection."

THE VISIT TO NIEHANS'S clinic was repeated in 1958, when Maugham was eighty-four, but in all other respects the pattern of Maugham's life remained much the same as before the war: winter and spring at the Mauresque, a few weeks of foreign travel (Austria, Italy, Spain) with a stay at a spa (Vichy, Abano, Vevey), an intensely social summer on the Riviera, followed by the autumn in London in his regular suite at the Dorchester Hotel. On the Riviera Maugham was a generous host—"It may interest you to know," he wrote to Frere in 1950, "that in three months, exclusive of breakfasts, we served 1060 meals"—and he enjoyed having people to stay, particularly if they were prepared to entertain themselves and not disturb his highly structured daily routine. Over the years he had encountered in his guests every type of delinquency, and now in old age he was fiercely intolerant of the slightest infringement of house rules. Like an experienced hotelier, he listed the offenses that annoyed him the most, the worst offenders treat-

---

★ Maugham's French doctor, Georges Rosanoff, strongly disapproved of the Niehans treatment, which he believed had had a deleterious effect on his patient. *"Une cure de cellules fraîches, très à la mode, qu'il avait suivie en Suisse . . . avait été très mal supportée,"* he wrote in his memoirs. *"J'eus beaucoup de difficultés à réparer les dégâts."* ("He had not reacted well to a fresh-cell treatment, very fashionable, that he had undertaken in Switzerland. I had much difficulty in repairing the damage.") (Rosanoff, *Racontez Docteur* [Guy le Prat, 1977], p. 142).

ing his house "as though they were gauleiters in a conquered province." These marauders left lights on, made cigarette burns in the sheets, borrowed books and never returned them, borrowed money that was never paid back, and sometimes arrived with three weeks' dirty laundry expecting it all to be washed and ironed before they went home.

From the guests' perspective, Maugham could be a daunting host. "One could never be quite certain of the reception one was going to get," his daughter recalled. "He might be kindness itself or he could on occasion be very crushing." Unpunctuality was the greatest sin, and he refused to wait a single second for anyone who was late arriving for a meal. Liza, for example, suffered agonies of nerves when staying with the children in case Camilla or Nic should delay proceedings and incur her father's displeasure; and the writer Peter Quennell, whose experience was typical of many, was not the only one to describe Maugham as a martinet. "He imposed a régime and demanded a standard of behaviour that his guests neglected at their peril; and a single ill-judged remark or minor misstep might plunge them into permanent disgrace." Such a misstep was taken by the producer Peter Daubeny, who as a young man recently engaged to be married was invited to spend a week at the Mauresque. On the first afternoon, Maugham took him for a walk along the Corniche, and as they rounded a corner a car roared by, loaded with small children, a pram strapped to the roof.

"That's what you'll be doing a year from now," commented Maugham, chuckling and slipping his hand into mine. . . . There was something faintly suggestive in his tone of voice, and in a reflex I pulled my hand away. I immediately sensed that I had done something foolish and gave him an uneasy smile. It was met by a face of freezing scorn and hostility. The walk continued in ominous silence. . . . From then on the week was pure disaster. At dinner, and every subsequent meal, Maugham made desultory conversation, but with an icy, withering malice, bitingly disparaging of anything I had done in the theatre.

Despite the risks involved and the many traps for the unwary, invitations were much sought after, with the Mauresque one of the prized landmarks of the Riviera. Inevitably stories of bad behavior and frightful gaffes were much prized and widely circulated, increasingly embellished as they did the rounds. There was the story of the "well-known peer" caught attempting to leave with a suitcase full of Maugham first editions, his bag conveniently "bursting open" at the bottom of the stairs as he was about to scuttle to safety through the front door. Then there was the story of Cyril Connolly famously caught filching three avocados from the orchard, an anecdote much relished and endlessly repeated, to Connolly's considerable annoyance, "[when] all I had done," as he plaintively explained, "was to bring him [Maugham] in an unripe windfall from the garden." Most famous of all was the story of Patrick Leigh Fermor and the stammer, which became one of the great set pieces, sure to be retold in certain circles whenever Maugham's name was mentioned. In the original version, the travel writer "Paddy" Leigh Fermor was taken to stay for a few days at the Mauresque by Ann Fleming, a great favorite of Maugham's. Lunch on the first day "went like a marriage bell," but at dinner an exuberantly tipsy Leigh Fermor found himself telling a funny story about a man with a stammer. Afterward "[when] we were enjoying a nightcap, Mr. Maugham got up, shuffled across the Aubusson, and with a limp handshake said . . . 'Well, I will say goodnight now and perhaps I should say goodbye too, as I expect that I will be in bed tomorrow when you leave,' and then ambled off." Leigh Fermor was instantly mortified, convinced he had been humiliatingly dismissed as a direct consequence of his lack of tact. Over the years he worked up this brief incident into an ornate melodrama in which Maugham is transformed into a gothic monster—"his face is the wickedest tangle of cruel wrinkles . . . alligator's eyes peer from folds of pleated hide and below them an agonizing snarl is beset with discoloured and truncated fangs"—who, mortally offended, brutally banishes the defenseless hero from his house. The fact that Maugham, by then more than a little deaf, may not even have heard the stammer story, nor cared very much if he had, seems never to have occurred to Leigh Fermor; nor the fact that with so many people brought to the Villa, Maugham probably had only the vaguest idea who he was or how long he intended to stay and genuinely believed him to be leaving the next morning.

Ann Fleming, who had married the writer Ian Fleming in 1952, provided exactly the kind of feminine company Maugham most enjoyed: like Barbara Back, she was chic and amusing and wrote witty, gossipy letters full of scabrous comment about their mutual friends; like Barbara, she was not in the least daunted by Maugham. Her husband, Ian, on the other hand, adopted a slightly deferential manner when in the presence of the older man, whom he much admired. When Fleming wrote his first novel, *Casino Royale,* he sent it to Maugham and was delighted to receive an enthusiastic letter in return: Maugham had been so absorbed by James Bond's adventures he had read into the early hours, he said; "It goes with a swing from the first page to the last & is really thrilling all through." Eager to make the most of such a valuable opinion, Fleming asked if he might use a quote from the letter to promote the book. "No," came the answer. "[It's] not that I didn't mean what I said, but that I am asked all the time to write something that can be used in such a way . . . & have always refused . . . I would not do it even for the author of the Book of Genesis." Soon after their wedding the Flemings came to stay at the Mauresque, and Maugham was touched to see how deeply the couple were in love. He was puzzled, however, by the large number of towels they used, upward of nine a day left in a damp pile on the bathroom floor. It later transpired that Fleming during sessions of highly inventive sex liked to whip his wife with a wet towel, then use another to wrap her in and soothe the smart.

With Fleming tied to his job at *The Sunday Times,* Annie often came to the Mauresque on her own, joining that group of old friends in whose company Maugham was happiest, friends such as Desmond MacCarthy, the Freres, Juliet Duff, Raymond Mortimer, and the charming and irascible Gerald Kelly. In 1948 Kelly had been elected president of the Royal Academy, and when Elizabeth II paid an official visit to the Academy, Kelly arranged for Maugham to be seated on her right at dinner. "I had wanted the Queen to be amused," Kelly explained to Bert Alanson, "and I asked her whether I could put Willie to sit next to her, and she said she would be too frightened, and I had to reassure her that he could, if he chooses, be the nicest company, and she agreed to take the risk."

One of the less congenial figures to be found sitting on the terrace at the Mauresque was that of F.H. Unlike his son and daughters, F.H. was a rare visitor to Cap Ferrat, but although very frail he was there on the occasion of his brother's seventy-sixth birthday in 1950. Throughout his stay he irritated Maugham by addressing him as "my boy," and true to form gave little sign of enjoying the celebrations. "Your father," Maugham reported to Robin, "bore with grim disapproval the various festivities which my friends & neighbours had arranged." The antagonism between the pair was real, and when in 1954 F.H. published an autobiography, *At the End of the Day,* he made in six hundred pages only three brief references to his younger brother, the longest comprising the book's last sentence: "I need not describe the works of my brother William Somerset Maugham."

More cheerful company was provided by some of the regular visitors from America, George Cukor, for instance, Garson Kanin and his actress wife Ruth Gordon, the playwright Sam Behrman, and a rich, amusing man about town, Jerry Zipkin. Zipkin, who divided his time between escorting prominent ladies to fashionable soirées and pursuing a hedonistic homosexual career undercover, had met Maugham at the bridge table in New York. Like Maugham, he was addicted to the game, and when on the Riviera played regularly with Maugham and his coterie of wealthy widows, his bunch of "old baguettes," as Zipkin unchivalrously called them. Chief among them was the brightly painted, heavily bejeweled Marion Bateman, who had her maid brush her white hair with cornstarch every night to make it shine. Lady Bateman liked to add tone to her table with blue blood, the aura of anciens régimes, and she was proud of her biggest catch, the exiled queen of Spain, a granddaughter of Queen Victoria. Maugham often entertained Queen Ena, inviting her to lunch to meet Charlie Chaplin and arranging bridge parties for her. Ena loved to play, although she was no good at the game and drove Maugham and other serious players frantic by her habit of looking at her cards and giving away what was in her hand by absentmindedly muttering to herself "Only two hearts," or "Quite a nice lot of spades."

Since the war, the Sporting Club in Monte Carlo had more than regained its international luster, and with Princess Grace as patron there was every summer a program packed with world-famous performers. In June 1958 Maugham attended a gala dinner at the Sporting Club at which Frank Sinatra was to sing, with Noël Coward as compère. Both Coward and Garson Kanin were staying at the Mauresque for the occasion, and both left descriptions of the event. On the night, Maugham and his party sat at a table with the New York columnist Leonard Lyons and his wife. According to Kanin, Sinatra stopped by on his way from the stage, and Noël introduced him to Maugham. "Frank says, 'Hiya, baby!' Maugham replies, 'Very well, indeed, but hardly a b-b-baby.' I have never seen Maugham in circumstances as strange as these," Kanin continued.

> There are too many people, too much noise. . . . But he takes it all in good part and sees to it that he has a good time. He has a positive gift for enjoying himself. He stays as long as he wants to, then takes his leave, making certain to stop at the main table in the middle of the room on his way out to pay his respects to the Prince and Princess.

The more observant Coward gives a slightly different version, unlike Kanin alert to Maugham's impatience underneath the bonhomous veneer. The evening was chaotic, he noted in his diary:

> Far too many people and suffocating. . . . Willie was getting more and more fractious as the evening wore on. . . . Finally I went on and introduced Frankie in French and English, then he hopped up on to the stage and sang for an hour, enchantingly. Willie was off home like a shot the moment Frankie's last note had died away. I don't think he enjoyed it much. . . .

Naturally such society was anathema to the more cultural among Maugham's friends, among them the historian and diarist James Lees-Milne, whose wife, Alvilde, had a house at Roquebrune; Christopher Isherwood, who with his very young lover, Don Bachardy, had an open invitation to stay at Cap Ferrat; and that exquisite bird of paradise, Jean Cocteau, who with his fabulously good-looking boyfriend, "Doudou," stayed often at the Villa Saint-Sospir, only a short distance down the road from the Mauresque. An artist as well as a writer, a close friend of Picasso, a celebrity in literary and theatrical circles in Paris, Cocteau should have had a great deal to offer Maugham; and yet although they continued to meet from time to time it was clear from the first that the friendship would never prosper. Cocteau had little regard for "Somerset," as he always addressed him, regarding his work as facile and populist, while Maugham was highly resistant to the flamboyant Frenchman's dazzling conversational flights of fancy, irritated by what he dismissively described as his "long-winded insincerity" and by his determination always to hold center stage. Maugham had recently bought two fine Picassos, *La Mort d'Harlequin* and *La Grecque,* and Cocteau as he was leaving one day stopped to admire them. He asked Maugham if he knew Picasso, and when Maugham said he did not, offered to arrange a meeting. "D-d-does he play b-b-bridge?" came the quizzical response.

During the 1940s and '50s Maugham added substantially to his picture collection. "It has always been an ambition of mine . . . to make a small collection of Impressionist pictures," he wrote to Bert Alanson while on a postwar shopping spree in New York. It was here that he bought some of his most important works, the *Femme assise dans un fauteuil jaune* by Matisse,* *Bateaux à Argenteuil* by Renoir, and Rouault's powerful *Christ crucifié,* as well as a small Pissarro, a Bonnard, a Monet, and a Utrillo. Maugham has been condemned by much of the art establishment for his pedestrian taste in

---

* Maugham used occasionally to visit Matisse, a neighbor of his on the Riviera. *"J'achète des tableaux pour fleurir ma maison* [I buy pictures to make my house blossom]," he once told Matisse. In response Matisse gave a snort of disgust. *"Ça, c'est la decoration!* [That's mere decoration!]," *Purely for My Pleasure,* p. 6

painting, marked down for his primarily literary approach to the visual arts. "He liked a picture for what he could read into it and write out of it rather than for any aesthetic reason," commented Harold Acton, an opinion that Maugham's own writing on the subject undeniably supports. "I do not think Utrillo is a great painter," he stated in a magazine article in 1941, "but I have occasionally seen a picture of what is called his white period that has wrung my heart. To someone who knows Paris, those street scenes of sordid suburbs, with their air of desolation and their hostile silence, are of an infinite sadness." During this same period further purchases were made in Paris and London, *La neige à Louveciennes* by Camille Pissarro, *Femme à l'ombrelle verte* by Matisse, Sisley's *Le Loing à Moret,* and a luscious nude by Renoir, "rather buxom & a bright tomato colour, not very big, but very beautiful," as Maugham delightedly described it. The last painting Maugham bought was a river scene, *La Seine à Paris,* by Lépine. He and Alan were passing a well-known gallery in Bond Street when they saw two men carrying in a picture covered by a sheet. Following them, they watched while the canvas, dirty and unframed, was unwrapped. "It was the picture I had been looking for in vain for years," Maugham wrote. He asked the price, and a formidable sum was named. " 'All right,' I said. 'I'll buy it.' " Another favorite work was by Toulouse-Lautrec, *Le polisseur,* a painting of a naked man on his hands and knees polishing a stone floor. The dealer told Maugham he could have asked three times the price had it been a nude woman, "[but] buyers jibbed at a male nude and I was able to buy it for a very reasonable sum." Raw, brutal, and disturbing, *Le polisseur* is untypical Lautrec, far removed from his courtesans and can-can dancers, and it amused Maugham to ask visitors to the Villa to guess the artist: only once was the correct answer given.

Much as he loved the visual arts, Maugham knew he was an amateur with a comparatively uninformed taste, and when spending large sums of money he looked to others to advise him. In the early days he had been guided by Gerald Kelly and Hugh Lane; he had also consulted the great Parisian collector and connoisseur Alphonse Kahn. It was Kahn who introduced him to Fernand

Léger, from whom he bought the abstract *Les toits de Paris,* which Léger had painted in homage to Cézanne. Subsequently Maugham turned for advice to Monroe Wheeler, to Jean Cocteau, and to one of the greatest of British art historians, Sir Kenneth Clark. Before the war a pupil of Bernard Berenson's, Surveyor of the King's Pictures, director of the National Gallery, "K" Clark was recognized in his field as one of the foremost scholars of the age, admired as much for his lucid, lapidary style of writing as for his formidable intellect. He and Maugham formed a firm friendship, Maugham much appreciating Clark's dry wit, fastidiousness, and urbanity, and becoming fond, too, of his elegant wife, Jane. The first time the Clarks came to the Mauresque, Maugham, as usual, challenged his guest to name the painter of *Le polisseur.* "Toulouse-Lautrec," Clark replied with barely a moment's hesitation. Unlike his mentor, Berenson, Clark respected Maugham's response to painting. Berenson, on the one occasion on which Maugham visited him at I Tatti, remarked afterward that the writer had displayed "a fantastic absence of feeling for visual art. In so far as he praised anything here, it was the poorest stopgap paintings." "K" Clark, on the other hand, thought that Maugham "was remarkably perceptive of excellence in all the arts," including painting.

> In the big sitting-room were pictures by Renoir and Monet in richly carved frames; on the staircase pictures by Matisse; but if one showed him reproductions of work by a painter unknown to him, like Paul Klee, his response was surprisingly quick and just. I once tried him to the limit with a Mondrian. To my astonishment he said "Yes, it is very fine."

It was through an introduction from Monroe Wheeler that Maugham met a protégé of "K" Clark's, the painter Graham Sutherland. In 1947 Sutherland and his wife while staying in the south of France were invited to the Mauresque, where Sutherland, like many before him, was immediately struck by the "paintability" of Maugham. He had never attempted a portrait before, but Maugham agreed to sit, and the Sutherlands moved into the villa for a week so that the painter could give himself over to his work, making pencil studies of his sitter's head, sketching his arms, hands, and legs, and making notes about his clothes, a brown velvet smoking jacket, a rose-colored silk foulard, gray flannels, a pair of suede slippers. On a tall, narrow canvas, the now famous picture, creating the image by which Maugham is most widely identified, shows the subject seated on a bamboo stool, the figure set against a thickly painted yellow background, with a few palm fronds above his head making a delicate reference to the Orient. The posture is slightly hunched, the eyes are melancholy, the mouth downturned, and yet there is a glimmer of sardonic amusement, the impression of a detached observer quietly enjoying the spectacle of human frailty. "The first time I saw it I was shocked," Maugham said in an interview, "and then I began to realize that here was far more of me than I ever saw myself." Others, too, claimed to see in the portrait a different side to the man they thought they knew. Gerald Kelly joked that Sutherland had made his old friend look like the madam of a brothel in Shanghai, while Max Beerbohm was revolted by the painting and thought the subject appeared to have been tortured. Maugham himself, however, was so taken with the work that he offered to buy it, agreeing with Sutherland on a price of £500. The next day Alan turned up with £300 in his hand, explaining that as the payment was in cash a £200 discount was expected, a cut that the disgruntled artist felt forced to accept. Sutherland did well from the portrait nevertheless: *Time* magazine carried a photograph of it, with other publications quickly following suit, and the picture was exhibited at the Tate, with the result that the painter found himself much in demand, commissioned to portray, among others, the press baron Lord Beaverbrook and Winston Churchill.

As became widely known, when Churchill saw his portrait, which had been commissioned by Parliament to hang in the House of Commons, he was appalled by the image represented, by the sadness and sense of defeat, and the canvas was destroyed on his wife's orders. Interestingly, Maugham, too, grew to dislike his Sutherland portrait, and before long found an excuse to have it moved out of the villa. "Although I wouldn't like Graham to know it for worlds,

I found it a terribly difficult picture to hang," he explained to "K" Clark. "It is a museum picture rather than a picture for a private house." But the truth was that he came to be haunted by it, haunted by its merciless vision and by the terrifying vista it revealed of an inexorably approaching and miserable old age.

CHAPTER 16

BETRAYAL

. . .

O N THE DAY AFTER HIS SEVENTIETH BIRTHDAY IN JANUARY 1944, Maugham had written in his notebook, "On the continent of Europe they have an amiable custom when a man who has achieved some distinction reaches that age. His friends, his colleagues, his disciples . . . join together to write a volume of essays in his honour." But when Maugham turned seventy the war was on and he was in America, and there was no opportunity for any such act of homage; and so it was not until ten years later, when he reached the age of eighty, that just such a plan was put into action. Heinemann commissioned the novelist Jocelyn Brooke to put together a Festschrift, a collection of essays on Maugham by fellow writers to be presented to him as a birthday tribute. Brooke solicited contributions from many of the most distinguished literary figures of the day, from poets, publishers, novelists, critics, from Elizabeth Bowen, Angus Wilson, Rosamond Lehmann, Anthony Powell, William Plomer, Rose Macaulay, Rupert Hart-Davis, William Sansom, Raymond Mortimer, Peter Quennell, J. R. Ackerley, Noël Coward. But to Brooke's dismay, one after the other the polite excuses came flowing in: "not a great fan of his . . . obliged to decline" (William Plomer), "don't think I'm at all the person to write about [him]" (Angus Wilson), "May I be excused?" (William Sansom), "[cannot] because of the novel which I *MUST* finish" (Elizabeth Bowen), "truly and deeply sorry to say that I cannot contribute" (Noël Coward). The only two acceptances came from

Anthony Powell and Raymond Mortimer. "[I] shall produce 2000 words for you if I possibly can," wrote Mortimer, "[but] I don't myself think that there is a great variety of things to say about Maugham [and] a devastating paper could be written on the limitations of his taste. . . . I am the last person, however, to emphasise such deficiencies . . . for he is a very old friend whom I regard with grateful affection." But two contributions were not enough, and in the face of this fastidious flinching, of this general lack of respect for Maugham's work, Brooke had no option but to abandon the project.

The birthday did not pass unnoticed, however: it was given extensive coverage in the press, and *Punch* ran a caricature of the writer by Ronald Searle accompanying a ditty by the magazine's assistant editor, B. A. Young:

> I bask in Antibes and in honour, and consider the works of
>> my pen
> That have made me in one full lifetime all things to all
>> literate men:
> The rich man's MARIE CORELLI, the poor man's ANDRÉ GIDE,
> A STEVENSON told of the facts of life, a KIPLING shorn of
>> his creed.
> O, I was TERENCE RATTIGAN when TERENCE was still in his cot,
> And the films and TV will call on me when USTINOV's
>> long forgot.
> Though the Ale I brewed was bitter, my Cakes were as sweet
>> as sin,
> And they brought me the Moon I sighed for, with a bit over
>> Sixpence thrown in.
> The world's most delectable secrets turned to Ashenden in
>> my mouth,
> And the fetters of Human Bondage hold me fast in the suns of
>> the south.

Among the most generous accolades was one from Maugham's old friend Compton Mackenzie, who wrote an open letter in *The Au-*

thor, the journal of the Society of Authors, speaking not only on behalf of Maugham's fellow writers but also for "those thousands of readers and playgoers all over the world whom you are still entertaining as you entertained their fathers [and] grandfathers." Mackenzie referred to his lifelong admiration for Maugham, which, he said, dated back to 1897 and his first reading of *Liza of Lambeth,* when "I regarded you with reverence as one of those fearless spirits who were liberating us from the shackles of Victorianism." As well as this, there was an exhibition of Maugham's manuscripts and first editions at the Times Bookshop in Wigmore Street, and a dinner given for him at the Garrick, during which a toast was proposed by the playwright St. John Ervine, followed by a speech from Maugham himself. This turned out to be a harrowing experience. Maugham gave a most impressive performance, Ervine recalled, his speech, which he had learned by heart, "full of wit, humour, well-turned phrases, and, surprisingly to some people, but not to me, full of feeling." But then toward the end he suddenly dried up:

> Anybody else would have sat down in confusion. . . . But Maugham stood perfectly still, though his fingers were trembling. After a few moments, he said, "I'm just thinking of what I shall say next!" Then he lapsed into silence again. A little later, he said, "I'm sorry to keep you waiting!" and became silent once more. Then, suddenly the machine of his mind moved again, and he finished the speech finely. He must have had a dry-up for about a couple of minutes, rather more than that, I should say, but remained imperturbable apparently, throughout what must have been a dreadful ordeal. And the company sat absolutely still.

Inevitably with such a world-renowned writer, Maugham had long been targeted by would-be biographers. Since the late 1920s there had appeared a number of critical studies of his work, and to those who wrote to him for information he was unfailingly helpful and courteous; for such a reticent man he answered questions with surprising frankness and often at length: as Sam Behrman remarked, "he will tell you everything, up to a point." Maugham nevertheless made it clear to these authors that they must not expect him to read the results of their research. "I really cannot stand reading about myself unless I am absolutely forced to do so," he explained to an American academic, Richard Cordell, who published a critical study in 1961. "It is a pathological defect [but] it is as uncomfortable for me to read praise . . . as it is to read censure." On biography, however, Maugham took a tougher stance, implacably opposed to any revelations about his personal life. In 1959 there had been one biographical work, *W. Somerset Maugham: A Candid Portrait,* by Maugham's old acquaintance Karl G. Pfeiffer, then a professor of English at New York University; it was gossipy, inaccurate, mildly malicious, and on the whole harmless, but Maugham had disliked it exceedingly, not only because of the invasion of privacy but because he felt betrayed: he had known Pfeiffer, had even had him to stay at the Mauresque, and had had no idea that their conversations were being secretly recorded for a book.

Now in his old age there were frequent requests from writers known and unknown hoping that he would agree to cooperate in, or at the very least not oppose the writing of, the big biography. Such a man, such a life presented an irresistible subject, but Maugham was determined to allow none of it, and he went to great lengths to protect himself. He instructed his literary executors (Frere, until he retired from Heinemann in 1961, when his place was taken by the literary agent Spencer Curtis Brown) that after his death they should continue to refuse information and access to all applicants, deny permission for the publication of letters, and where possible urge any person in possession of letters to destroy them. Further to cover his tracks, Maugham burned every scrap of documentary evidence he could lay his hands on. For years he had been ruthless with his own correspondence; Glenway Wescott remembered watching him answering letters at Yemassee, how "he tears everything into small scraps with a kind of spiteful haste and energy," and how, in a series of great bonfires at the Mauresque, Maugham threw into the flames every morsel he could find, including letters he had overlooked from long ago, letters from Sue Jones, from Arnold Bennett, Ada Leverson, H. G. Wells, Gerald Kelly, Desmond MacCarthy. Into the bonfire, too, at Maugham's insistence, went almost everything of Alan Searle's, including, to Alan's dismay, his love letters from Lytton Strachey. "I had held on to those letters," he pathetically recalled, "[because] I thought if something happened to Willie I might sell them."*

In the last years of Maugham's life, attitudes in England toward homosexuality were beginning to grow more tolerant, although the homosexual law reform bill was not to be passed until two years after his death. Yet Maugham was very much a product of his age, and his deviant sexuality, as it was then regarded, was an aspect of his life he strongly felt should be kept concealed. The outward appearance of respectability had always been of the utmost importance to him: when in 1954 Terence Rattigan asked for signatures on a petition supporting the young peer Edward Montagu, on trial for homosexual offenses, Maugham and Noël Coward were the only two who refused. With the gate firmly barred against bona fide biographers, Maugham might have felt relatively secure, but he still had to deal with the threat of blackmail. The first such approach was fairly easy to brush off, from Gerald's boyfriend, Louis Legrand, who in middle age had gone out to Australia to seek his fortune. When he failed to prosper, it occurred to Loulou that he was in possession of some valuable property in the form of letters not only from Haxton and Maugham, but also from a number of distinguished gentlemen whose acquaintance Loulou had made at the Mauresque and who might not be entirely overjoyed if the nature of that relationship were to be revealed. Loulou sent a series of misspelled letters to Maugham himself, to Alan, to Robin and to Liza ("Your kids of Paravicini & Lord Hope, will not be pleased when I shall give my memoires at the public [*sic*]"), but fortunately he was found to be open to reason and the matter was satisfactorily settled by a lawyer's letter and a check. But then a far more insidi-

---

* Searle did, however, manage to keep back several dozen letters written to him by Maugham.

ous threat materialized, this time from within the family, from none other than Maugham's nephew, Robin.

Despite his sometimes questionable behavior, Maugham was fond of Robin, although it had long been clear that his nephew's high-flying ambitions for himself were unlikely to be realized. In 1941, when Robin had stayed with his uncle in South Carolina, he had talked a great deal about his plans for the future and his desire to write. Maugham had been supportive, if uneasy about certain facets of Robin's character, in particular a lack of application and a tendency toward showing off. "Robin's handicap has always been that he was not interested in people for their own sake but only for the impression he was making on them," he told Kate Bruce. "That's not the attitude that makes a good writer." Since the war, Robin had failed to make a success of anything: he had given up the law and had failed at farming, and despite a brief success with a novella, *The Servant,* later made into a film, his writing remained unremarkable, giving rise to a suspicion that it was not writing per se that attracted Robin so much as the lavish lifestyle with which a few practitioners, notably his uncle, were rewarded. "[Robin] is as frivolous & scatter-brained as he was as a boy," Maugham complained as Robin approached his fortieth birthday:

> He has never grown up. He mixes with very disreputable people & throws his money around in the most reckless fashion. . . . It is all a terrible pity; he was a nice lad [and] might have amounted to something if he hadn't been so self-satisfied and fond of the bottle.

For Maugham it was Robin's habitual heavy drinking that gave rise to the greatest anxiety, as he had seen at close quarters how effectively alcohol could wreck a career. "It has been my ill-fortune to live much among drunkards," he was to write in an essay published in 1951, "and for my part I have found them boring at their best and disgusting at their worst." When in his cups, Robin could be both, and his uncle's tolerance was wearing thin. On his father's death

Robin had inherited the viscountcy and, as the second Lord Maugham, had immediately begun throwing his weight around, spending heavily to impress his attendant court of rent boys and hangers-on, confident that on his uncle's death he would become a very rich man. However, his expectations in that direction were less secure than he knew. The trust that Maugham had set up for Robin before the war had increased considerably in value, but Maugham had grown so alarmed by his nephew's irresponsible behavior that he decided to reduce it, siphoning off a substantial part into the settlement he had made for Liza and her children. Maugham saw no reason to inform his nephew of his action: Robin would still have a capital sum of $50,000, the interest on which, he considered, would yield a more than adequate annual income.

Of all Maugham's relations, it was only Robin whom Alan regarded as a friend. The two had always been close, Robin lending a sympathetic ear to Searle's grievances, while Alan acted as an invaluable mediator and informant; he spoke up for him when Robin was in trouble with his uncle and he kept him in touch with what was going on at the Villa. Naturally Alan was privy to all Maugham's affairs, affairs about which Robin increasingly began to show a lively curiosity. It was Alan one day, while the two of them were sitting by the pool, who indiscreetly revealed that the old man, disapproving of an increasing fecklessness and self-indulgence in Robin's behavior, had substantially reduced the financial provision he had made for his nephew. Robin, who had long lived with the comforting prospect of inheriting a generous unearned income, had been appalled. "I must tell you that this has come as a terrible blow . . . one of the greatest blows I've ever known," he wrote to Searle after he returned to England.

> During all these long years, I have always been able to console myself with the thought that . . . I had a substantial amount to look forward to when I could no longer make much money from writing. . . . Please, dear Alan, if you possibly get the chance, do put in a word for me so that I can get the settlement made back to me now.

Alan promised to do what he could, but it would have to wait for the right moment. Meanwhile he expressed his readiness to help forward a more immediately lucrative project, the writing of a full-scale biography, with no holds barred. Robin had first suggested the idea of a biography more than ten years before, but Maugham had rejected the proposal out of hand; now, however, with Alan as his backstage informant, Robin had an immensely profitable proposition in view, and with his financial future suddenly diminished he could hardly be expected to let it go. With a certain amount of trepidation he wrote to Maugham. "Dearest Willie," his letter began,

> I've had an offer from the American publisher, Victor Weybright, of an advance of 50,000 dollars. . . . Obviously I can't afford to turn down such a good offer. But equally obviously I don't want to write such a book behind your back. As you know, although I earn enough from my writing to keep me going each year, I haven't a penny of capital. . . . So what I really need, if you will give it me, is first of all, your blessing that I should accept the offer to write a full-length biography, and secondly as much help as you could possibly give me. . . . It does seem to me that with my deep admiration and affection for you I am at least likely to produce a better biography of you than anyone else.

Despite the undoubtedly genuine expression of affection, Maugham had no trouble recognizing blackmail when he saw it. He instantly paid up, sending Robin a check for the exact sum he had been offered by Weybright, on the strict understanding that he drop all plans of writing about him. "I promise you here and now that I will keep my part of the bargain," Robin wrote with every appearance of sincerity.

> I give you my word that I shall not write any other biography about you—ever. . . . I can use part of the money to pay off my overdraft and I can use the rest to buy myself an annuity

which will make all the difference to my life because it will give me security. I'm really awfully shy about all this, but I'm also very grateful.

When after his eightieth-birthday celebrations Maugham returned to the south of France, he found over a thousand letters of congratulation awaiting him. This was in addition to the normal heavy volume of business and personal correspondence and of fan letters, often amounting to five hundred a week, nearly all of which had to be dealt with by Alan Searle. There were also frequent telephone calls, invitations, and requests for interviews, all filtered through Alan, who as Maugham's secretary reveled in his position as guardian of the gate, even if it sometimes left him feeling flustered and exhausted. "[Mr. Maugham's] celebrity in Europe has reached its peak, and I am hard put to it to protect him from the Press and all and sundry," he wrote to Bert Alanson. "I get insulted most days by all the people I keep at bay, but it's part of the job [and] I rather enjoy the reflected glory." But even with the stresses and strains, Alan relished the glamour and excitement, especially when staying in London at the Dorchester, where he met numbers of famous people and was constantly petitioned by sycophantic journalists all dependent on Alan for their access to Maugham. Indeed, Searle was usually happier when away from Cap Ferrat, where he had the responsibility of the whole household on his shoulders and where he often felt unwell. Alan suffered from a skin condition, psoriasis, that the heat in summer made worse; he was prone to hemorrhoids and also to frequent liver attacks: the food at the Mauresque was rich, Alan was very greedy, and as a result he frequently had to spend a day in bed overwhelmed by headaches and nausea. Against this, he loved the social life, the luncheon parties, the constant arriving and departing of guests from England and America. With most of Maugham's friends he quickly adopted a manner of cozy intimacy, and in many cases, because they in return were genial toward him, he came to believe that he was held in much higher regard than was in fact the case.

Generally speaking, visitors to the Mauresque liked Alan well enough. His good humor and desire to please, above all his obvious devotion to his master, won respect; but most people, although naturally they concealed it, also found him silly and a bit of a bore. "[Alan] was not in himself very interesting company," said Glenway Wescott, "a namby-pamby" said Jerry Zipkin, "muddleheaded [and] not very bright" according to the art critic Douglas Cooper. High-strung and emotional, Alan was quick to interpret a normal show of friendliness and good manners as a sign of deep and undying affection for himself, and for some it was faintly embarrassing when Searle, after typing a letter of his employer's, would add an effusive handwritten postscript of his own. On letters of Maugham's to Lady Clark, for instance, Alan nearly always wrote a sentimental, sometimes rather bold, personal message—"I think you are a darling, and I love you. XX [kisses] Get some nice chap to give you these for me"—while Jerry Zipkin was frequently and fervently told, "[You are] such a darling . . . I have few friends I love as much as I love you. . . ."

For Searle, the two greatest pleasures in life were sex and self-pity. He loved to wallow in self-pity, complaining about his health, his nerves, the pressure of work, and above all his anxiety about what was to happen after his employer's death, when, he claimed, he would be turned out of the house with nothing and left to starve. He talked endlessly about his expectations, or lack of them, his voice breaking as he described the pathos of his situation, the fact that he believed Maugham was going to leave him penniless, that he would be thrown out onto the street when he was too old and frail to make a fresh start. That all this was nonsense, that Maugham had made it clear from the beginning that he had generously provided for him, made not the slightest difference to the burden of Alan's song. Some of Maugham's old friends, George Cukor among them, weary of the endless litany, tried to make him see reason, but Alan refused to listen. The truth was, as Jerry Zipkin soon realized, "he enjoyed the complaining." Every summer when Zipkin came to the Mauresque he would be treated yet again to "Alan's annual speech of complaint about all the *objets* that were his or that Willie had promised him, and what would happen after

Willie died." Eventually, Zipkin suggested he draw up a list and get Maugham to sign it, which Maugham was perfectly willing to do, "but Alan never would, preferring to complain."

It was Zipkin who was central, also, to Alan's other hobby, as he arranged for regular supplies of pornographic material to be sent over from the States. Boxes of photographs and magazines (the parcels carefully disguised to avoid the attention of French Customs) arrived at intervals from a specialist firm in Arizona, from which Alan, alone in his bedroom, derived many hours of vigorous pleasure. "Thank you for all those wonderful picture books!" begins one enthusiastic letter. "They've nearly driven me mad, and I am in a state of complete exhaustion, and almost too weak to turn the pages." Any good-looking young man invited to the Mauresque was pounced on, and most nights after dinner, Alan, like Gerald before him, would go over to Villefranche on the prowl. Searle was known along the Riviera for his proclivities; he tipped generously and so was always made welcome, his stout figure a familiar sight in backstreet bars and on the quayside when the American fleet was in.

Yet for all his foolishness and neuroses, it was Alan who made Maugham's highly structured routine possible, who protected him, cared for him, and showed him infinite kindness and compassion. The two men were largely compatible and understood each other very well; "[Mr. Maugham] was generous to me & loved me with all my faults," wrote Alan in later life. Yet Maugham, irascible in his old age, was frequently impatient with Alan, and, a master of the lethal barb, he would sometimes lash out at him with a ferocity that sent Searle rushing from the room in tears. This could annoy Maugham more, or alternately overwhelm him with guilt so that he would treat Alan with particular tenderness for the following day or two. Guests at the Villa were often shocked at the treatment meted out to Alan. "Alan Searle was a knight," according to Liza, "[and] some of the crushing and cruel things my father said to him were devastating," a perception shared by Christopher Isherwood, who "said in his entire life he's never known anyone so mistreated as Alan, so pissed on, kicked and shamed and disbelieved." Yet it was also evident that Alan reveled in the drama of it: he loved to be petted and pitied, and Maugham's harshness provided him with ever richer material for his grievances.

There were, too, enormous advantages to living with Maugham, and among the most prized by Searle was the opportunity to travel. Every year they journeyed within Europe, to Germany, Austria, Italy, Portugal, and Spain; in 1950 they went to Morocco, in 1953 to Greece and Turkey, and in 1956 to Egypt, where they were sumptuously entertained by the Aga Khan. After the war Maugham went only twice more to the United States, in 1949 and in 1950, when he presented the manuscript of "The Artistic Temperament of Stephen Carey" to the Library of Congress; but in 1959, at the age of eighty-five, he returned to the Far East, to Japan, where he had long been enormously popular, revisiting en route many of the old ports of call, Singapore, Saigon, Manila, Hong Kong. On their arrival in Yokohama, a crowd of several thousand was waiting to greet the great English novelist, a scene that was repeated in Tokyo, to Alan's intense excitement. "Mr. M.'s popularity in Japan is quite fantastic, and we can't put our noses outside the door without being instantly recognised . . . it has been really staggering!" They were escorted during part of their stay by the English novelist Francis King, then living in Kyoto. King was impressed by Maugham's lively curiosity about Japanese life and culture. "He still felt he had something important to learn. . . . He was often almost dead from exhaustion but he was determined to see all that he could."

Until well into his eighties, Maugham made little change to the schedule he had established as a young man, every morning retiring to his study to write as he had done all his life, although now he had to wear an elastic brace on his right hand. While no longer producing fiction, Maugham was still an immense bestseller, and naturally enough was much sought after to write introductions to the works of others. He contributed to books about Robbie Ross, Eddie Marsh, Charlie Chaplin, and Gladys Cooper; he wrote a foreword to the autobiography of the Aga Khan and a preface to a translation of *The Letters of Madame de Sévigné* by his childhood friend from Paris, Violet Hammersley (née Williams-Freeman).

In 1951 Maugham brought out *A Choice of Kipling's Prose,* his personal selection of stories by a writer for whom his feelings had always been somewhat ambivalent. Maugham had known Kipling only slightly, meeting him first at a dinner party in the 1890s, during which he remembered thinking that if Kipling said "pukka sahib" one more time he would throw a decanter at him. During the 1930s Kipling was brought to lunch at the Mauresque, and Maugham was amused to find that little had changed. "He's a white man," Kipling declared of a chap he admired, and Maugham waited for the inevitable phrase to follow. "He's a pukka sahib all right," continued Kipling, exactly on cue. The writer's daughter, Elsie Bambridge, had asked Maugham to do the book, and before making his choice he reread all the short stories, as he reported to Peter Stern. "I have been reading Kipling, reading Kipling, reading Kipling (the repetition is designed to express endurance, constancy, perseverance, a will of iron, determination & bull-dog courage) & at his best I think he is grand (Caps); at his worst—O God!" Such facetiousness notwithstanding, Maugham's admiration was genuine, in particular for the Indian stories, and his appraisal is both generous and judicious. "[Kipling] is our greatest story writer," he concludes, "the only writer of short stories our country has produced who can stand comparison with Guy de Maupassant and Chekhov."

In his eighties Maugham continued to write because in a sense he had no choice. "The fact is that, like drinking, writing is a very easy habit to form & a devilish hard one to break," as he explained to Bert Alanson. And yet now in old age his inspiration was failing him; his imagination had run dry, and he could no longer inhabit the vivid interior landscape in which he had lived with such intensity and absorption for over half a century. "[My] fertile invention . . . is a thing of the past," he ruefully admitted, "[and] I am well aware that I have lost any talent I may have had. . . . Not being a creative writer anymore, is very lonely. Your characters don't exist with you anymore." In a newspaper interview Maugham gave in 1958, he said sadly, "Writing with me has been like a disease, but now I must be content with an hour a day, if my hand allows, of writing about books instead of people. It is not the same thing at all." He sounded, said the reporter,

> like a man about to be divorced from a woman he really loves but cannot live with any longer. . . . As he spoke he kept rubbing the muscle between the thumb and the first finger nervously. Then he said, seeing my interest: "That is where it hurts. The muscle has just given up after all these years."

Increasingly, memories of the past began to haunt him, memories of his vigorous young manhood, of his childhood, and of his love for his mother, the only fully requited love he had ever known; his mind dwelled on Gerald and of their years together and their travels in the South Pacific and the Far East. To H. E. Bates, who in 1953 dedicated a book of stories to him, Maugham wrote poignantly that "the last one 'The Delicate Nature' took me a long way back & my memory fizzled with all my half-forgotten recollections of the East. I was thrilled & at the same time rather unhappy. Oh, the past!" By comparison Maugham found his daily life colorless, and he grew increasingly restless and dissatisfied. "I could not stand the life for a month if I hadn't got a certain amount of work to do," he complained to his niece Kate, "but that occupies only my morning & I have the rest of the day to get through."

There was plenty of society available, but many of his old friends were gone: Emerald Cunard had died in 1948, Desmond MacCarthy in 1952, Eddie Marsh in 1953, Max Beerbohm, whom Maugham had last visited in Rapallo only months before, in 1956, Bert Alanson, profoundly mourned, in 1958. Rather less regretted were a couple of deaths within the family. On March 23, 1958, F.H., after suffering a stroke, died at his house in Cadogan Square, aged ninety-one. A widower for eight years, he had been looked after by his eldest daughter, Kate, and his death was neither unexpected nor greatly grieved over. Yet if the death of his brother left

Maugham largely unmoved, that of his ex-wife three years earlier had been a cause for positive rejoicing. Returning to London after the war, Syrie had moved into a flat on Park Lane, where she continued to conduct her business, although on a much smaller scale than before. In her seventies, Syrie's formidable energy had begun to fail her, and she spent much of her day in bed, talking on the telephone and rapping out orders to her long-suffering maid and secretary. Since the bout of tuberculosis a few years earlier, her health had been precarious: she suffered from angina, and this, coupled with a bad bout of bronchial pneumonia, brought about her death, at the age of seventy-six, on July 25, 1955. Maugham learned of it in a telegram from a heartbroken Liza. "It would be hypocrisy on my part to pretend that I am deeply grieved at Syrie's death," he told Barbara Back. "She had me every which way from the beginning & never ceased to give me hell." Indeed, his strongest emotion was one of relief that he would no longer have the financial burden of supporting a woman from whom he had been divorced for nearly thirty years. "Tra la la, no more alimony, tra la la," he would sing, tapping his fingers on the card table. He attended neither the funeral nor the memorial service at the Grosvenor Chapel, nor did he contribute to the purchase of the sculpture presented in her memory to the Victoria & Albert Museum.

In his own last years Maugham thought constantly about death and about what form his end would take. "I am like a passenger waiting for his ship at a war-time port," he had written on the last page of *A Writer's Notebook*. "I do not know on which day it will sail, but I am ready to embark at a moment's notice." He became obsessed with his aging appearance, standing in front of the looking glass and deploring his hooded eyes and deeply lined face. And indeed there are many descriptions of Maugham in diaries and memoirs of this period in which the same saurian similes are repeated again and again, a crocodile, a tortoise, "an iguana sunning itself on a rock"; the diarist Frances Partridge compared Maugham to a chameleon, "with his pale deeply furrowed face, sunken glittering eyes and the mouth that opens deliberately and sometimes sticks there," while Harold Nicolson was "reminded of the lizards that creep slowly over the dry boulders of the Galapagos Islands"; Glenway Wescott conjured up a more cheerful image after seeing his host wearing nothing but a straw hat poised to jump into his swimming pool: "[Willie] was shapely but tiny and with his little potbelly he looked like the King of the Frogs in the fairy tale." Yet Maugham in old age remained nimble and fit; he was still sexually active, not only with Alan but with boys brought by Alan to the Villa: he saw sex as one of the physical appetites it was healthy to indulge, he told Wescott; and he still enjoyed his food and drink, looking forward to the preprandial cocktail (the martinis now made with a dash of absinthe) and continuing to take an informed interest in the ordering of menus for lunch and dinner.

As he neared the end of the 1950s, "a seedy relic of the Edwardian era," as he wryly described himself, Maugham rarely invited his friends to stay. "Things I could do with pleasure years ago now exhaust me," he wrote, aged eighty-five, to Gerald Kelly. "I am always (or nearly always) glad if people I like will come & lunch with me, but that is all the entertaining I can do." Among his favorites as luncheon guests were two men also far from their first youth, Winston Churchill and the Canadian press baron Lord Beaverbrook, proprietor of the *Express* newspapers. Churchill, who was often on the Riviera, was an exact contemporary, and Maugham could not resist remarking on how much fitter he was than his old friend, who, with his pink complexion and wispy white hair, looked like "a poor old celluloid doll," walking with great difficulty and taking in little of what was said. "If you think I'm g-g-g-ga-ga," Maugham would crow, "you should see W-W-W-Winston." Max Beaverbrook, on the other hand, five years younger, was still vigorous and spry, and when he was in residence at his villa on Cap d'Ail, the two men regularly visited each other, in between sending their chauffeurs to ferry over little gifts of figs and pots of marmalade.

IF FEW FRIENDS WERE invited to stay, an exception was always made for members of the family, and Liza's visits every summer were always an agreeable distraction. Maugham, who adored babies and young children, had been infinitely beguiled by Nic and Camilla when they were small, and he was equally charmed by the two little boys of Liza's second marriage, Julian, born in 1950, and Jonathon two years later. With his son-in-law he had never got on: he and John maintained the civilities, but privately Maugham found the man a bore, a dry stick, and it was tacitly agreed that whenever possible Liza should come without him. Especially for the two elder children the Mauresque was a magical place: they knew they had to be on their best behavior with their grandfather, whose patience might suddenly give way and whose temper could be terrifying, but there were the enormous garden, the tennis court, the swimming pool—and there was Alan. Alan had become a playmate, a confidant, ever ready with a giggle and a joke, making them collapse with laughter as he gave them a comic rendition of his exploits with the sailor boys down at the port the night before. As Maugham in his old age grew increasingly unpredictable, it was good, devoted Alan to whom everyone turned, Alan who seemed so kind and capable, soothing his employer, reassuring the visitors, and making everything all right. None of the family, not the children, not Liza herself had any inkling that he detested them and was determined to do them down. And yet with hindsight there are a few indications that all was not quite as it appeared. In retrospect both Nic and Camilla remembered occasions when Alan tried to coax them into naughty behavior that would have gotten them into serious trouble; and several of Maugham's friends detected a more complex personality behind the cheeky-chappy façade, saw something unctuous and moneygrubbing in his demeanor. One observer described Alan as a "cockney Mephistopheles," while Christopher Isherwood's boyfriend, Don Bachardy, wrote that "[Alan] is not nearly as simple and unimpressive as he pretends to be," a view endorsed by Alan Pryce-Jones, who defined Searle as "an intriguer, a schemer with a keen eye to his own advantage, a troublemaker."

The origins of Alan's vindictiveness toward Maugham's family are obscure. Alan Searle was a sweet-natured man who, as his previous career demonstrated, genuinely loved to do good; his devotion to Maugham was absolute; he had never been a gold digger, out to amass a fortune; and yet from the moment he arrived at the Mauresque he became obsessed, dangerously and irrationally obsessed, by a conviction that Liza and John Hope were scheming to cheat him, to grab for themselves what rightly belonged to him. Maugham had always been generous with Alan. He had set up a trust, as he had done for Gerald, that would provide him with a comfortable income for life, and he frequently made him presents, not only of money and clothes—a mink-lined overcoat, on one occasion—but also of paintings and even his own manuscripts, which were fetching high prices at auction in London and New York. And yet none of this reassured Searle. There must have been some profound insecurity embedded in his past that led him so bitterly to resent Liza's position as Maugham's only child. Perhaps a clue is to be found in a line written in an autobiographical memorandum discovered after his death: "Parents subjected me to appalling mental cruelty." Whatever the origins of his delusion, Alan over the years worked himself up into a state of bitter hatred for Liza, and by extension for her husband and children, a hatred he continually harped on to several of Maugham's closest friends. "I'm always thinking about the future and getting scared as to what will happen to me after I no longer have Willie to care for me . . . his family, of course, are longing to cut my throat, so I am afraid . . . I am in for a pretty rough time." Occasionally and in diluted form he expressed his anxieties to his employer, but Maugham, bored by his companion's endless complaining, was briskly dismissive. "What will become of me when you die?" Alan would whine. "You'll have to go into lodgings," Maugham teased him, and when Alan's eyes welled with tears, he would snap at him, "Oh, stop it, you silly cunt."

In his determination to defeat what he saw as the Hopes' wicked plans, Searle now determined do everything he could to turn Maugham against them. Yet here he had to tread carefully. Maugham was no fool, and it would be self-defeating to openly criticize Liza in front of him. But then by chance the ideal occasion presented itself, and there fell into Alan's lap the perfect opportunity to make trouble, trouble that was eventually to grow, to dominate and wholly destroy not only the end of Maugham's life and his relationship with his daughter but his standing in the eyes of the world before and after his death and for years to come.

BY THE MID-1950S, Maugham's picture collection had grown enormously in value. Of the thirty or so works of art bought since the beginning of the war, nine had been purchased in Liza's name, including the Renoir nude and a Picasso: legally they were hers, but it was understood that they should remain at the villa for her father's lifetime. During Liza's visits in the summer, Maugham enjoyed talking to her about her pictures and about his will, in which he had left her almost everything; since 1954 she had been the majority shareholder in the company that owned the Mauresque, formed in order to bypass death taxes, but he also wanted the Villa's contents, his money, and his royalties to go to her and the children. "I want you to know that you are going to be extremely well off," he would tell her. "You are going to be an extremely rich woman." Liza was a little embarrassed by these conversations, she said, "[but] it was always a friendly atmosphere and I thought it was very generous, naturally." Her father took care to go over with her every detail of her substantial inheritance, and it was during one of these conversations that he shocked her by revealing that she was born before he had married her mother, a fact of which she had been unaware. Recounting the circumstances of her birth, he explained that in his will he had deliberately referred to her not only by name but specifically as "my daughter," in case anyone should question her status after his death.

And so matters might have rested had it not been for Maugham's sudden decision to sell his collection. In 1960 there had been a series of well-organized art thefts along the Côte d'Azur, and these had alarmed him, his disquiet increased by a visit from the mayor of Saint-Jean, who came to warn him that his paintings were bound to be targeted. Alarmed, he contacted Sotheby's, the Bond Street auction house, and plans were put in place for a high-profile sale to be held in the spring of 1962; this would be accompanied by a short essay by Maugham about his pictures, "Purely for My Pleasure," handsomely bound and illustrated with color plates. Everything was to go, including the Gauguin on the glass panel in Maugham's study, and to increase the impact of the sale even further, Maugham persuaded the Hopes to include Liza's nine pictures with the rest. "It will also be very nice for you both," he said, "as you can have the money now and not wait for my death." This was amicably agreed between them during his daughter's annual visit to the Mauresque in August 1961. After she had returned home, Liza wrote to thank him for her stay, as she always did, and she also confirmed her consent to the selling of her paintings with his.

In October, Maugham as usual came to London, and Liza telephoned him at the Dorchester to arrange a meeting. But instead of her father, Alan answered, sounding strangely overwrought: he must come over and see her at once, he said, as there was something he needed urgently to discuss. On arrival at the Hopes' house in Chelsea, Alan abruptly informed Liza that her father had been made so angry by her "aggressive" letter that he refused to either speak to or see her. She must on no account try to contact him, said Searle, but meanwhile he himself would try to calm the old man down and do his best to effect a reconciliation. Stunned, Liza at first agreed to do as she was told, but when after a week she had heard nothing she again telephoned the Dorchester. Again Alan answered, this time telling her that her father was beside himself with rage, still refused to see her, and was now insisting that she give up at least half her share of the proceeds of the sale. She must obey, said Alan, as Maugham was in a terrible state, his condition was fast deteriorating, and if there were any recalcitrance on her part he could not answer for the consequences. Appalled by Alan's account and seriously worried, Liza wrote to her father. "Dearest Daddy, You really are making me quite miserable by refusing to see me," she began,

> when I think how well we have got on, and what happy times
> we have had even as recently as six weeks ago when you were
> so sweet to the children, and we all had such fun at the Mau-

resque. . . . How can you suddenly turn on me when I have done absolutely nothing? Please let me come and see you and don't let's have any more of this awful rift.

In reply she received an attorney's letter insisting that it was not possible for Mr. Maugham to meet Lady John while there were certain matters under dispute between them. Mystified and disturbed, Liza wrote a note to her father asking him please to explain what was going on. This note she attached to the lawyer's letter, giving both to Searle, who had again been to see her and had again pressed her to take just half the proceeds of the sale.

This second visit of Searle's was on a Friday. On Monday, Liza was telephoned by Alan, who to her astonishment said that her father would like her to come to tea. Searle gave her strict instructions, however, not to mention the pictures. "As far as he's concerned the whole thing is forgotten."

Or could it be that Maugham knew nothing of the matter? Certainly the subject of the sale was never mentioned. Liza found her father "very pleasant and friendly," and, extraordinarily, it was as though he were unaware that anything disagreeable had passed between them. A few days later he and Alan returned to the south of France.

The sale, which realized $1,466,864, took place at Sotheby's on April 10, 1962. Maugham remained at the Mauresque, but Searle, who had been much involved with the preparations, came over to London for the occasion. The night before the auction he called on Liza and talked to her in a manner that both shocked and frightened her. Red in the face and highly emotional, he said her father was determined not to let her have a penny of the picture money, and that if she pressed for it he would disinherit her children. But Liza was not Syrie's daughter for nothing: by now furious, she told Searle that if any attempt were made to deprive her of what was rightly hers she would fight it in court, at which Alan shouted that she was "a damn fool" and slammed out of the house.

From that moment open war was declared between Maugham and his only child, a source of profound unhappiness to them both.

It was only after Maugham's death that Liza began to suspect how deeply implicated Alan Searle must have been in the traumatic breakdown of her relationship with her father; only later, she said, that she realized "Alan must have had a hand in it."* Now nearly ninety, Maugham was a very old man, his mind deteriorating, his grip on reality becoming increasingly fragile. With Alan by his side, a podgy Iago constantly briefing against the family, it is hardly surprising that Maugham became convinced of their treachery and greed. Searle's letters to his cronies on the subject give a startling insight into the depth of his hostility. Liza, "his vile so-called daughter," was "a scavenger . . . a bitch [who] fills my heart with murder. She goes around saying 'I love my daddy, and I want to be with him.' I wonder she doesn't drop dead . . . she's only interested in what she can get out of him. . . . The greed of these people and their callousness is beyond belief." He told Maugham that Liza and her husband had been seen at the Mauresque counting the silver, making inventories, and walking around as if they owned the place, that Liza was interested only in his money. As Alan knew, Maugham was vulnerable to such propaganda because of his past history—since his prewar trip to India he had held a grudge against John Hope's family—but more crucial was his miserable marriage and his loathing of Syrie that was as virulently alive as ever: Liza was Syrie's daughter, and he saw too much of Syrie in her ever to forget the association.

By now there seemed little chance of resolution. "Alan incites Willie against Liza, Willie loathes Lord John Hope, and poor Liza is ill at ease but a cautious, discreet, ambitious girl," Ann Fleming reported to Evelyn Waugh. Maugham's niece Diana was another who saw faults on both sides, believing that Liza, too, was becoming unreachable by reason. "There is something in her—perhaps a coldness . . . to do with money," she observed, and she tried to persuade Liza to show more understanding toward her father. But any retrac-

* In a letter to *The Times* more than thirty-five years later, on January 16, 1999, Nicolas Paravicini recalled that "my mother's repeated attempts to see or even speak to her father when he became ill were continually thwarted by Alan Searle, thus making any reconciliation impossible, to my mother's lasting sadness."

tion was now out of the question. Liza was determined to sue, lawyers were called in, and Alan for one looked forward to his day in court. "I only hope that [Maugham] will say all the things that he has kept hidden all these years," he wrote to Robin. "It will ruin [the Hopes] completely . . . and serve them right too."

The "hidden things" so ominously hinted at by Alan was a reference to a sensational revelation he had up his sleeve regarding Liza's true paternity: the scandal was not that she had been born out of wedlock, which she now knew, but that Maugham was not her father. Taking full advantage of Maugham's increasing senility, Alan easily convinced him that Syrie had deceived him, that it was not he but any one of half a dozen lovers who might have fathered the child. From there it was a small step to persuade the eighty-nine-year-old Maugham that he should disown Liza and adopt Frank Alan Searle, aged fifty-seven, as his son; and once the adoption had been made official, the obvious next step would be to disinherit Liza and make Alan his heir. On counsel's advice, and to simplify the paternity case, it was decided not to bring up the subject of several lovers, but to argue that because Syrie was still married to Henry Wellcome when Liza was born, and because Wellcome had never disclaimed her as his daughter, then legally Liza was his child, not Maugham's. To make doubly sure that Liza would be left with nothing, Maugham, who by now had been worked up into a state of fury against his daughter, intended also to sue for the return of all gifts made to her on the grounds that over the years she and her children had clearly demonstrated "gross ingratitude."

This complicated case was complicated further by the fact that with Maugham domiciled in France it involved both French and English law, with the opposing sides each obliged to hire two teams of lawyers. The process was lengthy, distressing, and horrifyingly expensive; inevitably it attracted a great deal of media attention, with the press turning the whole affair into a freak show, a circus of scandal, gossip, and sanctimonious morality, embellished by irreverent jokes and jocular cartoons. The French hearing took place in camera at the Palais de Justice in Nice, at the end of which, on July 3, 1962, the court ruled in Liza's favor, declaring that there was no

evidence to show Lady John Hope was not the daughter of Somerset Maugham; that under British law a child born out of wedlock
becomes legitimate when the parents marry, and in France a legitimate child cannot be disinherited; and that the attempted adoption
of Alan Searle was invalid. In London, after much wrangling, the
quarrel over the ownership of the villa and the proceeds of the
Sotheby's sale was settled out of court: Maugham agreed to pay
Liza 50 percent of the money raised by the sale of her nine pictures,
as well as her considerable court costs, and she would also retain her
right of ownership of the Mauresque. Everything else, the contents
of the house, money, royalties, which had always been destined for
her and her children, Maugham was now free to leave to whomever
he chose.

The legal hearings and accompanying publicity had imposed an
enormous strain on Alan. ("I am peace-loving, so you can imagine
what a torment all these dreadful law-suits are," he unblushingly
complained. "None of the quarrels are mine, but I seem to get all
the knocks and the odium.") Yet for Maugham it was much worse.
Already half demented, he was plunged into a maelstrom of anger
and fear, haunted by all the most sulfurous memories of the past
and of the torment of his marriage to Syrie. Several of his friends
were disturbed by his state of mind, Noël Coward among them.
"He is devoured by retrospective hate of poor Syrie and it has become an obsession," Noël noted in his diary. The obsession was
now to take a material form, following an innocent suggestion of
Glenway Wescott's that Maugham should write an autobiography.
At first dismissive of the idea, Maugham began to consider it, and
during the period of the hostilities with Liza he set to work. Naturally enough, the project was vigorously encouraged by his publishers, and also by Maugham's neighbor, Max Beaverbrook, who
scented a richly rewarding subject for serialization in the *Sunday
Express*. When finished, the book was everything Beaverbrook
could have hoped, but its content appalled Frere, who was the first
to see a typescript of *Looking Back*. It was quite clear to him that its
central theme, a vitriolic account of the author's marriage, was the
product of an unsound mind, that Maugham, in short, had taken

leave of his senses, and that he must be protected from having his dotage exposed. Honorably, he refused to publish *Looking Back,* and he persuaded Doubleday to do the same. But Beaverbrook had no such qualms. Working with the eager cooperation of Alan Searle, the work's dedicatee, Beaverbrook played his hand cleverly, persuading Maugham to add yet more revelations and organizing a sensational publicity campaign. Alan, to whom the proceeds had been made over, was delighted to have done so well out of the deal, being paid £35,000 for the serialization by the *Express* newspapers and $250,000 by *Show* magazine in America. "I am thrilled," he wrote to Beaverbrook. "It is a very pleasant feeling to have something secure for the future."

LOOKING BACK IS VISIBLY the product of a failing intelligence. In it Maugham rambles over episodes of his life, describing fairly cursorily his childhood and education, his career as a dramatist, his travels, his work in espionage; he ponders religion and philosophy, and talks a little of the visual arts; he fondly recalls his affair with Sue Jones; but it is the account he gives of his relationship with Syrie, unfettered and envenomed, that in the eyes of the world made the work both so fascinating and so shocking. His description of Syrie's relentless pursuit of him, of her giving birth in Rome under an assumed name, her attempted suicide in the face of his reluctance to marry her, the frightful quarrels during their time together, her dishonesty in her business dealings—all is retailed in a strangely bland and monotonous tone. At the end of the book, Maugham, describing himself as "a very imperfect and tormented creature," admits that "I cut a very poor figure" before adding his familiar mantra, inscribed so often before: "If I have written it, it is to rid myself of recollections which too often have given me sleepless nights, for I have learned by experience that a sure way to free myself of haunting memories is to set them down in black and white."

This time, however, the fail-safe formula failed. During the seven weeks that *Looking Back* ran in the *Sunday Express,* in September and October 1962, "All hell," as Frere remarked, "was let loose." Maugham was inundated by abusive letters, many of them anonymous. "Everyone is fully aware of the stinking, filthy life you have led," runs one typical example. "You are a perfect disgrace to Britain and the sooner you leave this island of ours, the better, together with that boy-friend of yours." But far more personally wounding was the reaction of many of his friends, to the fore those who had been also friends of Syrie's. "Entirely contemptible," said Noël Coward; "a senile and scandalous work," Graham Greene wrote in a letter to the *Daily Telegraph;* Maugham was "an obscene little toad," according to Rebecca West; Garson Kanin described the work as "shabby, sordid, embarrassing [and] a wildly faggoty thing to have done." In October, Maugham came over to London as usual, and as usual went to the Garrick. As he entered the bar on the first floor, everyone stopped talking, and after a couple of seconds several members ostentatiously walked out. Maugham was devastated. It was borne in upon him that he was to be ostracized, that he had gravely offended, had broken the English gentleman's code of conduct, a code that no one understood better than he, that he had admired, analyzed, sometimes mocked, and on the outward observance of which he had based his entire existence. With the publication of *Looking Back,* said Gore Vidal, "the ancient Maugham mined his own monument, and blew it up." Alone with Alan, he wept and wept, tortured by guilt, overcome with remorse. The two of them returned to the Mauresque in December, and Maugham never came to England again.

FOR A MAN WHO had achieved such success in life as Somerset Maugham, who had shown such wisdom, such perception in his understanding of human nature, few would have predicted an old age of almost unrelieved anguish. He began to have nightmares from which he awoke terrified, and Searle now slept in Maugham's bedroom so he could comfort him when he awoke, getting up as many as six times in the night; during the day Maugham sat for hours at a time immobilized by despair, crying uncontrollably, refusing to be consoled. Wretchedly unhappy, he was unable to find relief anywhere or in anything. Toward the end of *Looking Back* he states uncompromisingly, "I believe neither in the existence of God nor in the immortality of the soul," yet the subject of religion continued to attract and mystify him while offering neither comfort nor conviction. As he neared his ninetieth year he grew more miserably restless, compelled to travel, as though searching for the safe haven which his own home no longer provided. "The maps are out," Alan would report with a sinking heart. "He is very frail, but longs to be on the move. It is a great anxiety for me." And indeed, with Maugham confused and increasingly incontinent, it was becoming impossible to cope, even in the grandest hotels. There had been some nightmarish incidents while staying at the Vier Jahreszeiten in Munich in October 1963, leading Alan to swear, "Never again will I stir an inch without the valet and a male nurse"; and the following year a trip to Venice was such a disaster that "we had to come home two weeks early. It has finally taught me that our travelling days are over."

And yet returning to the Mauresque offered little respite. "Rarely sensible, and in acute misery," as Searle described him, Maugham knew he was dying and he longed to depart. "Poor, poor Willie," Alan wrote to Robin. "He takes his medicines with reluctance. "'Don't try to keep me alive' he begs. 'Just let me slip away.'" On his ninetieth birthday, January 25, 1964, he was photographed shuffling along the terrace well wrapped up, accompanied by a beloved dachshund, George, a present from the Freres. In a birthday interview published in the *Sunday Express,* Maugham was quoted as saying that he still grieved for his mother ("even today the pain of her passing is as keen as when it happened in our home in Paris") and that he longed for death: "I am drunk with the thought of it. It seems to me to offer me the final and absolute freedom." Occasionally old friends dropped in to see him, among them Noël Coward, who was staying nearby. "I called on Willie Maugham," he wrote in his diary on August 25, 1965, "and I am glad I did because he was wretchedly, pathetically grateful. He is living out his last days in a desperate nightmare, poor beast. He barely makes sense and, of course, he *knows* his mind has gone. I managed to cheer him a bit and certainly helped poor Alan who is going through hell."

Alan was indeed going through hell. Having cried wolf for so many years, he now had serious cause for complaint. Maugham, deaf and with failing eyesight, was helpless, hopeless, and entirely dependent on Alan for everything. To make matters worse, the old man was subject to violent changes of mood, sometimes tearful and whimpering for sex, on other occasions seemingly possessed by furies, physically attacking Searle with a strength that hardly seemed possible from such a frail and shrunken body. "I have been shut up with a madman," Alan wrote desperately to Robin. "His beastliness is beyond endurance. . . . He lives in some terrifying world of his own which must be grim if his screams and terror are anything to go by." It was Robin who came most often to the Villa, an immense comfort to Searle, who, unless there was someone else prepared to sit with Maugham, was literally a prisoner in the house; the servants refused to be left alone with their master and would have nothing to do with any nursing, feeding, washing, or cleaning up. "I have a good many very unpleasant chores to perform," Alan told Glenway Wescott. "Poor old darling, how he would have hated and loathed it all in the old days." The staff were also afraid of him: as the old man seemed physically to shrivel, so his rages became more ferocious; he was "like a malignant crab," said Robin, and even he had to summon all his courage to face his uncle at his most maniacal. Yet for Robin these last days at the Mauresque yielded their own rewards. During the hours when the old man was in his right mind, Robin questioned him industriously about his life and the people he had known, scurrying upstairs to his room afterward to write down every word of the conversation for future use. He also carefully recorded details of the clothes Maugham wore, his moods, his appearance, and even the dishes that were served at meals:

[B]lack double-breasted quilted smoking jacket with purple design. White silk shirt open at neck. Narrow black trousers. Black velvet shoes with his monogram on toes in gold braid. . . . Lace table cloth. Pink champagne . . . pea soup, chicken in aspic and green salad, figs in strawberry sauce, cheese. Dates and nuts.

And after Maugham had been put to bed, Robin would interrogate Alan, who needed little persuading to reveal the secrets that over the years Maugham had confided in him, as well as the many episodes that he himself had witnessed.

Robin's last visit was in July 1965, and it was shortly after this that Alan reached the end of his tether. "Willie is now completely out of his mind and is in a constant state of terror and misery," he wrote to Ellen Doubleday.

He rarely knows me now and wanders about the house muttering, muttering and muttering. Sometimes he talks for two or three days and nights without ceasing, and his energy is frightening.

It was now that Alan in desperation decided to make contact with Liza, begging her to come down to the Mauresque. Liza, who had not seen her father in more than four years, arrived on November 3, met at the station by Searle, who warned her that she would find Maugham "absolutely mad" and possibly violent. Despite the warning, Liza was appalled by the sight of her father, a tiny, wizened figure, his face contorted as he constantly bared his teeth and growled at her, sometimes lunging toward her, his hands like claws. It was plain he had no idea who she was. Alan told her he could no longer go on, that he was at breaking point, and they agreed that Maugham should be brought to England, where he could be certified as insane. That evening on the drive back to Beaulieu Alan burst into tears and was still crying as Liza's train drew out of the station.

Events moved swiftly after Liza's departure. At the beginning of December, Maugham, tripping on a corner of carpet, fell and cut his head, and shortly afterward he developed pneumonia. An ambulance was called and he was taken to the Anglo-American Hospital in Nice, where he could be looked after by his personal physician, Dr. Rosanoff. Here Maugham remained for more than a week, lying semicomatose in a ground-floor room whose French windows looked out onto a garden and a distant view of the Mediterranean. Camped outside the main entrance of the hospital was a growing crowd of reporters, photographers, and cameramen, to whom a daily briefing was delivered with considerable élan by the flamboyant Dr. Rosanoff, proud of his sudden celebrity status and enjoying every moment of his performance. Meanwhile in his hospital room Maugham grew restless, disturbed by the strong mistral blowing outside that rattled the windows. A young English nurse who came in to sit with him found her patient anxious and confused, desperately in need of comfort. When she tucked in his blankets, he asked her to get into bed with him. "It wasn't sexual," she said, "he wanted comfort"; he wanted to be held as his mother had held him when he was a small child, and she fetched a soft bolster and laid it up against his back, which seemed to soothe him. During the early hours of December 16, Maugham died, barely a month short of his ninety-second birthday. The doctor on duty was summoned. *"Il est mort,"* he confirmed. Alan was telephoned and within the hour arrived from the Mauresque. Quickly and under cover of darkness Maugham's body was carried into the car and driven back to the villa, from where during the course of the morning it was announced to the world that Somerset Maugham had died in his bed at home, thus avoiding the autopsy that would otherwise have been required by French law.

The body was laid out, and for several days neighbors came in to pay their respects as the press descended en masse. The cremation took place in Marseilles on December 20, with only Alan present. In a stupor of weariness and grief he sat in a waiting room at the crematorium for what seemed like hours, holding the small urn he had brought to receive the ashes. Eventually a man appeared carrying a tray covered by a linen cloth. Removing the cloth, he revealed several long grayish-white bones, too big to have been consumed in the fire, and asked if he might break them up so that they would fit into the casket. Producing a hammer from his pocket, he went to work with enthusiasm, at which point Searle, overcome, ran out into the street and vomited. Two days later, on December 22, Maugham's ashes were interred outside the Maugham Library at the King's School, Canterbury, the ceremony presided over by the headmaster and by the dean of Canterbury, in the presence of boys from the school and a small group of mourners led by Liza, her husband, and her four children.

When Maugham's will was read, Alan Searle learned he was to be a very rich man. The Villa Mauresque went to Liza, who also kept the original financial settlements made for herself and her family. Robin, too, retained his trust fund, the income from which he supplemented by writing a series of memoirs of his uncle; within weeks of Maugham's death he had outed him as a homosexual in a mass circulation Sunday newspaper, and continued to supply the market with more of the same, in *Conversations with Willie, Somerset and All the Maughams, Escape from the Shadows,* and so on. There were bequests of £2,000 each for Annette and for Jean the chauffeur, and Maugham's portrait by Edouard MacAvoy was willed to the city of Nice. Everything else, the contents of the villa, all money, all investments, all royalties, all proceeds from the sale of manuscripts, was left to Alan for his lifetime, the residue after his death to go to the Royal Literary Fund in London for the relief of impoverished writers. Yet despite all his scheming, Alan derived little pleasure from his immense bequest. With a manservant to look after him he moved into an expensive apartment in Monte Carlo, which he filled with treasures from the Mauresque; as he had done with his employer, he continued to travel, staying in luxurious suites at the best hotels in London, Venice, and New York, where he spent extravagantly on boys, clothes, and enormous meals. And yet Alan was not happy: he was lonely, he missed Maugham and the glamorous life they had led together, and he soon succumbed to ill health; he grew enormously fat and suffered painfully from arthritis and later from Parkinson's disease, which eventually confined him to a wheelchair. Shortly before he died in 1985, aged eighty, he confessed to Ann Fleming, one of the few of Maugham's friends who kept in touch, that he bitterly regretted having caused such trouble.

After his death, the reputation of Somerset Maugham suffered the inevitable decline of renowned writers, the decline that especially follows a long career that has been lived much in the public eye and in tune with its times. In the 1960s the times were rapidly changing, and few cared to read then of the old order, of the days of Empire, of District Officers in the jungle or the wiles of wives in repressive Edwardian marriages. Maugham would not have been surprised. "The first little splutter of interest that follows a person's death in the case of a writer is followed by some years of neglect," he wrote in 1946. "Then if there is in his work anything of enduring value, interest in him is renewed. But the dead period may well last twenty or thirty years." This was prescient, for the last couple of decades have seen a remarkable revival of the work of this extraordinary man. Maugham learned very young to be wary and secretive in his personal life, which was full of pain, but in his writing he found happiness and release. He described the act of creation as "the most enthralling of human activities," the one place where the writer can find solace, "can tell his secret yet not betray it." His love for his art, his single-minded dedication, made him one of the most popular and prolific writers who ever lived, and it is safe to say now that he will again hold generations in thrall, that his place is assured: Somerset Maugham, the great teller of tales.

ACKNOWLEDGMENTS

...

I am enormously grateful to the many people and institutions who have helped me during the writing of this biography. I would like in particular to express my gratitude to the Royal Literary Fund, holders of the copyright and executors of the literary estate of Somerset Maugham, and also to the trustees of the literary estate, for allowing me to quote freely from Maugham's work and correspondence. Second, I would like to put on record my heartfelt thanks for the generosity of Neil and Reiden Jenman, who offered me the most warmhearted hospitality while allowing me unrestricted access to their extensive Maugham collection. I also thank Harry Frere for his kindness in making available the transcripts of his mother's conversations with Liza Maugham.

I owe sincere thanks to the following for their contributions to this book: Kate Amcott-Wilson, Mark Amory, Alan Anderson, Prof. William Baker, Frith Banbury, Nicolas Barker, Jonathan Bates, Michael Bloch, Adrian Bridgewater, Katherine Bucknell, Michael Burn, Peter Burton, John Byrne, Comtesse Chandon de Briailles, Aleid Channing, Anne Channing, Colette Clark, John Clay, Lisa Cohen, John Coldstream, Sally Connely, Bryan Connon, Robert Conquest, Anthony Curtis, Caroline Cuthbert, Timothy D'Arch-Smith, Lady Daubeny, Richard Davenport-Hines, Mary Dawson, Winton Dean, Nelson Doubleday, Jr., Charles Duff, Lord Dunluce, Sue Fox, David Freeman, Jean Frere, Lord Glendevon, the Earl of Gowrie, John Haffenden, Nicholas Haslam, Doreen

Hawkins, Peter Haxton, Tim Heald, Belinda Hollyer, Jonathan Hope, Glenn Horowitz, Barry Humphries, Bruce Hunter, Paul Hunter, Alan Judd, Zbigniew Kantorosinski, P. J. Kavanagh, H. K. Kelland, John Kenworthy-Browne, Alice Leader, Andrew Lycett, Diana Marr-Johnson, Chris Maxse, James McDonnell, Joan Morley, Patrick O'Connor, Nicolas Paravicini, June Pearson, Paul Pollak, Tom Sargant, Prof. Lewis Sawin, Tony Scotland, David Shackleton, Stella Shawzin, Craig V. Showalter, Malcolm Sinclair, Tom Stacey, James Stourton, David Twiston-Davies, Hugo Vickers, C. M. Vines, Michael Watkins, Vivienne Waugh, Christopher Wilkinson, Lindy Woodhead, Howard Woolmer, David Worthington, and Samantha Wyndham.

Among the following libraries and archives I would like to single out for special thanks the Howard Gotlieb Archival Research Center at Boston University and the Harry Ransom Humanities Research Center at the University of Texas at Austin.

I also thank:

Bancroft Library, University of California, Berkeley
Barnardo's, London
Beinecke Rare Book and Manuscript Library, Yale University
Berg Collection, New York Public Library
Bodleian Library, Oxford University
British Library
Cornell University, New York
University of Delaware Library
Eton College Library
Fales Library, New York University
Garrick Club
Jacob Rader Center of American Jewish Archives
Keble College, Oxford University
Kent County Council Centre for Kentish Studies
King's School, Canterbury
Library of Congress, Washington, D.C.
Lilly Library, Indiana University, Bloomington, Indiana
London Library

Mander & Mitchenson Theatre Collection, Jerwood Library of the Performing Arts, Trinity College of Music, Greenwich

Margaret Herrick Library, Academy of Motion Picture Arts and Sciences, Beverly Hills, California

University of Maryland Libraries

McFarlin Library, University of Tulsa

National Trust

New York Public Library

Princeton University Library

Public Record Office, the National Archives, Kew

Random House Group Archive

Z. Smith Reynolds Library, Wake Forest University, Winston-Salem, North Carolina

St. John's College Library, Cambridge University

Stanford University Library

University of Sussex Library

Texas A&M University

Victoria & Albert Museum Theatre Collections

Wake Forest University Library, North Carolina

Warburg Institute

Wellcome Library

Whitstable Museum

I am immensely grateful to Julie Kavanagh for her kind support during the writing of this book and for her unfailing editorial eye. I would also like to give warm thanks to Professor T. F. Staley and Professor R. F. Foster for their invaluable criticism, encouragement, and advice.

Every effort has been made to trace the holders of copyright, and I very much regret if inadvertent omissions have been made; these can be rectified in any future editions.

SOURCE NOTES

...

ABBREVIATIONS

Bancroft: Bancroft Library, University of California, Berkeley

Beinecke: Beinecke Rare Book and Manuscript Library, Yale University

Berg: The Henry W. and Albert A. Berg Collection of English and American Literature, New York Public Library, Astor, Lenox, and Tilden Foundations

Bodleian: Bodleian Library, Oxford

Cornell: Cornell University, New York

Delaware: University of Delaware

Fales: Fales Library, New York University

Garrick: The Garrick Club, London

HGARC: Howard Gotlieb Archival Research Center, Boston University

HRHRC: Harry Ransom Humanities Research Center, University of Texas at Austin

Jenman: Neil and Reiden Jenman Collection, New South Wales, Australia

KSC: The King's School, Canterbury

Lilly: Lilly Library, University of Indiana

Margaret Herrick Library: Margaret Herrick Library, Academy of Motion Picture Arts and Sciences, Beverly Hills, California

Maryland: Glenway Wescott Collection, Special Collections, University of Maryland Libraries

NYPL: Manuscripts and Archives Division, New York Public Library, Astor, Lenox, and Tilden Foundations

Princeton: Manuscripts Division, Department of Rare Books and Special Collections, Princeton University Library

PRO: Public Record Office, National Archives, Kew

Random House: Random House Group Archive, Northamptonshire

Stanford: Department of Special Collections and University Archives,

Stanford University Libraries, Maugham (William S.) Collection
1921–1979 (M0013)
Texas A&M: Texas A&M University, Texas
Wake Forest: Z. Smith Reynolds Library, Wake Forest University,
Winston-Salem, North Carolina

CHAPTER 1: A BLACKSTABLE BOYHOOD

6   *"une femme charmante" Gil Blas: Hebdomadaire Illustré* (Paris), February 6, 1882.
8   "[The servant] took the child" *Of Human Bondage,* 5.
9   *"cher papa, chere maman" Somerset Maugham,* Jeffrey Meyers, 10.
12 "My father was a stranger" *Somerset and All the Maughams,* 110.
13 "It was the end of a home" *At the End of the Day,* 19.
     "[the] one link" *Somerset and All the Maughams,* 118.
14 "I shall never forget the misery" Ibid., 117.
     "He had had so little love" *A Writer's Notebook,* 261.
     "he was very narrow-minded" *At the End of the Day,* 19.
15 "The vicar, having said grace" Ibid., 17.
16 "I'll hear you say it at tea time" *Looking Back,* 10.
17 "His aunt was not sorry" *Of Human Bondage,* 29.
18 "His guardians would rigidly take care" letter of Hubert Collar to Robert Cordell, August 2, 1961, Texas A&M.
18 "There was a long queue" *Somerset and All the Maughams,* 121.
21 "the most delightful habit in the world" *Of Human Bondage,* 38.
22 "He did not know" Ibid., 38.
23 "Tell him I stammer, Uncle" *Looking Back,* 11.
     "His heart beat so" *Of Human Bondage,* 45.
     "I have never forgotten the roar of laughter" *Somerset and All the Maughams,* 117.
24 "that engaging come-hitherness" *The Summing Up,* 46.
25 "that he seemed for a moment" *Of Human Bondage,* 78.
     "He began his work," Ibid., 68.
     "got a cup of coffee" Ibid., 60.
26 "I adored him" *The Cantuarian,* December 1965.
     "There was a wonderfully cobwebbed feeling" *The Vagrant Mood* (Mandarin 1998), 192.
27 "In fact, I did not like either" *Cakes and Ale,* 64.
     "accepted the conventions" Ibid., 87.
     "We thought London people vulgar" Ibid., 36.
28 "He prayed with all the power of his soul" *Of Human Bondage,* 57.
29 "someone I went to bed with" Alan Searle interview with Robert Calder, March 16, 1977, Jenman.

29 "I chose the name Ashenden" WSM to Mollie Ashenden, February 2, 1954, KSC.
30 "I made up my mind" *Looking Back,* 13.
    "I was small for my age" Ibid., 13.
    "His school-days were over" Ibid., 13.

CHAPTER 2: AT ST. THOMAS'S HOSPITAL

31 "He did not much like me" *The Summing Up,* 58.
35 "the delights of those easy" Ibid., 187.
36 "the glitter of cheap restaurants" Ibid., 85.
38 "a good deal of gossip" *The Gentleman in the Parlour,* 189.
39 "I tried to persuade myself" *Escape from the Shadows,* Robin Maugham, 232.
    "I complained of the abnormality" *The Summing Up,* 67.
    "[I] made few friends there" Ibid., 60.
40 "I was writing" WSM to *The Academy,* September 13, 1997, Princeton.
    "[James] was greeted with such an outburst" *The Vagrant Mood,* 163.
41 "I can never forget how kind" WSM to Wentworth Huyshe, August 30, 1997, HRHRC.
43 "treated like a crowned head" WSM to Norman Horne, March 19, 1937, Lilly.
    "I was bitterly disappointed" *Purely for My Pleasure,* 6.
    "I lived laborious days" *The Painted Veil,* viii.
    "such was my innocence" Ibid.
46 "The other day I went into the theatre" *A Writer's Notebook,* 31.
    "the most enchanting spot" *The Summing Up,* 96.
47 "I thought it all grand" Ibid., 96.
    "Its reputation as a decomposer" *Extraordinary Women,* Compton Mackenzie (Secker, 1929), 25.
49 "dear companion of my lonely youth" *A Bibliography of the Writings of William Somerset Maugham,* Frederick T. Bason, 9.
50 "woman is an animal that micturates" *A Writer's Notebook,* 13.
    "up stinking alleys" *Liza of Lambeth,* vi.
52 "There is some ability in this" Edward Garnett, July 20, 1996, Berg.
53 "I had at that time a great admiration" *Liza of Lambeth,* vii.
    "I described without addition" *The Summing Up,* 161.
    "the first of the realistic descriptions" WSM to Paul Dottin, September 14, 1926, HRHRC.
    "A very clever realistic study" *W. Somerset Maugham: The Critical Heritage,* ed. Anthony Curtis and John Whitehead, 22.
54 "Unwin is indeed a most troublesome person" Charles Scribner, June 14, 1997, Princeton.

54   "The whole book reeks of the pot-house" *Daily Mail,* September 7, 1997.
      "great and well-deserved success" *The St. Thomas's Hospital Gazette,* June
      1898.
      "I've just finished reading *Liza*" July 20, 1997, *The Collected Letters of
      Joseph Conrad,* vol. I, 1861–1897, ed. Frederick R. Karl and Laurence
      Davies (Cambridge University Press, 1983), 361.

55   "I have not yet had an opportunity" WSM to *Academy* September 13,
      1997, Princeton.

56   "a most unpleasant book" private collection.
      "He had no feeling for the old man" *Of Human Bondage,* 626.
      "I learned pretty well everything I know" WSM to Barbara Kurz, April
      1961, HGARC.
      "I am sorry I abandoned medicine" *The Merry-Go-Round* (Penguin,
      1976), 126.
      "I told him that I was throwing up medicine" *Liza of Lambeth,* viii.

57   "I was no longer interested in the slums" *The Summing Up,* 161.

CHAPTER 3: A WRITER BY INSTINCT

58   "Life was before him" *Of Human Bondage,* 671.

59   "I came to it after weary years" *The Land of the Blessed Virgin,* 51.

60   "In Spain the blood of youth is very hot" Ibid., 48.

61   "But when I write of Spanish women" Ibid., 84.
      "a young thing with green eyes" *The Summing Up,* 98.
      "life was too pleasant" Ibid.

62   "[Unwin] did me thoroughly in the eye" WSM to J. B. Pinker,
      September 22, 1909, HRHRC.
      "Seduced by this bad advice" *The Summing Up,* 163.

63   "So far as we can see" Edward Garnett readers' reports, Berg.
      "[Mr. Maugham] has written a good novel" *Spectator,* August 6, 1898.
      "He [Payne] was very good-looking" *Looking Back,* 25.

64   "I had a natural lucidity" *The Summing Up,* 22.
      "It is true that 'Stephen Carey' " WSM to Maurice Colles, November
      10, 1898, Berg.

65   "are all a little flat" Edward Garnett readers' reports, Berg.
      "at the time was not very familiar" *Liza of Lambeth,* xvi.

66   "an average book, fairly readable" *London Bookman,* July 1899.
      "The best writing we have yet seen" *Athenaeum,* June 17, 1899.
      "Mr. Maugham begins to be interesting" *Academy,* July 1, 1899.
      "The world is an entirely different place" *A Writer's Notebook,* 221.
      "almost continuously in love" WSM to Kate Bruce, April 3, 1929, Berg.
      "He is a fearfully emotional man" *Violet: The Story of the Irrepressible
      Violet Hunt,* Barbara Belford (Simon & Schuster, 1990), 116.

67   "a little strong" WSM to Maurice Colles, November 10, 1898, Berg.

67   "too indecent for publication" *Colles v. Maugham* in the High Court of
       Justice, King's Bench Division, 1908, HRC.
       "finally I have erased" WSM to Maurice Colles, July 31, 1899, Berg.
       "I should have lost a subject" *The Summing Up*, 187.
       "as merely an insignificant curiosity" speech to the Library of Congress,
       1950.

68   "the most interesting and consistently amusing" *The Summing Up*, 4.
       "I never ceased to be fascinated" *The Moon and Sixpence*, 10.

69   "a curious little home life" *The Water Beetle*, Nancy Mitford (Hamish
       Hamilton, 1962), 41.
       "He was not what people call a man's man" *The Vagrant Mood*, 28.
       "innately and intensely frivolous" WSM to Dean, February 10, 1950,
       Maryland.

70   "I prefer to call the conveyance" *The Vagrant Mood*, 39.
       "Do you like cigars?" Ibid., 38.

71   "Often it turned out to very pleasant" Raymond Mortimer interview
       with Robert Calder, November 2, 1972, Jenman.
       "You were different" *Looking Back*, 27.

72   "the first rent" *A Choice of Kipling's Prose*, xx.
       "The touch of her fingers" *The Hero*, 40.
       "is ugly and beastly" Ibid., 208.

73   "Maugham will doubtless" *The Maugham Enigma*, 141.

74   "Women are like chickens" *Mrs. Craddock*, 88.

75   "My recollection lingers with most pleasure" *Books and Bookmen*, May 1922.
       "[Gerald] was certainly not at all shy" *Mrs. Craddock*, 224.
       "[If] you are afraid to look life in the face" *Bookman*, December 1902.
       "a substantial success" *Liza of Lambeth*, xviii.

CHAPTER 4: LE CHAT BLANC

77   "it seemed less difficult" *The Summing Up*, 109.

79   "The shriek of execration" *Ibsen*, by Michael Meyer (Penguin 1985), 686.
       "Went to the first night" Kate Bruce unpublished ms, private collection.
       "Not for a long time" *Sunday Special*, March 1, 1903.

80   "[The second act] is admirably conceived" *Saturday Review*, February 28,
       1903.
       "I was not satisfied" *The Summing Up*, 111.
       "There is no reason to suppose" *Saturday Review*, March 5, 1904.
       "I can see now the shy young author" *Theatrical Companion*, by
       Raymond Mander and Joe Mitchenson, 20.

81   "Harry told me that my plays" *Conversations with Willie*, 56.
       "He needed a lot of understanding" *Somerset and All the Maughams*, 163.
       "Very much homosexual" Rebecca West interview with Robert Calder
       September 14, 1976, Jenman.

82   "I'm sure it wasn't only failure" *Somerset and All the Maughams,* 165.
"pale and grave" unpublished ms, private collection.
"violently pessimistic" *The Summing Up,* 27.
"perhaps they had insulated" unpublished ms, private collection.

83   "Times are very hard" WSM to Huyshe, nd, HRHRC.
"If you hear of anyone" WSM to Maurice Colles, nd, HGARC.
"Behold three short stories" WSM to Maurice Colles, July 3, 1904, Berg.

84   "an honourable condition" *The Magician,* vi.
"The whole thing was, of course" *The Unexpected Years,* Laurence Housman (Cape, 1937), 202.

85   "chiefly, I think, because it was called" WSM to Edward Marsh, April 1, 1943, Berg.
"She combined a masculine intelligence" *The Moon and Sixpence,* 12.

86   "If she had been beautiful and sane" *Henry James,* Leon Edel (Collins, 1987), 226.

87   "didn't quite come off" WSM to David Cecil, September 1957, Jenman.
"you, my boy, are not one" *Saturday Review,* April 4, 1908.
"He little knew" *Plays,* vol. I, vii.

88   "a strong man, of no very easy temper" *The Merry-Go-Round,* 35.
"Most of what one writes" WSM to Violet Hunt, nd, Cornell.
"because I was at the time much taken" *The Summing Up,* 164.

89   "quite the most dazzling figure" *Odd Man Out,* Douglas Goldring (Chapman & Hall, 1935), 54.
"We took a great liking to each other" Harry Philips to Joseph Dobrinsky; September 16, 1966, Texas A&M.
"She had a certain hold over him" *The Merry-Go-Round,* 171.
"Money was like a sixth sense" *The Summing Up,* 112.
"I see that you have charged me" WSM to Maurice Colles, August 28, 1904, Lilly.

90   "[Mr. Maugham] has his pen well under control" *Times Literary Supplement,* May 26, 1905.
"I wrote with jealousy gnawing" *Liza of Lambeth,* xiii.
"It was all very nice" *The Magician,* vi.

91   "When I am with my brother" WSM to Violet Hunt, nd, Berg.

92   "his whole face was just one colour" *Sunday Times,* January 24, 1954.
"Both of us obstinately refused" Ibid.
"to my shame" *The Magician,* vii.

93   "I am very sorry, though by no means surprised" WSM to Gerald Kelly, July 26, 1905, HGARC.
"Willie was a duck" *Times,* March 18, 1969.
"who has the ingenious idea" WSM to Gerald Kelly, nd, HGARC.
"I cannot say that I was his secretary" Harry Philips to Joseph Dobrinsky, September 16, 1966, Texas A&M.

94   "He was exceedingly kind" Ibid.

95   "I suspect he was a tragic figure" *Old Friends,* Clive Bell (Chatto &
     Windus, 1956), 164.
     "but unfortunately he took an immediate dislike" *Looking Back,* 28.
     "coldly and bitingly virulent" *The Vagrant Mood,* 183.
     "After a moment's hesitation" *Looking Back,* 28.
     "a bed bug, on which a sensitive man" *The Spirit of Solitude: An
     Autohagiography,* vol. II, Aleister Crowley (Mandrake Press, 1929), 243.

96   "I took an immediate dislike to him" *The Magician,* viii.
     "like a managing clerk" *The Vagrant Mood,* 183.

97   "Willie—with his impeccable French accent" *Sunday Times,* January 24,
     1954.
     "I am dreadfully afraid of being ridiculous" WSM to Arthur St. John
     Adcock, May 14, 1908, Lilly.
     "I've told her about you" *The Vagrant Mood,* 186.
     "a very lovable man" Ibid., 183.

98   "I never saw Maugham moved" *Violet,* 116.
     "I was somewhat ashamed" Harry Philips to Joseph Dobrinsky,
     September 16, 1966, Texas A&M.
     "I miss you sadly" WSM to Gerald Kelly, April 15, 1905, HGARC.

99   "I think I have got you a new client" Arnold Bennett to J. B. Pinker,
     June 11, 1905, HRHRC.

100 "I think we must agree to differ" WSM to Maurice Colles, July 29,
     1905, Beinecke.
     "& I imagine they will" WSM to J. B. Pinker, July 9, 1905, HRHRC.
     "We have been here nearly a week" WSM to Gerald Kelly, nd, HGARC.

102 "In the process of making a complete failure" *Final Edition,* E. F. Benson
     (Longmans Green, 1940), 106.
     "I'm sure a lot of people will think you" WSM to Gerald Kelly,
     September 19, 1905, HGARC.

103 "It was there I decided" Harry Philips to Joseph Dobrinsky, September
     16, 1966, Texas A&M.
     "one places all one's love" *A Writer's Notebook,* 42.
     "By the time I received the money" *The Summing Up,* 164.

104 "Has *The Lady's Realm*" WSM to J. B. Pinker, July 3, 1906, HRHRC.
     "I *do not like* it" WSM to Violet Hunt, April 10, 1907, Berg.

105 "The people were too heroic" WSM to Gerald Kelly, March 25, 1907,
     HGARC.
     "[and] Maugham told me afterwards" *Whatever Goes Up,* George C.
     Tyler (Bobbs-Merrill, 1934), 208.

106 "feeling pretty melancholy" Ibid., 209.
     "I began to think" *Plays,* vol. I (Heinemann, 1931), viii.
     "Your letter filled me with exultation" WSM to Golding Bright,
     September 16, 1907, HRHRC.

106 "I went to Cook's" *Plays,* vol. I (Heinemann, 1931), ix.

107 "[I was] very short of money" *A Bibliography,* Raymond Toole Stott, 274.

CHAPTER 5: ENGLAND'S DRAMATIST

108 "The years between the beginning" *A Short View of the English Stage 1900–1926,* James Agate (Herbert Jenkins, 1926), 68.

"I reflected upon the qualities" *Plays,* vol. I, vii.

109 "Now for the delicate soft bloom" Ibid., 73.

"D'you suppose I don't know" Ibid., 89.

110 "Exhilarating entertainment" *Times,* October 28, 1907.

"a delicious evening" *Academy,* November 2, 1907.

"as an accomplished dramatist" *Twenty-Five,* Beverley Nichols (Penguin, 1935), 233.

"ate crow" *Whatever Goes Up,* 210.

111 "I happened to look up" *The Summing Up,* 115.

"My success was spectacular" Ibid., 115.

"I was much photographed" Ibid., 116.

112 "I thoroughly enjoyed myself" *Looking Back,* 36.

"Great ladies cultivate those" *Plays,* vol. III, viii.

"Who is Edgar Wallace?" *The Vagrant Mood,* 197.

"When the ladies retired" *Cakes and Ale,* 3.

113 "One has to go back" *Sunday Times,* May 3, 1908.

"the hero of the year" *Saturday Review,* June 20, 1908.

"light as a feather" *Sunday Times,* March 29, 1908.

"suddenly became much sought after" Harry Philips to Joseph Dobrinsky, September 16, 1966, Texas A&M.

114 "I tried to get a small part" WSM to Gerald Kelly, February 20, 1908, HGARC.

"she had the most beautiful smile" *Looking Back,* 30.

115 "I have often acted a passion" *The Summing Up,* 77.

116 "a woman of whom I had been extremely fond" "Somerset Maugham," Graham Young, *Daily Mail,* January 27, 1953.

"came of common family" *For Love of Painting: The Life of Sir Gerald Kelly KCVO, PRA,* Derek Hudson (Peter Davies, 1975), 51.

"had a very happy love affair" Gerald Kelly to Richard Cordell, August 20, 1959, Lilly.

"the most perfectly realized woman" Gerald Kelly to WSM, nd, HGARC.

"I opened the door" *Cakes and Ale,* 139.

117 "desperately in love" *For Love of Painting,* 51.

"She posed beautifully" Gerald Kelly interview with Robert Calder, February 4, 1970, Jenman.

118   "Noticed in myself" *Journals,* vol. I, 287.
      "D'you know him at all?" *The Summing Up,* 117.
119   "I regularly wrote one act" WSM to Dobrinsky, August 1, 1957, Texas
      A&M.
      "I hated poverty" *A Writer's Notebook,* 73.
      "the great, the insinuating" *Two Made Their Bed,* Louis Marlow
      (Gollancz 1929), 9.
      "Sometimes after an evening with Willie" *Books and Bookmen,* May 1980.
120   "Practically nothing remains" WSM to Maurice Colles, November 29,
      1907, Jenman.
      "I have always thought that publishers" *Liza of Lambeth,* xii.
121   "I, as you know, make a point" WSM to Gerald Kelly, March 25, 1907,
      HGARC.
      "I wanted to consult you" WSM to J. B. Pinker, October 5, 1906,
      HRHRC.
      "[*The Magician*] would never" *Liza of Lambeth,* xx.
122   "I hear that Maugham has crucified us" *Roderic O'Conor,* Jonathan
      Benington (Irish Academic Press, 1992), 95.
      "an appreciation of my genius" *The King of the Shadow Realm: Aleister
      Crowley, His Life and Magic,* John Symonds (Duckworth, 1989), 129.
      "I had never supposed" *The Spirit of Solitude,* 242.
123   "the many things in the East" *The Magician,* 35.
      "I daresay you are quite right" WSM to Violet Hunt, December 31,
      1906, Berg.
      "with the title SON OF A BITCH" WSM to Gerald Kelly, nd, HGARC.
      "a real thrill of horror" *Spectator,* December 12, 1908.
124   "I am amorous of thy body" *The Magician,* 98.
      "You are a perfect dear" *Robbie Ross: Oscar Wilde's True Love,* Jonathan
      Fryer (Constable, 2000), 200.
125   "The most amusing man" *The Vagrant Mood,* 173.
      "I didn't want to hurt his feelings" WSM to David Cecil, nd, Jenman.
      "I received the impression" *The Vagrant Mood,* 174.
126   "They were very gay parties" WSM to David Cecil, nd, Jenman.
      "Her conversation was artificial" *Noble Essences,* 130.
      "*Write a light comedy at once*" *Wonderful Sphinx: The Biography of Ada
      Leverson,* Julie Speedie (Virago, 1993), 166.
127   "My dear Sphynx, It is too kind" WSM to Ada Leverson, July 2, 1909,
      Beinecke.
      "a great honour" Ibid., April 23, 1908.
      "[Maugham's] visits were looked forward to" *The Sphinx and Her Circle:
      A Biographical Sketch of Ada Leverson 1862–1933,* Violet Wyndham
      (Deutsch, 1963), 77.
      "I wish you would ask me" WSM to Ada Leverson, nd, Beinecke.
      " 'something nice' . . . because the author" *The Sphinx and Her Circle,* 167.

128   "My dear Sphinx, I am very sorry" Ibid.

129   "I want to tell you how glad I am" WSM to Charles Frohman, January 28, 1909, HRHRC.
"the hurried lunch at a restaurant" *The Summing Up*, 101.
"I tried to go to my own first nights" Ibid., 105.

130   "I read that I had neither decorum" *Plays,* vol II, vi.
"I have never been able" *The Summing Up* ms, HRHRC.
"she was not a particularly good actress" *Looking Back*, 48.
"the stoic and impeccable maid" *Sunday Times,* January 10, 1909.

131   "All my friends had been to bed with her" *Looking Back,* 49.
"[was] the only man she ever really loved" *For Love of Painting,* 51.
"There was no one I liked better" *Looking Back,* 49.

133   "He behaved like anybody else" *The Limit,* Ada Leverson (Grant Richards, 1911), 51.
"who is coarse and common" Ibid., 219.

134   "I am neither so happy" WSM to Gerald Kelly, nd, HGARC.
"Really it is with the greatest difficulty" Ibid., April 23, 1909.

135   "the fantastic conventions and prejudices" Gerald Kelly to Reginald Pound, Janury 26, 1953, Berg.
"To me England has been a country" *The Summing Up,* 95.
"An amiable person has offered" WSM to Gerald Kelly, March 25, 1907, HGARC.
"I met an Egyptian pasha" Ibid., September 9, 1907.
"a living link with Oscar" Louis Wilkinson to Llewellyn Powys, March 8, 1939, private collection.

136   "If light comedy is the only form" *Saturday Review,* January 9, 1909.
"They were just cynical enough" *William Somerset Maugham: The English Maupassant,* Desmond MacCarthy (Heinemann, 1934), 4.
"The critics accused me" *The Summing Up,* 116.
"The intelligentsia, of which" Ibid.

137   "I am tired & bored" WSM to Golding Bright, October 20, 1909, HRHRC.
"I was happy, I was prosperous" *Of Human Bondage,* 2.
"one of London's wittiest bachelors" *The Celebrity Circus,* Elsa Maxwell (W. H. Allen, 1964), 20.
"[He] had started to dress himself" *The Pleasant Years,* 135.

138   "You will not know 6 Chesterfield Street" WSM to Charles Frohman, nd, HRHRC.
"with the reserve and detachment" *William Somerset Maugham: The English Maupassant,* 4.
"still talked as though" *The Summing Up,* 2.
("My dear Mrs. Allhusen, You are a faithless woman") WSM to Dorothy Allhusen, nd, Beinecke.

139   "Thank you so much" Ibid., nd, Garrick.

139   "I want to make a compact with you" *Looking Back,* 36.
       "My dear Sphynx, Pray thank your friend" WSM to Ada Leverson,
       February 21, 1910, Beinecke.

140   "during the dreary time of public mourning" WSM to Violet Hunt, nd,
       Berg.
       "is one of the greatest successes" WSM to J. B. Pinker, February 12,
       1909, HRHRC.
       "I am sailing by the Caronia" WSM to Charles Frohman, October 9,
       1910, HRHRC.
       "like Christopher Columbus" WSM to Golding Bright, October 16,
       1909, HRHRC.

CHAPTER 6: SYRIE

142   "host of social entertainments" *New York Times,* November 5, 1914.
       "We were not members" *With a Feather on My Nose,* Billie Burke (Peter
       Davies, 1950), 91.

143   "there was never the least frankness" *Continual Lessons,* 93.
       "The great novelists, even in seclusion" *The Vagrant Mood,* 168.
       "I protested that I was perfectly capable" Ibid., 166.

144   "I think it possible" WSM to Gerald Kelly, nd, HGARC.

145   "I shall still be able" Ibid.
       "Howard has been very kind" Ibid.
       "one of the best things you have done" Ibid.
       "I have never been so comfortable" Ibid.

146   "I have half a mind to join you in Burmah" WSM to Gerald Kelly, nd,
       HGARC.
       "After submitting myself for some years" *Of Human Bondage,* 2.
       "I had all that stuff choking me" WSM to Joseph C. Smythe, nd,
       Jenman.

147   "It is a great satisfaction" WSM to Gerald Kelly, nd, HGARC.

148   "He simply couldn't believe" Robin Maugham unpublished diaries,
       Beinecke.
       "The teeming memories" *Of Human Bondage,* 2.

149   "His insignificance was turned to power" Ibid., 603.
       "it was absurd to care" Ibid., 309.

150   "Willie used my stuff" Gilbert Clark, May 1914, Jenman.

151   "he exercised peculiar skill" *Of Human Bondage,* 259.
       "I am aware that in the past" WSM to William Heinemann, August 6,
       1914, Random House.

152   "I am sorry to have been so fussy" Ibid.
       "Were I given freedom of choice" *Chronicles of Barabbas 1884–1934,*
       George H. Doran (Harcourt, Brace, 1935), 148.
       "Here is a novel" *New Republic,* December 25, 1915.

153   "partly on account of the weather" *Charles Frohman,* 407.
        "I want a new play from you" Ibid., 270.
        "I well remembered the shock" *Plays,* vol. II, xiii.
154   "a good deal of discomfort" WSM to Gerald Kelly, June 1, 1913,
        HGARC.
        "that curious and intense life" *Plays,* vol. II, xiii.
        "My God, what a life they lead" WSM to Mabel Beardsley, December
        29, 1912, Jenman.
155   "I give her board and lodging" *Plays,* vol. II, 247.
        "For God's sake take it" Ibid., 298.
156   "the audience of course knew nothing" WSM to Gerald Kelly,
        December 3, 1913, HGARC.
        "the leading part loses" Ibid.
        "was a beautifully written but dreary" *With a Feather on My Nose,* 98.
        "No Canadian man would dream" *Daily Bulletin* (Edmonton), April 10,
        1914.
157   "If I meant to marry" *The Summing Up,* 190.
158   "I've come to ask you" *Looking Back,* 48.
        "My schemes for going round the world" WSM to Gerald Kelly,
        December 3, 1913, HGARC.
159   "I guessed at once" *Looking Back,* 48.
        ("I knew how careless she was") Ibid.
160   "It happened that I had nothing" Ibid., 56.
        "I wish we didn't have to go" Ibid.
161   "She hoped I would come" Ibid., 57.
        "After that I saw Syrie" Ibid., 58.
166   "a courtesan just past her prime" Glenway Wescott interview with Ted
        Morgan, Jenman.
        "the most charming man in London" Ibid.
167   "It was all very delightful" *Looking Back,* 61.
        "Uncle Willie brought Mrs. Welcome" Kate Bruce unpublished ms,
        private collection.
168   "I didn't want to tell you" *Looking Back,* 61.
169   "I have got a great deal to tell you" WSM to Gerald Kelly, May 4, 1914,
        HGARC.
        "they had tastes in common" *Always Afternoon,* Faith Compton
        Mackenzie (Collins, 1943), 90.
170   "The bundle of papers that arrived" *As Much As I Dare,* Faith Compton
        Mackenzie (Collins, 1938), 269.
        "treated poor Brooks very badly" Compton Mackenzie to Grenville
        Cook, May 1, 1966, Lilly.
        "He had fine perceptions" *Final Edition,* 243.
171   "I don't know what I shall do" *My Life and Times: Octave Four 1907–1915,*
        Faith Compton Mackenzie (Chatto & Windus, 1965), 233.

171 "To me the very shape of England" *A Writer's Notebook,* 128.

172 "She made me feel a brute" *Looking Back,* 64.

173 "There are no candles" WSM to Gerald Kelly, nd, HGARC.

174 There was one German prisoner" *A Writer's Notebook,* 75.
"Conversation mingled with groans" Ibid., 78.
"Mais non, mon vieux" Looking Back, 63.
"I saw a battle between aeroplanes" WSM to Alfred Sutro, nd, private collection.

175 "I was lucky enough" WSM to William Heinemann, December 27, 1914, Random House.
"I had done no work of this kind" *A Writer's Notebook,* 76.
"The war had a most important influence" *William Somerset Maugham: The English Maupassant,* 14.

176 "We are either rushed off our legs" WSM to M. L. Fleming, nd, Jenman.
"It makes sightseeing a matter" WSM to Gerald Kelly, nd, HGARC.
"The work was hard and tedious" *A Writer's Notebook,* 82.
"When I remarked on it" *William Somerset Maugham: The English Maupassant,* 5.

177 "She took no notice" *Looking Back,* 64.

CHAPTER 7: CODE NAME "SOMERVILLE"

178 "I'm sorry, but is there anything else" *Conversations with Willie,* 18.

179 "From you or from life?" Ibid., 20.

180 "[he] charmed the birds from the trees" Arthur Marshall interview with Robert Calder, Jenman.
"jolly and delightful" *The Listener,* February 7, 1974.
"very masculine . . . with a hard tarty face" Peter Quennell interview with Robert Calder, Jenman.
"He had an air of dissipation" *Up at the Villa,* 17.

181 "without anyone knowing anything" *Looking Back,* 64.
"It is bitterly cold here" WSM to William Heinemann, February 10, 1915, Random House.
"If only I am able to write" WSM to Gerald Kelly, February 1, 1915, HGARC.

182 "She took it as the most natural thing" *Looking Back,* 68.
"She cried bitterly" Ibid.

183 "I am very glad to know" WSM to Al Hayman, June 10, 1915, Fales.
"a dazzling icy glitter" *Theatrical Companion to Maugham,* 8.

184 "mercilessly amusing" *New Statesman,* October 6, 1923.
"one of the most brilliant plays" *Short View of the English Stage,* 107.
"various rumours" *Theatrical Companion to Maugham,* 122.
"She was very amusing" *Looking Back,* 65.

185   "Pearl: I wish you wouldn't call me girlie" *Plays,* vol. III, 63.

"[Mr. Maugham] and Mrs. Wellcome" Wellcome Library collection.

186   "I was at a loose end" *Looking Back,* 69.

187   "You'd be a fool to marry her" Ibid., 74.

"If we were married" *Conversations with Willie,* 35.

188   "Tu n'as pas encore perdu" *Amoureuse: Théâtre d'Amour,* tome III,
Georges de Porto-Riche (Albin Michel, 1928), 87.

"It positively made my blood run cold" WSM to Gerald Kelly,
November 12, 1915, HGARC.

189   "You will be doubtless seeing her" Ibid., February 28, 1916.

"The whole matter has been a great distress" WSM to F. H. Maugham,
March 12, 1916, HRHRC.

"I have never had such an enormous success" WSM to F. H. Maugham,
March 12, 1916, HRHRC.

190   "Light as a feather" *Sunday Times,* February 13, 1916.

"Cooper: Well, ma'am, my belief" *Plays,* vol. III, 158.

191   "If you do well" *Ashenden,* 4.

192   "I know nothing so tedious as coding" Ibid., 215.

193   "as orderly and monotonous" Ibid., 109.

"Geneva, the centre of all rumours" WSM to Gerald Kelly, November
12, 1915, HGARC.

"it was absurd to think" *Ashenden,* 108.

194   "had been doing us down" *Secret Service: The Making of the British
Intelligence Community,* Christopher Andrew (Heinemann, 1985), 152.

"[Ashenden] gave him his orders" *Ashenden,* 19.

195   "no more than a tiny rivet" Ibid., 7.

"I wanted to recover my peace of mind" *The Summing Up,* 192.

"I was willing to marry Syrie" *Looking Back,* 75.

196   "There is a great deal of sympathy" WSM to Gerald Kelly, October 15,
1916, HGARC.

197   "[to look] for beauty and romance" *The Summing Up,* 193.

"I was convinced that by going to Tahiti" *Looking Back,* 76.

198   "On a journey by sea" Ibid., 90.

"not a tramp, not a sailing vessel" *A Writer's Notebook,* 90.

"it is an empty desert" *The Trembling of a Leaf,* 14.

199   "a more devoted, generous" WSM to Klaus Jonas, August 29, 1956,
HRHRC.

200   "hot lallapalooza from Honolulu" *The Two Worlds of Somerset Maugham,*
307.

201   "rather handsome travelling companion" Ibid., 316.

"I entered a new world" *The Summing Up,* 193.

202   "I rarely went to my ship's cabin" Wilmon Menard, *After Dark,*
December 1975.

"from a hint or an incident" *The Summing Up,* 195.

202   "the writer cannot afford to wait" WSM to Michael Watkins, July 4, 1954, private collection.

203   "[Mrs. Woodrow] spoke of the depravity" *A Writer's Notebook,* 94.
      "to have Sadie [Thompson]" *The Two Worlds of Somerset Maugham,* 108.

204   "After supper we went on deck" *A Writer's Notebook,* 96.

205   "a flat-nosed, smiling dark native" Ibid., 117.
      " 'How much will it cost?' I asked" Ibid., 118.

206   "the first completely beautiful" Glenway Wescott interview with Robert Calder, Jenman.
      "he was noisy and boastful" *Up at the Villa,* 28.
      "But for him I should never have got" *Looking Back,* 90.

207   "a sheer masterpiece of sardonic horror" *Saturday Review,* November 5, 1921.
      "One of the evil limitations" James Michener to Klaus Jonas, February 13, 1905, HRHRC.

208   "There is no object more deserving of pity" *The Moon and Sixpence,* 160.
      "I felt that I had been put" *Looking Back,* 97.

209   "who first sentenced the drunk" *Saturday Review,* October 14, 1961.

210   "I do not know whether it is intended" WSM to William Wiseman, July 7, 1917, Jenman.

211   "It was tantalizing" WSM to Gerald Kelly, September 25, 1917, HGARC.

212   "Mr. Somerset Maugham is in Russia" Wiseman mss file 90-42, E. M. House Collection, Yale University Library.

213   "In his cold and uninteresting way" *Ashenden,* 220.
      "I realized that I could not count" *Looking Back,* 80.

214   "[Kerensky] looked very unhealthy" *A Writer's Notebook,* 165.
      "in the middle of his speech" *Six Red Months in Russia,* Louise Bryant (Heinemann, 1918), 117.
      "I've never seen a man" Glenway Wescott interview with Robert Calder, Jenman.
      "With Sasha acting as hostess" *Looking Back,* 82.

215   "I am receiving interesting cables" *W. Somerset Maugham and the Quest for Freedom,* 282.

216   "The endless talk when action was needed" *The Summing Up,* 197.

217   "I felt homesick" *A Writer's Notebook,* 154.
      "I am longing for news" WSM to Edward Knoblock, October 1, 1917, Berg.

218   "we in the Hotel Europa" *Spy and Counterspy,* Emanuel Victor Voska (Doubleday, Doran, 1940), 232.

219   "You won't reveal you had lunch" www.ochcom.org.
      "Delightful lunch with Willie Maugham" Hugh Walpole ms diary, HRHRC.

220   "I am very sensual" Ibid.

220   "He watched Russia as we would watch a play" "William Somerset Maugham," Hugh Walpole, *Vanity Fair,* 1920.

"the secret agent of reactionary imperialism" *American Espionage: From Secret Service to CIA* by Rhodri Jeffreys-Jones (Collier Macmillan, 1977), 96.

221   "I must make the Russian soldiers understand" WSM to Wiseman, November 18, 1917, Wiseman mss, Yale University Library.

222   "I can't do that" *Looking Back,* 85.

"I fear this [is] of only historical interest" Private Secretary Archives 1917–24: Balfour, FO 800/205, Public Record Office.

"I failed lamentably" *The Summing Up,* 196.

223   [I thought] that it was only sensible" *Looking Back,* 86.

CHAPTER 8: BEHIND THE PAINTED VEIL

225   "I delighted in the privacy" *The Summing Up,* 197.

"There is something that would appeal" WSM to Edward Knoblock, February 24, 1918, Berg.

"The post is always the great thrill" WSM to Alfred Sutro, nd, private collection.

226   "Meant to be nothing" WSM to Paul Dottin, nd, HRHRC.

"a play so negligible" *New Statesman,* October 6, 1923.

"a very truthful account" WSM to Paul Dottin, nd, HRHRC.

"[Willie's] mysterious bosses" A. S. Frere to Ted Morgan, March 11, 1978, Jenman.

"[Maugham] often spoke" Kenneth Clark to Robert Calder, December 29, 1981, Jenman.

227   "They desired the end" *Ashenden,* 263.

228   He was travelling with a brand-new passport" Ibid., 171.

"The modern spy story began" *New York Times Book Review,* September 13, 1981.

"The Ashenden stories were certainly" *Maugham,* 313.

229   "*Ashenden* is unique" Raymond Chandler to WSM, January 13, 1950, HRHRC.

"a specimen of Somerset Maugham" *New York Times,* April 15, 1928.

"We find they are nothing" *Vogue* (London), July 20, 1928.

230   "a strange outcome for a series" WSM to Desmond MacCarthy, nd, Lilly.

231   "What will happen in the future" WSM to M. L. Fleming, nd, Jenman.

"[as] I should have thought" Hugh Walpole ms diary, HRHRC.

232   "They must be very pleasant" *The Moon and Sixpence,* 212.

233   "I am always sure" *Sunday Times,* January 24, 1954.

"hackneyed and vulgar beyond belief" *The Moon and Sixpence,* 66.

233   "had the true instinct" Ibid., 213.
234   "We must be shown something" *Athenaeum*, May 9, 1919.
      "I am making my plans" WSM to Gerald Kelly, October 14, 1918,
      HGARC.
235   "He wasn't nasty about it" *Listener*, February 7, 1974.
      "in which all the characters" *Plays*, vol. V, vi.
236   "gave dinner parties to end all" Glenway Wescott interview with Ted
      Morgan, Jenman.
      "I had naturally bad taste" Kate Bruce, unpublished ms, private
      collection.
237   "Syrie simply didn't understand" *Conversations with Willie*, 33.
      "You have driven me to talk to you" *Looking Back*, 100.
238   "I didn't have a voice in it" *Listener*, February 7, 1974.
      "I think that if Syrie hadn't fallen in love" Glenway Wescott interview
      with Ted Morgan, Jenman.
239   "I was forty-three when we married" *Looking Back*, 100.
240   "[Willie] looks ill and bored" Hugh Walpole ms diary, HRHRC.
241   "The difference between men and women" *Plays*, vol. III, 235.
      "style, wit, elegance" *Times*, September 1, 1919.
      "succeeded in turning herself" *Gladys Cooper*, Sheridan Morley
      (Heinemann, 1979), 79.
      "more or less unconsciously" Ibid., 79.
242   "gives you everything" WSM to Robin Maugham, June 10, 1937,
      HRHRC.
      "You have thrust your hideous inventions upon us" *On a Chinese Screen*,
      95.
243   "At its foot were a number" Ibid., 106.
244   "an experience that really enriches the soul" WSM to Robin Maugham,
      June 10, 1937, HRHRC.
      "one of the pleasantest places" WSM to David Horner, June 15, 1935,
      HRHRC.
      "very nasty smells" *On a Chinese Screen*, 88.
245   "I have got a good deal of material" WSM to Golding Bright, January
      12, 1920, HRHRC.
      "p. 124 I am inclined to criticize" WSM to H. I. Harding, October 7,
      1921, private collection.
246   "His descriptions are not so much natural" *Saturday Review*, January 13,
      1923.
      "the only novel I have written" *The Painted Veil*, ix.
248   "He was self-conscious" Ibid., 26.
      "Convivial amusement has always" *The Summing Up*, 76.
      "willing to chatter all day long" *The Painted Veil*, 26.
249   "I seem to live in an atmosphere" *Looking Back*, 96.

249   "You are very pleasant to travel with" Ibid., 95.

250   "Syrie had a very heartless side" Glenway Wescott interview with Ted Morgan, Jenman.

"it was easy to be fascinated" *Syrie Maugham,* 47.

"Her hospitality did not spring" *Childhood at Oriol,* Michael Burn (Turtle Point Press, 2005), 242.

"a little dull and lacking in drama" *Times,* August 10, 1920.

"I was a little frightened of him" Liza Maugham in conversation with Pat Wallace, Frere Family Archive.

251   "I think he must have had a picture" Ibid.

"He never stammered" Ibid.

252   "There are only two courses" *Looking Back,* 95.

CHAPTER 9: A WORLD OF VERANDA AND PRAHU

253   "I cannot imagine that anything is likely" WSM to Fred Bason, September 28, 1923, Lilly.

254   "Words fail to describe" *The Parade's Gone By,* Kevin Brownlow (Secker & Warburg, 1968), 277.

"the obscene Cecil" WSM to Edward Knoblock, August 17, 1921, Berg.

"I look back on my connection" Ibid.

255   "I was shoved roughly" Wilmon Menard, *After Dark,* December 1975.

256   "Say, this is the real life" *A Writer's Notebook,* 177.

257   "more bother than you can imagine" WSM to Alanson, May 17, 1925, Stanford.

258   "If all else perish, there will remain" *Sunday Times,* December 19, 1965.

"He tells us—and it had not been said before" *100 Key Books of the Modern Movement,* chosen by Cyril Connolly (Alison & Busby, 1986), 73.

"Most English households of the day" *Pattern of Islands,* Arthur Grimble (John Murray, 1969), 1.

259   "A sahib has got to act like a sahib" *Collected Essays* by George Orwell (Secker & Warburg, 1961), 19.

260   "a combination of awe, envy" *A Writer's Notebook,* 213.

"Most people living in out-of-the-way places" *The Casuarina Tree,* 130.

261   "they were more lonely than in the jungle" *First Person Singular,* 10.

262   "They are bored with themselves" *A Writer's Notebook,* 188.

263   "[Izzart] wondered whether" *The Casuarina Tree,* 216.

"to get a boy was easier" *Britain's Imperial Century, 1815–1914,* Ronald Hyam (Batsford 1976), 137.

264   "The blinds on the verandah" *The Casuarina Tree,* 165.

265   "It was the elder of his two sons" Ibid., 201.

"had real trouble on their hands" *The Two Worlds of Somerset Maugham,* 36.

265   "The chief disadvantage for ladies" *Handbook to British Malaya 1926,*
      Capt. R. L. German MCS (Malay States Information Agency), 46.
266   "Crosbie grew very red" *The Casuarina Tree,* 293.
267   "[it] was clearly marked" *The Memoirs of a Malayan Official,* Victor
      Purcell (Cassell, 1965), 271.
      "Some of the smaller communities" *The Casuarina Tree,* 309.
268   "It is interesting to try" *Straits Budget,* June 7, 1938.
      "masterpieces of disloyalty" *A Chime of Words,* ed. Edwin Tribble
      (Ticknor & Fields, 1984), 86.
      "I tried to make use of them" *The Two Worlds of Somerset Maugham,* 31.
269   "sitting over a siphon" *The Gentleman in the Parlour,* 32.
      "I'm sorry, I'm sorry" *The Two Worlds of Somerset Maugham,* 35.
      "was suggested by a misadventure" *The Casuarina Tree,* 309.
270   "a bit dreary" *Ah King,* 185.
271   "I thought the best thing" *A Writer's Notebook,* 184.
272   "a necessity, and if I am deprived" *The Summing Up,* 88.
      "I have the greatest admiration for Racine" *Ah King,* 165.
273   "I am dreadfully put out" WSM to M. L. Fleming, October 10, 1921,
      Jenman.
      "You are a wonderful friend" WSM to Bert Alanson, February 26, 1921,
      Stanford.
      "You were as ever wonderfully good" Ibid., February 9, 1949.
274   "one of the very few" *The Thread of Laughter,* Louis Kronenburger
      (Knopf, 1952), 294.
      "his technique is flawless" *A Short View of the English Stage,* James Agate
      (Herbert Jenkins, 1926), 86.
275   "One sacrifices one's life" *Plays,* vol. IV, 78.
      "[a] gift [that] sprang from a clear-sighted" *New Statesman,* October 6,
      1923.
      "*The Circle* is one of the best plays" Ibid., March 19, 1921.
      "each separate tale is begun" *Saturday Review,* November 5, 1921.
276   "My short stories have been a very great success" WSM to Bert Alanson,
      January 28, 1922, Stanford.
      "one of the most agreeable persons" WSM to Edward Knoblock,
      October 16, 1924, Berg.
277   "I think you have done a very clever thing" WSM to Gerald Kelly,
      May 5, 1920, HGARC.
      "in their ill-fitting, ready-made clothes" *A Writer's Notebook,* 171.
278   "restless, clownish, and intense" *Paint and Prejudice,* C.R.W. Nevinson
      (Methuen, 1937), 179–80.
279   "Thank you very much *indeed*" WSM to Edward Marsh, July 5, 1919, Berg.
      "Heavens! you *can't* be enjoying" *Edward Marsh,* Christopher Hassall
      (Longmans, 1959), 483.

280 "With the strength of a typhoon" *The Glass of Fashion,* Cecil Beaton (Weidenfeld & Nicolson, 1954), 204.

281 "She has exquisite taste" *A Writer's Notebook,* 174.

282 "I have a notion that children" *The Gentleman in the Parlour,* 35.
"my constant companion" WSM to Reginald Turner, December 12, 1921, Craig V. Showalter Collection.
"I left England" Robin Maugham unpublished diaries, Beinecke.

283 "of attaching himself" Rebecca West interview with Robert Calder, Jenman.
"a little arid" *Reggie,* 159.
"charming, full of kindness" Hugh Walpole ms diary, HRHRC.
"You cannot think how impatient I am" WSM to Bert Alanson, July 25, 1922, Stanford.

284 "Another piece of work like this" *Spectator,* September 9, 1922.
We have got quite an arsenal with us" WSM to Bert Alanson, October 25, 1922, Stanford.
"cherishing and fortifying" *Burmese Days* (Penguin, 1989), 69.
"I cock a snook" *The Gentleman in the Parlour,* 9.

285 "narrow alleys [and] devious ways" Ibid., 21.

286 "the staple sweets" Ibid., 93.
"I trusted that after he left me" Ibid., 93.
"A great deal of course was exquisitely boring" Ibid., 62.
"the harsh, the impetuous, the flamboyant" Ibid., 105.

287 "I felt extraordinarily happy" Ibid., 127.
"looming gigantic and black" Ibid., 159.

288 "I am often tired of myself" Ibid., 9.
"I guess Egbert would like" Ibid., 144.

289 "the bamboos, the Chinese bamboos" *On a Chinese Screen,* 41.
"[I used] to catch minnows" *The Gentleman in the Parlour,* 159.
"Never was Mr. Maugham more readable" *New York Herald Tribune,* April 20, 1930.
"sombre and beautiful" *William Somerset Maugham: The English Maupassant,* 16.
"Will you invest $5,000" WSM to Bert Alanson, May 25, 1923, Stanford.

CHAPTER 10: SEPARATION

290 "middle age has its compensations" *Vanity Fair,* December 1923.

291 "It is simply magnif" *Arnold Bennett's Letters to His Nephew* (Heinemann, 1936), 141.
"so roomy and spacious" WSM to Bert Alanson, October 6, 1923, Stanford.
"You must expect to pay something" WSM to M. L. Fleming, nd, Jenman.

292   "charming but *very* naughty" Norman Douglas, Robin Maugham
        unpublished diaries, Beinecke.
        "He was a naughty boy" *A Case of Human Bondage,* 147.
        "[Haxton] was probably the only person" Rebecca West to Beverley
        Nichols, May 4, 1966, Delaware.
        "the handsome young man" *A Case of Human Bondage,* 144.
293   "Willie's sex life was not necessarily" Glenway Wescott interview with
        Ted Morgan, Jenman.
        "Gerald Haxton was wonderful for Willie" George Cukor unpublished
        interview with Jesse Hill Ford, Margaret Herrick Library.
294   "I personally had much affection" WSM to Bert Alanson, August 27,
        1923, Stanford.
        "a very substantial, comfortable sum" WSM to Alanson, October 25,
        1923, Stanford.
        "It was quite an experience" Ibid., October 6, 1923.
295   "Take your freedom" *The Gentleman in the Parlour,* 137.
        "I cannot tell you how much" Ibid., January 14, 1924.
296   "a perfectly amazing letter" *The Letters of Carl Van Vechten,* ed. Bruce
        Kellner (Yale University Press, 1987), 72.
        "I must confess that I am disappointed" WSM to Edward Knoblock,
        October 16, 1924, Berg.
        "I feel that two such literary Englishmen" D. H. Lawrence to WSM,
        October 24, 1924, Jenman.
297   "Damn his eyes" D. H. Lawrence to Willard Johnson, October 25, 1924,
        Letters of D.H. Lawrence, vol. 5, eds. James T. Boulton and Lindeth Vasey
        (Cambridge University Press, 1989), 155.
        "He answered crossly" *Not I, but the Wind,* Frieda Lawrence
        (Heinemann, 1935), 139.
298   ("just like Atlantic City") WSM to Edward Knoblock, February 1, 1925,
        Berg.
        "[I have] arrived at the conclusion" Ibid.
299   "I am not so anxious" WSM to Charles Towne, November 23, 1924,
        Beinecke.
        "He just sent it out like a parcel" Ibid., September 25, 1925.
300   "My father was fifty years old" *Somerset and All the Maughams,* 172.
301   "Needless to say I could not work" WSM to Golding Bright, March 18,
        1925, HRHRC.
        "I do not of course know" WSM to Edward Knoblock, nd, Berg.
302   "Don't expect us to be two roses" *Letters of D. H. Lawrence,* vol. 5, 445.
        "she did desperately mind" Liza Maugham conversation with Pat
        Wallace, Frere Family Archive.
303   "I realized that what she was chiefly" *The Scandal of Syrie Maugham,* 122.
        "[Syrie] was incapable of realising" Frank Swinnerton to Robert Calder,
        September 28, 1976, Jenman.

304 "Did you have a nice day" Liza Maugham conversation with Pat Wallace, Frere Family Archive.
     "I had a great feeling of insecurity" Ibid.
305 "S-S-Syrie d-d-didn't really imp-p-prove matters" Rebecca West to Beverley Nichols, May 4, 1966, Delaware.
     "Willie took this without protest" Ibid.
306 "writing like a chambermaid" A. S. Frere interview with Ted Morgan, Jenman.
     "She had a miniature, rather touching dignity" *Childhood at Oriol,* 177.
     ("I think I should warn you") *A Case of Human Bondage,* 82.
     "[Syrie] for a time" *A Little Love and Good Company,* Cathleen Nesbitt (Faber 1975), 142.
307 "She was tricky in business" H. K. Kelland conversation with WSM, March 13, 1906.
     "I knew Syrie slightly" "Angus" to Ted Morgan, nd, Jenman.
     "a tough old rogue" *The Scandal of Syrie Maugham,* 159.
     "I don't know how to tell you" *Looking Back,* 92.
308 "I knew them both" Ibid., 105.
     "a disaster from the start" Liza Maugham conversation with Pat Wallace, Frere Family Archive.
309 "is really a very charming little place" WSM to Bert Alanson, May 17, 1925, Stanford.
310 "Gerald makes the *best* sidecars" *A Case of Human Bondage,* 73.
     "She'll pickle it" Ibid., 20.
     "Mon cher ami, il paraît" Ibid., 21.
     "He caught my eye and shouted" Ibid., 27.
311 "I am so thrilled at getting [away]" WSM to John Ellingham Brooks, October 3, 1925, HRHRC.
312 "He could cook, he could valet" *Ah King,* 2.
313 "I seemed to develop the sensitiveness" *The Summing Up,* 200.
     "I felt that all the depictions" WSM to Klaus Jonas, July 3, 1951, HRHRC.
     "The width of observation" *Listener,* December 23, 1965.
314 "Maugham achieves an unspoken ferocity" *100 Key Books,* 73.
     "The journey on a French boat" WSM to Bert Alanson, March 15, 1927, Stanford.
     "I cannot but think" WSM to Edward Knoblock, nd, Berg.
315 "I have made a very agreeable arrangement" WSM to Bert Alanson, May 20, 1926, Stanford.
316 "I will not conceal from you" WSM to Charles Towne, July 2, 1926, NYPL.
     "You seem now to have bound me hand and foot" Ibid., April 24, 1926, Beinecke.
     "I am sure you will make an excellent editor" Ibid., July 2, 1926, NYPL.
317 "Twenty minutes before starting" WSM to Bert Alanson, nd, Stanford.

CHAPTER 11: THE VILLA MAURESQUE

319   "I have at last found a place" WSM to Gerald Kelly, nd, HGARC.
      "I hadn't reckoned on the temptation" *Strictly Personal,* 3.
320   "The great luxury on the Riviera" Ibid., et seq.
      "I place Somerset Maugham" *Gladys Cooper* (Hutchinson, 1931), 245.
      "The majority of authors" Ibid.
321   "[We] have to content ourselves" *The Letters of Nöel Coward,* ed. Barry
      Day (Methuen, 2007), 227.
      "Maugham lacked genuine enthusiasm" *Seven Ages,* Basil Dean
      (Hutchinson, 1970), 177.
322   "I'm tired of being the modern wife" *Plays,* vol. IV, 157.
      "Constance: Are you as great a fool" Ibid., 180.
      "Refuse to speak to him" Ibid., 146.
323   "I suffered agonies" WSM to George Cukor, nd, Margaret Herrick
      Library.
      "Quite early in rehearsals" *Seven Ages,* 304.
324   "Maugham and his wife" Ibid., 304.
      "Mr. Maugham was out of form" *Saturday Review,* April 16, 1927.
      "nice enough but it had the disadvantage" *Looking Back,* 108.
325   "Crowds and crowds at the party" *Arnold Bennett's Letters to His Nephew,*
      188.
      "spent three whole nights in Central Park" unpublished ms, copyright
      the literary estate of the late Sir Cecil Beaton.
      "My mother had a very bad nervous breakdown" Liza Maugham
      conversation with Pat Wallace, Frere Family Archive.
326   "I always hated Gerald Haxton" Ibid.
      "I was hysterical" Ibid.
      "We lunched tête à tête" *Looking Back,* 108.
327   ("Your mother dragged me through the mud") Liza Maugham
      conversation with Pat Wallace, Frere Family Archive.
      "Everything is absolutely finished" WSM to Barbara Back, May 16,
      1929, HRHRC.
      "I made a mistake" *Looking Back,* 110.
328   "She made my life utter hell" Robin Maugham unpublished diaries,
      Beinecke.
      "abandoned liar" WSM to Barbara Back, April 22, 1929, HRHRC.
      "[the] tart who ruined my life" Robin Maugham unpublished diaries,
      Beinecke.
      "[opening] her mouth as wide" WSM to Kate Bruce, January 16, 1931,
      Berg.
      "For those who seek a moral" Harold Acton, *Washington Post,* March 2,
      1980.
329   "He wrote it at my request" *A Case of Human Bondage,* 102.
      "help one up one's little ladder" Ibid., 70.

329   "With drink Beverley's tongue" unpublished ms, copyright the literary estate of the late Sir Cecil Beaton.

330   "I have been very fortunate" *The Infirm Glory,* Godfrey Winn (Michael Joseph, 1967), 92.
"that Willie had fallen for him" *A Lion in the Bedroom,* Pat Cavendish O'Neill (Jonathan Ball, 2004), 295.
"Don't be a fool" *Last Words,* Anton Dolin (Century, 1985), 74.

331   "a delicious creature" *Continual Lessons: The Journals of Glenway Wescott 1937–1955,* ed. Robert Phelps (Farrar, Straus & Giroux, 1990), 91.
"You don't know the kind of life" Hugh Walpole to Virginia Woolf, *Letters of Virginia Woolf,* vol. 4 (Hogarth Press, 1978), 250.
"a modified version of rough trade" Glenway Wescott interview with Ted Morgan, Jenman.

332   "He was wonderful with elderly gentlemen" Raymond Mortimer interview with Robert Calder, Jenman.
"my starry eyed little friend" Guy Little to Alan Searle, January 16, 1934, HGARC.
"but if you'll have dinner with me" Alan Searle interview with Robert Calder, Jenman.

333   "the less Syrie knows" Ibid.
"Mr. Maugham wouldn't have" Liza Maugham conversation with Pat Wallace, Frere Family Archive.
"Perhaps we should all look" *Plays,* vol. V, 298.

334   "Stage dialogue has been simplified" Ibid., x.
"another of Mr. Maugham's" *New York Times,* November 20, 1928.

335   "[that] our business went up" *Gladys Cooper,* 270.

336   "For some reason (chiefly I suppose" WSM to Bert Alanson, September 15, 1928, Stanford.

337   "I was prepared to spend the rest of my life there" *Strictly Personal,* 3.

338   "the raffinement de luxe" *A Leaf from the Yellow Book: The Correspondence of George Egerton,* ed. Terence de Vere White (Richards Press, 1958).
"a haven of comfort" Ann Fleming, *Spectator,* May 17, 1980.
"The arms would drop back again" *The Golden Riviera,* Roderick Cameron (Weidenfeld & Nicolson, 1975), 42.

339   "I am silent with pleasure" *Clever Hearts,* Hugh and Mirabel Cecil (Gollancz, 1990), 294.

340   "[Willie] always had a genius for food" Christabel Aberconway to Alan Searle, September 2, 1964, HGARC.
("He had about him") *A Case of Human Bondage,* 19.
"It was Gerald Haxton" *Escape from the Shadows,* Robin Maugham, 96.

341   "Fundamentally Maugham was a formal man" *The Golden Riviera,* Roderick Cameron (Weidenfeld & Nicolson, 1975), 45.

342   "I have never been able to persuade myself" *The Summing Up,* 229.
"word followed word" *Looking Back,* 5.

342   "[As Darwin] never worked" article by Kenneth Allsop, *Daily Express,* nd.
"I have always had more stories in my head" Ibid., 80f.

343   "Then I go over very carefully" WSM to Paul Hackbest, November 15, 1930, Lilly.
"the most enthralling of human activities" *The Summing Up,* 222.
"the useful little imp" *Plays,* vol. 5, viii.
"I am no longer interested" WSM to Klaus Jonas, May 14, 1956, HRHRC.

344   "who had lingered in my mind" WSM to Paul Dottin, January 1, 1931, HRHRC.
"I swear I never thought of Hardy" *Daily Telegraph,* September 29, 1930.
"Oh, I don't know" *Remembering Mr. Maugham,* 101.

345   "I am just finishing a novel" WSM to Gerald Kelly, May 30, 1929, HGARC.
"I have noticed that when someone asks" *Cakes and Ale,* 7.

346   "[Her] manner with Mrs. Driffield" Ibid., 128.

347   "She told me the hardest job she had" Ibid., 178.

348   "I had long had in mind" Ibid., 1.
"the yellow hair of a girl" *The Gentleman in the Parlour,* 46.
"who neither read the books" *Cakes and Ale,* 41.
"was very amiable to the authors" Ibid., 154.

349   "in which he showed quite definitely" Ibid., 123.
"viceroy of the literary world" *My World of Theatre,* Peter Daubeny (Cape, 1971), 34.
"he was mean as cat's meat" "The Eighty Years of Mr Maugham," Thomas Brady, *New York Times Magazine,* January 24, 1954.

350   "I knew Hugh Walpole" *William Heinemann: A Century of Publishing, 1890–1990,* John St. John (Heinemann, 1990), 358.
"[I had] a considerable affection" *Cakes and Ale,* 8.
"I'll tell you the sort of book" Ibid., 98.

351   "[Alroy Kear's] views on marriage" Ibid., 18.

352   "one of the most memorable literary dissections" Anthony West, *New Yorker,* August 23, 1952.
"Read on with increasing horror" Hugh Walpole unpublished diaries, HRHRC.
"I can't see any resemblance" A. S. Frere interview with Ted Morgan, Jenman.
"[*Cakes and Ale*] contains a most envenomed portrait" *Lytton Strachey,* vol. 2, Michael Holroyd (Heinemann, 1968), 680.
"your laudable fiendishness" E. M. Forster to WSM, November 11, 1930, HGARC.

353   "I hear poor Hugh says" *Francis Brett Young,* Jessica Brett Young (Heinemann, 1962), 172.

353 "the red-hot poker" *A Chime of Words,* Edwin Tribble, ed. (Ticknor & Fields), 86.

"cried aloud to be caricatured" *All I Could Never Be,* Beverley Nichols (Cape, 1949), 232.

"No English writer" *New York Times,* October 12, 1930.

"supreme adroitness and ease" *Graphic,* October 15, 1930.

"a model of construction" *William Somerset Maugham: The English Maupassant,* 9.

"perfect novel" *United States,* Gore Vidal (Deutsch, 1993), 250.

"superb" *Listener,* December 23, 1965.

"[Driffield] gave you the impression" *Cakes and Ale,* 89.

354 "I am really very unlucky" WSM to Hugh Walpole, nd, HRHRC.

355 "piteous, writhing & wincing" *The Diary of Virginia Woolf,* vol. 3 (Hogarth Press, 1980), 328.

356 "[After *Cakes and Ale*] Maugham's reputation" *Figures in the Foreground,* Frank Swinnerton (Hutchinson, 1963), 35.

CHAPTER 12: MASTER HACKY

357 "As what I have was invested" WSM to Messmore Kendall, January 13, 1929, HRHRC.

358 "He was warm, affectionate" A. S. Frere to Anthony Curtis, December 31, 1973, private collection.

"[Maugham] had an inestimable gift" A. S. Frere interview with Ted Morgan, Jenman.

"I don't *read* books" Hamilton Basso, *New Yorker,* December 30, 1964.

"but Willie . . . can back Nelson into a corner" Ibid.

359 "as a St. Bernard towers over a beagle" Ibid.

360 "last of the great professional writers" *Enemies of Promise,* Cyril Connolly (Penguin, 1961), 93.

"He has a sense" *William Somerset Maugham: The English Maupassant,* 8.

"I can tell you nothing" David Garnett to Ted Morgan, January 25, 1978, Jenman.

"I know just where I stand" *Seven Friends,* Louis Marlow (Richards Press, 1953), 160.

361 "If you have a snap-shot" WSM to Fred Bason, December 25, 1930, Lilly.

"We Cockneys try to repay" attached to WSM to Fred Bason, September 28, 1934, Lilly.

"No, I do not think" Ibid., November 13, 1931.

362 "You know quite well" WSM to Fred Bason, October 25, 1935, Lilly.

"you are at perfect liberty" Ibid., May 11, 1926.

363 "the toil and struggle" *Plays,* vol. VI, viii.

"I haven't the desire" Ibid.

"[With a play] you cannot have" Ibid.

363 "Fashions change in the theatre" *The Infirm Glory*, 249.

"led by the brisk but determined form" *A Traveller in Romance*, 27.

"a picture of a gentleman on a shelf" reproduced in *Noël Coward and His Friends*, Cole Lesley, Graham Payn, and Sheridan Morley (Weidenfeld & Nicolson, 1979), 209.

364 "red-eyed and miserable" *Anything for a Quiet Life*, Jack Hawkins (Hamish Hamilton, 1973), 43.

"to see the brilliant castigator" *Writers at Work*, Louise Morgan (Chatto & Windus, 1931), 58.

"I dote really on the smell" WSM to David Horner, August 19, 1937, HRHRC.

"the most entertaining game" *The Traveller's Library*, 1.

365 "I've lost hundreds" *Celebrity Circus*, 19.

"The student of human nature" *The Traveller's Library*, 1.

"I do not flatter myself" WSM to Karl Pfeiffer, September 26, 1931, HRHRC.

"I wish I could make a novel" Charles Goren, *Sports Illustrated*, January 17, 1966.

366 *"Qu'importe sa vie"* Sibyl Colefax Collection, Bodleian.

"she was like a little parrot" *Glenway Wescott Personally*, Jerry Rosco (University of Wisconsin Press, 2002), 97.

"The talk goes rocketing round" Basil Bartlett unpublished diaries, private collection.

"I have to keep my youth" *Great Hostesses*, Brian Masters (Constable, 1982), 137.

367 "I remember being terribly hurt" Liza Maugham conversation with Pat Wallace, Frere Family Archive.

"It was the most terrible shock" Ibid.

368 "There was a trace of subservience" *Chips: The Diaries of Sir Henry Channon*, ed. Robert Rhodes James (Weidenfeld & Nicolson, 1967), 32.

"A strange little gathering" *The Pool of Memory*, E. Phillips Oppenheim (Hodder & Stoughton, 1941), 85.

369 *"J'ai un secrétaire"* *Adieu à mon ami anglais*, Horace de Carbuccia (Éditions de France), 5.

370 "He was a gangster" *Strictly Personal*, 29.

"My dear William . . . During a time" *I Discover the English*, John Lane (The Bodley Head, 1934).

371 "It is not true" Odette Keun to WSM, January 4, 1934, HGARC.

"For Barbara, because she never calls" *The Narrow Corner*, Sotheby's catalogue of the sale of the Villa Mauresque, November 20, 1967.

372 "Your letters are a boon" WSM to Barbara Back, nd, HRHRC.

"She is the least self-centred writer" WSM to Kate Bruce, nd, Berg.

"I think they all enjoyed themselves" WSM to Barbara Back, nd, HRHRC.

372   ("so nice, gay & easy to please") WSM to Alan Searle, nd, HGARC.
       "Oh, Mr. Maugham" *Tribulations and Laughter,* S. N. Behrman (Hamish
       Hamilton, 1972), 302.

373   "This is the South of France" *The Infirm Glory,* 263.
       "odious" Robin Maugham unpublished diaries, Lilly.
       "Willie had told him" Alec Waugh interview with Ted Morgan,
       Jenman.
       "Somerset Maugham may have misunderstood" *Rylands,* introduction
       by Victor Rothschild (Stourton Press, 1988).

374   "his taste appeared to me faultless" *The Summing Up,* 21.
       "Lunch would have been going" *Life's Rich Pageant,* Arthur Marshall
       (Hamish Hamilton, 1984), 88.
       "marvellously entertaining" Arthur Marshall, *New Statesman,* February
       25, 1977.
       "he loved to make one laugh aloud" *The Pattern of Maugham,* 15.

375   "it would be idle to deny" Rebecca West, *Nash's Magazine,* October 1935.
       "It is exasperating" *A Bundle of Time,* Harriet Cohen (Faber, 1969), 180.
       "Willie hated to be touched" Glenway Wescott interview with Ted
       Morgan, Jenman.
       "carping at everyone" *Glenway Wescott Personally,* 45.

376   "I lead a peculiarly quiet life" WSM to Gerald Kelly, December 14,
       1933, HGARC.
       "The mental domination" Beverley Nichols, Foyle's luncheon speech,
       1966.
       "No matter how badly he behaved" Arthur Marshall interview with
       Robert Calder, Jenman.

377   "[Maugham] venait généralement" *Adieu à mon ami anglais,* 8.
       "And did you masturbate?" Arthur Marshall interview with Robert
       Calder, Jenman.

378   "just this side of being a crook" Kenneth McCormick interview with
       Ted Morgan, Jenman.
       "I'm p-p-perfectly aware" *Conversations with Willie,* 50.
       "Thank you again for your kindness" Gerald Haxton to Bert Alanson,
       August 6, 1928, Stanford.

379   "He was a bad, bad, loud drunk" Jerry Zipkin interview with Ted
       Morgan, Jenman.
       "*Why* do you have to drink" *Conversations with Willie,* 52.
       "You do not know what it is like" *The Infirm Glory,* 280.

380   "At times when I'm shut up" *Conversations with Willie,* 20.
       "Gerald couldn't help resenting" Ibid.
       "He has moods" Ibid., 21.

381   "Gerald now likes the bottle" Arthur Marshall interview with Robert
       Calder, Jenman.
       "I could not bear the thought" *A Writer's Notebook,* 217.

381   "I don't know about you, ducky" *Escape from the Shadows,* 84.

382   "[Gerald] is getting more peaceful" WSM to Barbara Back, December 22, 1930, HRHRC.
       "It is really very pleasant here" Ibid., April 21, 1932.
       "Wretched creature, Why don't you write" WSM to Alan Searle, nd, HGARC.

383   "I am so very glad" Ibid.
       "makes his relations with H[axton" *The Letters of Lytton Strachey,* ed. Paul Levy (Viking, 2005), 639.
       "The artist should never allow" WSM to Tammy Ryan, October 26, 1946, private collection.

384   "One morning when he had been" *First Person Singular,* 140.

385   "After all, I am an Oriental" Ibid., 193.
       "Though he spoke facetiously" Ibid., 204.

386   "It was a large, square building" *The Narrow Corner,* 111.
       "Mainsail and foresail were hoisted" Ibid., 34.

387   "She was just aching for it" Ibid., 162.
       "I wanted him simply frightfully" Ibid., 202.
       "Maugham's one and only crypto-fag novel" *Sexually Speaking,* Gore Vidal (Cleis, 1999), 174.
       "a slim, comely youth" *The Narrow Corner,* 28.

388   "This matter, which I supposed" *Plays,* vol. VI, v.
       "I live on the Continent" *Daily Express,* November 3, 1932.
       "She wants a man" *Plays,* vol. VI, 126.

389   "The day's long past" *Ibid.,* 127.
       "We were the dupes" Ibid., 164.
       "of malevolent propaganda" *Daily Express,* November 17, 1932.

390   "Somerset Maugham's new play" November 17, 1932, private collection.
       "My dear Louis" Ibid.

391   "Sheppey: To tell you the truth" *Plays,* vol. VI, 300.
       "a perfectly straightforward" WSM to Raymond Mortimer, nd, Princeton.
       "so as to make it more palatable" WSM to Joseph Dobrinsky, August 1, 1957, Texas A&M.
       "It seemed to be conceived" *Early Stages,* John Gielgud (Macmillan, 1939), 220.
       "I almost bowed in acknowledgement" Noël Coward to WSM, nd, HGARC.

392   "[It] was the last play" WSM to Joseph Dobrinsky, August 1, 1957, Texas A&M.
       "I cannot tell you" *The Letters of Noël Coward,* 227.
       "With all its glamour" *Remembering Mr. Maugham,* 45.
       "I can never get over" WSM to Alan Searle, April 8, 1944, HGARC.
       "I want to write novels & stories" WSM to Bert Alanson, January 21, 1933, Stanford.

CHAPTER 13: THE TELLER OF TALES

395   "Beloved by unliterary, unofficial" *Images of Truth,* Glenway Westcott
(Hamish Hamilton, 1963), 65.
"the mahatma of middlebrow culture" Robert Mazzocco, *New York
Review of Books,* November 23, 1978.
"Mr. Maugham's short stories" *Spectator,* September 29, 1933.
"His extraordinary knowledge" *New Statesman,* August 25, 1934.
"Maughamesque short story" *The Journals: John Fowles, vol. 1, 1949–1965,*
ed. Charles Drazin (Knopf, 2003), 165.
"the transforming passion" V. S. Pritchett, *New Statesman,* October 8, 1949.
"I have never pretended" *Selected Prefaces and Introductions,* 69.

396   "I find it often" *A Writer's Notebook,* 219.
"She is not mondaine" Rebecca West to WSM, nd, HGARC.
"sunny place for shady people" *Strictly Personal,* 156.
"He had a certain dreadful circle" George Rylands interview with
Robert Calder, Jenman.

397   "He was too much impressed by money" *Sunday Times,* December 19, 1965.
"It was a representative Riviera party" *Collected Short Stories,* vol. I, 265.

398   "It was their fat that had brought them together" Ibid., 227.
"an enclosure covered with glass" Ibid., 231.
"In front of Beatrice" Ibid., 239.

399   "The cure at Bad Gastein" WSM to Sibyl Colefax, August 28, 1934,
Bodleian.
"We went to a lovely performance" et seq. WSM to Alan Searle, nd,
HGARC.

400   "easily the nicest character" Robin Maugham unpublished diaries, Lilly.

401   "JUDGE AND AUTHOR BEREAVED" *Daily Telegraph,* July 27, 1935.
"Charley's death was expected" WSM to Gerald Kelly, August 4, 1936,
HGARC.
" 'kinky clients' . . . the only time" unpublished ms, private collection.
"a well-dressed attractive man" *Escape from the Shadows,* 26.

402   "I'm not saying I think there was incest" Glenway Wescott interview
with Ted Morgan, Jenman.
"This is only to say" WSM to Robin Maugham, June 5, 1934, HRHRC.

403   "We met him the first night" *Escape from the Shadows,* 84.
"I learned many things in Vienna" Ibid., 86 et seq.

404   "I had a lovely party" Liza Maugham conversation with Pat Wallace,
Frere Family Archive.
"She was wrapped up in cotton-wool" *The Scandal of Syrie Maugham,* 137.
"What do you think" WSM to Barbara Back, March 28, 1934,
HRHRC.

405   "[a] distinctive trait of the homosexual" *Don Fernando,* 141.

406   "St. John of the Cross" *New Statesman,* June 29, 1935.
      "kind, very considerate" WSM to Barbara Back, nd, HRHRC.
      "I have been playing golf today" WSM to Alan Searle, February 11,
      1935, HGARC.
407   "Things are going very badly here" WSM to Alan Searle, nd, HGARC.
      "The doctor tells me" Ibid., et seq.
408   "fantastic contracts" WSM to Alan Searle, November 18, 1935,
      HGARC.
      "small, neat, impeccably dressed" Leon Edel, *Saturday Review,* March 15,
      1980.
      "Gerald has been behaving" WSM to Alan Searle, November 24, 1935,
      HGARC.
      "The place is picturesque enough" WSM to Alan Searle, December 16,
      1935, HGARC.
409   "The West Indies are disappointing" WSM to Juliet Duff, February 23,
      1936, HGARC.
410   "& gave me a couple of murderers" Ibid.
      "The guillotine is in a small room" *A Writer's Notebook,* 232.
      "[but] of all the men I questioned" WSM to Juliet Duff, February 23,
      1936, HGARC.
      "I got one very good story" WSM to Alan Searle, February 6, 1936,
      HGARC.
411   "I have been thinking much of you" Ibid., nd.
      ("My happiness would be complete") Ibid., December 22, 1935.
      "I can quite see that the prospect" Ibid.
412   "I am only coming to see you" Ibid., February 11, 1936.
      "Of course what I should like" WSM to Alan Searle, November 24,
      1935, HGARC.
413   *"Ses Laurencins étaient jolis" Marie Laurencin,* Flora Groult (Mercure de
      France, 1987), 233.
      "but felt it only right to remind her" *Looking Back,* 114.
      "J'ai dû être remplacée" Marie Laurencin, 233.
414   "fought like a steer" Liza Maugham conversation with Pat Wallace,
      Frere Family Archive.
      "I found myself positively in danger" *The Lady and the Law,* Ted
      Berkman (Little, Brown, 1976), 215.
416   "[and the] very serious rumours" *Harold Nicolson: Diaries & Letters
      1930–1939,* ed. Nigel Nicolson (Collins, 1966), 276.
      "I am a writer . . ." WSM to Juliet Duff, December 10, 1936, HGARC.
417   "I'm afraid I am not a very good partner" *Boothby: Recollections of a Rebel,*
      Robert Boothby (Hutchinson, 1978), 195.
      "I think she had a very difficult role" WSM to Charles Towne, March
      18, 1937, NYPL.

417   "I am leaving Cannes tomorrow" Wallis Simpson to WSM, March 7,
         1937, HGARC.
         "What many people did not understand" *The Infirm Glory,* 337.
         "Gerald is in bed" WSM to Alan Searle, December 24, 1936, HGARC.

418   "[Alan] is being very sweet" WSM to David Horner, January 15, 1937,
         HRHRC.
         "Searle was more pussy-cat" *Never a Normal Man,* Daniel Farson
         (HarperCollins, 1996), 77.
         "So far as I am concerned" WSM to Barbara Back, March 24, 1937,
         HRHRC.

419   *"Mon cher Lulu"* Harold Nicolson to Louis Legrand, October 13, ?,
         Stanford.
         "is a ghastly mess" WSM to Robin Maugham, February 9, 1935,
         HRHRC.

420   "You are quite attractive" *Conversations with Willie,* 22.
         "It is very wonderful" WSM to Bert Alanson, March 15, 1938, Stanford.
         "There is no reason why your father" WSM to Robin Maugham, May
         6, 1938, Lilly.

421   "Well-dressed, attractive and slim" *Search for Nirvana,* 52.
         "I am tired & want a change" WSM to Charles Towne, October 27,
         1937, NYPL.

422   "Yesterday Anthony Blunt & a friend" WSM to Alan Searle, nd,
         HGARC.
         "I have put into it" WSM to Charles Towne, October 27, 1937, NYPL.
         "I caught the colloquial note" *The Summing Up,* 109.

423   "Never have I read an autobiography" *And Did He Stop to Speak to You?*
         G. B. Stern (Henry Regnery, 1958), 164.

424   ("There's glory for me!") *Edward Marsh,* 640.

425   "I think you must know grammar" WSM to Edward Marsh, January 27,
         1937, Berg.
         "p. 28 Has 'massivity' any advantage" *Edward Marsh,* 692.
         "I like to think they may have adorned" WSM to Edward Marsh,
         October 8, 1938, Berg.
         "immensely readable" *Christian Science Monitor,* March 23, 1938.
         "continuously entertaining" *Spectator,* January 14, 1938.

426   "Never before were so many celebrities" Hugh Walpole unpublished
         diaries, HRHRC.
         "[who has] been to pretty well" WSM to Alan Searle, nd, HGARC.

427   "so far as stories were concerned" WSM to Karl Pfeiffer, February 26,
         1938, HRHRC.
         "[I] only regret that the shadow of Kipling" WSM to E. M. Forster,
         February 24, 1938, King's College, Cambridge.

428   I can understand that when people say" *A Writer's Notebook,* 261.
         "I have seldom seen a sight more thrilling" Ibid., 257.

428 "[We] are living in the lap of luxury" WSM to Alan Searle, nd, HGARC.
     "we are on our way to Madras" WSM to Juliet Duff, January 25, 1938,
     HGARC.

429 "Of course no larks" WSM to Alan Searle, nd, HGARC.
     "as soon as the maharajas realized" *My Brother Evelyn,* Alec Waugh
     (Cassell, 1967), 285.
     "Oh the doddering old fools" WSM to Barbara Back, March 26, 1938,
     HRHRC.
     "and when I told her that I had spent" *The Memoirs of the Aga Khan*
     (Cassell, 1954), foreword, ix.
     "I was enthralled to meet him" *Enchanted Evening,* M. M. Kaye (Penguin,
     1999), 227.

430 "As for getting any insight" WSM to Karl Pfeiffer, February 26, 1938,
     HRHRC.
     "I remained in that state for so long" *A Writer's Notebook,* 252.

431 "Bhagavan [the maharshi] and Somerset Maugham sat"
     www.beezone.com/Ramana/somerset_maugham.html.

432 "We have been much disturbed" WSM to Alan Searle, March 15, 1938,
     HGARC.
     "while Gerald painted the town red" *More Memoirs of an Aesthete,* Harold
     Acton (Methuen, 1970), 335.

433 "It really is the perfect holiday" *Harold Nicolson: Diaries and Letters
     1930–1939,* 351.

434 "I do not think there is any danger of war" WSM to Bert Alanson, May
     13, 1938, Stanford.
     "I have not waited until I received" WSM to Herman Ould, June 26,
     1938, HRHRC.
     "Alan has been an angel" WSM to Barbara Back, September 24, 1938,
     HRHRC.

435 "That young man holds the future" *The Diary of Virginia Woolf,* vol. V,
     ed. Nigel Nicolson (Hogarth Press, 1984), 185.
     "like a dead man" Ibid., 185.
     "Well, we've escaped war" WSM to Bert Alanson, October 23, 1938,
     Stanford.

CHAPTER 14: AN EXERCISE IN PROPAGANDA

436 "I think it an abuse" *Selected Prefaces,* 10.

437 "had a fearful reality" *Christmas Holiday,* 250.
     "I am now advised" David O. Selznick to Daniel T. O'Shea, March 24,
     1939, HRHRC.

438 "Here in Italy everyone seems convinced" WSM to Bert Alanson, June
     12, 1939, Stanford.
     "there was a feeling of gentle excitement" *Strictly Personal,* 26.

439   "I am hoping [to] get some sort of work" WSM to Desmond
MacCarthy, September 5, 1939, Lilly.

440   "I much fear that I shall be left" WSM to Robin Maugham, October 7,
1939, HRHRC.
"Willie and I are . . . feeling very aged" Gerald Haxton to Robin
Maugham, September 28, 1939, HRHRC.
"This raised my spirits" *Strictly Personal,* 60.

441   "private reports" Ibid., 136.
"What difference will it make" "The English Family," unpublished
typescript, Jenman.
"Méfiez-vous de cet Anglais" Adieu à mon ami anglais, 40.
"I was entertained by generals" *Looking Back,* 146.

442   "The officer in command told me" *Strictly Personal,* 88.
"I was determined to write" Ibid., 108.
"The impression I received" Ibid., 80.

443   "I cannot attempt to describe" *France at War,* 41.
"There are plenty of empty houses" Ibid., 29.
"These wretched people" *Strictly Personal,* 105.

444   "pleasantly democratic . . . Orders are given" *France at War,* 65.
"I had not been able to help" *Strictly Personal,* 115.
"arrived in London" Ibid., 124.

445   "It means that the second Viscount" WSM to Bert Alanson, April 4,
1939, Stanford.
"I am settling $25000 on you" WSM to Robin Maugham, November
20, 1939, Berg.

446   "I am very glad" WSM to Robin Maugham, February 11, 1939,
HRHRC.
"I am told on all sides" WSM to Robin Maugham, November 20, 1939,
Berg.
"It was very quiet on the Riviera" *Strictly Personal,* 137.
"Everyone is bored" WSM to Ellen Doubleday, nd, Princeton.

447   "It never struck any of us" *Strictly Personal,* 152.

449   "Don't struggle. Open your mouth" *Strictly Personal,* 162.
"Many broke down then" Ibid., 171.

450   "Willie got home!" unpublished, private collection.

451   "is to London what the Ritz bar" *Daily Express,* October 1, 1940.

452   "Willie! Thank God you're safe" Liza Maugham conversation with Pat
Wallace, Frere Family Archive.
"But it didn't work that way at all" Ibid.
"After my three weeks" *Strictly Personal,* 239.

453   "Willie Maugham was palpably bored" *The Diaries of Sir Robert Bruce
Lockhart, Vol. II, 1939–1965,* ed. Kenneth Young (Macmillan, 1980), 79.
"[I] shouted at [Virginia] to take cover" *Ilex and Olive,* Michael Swan
(Home & Van Thal, 1949), 75.

453   "You know we've had some air raid warnings" WSM to Alan Searle, nd,
HGARC.

454   "W. Somerset Maugham is in this country" *New York Times Book Review,*
November 24, 1940.

455   "Just as the best novel" *Writers and Friends,* Edward Weeks (Little,
Brown, 1981).
"When, in this war" *New York Times,* Ocober 24, 1940.
"the crisis was destroying" *Strictly Personal,* 261.

456   "On his arrival Maugham was given" *Beware the British Serpent,* 121.
"looking old, tired and shrivelled" *The Vagrant Mood,* 181.
"[where] she managed to create" WSM to David Horner, October 11,
1944, HRHRC.

457   "though frequently complimenting me" *Continual Lessons,* 97.
"I said that for my part" Ibid., 91.
"I had the feeling" Liza Maugham conversation with Pat Wallace, Frere
Family Archive.

458   "I can't bear this"" Glenway Wescott interview with Ted Morgan,
Jenman.
"a large ginger moustache" *Never a Normal Man,* 41.

459   "The vast majority are ready" WSM to F. H. Maugham, January 14,
1941, private collection.
"If by any chance we are beaten" "The English Family" unpublished
typescript, Jenman.

460   "in his hardest, narrowest voice" Glenway Wescott interview with Ted
Morgan, Jenman.

461   "Naturally we should keep confidential" David O. Selznick to Daniel T.
O'Shea, March 14, 1941, HRHRC.
"So far I have only been allowed" WSM to Alan Searle, April 1, 1941,
HGARC.
("poor & poorly acted") WSM to Alan Searle, April 15, 1941, HGARC.
"fictional drivel" *Nation,* May 3, 1941.
"worst novel" *New Republic,* May 19, 1941.
"talking in his sleep" *Newsweek,* April 7, 1941.
"an unscrupulous scamp" *Up at the Villa,* 105.
"He had immense vitality" Ibid., 28.

462   "Why didn't you leave him?" Ibid., 29.
"the most tedious job" WSM to Robin Maugham, June 4, 1942, HRHRC.
"It is two miles from the sea" WSM to Ellen Doubleday, June 3, 1941,
Princeton.

463   "Of course it wasn't true" Liza Maugham conversation with Pat
Wallace, Frere Family Archive.
"J'étais dans une grande soirée" Gerald Haxton to Louis Legrand, February
24, 1941, Stanford.

464   "fast-disappearing career" *Film Weekly,* March 29, 1935.

464   "I see something of the stars" WSM to Kate Bruce, June 27, 1941, Berg.
"one little ray of sunshine" WSM to Osbert Sitwell, October 9, 1941,
HRHRC.
"I meet few people who interest me" WSM to Karl Pfeiffer, July 20,
1941, HRHRC.
"You mean about Mickey Rooney?" *W. Somerset Maugham: A Candid
Portrait,* 69.

465   "Which one is he supposed to be now?" "Maugham in Hollywood,"
Wilmon Menard, *American Film,* April 1979.
"demure in black silk" *A Traveller in Romance,* 96.
"I was so pleased to see Willie again" *Christopher Isherwood Diaries, Vol. I:
1939–1960,* ed. Katherine Bucknell, 142.
"an old Gladstone bag" *Isherwood,* Brian Finney (Faber, 1979), 180.
"that delightful, strange man" *Ilex and Olive,* 70.
"[climbing] all over him" *Christopher Isherwood Diaries,* 142.

466   "I am afraid this is no more" WSM to Alan Searle, July 25, 1941, HGARC.
"I have read scripts and reviewed fiction" David O. Selznick collection,
April 25, 1941, HRHRC.

467   "I loathe the people" WSM to Kate Bruce, June 27, 1941, Berg.
"I know very well it was poor" WSM to Edward Marsh, March 1, 1943,
Berg.
"Writing, writing, writing" WSM to Alan Searle, October 24, 1941,
HGARC.
"the result so far" Ibid., November 13, 1941.

468   "Now that America is in the war" WSM to Glenway Wescott,
December 12, 1941, Maryland.
"The countryside [is] wild, lonely" WSM to Karl Pfeiffer, January 28,
1942, HRHRC.
"[They] have captured my sympathy" WSM to Robin Maugham, June
4, 1942, HRHRC.

469   "Ellen ran the worst household in America" Jerry Zipkin interview with
Ted Morgan, Jenman.

470   "I have grand gallops" WSM to Alan Searle, April 16, 1942, HGARC.
"It's no good your telling me" WSM to Edward Marsh, March 1, 1943,
Berg.

471   "Of course I should miss him" WSM to Alan Searle, May 10, 1942,
HGARC.
"I know that people used to come" Glenway Wescott interview with
Ted Morgan, Jenman.
"three long, long, long weeks" *You Might As Well Live,* John Keats
(Simon & Schuster, 1970), 237.

472   "Thank you very much for the recipe" WSM to Eleanor Roosevelt,
March 1, 1945, Library of Congress.

472   "What a distinguished profile" Ibid., nd.

"too hot to do anything" WSM to Alan Searle, June 26, 1942, HGARC.

"Our stock is falling lower" WSM to Alan Searle, June 30, 1942, HGARC.

473   "The book has been a great pleasure" WSM to Karl Pfeiffer, May 12, 1943, HRHRC.

"I will not pretend" WSM to Edward Marsh, June 1, 1944, Berg.

"It has given me a lot of satisfaction" WSM to Diana Marr-Johnson, October 18, 1944, private collection.

474   "Believe me, my dear fellow" *The Razor's Edge,* 63.

475   "I had written nothing more" Ibid., 340.

476   "[who] calls more countesses" *Our Betters,* 15.

"Gerald is working very hard" WSM to Robin Maugham, October 6, 1943, HRHRC.

477   "[He] is delighted really" WSM to Alan Searle, November 23, 1943, HGARC.

"[and] it is a wonderful relief" WSM to Karl Pfeiffer, November 24, 1943, HRHRC.

"who will give me, I think" Ibid., January 12, 1944.

478   "I was disappointed, but not distressed" WSM to Edward Marsh, June 1, 1944, Berg.

"I have been in great trouble" WSM to Barbara Back, July 9, 1944, HRHRC.

479   "Though I have long known" WSM to Ellen Doubleday, nd, Princeton.

480   "[began] to breathe a little better" WSM to Barbara Back, July 9, 1944, HRHRC.

"I think going to see him twice a day" WSM to Barbara Back, July 9, 1944, HRHRC.

"I am afraid he is growing weaker" WSM to Edward Knoblock, October 2, 1944, Berg.

481   "I have to face the prospect" WSM to Diana Marr-Johnson, October 18, 1944, private collection.

"There is a slight hope" WSM to Alan Searle, November 3, 1944, HGARC.

"Gerald's death has been a bitter blow" WSM to George Cukor, November 18, 1944, Margaret Herrick Library.

"Please don't write & sympathize" WSM to Charles Towne, November 28, 1944, NYPL.

"the tempestuous grief" WSM to Alan Searle, December 20, 1944, HGARC.

482   "I don't want to see you!" *Sunshine and Shadow, 1930–1946,* Cecil Roberts (Hodder & Stoughton, 1972), 376.

"He had his habitual composed" *Tribulations and Laughter,* 288.

"Mon pauvre Loulou" WSM to Louis Legrand, January 12, 1945, Jenman.

482   "I suppose I shall give it a trial" WSM to David Horner, October 11,
       1944, HRHRC.

CHAPTER 15: THE BRONZINO BOY

484   "For thirty years he has been" *The Letters of Noël Coward,* 229.
       "Tout me le rappelle" WSM to Louis Legrand, May 15, 1945, Jenman.
       "The best years of my life" WSM to Robin Maugham, June 26, 1944,
       HRHRC.
485   "I found Willie overwhelmed" *Escape from the Shadows,* Robin Maugham,
       140.
486   "It has happened to me from time to time" *New Yorker,* June 8, 1946.
487   "He has always disliked me" WSM to Ellen Doubleday, August 9, 1946,
       Princeton.
       "Everyone here is of course" WSM to Alan Searle, May 9, 1945,
       HGARC.
       "[Willie] was very, very kind to me" George Cukor interview with Jesse
       Hill Ford, Margaret Herrick Library.
488   "I'd never bought a picture" *Purely for My Pleasure,* 17.
489   "in grateful acknowledgement" *Traveller in Romance,* 132.
       "You would be doing me a great favour" WSM to the Earl of Halifax,
       July 6, 1945, Margaret Herrick Library.
       "I know that at one time" PRO, FO 371/44582, Donnelly minute,
       September 14, 1945, quoted in *Beware the British Serpent,* 132.
490   "Alan arrived, very heavy" Glenway Wescott interview with Ted
       Morgan, Jenman.
       "[Alan] is a great comfort to me" WSM to Bert Alanson, January 22,
       1946, Stanford.
       "it recalled a pain" *Traveller in Romance,* 132.
       "for the kindness and the generosity" Ibid.
       "I am very grateful to you" WSM to Ellen Doubleday, August 9, 1946,
       Princeton.
492   *"Voilà votre Colonel d'Amérique"* nd, Stanford.
       "[I lived] in Maugham's Paris apartment" David Posner to Ted Morgan,
       March 28, 1977, Jenman.
493   "gigantic Jewish poet" Glenway Westcott interview with Ted Morgan,
       Jenman.
       "I was starry-eyed" David Posner to Ted Morgan, February 22, 1977,
       Jenman.
       "Willie just cut his head off" Glenway Westcott interview with Ted
       Morgan, Jenman.
       "People are strangely apathetic" WSM to Nelson Doubleday, October
       20, 1946, Princeton.

494 "I hope I shall like her next husband" WSM to Bert Alanson, April 10, 1947, Stanford.

"said mother, aged 67" WSM to Nelson Doubleday, September 12, 1946, Princeton.

"In the last week I have had requests" WSM to Ann Fleming, nd, private collection.

495 "Millionaires & such like" WSM to Sibyl Colefax, December 15, 1944, Bodleian.

"Does Mr. Maugham realize" *Daily Telegraph,* April 17, 1947.

496 "overcome [by] the indifference" *The Artist and the Theatre,* Raymond Mander and Joe Mitchenson (Heinemann, 1955).

"I wish I could enlist your help" WSM to J. B. Priestley, January 12, 1948, HRHRC.

497 "I think you have been harsher" WSM to Edward Marsh, February 9, 1948, Berg.

498 "I cannot tell you what a relief" WSM to Glenway Wescott and Monroe Wheeler, August 22, 1948, Maryland.

"very much pleased" WSM to Ellen Doubleday, January 26, 1947, Princeton.

499 "as right as rain for William" *Continual Lessons,* 162.

500 "[the perfect] nanny" *Maugham,* 494.

"I loved him with all my heart" unpublished ms, Margaret Herrick Library.

"I am, I think, very happy" Alan Searle to Ellen Doubleday, December 27, 1946, Princeton.

"I'm so glad you're here" *Maugham,* 565.

"The family were all fond of Alan" Nicolas Paravicini to WSM.

"Liza and the children are here" Alan Searle to Bert Alanson, August 21, 1947, Stanford.

"He is a pompous donkey" WSM to Ellen Doubleday, September 11, 1953, Princeton.

501 "which adds greatly to the gaiety" WSM to Nelson Doubleday, August 19, 1948, Princeton.

503 "[The Queen] was very nicely dressed" WSM to Bert Alanson, July 23, 1954, Stanford.

"But don't you see" George Rylands interview with Robert Calder, Jenman.

"[and as] I am the greatest living writer" F. J. Shirley, *The Cantuarian,* December 1965.

504 "You will remember how astonished" WSM to Antony Darnborough, nd, Jenman.

"soulful damsels" WSM to Diana Marr-Johnson, nd, private collection.

505 "People I haven't seen" Robin Maugham unpublished diaries, Beinecke.

"I am not a monkey in the zoo" WSM to Kate Bruce, nd, Berg.

505 "When he emerges [from the pool]" *Remembering Mr. Maugham,* 27.
"Willie arrived punctually at eight" *The Diaries of Sir Robert Bruce Lockhart,* vol. II, 684.

506 "I feel strange" *Remembering Mr. Maugham,* 139.

507 "We had Willie Maugham and his catamite" *Mr. Wu and Mrs. Stitch: The Letters of Evelyn Waugh and Diana Cooper,* ed. Artemis Cooper (Hodder & Stoughton, 1991), 261.
"It may interest you to know" WSM to A. S. Frere, January 7, 1950, Frere Family Archive.

508 "as though they were gauleiters" *The Vagrant Mood,* 179.
"One could never be quite certain" Liza Maugham conversation with Pat Wallace, Frere Family Archive.
"He imposed a regime" *The Wanton Chase,* Peter Quennell (Collins, 1980), 162.
"That's what you'll be doing" *My World of Theatre,* Peter Daubeny (Cape, 1971), 98.

509 "[when] all I had done" *Sunday Times,* April 3, 1966.
"[when] we were enjoying a nightcap" *Paris Review* no. 165, 205.
"his face is the wickedest tangle" *In Tearing Haste: Letters Between Deborah Devonshire and Patrick Leigh Fermor,* ed. Charlotte Mosley (John Murray, 2008), 20.

510 "It goes with a swing" WSM to Ian Fleming, nd, Lilly.
"[It's] not that I didn't mean" Ibid.

511 "I had wanted the Queen" Gerald Kelly to Bert Alanson, March 3, 1953, Stanford.
"Your father bore with grim disapproval" WSM to Robin Maugham, February 3, 1950, HRHRC.

512 "Only two hearts" *Ena: Spain's English Queen,* Gerard Noel (Constable, 1984), 282.
"Frank says, 'Hiya, baby!' " *Remembering Mr. Maugham,* 191.
"Far too many people" *The Noël Coward Diaries,* ed. Graham Payne and Sheridan Morley (Papermac, 1982), 382.

513 "It has always been an ambition" WSM to Bert Alanson, April 30, 1949, Stanford.

514 "He liked a picture" *Memoirs of an Aesthete,* 189.
"I do not think Utrillo" *Life,* December 1, 1941.
"It was the picture" *Purely for My Pleasure,* 24.

515 "a fantastic absence of feeling" *Sunset and Twilight: From the Diaries of Bernard Berenson,* ed. Nicky Mariano (Hamish Hamilton, 1964), 439.
"was remarkably perceptive" *The Other Half,* Kenneth Clark (John Murray, 1977), 116.

516 "The first time I saw it" *Daily Express,* November 16, 1951.
"Although I wouldn't like Graham to know" WSM to Kenneth Clark, April 16, 1951, Wake Forest.

CHAPTER 16: BETRAYAL

518   "On the continent of Europe" *A Writer's Notebook,* 318.

"not a great fan of his" William Plomer to Jocelyn Brooke, May 14, 1953, Jenman.

"don't think I'm at all" Angus Wilson to Jocelyn Brooke, May 5, 1953, Jenman.

"May I be excused?" William Sansom to Jocelyn Brooke, May 5, 1953, Jenman.

"[cannot] because of the novel" Elizabeth Bowen to Jocelyn Brooke, March 24, 1953, Jenman.

"truly and deeply sorry" Noël Coward to Jocelyn Brooke, June 16, 1953, Jenman.

519   "[I] shall produce 2000 words" Raymond Mortimer to Jocelyn Brooke, April 27, 1953, Jenman.

"I bask in Antibes" *Punch,* January 1954.

520   "those thousands of readers" *The Author,* January 25, 1954, Lilly.

"Anybody else would have sat down" St. John Ervine to Richard Church, February 19, 1954, HRHRC.

521   "he will tell you everything" *New Yorker,* October 29, 1949.

"I really cannot stand" WSM to Richard Cordell, January 23, 1939, Lilly.

"he tears everything" *Continual Lessons,* 166.

522   "I had held on to those letters" Jerry Zipkin interview with Ted Morgan, Jenman.

("Your kids of Paravicini") Louis Legrand to Liza Maugham, April 15, 1964, private collection.

523   "Robin's handicap has always been" WSM to Kate Bruce, February 2, 1957, Berg.

"[Robin] is as frivolous" WSM to Bert Alanson, July 28, 1955, Stanford.

"It has been my ill-fortune" *A Choice of Kipling's Prose,* xxii.

524   "I must tell you that this has come" Robin Maugham to Alan Searle, December 28, 1962, HGARC.

525   "I've had an offer from the American" Robin Maugham to WSM, February 14, 1962, HGARC.

"I promise you here and now" Ibid., February 20, 1962.

526   "[Mr. Maugham's] celebrity in Europe" Alan Searle to Bert Alanson, January 29, 1953, Stanford.

527   "[Alan] was not in himself" *Continual Lessons,* 162.

"a namby-pamby" Jerry Zipkin interview with Ted Morgan, Jenman.

"muddle-headed [and] not very bright" Douglas Cooper to Robert Calder, September 10, 1978, Jenman.

"I think you are a darling" Alan Searle to Jane Clark, April 17, 1952, Wake Forest.

"[You are] such a darling" Alan Searle to Jerry Zipkin, March 10, 1959, HGARC.

527   "he enjoyed the complaining" Jerry Zipkin interview with Ted Morgan, Jenman.

528   "Thank you for all those wonderful picture books!" Alan Searle to Jerry Zipkin, December 28, 1954, HGARC.
"[Mr. Maugham] was generous to me" unpublished ms, Margaret Herrick Library.
"Alan Searle was a knight" Liza Maugham conversation with Pat Wallace, Frere Family Collection.
"said in his entire life" Glenway Wescott interview with Ted Morgan, Jenman.

529   "Mr. M.'s popularity in Japan" Alan Searle to Klaus Jonas, November 25, 1959, HRHRC.
"He still felt he had something" *Somerset Maugham: A Life,* 317.

530   "He's a white man" *Diaries, 1942–1954,* James Lees-Milne, ed. Michael Bloch (John Murray, 2006), 435.
"I have been reading Kipling" WSM to G. B. Stern, February 6, 1951, HRHRC.
"[Kipling] is our greatest story writer" *A Choice of Kipling's Prose,* xxviii.
"The fact is that, like drinking" WSM to Bert Alanson, September 5, 1954, Stanford.
"[My] fertile invention" WSM to Klaus Jonas, May 14, 1956, HRHRC.

531   "Writing with me" *Daily Express,* January 20, 1958.
"the last one 'The Delicate Nature' " WSM to H. E. Bates, September 22, 1953, private collection.
"I could not stand the life" WSM to Kate Bruce, January 18, 1951, Berg.

532   "It would be hypocrisy" WSM to Barbara Back, August 10, 1955, HRHRC.
"Tra la la, no more alimony" *Somerset and All the Maughams,* 20.
"I am like a passenger" *A Writer's Notebook,* 333.
"an iguana sunning itself" *Willie: The Life of W. Somerset Maugham,* 43.
"with his pale deeply furrowed face" *Everything to Lose: Diaries 1945–1960,* Frances Partridge (Little, Brown, 1985), 131.
"reminded of the lizards" Harold Nicolson to Robin Maugham, December 17, 1958, Lilly.

533   "[Willie] was shapely but tiny" Glenway Wescott interview with Ted Morgan, Jenman.
"a seedy relic of the Edwardian era" WSM to Douglas M. Black, January 30, 1957, Jenman.
"a poor old celluloid doll" *Beaton in the Sixties,* introduction by Hugo Vickers (Weidenfeld & Nicolson, 2003), 17.
"If you think I'm g-g-g-ga-ga" *Tribulations and Laughter,* 308.

534   "[Alan] is not nearly as simple" *The Isherwood Century,* ed. James J. Berg and Chris Freeman (University of Wisconsin Press, 2000).
"an intriguer, a schemer" *The Bonus of Laughter,* Alan Pryce-Jones (Hamish Hamilton, 1987), 224.

535   "Parents subjected me" unpublished ms, Margaret Herrick Library.
       "I'm always thinking about the future" Alan Searle to Bert Alanson,
       January 12, 1950, Stanford.
       "What will become of me" Alan Searle interview with Robert Calder,
       Jenman.
536   "I want you to know" Liza Maugham conversation with Pat Wallace,
       Frere Family Collection.
537   "It will also be very nice for you both" Ibid.
       "Dearest Daddy, You really are making me quite miserable" Ibid.
538   "As far as he's concerned" Ibid.
539   "Alan must have had a hand in it" Ibid.
       "his vile so-called daughter" Alan Searle to Klaus Jonas, April 17, 1963,
       HRHRC.
       "a scavenger . . . a bitch" Alan Searle to Jerry Zipkin, August 21, 1963,
       HGARC.
       "Alan incites Willie against Liza" *The Letters of Ann Fleming,* ed. Mark
       Amory (Collins Harvill, 1985), 184.
       "There is something in her" Diana Marr-Johnson to Alan Searle, April
       12, 1962, HGARC.
540   "I only hope that [Maugham]" Alan Searle to Robin Maugham, June 1,
       1962, HGARC.
541   ("I am peace-loving") Alan Searle to Sam Behrman, July 26, 1963,
       Jenman.
       "He is devoured by retrospective hate" *The Noël Coward Diaries,* 508.
542   "I am thrilled" Alan Searle to Lord Beaverbrook, November 11, 1961,
       Parliamentary Archives BBK/C/293.
       "a very imperfect and tormented creature" *Looking Back,* 144.
543   "All hell was let loose" A. S. Frere to Ted Morgan, March 11, 1978,
       Jenman.
       "Entirely contemptible" *The Noël Coward Diaries,* 511.
       a senile and scandalous work" *Yours, etc: Letters to the Press, 1965–1989*
       (Reinhardt, 1989).
       "an obscene little toad" Rebecca West to Beverley Nichols, March 30,
       1962, University of Delaware.
       "shabby, sordid, embarrassing" *Remembering Mr. Maugham,* 68.
       "the ancient Maugham mined his own monument" *United States,* Gore
       Vidal, 237.
544   "I believe neither in the existence of God" *Looking Back,* 128.
       "The maps are out" Alan Searle to Jane Clark, February 11, 1955, Wake
       Forest.
       "Never again will I stir an inch" Alan Searle interview with Ted
       Morgan, Jenman.
       "Rarely sensible, and in acute misery" Alan Searle to Jerry Zipkin,
       August 21, 1963, HGARC.

544 "Poor, poor Willie" Alan Searle to Robin Maugham, December 1, 1963, HGARC.

("even today the pain of her passing") *Sunday Express,* January 26, 1964.

"I called on Willie Maugham" *The Noël Coward Diaries,* ed. Graham Payn and Sheridan Morley (Papermac, 1983), 607.

545 "I have been shut up with a madman" Alan Searle to Robin Maugham, April 5, 1965, HGARC.

"He lives in some terrifying world" Alan Searle to Jerry Zipkin, April 5, 1965, HGARC.

"I have a good many" Alan Searle to Glenway Wescott, July 2, 1965, Maryland.

"like a malignant crab" Robin Maugham unpublished diaries, Lilly.

"[B]lack double-breasted quilted smoking jacket" Robin Maugham unpublished diaries, Lilly.

546 "Willie is now completely out of his mind" Alan Searle to Ellen Doubleday, November 27, 1965, Princeton.

547 "It wasn't sexual" Mary Dawson interview with author, May 18, 2006.

549 "The first little splutter of interest" WSM to Karl Pfeiffer, May 1, 1946, HRHRC.

"the most enthralling of human activities" *The Summing Up,* 222.

"can tell his secret yet not betray it" *Mrs. Craddock,* 221.

SELECT BIBLIOGRAPHY

. . .

EDITIONS OF THE WORKS OF SOMERSET MAUGHAM REFERRED TO IN THE TEXT:

Liza of Lambeth (Vintage, 2000)
The Making of a Saint (Farrar, Straus & Giroux, 1966)
Orientations (Fisher Unwin, 1899)
The Hero (Hutchinson, 1901)
Mrs. Craddock (Vintage, 2000)
A Man of Honour (Dramatic Publishing Company, 1903)
The Merry-Go-Round (Vintage, 2000)
The Land of the Blessed Virgin (Knopf, 1920)
The Bishop's Apron (Chapman & Hall, 1906)
The Explorer (Heinemann, 1922)
The Magician (Vintage, 2000)
The Tenth Man (Heinemann, 1913)
Landed Gentry (Grace) (Heinemann, 1913)
Of Human Bondage (Vintage, 2000)
The Moon and Sixpence (Vintage, 1999)
The Trembling of a Leaf (Heinemann, 1921)
On a Chinese Screen (Vintage, 2000)
Loaves and Fishes (Heinemann, 1924)
The Painted Veil (Vintage, 2001)
The Casuarina Tree (Oxford University Press, 1985)
The Letter (Heinemann, 1927)
Ashenden (Vintage, 2000)
The Gentleman in the Parlour (Vintage, 2001)
Cakes and Ale (Vintage, 2000)
First Person Singular (Heinemann, 1931)

The Narrow Corner (Vintage, 2001)

Ah King (Oxford University Press, 1986)

Don Fernando (Vintage, 2000)

Cosmopolitans (Doubleday, Doran, 1936)

Theatre (Vintage, 2000)

The Summing Up (Vintage, 2001)

Christmas Holiday (Vintage, 2001)

France at War (Heinemann, 1940)

Books and You (Doubleday, Doran, 1940)

The Mixture as Before (Heinemann, 1940)

Up at the Villa (Vintage, 2000)

Strictly Personal (Doubleday, Doran, 1941)

The Hour Before the Dawn (Doubleday, Doran, 1942)

The Razor's Edge (Vintage, 2000)

Then and Now (Vintage, 2001)

Creatures of Circumstance (Heinemann, 1947)

Catalina (Vintage, 2001)

Great Novelists and Their Novels (John C. Winston, 1948)

A Writer's Notebook (Vintage, 2001)

The Writer's Point of View (Cambridge University Press for the National Book
    League, 1951)

The Vagrant Mood (Vintage, 2001)

Points of View (Vintage, 2000)

Purely for My Pleasure (Heinemann, 1962)

Collected Short Stories, Vol. I (Vintage, 2000)

Collected Short Stories, Vol. II (Vintage, 2002)

Collected Short Stories, Vol. III (Vintage, 2002)

Collected Short Stories, Vol. IV (Vintage, 2002)

The Plays of Somerset Maugham (Heinemann, 1931–1934)

Vol. I: *Lady Frederick, Mrs. Dot, Jack Straw*

Vol. II: *Penelope, Smith, The Land of Promise*

Vol. III: *Our Betters, The Unattainable (Caroline), Home and Beauty*

Vol. IV: *The Circle, The Constant Wife, The Bread-Winner*

Vol. V: *Caesar's Wife, East of Suez, The Sacred Flame*

Vol. VI: *The Unknown, For Services Rendered, Sheppey*

The Traveller's Library, compiled and with notes by W. Somerset Maugham
    (Doubleday, Doran, 1937)

Tellers of Tales, selected and with an introduction by W. Somerset Maugham
    (Doubleday, Doran, 1939)

W. Somerset Maugham's Introduction to Modern English and American Literature
    (New Home Library, 1943)

A Choice of Kipling's Prose, selected and with an introductory essay by W.
   Somerset Maugham (Macmillan, 1952)

Selected Prefaces and Introductions of W. Somerset Maugham (Heinemann, 1963)
Seventeen Lost Stories by W. Somerset Maugham, compiled by Craig V. Showalter
   (Doubleday, Doran, 1969)
A Traveller in Romance: Uncollected Writings 1901–1964: W. Somerset Maugham,
   edited by John Whitehead (Anthony Blond, 1984)

SELECTED LIST OF WORKS ABOUT SOMERSET MAUGHAM

Aldington, Richard. *W. Somerset Maugham: An Appreciation.* Doubleday, Doran,
   1939.
Bason, Frederick T. *A Bibliography of the Writings of William Somerset Maugham.*
   Unicorn Press, 1931.
Brander, L. *Somerset Maugham: A Guide.* Barnes & Noble, 1963.
Brophy, John. *Somerset Maugham.* Longmans, 1952.
Brown, Ivor. *W. Somerset Maugham.* International Profiles, 1970.
Calder, Robert Lorin. *W. Somerset Maugham and the Quest for Freedom.*
   Heinemann, 1972.
———. *Willie: The Life of W. Somerset Maugham.* Heinemann, 1989.
———. *Beware the British Serpent: The Role of Writers in British Propaganda in the
   United States, 1939–1945.* McGill–Queen's University Press, 2004.
Connon, Bryan. *Somerset Maugham and the Maugham Dynasty.* Sinclair-
   Stevenson, 1997.
Cordell, Richard. *Somerset Maugham: A Biographical and Critical Study.*
   Heinemann, 1961.
Curtis, Anthony. *The Pattern of Maugham.* Quality Book Club, 1974.
———. *Somerset Maugham.* Weidenfeld & Nicolson, 1987.
Curtis, Anthony, and John Whitehead, eds. *W. Somerset Maugham: The Critical
   Heritage.* Routledge & Kegan Paul, 1987.
Dottin, Paul. *Somerset Maugham et ses romans.* Perrin, 1926.
———. *Le Théâtre de Somerset Maugham.* Perrin, 1937.
Fisher, Richard B. *Syrie Maugham.* Duckworth, 1978.
Jonas, Klaus W. *The Gentleman from Cap Ferrat.* New Haven, Connecticut,
   Centre for Maugham Studies, 1956.
———. *The World of Somerset Maugham.* Greenwood Press, 1959.
Jonas, Klaus W., ed. *The Maugham Enigma.* Peter Owen, 1954.
Kanin, Garson. *Remembering Mr. Maugham.* Hamish Hamilton, 1966.
MacCarthy, Desmond. *William Somerset Maugham: The English Maupassant.*
   Heinemann, 1934.
Mander, Raymond, and Joe Mitchenson. *Theatrical Companion to Maugham.*
   Rockliff, 1955.
Maugham, the Rt. Hon. Viscount. *At the End of the Day.* Heinemann, 1954.

Maugham, Robin. *Somerset and All the Maughams*. Heinemann, 1966.

———. *Escape from the Shadows*. Hodder & Stoughton, 1972.

———. *The Search for Nirvana*. W. H. Allen, 1975.

———. *Conversations with Willie*. W. H. Allen, 1978.

McKnight, Gerald. *The Scandal of Syrie Maugham*. W. H. Allen, 1980.

Menard, Wilmon. *The Two Worlds of Somerset Maugham*. Sherbourne Press, 1965.

Meyers, Jeffrey. *Somerset Maugham: A Life*. Knopf, 2004.

Morgan, Ted. *Maugham*. Simon & Schuster, 1980.

Nichols, Beverley. *A Case of Human Bondage*. Secker & Warburg, 1966.

Pfeiffer, Karl G. *W. Somerset Maugham: A Candid Portrait*. Norton, 1959.

Raphael, Frederic. *Somerset Maugham and His World*. Thames & Hudson, 1976.

Sanders, Charles. *W. Somerset Maugham: An Annotated Bibliography of Writings About Him*. Northern Illinois University Press, 1970.

Stott, Raymond Toole. *A Bibliography of the Works of W. Somerset Maugham*. University of Alberta Press, 1973.

INDEX

...

Note: The initials WSM refer to William Somerset Maugham. All works (novels, plays, short stories, and essays) are authored by WSM unless otherwise noted.

ILLUSTRATION CREDITS

. . .

Frontispiece. *Courtesy of the Cecil Beaton Studio Archive at Sotheby's.*

INSERT ONE

A lonely child. *Courtesy of the Harry Ransom Humanities Research Center, the University of Texas at Austin.*

Robert Maugham. *Courtesy of the Neil & Reiden Jenman Collection.*

Edith Maugham. *Courtesy of the Neil & Reiden Jenman Collection.*

The Rev. Henry Maugham. *Courtesy of the Estate of Robin Maugham/Eric Glass Ltd.*

Aunt Sophie. *Courtesy of the Neil & Reiden Jenman Collection.*

Willie and his uncle outside the vicarage. *Courtesy of the Harry Ransom Humanities Research Center, the University of Texas at Austin.*

"Life was before him . . ." *Courtesy of the Neil & Reiden Jenman Collection.*

At the King's School, Canterbury. *Courtesy of the Harry Ransom Humanities Research Center, the University of Texas at Austin.*

Willie, Charlie, and Harry Maugham. *Courtesy of Anne Channing.*

F. H. Maugham. *Courtesy of the Neil & Reiden Jenman Collection.*

Gerald Kelly. *From a private collection.*

Sue Jones. *From a private collection.*

Ethel Irving. *Courtesy of Mander & Mitchenson Theatre Collection/Foulsham & Banfield/Rotary Photo.*

Gladys Cooper. © *Getty Images.*

Syrie Wellcome. *Courtesy of Wellcome Library/London.*

The Maughams with Liza. *From a private collection.*

Gerald Haxton. *Courtesy of the British Library.*

Maugham aboard RMS *Aquitania.* © *Associated Press.*

In Hollywood. © *Time & Life Pictures/Getty Images.*

A. S. Frere. *Courtesy of the Frere family archive/National Portrait Gallery, London.*

Eddie Marsh. © *Time & Life Pictures/Getty Images.*

Liza's wedding. © *Keystone/Hulton Archive/Getty Images.*

The Villa Mauresque. © *Time & Life Pictures/Getty Images.*

Maugham and Haxton. *Photograph by Carl Van Vechten, courtesy of the Carl Van Vechten Trust.*

With Churchill and Wells. *Courtesy of Comtesse Chandon de Briailles.*

Henry James. © *Bettmann/Corbis*

Edith Wharton. © *Bettmann/Corbis*

Virginia Woolf. © *Hulton-Deutsch Collection/Corbis*

In Macy's. © *Leonard McCombe/Time & Life Pictures/Getty Images.*

On Cape Cod. © *Alfred Eisenstaedt/Time & Life Pictures/Getty Images.*

Robin Maugham. *Courtesy of the Estate of Robin Maugham/Eric Glass Ltd.*

Glenway Wescott. *Courtesy of the Estate of George Platt Lynes.*

Beverley Nichols. © *E. O. Hoppé/Corbis.*

Barbara Back. *Courtesy of the Neil & Reiden Jenman Collection.*

With G. B. Stern. © *Associated Press.*

Alan Searle. *From a private collection.*

With Rylands, Mortimer, Hyslop, Haxton, Back, and Marshall. *Courtesy of the Neil & Reiden Jenman Collection.*

By the pool. *Courtesy of the Raymond Mortimer Collection, Manuscripts Division, Department of Rare Books and Special Collections, Princeton University Library.*

Breakfast in bed. © *Mirrorpix.*

With Liza and Alanson. *Courtesy of the Stanford University Special Collection.*

With Ellen and Nelson Doubleday. © *J. C. C. Glass (photograph by Douglass Glass).*

Riding in South Carolina. © *Time & Life Pictures/Getty Images.*

Fishing on the Combahee River. © *Alfred Eisenstaedt/Time & Life Pictures/Getty Images.*

Evening on the Riviera. *Courtesy of Comtesse Chandon de Briailles.*

Bridge. © *Getty Images.*

With Alan. *Courtesy of the Estate of Robin Maugham/Eric Glass Ltd.*

With Robin. *Courtesy of the Neil & Reiden Jenman Collection.*

Writing. *Courtesy of the Harry Ransom Humanities Research Center, the University of Texas at Austin.*

ABOUT THE AUTHOR

...

SELINA HASTINGS worked at the *Daily Telegraph* before becoming the literary editor for *Harpers & Queen*.
She is the author of *Nancy Mitford: A Biography, Evelyn
Waugh: A Biography,* and *Rosamond Lehmann*. A fellow
of the Royal Society of Literature, she has been a
judge of the Booker, Whitbread, British Academy,
Ondaatje, and Duff Cooper prizes and of the UK
Biographers' Award. Her biography of Waugh won
the Marsh Biography Prize.

ABOUT THE TYPE

. . .

This book was set in Bembo, a typeface based on an
old-style Roman face that was used for Cardinal
Bembo's tract *De Aetna* in 1495. Bembo was cut by
Francisco Griffo in the early sixteenth century. The
Lanston Monotype Company of Philadelphia brought
the well-proportioned letterforms of Bembo to the
United States in the 1930s.